Commodity
Trading Systems
and Methods

Commodity Trading Systems and Methods

P. J. KAUFMAN

A RONALD PRESS PUBLICATION
JOHN WILEY & SONS, New York • Chichester • Brisbane • Toronto • Singapore

Copyright © 1978 by John Wiley & Sons, Inc.

All rights reserved. Published simultaneously in Canada.

Reproduction or translation of any part of this work beyond that permitted by Sections 107 or 108 of the 1976 United States Copyright Act without the permission of the copyright owner is unlawful. Requests for permission or further information should be addressed to the Permissions Department, John Wiley & Sons, Inc.

This publication is designed to provide accurate and authoritative information in regard to the subject matter covered. It is sold with the understanding that the publisher is not engaged in rendering legal, accounting, or other professional service. If legal advice or other expert assistance is required, the services of a competent professional person should be sought.

From a Declaration of Principles jointly adopted by a Committee of the American Bar Association and a Committee of Publishers.

Library of Congress Cataloging in Publication Data

Kaufman, Perry J.
    Commodity trading systems and methods.

    "A Ronald Press publication."
    Includes bibliographical references and indexes.
    1. Commodity exchanges.   I. Title.

HG6046.K34   332.6'44   77-28654
ISBN 0-471-03569-6

Printed in the United States of America

10 9 8 7

TO MY MOTHER

Preface

This book is for a commodities trader in need of more information. It is a book about systems and methods. It tries to help the reader decide which technique to apply to different situations. But it goes one step further than just presenting technical approaches to the commodities markets—it explains why these methods are used, and why they may or may not work. It is not the intention of this book to promote or sell any of the systems included in the discussions or examples—method and not profitability is of primary interest. Most of the systems are well known and more information can easily be located by obtaining a copy of one of the sources listed in the references at the back of this book. There is no doubt that some important work will have been overlooked in this writing, but to obtain and research all methods would be a monstrous task. Unfortunately, therefore, some material that was well worth studying has been slighted. It is hoped that this will be corrected at some future time.

Commodity traders have few means for expanding their knowledge. If you are not satisfied with your current trading approach and look for new ideas, you won't find them in elementary commodity books. If you're past the stage of learning what an OB order is and understand volume and open interest and have experienced the impact of a surprising USDA report, then you have exhausted the current market resources of educational materials. There are some interesting Horatio Alger stories of turning $5 into $5 million, or how to take a good position in cocoa and then go on a safari and return a millionaire! More often, commodity traders start with large fortunes and end up with small ones.

The problem is, how do you get new ideas and how do you test them to know their value? The first step is to develop a basic awareness of what information currently exists. To do that, you can read some of the elementary commodity books now available. Each author presents one or two interesting, although simple, methods for trading cocoa, silver, or some other item that is of importance to him. To get at the trading technique, you must reread sections on "how to place an order" and "what is it all about." Occasionally, the success stories convey some slight idea of a method. You might find these more interesting than the techniques presented explicitly by authors selling the *foolproof* trading system. In the first case, you feel that the now-millionaire is sharing his success with a hint of how he really did it;

in the second case, you are given the entire system but can't help thinking that if this really works, why is the author sharing it?

How else do you find trading methods? The two main sources are experienced traders and a creative partner in learning. The experienced, successful traders can be classified in the Horatio Alger group, telling you as little as possible of what they really do and talking around the issue. If you're a good friend, they may tell you more, but not all. More often, they may share an idea that they have considered for 20 years but would like to see someone else use first. Would you like to be the one? Often a successful trader cannot tell you what he is doing right. To sample a good cross section of experienced and beginning players, have a drink at *The Sign of the Trader* in the Board of Trade building in Chicago. Every afternoon there is a recap of the key events of the day followed by a session on "how I would have done it." For the younger traders, or those still aspiring to be members of the Exchange, it is a valuable learning experience. Many important observations are passed over; some are discussed but not followed up. There are comments on reactions to reports, slow trading times during the day, reversals after the open, Friday or holiday liquidation, commercial sales or purchases—what do you do with them?

You now know a little about a lot of systems; you have some ideas concerning elements of the markets that have not been applied to your satisfaction. What do you do? Very few speculators ever get an opportunity to find out whether a new system will work in advance. They do what they can using a pocket calculator, a lot of paper, and whatever data they can amass that they consider representative. Once their results seem reasonable, or they have developed a "feel" for the system, they place orders and hope. If the first few trades lose, the system is usually discarded or put aside until they gain more confidence.

Only a few organizations exist that have the facilities to test new systems. There is too much specialized talent necessary to perform the systems work, and speculators with valuable new ideas are not inclined to share them with the person doing the testing, who might end up competing with them. There have been some studies released by various individuals and firms on moving averages and other specific systems. The most comprehensive that I am aware of are on point-and-figure (by Davis and Thiel), moving averages (by Maxwell), and silver trading (by Turner and Blinn). Each study tests a relatively broad data base to find the best performers over a reasonable time period. Although they are incomplete in many ways, they are performed with more objectivity than was previously available.

This book contains a summary of selected currently known and used technical trading methods. It describes the purpose of each approach, its use, and some results and observations by experienced speculators. The methods are classified into general categories and then various modifications to the systems are taken up. Each section is developed from the simplest form to the more complex, with examples. Most of these combinations have been tested with different degrees of success, and some are discussed with their results. If every combination of ideas were tested, this work would never have been completed. In the presentation of the basic systems, no conclusions are implied—each method has good and bad features. Moving averages are categorized as time-series, each day serving as an implied interval in your calculations; a point-and-figure technique has no time element included in its concept. Both approaches succeed and fail because of these assumptions. We will try to study them in order to understand these features.

PREFACE

Some of the chapters include a lot of basic mathematics. It is not necessary to understand it all to benefit from the other sections, but the ability to know what *regression* means or to look at situations as *probabilistic* is implied in every system. Any decision to trade is one of favorable odds, and a clearer understanding of what those chances are can be of great help. The *regression analysis*, which might seem a very sophisticated tool for a trader, is the basis for determining the direction of prices—the trend, the seasonal or the cyclic movement. All the more complex mathematical methods for finding these elements are also discussed using simpler techniques.

The bad results as well as the good have been included. Some of the tests resulted in a high probability of success, whereas others were terrible. They were all included because they seemed like good ideas before we knew the results, and you may have been tempted to try them yourself. The unfortunate aspect of statistical studies is that there is rarely a situation of such overwhelming probability that you can borrow money on your house and family and pressure friends into borrowing on theirs in order to speculate with a 99% chance of quadrupling your money in 3 hours. Statistical techniques work by mass numbers—that is not the same as "the trend is up when prices are rising." In this work, there are many studies that show success 60–70% of the time. To succeed using statistically sound techniques still requires sound money management. If you lose all your money on the 30–40% chance of a bad trade, you can't continue the game no matter what the likelihood is for success.

The last question you might have is one that was asked before: if these methods are good, why are they being published?

There is a need for a more advanced commodities trading guide among the available literature. After years of looking hopefully on shelves of popular and university bookstores for a book of this sort, I have decided to put one there myself. But these techniques alone will not make you a success overnight. They must be combined with common sense, experience, and an equally sophisticated understanding of money management. Many sound systems lose money by poor handling of portfolios or by pyramiding at the wrong time. Experience also shows that no two traders will use the same system the same way. Like a good chef, each one adds spices to reflect his tastes and personality; the results cause the same basic ingredients to transform into a variety of unrecognizable dishes.

It is the simplest of all approaches included here that will be of the most value, but you will have to study them all to draw a valid conclusion. The key to the method that you choose may lie in its selection and testing strategy rather than in the trading method itself. This book will try to give you the knowledge to make that decision.

P. J. KAUFMAN

Decatur, Illinois
January 1978

Acknowledgments

This book involved many years of experimentation and writing, during which time many people contributed by helping me to formulate my ideas, by reviewing my efforts, and by their encouragement. At this time I would like to thank them for their invaluable assistance. My greatest appreciation goes to those who helped at the beginning: Stuart Myers, who remains a model of the right way to research a problem; Kermit C. Zieg, Jr., who introduced me to commodities; and Todd Lofton, who always had a good word.

The research effort was helped by the contributions of two eminently qualified mathematicians, Al Boyd and Helene Terris. Other generous people helped review my efforts and direct them toward areas of importance: Don Roberts, who also made available his collection of financial literature; Herb Lobel, who has reviewed most known systems; and Ted Hartley and Bill Requarth, both of whose judgment has been of immense help.

Special appreciation goes to Billy Jones for his generosity in providing all the W. D. Gann material available and to David Harahus for his direction in the area of phyllotaxis.

In preparing the manuscript, an effort of more than a year, my greatest thanks to Mischa Baldwin.

P. J. K.

Contents

CHAPTER

1 INTRODUCTION   1

     Technical Versus Fundamental, 2
     Professional and Amateur, 3
     Trends, 4
     Prerequisites, 5
     How To Read This Book, 6
     Research Skills, 8

2 BASIC CONCEPTS   9

     On the Average, 9
     The Practical Use of Data, 21

3 COMPONENTS OF COMMODITY PRICE MOVEMENT— THE TREND   25

     Characteristics of the Price Data Used, 27
     Precautions in the Variations of Time-Series, 27
     Regression Methods for Finding the Trend, 29
     Application of Linear Correlation, 36
     Nonlinear Approximations for Two Variables, 37
     Multivariate Approximations, 45
     Markov Chains, 49

4 COMMODITY-TRENDING MODEL   53

     The Moving Average, 58
     Geometric Moving Averages, 64
     Exponentially Smoothed Moving Averages, 64
     Relating Exponential and Standard Moving Averages, 67

| 5 | MOVING-AVERAGE SYSTEMS | 74 |

Basic Buy and Sell Signals, 74
Rules for Using Bands, 77
Applications of Single Moving Averages, 79
Techniques Using Two Moving Averages, 81
Multiple Moving Averages, 82

| 6 | MOMENTUM AND OSCILLATORS | 86 |

Momentum, 86
Oscillators, 91
Velocity-Acceleration, 95
Phasing (Synchronizing a Moving Average To Represent Cycles), 99

| 7 | LIVING WITH MOVING AVERAGES | 103 |

"Take Your Profits and Let Your Losses Run," 104
Selecting the Right Moving Average, 104

| 8 | CYCLES AND SECULAR TRENDS | 106 |

Trigonometric Curve-Fitting, 107
Complex Trigonometric Curve-Fitting, 114
Other Methods for Finding Seasonal Effects, 117
Seasonals for Trading, 130
The Cycle, 132

| 9 | ADVANCED CHARTING | 134 |

| 10 | INTERPRETING THE BAR CHART | 137 |

Trading Rules, 139
Tops and Bottoms, 140
Head and Shoulders, 141
Other Top-and-Bottom Formations, 142
Now You See It, Now You Don't! 143
Gaps, 144
Price Objectives for Bar-Charting, 145
Using the Bar Chart, 148

| 11 | THE POINT-AND-FIGURE METHOD | 150 |

The Point-and-Figure Box Size, 154
The Problem of Risk, 154
Trading Techniques, 158
Take It and Run . . . ! 160
Alternate Treatment of Reversals, 161
Price Objectives, 163
A Study in Point-and-Figure Optimization, 169

CONTENTS xv

12 SYSTEMS FOUNDED ON CHARTING PATTERNS   177

William Dunnigan and "The Thrust Method," 177
Nofri's Congestion-Phase System, 180
Keltner's Minor-Trend Rule, 181
Donchian's Four-Week Rule, 182
Action and Reaction, 183

13 BEHAVIORAL TECHNIQUES   187

Measuring the News, 187
Contrary Opinion, 190
Mathematics and the Mystic, 192
Elliot's "Wave Principle," 194
W. D. Gann, "Time and Space," 200

14 PATTERN RECOGNITION   207

Time of Day, 208
Relating the Opening Trade to the Prior Day, 213
Daily Price Variation, 215
Three Studies in Market Movement—Weekly, Weekend, and Reversal Patterns, 219

15 DAY TRADING   249

One-Day-Only Techniques, 249
Liquidity, 251
Point-and-Figure as a Day-Trading Method, 251
Moving Averages, 252
Interday Variations, 252
The Taylor Trading Technique, 254

16 PRACTICAL CONSIDERATIONS   259

Use and Abuse of the Computer, 260
Gambling Technique—The Theory of Runs, 267
Filtering, 274
Combining Trends and Trading Ranges, 277
Trading Limits—A Dampening Effect, 279
Going to Extremes, 282

17 SYSTEM MANAGEMENT   286

Capital, 286
Pyramiding, 288
Equity Cycles, 289
System Evaluation, 292
χ^2—Chi-Square Test, 295

18 PERSONAL MANAGEMENT   **298**

APPENDICES

1. Least-Squares Method Using Normal Equations, 303

    Corn–Soybean Solution 1956–1972, 304
    Corn–Soybean Solution 1965–1975, 304

2. Statistical Programs, 306

    a. FORTRAN Program for Least Squares (Two Variables), 306
    b. Programs for the Texas Instruments SR-52 Hand-Held Programmable Calculator, 306
    c. Programs Available on Computers, 340

3. Matrix Solution to Linear Equations, 341

    a. General Form, 341
    b. Solution to Weather Probabilities Expressed as a Markov Chain, 344

4. Construction of a Pentagon, 346

    a. Construction of a Pentagon from One Fixed Diagonal, 346
    b. Construction of a Pentagon from One Side, 347

5. Uniform Random-Number Table, 349
6. String Lengths (Sequences of Runs), 351
7. Annual Price Fluctuations, 355

    Source of Prices Used, 358

8. Weekly Pattern Tables, 359
9. Weekend Pattern Tables, 366
10. Tables of Price Variation, 374

BIBLIOGRAPHY   **393**
INDEX   **397**

If you have a minute, I'll tell you how to make money in stocks. Buy low and sell high. Now if you have five or ten years, I'll tell you how to tell when stocks are low and high.

                                                                       JRL June, 1966

Commodity Trading Systems and Methods

CHAPTER 1
Introduction

Commodity trading is a form of price forecasting that deals with the simple concept: where are prices going? The accuracy with which this question can be answered depends on the depth of the analysis and how far your predictions will reach into the future—the farther you look, the greater the possibilities for error. Most of the work that follows reduces the problem of direction to the simplest form, that of "where are prices going today with respect to previous days?" The only answers that are expected will be *up*, *down*, or *undetermined*. This may seem to be an oversimplification of the basic concept, but it solves the problem.

Price determination for speculating must consider *how* the price will get from where it is now to where it will be later. A cattle feeder will only care about what price he can expect at the time his steers are ready for market—fluctuations in price during the interval from purchase to delivery will have no effect on his income. To a speculator, the "how" is everything. If his prediction is for higher prices, but a decline comes first, his finances may not survive to take advantage of the final results.

Analysis of price movement is applicable to many markets, but has made the greatest advances in the stock market because of public interest. For this reason the New York Stock Exchange must be considered the "sponsor" for systems research in other areas of speculation. Until recently, the most recognition that commodities have received is to be found in a line from Angas, who summarized his work by saying: "All the rules outlined above can be applied not only to stocks, but also to deals in raw commodities." Offhand recognition hardly seems appropriate for the grain and soybean markets, which do more business in some weeks than the stock exchange does in a full year.

In 1973 and 1974 the commodities markets caught the attention of the public when food prices became so high that they deserved prime news coverage. Sugar climbed from its near lows of 7¢ per pound to a record high of 60¢. Food stores began to ration bags of sugar and restaurants only served small amounts on request. The speculators' interest peaked at a time when the stock market was in a slump that had begun in about 1967. Leverage in the commodities futures markets averages below 10% for speculators and near 5% for commercial traders. Sugar purchased at 7¢ that increases in value to 60¢ returns an 857% profit—on 10% margin that means 8570%. A $1000 investment could have been turned into $85,700. It is no wonder that commodities, which has always been the biggest business in town, became the only game for the speculator. The financial analysts also began to switch to where there was increasing demand.

A large portion of the foundation work that is covered in this book still belongs to the stock market, although those sections are explained using examples of commodities. The original research performed for this book and many of the other systems and ideas were only intended for use in commodities. The problems of economics that affect specific raw materials are easier to comprehend, yet more difficult to analyze mathematically, than are stock market problems. Commodities may interrelate and prices may move uniformly at some points, at which times they may be adequately represented by an index, similar to the Dow–Jones Industrial Average. At other times there are some specific demand and fundamental factors that cause the price of related commodities to move apart. Consequently, analysis of commodities tends to be on an individual basis, whereas studies in stocks are often directed toward the index.

TECHNICAL VERSUS FUNDAMENTAL

Two basic approaches for determining commodity-price objectives are fundamental and technical analysis. The fundamental approach is primarily goal-oriented; as was the case with the cattle feeder mentioned before, this approach is not concerned with the nature of the current price direction so much as with anticipated prices. It is a composite of supply-and-demand elements: statistical reports on production, anticipated use, political ramifications, labor influences, price support, industrial development—everything that makes prices what they are. Technical analysis is a study of patterns and motion. Its elements are limited normally to the prices as well as market volume and open interest. It is considered to be the study of the market itself. There seems to be dissension between advocates of these two methods, but in actuality there may be substantial overlapping. There will always be purists on either side, rigid fundamentalists and technicians, but a great number of professionals combine the two techniques. You will have to judge for yourself.

Fundamental analysis attempts to isolate and use the basic components of supply and demand, but these are complex and extensive. A fundamentalist must have complete and accurate information and must weigh it properly in order to draw a reasonable conclusion.

Technical analysis considers only the market and therefore must account for fluctuations that are behavioral and not necessarily part of the supply-and-demand cycles. This analysis is based on both patterns and trends and is subject to problems in determination of relevant time periods. Its advantage is that it is completely self-contained. One of the first great advocates of price analysis was Charles Dow, who said:

> The market reflects all the jobber knows about the condition of the textile trade; all the banker knows about the money market; all that the best-informed president knows of his own business, together with his knowledge of all other businesses; it sees the general condition of transportation in a way that the president of no single railroad can ever see; it is better informed on crops than the farmer or even the Department of Agriculture. In fact, the market reduces to a bloodless verdict all knowledge bearing on finance, both domestic and foreign.

A major difficulty with fundamental information is that the facts are not enough to determine the resulting price of a product. To profit in commodities speculation you must be able to anticipate what will happen next. Today's market prices already include all the known fundamental information, some forms of which are subtle and sophisticated:

- Government reports (USDA planting intentions, yield, carry-over, cattle on feed, etc.)
- Warehouse receipts
- Country grain movement and elevator prices
- Comparisons with previous stocks
- Export commitments
- Known weather problems
- International currency fluctuations
- Purchases and sales between other countries

Although most of this information is not precisely accounted for, it is accurate to a reasonable approximation. Information is immediately available to the professional through general information sources (Reuters, Commodity News Service) and specific services via Telex and other communications equipment for terminal market prices, and through political and economic decisions directly affecting a specific industry (grains, cotton, cattle, etc.).

Much of the price movement reflected in both commodity cash and futures markets is anticipatory, an approximation of the effects of an economic development. Because of this, it is subject to change without notice. For example, a hurricane bound for the Philippines will send sugar prices higher, but if the storm turns off course prices will return to prior levels. Also, a major scheduled crop report causes a multitude of professional guessing, which may correctly or incorrectly move prices just before the actual report is published. By the time the public is ready to act, the news is already part of the price.

PROFESSIONAL AND AMATEUR

Beginning speculators often find a system or technique that seems extremely simple and convenient to follow, one that they think has been overlooked by the professionals. Sometimes they are right, but most often that method has been rejected because of subtle problems. Reasons for not using this technique could be the inability to get a good execution, the risk/reward ratio, or the number of consecutive losses that occur. Speculation is a sophisticated business, and to be successful at it you must make it your business. As Wyckoff has said:"Most men make money in their own business and lose it in some other fellow's."

To compete with a professional speculator you must anticipate the next move better or be more accurate in predicting prices from current news—not the article printed in today's newspaper ("United States Buys Beef For School Lunch Program"), which was discounted weeks ago, and not the one on the wire service ("15% Fewer Soybeans and 10% More Fishmeal"), which went into the market two days ago, but the one that has not been published. You need the answers to "what if...?" Two possible approaches to the solution could be to:

1. Recognize recurring patterns in price movement, and determine the most likely results of such patterns; or
2. Determine the "trend" of the market by isolating the basic direction of prices over a predetermined time interval.

Pure pattern recognition over short intervals is a study of behavioral science. Within the commodities markets speculators and commercial traders will react in a similar manner over and over again given similar circumstances. After many years these patterns may vary or become more complex, but they exist and can be used to anticipate subsequent price moves. The exclusive use of patterns will divorce you from any long-term supply-and-demand factors, since the short-term move may be contrary to the ultimate direction of the prices.

The study of price patterns has come a long way since Jesse Livermore's time, but they are still only as successful as the person using them. The bar (or line) chart, which is discussed later in detail, is the simplest representation of the market itself. The forms of information most used by bar chartists are the same ones that were recognized by Livermore on the ticker tape. Because they are interpretive, more precise methods, such as point-and-figure charting, are frequently used, which adds a level of exactness to charting. Point-and-figure charts are popular because they offer both specific trading rules and formations similar to both bar charting and ticker-tape trading.

Mathematical modeling, using probability and statistics, is becoming an increasingly popular technique for determining price movement. Most of these methods are modifications of developments in *econometrics* (the science of economics), and basic statistical theory. They are precise because they are based entirely on numerical data.

TRENDS

It would be an injustice to leave the reader with the idea that a "price trend" is a universally accepted concept. There have been analytic studies published contending that trends, with respect to stock price movement, do not exist. The most authoritative papers on this topic are collected in Cootner's book, *The Random Character of Stock Market Prices*. This means that, when considered serially (one day after the other), there is no consistent mathematical relationship between today's price, yesterday's price, or any previous sequential combination of prices. This lack of "serial dependence" implies that you cannot use yesterday's prices to determine what will happen today. Since the publication of Cootner's book, numerous analysts have claimed that there is a positive correlation between successive days; most of these recent studies have been empirical, using price histories of commodities and computer analysis.

Realistically, the advocates of nonrandom (serially dependent) motion are arguing academically. The apparent relationship is so close to being random that is a pointless

INTRODUCTION 5

question. It is possible to accept the hypothesis that long-term price motion is random and consider the problem of trending in a different way. By varying the time intervals for analysis we find that over shorter time spans the price movement is abnormally prolonged, while over the longer interval the randomness dominates. The distortion of the shorter intervals may be caused by the behavioral aspects of the market, the use of technical systems, the overreaction of the traders to reports, and the speculators themselves. These moves allow trend-following systems to work.

Some aspects of technical analysis have already been accepted and used by all traders in different ways. One important concept is that "the magnitude of fluctuation of prices is in direct relationship to the price level." Very few professionals could tell you exactly what that relationship is, but they are aware of a corresponding increase in risk as prices climb. Based on recent research, it is possible that the relationship of price fluctuation (*volatility*) to price level over varied intervals for all commodities is the same. Certainly it is a measure of market behavior, and can be useful. The future will show a gradual acceptance of these relationships.

PREREQUISITES

The contents of this book assume an understanding of speculative markets, particularly the commodities futures markets. An ideal reader should have read one or more of the available commodity "trading guides" and understand the workings of a buy or sell order and the specifications of contracts. Experience in actual trading would be helpful. A professional trader, a broker, or a purchasing agent will already possess all the qualifications necessary. A farmer or rancher with some hedging experience will be well qualified to understand the risks involved.

The basic reference book for general contract information is the *Commodity Trading Manual* published by the Chicago Board of Trade. For beginning or reviewing the basics there is Powers, *Getting Started in Commodity Futures Trading*. Two other comprehensive books on the topic are Kroll and Shisko, *The Commodity Futures Market Guide*, and Teweles, Harlow, and Stone, *The Commodity Futures Game—Who Wins? Who Loses? Why?* The introductory material is not repeated here.

A good understanding of the two most popular charting methods can be developed by reading the classic by Edwards and Magee, *Technical Analysis of Stock Trends*, a comprehensive study of bar charting, and Zeig and Kaufman, *Point and Figure Commodity Trading Techniques*. The sections on advanced charting in the present volume only briefly review the elements of each before going on to develop the techniques further. Writings on other technical methods are more difficult to find. *Commodities Magazine* often has a technical article, and most other commodity books express a specific technical approach, although not necessarily completely. A comprehensive study on *Commodity Futures Trading with Moving Averages* by Maxwell would be worth studying. On general market lore, the one book which stands out is Lefevre, *Reminiscences of a Stock Operator*, but a few others are also worth reading. Wyckoff mixes humor and philosophy in most of his books, but *Wall Street Ventures and Adventures through Forty Years* may be of general interest.

A reader with a good background in high school mathematics can follow most of this book through its more complex parts. A technical analyst will work with numbers, and an aptitude in that area is expected. An elementary course in statistics is ideal, but a knowledge of the type of probability found in Thorp's *Beat the Dealer* is adequate. A good calculator, one with mathematical functions, preferably programmable, will be of great help. Many of the problems have been solved on a Texas Instruments SR-52 calculator, and the program solutions appear in the Appendix.

HOW TO READ THIS BOOK

The mathematical sections of this book assume only an elementary knowledge of mathematics but develop this knowledge to a high degree. Since it is not necessary to read the mathematical parts in order to understand the systems and trading sections, this reading guide will indicate what can be omitted by the nonmathematician.

Chapter 2 should be read by everyone either briefly or in detail, since it lays the foundation for the use of averages and data. It is intended to have you question the most elementary part of a system, and prevent you from accepting a conventional method that has been adopted by others without understanding its strong and weak points.

Chapter 3 is entirely mathematical and related to econometrics. It is useful in developing the relationship between two commodities or any two elements. Using the regression techniques given, you can find the formula that gives volatility as it relates to price, develop your own corn-hog ratio, or find the parity price for corn and soybeans. Most of these techniques help the long-term outlook of price direction.

Chapter 4 is a complete discussion of moving averages from a mathematical viewpoint. It relates standard moving averages with exponentially smoothed averages and introduces the geometric average.

Chapter 5 is the first nonmathematical discussion of trading systems, rules, and application. It includes examples of the most well-known systems of which most traders should be aware.

Chapter 6 continues the discussion of trading systems into momentum and oscillators, and other applications of time-related and moving average systems. The later sections contain substantially more complicated techniques than the ones that appeared in Chapter 5. The two areas of velocity-acceleration and phasing require a good knowledge of numbers.

Chapter 7 summarizes the chapters on moving average and time-related systems and poses some practical questions concerning the implementation of these techniques.

Chapter 8 is the last of the basic mathematical systems and includes both mathematical development in the first two sections and practical applications in the remainder of the chapter. Cycles and seasonal tendencies are basic elements of price motion that are forecasted with a more rigid method than the trend. To find the "wave" motion that simulates these patterns requires a working knowledge of trigonometry and a programmable calculator. The third through fifth sections solve the same problems in a much simpler and more practical manner, and then present some common trading approaches for profiting from seasonal and cyclic movement.

Chapter 9 introduces charting methods. Background information only is provided, as well as some rationale for its use, all in nonmathematical terms.

INTRODUCTION 7

Chapter 10 concentrates on the bar or line chart, emphasizing the trading implications of various formations. Although there is a summary of basic terms and patterns, the intention of this chapter is to present trading techniques in a practical vein.

Chapter 11 covers the point-and-figure system from a trader's view, discussing modifications to the basic rules that may improve overall performance or limit risks on selected trades. A prior knowledge of the method and the problems encountered during trading is required in order to take full advantage of it. The last section considers the problem of a variable-box point-and-figure chart. It is an attempt to combine the concept of a price-volatility relationship with point-and-figure box size, increasing the size as prices move higher. Although the discussion uses mathematics developed in Chapter 3, the concept and tests are easily understood.

Chapter 12 is a review of some famous systems that are based on chart patterns. Dunnigan's method was used in the stock market but relates well to commodities. The last section groups ideas common to many systems. There is no mathematics here.

Chapter 13 presents the most unique and interesting trading systems. Creativity is often a stumbling block when devising new methods for analyzing the market. These approaches break through many of the conventional ways of thinking.

Chapter 14 contains original research studies based on pattern recognition. The first three sections analyze the time of day at which price reversals are likely to occur. The remaining studies use daily prices and evaluate the pattern of reversals throughout the week and over the weekend. The research is presented in a rigorous, but non-mathematical way using simple tallies only and creating tables of probable happening.

Chapter 15 is a discussion of methods that are commonly used by professional traders for fast profits. There is a brief introductory look at the impact of commissions for those speculators who do not benefit from membership rates, and some guidelines for evaluating relative potential based on price levels. Included is a practical attempt to use the rigid techniques already developed for intraday trading, followed by more interpretive methods. The last part presents the Taylor trading technique.

Chapter 16 contains important indirect factors influencing trading, most of which contain no mathematics. For a trader interested in developing a computerized system, the first section is a *must*, containing the do's and don'ts. The gambling approach to management is evaluated in the second section. The next two sections are practical areas of technique that assume a knowledge of trading experience. The last sections discuss the controversial impact of daily trading limits and a classic example of the wrong way to operate.

Both Chapters 17 and 18 stress the management of your investment and yourself. The system management includes the capital requirements and effects on trading, pyramiding, and other methods for compounding results, and the means for evaluating whether or not your performance is meeting its expectations. There is no significant mathematics needed here, only arithmetic. The personal management, of equal importance, is expressed as market philosophy, with quotes and paraphrases of important techniques and classic comments.

For those readers interested in reviews of other *systems*, most of the information will be found in Chapters 5, 6, 12, 13, and 15. *Trading techniques* of a more general form will be additionally located in Chapters 7, 8 (second part), 10, 11, 12, 14, and 16. *General information* and *introductory material* are in Chapters 2, 9, and 18. *Mathematical development* is confined to Chapters 2, 3, 4, and 8.

RESEARCH SKILLS

Before starting on a learning process, a few guidelines may help make the task easier. They have been set down as rules to follow in research:

1. *Do not form conclusions before you begin.* Theories tend to obscure facts and often cause you to set out to prove your conclusion at all costs. Let the research and testing direct you to the answer.
2. *State your hypothesis or question in its simplest form.* It is always important to know exactly what it is that you are testing. It will be easier to evaluate the answer.
3. *Do not assume anything.* Many projects that fail do so on their basic assumptions and not necessarily on system testing. Be objective enough to exclude opinions and secondhand information and work with facts.
4. *Do the simplest things first.* Do not try to combine systems together before you show that each element of each system works independently. Two failing methods will not usually produce a good combined result.
5. *Build one step at a time.* Go on to the next only after the previous ones have been tested. If you start with too many combined steps and fail, you will have to start from the beginning to find out what went wrong.
6. *Be careful of errors of omission.* The most difficult part of research is identifying the components to be selected and tested. Because all the questions that were asked were answered to your satisfaction does not mean that all the right questions were there. The most important may be missing.
7. *Do not take shortcuts.* Sometimes others have tried to answer the same questions you pose. Check the method that was used in their work and ask yourself whether there were any flaws in their approach. Remember that your work is as good as its weakest point. You would not want to waste all your time by assuming another's research was as well done as your own without knowing for certain.
8. *Start at the end.* Start with the end result and work back to the beginning. That way you only look at the issues relevant to the result; otherwise you might be proving the existence of the universe before long. If your goal is a trend-following system that generates daily trading signals you might start by asking the questions:

    Q. What do I want as a result?

    A. A system that tells me when to buy and when to sell.

    Q. In what form do I want these answers?

    A. A statement of price based on the close-only.

From here you must examine the possible choices of systems, risk, computational difficulty, and other relevant factors.

The remainder of this volume will contain much of the material necessary to answer these questions.

CHAPTER 2
Basic Concepts

> ... *economics is not an exact science; it consists merely of Laws of Probability. The most prudent investor, therefore, is one who pursues only a general course of action which is "normally" right and who avoids acts and policies which are "normally" wrong.*
>
> L. L. B. Angas

ON THE AVERAGE

In talking about numbers, we often resort to representative values, rather than dealing with the individual items themselves. We can discuss the range of values or average those numbers that are related for the purpose of solving some predetermined problem. Not all data can be combined or averaged and have meaning. The average of all commodity prices taken on the same day would not necessarily be significant; you would have an "average price," but that price would tell you nothing about any individual commodity that comprised the result. The average of a group of values must meaningfully represent the individual items that were used for the calculation. Let's consider a single commodity whose price went from 40¢ per pound to $2.00 per pound in over a little more than 1 year (this may remind you of coffee). The *arithmetic mean*, which is commonly called the "average," is calculated by dividing the sum of the given values by the total number of elements in the sum. If we had recorded five prices, the arithmetic mean would be

$$A = \frac{40 + 80 + 120 + 160 + 200}{5} = 120$$

This shows that the mean price was $1.20. The general form for the arithmetic mean is

$$A = \frac{a_1 + a_2 + a_3 + \cdots + a_n}{n} = \frac{\sum^n a}{n}$$

where $\sum^n$ is a symbol representing the sum of n different a's.

While this is the most common way of calculating an average, it is not representative for many situations. If we look at the prices of our commodity again, we can show that the time intervals between each price varied, with the longer intervals at lower prices. Table 2-1 is a list of the changes in prices as well as the elapsed time for that change.

Table 2.1   Weighting an Average

Prices go from	to	Average during interval	Total days for interval	Weighted	1/a
40	80	$a_1 = 60$	100	6000	.01666
80	120	$a_2 = 100$	80	8000	.01000
120	160	$a_3 = 140$	60	8400	.00714
160	200	$a_4 = 180$	40	7200	.00555

When the time spent at each price level is included in our thinking, it can be seen that the "average" price should be lower than $1.20. One way we might calculate this, knowing the specific number of days in each interval, is by multiplying the average price in each interval by the number of days spent in that interval, then dividing by the total elapsed days. We get the weighted average

$$W = \frac{a_1 d_1 + a_2 d_2 + a_3 d_3 + a_4 d_4}{d_1 + d_2 + d_3 + d_4}$$

$$= \frac{6000 + 8000 + 8400 + 7200}{280}$$

$$= 105$$

Although this is not exact because of our use of average prices for intervals, it closely represents the *average price relative to time*. There are two other averages for which time is an important element—the *geometric* and *harmonic means*. The geometric mean represents a growth function in which a price change from 50 to 100 is as important as a change from 100 to 200. Table 2-1 does not use the intervals relating the time between elements, but it does give greater weight to changes occurring in smaller values:

$$G = \sqrt[n]{a_1 \times a_2 \times a_3 \times \cdots \times a_n}$$

The solution to the geometric mean can be either of two forms:

$$\ln G = \frac{\ln a_1 + \ln a_2 + \cdots + \ln a_n}{n} \qquad (1)$$

$$\ln G = \frac{\ln(a_1 \times a_2 \times a_3 \times \cdots \times a_n)}{n} \qquad (2)$$

BASIC CONCEPTS

The two solutions are different but equivalent forms, and the choice is personal preference. Using (1) and entering data from our first example we have

$$\ln G = \frac{\ln 40 + \ln 80 + \ln 120 + \ln 160 + \ln 200}{5}$$

$$= \frac{3.689 + 4.382 + 4.787 + 5.075 + 5.298}{5}$$

$$= 4.6462$$

$$G = 104.19$$

which is very close to the weighted average value. The geometric mean has other advantages in application to economics and prices. A classic example is comparing a rise in price of tenfold from 100 to 1000 compared to a fall of one tenth from 100 to 10. An arithmetic mean of 10 and 1000 is 505, while the geometric mean of the same number gives

$$G = \sqrt{10 \times 1000} = 100$$

which shows the relative distribution as a function of comparable growth. Due to this property, the geometric mean is the best choice when averaging ratios that can be either fractions or percentages. When we consider deviations in the next section, a geometric mean should be used with relative deviation for cases where the absolute data was so large that a percentage was used for convenience.

The geometric mean is the basis for the compounded growth associated with interest rates. If you start with $1000 and get back $1600 in 12 years there has been an increase of 60%. The arithmetic mean gives an average of $\frac{60}{12} = 5\%$ but the compounded growth is

$$P_n = P_0(1 + r)^n$$

or

$$r = \sqrt[n]{\frac{P_n}{P_0}} - 1$$

$$= \sqrt[12]{\frac{1600}{1000}} - 1$$

$$= .04 \text{ or } 4\%$$

Later in the study of cycles and seasonal trends we will extract the rate of inflation using this same formula for compounded growth.

The harmonic mean is more of a time-weighted average, not biased towards higher or lower values as in the geometric mean. A simple example is to consider the average rate of speed of a car that travels 4 miles at 20 mph and 4 miles at 30 mph. An arithmetic mean would result in 25, without consideration of the fact that 12 minutes were spent at 20 mph and 8 minutes at 30 mph. The weighted average would give

$$W = \frac{12 \times 20 + 8 \times 30}{(12 + 8)} = 24$$

The harmonic mean is

$$\frac{1}{H} = \frac{\frac{1}{a_1} + \frac{1}{a_2} + \cdots + \frac{1}{a_n}}{n}$$

which can also be expressed as

$$H = n \bigg/ \sum_{i}^{n} \left(\frac{1}{a_i}\right)$$

For two or three elements, the simpler forms can be used:

$$H_2 = \frac{2ab}{a+b} \qquad H_3 = \frac{3abc}{ab+ac+bc}$$

This allows the solution pattern to be seen. For the 20 and 30 mph rates of speed, our solution is

$$H_2 = \frac{2(20)(30)}{20+30} = 24$$

which is the same answer as the weighted average. Considering the original set of numbers again, we can apply the basic form of harmonic mean:

$$\frac{1}{H} = \frac{\frac{1}{40} + \frac{1}{80} + \frac{1}{120} + \frac{1}{160} + \frac{1}{200}}{5}$$

$$= \frac{.05708}{5} = .01142$$

$$H = 87.59$$

There is a general relationship between the three principal means that is reflected in the results that have just been calculated,

arithmetic mean > *geometric mean* > *harmonic mean*

with the exception that all are equal if all the data are equal.

Averages have specific implications. It would be a mistake to apply the arithmetic mean to a commodity that had a short-lived extreme price peak and say that the mean represented the value of that commodity *most of the time*. There are other mathematical techniques for dividing the price distribution.

The *median*, or "middle item," is helpful for establishing the "center" of a large group of elements. It effectively divides any group into two equal parts, with each item in one half greater than or equal to all items in the other half. For example, if you had a long list of prices for a particular commodity and you wished to know the median price, you would first sort the prices in either ascending or descending order. Once that had been completed, the price in the middle would be the median,

median $= a_{(n/2)}$

where the elements are $a_1, a_2, \ldots, a_n$. One advantage of the median is that it discounts any extreme values that might distort the arithmetic mean. For example, a

BASIC CONCEPTS   13

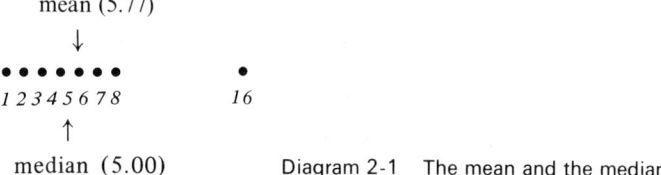

Diagram 2-1 The mean and the median.

group of points in Diagram 2-1 would result in a median value in the center of the cluster, while the arithmetic mean would be moved to the right due to some extreme data point that must be included in the calculation.

It could be that the extreme point (16) should have been part of the calculation, or that it was an error; the choice of the median or mean is up to the user. A simple and commonly used technique for eliminating unaccountable values is to drop the highest and lowest values as erroneous. An evaluation of your own data-collection technique will permit you to decide the validity of this method. If we take Diagram 2-1

Table 2.2 Frequency Distributions

May 76 Cocoa, 3-10-75 through 3-24-76							June 76 Live Cattle, January 28, 1976				
0	1⎤	105	5⎤	205	2⎤		41.35	2⎤3	41.85	67⎤82
5	5	110	8 25	210		4	.37	1	.87	15
10	5 ⎬16	115	8	215	2		41.40	5⎤6	41.90	62⎤73
15	3	120	4⎦	220	⎦		.42	1	.92	11
20	1⎦									
25	6⎤	125	6⎤	225	⎤		41.45	3⎤3	41.95	37⎤53
30	4 31	130	9 21	234	1 1		.47	0	.97	16
35	11	135	5	235			41.50	2⎤2	42.00	21⎤23
40	10⎦	140	1⎦	240	⎦		.52	0	.02	2
45	11⎤	145	2⎤	245	1⎤		41.55	1⎤2	42.05	11⎤12
50	19 51	150	5 13	250	1		.57	1	.07	1
55	8	155	4	255			41.60	9⎤11	42.10	10⎤12
60	13⎦	160	2⎦	260	⎦		.62	2	.12	2
65	13⎤	165	1⎤	265	2⎤		41.65	14⎤15	42.15	5⎤6
70	9 45	170	2 10	270	3		.67	1	.17	1
75	12	175	4	275	1		41.70	24⎤25	42.20	2] 2
80	11⎦	180	3⎦	280	⎦		.72	1		
85	7⎤	185	1⎤	285	⎤		41.75	19⎤23		
90	10 30	190	2 8	290	2 2		.77	4		
95	7	195	2	295			41.80	42⎤55		
100	6⎦	200	3⎦	300	⎦		.82	13		

Daily trading range
260 days

409 ticker prices

and disregard the lowest and highest points, we find that both the median and mean coincide at 5. Perhaps the high point was significant, perhaps not. Uses of larger quantities of data might eliminate the distinction between the mean and the median. The *mode* is another measurement of importance. Also called the *modal value*, it is the *most commonly occurring value*; it will be of great use in referring to the most frequent appearance of a specific value within a large group.

As an example of the use of three ways of measuring the center of a set of data elements, let's look at the daily trading range of May 76 Cocoa and analyze the averages. We present our results as a *frequency distribution*, a chart or plot of the relationship between the daily price range and the number of occurrences of that price range (called the *frequency density*).

For the purposes of our example, we looked only at the high minus the low of the day and disregarded the inclusion of gap openings or the relationship to the prior closing price. Diagram 2-2 shows a frequency distribution of the result for May 76 Cocoa from March 10, 1975, through March 24, 1976; a total of 260 trading days were used. The range of points (1 point = $\frac{1}{100}$ cent) was from 0 to 300, and we grouped the occurrences by 20-point intervals in order to consolidate the distribution. (The first interval

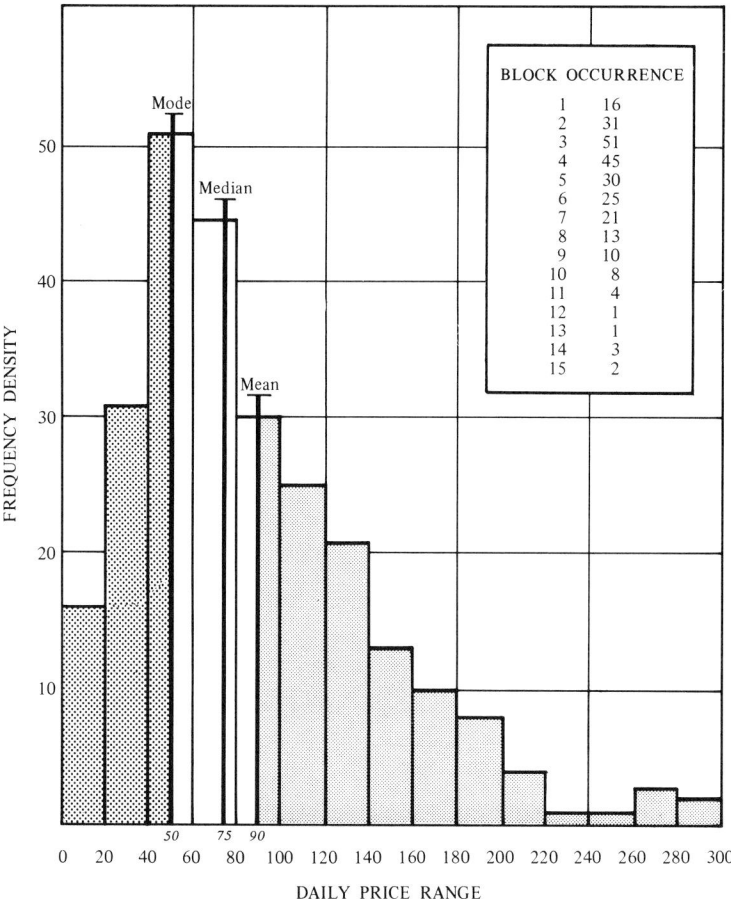

Diagram 2-2 May 76 Cocoa frequency distribution, 3-10-75 through 3-24-76.

BASIC CONCEPTS 15

includes the possible ranges 0–20, then 21–40, 41–60, etc., as in Table 2-2.) Other choices of groupings could have been made without affecting the relative positioning of our three measures. In Diagram 2-2 the mode occurred as the third bar, including a daily range above 40 points but not above 60 points. The median is identified within the bar containing the 130th element (midpoint of the total elements included). Since bars 1, 2, and 3 contain a total of 97 data points and 4 contained 45 more, the 130th item fell in the 4th bar. More specifically, if taken in smaller point intervals, the median can be shown to be at 75. *The median divides the area under the frequency distribution in half*, as you can see from Diagram 2-2. The total area of the bars to the left of the median is equal to the total area to the right. The long tail on the right end of the cocoa distribution may make this difficult to see.

The mean is simply the average of all the values included in the distribution; for May 76 Cocoa the mean is 90. There is a general relationship between the mode, median, and mean that will help approximate their values for standard distributions:

$$mean - mode \doteq 3 \times (mean - median)$$

For our example we have

$$90 - 50 \doteq 3(90 - 75)$$

or

$$40 \doteq 45$$

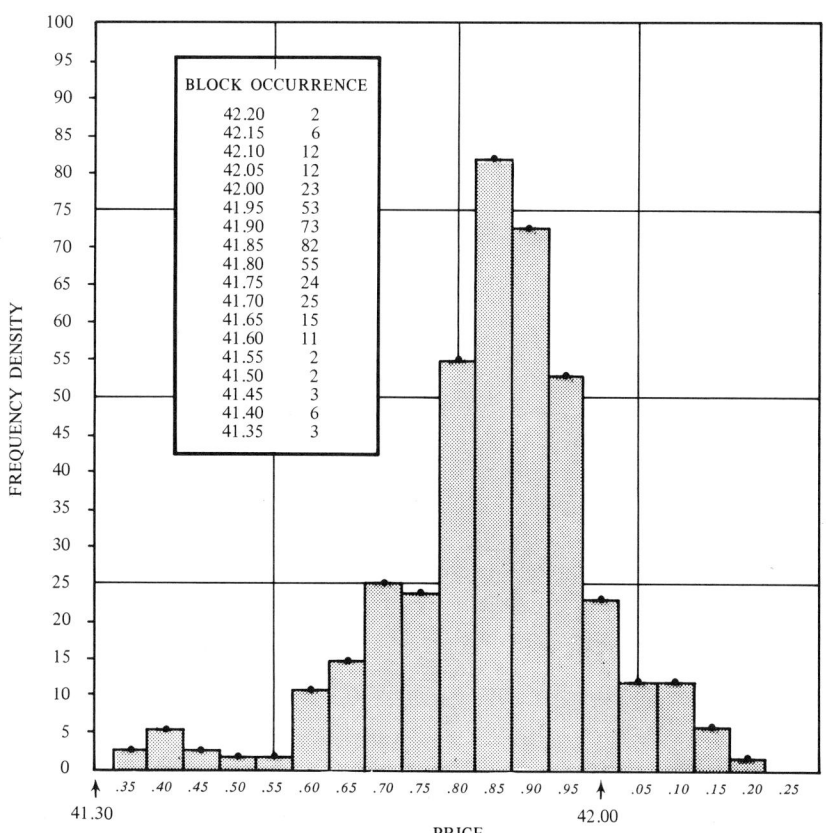

Diagram 2-3 June 76 Live Cattle frequency distribution.

Since a perfectly symmetric distribution would mean that the mode, median, and mean were all equal, the increased difference between the left and right elements of this approximation (40 and 45) might be considered as a measure of *skewness*.

Another frequency distribution can be created by looking at each price recorded on a ticker for June 76 Live Cattle on January 28, 1976. On that day, there were 409 individual ticks (each one resulting in one or more sales) ranging from a low of 41.35 to a high of 42.20.

In Diagram 2-3 we show the resulting distribution when the price occurrences were grouped into 5-point blocks (fractions between 5-point increments were included at the next higher level). The modal value was at 41.85, the median (the 205th ordered value) and the mean were also 41.85, resulting in a relatively symmetric frequency distribution. We can use both the cocoa and cattle distributions to show how to isolate important characteristics of price distribution.

Characteristics of the Principal Averages

Each averaging method has its unique meaning and usefulness. The following summary points out their principal characteristics:

The *arithmetic mean* is affected by each data element equally, but it has a tendency to emphasize extreme values more than other methods. It is easily calculated and is subject to algebraic manipulation.

The *geometric mean* gives less weight to extreme variations than the arithmetic mean and is most important when using data representing ratios or rates of change. It cannot always be used for a combination of positive and negative numbers but is also subject to algebraic manipulation.

The *harmonic mean* is most applicable to time changes and, along with the geometric mean, has been used in economics for price analysis. The added complications of computation has caused this to be less popular than either of the other averages, although also capable of algebraic manipulation.

The *mode* is not affected by the size of the variations from the average, only the distribution. It is the location of greatest concentration and indicates a typical value for a reasonably large sample. With an unordered set of data the mode is time consuming to locate and is not capable of algebraic manipulation.

The *median* is most useful when the center of an incomplete set is needed. It is not affected by extreme variations and is simple to find if the number of data points is known. Although it has some arithmetic properties, it is not readily adaptable to computational methods.

Deviation

The averages we have discussed are for the purpose of generalizing or standardizing a set of numbers that relate to one another. In the cocoa example, all the data plotted represented the daily trading range; for cattle each point was a price on the ticker.

BASIC CONCEPTS

For those sets the average is the range or price most likely to occur, although the exact value of the average does not have a high likelihood of occurrence (except the mode, which has the highest possibility by definition).

The average is used to determine the center of the data; it represents a typical occurrence only. There are practical uses of these averages, especially the mean, for determining in what region the largest portion of the data lies. If you could tell that 95% of all cocoa-trading days has a range of less than P points, then you might expect a reversal whenever that many points were spanned on any one day; historically, only 5% of prior trading ranges would have failed that conditions.

The *mean deviation* is a basic measuring tool for isolating the majority of data. If you add up the difference between the mean value and each data point (always considering the difference as a positive number), dividing by the total number of points will give you the average variance of all points from the mean:

$$\text{Mean deviation} = MD = \frac{\sum |\bar{x} - x|}{n}$$

By plotting the mean ± mean deviation as a vertical line on a frequency distribution, you can isolate the bulk of the data.

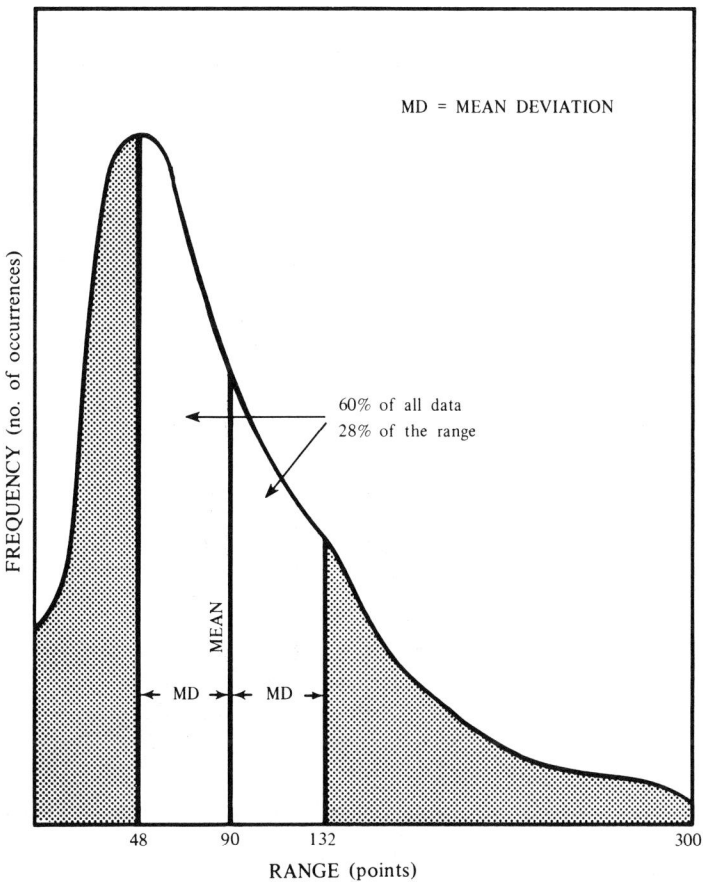

Diagram 2-4 Mean deviation for May 76 Cocoa.

According to the formula, the mean deviation for May 76 Cocoa was approximately 42 points, making the total range about the mean line (at 90) from 48 to 132. The significance of this calculation is that the range represented by twice the mean deviation is only 84 total points out of a maximum data span of 300 points (28%) but it includes 155 data points, or 60% of the total points. The mean deviation gives you a way of isolating the bulk of the data or eliminating the data points that are less likely to occur.

For June 76 Cattle the mean deviation was .088 points centering around 41.85, or from 41.76 to 41.94. That was 20% of the total range and contained 214 of 409 points, or 52%.

A more common measurement is called the *standard deviation* (also called the *root mean square*) and is calculated thusly:

$$SD = \sqrt{\frac{\sum (\bar{x} - x)^2}{n}}$$

where $(\bar{x} - x)$ is the difference between the mean and each of n data points. By squaring the results we always get a positive number, and so an absolute value as in the mean deviation is not necessary. The standard deviation serves the same purpose as the

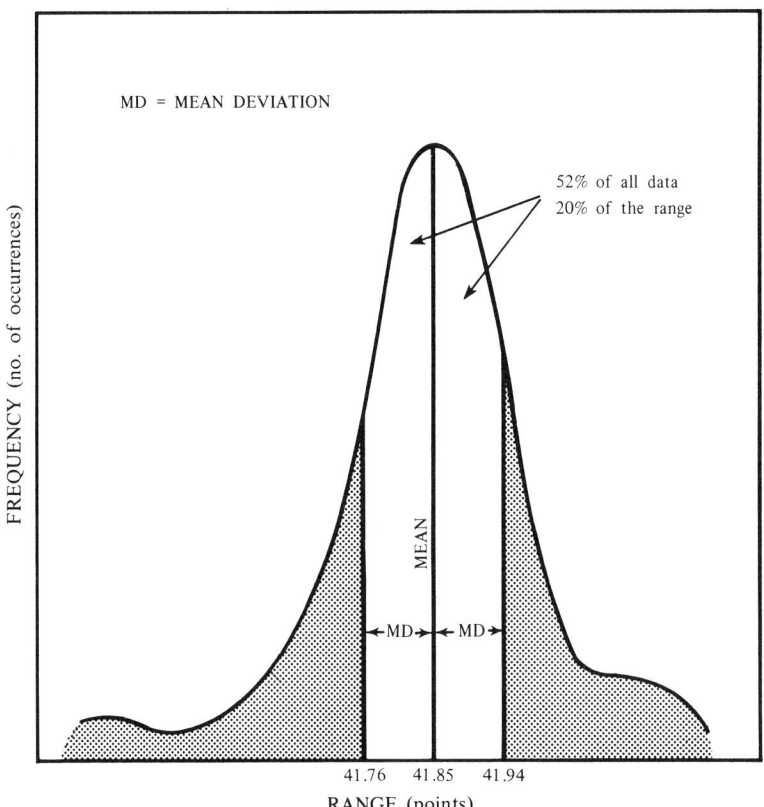

Diagram 2-5   Mean deviation for June 76 Cattle.

BASIC CONCEPTS

mean deviation, but is considered a better technique for defining the distribution of data points. If we calculate the standard deviation for cocoa and cattle and compare this with the mean deviation, we get the results shown in Table 2-3.

Table 2.3 Comparative Deviations

	Cocoa			Cattle		
	No. of points in range	Percentage of total range (300 pts)	Percentage of data included	No. of points in range	Percentage of total range (85 pts)	Percentage of data included
Mean deviation	84	28.0	59.6	17.6	20.7	52.3
Standard deviation	112	37.3	74.2	24.6	28.9	69.9
2 Standard deviations	202	67.3	95.8	49.2	57.9	89.0

The general rule for the standard deviation is that one standard deviation will contain about $\frac{2}{3}$ (66%) of the total data and two standard deviations will include about 95% of all the data. Cocoa shows that there were only 25.8 chances out of 100 (about 1 out of 4) that the daily range will exceed 112 points and only 4 chances out of 100 that it will exceed 202 points.

To have an objective measure of the differences between one distribution and another, we can compute a *coefficient of variability*:

$$V = \frac{100 \times \text{standard deviation}}{\text{mean}} = \frac{100 SD}{\bar{x}}$$

The larger the result, the more variable will be the distribution. When V is small, most of the data are grouped near the mean:

$$V(\text{cocoa}) = \frac{100 \times 56}{90} = 62.22$$

$$V(\text{cattle}) = \frac{100 \times 12.3}{85} = 14.47$$

These results show that the cattle data were significantly more consolidated about the mean than were the cocoa results.

In General

Before leaving our discussion of averages, it is necessary to look back at the implications of generalization. The purpose of an average was to transform individuality into a classification. When done properly, there is useful information to be gained.

Perhaps the index ranks as one of the greatest misused applications of the average. There are a number of popular indices relative to commodity prices: the Dow–Jones Spot Index, the Dow–Jones Futures Index, Reuters (United Kingdom) Index, and the CRB (Commodity Research Bureau) Futures Group Index. All these attempt to combine selected commodity prices into a composite, concluding that the "ABC Index rose two points today," and so on. The first question to ask yourself is: "How does the index rising two points relate to what I am doing?" If the index is a composite of metals, it certainly will not tell you much about grains. If there is a weighted importance to certain commodities, the results will be biased to reflect the movements of those weighted commodities rather than the others. Creating and following an index can be a great exercise, but its usefulness is subject to careful inspection. Of what importance is the rise or fall of a general index? It is usually only remotely related to the movement of one particular commodity that may be of interest to you. An index of commodities will give more insight into a general economic problem than to any of the individual commodities that comprise the index.

Without going into a subject of controversy, there are ways to evaluate the usefulness of an index, although you may never determine just what the index is measuring. Perform an empirical test or correlation between the commodity or portfolio of interest to you, and the index that seems to relate to your interest; if the index moves in such a way that it parallels or anticipates your moves, it will be useful to you.

The Index

If you have not been completely discouraged by the previous comments on the index, and are sufficiently wary of its misuse, you may proceed to a brief discussion of the development of an index.

An index is traditionally used to determine relative value, the increase or decrease in value over time. The most common examples of this are the Consumer Price Index, the Cost-of-Living Index, and so on, which have a starting value (1 or 100) on a specific year. The index itself is a ratio of the current value or composite values with the same calculation during the base year. The selection of the base year may serve a future purpose as a basis for comparison, but it is frequently subjective and not all representative. For commodities, most years prior to 1976 would be adequate, with certain key years as exceptions. If we select a set of commodities for our index and combine them using whatever weighting method we determine, the index value for a specific year is the ratio.

$$index\ (year\ t) = \frac{commodity\ values\ (year\ t)}{commodity\ values\ (base\ year)} \times 100$$

If the change in the value of the index is negative, the composite values are lower in year t than they were in the base year. The actual index value represents the percentage change.

A *simple aggregate index* is the ratio of unweighted sums of commodity prices in a specific year to the same commodities in the base year. Most of the popular indices known to us fall into this class. A *weighted aggregate index* uses an intentional bias toward certain commodities by weighting them to increase or decrease their effect on the composite value. The index is then calculated as in the simple aggregate index.

BASIC CONCEPTS   21

Weighting can be used to correct price distortions. In trying to determine true increases in price, each commodity could be weighted inversely by its production. Therefore, if the price of sugar increased 200% while its production remained constant, inflation or demand increased, but if production decreased 50% (over half), these prices must be adjusted to reflect a shorter supply and a natural increase in price. The sugar price increase of 200% could be divided by 2 (multiplied by $\frac{1}{2}$) to account for this. We are now getting into a very complicated area of study that would require a text of its own. Let it be said that an index can be both complex and useful and must be developed with care.

THE PRACTICAL USE OF DATA

Most applications of statistics are not as fortunate as commodity technical analysis because price evaluation has a set of perfect data. There is no error factor included in your calculations due to unknown quantities. Even econometrics, which uses the best data available, introduces error into its calculations when its data are not complete but *representative*. The average price received by all farmers for corn on the 15th of the month cannot practically be an exact number, although it may be so close that the error is insignificant. For both economic and practical considerations, most statistics are accumulated by *sampling*.

When using incomplete or representative sets of data, you should know the approximate error in the sample data. This can be done by finding the standard deviation and coefficient of variance, as discussed in the previous section. A large standard deviation means a large error or an extremely scattered and not consolidated set of points. This process is called the *testing of significance*. Sample data usually become more significant as the number of items sampled becomes larger; the measurement of deviation or error will become increasingly small as the sample becomes larger.

$$Error = \frac{1}{\sqrt{no.\ of\ items\ sampled}} = \frac{1}{\sqrt{N}}$$

Therefore, if only one item is sampled, the error is considered 100%; if two items, the error is 50%; nine items, 33%; and so on. The error calculation is an important concept for testing the reliability of a commodity-trading system. If your system has had four trades, whether profits or losses, there is a 50% error possibility in your conclusions. You must have enough tests to assure a comfortably small error factor. If you would like the error to be only 5%, you should have 400 trades.

The Law Of Averages

The law of averages is a greatly misunderstood and misquoted principle. Its most common use in commodity trading is in referring to an abnormally long series of profits or losses that is compensated by some other series or combinations of series of opposite successes whose effect is to offset the prior results "in the long run." That is not what is meant by the law of averages. Over a large sampling, the bulk of the data will be scattered close to the average in such a way as to overwhelm an abnormally distant set of data points and cause them to be insignificant.

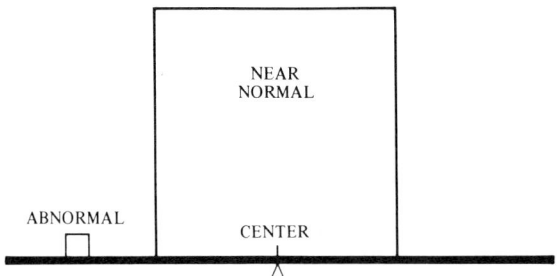

Diagram 2-6   The law of averages.

This principle can be seen in Diagram 2-6, where the addition of a small abnormal grouping to one side of an already balanced large group of near-normal data does not affect the balance. In a later section we discuss strings and the likelihood of a series of successive events occurring; the law of averages does not account for those situations.

Weighting of Samples

When sampling is used to obtain statistical data, it is common to divide the entire problem into discrete parts and attempt a representative sampling of each portion. These samplings are then weighted to reflect the impact of each part on the whole. Such a weighting will magnify or reduce the errors in each of the discrete sections. This problem is called an *error of bias* due to the result of such weighting adding emphasis to one or more parts of the entire data set. It is important to note that even large numbers within a sampling cannot overcome the implications of bias introduced by weighting.

Commodity-price analysis and trading techniques often introduce bias in both implicit and explicit ways. A *weighted average* is an overt way of adding what is considered a positive bias (positive because it is intentional), while the use of two analytic techniques acting together may without notice rely doubly on one statistical element or aspect of the data; at the same time other characteristics of the data may be used only once or may be eliminated by offsetting use. The use of the daily high and low in one part of a program and the daily range (high − low) in another section would be considered duplicate use and weighting of the same data.

Chance Introduced

Calculation must measure the incalculable.

Dixon G. Watts

Chance is a term that causes great anxiety in many people. Chance can be neither predictable nor completely unpredictable, for if it were either it would have well-defined properties and we would not call it "chance." We can measure the effects of chance or its significance, but we cannot predict it. We will be able to use the notion of

BASIC CONCEPTS

chance for our smoothing techniques; we will define the noise or perturbations around a "trend" as the result of events or combinations of events working together or in conflict in such a way as to make their determination impractical and unnecessary.

Rather than attempting to explain each incident or solve the complex equations for the perturbations that cause apparent erratic movement, we can attribute them all to chance and measure their net effect about a known pattern or a fitted curve. The arrival at a calculation of standard error will help us distinguish between the price changes that can be attributed to chance and those that are part of the basic directional move.

When measuring chance, we include other price deviations caused by both personal bias and experimental error. There is very little control over these other elements and they cannot be measured separately, and so it is best to attempt only to keep them as small as possible.

Probability

Although probability is a field of mathematical specialization, for us it will be an extension of the previous comments on averages and frequency distribution. Everyone uses probability in daily thinking and actions. When you tell someone that you will be there in 30 minutes, you are assuming:

- Your car will start
- You will not have a breakdown
- There will be no unnecessary delays
- You will drive at some specific speed
- You will have the appropriate number of green lights

All these circumstances are extremely probabilistic and yet everyone makes the same assumptions. Actually, your 30-minute arrival is only an estimate of the average time it should take for the trip. If your arrival time were critical you would extend that estimate to 40 or 45 minutes to account for extreme circumstances. You would not generally raise the time to 2 hours because the likelihood of such a delay would be too remote. But all estimates or averages include an allowable variation, all of which is considered normal.

In mathematics, probability is a well-defined way of measuring or referring to the uncertainty surrounding an average value. Any element that has no uncertainty is called *definitive* and is no longer probabilistic. Probabilities are measured in percent of likelihood; for example, if you expect M numbers out of a total of N to fall within a specific area, the probability P of any one number satisfying the criteria is

$$P = \frac{M}{N} \qquad 0 < P < 1$$

There are two important basic principles in probability that will be easy to explain using examples with playing cards. Within a deck of 52 cards there are 4 suits of 13 cards each. The probability of drawing a specific card on any one turn using the entire deck is $\frac{1}{52}$. Similarly, the likelihoods of drawing a particular suit or card number are $\frac{1}{4}$ and $\frac{1}{13}$, respectively. The *probability of any one of these three possibilities occurring is the sum of their individual probabilities.* If you can choose either a numbered card or a suit or a specific card, the probability of success is

$$P = \tfrac{1}{13} + \tfrac{1}{4} + \tfrac{1}{52} = \tfrac{18}{52} = 35\%$$

The other basic principle is that the *probability of two occurrences happening simultaneously or in succession is equal to the product of their separate probabilities.* The likelihood of drawing a three and a club from the same deck in two consecutive turns (replacing the card after each draw) or of drawing the same cards from two decks simultaneously is

$$P = \tfrac{1}{13} \times \tfrac{1}{4} = \tfrac{1}{52} \doteq 2\%$$

Probability is another way of looking at the frequency distribution of cocoa and cattle in the previous sections. For cocoa, Table 2-3 shows that one standard deviation contained 74.2% of all data, or there was a 74.2% probability of the next day's trading having a high-low range of 112 points or less. When expressed in those terms, the frequency distribution is called a *probability distribution.*

CHAPTER 3
Components Of Commodity Price Movement — The Trend

Commodity prices are the composite of many complex factors. The reasons for the changes in price are highly dependent on the length of the observed time period, the fundamentals of supply and demand, inflation, and government programs of long-term significance. Emotion and speculation, along with short-term production requirements and public demand cause variations that appear as "noise" around the long-term movement. But commodity prices have a property that allows the mathematical decomposition of the factors that make up the movement—each price occurs sequentially as related to time. Commodity prices comprise a *time-series*.[1]

---

[1] An important trait of the time-series is its *sequential dependence*, which means that the values of successive elements in the time-series are somehow dependent on the values of prior elements. In mathematical terms, one may say that a relationship exists such that

$$P_i = F(P_{i-1}, P_{i-2}, \ldots, P_1)$$

where P_i is a price at time $= i$
P_1 is a price at time $= 1$
F is a mathematical formula combining P_1 through P_{i-1}

If a time-series does not have this property, it is called *sequentially independent* and we will consider the numbers $P_1, \ldots, P_i$ as random. There is an ample number of classic studies on this topic in many sources, some of which are listed in the reference section of this book. Other characteristics of time-series will be looked at here.

A time-series is considered to have four elementary components:

- A trend
- A cyclic variation
- A seasonal pattern (or secular trend)
- Chance movement

Trends are the subject of many commodity-trading methods, but the primary trend of an economic time-series is inflation. As prices fluctuate yearly, the rate of inflation must cause an upward bias that forces the lowest prices to increase steadily. Because the annual compounded inflation rate since 1928 was 2.9%, but more recently 5.5%,[2] this would have a noticeable effect on any predictive method. Trends can be related to a time interval; as the span becomes shorter the predictive quality will tend to lessen and the deviation from the prediction will increase. Other longer trends that may be considered for later study are in the Wholesale Price Index, the value of real estate, and the population growth.

Cycles are responsible for the major price fluctuations about the trend. Cycles do not necessarily have uniform periods; that is, the peaks and valleys of the waves are not always at equal distances. Business and industrial cycles are usually reactions to supply and demand reflected by prices. If the price of copper were high, mining operations would step up production to take advantage of the better prices; consequently, demand would be satisfied and prices would decline as the surplus stocks increased. Once prices were too low, mining production would be cut back, supply would dwindle, and prices would rise. If the reduction and increase in production and stocks each took 2 years, we would have a 4-year copper cycle, which would cause prices to fluctuate above and below the trend.

The *seasonal effect* is easier to isolate since it relates to a specific one-year period, usually a growth cycle. The seasonality of the grains causes fluctuations due to the change in supply throughout the crop year. During the harvest season the plentiful supply causes depressed prices, while for the remainder of the season prices rise as the stored supply is diminished. The consumer can also cause a seasonal effect, increasing the demand for a commodity at the same time each year. For example, crude oil is produced and processed with regularity throughout the year but used more in the winter for heating. The seasonal effect based on demand may not conform to a specific calendar year but it is present, as is the crop seasonal effect, and will bias prices regardless of the apparent trend.

The *chance* element of price movement is a composite of everything we do not know and cannot or will not measure. Any variations from our predictive models we will attribute to chance. The economics and practicality of every situation require that research and analysis should continue only until a solution of reasonable accuracy is reached. In later sections we will refer to studies by Box and Jenkins, who have recently consolidated and analyzed material that emphasizes the dependency of sequential elements of a time-series, the results of which enable us to decompose the chance component and thereby reduce the magnitude of the unknown items.

The trend will be the subject of the remainder of this chapter, since it is the area of heaviest concentration by analysts. The trend may appear to be a cycle or a seasonal

---

[2] Based on the Consumer Price Index for 1928–1977 and 1967–1977, respectively.

COMPONENTS OF COMMODITY PRICE MOVEMENT—THE TREND

pattern when taken for intermediate time intervals, but only if that pattern is dominant during the interval chosen and only if the phasing of the trend is "in step." Later sections will discuss the cyclic and seasonal variations specifically.

We will start by using linear regression, a technique for representing a trend with a straight-line approximation, and then proceed to find nonlinear trends and higher-order relationships. Since a trend can also take the form of any curve, all techniques for fitting data have been included together. The following two chapters expand the analysis of the trend to its prediction and use in commodity trading. The statistical methods presented first are not the flexible ones used for trading, but they are important for any long-term price analysis.

CHARACTERISTICS OF THE PRICE DATA USED

A time-series is represented by an ordered pair of numbers, a price and its related time of occurrence. They must be ordered by time and the intervals must be equally spaced —otherwise the continuity of change over time is lost. Other price data used in the regression section will be pairs of prices taken at the same time, although the time ordering will not be used. For example, on the same day we may record the hog-corn or gold-silver ratio or we may compare the price of corn and soybeans as crop substitutes.

PRECAUTIONS IN THE VARIATIONS OF TIME-SERIES

There are two important variables in a time-series; the elapsed time between data elements, and the total number of elements in the set. By changing either, you could materially changes the patterns. In Diagram 3-1 we have some data points in a continuous series, from t_1 through t_{25}. By using all the data points, we get a very distinct wave effect, but as we select every second, third, ... point, the pattern changes.

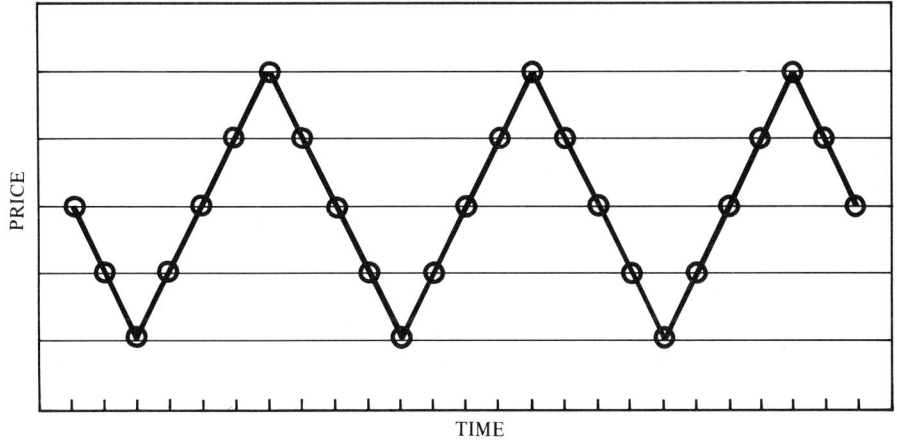

Diagram 3-1 Time-series.

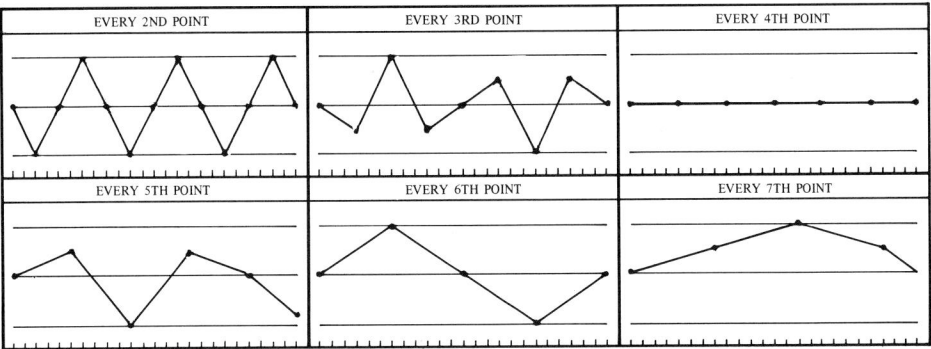

Diagram 3-2   Variations in time-series patterns using selected time intervals.

Some of these new patterns are easily compared with the original wave formation: (2) is identical, (6) and (7) seem to be elongations or "smoothings" of the same pattern, and (4) is the ultimate smoothing. But (3) and (5) are severe alterations of the original wave—and yet they are produced by the continual extension of the time interval.

In the use of statistics and commodity prices, this possible distortion might readily occur when the use of data is not continuous. A daily price pattern cannot be studied by using anything but continuous daily prices. Examination of longer historic periods using time intervals other than the one to which the ultimate solutions will be applied may prove to be a disaster. The success of a system tested using only the prices each Friday does not preclude its success using daily prices during the same time period. We will refer to this concept again in a later discussion of smoothing techniques.

The second variation of a time-series that is equally significant is the length of the series. A shorter series of points has the advantage of satisfying many correlation methods and approximating techniques, but with a great error factor. As you add points, you define the pattern more clearly and make the interpretation more precise.

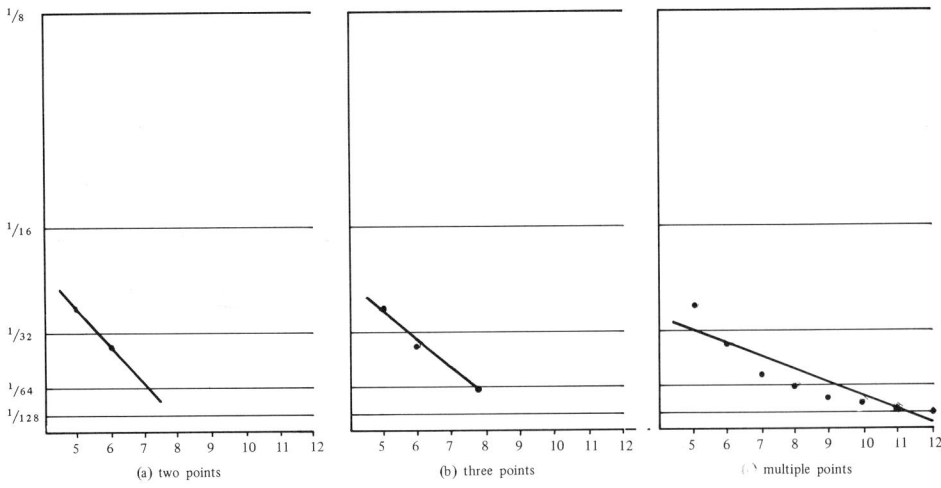

Diagram 3-3   Development of a time-series pattern.

COMPONENTS OF COMMODITY PRICE MOVEMENT—THE TREND

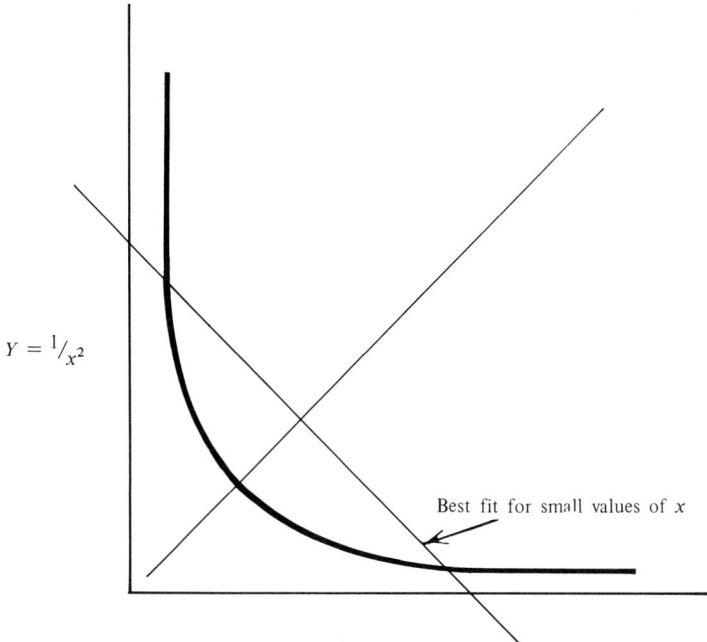

$Y = 1/x^2$

Best fit for small values of x

Diagram 3-4   Development of a time-series pattern (the complete curve).

If you started at any two points, t_i and t_{i+1}, of a well-defined relationship between x and y, where $x = 5$, $y = \frac{1}{25}$, and $x = 6$, $y = \frac{1}{36}$, you could get a straight-line approximation that would be perfect for those two points but would not necessarily be representative of points outside the range (Diagram 3-3a). Adding a third point t_{i+2}, where $x = 7$, $y = \frac{1}{49}$, you can also approximate the points closely with a straight line (Diagram 3-3b), and as you add more points a straight-line approximation still seems reasonable for larger values of x (Diagram 3-3c); but using the smaller values of x, the linear approximation looks like Diagram 3-4, not a useful representation.

A small number of data points can be misleading. Just as in the examples of varying time intervals, the range of the data selected can distort the overall pattern.

REGRESSION METHODS FOR FINDING THE TREND

The results of most regression techniques are called the "best fit" because the trend line or curve that has been calculated to approximate the price movement comes the closest to being successful. The best fit is used to fill gaps where no data were available, and to forecast a continuation of the same pattern that approximates the existing data. Both the determination of a relationship between two elements and the forecasting ability have important applications.

A widget manufacturer has found that his quarterly sales are increasing rapidly and he will have to expand to maintain production in excess of sales. What should the output capacity of his factory be if he expects the continued increase for the next 3 years? A curve or line representing past growth will serve to help predict future demand.

A farmer must decide whether to plant corn or soybeans this year. He knows his relative yields and the average price of each crop for many years. By using regression analysis he can determine the relationship of corn prices to soybean prices and decide whether his relative yield favors the planting of one or the other (all other factors being equal). We will begin with straight-line relationships between two elements and work up to the more complex.

Linear Relationships

The first step in statistical analysis is to be able to determine the relationship, if any, between two distinct products. To do this we need data on both products, taken at the same time.

Table 3.1 Annual Average Corn and Soybean Prices[a]

	1956				1960					1965
Corn	1.27	1.19	1.10	1.10	1.05	1.00	.98	1.09	1.12	1.18
Soybeans	2.43	2.26	2.15	2.07	2.03	2.45	2.36	2.44	2.52	2.74

	1966				1970					1975
Corn	1.16	1.24	1.03	1.08	1.15	1.33	1.08	1.57	2.55	3.02
Soybeans	2.98	2.93	2.69	2.63	2.63	3.08	3.24	6.22	6.12	6.33

[a] Source: 1956–1965—Illinois Statistical Service
1966–1975—CRB Commodity Yearbook

We need to find a straight line that best fits between all the points. If we look at the first two entries only, 1956 and 1957, we can easily apply the equation for a straight line (first-order equation)

$$y = a + bx$$

where y is the price of corn and x is the price of soybeans. Then we have to find a and b by solving the same equation with the substituted values

$$(1956) \quad 1.27 = a + b \times 2.43$$

$$(1957) \quad 1.19 = a + b \times 2.26$$

We find the value of a in 1956 as $1.27 - b \times 2.43$ and substitute it into the 1957 equation to get

$$1.19 = 1.27 - b \times 2.43 + b \times 2.26$$

Then we can solve for b:

$$b = \tfrac{8}{17} = .47 \quad (approximate)$$

COMPONENTS OF COMMODITY PRICE MOVEMENT—THE TREND

Substituting back into the 1956 equation, we can now solve for a:

$$1.27 = a + .47 \times 2.43$$

$$a = .1279$$

Then the equation for a straight line through the first two points is

$$y = .1279 + .47x$$

In order to see the results more clearly, we plot the relationship of corn to soybeans using this equation by substituting values of x (soybeans) and finding the corresponding value of y (corn).

Table 3.2 Linear Relationship of Corn and Soybean Prices

Soybeans x	1.00	2.00	3.00	4.00	5.00	6.00
Corn y	.60	1.07	1.54	2.01	2.48	2.95

Diagram 3-5 shows the straight-line relationship of corn and soybeans.

It is evident that two points are not necessarily representative of a complex relationship over many years. The problem with fitting more than two points is that a straight line will no longer pass through all three points, and the simple solution of linear equations cannot be used. In addition, no matter where the line is drawn, we know from our data that the actual price relationship can vary on either side of our straight line approximation. Our goal is to find a line that *best* fits the situation, since no line will fit exactly. To do this we want the line to be placed at the most frequent occurrence of price relationship at any point. For example, when soybean prices were in the range of $2.43–2.45 (1956, 1961, and 1963) corn prices ranged between $1.00–1.27; when soybeans were $6.12–6.33 (1973–1975), corn was $1.57–3.02. We will try to

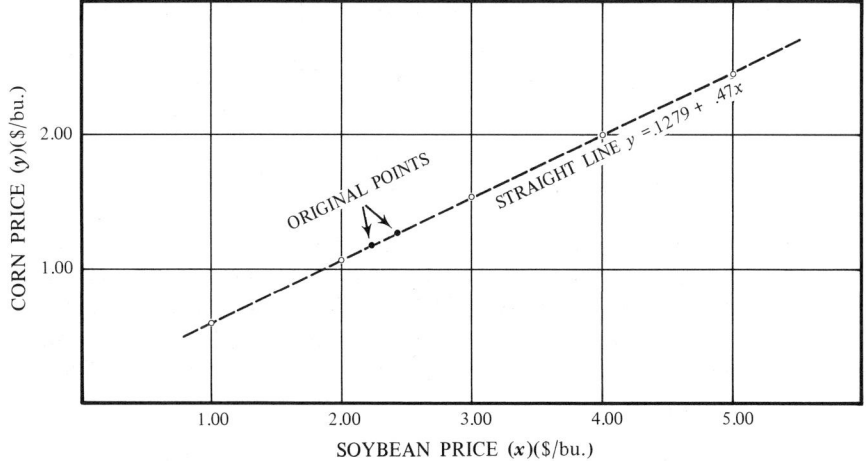

Diagram 3-5 Straight-line approximation.

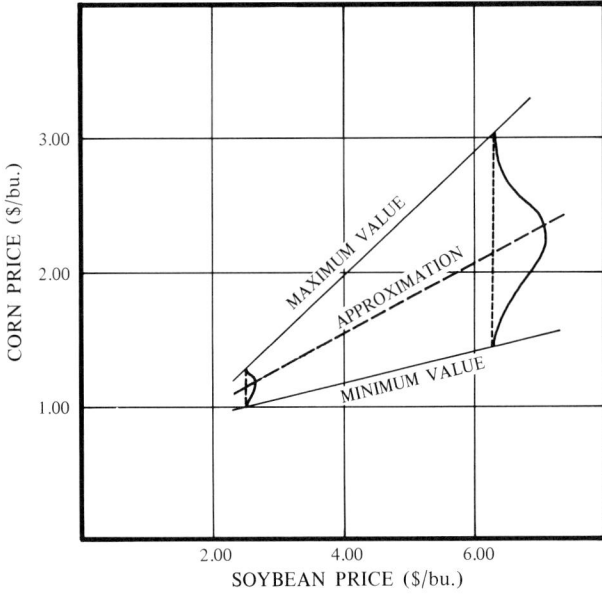

Diagram 3-6 Probabilistic model.

locate the center of this range in such a way that our approximation will have the greatest likelihood of occurring.

In Diagram 3-6 the broken line represents the conceptualized relationship of corn to soybeans; the solid lines connect the extreme price relationships between the two commodities. With proper calculations, the approximated relationship will cross through the center of a bell-shaped distribution at each point on the soybean axis. This means that for each soybean price, the price of corn will most likely be the value of the approximation line; it could be as high or as low as the extreme occurrences, but will probably fall towards the center. This representation is called a *probabilistic model*. It differs from most other methods we will use, called *deterministic*, because it allows for error.

In order to move from a simple line through two points to a line through many points, we must find a method for weighting each point on the chart so that we can draw a straight line through the center of all the data points and measure its accuracy. Once this is done we will have a relational equation called a *regression line*.

Method of Least Squares

The most popular technique in statistics for finding a "best fit" is the *method of least squares*. Using this approach we will try to find a line for which the actual data points deviate the least from the line approximation. To do this we calculate the *sum of the squares* of all the deviations and choose the line that results in the smallest sum, where this sum represents the error involved in the selection of a specific line. The mathematical expression for this is

$$S = \sum (y_i - \hat{y}_i)^2 \qquad \text{where all uses of } \sum \text{ implies } \sum_{i=1}^{n} \qquad (1)$$

COMPONENTS OF COMMODITY PRICE MOVEMENT—THE TREND

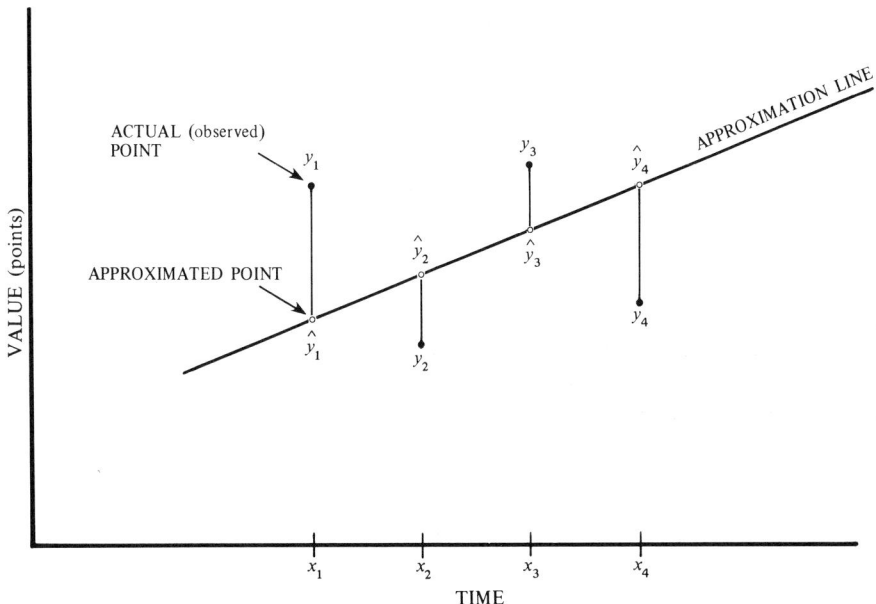

Diagram 3-7 Error deviation for method of least squares.

S is the sum of the squares of the error of each of the data sets and the value of $y_i - \hat{y}_i$ is the difference between the actual value of y_i at x_i and the predicted value ($\hat{y}_i$). Graphically, the individual deviations or errors for four points may look like Diagram 3-7.

Each actual data point is (x_1, y_1), (x_2, y_2), (x_3, y_3), and (x_4, y_4), and the approximated position on the line is $(x_1, \hat{y}_1)$, $(x_2, \hat{y}_2)$, $(x_3, \hat{y}_3)$, and $(x_4, \hat{y}_4)$. The sum of the squares of the errors is

$$S = \sum (y_i - \hat{y}_i)^2 = (y_1 - \hat{y}_1)^2 + (y_2 - \hat{y}_2)^2 + (y_3 - \hat{y}_3)^2 + (y_4 - \hat{y}_4)^2$$

The line that causes S to be the smallest possible will be the best choice for approximating these data points. Since the square of $y_i - \hat{y}_i$ is always positive, this technique magnifies the importance of the error of data points that are far from the line approximation in either direction and reduces the significance of those points for which the approximation is good.

To use the least-squares method for solving our corn-soybean price relationship, we again will be looking for a solution to the equation for a straight line, $y = a + bx$. Without going into the mathematics of the solution, we get the following formulas for a and b through a sophisticated process of differential calculus:[3]

$$b = \frac{N \sum xy - \sum x \sum y}{N \sum x^2 - (\sum x)^2} \qquad (2)$$

$$a = \frac{1}{N} \left(\sum y - b \sum x \right) \qquad (3)$$

[3] Appendix 1 shows another solution to this problem developed from the normal equations for a straight line.

Here N is the number of data points and $\sum$ represents $\sum_{i=1}^{n}$, the sum over N points. For example, using soybean values from 1956–1975 we get the 20-year sum as

$$\sum X = \sum_{i=1}^{20} x_i = x_1 + x_2 + \cdots + x_{19} + x_{20}$$
$$= 2.43 + 2.26 + \cdots + 6.12 + 6.33$$
$$= 62.30$$

In order to solve these equations in an organized manner, we construct a table of corn and soybean values and calculate the unique expressions in formulas (2) and (3) individually with a calculator. We total each column in two places, after 1972 and 1975, in order to compare the impact of the past 3 years on the price relationship. We can now substitute our values into the formulas and solve for a and b.

Table 3.3 Totals for Least-Squares Solution

		Corn	Soybeans			
	i	y_i	x_i	x_i^2	$x_i y_i$	y_i^2
1956	1	1.27	2.43	5.90	3.09	1.61
1957	2	1.19	2.26	5.11	2.69	1.42
1958	3	1.10	2.15	4.62	2.36	1.21
1959	4	1.10	2.07	4.28	2.28	1.21
1960	5	1.05	2.03	4.12	2.13	1.10
1961	6	1.00	2.45	6.00	2.45	1.00
1962	7	0.98	2.36	5.57	2.31	.96
1963	8	1.09	2.44	5.95	2.66	1.19
1964	9	1.12	2.52	6.35	2.82	1.25
1965	10	1.18	2.74	7.51	3.23	1.39
1966	11	1.16	2.98	8.88	3.46	1.34
1967	12	1.24	2.93	8.58	3.63	1.54
1968	13	1.03	2.69	7.24	2.77	1.06
1969	14	1.08	2.63	6.92	2.84	1.17
1970	15	1.15	2.63	6.92	3.02	1.32
1971	16	1.33	3.08	9.49	4.10	1.77
1972	17	1.08	3.24	10.50	3.50	1.17
$\sum$ Sums		19.15	43.63	113.94	49.34	21.71
1973	18	1.57	6.22	38.69	9.76	2.46
1974	19	2.55	6.12	37.45	15.61	6.50
1975	20	3.02	6.33	40.07	19.12	9.12
$\sum$ Sums		26.29	62.30	230.15	93.83	39.79

COMPONENTS OF COMMODITY PRICE MOVEMENT—THE TREND 35

The 1956–1972 relationship:

$$b = \frac{17(49.34) - (43.63)(19.15)}{17(133.94) - (43.63)^2}$$

$$= \frac{838.78 - 835.51}{1936.98 - 1903.58}$$

$$= \frac{3.27}{33.4} = .0979$$

$$a = \frac{19.15 - .0979(43.63)}{17} = \frac{14.88}{17} = .875$$

The equation for the least-squares approximation is

$$y = .875 + .0979x$$

Using even values of x we get

Table 3-4 Least-Squares Relationship for Corn and Soybeans 1956–1972

Soybeans	x	1.00	2.00	3.00	4.00	5.00	6.00
Corn	y	0.97	1.07	1.17	1.27	1.36	1.46

This shows a relatively horizontal approximation for 17 years (1956 through 1972).

The 1956–1975 relationship:

$$b = \frac{20(93.83) - (62.30)(26.29)}{20(230.15) - (62.30)^2}$$

$$= \frac{1876.6 - 1637.867}{4603.0 - 3881.290}$$

$$= \frac{238.722}{721.710} = .331$$

$$a = \frac{26.29 - (.331)(62.30)}{20} = \frac{5.6687}{20} = .283$$

The equation for the least-squares approximation is

$$y = .283 + .331x$$

and selecting values of x and solving for y we get

Table 3-5 Least-Squares Relationship for Corn and Soybeans 1956–1975

Soybeans	x	1.00	2.00	3.00	4.00	5.00	6.00
Corn	y	0.61	0.94	1.28	1.61	1.94	2.27

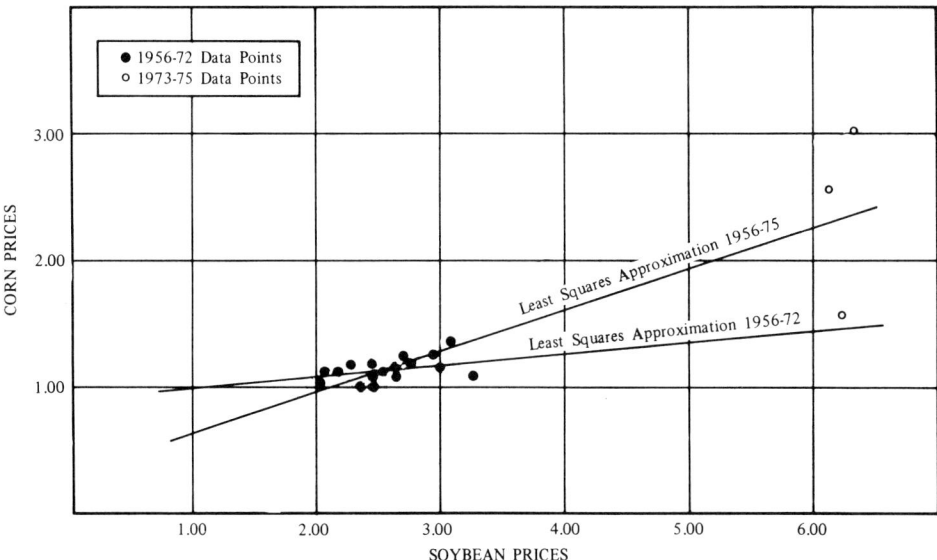

Diagram 3-8 Least-squares approximations.

The results of both linear approximations are shown in Diagram 3-8. The addition of the 3 years 1973–1975 causes the relationship to be noticeably more oblique. It becomes necessary to check the answers in order to determine whether the relationship is changing and the 3 later years cause the approximation to become nonlinear, or whether the earlier data was not reliable due to clustering.

APPLICATION OF LINEAR CORRELATION

Solving the least-squares equation for the "best fit" does not mean that the answer is usable in the practical sense. It may be that the relationship between the scattered points was not linear.

For example, Diagram 3-9 shows four possible distributions of points, where (1) is definitely linear, (2) is somewhat linear and (3) and (4) are nonlinear. Lines drawn through (3) and (4) may be the least-squares solution of smallest error, but this will not solve any forecasting problems.

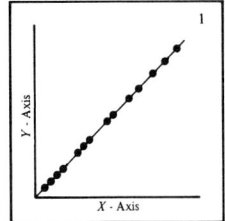 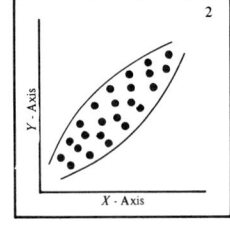 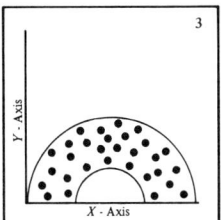 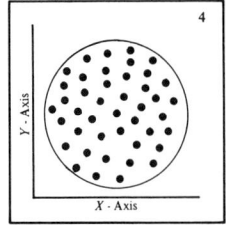

Diagram 3-9 Degrees of correlation. From STATISTICS FOR MANAGEMENT AND ECONOMICS, second edition, by William Mendenhall and James E. Reinmuth. © 1974 by Wadsworth Publishing Company, Belmont, California 94002. Reprinted by permission of the publisher, Duxbury Press.

COMPONENTS OF COMMODITY PRICE MOVEMENT—THE TREND

To determine the linear correlation of a set of data points, we need another formula, namely

$$R = \frac{N \sum xy - \sum x \sum y}{\sqrt{(N \sum x^2 - (\sum x)^2)(N \sum y^2 - (\sum y)^2)}} \quad (4)$$

This is simple to calculate since it requires only one addition sum more than the solution to the least-squares problem itself. The results, R, are interpreted as follows:

$R = 0$ no linear correlation at all (as in Diagram 3-9, 3 and 4)

$R = +1$ a perfect positive linear correlation. The data points are along a straight line going upward to the right (as in Diagram 3-9, 1)

$R = -1$ a perfect negative linear correlation, the line going downward to the right

$+1 > R > 0$ the scattered points become more uniformly distributed about a positive approximation line as the value of R becomes closer to $+1$

$-1 < R < 0$ the scattered points become more uniformly distributed about a negative approximation line as the value of R becomes closer to -1

Applying the formula for correlation to the 1965–1972 results gives

$$R = \frac{17(49.34) - (43.63)(19.15)}{\sqrt{(17(113.94) - (43.63)^2)(17(21.71) - (19.15)^2)}}$$

$$= \frac{3.2655}{\sqrt{(33.4031)(2.3475)}} = \frac{3.2655}{\sqrt{78.4137}} = \frac{3.2655}{8.855}$$

$$= .369$$

And again applying the formula, this time to the 1956–1975 results, gives

$$R = \frac{20(93.83) - (62.30)(26.29)}{\sqrt{(20(230.15) - (62.30)^2)(20(39.79) - (26.29)^2)}}$$

$$= \frac{238.733}{\sqrt{(721.71)(104.6359)}} = \frac{238.733}{\sqrt{75516.78}} = \frac{238.733}{274.8032}$$

$$= .869$$

The results show that the addition of the years 1973 through 1975 caused the relationship to be significantly more linear by elongating the set of data points. The correlation of corn and soybean prices for 20 years is extremely high.

NONLINEAR APPROXIMATIONS FOR TWO VARIABLES

Data points that cannot be related linearly may be approximated using a method of curve fitting. These techniques vary primarily in the rate of increase of the curve. There is a general polynomial formula that can be used to approximate any curve, when enough terms are used:

$$y = a_0 + a_1 x + a_2 x^2 + \cdots + a_n x^n \quad (5)$$

When the first two terms are taken we have the first-order equation for a straight line, $y = a_0 + a_1 x$. Each additional term, $a_i x^i$, alters both the rate of change of the curve and its direction (increasing if $a_i > 0$ and decreasing if $a_i < 0$). The magnitude of each coefficient a_i weights the significance of its corresponding element x_i.

Since Diagram 3-8 shows that the slope of the linear approximation increased in angle as the value of the data points got larger in 1973 through 1975, it is possible that the relationship between corn and soybeans can be approximated using a curve. In the following examples, we will apply the 20 years of average prices to the most popular types of nonlinear methods.

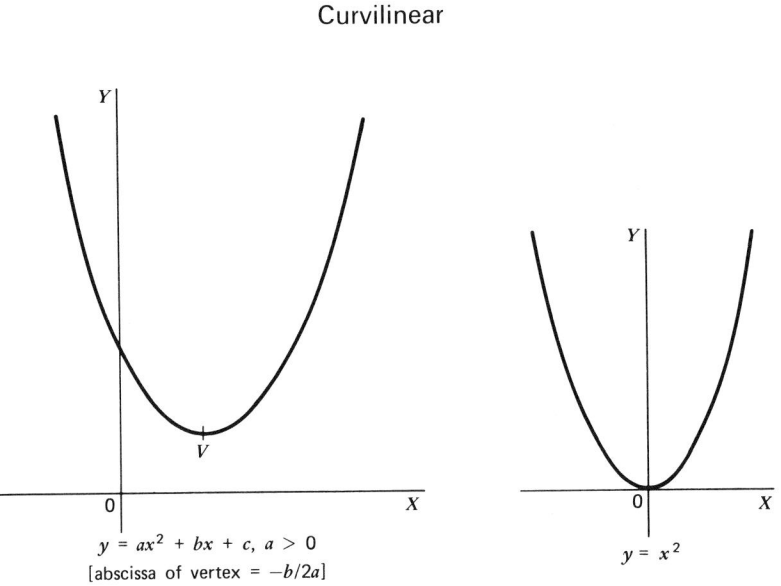

Diagram 3-10 Curvilinear (parabolas). Reprinted with permission from *Standard Mathematical Tables*, 24th ed., pp. 321, 322. Copyright 1976, CRC Press, Inc.

Curvilinear refers to a first-order curve, derived from the first three terms of the general equation (5). Using a, b, and c for a_0, a_1, and a_2 we have the equation

$$y = a + bx + cx^2 \tag{6}$$

which must be solved for coefficients a, b, and c. The answer can be arrived at by solving the simultaneous equations

$$Na + b \sum x + c \sum x^2 = \sum y \tag{7}$$

$$a \sum x + b \sum x^2 + c \sum x^3 = \sum xy \tag{8}$$

$$a \sum x^2 + b \sum x^3 + c \sum x^4 = \sum x^2 y \tag{9}$$

These equations are derived in the same manner as the linear equations in Appendix 1.

We can use the calculations in Table 3-3 for substitution into equations (7), (8), and (9) and add the terms shown in Table 3-6.

COMPONENTS OF COMMODITY PRICE MOVEMENT—THE TREND

Table 3-6 Totals for Curvilinear Solution

y	x	x^2	x^3	x^4	xy	x^2y
1.27	2.43	5.90	14.35	34.87	3.09	7.50
1.19	2.26	5.11	11.54	26.09	2.69	6.08
1.10	2.15	4.62	9.94	21.37	2.36	5.08
1.10	2.07	4.28	8.87	18.36	2.28	4.71
1.05	2.03	4.12	8.36	16.98	2.13	4.33
1.00	2.45	6.00	14.71	36.03	2.45	6.00
.98	2.36	5.57	13.14	31.02	2.31	5.46
1.09	2.44	5.95	14.53	35.44	2.66	6.49
1.12	2.52	6.35	16.00	40.33	2.82	7.11
1.18	2.74	7.51	20.57	56.36	3.23	8.86
1.16	2.98	8.88	26.46	78.86	3.46	10.30
1.24	2.93	8.58	25.15	73.70	3.63	10.64
1.03	2.69	7.24	19.46	52.36	2.77	7.45
1.08	2.63	6.92	18.19	47.84	2.84	7.47
1.15	2.63	6.92	18.19	47.84	3.02	7.95
1.33	3.08	9.49	29.22	89.99	4.10	12.62
1.08	3.24	10.50	34.01	110.20	3.50	11.34
1.57	6.22	38.69	240.64	1496.79	9.76	60.74
2.55	6.12	37.45	229.22	1402.83	15.61	95.51
3.02	6.33	40.07	253.64	1602.52	19.12	121.01
$\sum$ 26.29	62.30	230.15	1026.19	5322.78	93.83	406.65

Replacing the sums in equations (7), (8), and (9) and letting $N = 20$ gives

$$20a + 62.30b + 230.15c = 26.29 \quad (7')$$

$$62.30a + 230.15b + 1026.19c = 93.83 \quad (8')$$

$$230.15a + 1026.19b + 5322.78c = 406.65 \quad (9')$$

This system of simultaneous linear equations can be solved by matrix elimination:

$$\begin{pmatrix} 20.00 & 62.30 & 230.15 & 26.29 \\ 62.30 & 230.15 & 1026.19 & 93.83 \\ 230.15 & 1026.19 & 5322.78 & 406.65 \end{pmatrix}$$

$$\begin{pmatrix} 1 & 3.115 & 11.5075 & 1.3145 \\ 0 & 36.086 & 309.273 & 11.94 \\ 0 & 309.273 & 2674.329 & 104.118 \end{pmatrix}$$

$$\begin{pmatrix} 1 & 0 & -15.1898 & .28409 \\ 0 & 1 & 8.5706 & .33079 \\ 0 & 0 & 23.6899 & 1.81411 \end{pmatrix}$$

$$\begin{pmatrix} 1 & 0 & 0 & 1.4473 \\ 0 & 1 & 0 & -.3255 \\ 0 & 0 & 1 & .0766 \end{pmatrix}$$

The results give $a = 1.4473$, $b = -.3255$, $c = .0766$, and the curvilinear equation

$$y = 1.4473 - .3255x + .0766x^2$$

Using the selected values of x we get

Table 3-7 Curvilinear Relationship for Corn and Soybeans 1956–1975

Soybeans	x	1.00	2.00	3.00	4.00	5.00	6.00
Corn	y	1.20	1.10	1.16	1.37	1.73	2.25

Logarithmic (Power)

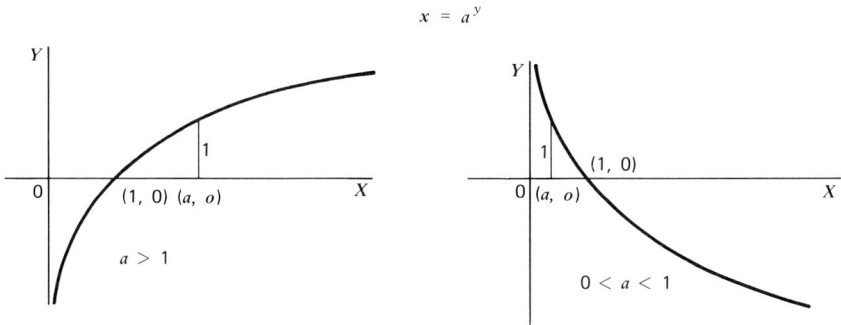

Diagram 3-11 Logarithmic. Reprinted with permission from *Standard Mathematical Tables*, 24th ed., p. 320. Copyright 1976, CRC Press, Inc.

A relationship between two variables x and y of the general form

$$y = ax^b \quad \text{or} \quad \ln y = \ln a + b \ln x$$

is called *logarithmic*. The coefficient a will determine where the curve will cross the y-axis, and b will be the slope, or angle of incline. We can solve for a and b using the equations

$$b = \frac{N \sum \ln x \ln y - \sum \ln x \sum \ln y}{N \sum (\ln x)^2 - (\sum \ln x)^2}$$

$$\ln a = \frac{1}{N} \left(\sum \ln y - b \sum \ln x \right)$$

We follow the same procedure of substitution for solving these equations as in the other methods. First we create a table of elements in the equations; a pocket calculator

COMPONENTS OF COMMODITY PRICE MOVEMENT—THE TREND

Table 3-8   Totals for Logarithmic Solution

	y	x	ln x	ln y	(ln x)²	ln x ln y	x ln y
1	1.27	2.43	.888	.239	.788	.212	.5808
2	1.19	2.26	.815	.174	.665	.142	.3931
3	1.10	2.15	.765	.095	.586	.073	.2049
4	1.10	2.07	.728	.095	.529	.069	.1973
5	1.05	2.03	.708	.049	.501	.035	.0990
6	1.00	2.45	.896	.000	.803	.000	.0000
7	.98	2.36	.859	−.020	.737	−.017	−.0477
8	1.09	2.44	.892	.086	.796	.077	.2103
9	1.12	2.52	.924	.113	.854	.105	.2856
10	1.18	2.74	1.008	.166	1.016	.167	.4535
11	1.16	2.98	1.092	.148	1.192	.162	.4423
12	1.24	2.93	1.075	.215	1.156	.231	.6303
13	1.03	2.69	.990	.030	.979	.029	.0795
14	1.08	2.63	.967	.077	.935	.074	.2024
15	1.15	2.63	.967	.140	.935	.135	.3676
16	1.33	3.08	1.125	.285	1.265	.321	.8784
17	1.08	3.24	1.176	.077	1.382	.090	.2494
18	1.57	6.22	1.828	.451	3.341	.824	2.8057
19	2.55	6.12	1.812	.936	3.282	1.696	5.7289
20	3.02	6.33	1.845	1.105	3.405	2.040	6.9963
$\sum$	26.29	62.30	21.3588	4.4616	25.148	6.4652	20.7575

with scientific functions will make this simple.

$$b = \frac{(21.359)(4.4616) - 20(6.4652)}{(21.359)^2 - 20(25.148)}$$

$$= \frac{95.295 - 129.304}{456.207 - 502.96} = \frac{-34.009}{-46.753}$$

$$= .7274$$

$$\ln a = \frac{4.4616 - (.7274)(21.359)}{20}$$

$$= \frac{4.4616 - 15.5365}{20} = \frac{-11.0749}{20}$$

$$= -.5537$$

$$a = .5748$$

The resulting equation for the logarithmic approximation is

$$y = .5748 x^{.7274}$$

To plot the results, we select values for x as before, and apply natural logarithms again to the preceding equation:

$$\ln y = \ln(.5748) + .7274 \ln x \quad \text{where } \ln(.5748) = -.5537$$

Table 3-9 Logarithmic Relationship for Corn and Soybeans 1956–1975

Soybeans	x	1.00	2.00	3.00	4.00	5.00	6.00
Corn	y	.57	.95	1.28	1.58	1.85	2.12

Exponential

$$y = ae^{bx}$$

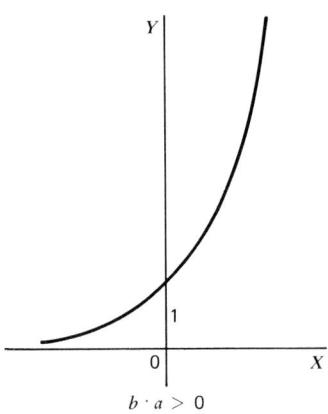

$b \cdot a > 0$

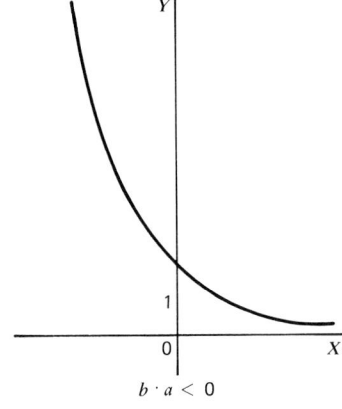

$b \cdot a < 0$

Diagram 3-12 Exponential. Reprinted with permission from *Standard Mathematical Tables*, 24th ed., p. 316. Copyright 1976, CRC Press, Inc.

An exponential relationship between two variables is expressed as

$$y = ae^{bx} \quad \text{or} \quad \ln y = \ln a + bx$$

where a is the point at which the curve crosses the y axis and b is the slope. To find a and b we solve the equations

$$b = \frac{\sum x \sum \ln y - N \sum x \ln y}{(\sum x)^2 - N \sum x^2}$$

$$\ln a = \frac{1}{N} \left(\sum \ln y - b \sum x \right)$$

COMPONENTS OF COMMODITY PRICE MOVEMENT—THE TREND

We can apply the totals from both Tables 3-3 and 3-8 and substitute into the equations

$$b = \frac{(62.30)(4.4616) - 20(20.7575)}{(62.30)^2 - 20(230.15)}$$

$$= \frac{277.9577 - 415.15}{3881.29 - 4603} = \frac{-137.1923}{-721.71}$$

$$= .19009$$

$$\ln a = \tfrac{1}{20}(4.4616 - (.19009)(62.30))$$
$$= \tfrac{1}{20}(4.454 - 11.8426)$$
$$= -.36905$$
$$a = .69139$$

The equation for the exponential approximation is

$$y = .69139 e^{.19009x}$$

To enter values of x and solve for y, we use natural logarithms:

$$\ln y = \ln(.69139) + .19009x$$
$$= -.36905 + .19009x$$

Table 3-10 Exponential Relationship for Corn and Soybeans 1956–1975

Soybeans	x	1.00	2.00	3.00	4.00	5.00	6.00
Corn	y	.84	1.01	1.22	1.48	1.79	2.16

Evaluation of Two-Variable Techniques

Of the three curve-fitting techniques, the curvilinear and exponential results are very similar, both curving upward and passing through the main cluster of data points at about the same incline. The exponential approximation curves downward after all three pass through the main cluster of data points at about the same point as the other approximations. At the highest values the three nonlinear techniques all have values lower than the linear value. For the smallest values of x the linear is close to the bottom. Because of the lack of data in the range between $4.00 and $6.00, and below $2.00, in soybeans, the curves show the greater variance from one another there.

To objectively evaluate whether any of the nonlinear methods are a better fit than the linear approximation, we perform the tedious task of computing the sums of the squares of the errors, presented in Table 3-11. The sums have been totaled for the

Table 3-11 Error Analysis

	Soybeans	Corn	Linear		Curvilinear		Logarithmic		Exponential	
	x	y	$\hat{y}$	$(y-\hat{y})^2$	$\hat{y}$	$(y-\hat{y})^2$	$\hat{y}$	$(y-\hat{y})^2$	$\hat{y}$	$(y-\hat{y})^2$
1	2.43	1.27	1.09	.03337	1.11	.02617	1.10	.03010	1.10	.02980
2	2.26	1.19	1.03	.02526	1.10	.00765	1.04	.02246	1.06	.01150
3	2.15	1.10	.99	.01110	1.10	.00000	1.00	.00940	1.04	.00355
4	2.07	1.10	.97	.01738	1.10	.00000	.98	.01543	1.02	.00566
5	2.03	1.05	.95	.00904	1.10	.00268	.96	.00774	1.02	.00109
6	2.45	1.00	1.09	.00883	1.11	.01192	1.10	.01062	1.10	.01030
7	2.36	.98	1.06	.00708	1.11	.01571	1.07	.00873	1.08	.01057
8	2.44	1.09	1.09	.00000	1.11	.00035	1.10	.00010	1.10	.00009
9	2.52	1.12	1.12	.00001	1.11	.00005	1.13	.00004	1.12	.00001
10	2.74	1.18	1.19	.00010	1.13	.00249	1.20	.00027	1.16	.00026
11	2.98	1.16	1.27	.01196	1.16	.00001	1.27	.01253	1.22	.00339
12	2.93	1.24	1.25	.00017	1.15	.00797	1.26	.00027	1.21	.00111
13	2.69	1.03	1.17	.02056	1.13	.00913	1.18	.02269	1.15	.01510
14	2.63	1.08	1.15	.00541	1.12	.00165	1.16	.00631	1.14	.00358
15	2.63	1.15	1.15	.00001	1.12	.00086	1.16	.00013	1.14	.00010
16	3.08	1.33	1.30	.00076	1.17	.02530	1.30	.00074	1.24	.00781
17	3.24	1.08	1.36	.07587	1.20	.01352	1.35	.07383	1.27	.04000
18	6.22	1.57	2.34	.59571	2.39	.66447	2.17	.36277	2.26	.46970
19	6.12	2.55	2.31	.05822	2.32	.05144	2.15	.16254	2.21	.11360
20	6.33	3.02	2.38	.41187	2.46	.31916	2.20	.67211	2.30	.51410
			1956–1972	.22691		.12546		.22139		.14392
			1973–1975	1.06580		1.03507		1.19742		1.09740
			1956–1975	1.29271		1.16053		1.41881		1.24132

Linear $y = .283 + .331x$
Curvilinear $y = 1.447 - .3255x + .07658x^2$
Logarithmic $y = .5748x^{.7274}$
Exponential $y = .691e^{.19x}$ or $\ln y = \ln .691 + .19x$

separate and combined periods of 1956–1972 and 1973–1975. The results show that the curvilinear approximation is best for all periods. The exponential approximation is a close second place for the first 17 years, while the logarithmic (power) approximation is noticeably the worst for the full 20 years.[4]

Direct Relationships

Many products are strongly dependent on the prices of other commodities in either the cost of production or as substitute products. These relationships are directly applicable to the regression methods just discussed.

---

[4] Appendix 2 contains a computer regression program and programmable-calculator solutions for a least-squares approximation.

COMPONENTS OF COMMODITY PRICE MOVEMENT—THE TREND

Basic Product	Dependent	Reason
All crops	All crops	Relative income for farmers
Grain	Other grains	Protein substitution for feed
Hogs	Corn	Feed, cost of production
Cattle	Grains	Feed, cost of production
Silver	Silver coins	Substitute product if melted
Sugar	Corn	Corn sweetener substitution
Bellies	Hogs	Product dependence
Hogs	Cattle	Food substitutes
Price	Volatility	Risk analysis

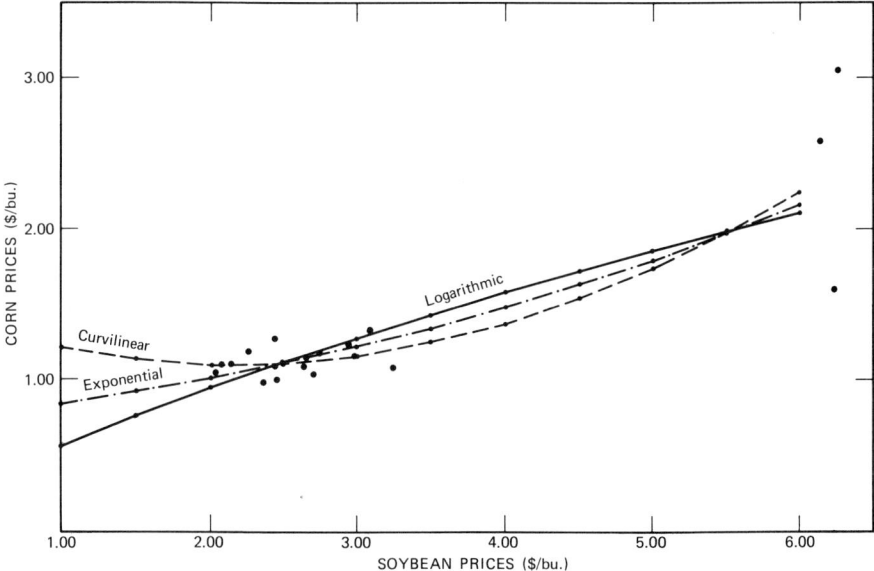

Diagram 3-13   Results of nonlinear approximations.

Other interesting relationships that can be analyzed are production-storage-consumption-price combinations. Knowing the mathematical relationships between any of these elements can play an important role in your trading plan.

MULTIVARIATE APPROXIMATIONS

Although there is a risk of treading very close to the fringes of econometrics, we should look at relationships between more than two variables; but for our purposes, we will try to find the relationship between the price, production, and distribution of soybeans on an annual basis. The results of this examination will determine whether or not other factors are significant in determination of soybean prices. Since we know already that the demand for soybeans and products is complex, we should not expect a high correlation between the data, but we have no way of knowing how much impact these other factors have on the prices over a long term.

We approach the problem using the method of least squares that we employed for a simple linear regression. We will define our new equation as

$$y = a + bx_1 + cx_2$$

where y is the resulting price
 x_1 is the total production (supply)
 x_2 is the total distribution (demand)
 a, b, c are constants to be calculated

As in the linear approximation, the solution to this problem will be chosen by minimizing the sum of the squares of the errors at each point:

$$S = \sum_{i=1}^{n} (y_i - \hat{y}_i)^2$$

Substituting for $\hat{y}$ from the previous equation,

$$S = \sum_{i=1}^{n} (y_i - (a + bx_1 + cx_2))^2$$

Table 3-12 Totals for Multivariate Solution

		Soybeans						
			Supply	Demand					
		y	x_1	x_2	x_1^2	x_2^2	$x_1 x_2$	$x_1 y$	$x_2 y$
			(Bil)		(Bil)			(Mil)	
1964	1	2.67	.700	.677	.490	.458	.474	1.869	1.808
1965	2	2.88	.845	.738	.714	.545	.624	2.434	2.125
1966	3	2.98	.928	.839	.861	.704	.779	2.765	2.500
1967	4	2.93	.976	.874	.953	.764	.853	2.860	2.561
1968	5	2.69	1.107	.900	1.225	.810	.996	2.978	2.421
1969	6	2.63	1.133	.946	1.284	.895	1.072	2.980	2.488
1970	7	2.63	1.127	1.230	1.270	1.513	1.386	2.964	3.235
1971	8	3.08	1.176	1.258	1.383	1.583	1.479	3.622	3.875
1972	9	3.24	1.271	1.202	1.615	1.445	1.528	4.118	3.894
1973	10	6.22	1.547	1.283	2.393	1.646	1.985	9.622	7.980
1974	11	6.12	1.215	1.435	1.476	2.059	1.744	7.436	8.782
1975	12	6.33	1.521	1.200	2.313	1.440	1.825	9.628	7.596
$\sum$		44.40	13.546	12.582	15.977	13.862	14.745	53.276	49.265

COMPONENTS OF COMMODITY PRICE MOVEMENT—THE TREND

The solution to the multivariate problem of two independent variables x_1 and x_2 requires the following three least-squares equations:

$$an + b\sum x_1 + c\sum x_2 = \sum y$$
$$a\sum x_1 + b\sum x_1^2 + c\sum x_1 x_2 = \sum x_1 y$$
$$a\sum x_2 + b\sum x_1 x_2 + c\sum x_2^2 = \sum x_2 y$$

where every use of $\sum$ implies $\sum_{i=1}^{n}$.

The procedure for solving the three simultaneous equations is the same as the curvilinear method of coefficient elimination. The sums are calculated in Table 3-12, then substituted into the last three equations:

$$12.00a + 13.546b + 12.582c = 44.4$$
$$13.55a + 15.980b + 14.75c = 53.28$$
$$12.58a + 14.75b + 13.86c = 49.264$$

The coefficient matrix solution is

$$\begin{pmatrix} 12.00 & 13.55 & 12.58 & 44.40 \\ 13.55 & 15.98 & 14.74 & 53.28 \\ 12.58 & 14.74 & 13.86 & 49.26 \end{pmatrix}$$

$$\begin{pmatrix} 1 & 1.129 & 1.048 & 3.700 \\ 0 & .6798 & .5451 & 3.145 \\ 0 & .5451 & .6720 & 2.714 \end{pmatrix}$$

$$\begin{pmatrix} 1 & 0 & .1429 & -1.5240 \\ 0 & 1 & .8018 & 4.6264 \\ 0 & 0 & .2349 & .1922 \end{pmatrix}$$

$$\begin{pmatrix} 1 & 0 & 0 & -1.641 \\ 0 & 1 & 0 & 3.9703 \\ 0 & 0 & 1 & .8183 \end{pmatrix}$$

The results show $a = -1.641$, $b = 3.9703$, and $c = .8183$, so that the multiple linear approximation of the price is

$$\hat{y} = -1.641 + 3.9703x_1 + .8183x_2$$

where x_1 is the production in billions of bushels and x_2 demand in billions of bushels. The coefficient of supply is the principal factor in the determination of price. Had either coefficient of x_1 or x_2 been small, it would have indicated a lack of significance. The selection of which data to try when determining price components is not obvious and may result in a useless answer. In our example we chose supply-and-demand figures to determine price, but perhaps supply and inflation or demand and inflation would have been better. To find out which sets of data are best, each combination would have to be tested and the results compared.

Generalized Multivariate

In general, we can express the relationship between n independent variables as

$$y = a_0 + a_1 x_1 + a_2 x_2 + \cdots + a_n x_n$$

The solution to this equation is an extension of the problems in two variables previously presented. In this case, we get $n + 1$ equations in $n + 1$ variables by summing the $n + 1$ equations developed from the general equation by multiplying the second by x_1, the third by x_2, and so on:

$$a_0 n + a_1 \sum x_1 + a_2 \sum x_2 + \cdots + a_n \sum x_n = \sum y$$
$$a_0 \sum x_1 + a_1 \sum x_1^2 + a_2 \sum x_1 x_2 + \cdots + a_n \sum x_1 x_n = \sum x_1 y$$
$$a_0 \sum x_2 + a_1 \sum x_1 x_2 + a_2 \sum x_2^2 + \cdots + a_n \sum x_2 x_n = \sum x_2 y$$
$$\vdots$$
$$a_0 \sum x_n + a_1 \sum x_1 x_n + a_2 \sum x_2 x_n + \cdots + a_n \sum x_n^2 = \sum x_n y$$

The solution to this system of equations can be calculated on most computers using a standard program available for this purpose (see Appendix 2). Some words of caution for those with only a little experience in regression analysis: the calculated prediction (model) is most accurate within the range of the data points; as you progress outside the bounds of the sample data, the predictive qualities of the regression formula decrease with distance.

It is also possible to try as many dependent variables (x_i) as are needed to make it likely that you will succeed in finding a good total correlation. The predictive quality of this solution will depend on the relevance of the independent variables. It is best to start with the obvious components of a time series: inflation, using the Wholesale Price Index or Consumers Price Index; the industrial cycle, often represented by the accumulation of stocks or overall production; and a seasonal variation measured as an index of adjustment. Measuring the error of the estimates will help determine whether additional factors are necessary.

Least-Squares Sinusoidal

A special case of the multiple linear predictor occurs when periodic peaks can be observed in the sample data taken at specific time intervals (time-series). These peaks and valleys suggest that the time-series may have a cyclic pattern. One of the more well-known uses of cyclic analysis was performed by J. M. Hurst in *The Profit Magic of Stock Transaction Timing*, in which there is an interesting example of Fourier analysis applied to the Dow Jones Industrial Averages.

The equation for the approximation of a periodic movement is

$$y_t = a_0 + a_1 t + a_2 \cos \frac{2\pi t}{P} + a_3 \sin \frac{2\pi t}{P} + a_4 t \cos \frac{2\pi t}{P} + a_5 t \sin \frac{2\pi t}{P}$$

which is a special case of the generalized multivariate approximation

$$y = a_0 + a_1 x_1 + a_2 x_2 + a_3 x_3 + a_4 x_4 + a_5 x_5$$

where P is the number of data points in each cycle

$x_1 = t$, the incremental time element
$x_2 = \cos(2\pi t/P)$, a cyclic element
$x_3 = \sin(2\pi t/P)$, a cyclic element
$x_4 = t \cos(2\pi t/P)$, an amplitude-variation element
$x_5 = t \sin(2\pi t/P)$, an amplitude-variation element

The term $a_1 t$ will allow for the linear tendencies of the sequence. You will notice that the term 2π refers to an entire cycle and $2\pi t/P$ designates a section $(1/P)$ of a specific cycle t; this in turn adds weight to either the sin or cos functions at different points within a cycle.

The solution is calculated in the tabular manner of the other methods, using simultaneous linear equations derived in the same way as the generalized multivariate equation, substituting from the table of sums and solving the coefficient matrix for $a_0, \ldots, a_5$. A complete discussion of curve fitting using trigonomometric functions appears in Chapter 8.

MARKOV CHAINS[5]

Most of the probability functions that we deal with are based on sequentially independent action, where the results of the current event is not related to any past event. Under ideal conditions a coin coming up heads or tails is not connected with any prior toss. A Markov process or chain is a more complex probability function that considers the dependence of one event on the next. Although it appears theoretical, it is used in a great number of business applications to solve problems of interaction and has been hinted to be the key to the solution of stock-price forecasting. Examples of sequentially dependent events are more descriptive of the nature of the process. Consider the following example:

> The chances of an Olympic swimmer breaking the world record can be initially calculated from his timing in trial events. Once the race starts, if he falls behind at the beginning, his chances decrease; the longer he stays ahead of the world record the greater his chances of success. At each point in the race his performance relative to his goal is significant in judging potential success.

The weather may be difficult to predict without a meteorological service, but the possibility of a clear, cloudy, or rainy day tomorrow might be related to today.

The different combinations of dependent possibilities can be given by a switching matrix. In our weather prediction, a clear day has a 70% chance of being followed by another clear day, a 25% chance of a cloudy day, and only a 5% chance of rain. Each possibility today is shown on the left and its probability of changing tomorrow is indicated across the top. Each row totals 1.00, accounting for all weather combinations.

---

[5] A full mathematical treatment of Markov chains can be found in Kemeny (1976).

Table 3-13 Switching Matrix

		Tomorrow		
		Clear	Cloudy	Rainy
Today	Clear	.70	.25	.05
	Cloudy	.20	.60	.20
	Rainy	.20	.40	.40

The relationship between these events can be shown as a network to give you an idea of the continuity of the process.

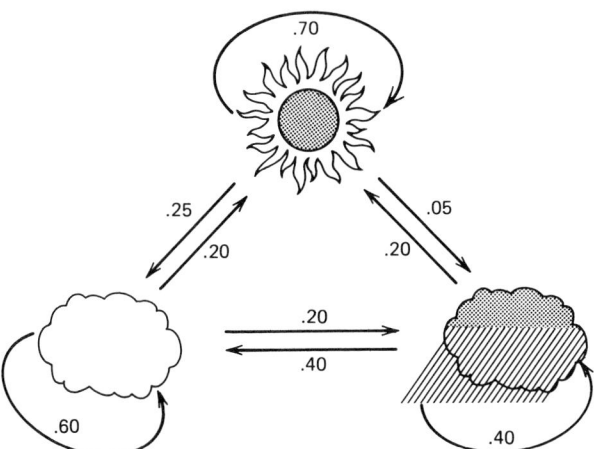

Diagram 3-14 Probability network.

The Markov process will help you reduce intricate relationships to a simpler form. But first consider a simpler two-state process. Using the commodities markets as an example, what is the probability of an up or down day following an up day or following a down day? It would be easy to count some contracts and arrive at an historic probability for these two situations. Let's say that following an up day there was a 70% chance of another up day and following a down day there was a 55% chance of an up day. We would like to know how many up days and down days to expect and what the probability is of any day being up.

We start with either an up or down day and look at the probability of the next day being up or down. Since we have the choice of assigning the original day as up or down, it is an exception to the general rule and therefore the first day is given the weight of 50%. The probability of the following day (second day) being up or down is the sum of the joint probabilities:

$$P(\text{UP})_2 = (.50 \times .70) + (.50 \times .55)$$
$$= .625$$

The probability of the second day being up is 62.5%. Continuing along the same line we use the probability of an up day as .625 and the down as .375 and calculate the third day,

$$P(UP)_3 = (.625 \times .70) + (.375 \times .55)$$
$$= .64375$$

and the fourth day,

$$P(UP)_4 = (.64375 \times .70) + (.35625 \times .55)$$
$$= .64656$$

which can now be seen to be converging. To generalize the probability of an up day we look at what happens on the ith day:

$$P(UP)_{i+1} = (P(UP)_i \times .70) + ((1 - P(UP)_i) \times .55)$$

But because the probability is converging we can use the relationship

$$P(UP)_{i+1} = P(UP)_i$$

and solve the simple equation

$$P(UP)_i = (P(UP)_i \times .70) + (.55 - P(UP)_i \times .55)$$

until we get

$$P(UP)_i = .64705$$

This is the probability of any day being up.

Going back to predicting the weather, we see a more involved case of multiple situations converging. By approaching the problem in the same manner as the two-state process we assign a 1/3 probability to each situation for the first day and predict the second day:

$$P(CLEAR)_2 = (.333 \times .70) + (.333 \times .20) + (.333 \times .20)$$
$$= .3663$$

$$P(CLOUDY)_2 = (.333 \times .25) + (.333 \times .60) + (.333 \times .40)$$
$$= .41625$$

$$P(RAINY)_2 = (.333 \times .05) + (.333 \times .20) + (.333 \times .40)$$
$$= .21645$$

Then using the second day results we can get the third day:

$$P(CLEAR)_3 = (.3663 \times .70) + (.41625 \times .20) + (.21645 \times .20)$$
$$= .38295$$

$$P(CLOUDY)_3 = (.3663 \times .25) + (.41625 \times .60) + (.21645 \times .40)$$
$$= .42791$$

$$P(RAINY)_3 = (.3663 \times .05) + (.41625 \times .20) + (.21645 \times .40)$$
$$= .18815$$

The general form for solving these three equations is

$$P(CLEAR)_{i+1} = (P(CLEAR)_i \times .70) + (P(CLOUDY)_i \times .20) + (P(RAINY)_i \times .20)$$

$$P(CLOUDY)_{i+1} = (P(CLEAR)_i \times .25) + (P(CLOUDY)_i \times .60) + (P(RAINY)_i \times .40)$$

$$P(RAINY)_{i+1} = (P(CLEAR)_i \times .05) + (P(CLOUDY)_i \times .20) + (P(RAINY)_i \times .40$$

where each $i + 1$ element can be set equal to the corresponding ith values; we then have three equations and three unknowns, which can be solved directly or by the matrix method of simultaneous linear equations as shown in the appendix. In solving this yourself it will be necessary to use the additional relationship

$$P(CLEAR)_i + P(CLOUDY)_i + P(RAINY)_i = 1.00$$

The results are

$$P(CLEAR) = .400$$

$$P(CLOUDY) = .425$$

$$P(RAINY) = .175$$

You might want to try this yourself. If you have any problems the matrix solution can be found in Appendix 3, Part 2.

CHAPTER 4
Commodity-Trending Model

The linear and nonlinear techniques used for correlation in the previous sections have used data recorded at equal time intervals, but have not taken advantage of the properties of a time-series. The data sets were evaluated with respect to the relative dependence of one value on one or more independent variables. The predictive qualities of these methods are best within the area bounded by existing data and decrease sharply as we extrapolate values outside the previous realm of occurrences. The techniques most commonly used for evaluating the direction or tendency of commodity prices are classified as *autoregressive* forecasting. Unlike the other models, which are often used for business applications involving growth, we will only concern ourselves with evaluating the current direction of prices. This analysis will result in one of three conclusions: prices are moving in an upward, downward, or sideways direction. Later we will make relative distinctions between these possibilities, form rules of action, and develop complex strategies of anticipation.

In an autoregressive model, we use one or more of the previous day's prices (we will use "price" interchangeably with "data" in this discussion) to determine the next sequential price. If t represents today's price, $t-1$ yesterday's and so on, then tomorrow's price will be

$$P_{t+1} = a_0 + a_1 P_t + a_2 P_{t-1} + \cdots + a_t P_1 + \varepsilon$$

where each price is given a corresponding weighting a_i and combined to give the resultant price for tomorrow $P_{t+1} \pm \varepsilon$ (ε represents an error factor). The simplest example is the use of yesterday's price alone to generate tomorrow's price:

$$P_{t+1} = a_0 + a_1 P_t + \varepsilon$$

The autoregressive model does not have to be linear; each prior day can have a nonlinear predictive quality. Thus P_t could be represented by a curvilinear expression, P_{t-1} by an exponential or logarithmic formula and so on. All of these expressions would then be combined to form an autoregressive forecasting model for P_{t+1}. In going from the simple to the complex, it is natural to want to know which of these choices will perform best. The answer can only be found by experimentation and application to a specific problem. Various methods must be attempted and applied to actual data in a real-time or extrapolated situation to determine the predictive quality of any model.

One of the basic autoregressive models is the application of the least-squares technique on sequential prices. This method allows us to use a simple error analysis to determine its predictive qualities. Assume we have some number of sequential prices for any commodity and that we would like to know how many prior days is optimum for predicting the next day's price. We then will get our answer by looking at the average error in our predictions. If we increase the number of days in our calculation and the predictive error decreases, we are on the right track; if the error stops decreasing, we have reached the limit of our accuracy. As an example we will start by using only one prior day,

$$P_{t+1} = a_0 + a_1 P_t$$
$$P_t = a_0 + a_1 P_{t-1}$$
$$P_{t-1} = a_0 + a_1 P_{t-2}$$
$$\vdots$$
$$P_2 = a_0 + a_1 P_1$$

and work our way up to a large number of days:

$$P_{t+1} = a_0 + a_1 P_t + a_2 P_{t-1} + \cdots + a_n P_{t-n+1}$$
$$P_t = a_0 + a_1 P_{t-1} + a_2 P_{t-2} + \cdots + a_n P_{t-n}$$
$$P_{t-1} = a_0 + a_1 P_{t-2} + a_2 P_{t-3} + \cdots + a_n P_{t-n-1}$$

In the last case it takes n days of prior prices to generate each new prediction. In all cases, we can develop $n + 2$ equations to solve the $n + 1$ coefficients $a_0, a_1, \ldots, a_n$ using matrix elimination (see Appendix 3). As a result we get predicted prices $\hat{P}_t$ for each actual price P_t. We will use the notation $\hat{P}(n)_t$ to mean the predicted price for day t using an n-day linear regression; therefore, $\hat{P}(3)_{25} = 58.00$ means that the predicted value of P on the 25th day was 58.00 using a 3-day linear regression analysis (a straight-line fit of the 3 prior days). The error occurring from each prediction can be defined as

$$\hat{E}(n)_t = P_t - \hat{P}(n)_t$$

the difference between the actual and predicted values for that day using an n-day linear regression. As an example of error analysis we selected the May 77 Copper contract from November 1, 1976, through November 30, 1976, a period of 20 trading days showing a slight upward move and a slight downward move, with some intermediate changes of direction.

Table 4-1a shows the actual predictions using linear regressions with from two through seven prior prices and prediction 1 day forward. Table 4-1b shows the relative error in these predictions and a statistical analysis of the errors. The *mean* is a simple arithmetic average of all the points, where $+.10$ and $-.10$ would result in an average of .00. The mean can show that the errors were equally balanced on both sides of the predicted price, but does not tell you anything of the distribution about the line.

COMMODITY-TRENDING MODEL

Table 4-1a Analysis of Predictive Error, May 77 Copper, November 1, 1976 through November 30, 1976

Date	Sequence t	Price P_t	Price predictions for $P(n)$-day linear regression					
			$\hat{P}(2)_t$	$\hat{P}(3)_t$	$\hat{P}(4)_t$	$\hat{P}(5)_t$	$\hat{P}(6)_t$	$\hat{P}(7)_t$
10-21	1	60.30						
10-22	2	59.30						
10-25	3	58.70						
10-26	4	57.80						
10-27	5	59.80						
10-28	6	58.20						
10-29	7	58.40						
11-01	8	58.90	58.60	57.40	58.60	58.52	58.30	57.95
11-03	9	59.10	59.40	59.20	58.20	58.86	58.75	58.53
11-04	10	61.00	59.30	59.50	59.45	58.67	59.10	58.98
11-05	11	62.10	61.90	61.77	61.35	60.15	60.15	60.30
11-08	12	62.00	63.20	63.73	63.15	62.75	62.37	61.53
11-09	13	62.50	61.90	62.70	63.50	63.38	63.20	62.94
11-10	14	63.50	63.00	62.60	63.00	63.68	63.71	63.64
11-11	15	61.30	64.50	64.16	63.70	63.84	64.34	64.38
11-12	16	61.70	60.10	61.23	62.05	62.25	62.69	63.36
11-15	17	62.00	62.10	60.36	61.10	61.66	61.87	62.30
11-16	18	62.20	62.30	62.37	61.10	61.36	61.71	61.86
11-17	19	61.70	62.40	62.47	62.55	61.57	61.64	61.85
11-18	20	61.50	61.20	61.67	61.95	62.17	61.47	61.51
11-19	21	62.40	61.30	61.10	61.35	61.61	61.85	61.31
11-22	22	61.40	63.30	62.57	62.05	61.99	62.07	62.20
11-23	23	59.90	60.40	61.67	61.75	61.57	61.61	61.73
11-24	24	59.80	58.40	58.73	59.85	60.29	60.37	60.58
11-26	25	59.10	59.70	58.76	58.85	59.22	59.59	59.71
11.29	26	59.50	58.40	58.85	58.30	58.06	58.55	58.87
11-30	27	59.10	59.90	59.17	59.10	58.56	58.20	58.48

Diagrams 4-1a and b show two situations where the mean would be zero and yet the linear regression would be a poor fit. In both cases the correlation coefficient would be zero.

Diagram 4-1a shows the fitted line as a perpendicular bisector of the actual price line, giving offsetting positive and negative errors, resulting in a net value of zero and a mean of zero. Diagram 4-1b shows a symmetric curve fit by a horizontal line cutting the top and bottom parts into equal sections, also resulting in a mean value of zero. The mean alone is not a sufficient tool for determining a good line fit.

The standard deviation and coefficient of variance are both measurements of the distribution of points about the approximation line. As discussed in Chapter 2, the standard deviation measures the occurrence of points near the predictions, the smaller the value the closer being the grouping. The variance is a tool for comparing deviations; the smaller the variance the better the calculation of standard deviation. The copper error analysis shows all three values are smallest for $\hat{E}(4)_t$, the 4-day

Table 4-1b Analysis of Predictive Error, May 77 Copper, November 1, 1976 through November 30, 1976

Date	Sequence t	Price P_t	Predictive error for $E(n)_t$-point linear regression					
			$\hat{E}(2)_t$	$\hat{E}(3)_t$	$\hat{E}(4)_t$	$\hat{E}(5)_t$	$\hat{E}(6)_t$	$\hat{E}(7)_t$
10-21	1	60.30						
10-22	2	59.30						
10-25	3	58.70						
10-26	4	57.80						
10-27	5	59.80						
10-28	6	58.20						
10-29	7	58.40						
11-01	8	58.90	−.30	−1.50	−.30	−.38	−.60	−.95
11-03	9	59.10	.30	.10	−.90	−.24	−.35	−.57
11-04	10	61.00	−1.70	−1.50	−1.55	−2.33	−1.90	−2.02
11-05	11	62.10	−.20	−.33	−.75	−1.95	−1.95	−1.80
11-08	12	62.00	1.20	1.73	1.15	.75	.37	−.47
11-09	13	62.50	−.60	.20	1.00	.88	.70	.44
11-10	14	63.50	−.50	−.90	−.50	.18	.21	.14
11-11	15	61.30	3.20	2.86	2.40	2.54	3.04	3.08
11-12	16	61.70	−1.60	−.47	.35	.55	.99	1.66
11-15	17	62.00	.10	−1.64	−.90	−.34	−.13	.30
11-16	18	62.20	.10	.17	−1.10	−.84	−.49	−.34
11-17	19	61.70	.70	.77	.85	−.13	−.06	.15
11-18	20	61.50	−.30	.17	.45	.67	−.03	.01
11-19	21	62.40	−1.10	−1.30	−1.05	−.79	−.65	−1.09
11-22	22	61.40	1.90	1.17	.65	.59	.67	.80
11-23	23	59.90	.50	1.77	1.85	1.67	1.71	1.83
11-24	24	59.80	−1.40	−1.07	.05	.49	.57	.78
11-26	25	59.10	.60	−.34	−.25	.12	.49	.61
11-29	26	59.50	−1.10	−.70	−1.20	−1.44	−.95	−.63
11-30	27	59.10	.80	.07	.00	−.54	−.90	−.62
σ (Standard deviation)			1.209	1.217	1.069	1.151	1.149	1.220
M (Mean)			.030	−.037	.012	−.027	.037	.065
V (Variation)			1.389	1.406	1.086	1.260	1.255	1.415

linear regression. Because of the short test period of 20 days, we would expect a good fit using a small number of days. As you choose larger values, your approximation will become less sensitive.

Determination of the best predictive model using error analysis can be applied to any of the techniques discussed. Your results must be coordinated with the solution of the problem of how to use the results effectively. A system that has been chosen for its predictive quality must look at how those predicted results varied from the subsequent actual results for one or more days of prediction. Having calculated your straight-line equation using 4 days or n days (or any other nonlinear equation), predict the value for the next day $t + 1$, then $t + 2$, $t + 3$, and so on. You might find your ability to predict two or three days in advance important in devising a trading program.

COMMODITY-TRENDING MODEL

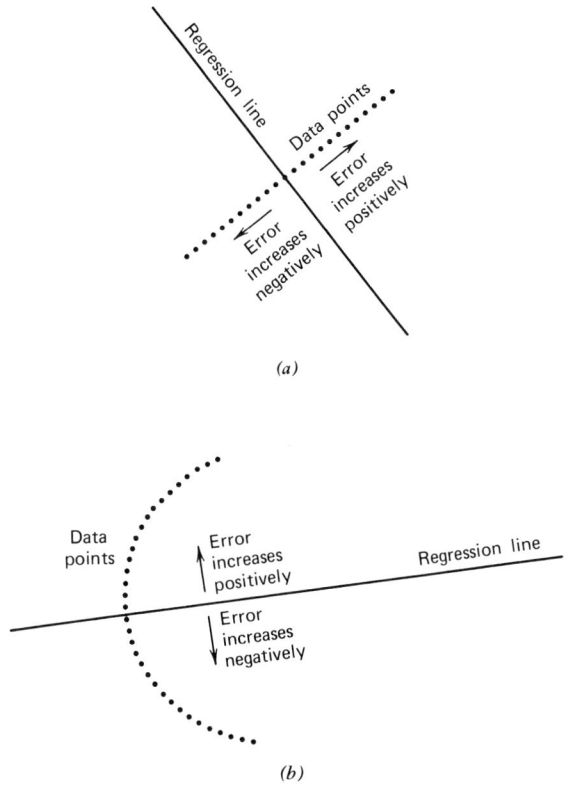

Diagram 4-1 Examples of the mean = 0 with no correlation.

Your predictions will be easier to calculate than to apply to trading. The situations that occur once your calculation is complete are:

1. The prediction and the actual price are very close.
2. The prediction is within one standard deviation from the actual price.
3. The prediction is greater than one standard deviation from the actual price.

In the first case, your current trend is continuing (you must determine whether that is up or down, good or bad). The second case leaves you with some doubt, but one standard deviation is a valid prediction error and you must conclude that the predictive ability of your approximation is still intact. The third case is a problem, since some situations are always going to violate the range of probability. You can refer to a table of normal distribution (Appendix) to find the probability of variance of a single occurrence and decide whether this situation is still reasonable, or you can retest your regression analysis to see whether the price patterns have changed and you are in need of more or less days in your calculation. Regardless of what direction you take, there are two elements necessary: a smoothing technique to determine the trend of prices, and rules to apply as prices vary from the prediction for both up, down, and sideways trends. In order to choose properly you must know what selections are available.

THE MOVING AVERAGE

The simplest and most well-known of all smoothing techniques is called the *moving average*. Using this method, the number of elements to be averaged remains the same, but the time interval advances. Using a generalized time-series as an example we have $P_1, P_2, \ldots, P_t$ as a set of time-sequential elements. A moving average measured over n of these points at time t would be

$$M_t = \frac{P_t + P_{t-1} + \cdots + P_{t-n+1}}{n} = \frac{\sum_{i=1}^{n} P_{t-i+1}}{n} \qquad n \leq t$$

In other words, the most recent moving-average calculation is the average (arithmetic mean) of the prior n data points. Consider the use of three points ($n = 3$) to generate a moving average:

$$M_3 = \frac{P_1 + P_2 + P_3}{3}$$

$$M_4 = \frac{P_2 + P_3 + P_4}{3}$$

$$\vdots$$

$$M_t = \frac{P_{t-2} + P_{t-1} + P_t}{3}$$

If P_t represented a commodity price at a specific time, then the moving average would smooth the price movement. The more prices that are used the less effect a new price will have. If five successive prices are used, we have a *5-day moving average*. When we add the next sequential price and drop off the oldest we change the prior average by $\frac{1}{5}$ of the difference between the old and the new values. If

$$M_5 = \frac{P_1 + P_2 + P_3 + P_4 + P_5}{5}$$

and

$$M_6 = \frac{P_2 + P_3 + P_4 + P_5 + P_6}{5}$$

we can substitute $C = P_2 + P_3 + P_4 + P_5$ for the common part of the moving average, solve for C, and substitute to get

$$M_6 = M_5 + \tfrac{1}{5}(P_t - P_{t-n})$$

This also gives you a faster way to calculate a moving average. By generalizing we see that the more terms in the moving average the less effect the addition of a new term is likely to have:

$$M_t = M_{t-1} + \frac{1}{n}(P_t - P_{t-n})$$

The selection of the proper number of terms is a complex decision based on both the technical consideration of the predictive quality of the choice (measured by the error) and the need to determine price trends over specific time periods for commercial

COMMODITY-TRENDING MODEL

use. The more days or data points used in the moving average the more *smoothing* will occur, and variation lasting only a short while will have less effect. There is also a danger of losing cyclic or seasonal variations in prices by the choice of the wrong value of n. For example, a repeating cycle of four data points 5, 8, 3, 6, 9, 4, 7, ..., which advances by one each complete cycle, will appear as a straight line if a moving average of 4 days is used. If there is a possibility of a cyclic or seasonal pattern within the data, care should be taken to select a moving average that is out of phase with the possible pattern.

The length of the moving average must also correspond to its use. A purchaser of silver for jewelry may need to buy each week and would like to wait as long as possible while prices continue to trend downward during that week but will buy immediately when an upward turn is identified. A 6-month trend cannot help his problem, but a 5-day moving average may.

What Do You Average?

The most obvious price to apply to a moving average is the closing or daily settlement price of any commodity. It is generally accepted as the "true" price of the day and is used by many analysts for calculation of trends. But other alternatives exist. The average of the high and low price of the day will itself act as a smoothing device by preventing the maximum difference from occurring when the close is also the high or low. A similar approach that also gives weight to the closing price is the average of these three values: high, low, and close. Any selection will be meaningful but each will serve a different purpose.

Another perfectly valid component of a moving average can be other averages. For example, the elements P_1, P_2, and P_3 to be used in a 3-day moving average can actually be

$$P_1 = \frac{P_1 + P_2 + P_3}{3}, \qquad P_2 = \frac{P_4 + P_5 + P_6}{3}, \qquad P_3 = \frac{P_7 + P_8 + P_9}{3}$$

and so the moving average will be "doubly smoothed."

Another popular use of the moving average is to smooth the highs and the lows independently. The result is a band representing the daily trading range, or volatility, over a specified time interval. This can be important for the development of a trading system.

Types of Moving Averages

Besides varying the length of the moving average and the elements that are to be averaged, there are a great number of other modifications of the moving average.

An *accumulative average* may be used for a long-term trend. It does not satisfy our strict definition of a moving average since it adds data but does not discard any and, hence, is cumulative. It is traditionally started at the beginning of a contract and continued until the contract expires. Since there is a constant accumulation of prices and an increase in the length of the average we can easily see that the effect of the additional price at day t on the old moving average will be P_t/t, which becomes very small later in the contract. (A 1-year contract has approximately 250 trading days.) A *reset accumulative average* is a modification of the standard accumulative average and attempts to correct for the loss of sensitivity as the number of trading days becomes large. This alternative allows you to reset or restart the moving average whenever a new trend has started or at some other specified time. The use of this technique is combined with trend lines to develop a trading system.

Truncated moving averages are the most familiar to us; we will refer to them simply as *moving averages*. The most basic has already been discussed in detail in the introduction to smoothing. Once you have made longhand calculations of moving averages, you will discover that the simplest way of continuing your daily calculation is to keep the total of the past n days necessary for your calculation. Each new day requires the addition of the new value and subtraction of the oldest value. That number is saved for the next day while it is also divided by n to get the new moving average value. An interesting twist to this technique is called the *average-modified method*, in which you add the new day but subtract the last moving average value. If we go back to our example of a 5-day moving average, the 6th day was

$$M_6 = M_5 + \tfrac{1}{5}(P_6 - P_1)$$

This will become

$$M_6 = M_5 + \tfrac{1}{5}(P_6 - M_5)$$

The average-modified version is more convenient for the user since he no longer must keep the individual components of the average; only the prior moving average value and the new price are necessary. The substitution of the moving average value tends to smooth the results even further. Its use prevents the difference $(P_6 - P_1)$ from becoming too extreme; it effectively cuts the possible range in half and dampens the end-off impact.

The *weighted moving average* opens up a large area of study. When we discussed representative sampling, we included the notion of weighting as a means for restoring proper significance to a component of a sampling that is taken in parts. In doing this we introduced the possibility of bias, which is impossible to remove if incorrect. A weighted moving average is expressed in its general form as

$$W_t = \frac{w_1 P_t + w_2 P_{t-1} + \cdots + w_n P_{t-n+1}}{w_1 + w_2 + \cdots + w_n} = \frac{\sum_{i=1}^{n} w_i P_{t-i+1}}{\sum_{i=1}^{n} w_i}$$

This gives the weighted moving average at time t as the average of the previous n prices, each one weighted by w_i according to its position relative to t. The two forms most commonly used are both called "front-loaded" because they give more weight to the most recent data and reduce the significance of the older elements. Therefore, for a front-loaded weighted moving average

$$w_1 \geq w_2 \geq \cdots \geq w_n.$$

The first case of possible weighting is one in which the w_i have been determined by a regression analysis; but here the weighting factors may not always qualify as front-loaded. Other selected w_i may satisfy this condition with no set relationship between any two of the weighting factors. The second situation, which is more common but

COMMODITY-TRENDING MODEL   61

not necessarily as well-founded, is called *step-weighting*, in which each successive w_i differs from the previous elements by a fixed increment

$$C = w_i - w_{i-1}$$

The simplest case takes integer values for an *n*-day step-weighted moving average:

$$w_n = n$$
$$w_{n-1} = n - 1$$
$$\vdots$$
$$w_1 = 1$$

This gives the weighting factors the values of 5, 4, 3, 2, and 1 for a 5-day average. Another approach to step-weighting would be a percentage relationship between w_i elements,

$$w_{i-1} = a \cdot w_i$$

where $a = .9$. Then if $w_5 = 5$, $w_4 = 4.5$, $w_3 = 4.05$, $w_2 = 3.645$, and $w_1 = 3.2805$.

Table 4-2 Sample Moving Averages Using May 77 Copper (NY).

	Date	Price	3-day	5-day	10-day	5-day average modified	Accumulative	10-day step-weighted
				60.60	61.40	60.30	59.30	58.70
1	11-01	58.90	58.50	58.56	59.31	58.56	59.31	58.90
2	11-03	59.10	58.80	58.48	59.08	58.67	59.29	58.84
3	11-04	61.00	59.67	59.04	59.15	59.13	59.43	59.18
4	11-05	62.10	60.73	59.78	59.43	59.73	59.64	59.72
5	11-08	62.00	61.70	60.40	59.76	60.18	59.81	60.21
6	11-09	62.50	62.20	61.08	60.23	60.65	59.99	60.74
7	11-10	63.20	62.57	61.52	60.60	61.16	60.19	61.33
8	11-11	61.30	62.33	61.36	60.91	61.18	60.26	61.48
9	11-12	61.70	62.07	61.30	61.24	61.29	61.34	61.67
10	11-15	62.00	61.67	61.20	61.55	61.43	60.42	61.85
11	11-16	62.20	61.97	61.00	61.86	61.58	60.49	62.00
12	11-17	61.70	61.97	61.08	61.93	61.61	60.55	62.00
13	11-18	61.50	61.80	61.04	61.87	61.59	60.59	61.91
14	11-19	62.40	61.87	61.12	61.91	61.75	60.67	61.98
15	11-22	61.40	61.77	60.96	61.80	61.68	60.70	61.86
16	11-23	59.90	61.23	60.60	61.47	61.32	60.67	61.48
17	11-20	59.80	60.37	60.26	61.32	61.02	60.64	61.13
18	11-26	59.10	59.60	59.60	61.06	60.63	60.58	60.71
19	11-29	59.50	59.47	59.22	60.81	60.41	60.54	60.41
20	11-30	59.10	59.23	59.06	60.50	60.15	60.49	60.07
21	12-01	58.70	59.10	58.84	60.20	59.86	61.43	59.72
22	12-02	58.70	58.83	58.76	59.92	59.62	60.37	59.42
23	12-03	59.50	58.97	58.76	59.63	59.60	60.35	59.33
24	12-06	59.60	59.27	58.86	59.45	59.60	60.32	59.29
25	12-07	59.50	59.53	59.02	59.41	59.58	60.30	59.30

A popular modification to the weighting of individual prices is the weighting of a group of prices. If we allowed every two consecutive data elements to have the same weighting factor, we would get

$$W_t = \frac{w_1 P_t + w_1 P_{t-1} + w_2 P_{t-2} + w_2 P_{t-3} + \cdots + w_{n/2} P_{t-n+1}}{w_1 + w_2 + \cdots + w_n}$$

or, grouped with n even,

$$W_t = \frac{w_1(P_t + P_{t-1}) + w_2(P_{t-2} + P_{t-3}) + \cdots + w_{n/2}(P_{t-n+2} + P_{t-n+1})}{w_1 + w_2 + \cdots + w_n}$$

Any number of consecutive data elements can be grouped and still satisfy the criteria for a step-weighted moving average.

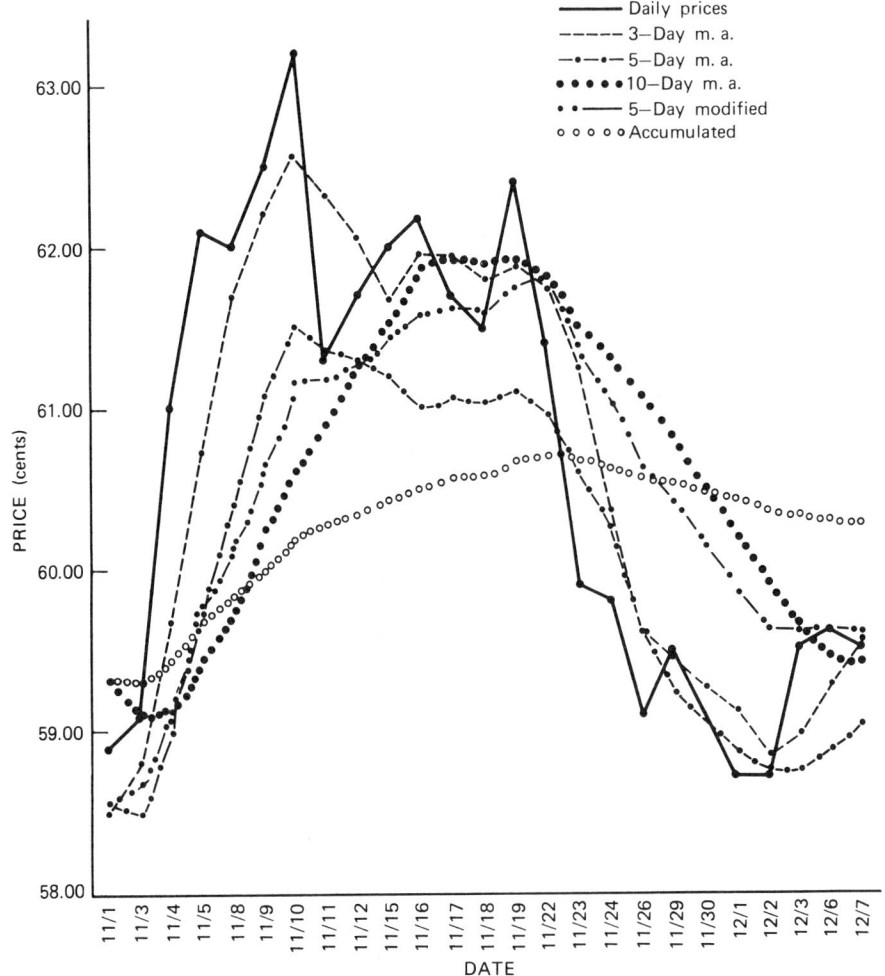

Diagram 4-2   A comparison of moving averages (May 77 Copper, November–December 1976).

COMMODITY-TRENDING MODEL   63

These moving averages can also be plotted in different ways, each way having a major impact on their interpretation. The conventional plot places the moving average value M_t on the same vertical line as the last entry P_t of the moving average. When prices have been trending higher over the period of calculation, this will cause the value M_t to lag behind (or below) the actual prices; when prices are declining, the moving average will be above the prices.

The plotted moving average can either *lead* or *lag* the last price recorded. If it is to lead by 3 days, the value M_t is plotted on the vertical line $t + 3$; if it is to lag by 2 days it is plotted at $t - 2$. In the case of leading moving averages, the analysis attempts to compensate for the time delay and force the prices to continue at the previous rate of increase or decrease or also violate or penetrate the moving average line by changing direction. The lag technique serves the more sophisticated purpose of *phasing* the moving average. A 10-day moving average, when lagged by 5 days, will be placed in the midst of the actual price data. This technique will be covered later.

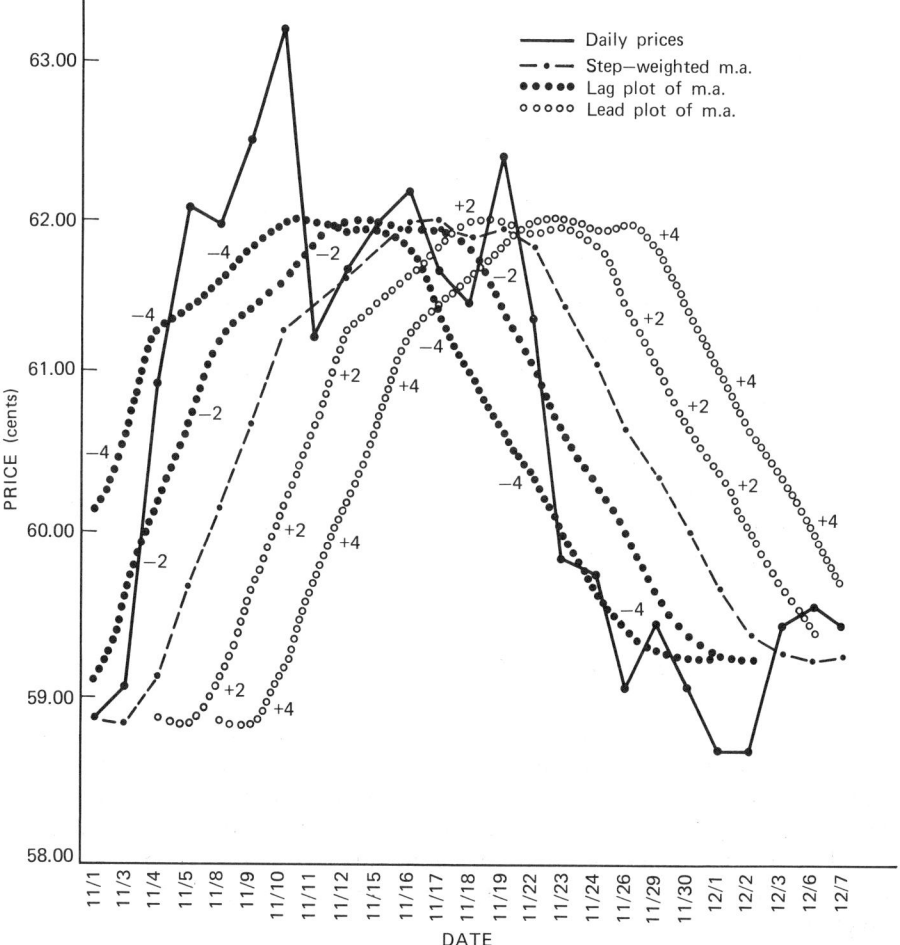

Diagram 4-3 Plotting lag and lead for a 10-day step-weighted moving average (weighting 10, 9, 8, . . . , May 77 Copper, November–December 1976).

GEOMETRIC MOVING AVERAGES

The previous discussion could equally apply to a geometric average, in which case the basic equation for the last n points at time t would be

$$G_t = (P_t \times P_{t-1} \times \cdots \times P_{t-n+1})^{1/n} = \left(\prod_{i=1}^{n} P_{t-i+1}\right)^{1/n}$$

The daily calculation is more complicated but, as shown in the discussion of averages, could be rewritten as

$$\ln G_t = \frac{\ln P_t + \ln P_{t-1} + \cdots + \ln P_{t-n+1}}{n}$$

$$= \frac{1}{n}\left(\sum_{i=1}^{n} \ln P_{t-i+1}\right)$$

This is similar in form to the summation of a standard moving average based on the arithmetic mean. A weighted geometric moving average would have the form

$$\ln G_t = \frac{w_1 \ln P_t + w_2 \ln P_{t-1} + \cdots + w_n \ln P_{t-n+1}}{w_1 + w_2 + \cdots + w_n}$$

$$= \frac{\sum_{i=1}^{n} w_i \ln P_{t-i+1}}{\sum_{i=1}^{n} w_i}$$

The geometric moving average itself would give greater weight to lower values without the need for a discrete weighting function. In applying the technique to actual commodity prices this distinction is not as apparent. For widely ranging values such as 1000 and 10 the simple average is 505 and the geometric average is 100, but for these three sequential cocoa prices—56.20, 58.30, and 57.15—the arithmetic mean is 57.2166 and the geometric is 57.1871. A similar test of 5, 10 or 20 days of commodity prices will show a negligible difference between the results of the two averages. If the geometric moving average is to be helpful, it would be best applied to long-term historic data with wide variance, using yearly or quarterly average prices.

EXPONENTIALLY SMOOTHED MOVING AVERAGES

Exponential smoothing will appear to be more complex than other techniques but it is only another form of a weighted moving average. It has the added advantage of being simpler to calculate than any other method discussed; only the last *exponentially smoothed value* E_{t-1} and the *smoothing constant a* are necessary to compute the new value. The technique of exponential smoothing was developed during World War II for tracking aircraft and projecting their position—the immediate past is used to predict the immediate future.

By using a geometric progression

$$1, a, a^2, a^3, \ldots, a^{n-1}$$

COMMODITY-TRENDING MODEL

applied to the terms of a weighted moving average

$$W_t = \frac{w_1 P_t + w_2 P_{t-1} + \cdots + w_n P_{t-n+1}}{w_1 + w_2 + \cdots + w_n}$$

we get $w_1 = 1, w_2 = a, w_3 = a^2, \ldots, w_n = a^{n-1}$. If $a = \frac{1}{2}$, also said to be 50% smoothed, we have the sequence

$$1, \tfrac{1}{2}, \tfrac{1}{4}, \tfrac{1}{8}, \ldots, (\tfrac{1}{2})^{n-1}$$

This shows the rapidly decreasing importance of each older price. Substituting the geometric progression into the equation for the weighted moving average we get

$$E_t = \frac{1 P_t + a P_{t-1} + a^2 P_{t-2} + \cdots + a^{n-1} P_{t-n+1}}{1 + a + a^2 + \cdots + a^{n-1}}$$

By a lengthy arithmetic process using the formula for the sum of a geometric progression we can state the same equation as

$$E_t = (1 - a)P_t + a E_{t-1}$$

where P_t is the most recent price and $0 \leq a \leq 1$. It can be seen that 100% of the combined value of past prices are distributed such that $a \times 100$ goes towards the previous exponential moving average and the balance towards the most recent price. If $a = .70$ then the current price P_t will receive a weighting of 30% of the total moving average. A more popular form, and one which reverses the weighting natations is:

$$E_t = E_{t-1} + a(P_t - E_{t-1})$$

We can start the smoothing process at P_2 by letting $E_1 = P_1$ and calculate our next value:

$$E_2 = E_1 + a(P_2 - E_1)$$

The interpretation of this last equation can be seen from the following:

new exponential value = prior exponential value + some % of (today's price − prior exponential value)

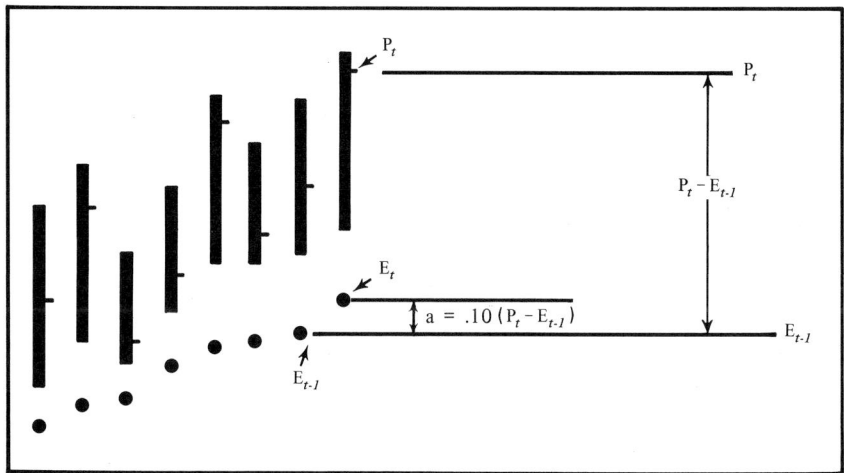

Diagram 4-4 Exponential smoothing.

An important feature of the exponentially smoothed moving average is that all data previously used is always part of the new result, although with diminishing significance. In general:

$$E_i = a(P_i + (1-a)P_{i-1} + (1-a)^2 P_{i-2} + \cdots + (1-a)^n P_{i-n} \cdots)$$

For example, if the smoothing constant $a = .10$, we will add 10% of the new difference to the old average:

$$E_t = E_{t-1} + .10(P_t - E_{t-1})$$

That in effect will reduce all data from point 1 through $t-1$ by 10%; the next calculation for $t+1$ will cause the data from t back to be reduced again by 10%. Therefore, at any time t the impact of data used at time k is based on the number of days elapsed, $t-k$, and the smoothing constant a. Let the significance of $P_k - E_{k-1} = k = D_k$. Then on day k we have

$$k = a \cdot D_k$$
$$k + 1 = a \cdot D_k - a \cdot a \cdot D_k$$
$$\vdots$$
$$k + n = a \cdot D_k - (a^2 \cdot D_k + a^3 \cdot D_k + \cdots + a^{n+1} D_k)$$
$$= a \cdot D_k - \sum_{i=2}^{n+1} a^i D_k \quad \text{(written in summation form)}$$
$$= D_k \left(a - \sum_{i=2}^{n+1} a^i \right) \to 0 \quad \text{as } n \to \infty$$

This shows that the significance of the data on day k goes to zero as n gets infinitely large. Consider the following example. You are an investor with 10% of the shares of stock in a corporation where there are t investors. The corporation decides to take in another investor and give him 10% of the total outstanding shares. There are now $t + 1$ investors and your shares are diluted to 9% of the total. Another investor buys in at 10% of the total; there are now $t + 2$ investors and you now have 8.1% of the stock (10% less). As three investors are added, your stock holdings dwindle to 7.29%, 6.561%, and 5.9049%. While the number of shares that you hold remain the same, their significance to the whole has been reduced. No matter how many investors are added at 10%, you will always retain your shares and will always have some minor percent of the whole. In exactly the same way the original price used in an exponentially smoothed moving average always retains some relevance, while with a standard moving average of n days, the $(n + 1)$th day is dropped off and ceases to have any impact.

Double Exponential Smoothing

As a trend continues in its direction, the exponentially smoothed moving average will lag farther behind. By selecting a smoothing constant nearer to 1 the magnitude of this lag will be lessened, but it will still increase. If we consider the lag as the predictive error in our calculation, we get

$$\varepsilon_t = P_t - E_t \quad \text{(error)}$$

where E_t is the exponential smoothing approximation of the price P_t. We can apply the same exponential smoothing technique to the pattern of increasing or decreasing error to get

$$\Sigma_t = \Sigma_{t-1} + a(\varepsilon_t - \Sigma_{t-1})$$

and then add the difference between the original smoothing value and the double (second-order) smoothing back into the approximation:

$$EE_t = E_t + \Sigma_t$$

The effect of error due to lag will be corrected so that instead of the lag increasing it will decrease. This method can be extended to "third-order" smoothing as necessary.

RELATING EXPONENTIAL AND STANDARD MOVING AVERAGES

Most people grasp the time relationship of a standard moving average much more rapidly than an exponential. Because of the diluting effect of the exponential smoothing, a comparison with respect to days is based on both the smoothing constant and the elapsed time. Intuitively, we know that a 50% smoothing is somewhat slower than a 2-day moving average, a 10% smoothing is slower than a 10-day moving average, and a 5% smoothing is slower than a 20-day moving average. The important factor is that for any specified smoothing constant the exponential moving average includes all prior data. If we were to compare a 5-day moving average with an exponential with only 5 total days included, our relationship would be closer to a straight moving average than if the exponential had 10 or 20 days of elapsed calculation.

Look at the situation of continuously increasing numbers from 1 through 15 and back to 1. Comparing a 5-day moving average with an exponential moving average will show the relationship. The exponential is calculated two ways: once using only the last five prices (a modified approach for our example); the other using all prices from the beginning (the standard method).

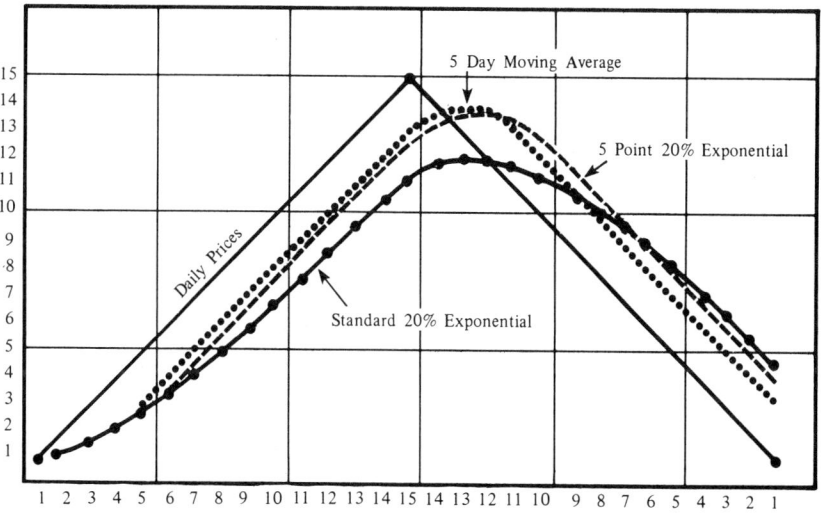

Diagram 4-5 Daily price with moving averages.

Diagrams 4-5 and 4-6 and Table 4-3 show the relationship between the standard exponential and the modified exponential using five points. During the period of constant increase and decrease of at least 5 consecutive days, both the 5-day standard and exponential five points stabilize, since those 5 days represent their entire realm of calculation values. At the peak the standard moving average reacts faster than the other methods in staying closer to the current price; the 5-point exponential gives 20% of its weight to the most recent price, and less to prior prices, causing it to react slower than the standard moving average.

The standard exponential smoothing is different, lagging farther behind each day, but increasingly *approaching* the value of one, as the data increase by one, for long time periods. The weighting of the near values is offset by the retained significance of the oldest data, which is never fully lost, causing the exponentially smoothed moving average to lag the farthest behind the current prices. Although there are 14 days of

Table 4-3 Comparison of Lag Between Standard and Exponentially Smoothed Moving Averages

Price	Standard 5-day	5-point 20% exp	Standard 20% exp	Change 5-day	5–20% exp	20% exp
1	—	1.00	1.00	—	—	—
2	—	1.20	1.20	—	—	—
3	—	1.56	1.56	—	Not enough	—
4	—	2.05	2.05	—	data	—
5	3	2.64	2.64	—	—	—
6	4	3.64	3.31	1.00	1.00	.67
7	5	4.64	4.05	1.00	1.00	.74
8	6	5.64	4.84	1.00	1.00	.79
9	7	6.64	5.67	1.00	1.00	.83
10	8	7.64	6.54	1.00	1.00	.87
11	9	8.64	7.43	1.00	1.00	.89
12	10	9.64	8.34	1.00	1.00	.91
13	11	10.64	9.27	1.00	1.00	.93
14	12	11.64	10.22	1.00	1.00	.95
15	13	12.64	11.17	1.00	1.00	.95
14	13.6	13.24	11.74	.60	.60	.57
13	13.8	13.52	11.99	.20	.28	.25
12	13.6	13.54	11.99	−.20	.02	.00
11	13	13.36	11.79	−.60	−.18	−.20
10	12	12.36	11.43	−1.00	−1.00	−.36
9	11	11.36	10.95	−1.00	−1.00	−.48
8	10	10.36	10.36	−1.00	−1.00	−.59
7	9	9.36	9.69	−1.00	−1.00	−.67
6	8	8.36	8.95	−1.00	−1.00	−.74
5	7	7.36	8.16	−1.00	−1.00	−.79
4	6	6.36	7.33	−1.00	−1.00	−.83
3	5	5.36	6.46	−1.00	−1.00	−.87
2	4	4.36	5.57	−1.00	−1.00	−.89
1	3	3.36	4.65	−1.00	−1.00	−.92

COMMODITY-TRENDING MODEL

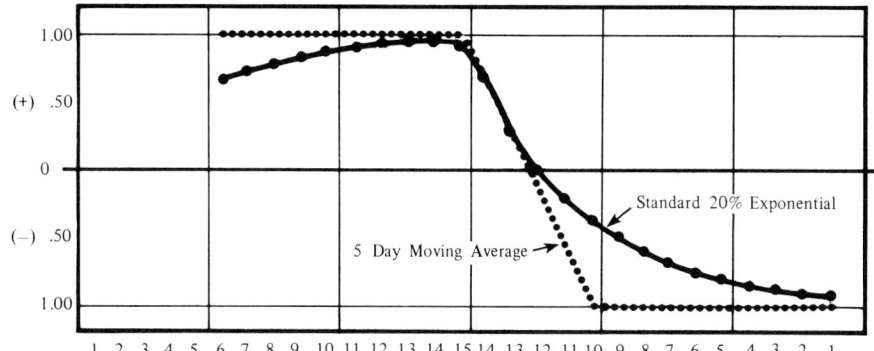

Diagram 4-6 Comparative changes in straight and exponential moving averages.

constant decline, the standard exponential has not yet stabilized, still reflecting the turning of prices from up to down at 15.

In order to form the specific relationship between exponential smoothing and standard moving averages, we create a table showing the significance of each oldest day in the exponential calculation. In Table 4-4, the .50 smoothing constant gives 50% of the total value to the current price, 25% to the prior day, $12\frac{1}{2}\%$ to the next oldest, until the 7th oldest day adds only .8% to the total value of the exponential moving average. Table 4-5 accumulates these weights to show how much of the calculation has been completed by the elapsed days printed across the top. Table 4-5 is plotted in Diagram 4-7. You can see how the most recent days (on the left) receive the bulk of the significance while the oldest prices are of little impact. The .10 smoothing calculation is 90.1% complete by the 22nd day; the total remaining days added together only account for 9.9% of the value.

Diagram 4-7 relates the fully calculated exponential smoothing (to within 1%) to the standard moving average. By finding the smoothing constant on the left you can relate the number of days in a standard moving average along the bottom. You should observe that testing various equally distant smoothing constants may give you an unexpected distribution relative to past days.

Equating Standard Moving Averages to Exponential Smoothing

Smoothing constant (%)	.10	.20	.30	.40	.50	.60	.70	.80	.90
Standard (n-day avg)	20	10	6	4	3	2.25	1.75	1.40	1.15

If you test the smoothing constants shown above, half of your tests will analyze moving averages of 3 days or less. If you would like a testing program more easily related to the standard moving average, reverse the process, finding the smoothing constant relating to a known number of days.

Equating Exponential Smoothing to Standard Moving Averages

Standard (n-day avg)	2	4	6	8	10	12	14	16	18	20
Smoothing constant (%)	.65	.40	.30	.235	.20	.165	.14	.125	.11	.10

Table 4-4 Evaluation of Exponential Smoothing—Significance of Prior Data

Weighting (%)	Past number of days																						
	1	2	3	4	5	6	7	8	9	10	11	12	13	14	15	16	17	18	19	20	21	22	23
1.00	100.0	—	—	—	—	—	—	—	—	—	—	—	—	—	—	—	—	—	—	—	—	—	—
.90	90.0	9.0	.9	—	—	—	—	—	—	—	—	—	—	—	—	—	—	—	—	—	—	—	—
.80	80.0	16.0	3.2	.6	—	—	—	—	—	—	—	—	—	—	—	—	—	—	—	—	—	—	—
.70	70.0	21.0	6.3	1.9	.6	—	—	—	—	—	—	—	—	—	—	—	—	—	—	—	—	—	—
.60	60.0	24.0	9.6	3.8	1.5	.6	—	—	—	—	—	—	—	—	—	—	—	—	—	—	—	—	—
.50	50.0	25.0	12.5	6.3	3.1	1.6	.8	—	—	—	—	—	—	—	—	—	—	—	—	—	—	—	—
.40	40.0	24.0	14.4	8.6	5.2	3.1	1.9	1.1	.7	—	—	—	—	—	—	—	—	—	—	—	—	—	—
.30	30.0	21.0	14.7	10.3	7.2	5.0	3.5	2.5	1.7	1.2	.8	—	—	—	—	—	—	—	—	—	—	—	—
.20	20.0	16.0	12.8	10.2	8.2	6.5	5.2	4.2	3.3	2.7	2.1	1.7	1.4	1.1	.9	—	—	—	—	—	—	—	—
.10	10.0	9.0	8.1	7.3	6.6	5.9	5.3	4.8	4.3	3.9	3.5	3.1	2.8	2.5	2.3	2.1	1.8	1.7	1.5	1.3	1.2	1.1	1.0

Table 4-5 Evaluation of Exponential Smoothing—Significance of Prior Data

| Weighting (%) | Total inclusion through Nth day ||||||||||||||||||||||||
	1	2	3	4	5	6	7	8	9	10	11	12	13	14	15	16	17	18	19	20	21	22	23
1.00	100.0	—	—	—	—	—	—	—	—	—	—	—	—	—	—	—	—	—	—	—	—	—	—
.90	90.0	99.0	99.9	—	—	—	—	—	—	—	—	—	—	—	—	—	—	—	—	—	—	—	—
.80	80.0	96.0	99.2	—	—	—	—	—	—	—	—	—	—	—	—	—	—	—	—	—	—	—	—
.70	70.0	91.0	97.3	99.2	99.8	—	—	—	—	—	—	—	—	—	—	—	—	—	—	—	—	—	—
.60	60.0	84.0	93.6	97.4	99.0	99.6	—	—	—	—	—	—	—	—	—	—	—	—	—	—	—	—	—
.50	50.0	75.0	87.5	93.8	96.9	98.5	99.3	—	—	—	—	—	—	—	—	—	—	—	—	—	—	—	—
.40	40.0	64.0	78.4	87.0	92.2	95.3	97.2	98.3	99.0	—	—	—	—	—	—	—	—	—	—	—	—	—	—
.30	30.0	51.0	65.7	76.0	83.2	88.2	91.8	94.2	96.0	—	—	—	—	—	—	—	—	—	—	—	—	—	—
.20	20.0	36.0	48.8	59.0	67.2	73.8	79.0	83.2	86.6	89.3	91.4	93.1	94.5	95.6	96.5	—	—	—	—	—	—	—	—
.10	10.0	19.0	27.1	34.4	41.0	46.8	52.2	57.0	61.3	65.1	68.6	71.8	74.6	77.1	79.4	81.5	83.3	85.0	86.5	87.8	89.1	90.1	91.1

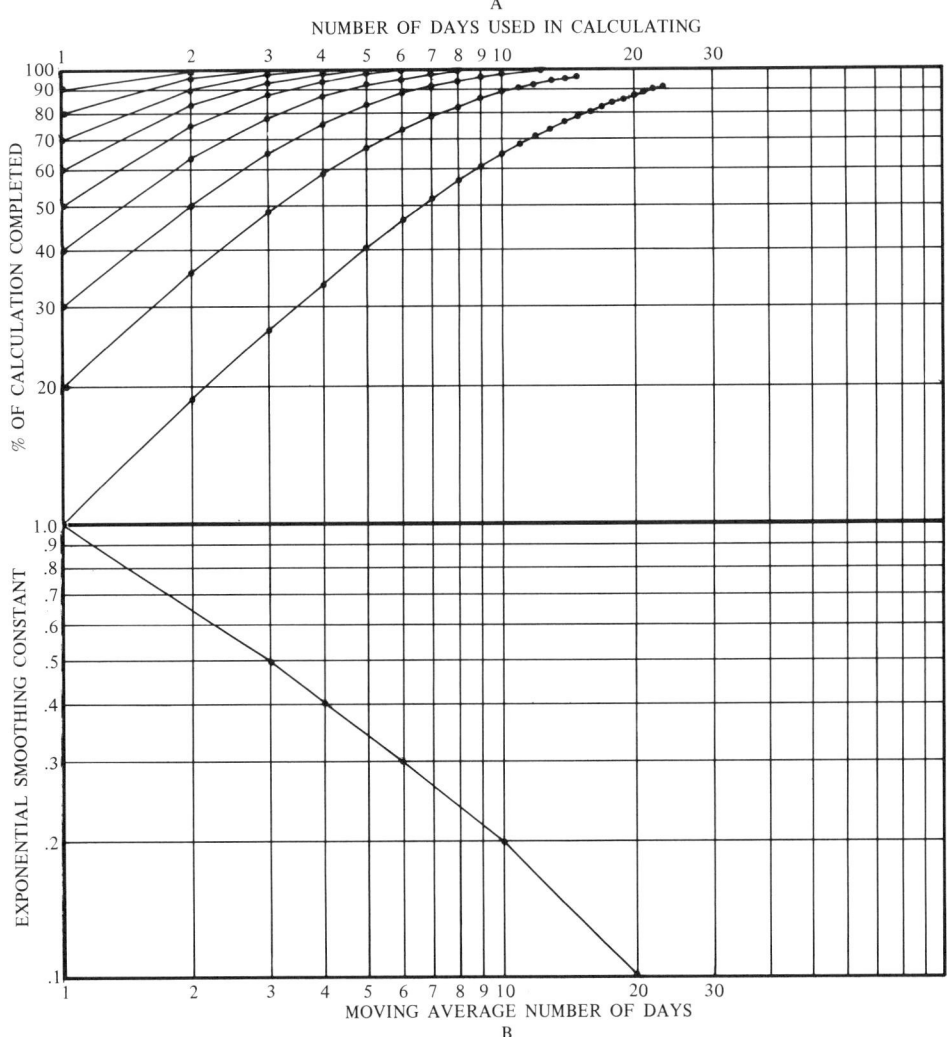

Diagram 4-7 Evaluation of exponential smoothing.

The distribution of smoothing constants is very close to logarithmic and is plotted on log paper for emphasis. To test a range of days using exponential smoothing, use a logarithmic distribution of tests across the range, with closer values taken at the smaller numbers. This may seem like an unnecessary precaution, but it is essential when using this smoothing technique.

Complex Exponential Smoothing Techniques

Exponential smoothing can also be used for predicting more than a day (or time period) in advance of the most recent price. The mathematical elaboration needed for this is too advanced for our discussions, but can be found in the references related to mathematical statistics. It is important to know that forecasts can be made with respect to long-term characteristics of the data. For example, if the price of a commodity or acreage planted seems constant over time, a simple exponentially smoothed value can be used; if the price seems to be increasing or decreasing at a constant rate we apply a linear smoothing; and if neither is apparent, there is a more complex formula. Commodity prices do not appear to fall into the category of long-term unchanged values, but they might follow a somewhat direct relation to the cost of living or the buying power of the United States dollar. If none of these assumptions is satisfactory, the only alternative is a lengthy solution.

CHAPTER 5
Moving-Average Systems

Now that we have the tools for calculating any sort of moving average—standard, weighted, or exponentially smoothed—we have to establish rules for using them. There are so many possible combinations of rules that this may be just as challenging as the selection of the moving-average technique. We will first cover the simplest methods before classifying the variations.

BASIC BUY AND SELL SIGNALS

Regardless of the selection of moving averages, the value of the calculation will lag behind the actual current market price. In bull markets this lag will cause the moving average to be below the price; in bear markets it will be above. When prices change direction, the moving average and the actual commodity prices cross; the moving average still reflects the previous trend. When this crossing occurs, we have a basic trading signal.

Buy when the rising price crosses the moving average.
Sell when the declining price crosses the moving average.

These rules are straightforward and are well-defined. The next step is to decide "when what price crosses the moving average." The answer depends greatly on the construction of the average and the testing of the system. If your average is composed only of closing prices, then it is reasonable to start testing with the modified signals.

Buy when the rising price closes above the moving average.
Sell when the declining price closes below the moving average.

If you used an average of high and low prices, you would want to buy or sell when the new average (*high* + *low*)/2 was above or below the previous average. In all cases,

MOVING-AVERAGE SYSTEMS 75

consistency is important. The system that you test and the one that you trade should be the same. When we use the term "close" in our explanation, we really mean whatever value was used to create the average. To find out whether your signal was generated according to these rules, wait until the close of trading, calculate your new moving average, then see whether a crossing occurred relative to the new value. This means that you cannot act on the signal until the next trading day. You can modify your approach and buy or sell on today's market close if that close is above or below yesterday's moving average value. A small amount of testing by longhand calculation can tell you which approach will work best. Still another modification would be to test today's close against yesterday's projected moving average, so that if that moving average for the past 3 days were

$$M_{t-1} = 432$$

$$M_{t-2} = 429$$

$$M_{t-3} = 427$$

we would take the difference $M_{t-1} - M_{t-2} = 3$, and add that to M_{t-1} to get our turning criterion of 435 for M_t today. That means that the *rate of change* must differ for a signal to occur. More sophisticated approaches to projecting the moving average can be considered.

Lead and *lag* are features of two of the comprehensive moving-average analyses covered later in this chapter. The opposite in construction, a lead time of n days, advances the plotted value of the moving average M_t from beneath the current price P_t to the position P_{t+n} columns ahead (see Diagram 4-3). Lag time does the opposite, plotting the moving average in the column with P_{t-n} for n-day lag. Both techniques attempt to adjust the time of the signal. The lead plot catches the price-trend change sooner to get the maximum out of a trend; the lag waits until the trend is well-defined to prevent whipsaws from occurring while a new direction is being established. Both lead and lag techniques may use the same basic buy and sell signals as standard plotting.

Entry and exit timing may be improved by a *delay* in taking action on a signal, usually from 1 to 3 days. This technique allows a number of days for the newly developed trend to reverse and show a "false signal" at the cost of missing the beginning of the trend. One of the most important features of a system is whether it is committed to being continually in the market. A system that always enters a new long position when a short trade is closed out will always be committed. It will generally capture more profits when the trade is successful, but show more frequent losing trades because of constant commitment during trend changes in whipsaw periods. You can make your own evaluation by taking any system that always reverses its position and liquidate, but do not reverse. Test the results for 1, 2, and 3 days of delay and decide yourself. It's a simple exercise that could be worth a great deal.

So far, these modifications have been concerned with a simple moving-average line. We can adjust our plot forward or backward, reverse our position, or delay our entry or exit, in an attempt to begin our new trade at the time the trend has decidedly taken a new direction. Even if prices have begun what will become a major downtrend, an entry into a short position too soon may be subject to sharp reversals caused by conflicting fundamental and technical elements at these turning points. The simplest way to avoid these price variations is by using a band.

A *band* is an area surrounding a trend line above and below that acts as a zone of commitment for the trader and allows time, as measured by movement and risk, for prices to settle into their new direction. Bands can be created in many ways, the most popular being a percentage of the current price or the current trend line value. A band that is formed from the trend line will be

(upper band) $\quad B_U = M_t + cM_t$

(lower band) $\quad B_L = M_t - cM_t$

where c is a percentage, $0 \leq c \leq 1$. Since the moving average is a smoothing, the band will be uniform as well. If the current price is used instead of the moving average we get

$$B_U = M_t + cP_t$$
$$B_L = M_t - cP_t$$

The band will vary in width at a much faster rate using price. During an uptrend, if a slow moving average falls far behind current prices the band based on prices will get very wide. Another popular type of band is based on *absolute point value* with, for example, silver being 5¢ or corn 5¢ or cattle 25 points, each representing a dollar risk to the trader. The use of this type of band is usually found coordinated with a money-management program that limits losses on trades to a specific number or to a maximum percentage of the portfolio being managed.

The *independent smoothing* of the high and low daily prices forms a *volatility band*. While it may be practical to use the same technique or the same relative smoothing (e.g., 10-day or 10% smoothing constant) for the high, low, and closing prices, it is not a requirement. If the same smoothing criterion is used, the band will be uniform with respect to the moving average of the closing price; if not, you might find all three trend lines weaving around one another. A *volatility function* can also be used to create a band. Rather than the simple percentage calculation shown first, we can increase the band at rates equal to the price-volatility relationship discussed earlier in this book. All of the methods of forming bands are subject to *scaling*. Scaling will increase or reduce the sensitivity of any technique used for calculating the band. If S is a scaling factor we have

$B = M_t \pm S \times c \times M_t$ (percentage smoothing)
$B = M_t \pm S \times c \times P_t$ (percentage smoothing using price)
$B = M_t \pm S \times R$ (fixed risk using absolute point value)
$B_U = S \times f(H_t)$
$B_L = S \times f(L_t)$ } (independent smoothing of highs or lows)
$B = M_t \pm S \times (H_t - L_t)$ (volatility of high-low)
$B = M_t \pm S \times V(P_t)$ (volatility function at price level)
$B = M_t \pm S \times V(M_t)$ (volatility at moving average level)

When $S = 1$, the scaling effect is nullified; for $S > 1$ it magnifies the band; and for $S < 1$ it reduces the band.

MOVING-AVERAGE SYSTEMS

RULES FOR USING BANDS

Regardless of the type of band that is constructed, techniques for its use in generating trading signals are limited. First a decision must be made concerning whether or not a liquidation of a current position will be reversed, causing the entry into a new position in the opposite direction. Assuming that we always reverse from long to short and from short to long we have the following rules:

Buy (close out shorts and go long) when the price penetrates the upper band.
Sell (close out longs and go short) when the price penetrates the lower band.

This technique always keeps you in the market with a maximum risk (without skids and gaps) equal to the width of the band on entry. If you would like a neutral position or choose not to reverse your position when you close out a prior trade, you have more alternatives:

Buy (go long) when prices penetrate the upper band and close out that long position when prices reverse and go below the moving-average value.
Sell (go short) when prices break below the lower band and cover your short when prices penetrate back through the moving-average value.

The band is then used to enter into either new long or short trades and the moving average within the band is used only for liquidation. If prices do not continue with enough strength to penetrate the opposite band on the close, you remain neutral after closing out your trade. The next day you use both upper and lower bands to reenter either a long or short trade, respectively. No new trades are entered as long as those bands are not violated.

This technique has two advantages and one disadvantage. It allows you to close out a trade and reenter a new one in the same direction in the event of a "false breakout." Or, if a pullback occurs after a closeout, before a reverse position can be entered

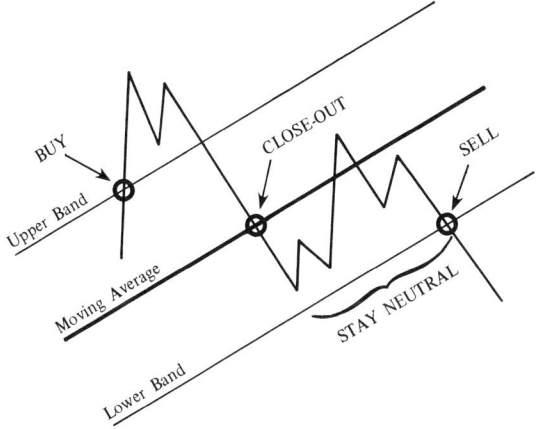

Diagram 5-1 Basic rules for using bands.

(as in Diagram 5-1) an entry at a later date might be a better price. The disadvantage occurs which the price changes direction and moves so fast that both the closeout and new signal occur on the same day. Reversing your position at one price would have been better in that situation.

A second approach to entry-exit requires the use of the high and low of the day as penetration criteria. Again using the outer bands for entry and the moving average for exit apply the following rules:

Buy when the high of the day penetrates the upper band and close out longs when the low of the day penetrates the moving average.

Sell when the low of the day penetrates the lower band and cover shorts when the high penetrates the moving average.

With both the first and second set of rules, risk is limited to half of the full band. In the second case, the chances of exiting one trade and remaining neutral are greater than the first.

The type of order placed when following your system will have a long-term effect on your results. The use of a band with a single moving average identifies change of trends when a breakout occurs. Buying during an upside break or selling during a downside break often causes poor entry prices and has been known to place the trader in a new trend at the point where prices are ready for a "technical adjustment." The most frequent complaints of trend followers is that their new positions usually show losses and that it takes a long time before the technical adjustment ends and the new trend returns to its entry price level. This reasoning has caused many variations from the original rules:

Buy (or *Sell*) on the close after an entry signal has been indicated.

Buy (or *Sell*) on the next market open following a signal.

Buy (or *Sell*) with a delay of 1, 2, or 3 days after the signal.

Buy (or *Sell*) after a price retracement of 50% (or some other value) following a signal.

Buy (or *Sell*) when prices move to within a specified risk relative to a stop-loss point.

These modifications are for the purpose of entering a new position with an immediate profit or preventing excessive risk. Some can be categorized as "timing" and others as "risk management." If you are using intraday prices to signal new entries and exits, you can add a rule that states:

Only one order can be executed in one day, either the liquidation of a current position or an entry into a new position.

An entire area of study has been devoted to the problem of exit and entry with good cause. The speculator has limited capital and conservation of his investment is important when the greater number of trades are expected to lose money. Better entry points will reduce the risk on a larger part of his trades and allow him to suffer longer strings of poor performance with less discomfort.

It may be found when a careful study of delay tactics has been completed that waiting for the "right time" has more disadvantages than is apparent. In tests on one system conducted over a year and a few hundred actual commodity trades (unpublished study by P. J. Kaufman (1975)) it was shown that positions entered on the market opening on the day following the system signal improved fill prices about 75% of the time but overall caused smaller profit for the year. Why? The year was 1974 and many breakouts never adjusted back to allow the trader to enter at a better price. The three out of four better fills were more than offset by the one bad one. Of course, 1974 may not be typical of commodity-price patterns since a year of fast market movement would defeat the delay methods. Each commodity may be subject to individual analysis to determine which strategy is best applied in today's market.

APPLICATIONS OF SINGLE MOVING AVERAGES

The selection of the speed of the moving average is as important as any of the rules of the system. The speed determines the activity of trading and the nature of the trend to be isolated. To help this decision some of the preceding sections have shown comparisons of the different speeds as well as a predictive approach, based on reducing the magnitude of errors. Without a computer or other powerful calculating tools, extensive examination of alternatives is impossible.

The precedent for selection has been choosing multiples of calendar periods, expressed as trading days. In doing this there is an opportunity to be in phase with behavioral patterns of traders and brokerage houses, who may work within weekly or monthly spans. The most popular intervals for selection have been: 3 days, the expected duration of a short price move; 5 days, a trading week; 20 to 21 days, a trading month, and so on. Included in the next headings are well-known systems using single moving averages, followed by examples of multiple-average systems. By studying these systems it may help formulate your own ideas on how best to use a moving average.

MPTDI (A Step-Weighted Moving Average)

In 1972 Robert Joel Taylor published the description of a system called the Major Price Trend Directional Indicator, which was reprinted in summary form in the September 1973 *Commodities Magazine*. The system was promoted and implemented through Enterex Commodities in Dallas. MPTDI was historically tested by Dunn and Hargitt Financial Services in West Lafayette, Indiana, in 1972 and the results made available to the public. Since it was also one of the few well-defined published systems it served as the basis for much experimentation for current technicians and aspiring analysts.

MPTDI is based on a step-weighted moving average of varying lengths, with an effective band of designated widths relative to volatility. It is unique among known systems for its complete dependence on incremental values for all aspects of the system: the moving average, entry, and stop-loss points. For example, if gold were part of the system, it might be assigned the following conditions:

Table 5-1   MPTDI Variables

Average trading range	Number of days in calculation	Weighting-factors progression	Entry-signal penetration	Approximate stop-loss point
50–150	25 days	TYPE A	100 pts	150 pts
150–250	20 days	TYPE B	200 pts	300 pts
250–350	15 days	TYPE C	250 pts	350 pts
350–450	10 days	TYPE D	350 pts	450 pts
450+	5 days	TYPE E	450 pts	550 pts

If gold were trading in an average range of 250 to 350 points each day, then the weighting factor for the moving average would be TYPE C, indicating medium volatility (TYPE A is lowest). Using TYPE C with a 15-day moving average, the most recent 5 days are given the weight 3, the next 5 days 2, and the last five days are weighted by 1. The buy and sell signals use the corresponding entry-signal penetration of 250 points above the moving average as a buy signal and below as a sell entry. The highs or lows of intraday trading are used to activate the entry based on values calculated after the close of trading on the prior day. A stop-loss point is fixed at the time of entry equal to the value on the same line as the proper volatility. The penetration of the stop-loss will cause the liquidation of the current trade while a new signal in the reverse direction will serve as both a stop-loss and reentry point.

There is a lot to say in favor of the principles of MPTDI. It is individualized with respect to commodities and self-adjusting with changing volatility. The stop-loss serves to limit the initial risk of the trade and allow the coordination of a money-management approach. The fixed risk differs from moving averages using standard bands, since a moving average and its band can back away from system-entry points on a gradual reversal of the price trend. But there are some rough edges to the system. The incremental ranges for volatility, entry points, and stops seem a crude measure. Even if they are accurate in the center of the range, they must get doubtful at the extremes when there is a change from one range to another. MPTDI is an interesting system; it is easy to understand and well-defined, and perhaps it works.

The 10-Day Moving-Average Rule

The most basic application of a moving-average system was proposed by Keltner in his 1960 publication, *How to Make Money in Commodities*. Of the three mechanical systems chosen by Keltner, his choice of a moving average was based on performance and experience. The system itself is quite simple: a 10-day moving average based on the average of the daily high, low, and closing prices, with a band on each side formed from the 10-day moving average of the high-low range. A buy signal occurs on

MOVING-AVERAGE SYSTEMS 81

penetration of the upper band and a sell signal when the lower band is broken; positions are always reversed.

The 10-day moving-average rule is basic, but it does account for the fundamental volatility principle and serves as an example of the actual use of moving averages. Keltner expresses his preference for this particular technique because of its identification of minor rather than medium or long-term trends, and there are some performance figures that substantiate his conclusion. As an experienced trader, he prefers the speed of the 10-day moving average, which follows the market prices with more reasonable risk than other methods. A side benefit to the selection is that the usual division required by a moving-average calculation can be substituted by a simple shift of the decimal place; and who knows how much impact that convenience had on Keltner's choice?

TECHNIQUES USING TWO MOVING AVERAGES

Since this section is restricted to applications of moving averages, do not assume that these constitute the only timing methods. Any secondary system used in conjunction with another, analyzing a shorter term than the primary, can be considered as a timing device. For example, a 3-day moving average could act as a timing technique for a 10-day average. The delays of 1, 2, 3, or more days, discussed earlier, are for timing; but you would not use a 5-day delay with a 3-day moving average since the two would not be complementary. Plotting of lag and lead moving-average values was another timing method from the discussion of moving averages. At this point we will look at the use of more than one moving average (any type of moving average would apply) to create a system; our choice will be a standard moving average.

In using two averages the slower one, requiring more days in its calculation, will define the long-term trend and the faster average will be used for timing. A long-term moving average generates a signal with respect to the long-term trend, regardless of recent patterns. A trader would be more comfortable knowing that there is a recent short-term surge of prices in the direction of his new position at the moment of entry. To resolve this problem, select two moving averages, one noticeably faster or slower than the other and apply either of the two following rules:

1. *Buy* when the faster moving average crosses the slower moving average going up.
   Sell when the faster moving average crosses the slower moving average going down.
2. *Buy* when the current price crosses above both moving averages and close out your long position when prices cross below either moving average.
   Sell when the current price crosses below both moving averages and close out your short position when prices cross above either moving average.

With the first you are always in the market, going from long to short and back as the long-term trend is violated by the faster trend. The second set of rules allows you to remain neutral when you close out your current position while the long-term trend is not penetrated. One problem with this second approach is that the faster moving average subjects you to possible whipsaws by being too close to the current price.

Double Moving Averages Applied

The combined use of two moving averages has been popular among professional advisors. Of these, one of the most well-known is *Donchian's 5- and 20-day moving averages*,[1] a method claiming one of the longest recorded operational results, beginning January 1, 1961. There is no explanation as to the reason behind the selection of these two values, but in 1961 when moving averages were more the state-of-the-art than now, they were a reasonable choice. We can justify the selection because of their close relationship to the trading days in a week and a month; even now the calendar periods might add some desirable features to a system.

Donchian's idea is to use a volatility-penetration criterion relative to the 20-day moving average, but with some added complication. The current penetration must not only cross the 20-day moving average, but exceed any previous 1-day penetration of a closing price by at least one volatility measure. His use of combined volatility and moving averages is still unique in trading systems.

The 5-day moving average serves as a liquidation criterion (along with others) and is also modified by prior penetration and volatility. These features tend to make Donchian's volatility measurement "self-adjusting." Even if selected poorly, the new penetration must exceed prior breakouts; without thorough testing it may be difficult to determine which rule has more significance. Not to forget the human element, Donchian adds a level of complication by requiring execution of certain orders to be delayed a day if the signals occurred on specific weekdays or before a holiday. The combination of different factors is generally the result of refinement over years of actual operation, but neither complexity nor sophistication guarantees success; only the results will tell.

MULTIPLE MOVING AVERAGES

If two moving averages improve trading then it should follow that three or more are even better—but it doesn't. With the use of two moving averages we have a main-trend identifier and a timing device; the addition of one or more averages or indicators must fill a distinct purpose. The more moving averages that must agree on the same signal, the less chance you will have to trade and the shorter will be the length of the trade. The elements of this problem are discussed in the chapter on filtering. At this point only consider the importance of each moving average existing for an individual purpose: a seasonal tendency, a long-term trend, timing an entry or exit.

Comprehensive Studies

At this time, there are only three known comprehensive studies of moving-average systems: Maxwell's, Davis and Thiel's, and Turner and Blinn's. They are all worth

---

[1] Donchian (1974).

MOVING-AVERAGE SYSTEMS

reading because they emphasize different features of trading that were important to the authors and would help someone whose interest is directed towards testing. But along with completeness in one area often comes a deficiency in another. Davis and Thiel analyze the greatest variety of commodities, covering virtually all of the United States crops as well as cattle, eggs, and the soybean complex. They include about 5 years of data and use relatively fast moving averages (up to 10 days); they introduce variations in lead-oriented plotting and in testing nonconsecutive days; the data used is close-only. The results are clearly presented in both detail and summary, and yield generally good returns. If we had a choice, we would have liked to have had them do more.

The authors R. E. Davis and C. C. Thiel, Jr., present excellent credentials and experience in systems testing. Their study of moving averages uses combinations of simple buy and sell signals, leading plots, and skips in the slection of sequential prices used (e.g., a skip of two uses every other price). They test a total of 100 combinations of these three factors:

- a *skip* from 1 day (none) to 5 days (1 week)
- an *average* of 5, 6, 7, 8, or 10 days
- a *leap* of 0 or 2 days.

Commodities tested were soybeans, bellies, cattle, cocoa, copper, corn, eggs, soybean meal, oats, soybean oil, potatoes, rye, sugar, and wheat.

Maxwell's study is extremely comprehensive but limited by its application to only one commodity, pork bellies. His idea was to apply combinations of features and test the results. The first feature was the choice of trend and included the possibilities of a simple mean, or a moving average of 3, 5, or 10 days, of either a conventional, average-modified, or weighted type. The second feature was the delay factor, used to improve timing of both entry or exit. Some of the possibilities were: (1) act without delay; (2) act if the signal condition persists for one additional day; (3) initiate if the signal condition persists for two additional days, but liquidate without delay; and others. Combinations of two types of moving averages and a delay factor were tested, with and without fixed or moving stops. With ten types of averages, six delay factors, and different stops, Maxwell has a lot of combinations to examine.

The study is then expanded to three-factor systems with a list of eighteen combinations of rules to generate 324 systems of which the results of 285 are recorded, with 48.77% profitable and 51.22% losers. The largest loss was generated by a system with the rules:

Enter a new position when both the weighted 3-day and weighted 10-day moving averages cross the price-mean, as long as the signal condition persists for two additional days (buy if averages cross moving down, sell if up).

Liquidate positions when the 3-day average reverses its direction through the price-mean as long as it continues for one additional day.

No fixed stops are used.

The best profits in the 3-factor system required both a 5-day average-modified and a 10-day weighted average to move across the price-mean, provided the 5-day average lagged behind the 10-day. The current position was liquidated when the shorter-term average crossed the longer term. No fixed stops were used.

Maxwell's study represents a great amount of work and some simple and sound philosophy, but does not cover an adequate sampling of data to justify most of his conclusions. Conclusions were drawn based on a selected 50-day test period using May 72 Pork Bellies, leaving many questions regarding the success of this system or any other system when applied to this short test interval. Maxwell does test four other selected 50-day periods, but the reader cannot know how these periods were chosen. Considering the effort in outlining a testing program and establishing rules, the actual magnitude of the system testing is disappointing.

Turner and Blinn study silver, recording thirteen computer-tested methods with professional competence. The systems they present are classified as:

A. Five profitable trading methods

　1. 40- and 5-day moving average
　2. 30- and 8-day moving average
　3. 30- and 5-day moving average
　4. 25- and 8-day moving average
　5. 25- and 5-day moving average

These double moving-average systems always have a position in the market, going from short to long when the faster moving average crosses above the slower one and from long to short when the opposite occurs.

B. Three terrible trading methods

　1. 10- and 1-day moving average
　2. 10- and 5-day moving average
　3. 15- and 2-day moving average

C. Two mediocre methods

　1. 40- and 2-day moving average
　2. 25- and 1-day moving average

A total of fifteen combinations of "extreme price channel" breakouts and delays were then tested. The n-day channel was defined as bounded by the highest and lowest prices reached during the prior n days. A delay of m days means that the most recent m days are not included, but used to determine whether a signal has occurred. Using this technique the authors were noticeably successful with two choices, unsuccessful with two others, and mediocre with two, concluding that the waiting period seemed to be more significant than the length of the channel and that risks could be quite large. To improve the problems of the "extreme price channel" method, only the closing prices were used and the contracts retested in hopes of reducing the give-ups. This time shorter channels outperformed longer channels.

With the loss on exit still too large, Turner and Blinn moved to price objectives, using the theory that a price goal captures more profits and maintains the integrity of the system. Accordingly, various objectives ranging from 1000 to 2000 points were tested with some improvement and some reduction in profits. Additional testing included protective stops, which did not improve otherwise successful methods.

Trading Silver Profitably is clear and informative and covers good samplings of moving-average systems. It is difficult to tell how thoroughly each system was tested because only a few results are presented. If testing were complete but profitable results were few and intermittent, these results would not be reassuring; if only a few tests were performed, there would not be an adequate sample. The important question becomes: why did the authors choose to select to publish *those* results?

CHAPTER 6
Momentum And Oscillators

The study of momentum is an analysis of changes in price rather than price levels. Among technicians momentum establishes the pace of the commodity, the rate of ascent or descent. In geometry momentum is analogous to slope, the angle of inclination as measured from a horizontal line representing time. Momentum is also thought of as force or impact, and as in Newton's law once started it tends to remain in motion in a straight line.

MOMENTUM

Momentum is usually calculated by taking the continuous difference between prices at a fixed interval. For example, today's 5-day momentum value $M(5)$ would be the difference between today's price P_t and the price 5 days ago:

$$M(5)_t = P_t - P_{t-5}$$

The momentum value $M(5)_t$ will increase as the change in price increases over a fixed number of days (5 for a 5-day momentum). Diagram 6-1 shows that a price increase will cause both angle "a" to become larger and the hypotenuse of the triangle, marked "momentum," to increase. A price rise of 100 points in 5 days can be expressed as the slope of the momentum line, or $\frac{100}{5} = 20$ and a momentum value of $(P_{t-5} + 100) - P_{t-5} = 100$. If prices had increased 150 points the slope would be $\frac{150}{5} = 30$ and the momentum 150. Since the momentum will always be 5 times greater than the slope using a 5-day evaluation, there is no need to divide every value.

$M(5)_t$ can range in value from the maximum upward move to the maximum downward move that the commodity can make in 5 days; the momentum is zero if prices are unchanged after 5 days. Diagram 6-2 shows the possible moves in the momentum calculation. Consider a commodity with a 20 point limit move. Starting at point A the 5-day price change *increased at a faster rate* for 8 days (up 2, up 4, etc.) until at point B prices had increased their fastest for the past 5 days. At point B the 5-day price

MOMENTUM AND OSCILLATORS

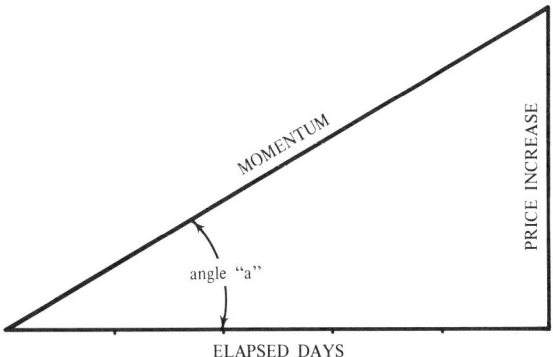

Diagram 6-1   Geometric representation of momentum.

change was $\frac{3}{5}$ of the maximum 100 point change, or 60 points. From point B to C prices still increased but at a slower rate, until the 5-day difference at point C was zero. Prices then declined at an increasing rate until at point D the maximum 5-day decline of 40 points was reached; at point E the 5-day difference was again zero. Note that at point B prices did not start down; they only increased at a slower rate. Also at C prices first began their 5-day relative decline.

The difference between a 5-day momentum plot and a 5-day moving average is not immediately apparent, but can be shown mathematically. If a 5-day momentum indicator is

$$M(5)_t = P_t - P_{t-5}$$

a corresponding moving average is

$$MA(5)_t = \tfrac{1}{5}(P_t + P_{t-1} + P_{t-2} + P_{t-3} + P_{t-4})$$

We can also express the moving average as

$$MA(5)_t = \tfrac{1}{5}(5MA_{t-1} + P_t - P_{t-5})$$
$$= MA_{t-1} + \tfrac{1}{5}(P_t - P_{t-5})$$

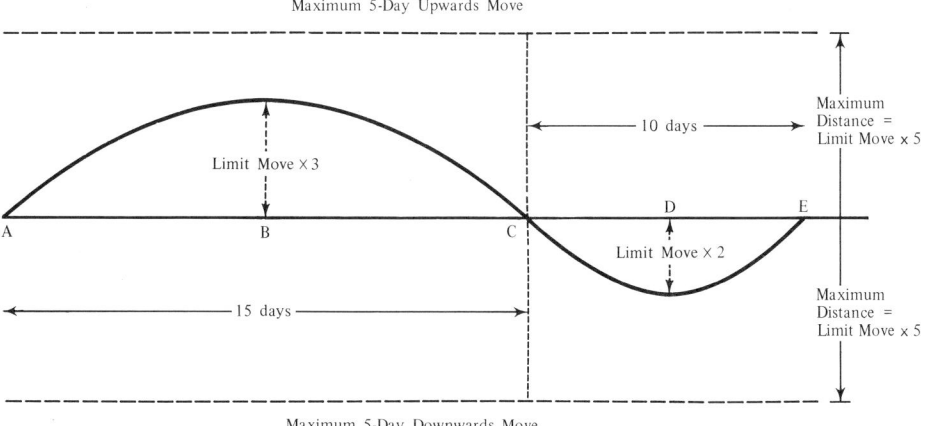

Diagram 6-2   Momentum range.

where we calculate the new moving average by subtracting the oldest value (P_{t-5}) and adding the newest (P_t). Then we can substitute into the last equation and solve for $M(5)_t$:

$$MA(5)_t = MA(5)_{t-1} + \tfrac{1}{5}(M(5)_t)$$

$$M(5)_t = 5(MA(5)_t - MA(5)_{t-1})$$

The 5-day momentum is equal to five times the difference between the last two 5-day moving-average values. We can see that $M(5)_t = 0$ if the last two moving-average points are equal, which can only happen if the oldest value to be dropped and the newest value to be added (P_t and P_{t-5}) are also equal. At first glance, it may seem that point C in Diagram 6-2 might also represent the point at which the corresponding moving average would cross the current prices to indicate that the trend has turned down. This turns out not to be the case, although a specific relationship can be found.

The use of a momentum index is straightforward. The momentum span is selected and plotted as in Diagram 6-3. A buy signal occurs whenever the value of the momentum index turns from negative to positive and a sell signal when the opposite occurs. If a band is preferred in order to establish a neutral position or a commitment zone, it should be drawn around the horizontal line representing the momentum value of zero.

In order to find that best choice of a momentum span a sampling of different values could be tested for optimum performance or a chart could be examined for some natural price cycle. Identify the significant tops and bottoms of any bar chart and average the number of days between these cycles, or find the number of days that would closely approximate the occurrences of these peaks and valleys. These natural cycles will often be the best choice of momentum span (Diagram 6-4).

An equally popular and more interesting interpretation of the momentum chart is based on an analysis of tops and bottoms. All momentum values are bounded on the top and bottom by the maximum move that could be made in the time interval represented by the span of the momentum. Faster momentum indices will reach these maximum values and stay there for extended periods of high upward or downward

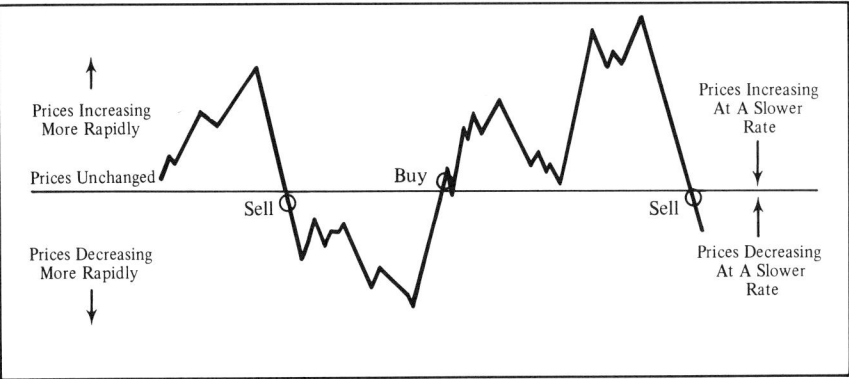

Diagram 6-3 Price momentum signals.

MOMENTUM AND OSCILLATORS

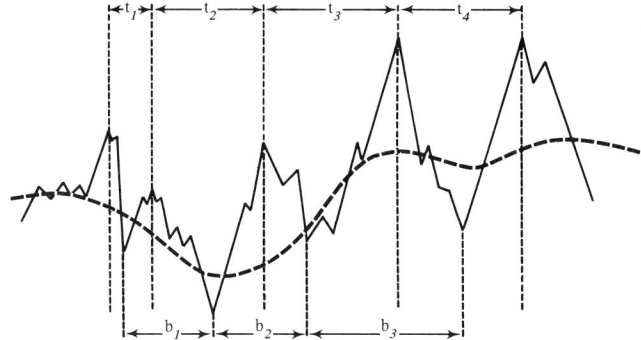

Tops and Bottoms Determine Momentum Value

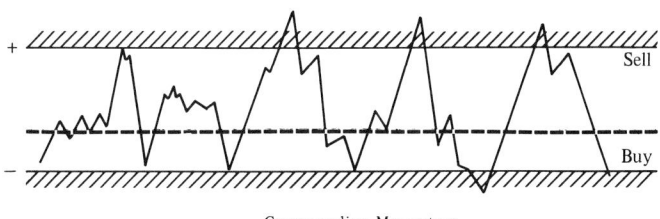

Corresponding Momentum

Diagram 6-4 Relationship of momentum to prices

momentum, while a very slow momentum index will probably never test its bounds. If the momentum system uses the horizontal zero line to enter and exit trades, then it is of no consequence whether the bounds are touched or not. Once a position is entered the high momentum condition will serve as positive reinforcement for the trade. However, the maximum positive and negative momentum values can be measured and used to anticipate the end of a trend.

The conditions at the points of maximum positive and negative momentum are called *overbought* and *oversold*, respectively. A market is overbought when it can no longer sustain the strength of the current trend, and a downward price reaction is imminent; an oversold market is ready for a upward move. A short-span momentum indicator may have disadvantages when used to determine an overbought/oversold condition since the tops and bottoms of the graph may be cut off—the momentum index must be allowed to reach its full value.

A system that takes advantage of the momentum extremes must be able to measure them. The simplest way would be to draw two horizontal lines on the momentum graph (Diagram 6-4) above and below the zero line in such a way that the tops and bottoms of the major moves are isolated. You might select these lines visually in such a way that once your new line is penetrated, a simple top or bottom is formed before momentum reverses, and that no "false" penetrations occur. Another selection might simply be a percentage of the maximum possible momentum value. A third statistical approach would be to use a multiple of the standard deviation or some other probability distribution function so that your band is formed by the zero line plus/minus 2σ (two standard deviations), meaning that about 95% of all values will be within the area bounded by the two horizontal lines. Once these lines have been drawn, the trading rules will be the following:

> Enter a new long position when the momentum index penetrates the lower bound and a new short position when the index penetrates the upper bound
>
> or
>
> Enter a new or short position on the first day the momentum index value turns down after penetrating the upper bound (the opposite for longs)
>
> or
>
> Enter a new short position when the momentum index value penetrates the upper bound coming down (the opposite for longs)
>
> or
>
> Enter a new short position after the momentum index has remained above the upper bound for t days (the opposite for longs)

To close out a profitable position we have many alternatives:

> Close out of long positions or cover a short when the momentum index value satisfies the entry condition for a reverse position
>
> or
>
> Cover a short position when the momentum index penetrates the zero line minus 1 standard deviation (or some point—e.g., halfway—between the zero line and the lower bound)
>
> or
>
> Cover a short position if the index value recrosses the zero line moving up after penetrating it moving down.

Protective stops may be used to prevent giving up all profits (as in the last point) or for protecting the trader from a sustained move that causes the index value to remain on the outside of the bound or to attain new highs or lows.

> Place a protective stop above or below the most extreme high or low index values, respectively
>
> or
>
> Follow the reversing index with a nonretreating stop based on points, percentage, or such
>
> or
>
> Establish quadrants or divisions (horizontal lines) that act as levels of attainment and do not permit reverse penetrations once entered.

These precautions are due to both normal price variability and the relationship of momentum to volatility. As prices reach higher levels, momentum tops and bottoms will get further out; at lower levels they may not be active enough to penetrate the bounds. A boundary established when coffee prices were 50¢/lb and the maximum daily range was 2¢ would not work with coffee at $2.50/lb and limits of 4¢. A reasonable

MOMENTUM AND OSCILLATORS

modification to the momentum plot might be the index value as a percentage of price or as a percentage of the permissible limit move (a volatility function). Tops and bottoms would remain more in line, although the risk would increase appreciably.

When selecting your trading rules for selling into an overbought market and buying in an oversold one, timing will be the greatest problem. The first entry rule was to sell on penetration of the upper bound. To do this is to sell when the upward move is strongest, and if you do not get an immediate reversal you might need substantial reserves to hold your position. This situation has been tested on a computer—selling into strength and placing a tight nonretreating stop. The first results were thought to be outstanding in profits and consistency until it was discovered that the computer had done exactly the opposite of what it was thought to be doing. In fact, it had *bought* when the momentum crossed the upper bound and placed a close stop *below* the entry. It did prove for a good sampling of commodities that high momentum periods carried through for enough time to capture consistent profits. It also shows that anticipating a reversal too early could be a disaster.

OSCILLATORS

Because the representation of the momentum index is that of a line fluctuating above and below a zero value, this technique has often been termed an *oscillator*. Even though it does oscillate, the terminology regarding this is confusing. In this presentation we will restrict the use of the term oscillator to a specific form of momentum, that which is normalized, expressed in terms of values ranging between $+1$ and -1 or $+1$ and 0.

To transform a standard momentum calculation into the normalized form (maximum value of $+1$, minimum value of -1) we can divide the momentum calculation by the maximum attainable value of the momentum index. A 5-day index for silver with a 20¢ limit move could be divided by $1.00 to get the normalized value. If silver were to move its limit up for 5 days, the oscillator would have the value $+1$ rather than the momentum value 100. If the limits were to change the divisor would change as well, giving the technique a means of adjusting for varying volatility. Using the normalized momentum, or oscillator, we have a well-defined top and bottom without changing any of the other good and bad features of a momentum index.

In 1972 Jim Waters and Larry Williams published a description of their A/D oscillator in *Commodities Magazine*. For their system A/D stands for Accumulation/Distribution rather than the usual notation of Advance/Decline, a well-known interpretive index for stocks. They used a unique form of relative strength, defining buying power *BP* and selling power *SP* as

$$BP = high - open \qquad SP = close - low$$

where the values used were today's open, high, low, and closing prices. The two values *BP* and *SP* show the additional buying strength (relative to the open) and selling strength (compared to the close) in an effort to measure the implications of the day's trading. The combined measurement, called the *Daily Raw Figure* (*DRF*), is calculated thusly:

$$DRF = \frac{BP + SP}{2 \times (high - low)}$$

Table 6-1 A/D Oscillator—January 77 Soybeans

						DRF		30% *DRF* Smoothing		
1976 Date	Open	High	Low	Close	*DRF*	*DRF*[a] signal	Price	30% Smoothed *DRF*	30% Smoothed signal[a]	Price
11-01	682	686	674¾	678½	.34			.34		
11-03	679	683	655	658½	.13			.28		
11-04	658	676	658	671½	.87	Sell		.45		
11-05	674	678	665	673½	.48		674	.46		
11-08	673	685	671	674¼	.54			.48		
11-09	673	673	660	666	.23			.41		
11-10	667	676½	665	675	.85	Sell		.54		
11-11	660	662½	645	651	.24		660	.45		
11-12	652	658	650½	653	.57			.49		
11-15	652	652	627	632½	.11	Buy		.37	Buy	
11-16	639½	655	636½	654¼	.90	Sell	639½	.53		639½
11-17	653	671	649	668½	.85		653	.63		
11-18	667	674½	658	666½	.48			.58		
11-19	670	691	669½	678¾	.70			.62		
11-22	680	691	675½	690½	.84	Sell		.68	Sell	
11-23	689	696½	674½	675¾	.20	Buy	689	.54		689
11-24	681	686	678½	680	.43		681	.51		
11-26	678	681½	670½	671¾	.21	Buy		.42		
11-29	670	675	661½	672	.57		670	.46		
11-30	668	677½	666	674½	.78			.56		
12-01	676	681½	673	677	.56			.56		
12-02	678	681½	675	679½	.61			.57		
12-03	679	687	679	685¾	.92	Sell		.68	Sell	
12-06	690	698½	689	696½	.84		690	.73		690
12-07	700	700	690	690½	.02	Buy		.51		
12-08	691	708	691	706	.94	Sell	691	.64		
12-09	705	712	702	703	.40		705	.57		
12-10	704	704	696	696½	.03	Buy		.41		
12-13	693	695	690½	691½	.33		693	.38	Buy	
12-14	696	701½	694	701	.83	Sell		.52		696
12-15	701	702	684	687	.11	Buy	701	.39	Buy	
12-16	688½	692	685	690½	.64		688½	.47		688½
12-17	690	690	676	677½	.05	Buy		.34	Buy	
12-20	680	684½	679½	683¼	.82	Sell	680	.49		680
12-21	682	688	679	687½	.80		682	.58		
12-22	688	693	686½	689¼	.60			.59		
12-23	689	693	684½	692½	.71			.62		
12-27	695	705	694	700¾	.76			.66		
12-28	701	706½	697½	705¾	.76			.69	Sell	
12-29	708	710	699	699½	.11	Buy		.52		708
12-30	703½	708	698	706½	.65		703½	.56		

[a] Signals taken following day on open.

MOMENTUM AND OSCILLATORS

Table 6-1 (*continued*)

Basic *DRF* performance[b]		30% smoothed *DRF* performance[b]	
16 signals		7 signals	
4 compounded signals		3 compounded signals	
12 profits		5 profits	
Average profit	13.08¢	Average profit	22.10¢
4 losses		2 losses	
Average loss	14.25¢	Average loss	6.50¢
Net profit/loss	99.96¢	Net profit/loss	97.50¢

[b] No commissions have been deducted.

The maximum value of 1 is reached when a commodity opens trading at the low and closes at the high: $BP - SP = high - low$. When the opposite occurs and the market opens at the high and closes on the lows, *DRF* will be 0. Each commodity will develop its own patterns, which can be smoothed or traded in many ways similar to a momentum index. The Waters/Williams A/D oscillator solves problems of volatility and physical limits. *DRF* completely adjusts to higher or lower trading ranges because the divisor itself is a multiple of the day's range; and because each day is treated independently, the cumulative values of the momentum index are not part of the results. This day-to-day evaluation causes *DRF* to vary radically and requires some smoothing technique or cycle interpretation to make it useable. As an example, look at the January 77 Soybean contract for the two months before delivery, November and December 1976. Table 6-1 shows the calculations for the daily raw figure and for the smoothed *DRF* using an exponential moving average with a smoothing constant of 30% (selected arbitrarily). *DRF* is plotted as the solid line on a scale of .00 to 1.00 in Diagram 6-5 and is extremely erratic in its movements. The dotted line is the smoothed *DRF*. Once plotted, two horizontal lines can be drawn to isolate the peaks and bottoms of *DRF*; the top part becomes a zone representing an overbought condition and the bottom zone represents oversold. You should bear in mind that these lines were drawn after *DRF* was plotted and cannot be construed as predictive; however, in the article by Waters and Williams their example of soybean oil had lines drawn in a similar place. Corresponding broken lines were drawn to indicate the overbought and oversold state for the smoothed *DRF*.

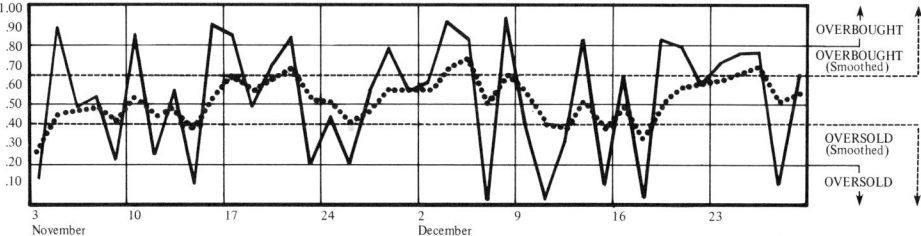

Diagram 6-5 A/D oscillator.

The rules for using the A/D oscillator were not defined in the *Commodities Magazine* presentation, but some simple rules could be:

Sell when *DRF* (or smoothed *DRF*) penetrates into the overbought zone. Close out all accumulated long positions if any and go short on the open of the next trading day.
Buy when the opposite condition occurs.

If *DRF* (or smoothed *DRF*) enters an overbought or oversold zone more than once without the opposite zone being entered, one additional position is added at each reentry. Following these rules the A/D oscillator showed excellent success for both the raw and smoothed values. Accepting the after-the-fact designation of zones, the results still show that the method is viable and that a smoothing technique can be applied to *DRF* to vary the speed of trading.

Waters and Williams used a simple 10-day momentum for their example of the A/D oscillator. The choice of interval can be determined by examining the tops and bottoms of a chart for the natural cycle of the prices.

In reviewing the A/D oscillator, there are modifications to be considered. Conceptually we want the value of the oscillator to be +1 when prices are rising rapidly. The most extreme example of that is a locked-limit no-trading day, representative of the strongest (or weakest) market. But for that case the open, high, low, and closing prices are all the same and *DRF* cannot be determined (since the divisor is zero). A more basic problem concerns gap openings. A much higher opening with a stronger close would also upset the resulting *DRF*. For example, the following trading occurs:

Example 6-1   Original *DRF* Calculations

	Open	High	Low	Close	DRF	ΔDRF	ΣΔDRF
Monday	43.00	44.00	40.00	41.00	.25		
Tuesday	42.00	42.00	39.00	40.00	.17	−.17	−.17
Wednesday	38.50	38.50	38.00	38.00	.00	+.17	.00
Thursday	42.00	42.00	39.00	40.00	.17	−.33	−.33
Friday	40.00	43.00	40.00	42.00	.83	+.50	+.17

Note that on Wednesday the Δ*DRF* indicates that the momentum has reversed, while in fact the price is falling rapidly and gives no indication of recovering; it may actually be gaining momentum. On Thursday the price soars up and closes in the midrange but the Δ*DRF* shows a new downward momentum. The problem seems to be related to lack of association with the prior closing price. The daily movement can take on different appearances if the entire range was above or below the closing price. To form this link, we will replace the current high or low with the prior closing price if that price was outside the current trading range. Example 6-2 shows the results smoothed out and leaves the trend intact.

MOMENTUM AND OSCILLATORS 95

Example 6-2 Adjusted *DRF* Values

	Open	High	Low	Close	DRF	ΔDRF	ΣΔDRF
Monday	43.00	44.00	40.00	41.00	.25		
Tuesday	42.00	42.00	39.00	40.00	.17	−.17	−.17
Wednesday	38.50	(40.00)	38.00	38.00	.37	+.04	−.13
Thursday	42.00	42.00	(38.00)	40.00	.25	−.12	−.25
Friday	40.00	43.00	40.00	42.00	.83	+.58	+.33

Another construction of an oscillator can be made using the highs and lows relative to the prior close:

$$O_t = \frac{H_t - C_{t-1}}{H_t - L_t}$$

The two days are linked together and the ratio of the high price relative to the prior close is measured against the total range for the day. For the normal case $H_t \geq C_{t-1} \geq L_t$; but if $C_{t-1} > H_t$ or $L_t > C_{t-1}$, then C_{t-1} replaces either H_t or L_t to extend the range. The value of O_t will be either 1 or 0 for these extreme cases. As with the A/D oscillator the values derived from this method may also be smoothed.

Oscillators are not the only tools for measuring momentum or for determining overbought or oversold conditions. Because it is very different from either a charting technique or a moving average it is valuable either on its own or as a confirmation of another method.

A word of caution. Trading against the trend can be exciting and profitable, but at considerably greater risk than a trend-following system. The problem with selling an overbought condition is that there is no way to hold your losses to a minimum. Once you sell, the momentum or the oscillator value could sustain its strength and move against your position. It didn't happen in the examples, but it might in actual trading.

VELOCITY-ACCELERATION

A method conceptually similar to momentum is derived from the concepts in physics of velocity and acceleration, elements of the science of motion. *Velocity*, as defined in the fundamental concepts of mechanics, is the rate of change of position with respect to time (also called *speed*). There are two types of velocity, *average* and *instantaneous*, where the average velocity is simply calculated as the mean velocity over a fixed distance and for a fixed time interval. In working with commodity prices our time interval is always in days and our distance is measured in points; so that if silver moved 40 points in 6 days, its average velocity is

$$\bar{v} = \tfrac{40}{6} = 6\tfrac{2}{3} \text{ points per day}$$

In general, the average velocity is expressed

$$\bar{v} = \frac{D}{T}$$

where D is the total elapsed distance over the time interval T. For a geometric interpretation of momentum, we can relate D to the change in price and T to the length of the momentum span and get exactly the same results for average velocity as we do for slope.

The instantaneous velocity v, which is the velocity calculated at a specific point in time, will be different. In order to determine the instantaneous velocity we use a mathematical technique called *differentiation*. It effectively allows you to look at smaller and smaller time intervals and consequently smaller distances on the price curve until you have reduced the slope calculation to a single point. The results of the process of differentiation is called the *derivative* and is expressed

$$v_t = \lim_{\Delta t \to 0} \overset{(1)}{\frac{\Delta D}{\Delta t}} = \overset{(2)}{\frac{dD}{dt}}$$

This shows that the velocity taken at a point (2) is the result of the time interval (Δt) becoming progressively smaller without reaching zero. The rules for differentiation can be found in any advanced mathematics book and we will only present the results of the process for the curves we have studied. The velocity v_t represents the speed or

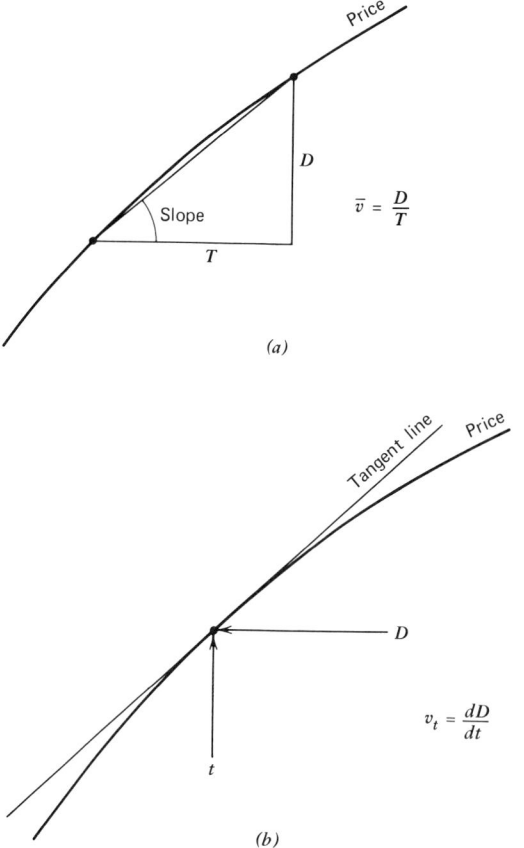

Diagram 6-6   (a) Average velocity; (b) instantaneous velocity.

Table 6-2 Equations for Velocity and Acceleration

	Basic equation	Velocity at x_t,[a]	Acceleration at x_t
Straight line	$y_t = a + bx_t$	$v_t = b$	$a_t = 0$
Curvilinear	$y_t = a + bx_t + cx_t^2$	$v_t = b + 2cx_t$	$a_t = 2c$
Logarithmic (base a)	$y_t = \log_a x_t$	$\begin{cases} v_t = (\log_a e)/x_t \text{ or} \\ v_t = 1/(x_t \ln a) \end{cases}$	$a_t = -1/(x_t^2 \ln a)$
Logarithmic (natural log)	$y_t = \ln x_t$	$v_t = 1/x_t$	$a_t = -1/x_t^2$
Exponential	$y_t = e^{ax_t}$	$v_t = ae^{ax_t}$	$a_t = a^2 e^{ax_t}$
Moving average	$y_t = \dfrac{x_t + x_{t-1} + \cdots + x_{t-n+1}}{n}$	$v_t = 1$	$a_t = 0$
Weighted moving average	$y_t = \dfrac{a_1 x_t + a_2 x_{t-1} + \cdots + a_n x_{t-n+1}}{n}$	$v_t = \dfrac{a_1 + a_2 + \cdots + a_n}{n}$	$a_t = 0$
Exponential smoothing	$y_t = y_{t-1} + c(x_t - y_{t-1})$	$v_t = c$	$a_t = 0$

[a] Since volocity and acceleration are time derivitives, all equations implicity include the factor $\dfrac{d(x_t)}{d_t}$ as part of the right member.

momentum of the price at the point in time t. If v gets larger for $t_0, t_1, t_2, \ldots$, then the velocity is increasing; if v gets smaller the velocity is decreasing. Since the velocity also denotes direction it can be both positive and negative in value and appear similar to a momentum indicator. Systems applied to momentum may equally be applied to velocity. Of course, some of the basic equations have constant velocity and cannot be used for a velocity trading plan since the values never change. The straight line, simple and weighted moving averages, and exponential smoothing all have constant velocities. To use these equations, we will apply filtering functions shown later.

When you reapply the processes of differentiation to the equation for velocity you get the rate of change of the speed with respect to time, or *acceleration*. This type of acceleration will tell you whether the velocity is increasing or decreasing at any point in time. The acceleration, also called the *second derivative*, adds another dimension to momentum, and may allow you to improve the timing of trades.

Let's assume that you could already calculate velocity and acceleration (Table 6.2). The following are the possible combinations that can occur:

Vel	Acc	Price movement
+	+	Price is moving up at an increasing rate
+	0	Price is moving up at a constant rate
+	−	Price is moving up at a decreasing rate
0	0	Price is static
−	+	Price is moving down at a decreasing rate
−	0	Price is moving down at a constant rate
−	−	Price is moving down at an increasing rate

Using the acceleration feature, we can determine when the velocity (or momentum) is about to change direction or we can confirm the strength of a current price move.

Filtering Functions

The first part of this discussion is for readers with solid mathematical background, while the second set of equations can be used by anyone capable of applying exponential smoothing. The formal equations for adapting the exponential smoothing method to velocity-acceleration requires the following filtering functions. Let

$$x(s)_n = \text{smoothed value of } x_n$$
$$x(o)_n = \text{observed value of } x_n$$
$$x(p)_n = \text{predicted value of } x_n$$
$$v = \dot{x}_n = \text{velocity (1st derivative)}$$
$$a = \ddot{x}_n = \text{acceleration (2nd derivative)}$$
$$\alpha = \text{weighting factor}, 0 \leq \alpha \leq 1$$
$$\beta^2 = 2\alpha\gamma$$
$$2\beta = \left(\alpha + \beta + \frac{\gamma}{2}\right)\alpha$$

MOMENTUM AND OSCILLATORS

The filtering functions are defined as:

$$x(s)_n = x(p)_n + \alpha(x(o)_n - x(p)_n)$$
$$x(p)_{n+1} = x(s)_n + \dot{x}_n t + \tfrac{1}{2}\ddot{x}(p)_n t^2$$
$$\dot{x}_n = \dot{x}_{n-1} + \ddot{x}_{n-1} t + \frac{\beta}{t}(x(o)_n - x(p)_n)$$
$$\ddot{x}_n = \ddot{x}_{n-1} + \frac{\gamma}{t^2}(x(o)_n - x(p)_n)$$

These formulas are presented in an iterative form to allow for adaptation to computer processing. Values for α and γ must be estimated and tested.

Velocity-Acceleration Applied

To interpret this for use in a daily trading calculation, we select a value for a by prior testing and then

$$a = \text{assigned by prior selection}$$
$$b = 4 - 2a - 4\sqrt{1-a}$$
$$c = \frac{b^2}{2a}$$

Let x_t be the closing price, mean, or other combination of prices that forms the basis for the smoothing function. Perform the following calculations in order:

$S_t = P_{t-1} + a(x_t - P_{t-1})$ smoothed trend
$V_t = V_{t-1} + A_{t-1} + b(x_t - P_{t-1})$ velocity
$A_t = A_{t-1} + c(x_t - P_{t-1})$ acceleration
$P_t = S_t + V_t + \tfrac{1}{2}A_t$ next value for trend smoothing (first step)

To start the operations assign the initial values of $V_0 = 0$, $A_0 = 0$, and $P_0 = x_0$.

PHASING (SYNCHRONIZING A MOVING AVERAGE TO REPRESENT CYCLES)

One of the most interesting applications of the cyclic element of a time-series is presented by J. M. Hurst in *The Profit Magic of Stock Transaction Timing*. This section will not try to replace an actual reading of the book, but will highlight some of the concepts and simplify the application. The cycle is one of the four basic components of a time-series. In order to isolate the cycle from the other elements, the trending and seasonal factors should be subtracted, reducing the resulting values to their cyclic and chance parts. In many cases the seasonal and cyclic components are similar, but

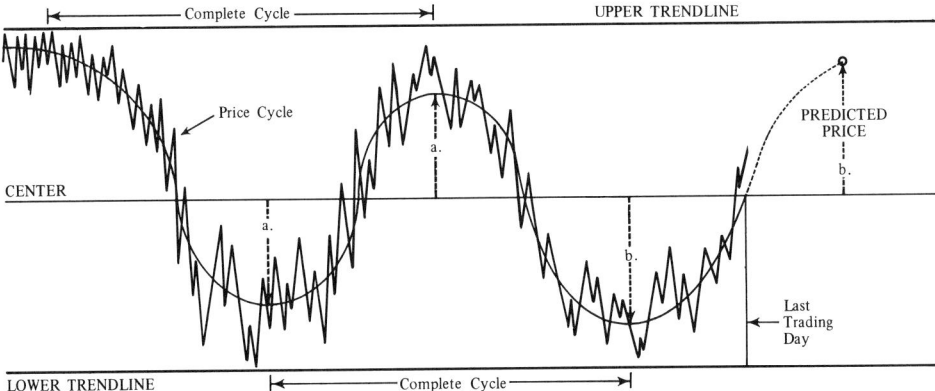

Diagram 6-7 Price cycle using a moving average.

the trend is unique. Hurst treats the cyclic component as the dominant component of price movement and uses a moving average in a unique way to identify the combined trend-cycle.

Graphically we see the system as measuring the oscillation about a straight-line approximation of the trend (center line), anticipating equal moves above and below. Prices have many long-term and short-term trends, depending on the interval of analysis. Since this technique was originally applied to stocks, most of the examples used by Hurst are long-term trends expressed in weeks. For commodities the same technique could be used by applying the nearest futures contract on a continuous basis; a short-term look at cycles can use one specific contract. Continuation charts are available through professional services.

As a simple example of the concept, we will choose a moving average of medium length for our trending component. A selection of the length of the moving average could be made by drawing a channel around the prices by connecting the tops and bottoms of the prior moves with trend lines. The number of elapsed trading days for one complete "cycle" to occur, where the prices touch the top and bottom of the band and return to the center of the channel, may be a good choice of the "full-span" moving average. The "half-span" moving average is then equal to half the days used in the full-span average.

The problem with using moving averages is that they always lag behind. A 40-day moving average is always 20 days behind the price movement. The current average is plotted under the most recent price, although it comes closer to representing the price pattern if the plot were lagged by half the value of the average. This method applies a process that will be called *phasing*, since it aligns the tops and bottoms of the moving average with the corresponding tops and bottoms of the price movement. To phase the full- and half-span moving averages, we lag each plot by half the days in the average, causing the curve to overlay the price movement (Diagram 6-8). We project the phased full- and half-span moving averages until they cross. A line or curve connecting two or more of the most recent intersections will be the major trend line. The more points used, the more complicated the regression formula for calculating the trend; Chapter 2 gives a variety of linear and nonlinear techniques for

MOMENTUM AND OSCILLATORS

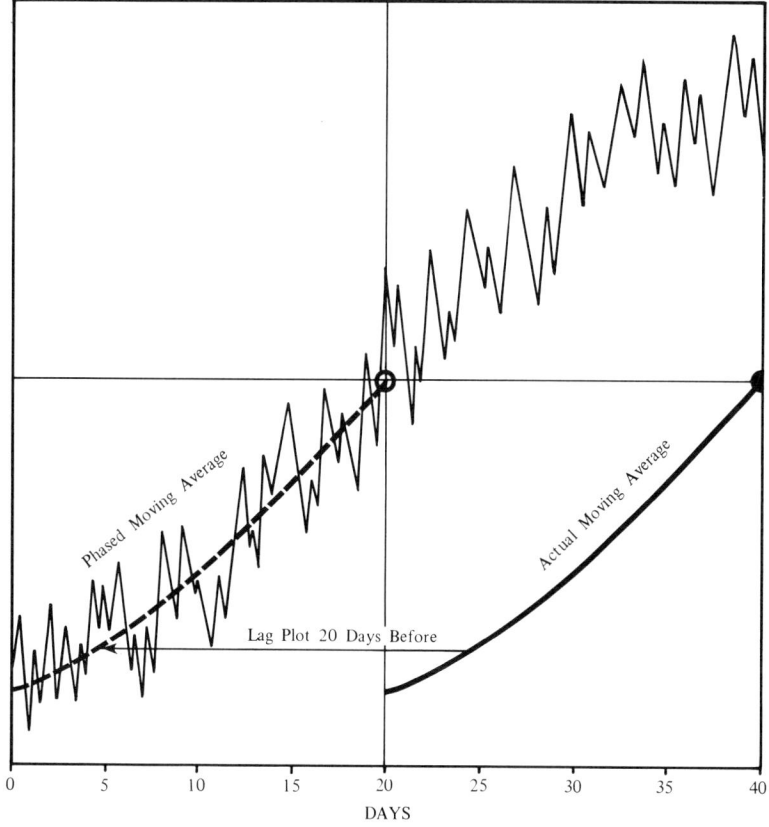

Diagram 6-8 Phasing.

finding a "best fit" of these intersections. Once the trend line is calculated we can also project it as the center of the next price cycle.

With the trend identified and projected, the next step is to reflect the cycle about the trend. When the phased half-span average turns down at point A (Diagram 6-9) we measure the greatest distance (D) of the actual prices above the projected trend line. The system then anticipates the actual price crossing the trend line at point X and declining an equal distance (D) below the projected trend line. Once the projected

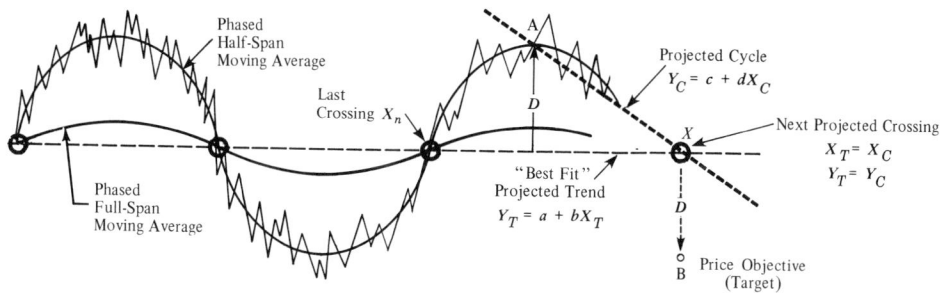

Diagram 6-9 Finding the target price.

crossing becomes an actual crossing, the distance D can be measured exactly and the price objective firmed. Rules for using this technique can be listed as follows:

1. Calculate the full-span moving average for the selected number of days; lag the plot by half the days. If the full-span moving average uses F days, the value of the average is calculated at $t - F/2$, where t is the current day. Call this phased point PH_t.
2. The half-span moving average is calculated for H days and plotted at $t - H/2 + PH_t$.
3. Record the points where the two phased averages PH_i and PF_i cross and call these points $X_n, X_{n-1}, \ldots$.
4. Find the trend by performing a linear regression on the crossing points $X_n, X_{n-1}, \ldots$. If a straight line, then $Y_T = a + bX_T$.
5. Record the highest (or lowest) values of the price since the last crossing, X_n.
6. Calculate the projection of the half-span by creating a straight line from the highest (or lowest) half-span value since the last crossing (A) to the last calculated half-span value. This equation will be $Y_C = c + dX_C$.
7. Find the point at which the projected trend line crosses the projected cyclic line by setting the equations equal to one another and solving for X and Y. At the point of crossing $(X_T, Y_T) = (X_C, Y_C)$, giving us two equations in two unknowns, which is easily solvable (X is time in days; Y is price).
8. If the half-span is moving down, the maximum price reached by the commodity since the last crossing is subtracted from the Y coordinate of the projected crossing. This distance D is subtracted again from the Y coordinate to determine the price objective. If the half-span is moving up, the price objective uses the minimum price and reflects the distance above the projected crossing. It should be noted that this calculation of distance is simplified because the trend is established by a straight line; for non-linear fits, the measurement of D will be more complicated.
9. Recalculate the moving averages, the half-span projection (6), the projected crossing (7), and price objective (8) each day until the actual crossing occurs at the time D is fixed.
10. Follow the trading rules:

    a. Enter a new long position when the half-span moving average turns up; cover any existing short positions regardless of the price objective.
    b. Enter a new short position when the half-span moving average turns down; close out any long positions.
    c. Close out both long and short positions if the price objective is reached. An allowable error factor is considered as 10% of the height of the full cycle (lowest to highest point).

This approach to cycles should be studied carefully, since it is a complex problem solved using elementary mathematics. There are many techniques for determining trends and a number of seasonally oriented systems, but a cyclic approach is rare. While Hurst's explanation is more complete and more sophisticated, the interpretation presented in this section should be considered a reasonable approximation.

CHAPTER 7
Living With Moving Averages

The advantages of moving averages are those of most well-defined or disciplined systems, and so are the disadvantages. The major points relative to the general inflexibility of systems are discussed in a latter section of Chapter 16. The present section refers specifically to moving averages. The first question that a trader should ask is: "What can I expect from a moving average?" Although the question might be vague, it requires a statement of the nature of the trades, profitability, and reliability. Trading on a moving average requires the development of a "feel" for its results. Fast moving averages enter into trades on the first strong reversal day; slower averages identify longer trends. No matter what speed or how well timed, a moving average can never be precise; consequently, watching the commodity prices with respect to the moving average will be aggravating. The moving average will rarely enter or close out a position at just the right place. It is intended to extract profits from the middle of a trend and hold losses to a minimum. The risks and magnitude of the rewards are intrinsic to the speed of the moving average, although the risk/reward ratio may be similar for many moving averages. Since the success of such a system can only be judged by its actual performance, users should study weekly or monthly accumulated results rather then confirm the accuracy of the current market position by observing the relative position of the trend line to the price.

The slower the moving average, the farther behind it will lag.[1] Professional traders lean towards the faster averages and portfolio managers towards slower. For trading only one commodity, individual risks on trades can be kept small using faster averages. The portfolio trader can offset a long-term adverse move in one commodity with an equally long favorable trend in another. The advantage of long diversified trades is that each one will move in the direction of the trend the majority of days, even if that only means 6 out of every 10 days. A portfolio with ten commodities, each with a 60% probability of a trend move, will generally result in six moving with you and four against you on any given day. It is highly unlikely that all ten will move

---
[1] This is for "first-order" moving averages.

against your positions on the same day, while it is possible that they will all move in a profitable direction.

The speed of a moving average determines the nature of the trend identified. The long-term moving average corresponds to inflation, production cycles, seasonal adjustments and other noticeable fundamental elements of prices. The faster average reflects momentum, market psychology, and short cycles. In addition, a fast moving average may work more successfully within a consolidation area, taking small profits within the range, whereas the slow moving average would retain the same position throughout the development and life of the intermediate trading range. A means for selecting the proper moving average could be based on its success in support-resistance ranges of a predetermined size. For example, if a moving average is required to return a profit for 50¢ swing in silver, which occurs over an average elapsed period of 10 days, you would want to identify the change in 2 days and exit 2 days after the market reversed, leaving 6 days of trending profit. A 2-day or 3-day moving average or .75 exponential-smoothing constant would be your choice. In this way the span of the average can be adjusted according to the current market patterns.

"TAKE YOUR PROFITS AND LET YOUR LOSSES RUN"

As ridiculous as that saying seems, many traders who use moving-average systems are guilty of exactly that. Moving averages cut losses short relative to the length of the moving average; they also lag behind a fast price move. It is inevitable for a trader who sees a $1,000 profit on a single contract to think of closing out his position because the stop is placed where his net return would be only $300. To do this would be to place an arbitrary limit on potential profits and to let losses remain at their natural size by following the rules exactly. A trend-following system makes up for a lot of losses when prices sustain a move in one direction—don't cut it short.

SELECTING THE RIGHT MOVING AVERAGE

Up to now we have introduced only general ways of selecting the right moving average, all of which may be unrealistic. The actual considerations in the choice are conceptually simple, but difficult to implement manually.

The selected moving average should be tested with an adequate sample to assure a small predictive error.

This is easy enough for shorter moving-average calculations that can generate 100 trades each year for a single contract, but for slow averages it may require 10 years of test data. For the number of trades necessary for accurate testing, you should refer to the earlier section on sampling. This may be a reason in favor of shorter trends.

Will the same moving average work for all commodities?

It may be that it does, but there is no reason to assume so. In addition, success over a long time period does not eliminate the possibility of a losing run of trades of sufficient length to cause ruin. Unfortunately, this may mean that the testing performed initially will have to be repeated periodically for each commodity traded. To make matters even worse, there is a good argument for differing patterns between old and new crop agricultural products or even near and deferred contracts of metals that may have diverse seasonal demand. Testing could become a full-time proposition.

How long can you expect a moving average to perform after it has been chosen from an adequate sample?

Certainly not forever. If price levels stay the same or the system accounts for volatility or some other variable factors, the useable life of the moving average can be extended. Consider a moving average tested over the past 2 years that generated a large number of short trades. If testing were completed yesterday, then today's price movement would relate strongly to the levels and patterns of the test. But in the next year prices may move to levels not part of the original test. It is unreasonable to expect continued success over a period of time equal to the length of the test; a 2-year historic test should not be used for the next 2 years. As in all price forecasting, accuracy declines sharply outside the ranges of the data upon which the forecast was based. The system analyst must decide on the frequency and necessity of retesting.

CHAPTER 8
Cycles And Secular Trends

In Chapter 3 we introduced the components of a time-series: the trend, the cycle, the seasonal pattern, and chance movement. We have explained various ways of finding the trend using statistical analysis and forecasting techniques and then the autoregressive methods of moving averages. At this time we turn our attention to the other two principal components, the cyclic and seasonal movements. The seasonal element appears in almost all commodities, whether crops or nonperishables. The essential habits of the consumer can cause a seasonal pattern in metals, as weather does for the crops. The seasonal component is a special case of a cycle and may cause difficulties in analysis if it is not treated separately. It has all the characteristics of a cycle, varying with a constant period of 12 months and fluctuating, when adjusted, equally above and below an average price.

The cycles in which we are interested are not as regular as seasonal patterns. Many are caused by factors that are specific to an industry. The storage and carry-over of large supplies of grain has a dampening effect on the farm prices; the shutting of mines will have an inflationary influence on a metal. The frequency of these cycles is usually variable; for example, the supply of corn is not always at its maximum every 4 years, nor is the supply of coffee reduced to a minimum in 3 years. The magnitude of the price increase during the high-demand periods is not measurable, while the base price during the high-surplus times of the cycle may be determined to some degree by government support programs.

It is important to be able to identify both cyclic and seasonal patterns. For this purpose, as with the trending component there are statistical and mathematical ways as well as heuristic methods. The mathematical means can use sophisticated trigonometric formulas or moving averages adapted to finding a specific pattern. Both methods will be discussed in this chapter, followed by some practical applications. This mathematical approach will not distinguish between the long-term cyclic component and the shorter seasonal pattern; methods discussed afterwards will differentiate them.

TRIGONOMETRIC CURVE-FITTING

The regression techniques using the general polynomial equation

$$y = a + bx + cx^2 + \cdots$$

as well as systems of simultaneous linear equations for solving the multivariate problem may represent a curve of a nonrepeating form. It is often convenient to study uniform waves to represent cycles of motion. Most of these cycles can be fitted using the trigonometric functions of *sine* and *cosine*. These functions are also called *periodic waves* because they nominally repeat every 360° or 2π radians (where $\pi = 3.141592$). Since we can convert all notation from degrees to radians using the relationship

$$1 \ degree = \frac{2\pi}{360}$$

all work will be performed in degrees. Some other terms that must be understood when discussing wave motion are:

1. *Amplitude* (a), the height of the wave from the center (x-axis) at any point.
2. *Frequency* (ω), the number of wavelengths that repeat every 360°, calculated as $\omega = 1/T$.
3. *Period* (T), the number of time units necessary to complete one wavelength (or cycle).

A simple sine wave fluctuates from 0 to $+1$, then back to 0, -1, and 0 again for each cycle (one wavelength) as the degrees increase from 0° to 360°. To relate the wavelength to a specific distance in boxes (on graph paper) simply divide 360° by the number of boxes in a full wavelength and you have the increments, in degrees, represented by each box. For example, a 100-box cycle would give a value of 3.6° to each box. To change the wavelength to other than 360° we introduce a constant ω, which is a multiplier of the angle of a standard sine wave and is written

$$\sin \omega \phi$$

If $\omega > 1$ the wavelength is less than 360°; if $\omega < 1$ it will be greater than 360°. Actually, as ω is the frequency, it gives the number of wavelengths in each 360° cycle. To change the *phase* of the wave we add the value b to the angle and write the new term

$$\sin(\psi \phi + b)$$

If b is 180° the sine wave will start in the second half of the cycle; b serves to shift the wave to the left. The last variation changes the *amplitude* by multiplying the resulting value by the constant a. Since the sine will range from $+1$ to -1 the new range will be $+a$ to $-a$. Diagram 8-1 shows a generalized sinusoidal wave.

Since there are few examples of commodity-price movement that can be represented by such a uniform wave, the concept of adding waves must be introduced. Two generalized sine waves can be added together to form a very different *compound wave*:

$$y = a_1 \sin(\omega_1 \phi + b_1) + a_2 \sin(\omega_2 \phi + b_2) \tag{1}$$

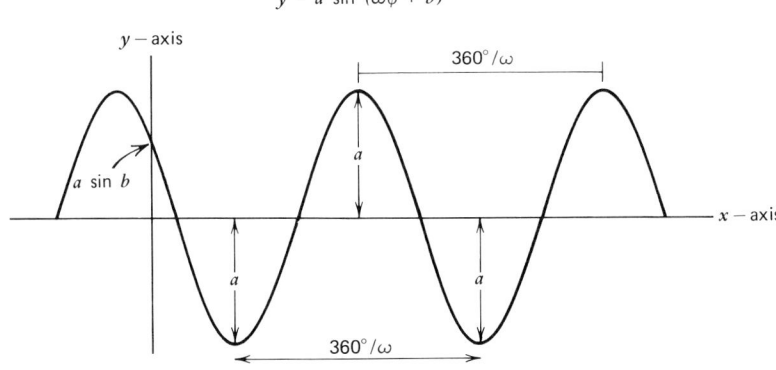

Diagram 8-1 Sinusoidal wave.

Each set of characteristic variables a_1, ω_1, b_1, and a_2, ω_2, b_2 can be different, but both waves are measured at the same point ϕ, at the same time. Consider an example that lets the phase constants b_1 and b_2 be zero:

$$y_1 = 3 \sin 4\phi$$
$$y_2 = 5 \sin 6\phi$$
$$y = y_1 + y_2$$

Diagram 8-2 shows the individual regular waves y_1 and y_2 and the degenerating wave y over the interval $0°$ to $180°$. Note that both y_1 and y_2 began the normal upward cycle at $0°$; but by $180°$ they are perfectly out of phase. During the next $180°$ the two waves come back into phase. When combining periodic waves, it is useful to know the maximum and minimum amplitude of the resulting wave. Since the peaks of the two elementary waves do not necessarily fall at the same point, the sum of $a_1 + a_2$ represents only the greatest value that may be reached.

A mathematical technique, called *differentiation*, allows you to find these values directly. The first derivative, with respect to angle ϕ, is written $dy/d\phi$ or y', where y is

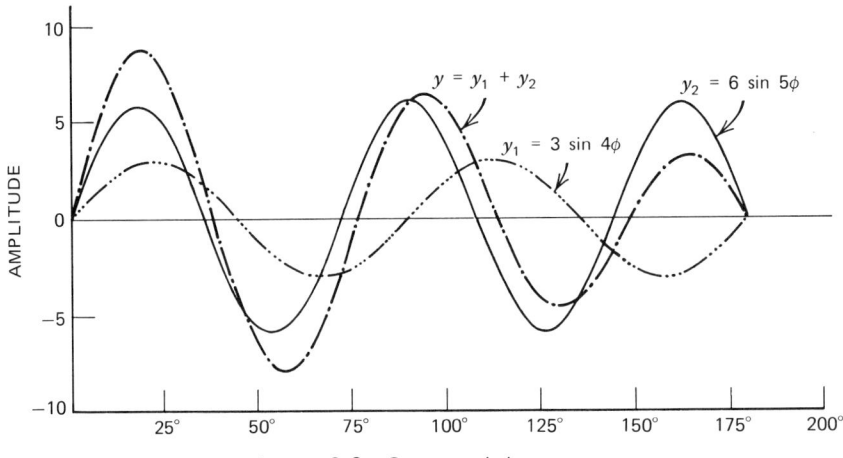

Diagram 8-2 Compound sine wave.

CYCLES AND SECULAR TRENDS 109

the formula to be differentiated. The simple rules to follow are

$$\frac{d}{d\phi}(\sin \phi) = \cos \phi; \quad \frac{d}{d\phi}(\cos \phi) = -\sin \phi$$

$$\frac{d}{d\phi}(\sin \omega\phi) = \omega \cos \omega\phi$$

$$\frac{d}{d\phi}(\sin(\omega\phi + b)) = \omega \cos (\omega\phi + b)$$

$$\frac{d}{d\phi}(a_1\sin(\omega_1\phi+b_1)+a_2\sin(\omega_2\phi+b_2)) = a_1\omega_1\cos(\omega_1\phi+b_1) + a_2\omega_2\cos(\omega_2\phi+b_2)$$

Applying this method to our previous example, we have

$$y = 3 \sin 4\phi + 6 \sin 5\phi$$

$$\frac{dy}{d\phi} = y' = 12 \cos 4\phi + 30 \cos 5\phi$$

The points of maximum and/or minimum value occur when $y' = 0$. Taken separately, with $y'_1 = 12 \cos 4\phi$ and $y'_2 = 30 \cos 5\phi$, we can see that $y'_1 = 0$ when $4\phi = 90°$ and $270°$ or when $\phi = 22\frac{1}{2}°$ or $67\frac{1}{2}°$, as seen in Diagram 8-2. For y'_2 the maximum and minimum values occur when $y'_2 = 0$ or $5\phi = 90°$ and $270°$, at $\phi = 18°$ and $54°$ respectively. While we are on the simpler component equations it should be pointed out that the first derivative tells where the extreme high and low points are, but does not tell which one is the maximum and which is the minimum. The second derivation, y'', calculated by taking the derivative of y', is used for this distinction as follows:

if $y'(x) = 0$ and $y''(x) > 0$, then $y(x)$ is a minimum

if $y'(x) = 0$ and $y''(x) < 0$, then $y(x)$ is a maximum

From this we can determine that $y_1 = 22\frac{1}{2}°$ and $y_2 = 18°$ are maxima and $y_1 = 67\frac{1}{2}°$ and $y_2 = 54°$ are minima.

Anyone interested in pursuing the analysis of maxima and minima (extrema) will find more complete discussions in a text on calculus. Rather than concentrating on these theoretical aspects of curves,[1] consider a practical example of finding any existing cycles in the price of scrap copper, shown in Table 8-1 and charted in Diagram 8-3. The price peaks seem somewhat evenly spaced, occurring at mid-1966, January 1970, and January 1974, about 4 years apart. The solutions to these problems are tedious; therefore, calculations will be performed on a programmable handheld calculator with the programs recorded in Appendix 2b.

The results obtained by using actual copper prices will not be as good as those obtained by using fictitious data, but they will be realistic. It is important to be able to understand the significance of practical results and use them effectively. This example will attempt to find the principal cycle in scrap-copper prices.

Since trigonometric curves fluctuate above and below a horizontal line of value zero, the first step in fitting the data points is to find a detrending line using the least-squares method. This will give the equation for a straight line representing the upward

---

[1] A more specific presentation of trigonometric curve fitting can be found in Cleeton (1976), Chapter 8. The material covered in this section is carried further in that work.

Table 8-1 Dealer's Buying Price, No. 2 Heavy Copper Scrap at New York[a]

| | Average quarterly price (¢/lb) | | | | |
Year	1st	2nd	3rd	4th	Yearly Average
1963	22.12	22.46	22.17	22.00	22.19
1964	23.18	24.56	25.57	30.59	25.98
1965	28.23	33.77	35.90	40.05	34.49
1966	46.22	51.48	40.76	40.16	44.66
1967	36.51	29.30	30.36	36.42	33.15
1968	39.75	30.07	29.08	32.13	32.76
1969	38.94	42.95	43.38	46.23	42.88
1970	47.70	46.98	35.78	27.35	39.45
1971	25.40	29.45	27.15	28.48	27.57
1972	32.74	33.53	30.01	29.25	31.38
1973	36.82	45.07	55.13	65.51	49.80
1974	66.56	70.06	27.30	35.62	54.88
1975	32.06	31.46	35.75	36.46	33.94
1976	38.22	43.24	45.46	38.96	41.47

[a] Based on prices from the American Metal Market.

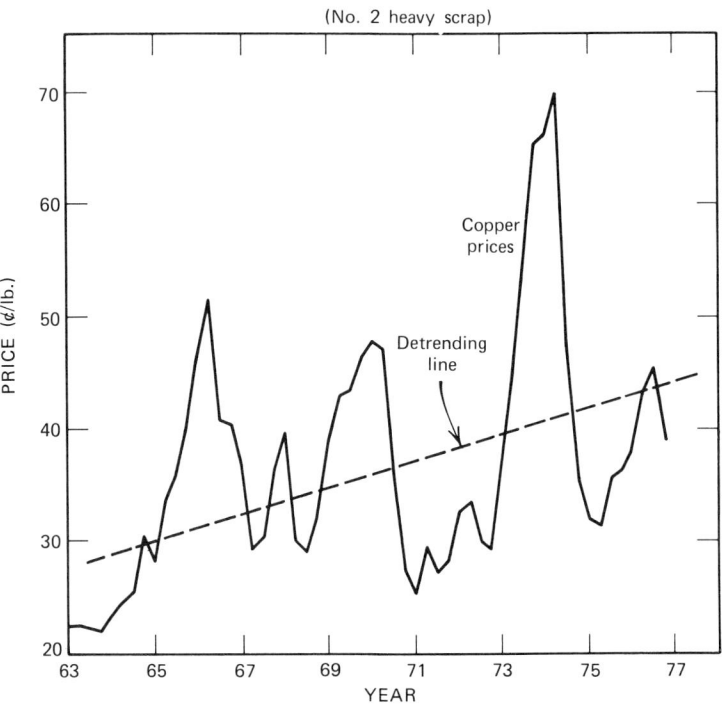

Diagram 8-3 Copper prices 1963–1976.

CYCLES AND SECULAR TRENDS

slant of the data. We will then be able to subtract the value of the detrending line from the original data and get copper prices that vary equally above and below the line from positive to negative values.

The technique for finding the "best fit" equation for a straight line $y = a + bx$ was to solve the least-squares equations

$$b = \frac{N \sum xy - \sum x \sum y}{N \sum x^2 - (\sum x)^2}$$

$$a = \frac{1}{N} \left(\sum y - b \sum x \right)$$

To do this we will let x be the date and y be the price on that date. For convenience, instead of letting $x = 1967, 1967\frac{1}{4}, 1967\frac{1}{2}, \ldots$, we will let $x = 1, 2, 3, \ldots$, and remember that when $x = 1$ we mean 1967, and so on. The method of solution can be found under linear regression techniques, discussed earlier.

All the problems in this section have been programmed and solved on a calculator, and all of the programs appear in Appendix 2b. As we proceed through these problems we will refer to Program #1, and so on. To find the least-squares approximation for a straight line we applied Program #2 using dates of value 1, 2, 3, and so on. The answer was the equation

$$y = 33.4117 + .2636x$$

Diagram 8-3 shows the original copper prices and the detrending line beginning at 33.67 for 1967 and ending at 43.95 for $1976\frac{3}{4}$ (values of x equal to 1 and 40).

The original prices can now be made horizontal from positive to negative values by subtracting the value of y, as calculated in the detrending line, from the corresponding original data point. We get the new resulting Table 8-2 by using Program #3.

Table 8-2 Detrended Scrap Copper (c/1b)[a]

Year	1st	2nd	3rd	4th
1963	−7.34	−7.26	−7.81	−8.24
1964	−7.33	−6.22	−5.50	−.71
1965	−3.34	1.94	3.81	7.69
1966	13.59	18.60	7.61	6.75
1967	2.83	−4.64	−3.84	1.95
1968	5.02	−4.92	−6.18	−3.39
1969	3.16	6.90	7.07	9.66
1970	10.86	9.88	−1.59	−10.28
1971	−12.49	−8.71	−11.27	−10.20
1972	−6.21	−5.68	−9.46	−10.49
1973	−3.18	4.80	14.60	24.72
1974	25.50	28.74	5.72	−6.22
1975	−10.50	−10.91	−6.89	−6.44
1976	−4.94	−.19	1.77	−5.00

[a] Based on 1967–1976.

We now must find the solution to the general trigonometric single-frequency wave:

$$y_t = a \cos \omega t + b \sin \omega t \qquad (2)$$

The variable t has replaced ϕ since we will consider the angle in units of 1, 2, 3, ..., rather than in degrees. This will be more convenient to visualize and to chart.

In order to find the frequency ω it will be necessary to first solve the equation

$$\cos \omega - \tfrac{1}{2}\alpha = 0$$

This can be done easily by solving the system of equations

$$\alpha y_2 = y_1 + y_3$$
$$\alpha y_3 = y_2 + y_4$$
$$\vdots$$
$$\alpha y_{n-1} = y_{n-2} + y_n \qquad (3)$$

using a least-squares method. This can be accomplished by finding the value for c and d in the equation

$$\alpha \sum c^2 = \sum cd \qquad (4)$$

where $c = y_n$ and $d = y_{n-1} + y_{n+1}$. Program #4 was used to find the value of α using the detrended data. When completed we got $\sum c^2 = 4149.57$ and $\sum ab = 6706.06$; then $\alpha = 1.6161$. We can now substitute the value for α into the intermediate equation and solve for the frequency ω:

$$\cos \omega - \tfrac{1}{2}(1.6161) = 1$$

$$\cos \omega = .80805$$

$$\omega = 36.1°$$

The period T is $360/36.1 = 9.97$ calendar quarters. The last step in solving the equation for a single frequency is to write the normal equations

$$a \sum \cos^2 \omega t + b \sum \cos \omega t \sin \omega t = \sum y_t \cos \omega t \qquad (5)$$
$$a \sum \sin \omega t \cos \omega t + b \sum \sin^2 \omega t = \sum y_t \sin \omega t \qquad (6)$$

and solve for a and b, where $t = 1, \ldots, 40$, and $\omega = 36.1°$. As in the other solutions, we can write a program for a calculator to find the sums necessary to solve the equations. Using Program #5 we get the values

$\sum \cos^2 \omega t = 20.045$ $\sum \sin \omega t \cos \omega t = .038$
$\sum \cos \omega t \sin \omega t = .038$ $\sum \sin^2 \omega t = 19.955$
$\sum y_t \cos \omega t = 82.476$ $\sum y_t \sin \omega t = -19.438$

Then the normal equations can be solved with $a = 4.1165$ and $b = -1.0509$. We get the resulting equation of our single-frequency curve:

$$y_t = 4.1165 \cos 36.1°t - 1.0509 \sin 36.1°t$$

Using $t = 1$ to be 1967 and $t = 40$ to be $1976\tfrac{3}{4}$ we can calculate and plot the periodic curve of the results. It is shown in Diagram 8-4. Program #6 was used to calculate the results.

CYCLES AND SECULAR TRENDS

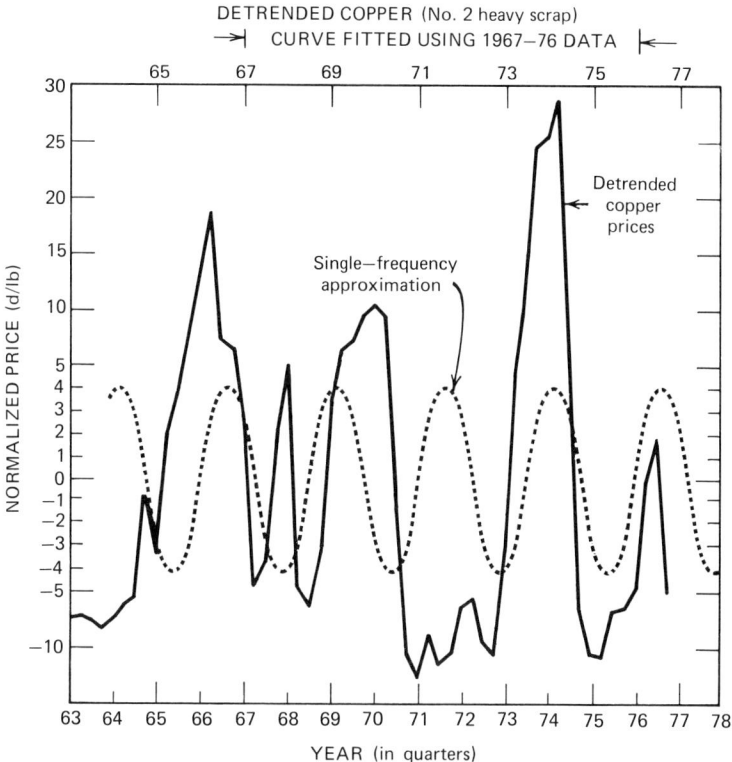

Diagram 8-4 Single-frequency trigonometric approximation.

The same results can also be expressed as a single sine wave by using the relationships $c = \sqrt{a^2 + b^2}$ and $\tan \phi = a/b$; then $c = 4.249$ and $\phi = -75.7°$ and the single-frequency sine wave can be written

$$y_t = 4.249 \sin(36.1°t - 75.7°)$$

The single-frequency curve is not as representative as we would have liked. Most of the peaks occur at the same point as a peak in the detrended copper prices, but the earlier data is somewhat out of phase and the 1968 peak is going in the wrong direction. This difficulty points out a fundamental problem of cycles—they are not as uniform as either the trending or seasonal components of a time-series. The copper-price charts show that there are three major peaks, of uneven height but uniform distance; between these peaks there are very different patterns, another peak in 1968, and a further dip in 1972.

There are two ways to improve on this problem. By using a longer time period the more dominant cycle will be identified; for this case either quarterly or average yearly data could be used. The yearly data would effectively smooth the fluctuations and help isolate the cycle. The second method is to attempt to fit a curve of a more complex form, and is the subject of the next section.

COMPLEX TRIGONOMETRIC CURVE-FITTING

The regular cyclic component of price movement is not likely to be accurately represented by a single-frequency trigonometric curve. A combination of more than one set of sine and cosine waves of varying amplitudes and frequencies is more likely to represent the patterns. We will try a simple two-frequency wave to see whether the results improve the single-frequency curve. The equation for the two-frequency curve is written

$$y_t = a_1 \cos \omega_1 t + b_1 \sin \omega_1 t + a_2 \cos \omega_2 t + b_2 \sin \omega_2 t \tag{7}$$

To find the results of this complex wave it is necessary to apply the same techniques used in the single-frequency approach to the detrended copper data in Table 8-2. The algebra for solving this problem is an expanded form of the previous solution and the use of a programmable calculator is almost a requirement. As in the other problem, all programs necessary to solve this one will appear in Appendix 2b. The frequencies ω_1 and ω_2 are found by solving the quadratic equation $2x^2 - \alpha_1 x - (1 + \alpha_2/2) = 0$, where $x = \cos \omega$, using the standard formula

$$x = \frac{\alpha_1 \pm \sqrt{\alpha_1^2 + 8(1 + \alpha_2/2)}}{4} \tag{8}$$

We can use the same least-squares method as before derived from the general form

$$\alpha_1(y_n + y_{n+2}) + \alpha_2 y_{n+1} = y_{n-1} + y_{n+3} \tag{9}$$

The least-squares equations for finding α_1 and α_2 are

$$\alpha_1 \sum c^2 + \alpha_2 \sum cd = \sum cp \tag{10}$$

$$\alpha_1 \sum cd + \alpha_2 \sum d^2 = \sum dp \tag{11}$$

where $c = y_n + y_{n+2}$, $d = y_{n+1}$, and $p = y_{n-1} + y_{n+3}$. Program #7 will give the necessary sums for the solutions. Once α_1 and α_2 are found, ω_1 and ω_2 are calculated from the two solutions of the quadratic equation (8). The next step is to solve the normal equations to get the amplitudes, a_1, b_1, a_2, and b_2:

$$a_1 \sum \cos^2 \omega_1 t + b_1 \sum \cos \omega_1 t \sin \omega_1 t + a_2 \sum \cos \omega_1 t \cos \omega_2 t \\ + b_2 \sum \cos \omega_1 t \sin \omega_2 t = \sum y_t \cos \omega_1 t \tag{12}$$

$$a_1 \sum \sin \omega_1 t \cos \omega_1 t + b_1 \sum \sin^2 \omega_1 t + a_2 \sum \sin \omega_1 t \cos \omega_2 t \\ + b_2 \sum \sin \omega_1 t \sin \omega_2 t = \sum y_t \sin \omega_1 t \tag{13}$$

$$a_1 \sum \cos \omega_2 t \cos \omega_1 t + b_1 \sum \cos \omega_2 t \sin \omega_1 t + a_2 \sum \cos \omega_2 t \\ + b_2 \sum \cos \omega_2 t \sin \omega_2 t = \sum y_t \cos \omega_2 t \tag{14}$$

$$a_1 \sum \sin \omega_2 t \cos \omega_1 t + b_1 \sum \sin \omega_2 t \sin \omega_1 t + a_2 \sum \sin \omega_2 t \cos \omega_2 t \\ + b_2 \sum \sin^2 \omega_2 t = \sum y_t \sin \omega_2 t \tag{15}$$

As before, the sums in these equations can be calculated using Program #8 or, in many hours, using a standard calculator. The final step is to create a 4 × 5 matrix to solve the four normal equations (12)–(15) for the coefficients a_1, b_1, a_2, and b_2. When

CYCLES AND SECULAR TRENDS

plotting the answer, it will be best to plot equation (7) in its components as well as in total:

$$y'_t = a_1 \cos \omega_1 t + b_1 \sin \omega_1 t$$
$$y''_t = a_2 \cos \omega_2 t + b_2 \sin \omega_2 t$$
$$y_t = y'_t + y''_t$$

The solution to the two-frequency problem will give the following values

$$\alpha_1 = .649269 \qquad x_1 = .8626$$
$$\text{and}$$
$$\alpha_2 = -.038532 \qquad x_2 = -.5380$$

We then get

$$\omega_1 = 30.39° \quad \text{and} \quad \omega_2 = 122.55°$$

or periods of

$$T_1 = 11.8 \ (3 \text{ years}) \quad \text{and} \quad T_2 = 2.9 \ (\tfrac{3}{4} \text{ year})$$

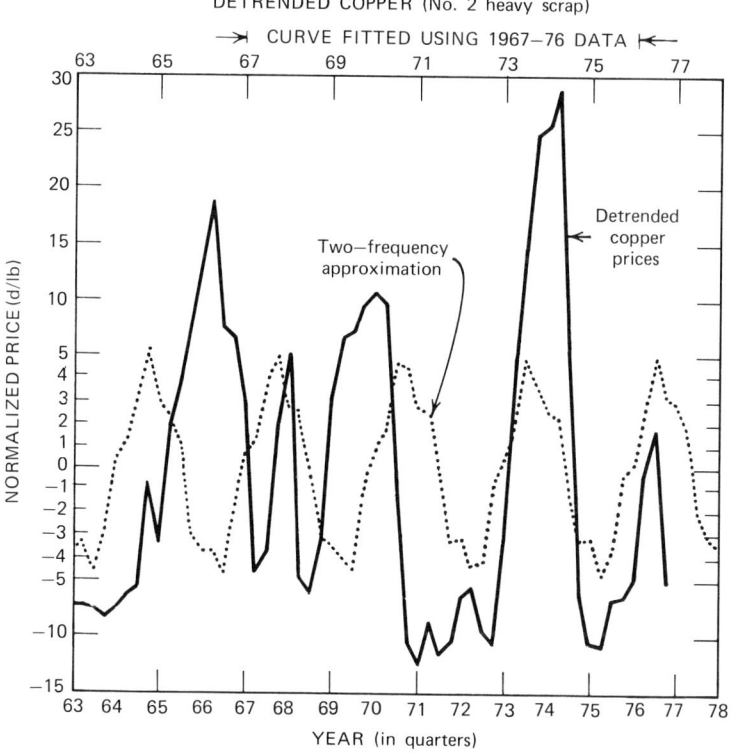

Diagram 8-5 Two-frequency trigonometric approximation.

The matrix solution gives the final results

$$y_t = -2.25 \cos 30.39t + 3.70 \sin 30.39t$$
$$+ .17 \cos 122.55t + .90 \sin 122.55t$$

The two-frequency curve is plotted in Diagram 8-5. It seems to be a better representation of the cycle than was the single-frequency curve and has a period of about 3 years. The tops and bottoms match fairly well, but the short span used for testing shows its limitation as soon as you extrapolate back to 1963, where it becomes out of phase with the 1966 peak.

Fourier Analysis

Assuming that we have a cycle, and that there are N data points in each repetition of this cycle, then the Fourier method of analysis will show that the N points lie on the regression curve

$$y_i = 1 + \sum_{k=1}^{(N/2)} \left(u_k \cos \frac{2\pi ki}{(N/2)} + v_k \sin \frac{2\pi ki}{(N/2)} \right) \qquad (16)$$

where the regression coefficients u_k and v_k are given by

$$u_k = \frac{1}{(N/2)} \sum_{i=1}^{N} y_i \cos \frac{2\pi ki}{(N/2)} \qquad k = 1, 2, \ldots, \frac{N}{2} \qquad (17)$$

$$v_k = \frac{1}{(N/2)} \sum_{i=1}^{N} y_i \sin \frac{2\pi ki}{(N/2)} \qquad k = 1, 2, \ldots, \frac{N}{2} \qquad (18)$$

$$v_{N/2} = 0$$

It is important to see that the mean of all the points on one cycle is equal to 1. The N values of y_i will have the property

$$\sum_{i=1}^{N} y_i = N \qquad (19)$$

The application of this method to the seasonal component will help clarify it. Seasonal data form the most obvious cycle; using average monthly prices, detrended to avoid any skew, we can let $N = 12$. We also know from our nonrigorous studies of seasonals, that seasonally adjusted prices will vary about the mean value; hence the weighting factors will have the same property as (19). While this is a simple example, it will be easy to generate the trigonometric curve to approximate seasonals and compare the results against the other methods used.[2]

Spectral Analysis

Spectral analysis, an application of Fourier analysis, is considered to be more adaptable to price cycles and not as restricted to deterministic models. The most important

---

[2] A continuation of this development can be found in Gilchrist (1976) pp. 139–148; a more theoretical approach is to be found in Chatfield (1975), Chapter 7.

CYCLES AND SECULAR TRENDS

aspect of the analysis is to find the proper estimators, or weighting factors, of single-frequency series of cosine waves. When looking for long-term cycles it is worth being reminded that the trend and seasonal components must be removed, since the method of spectral analysis will consider these the dominant characteristics and any other cycle desired will be obscured.

As in our other trigonometric formulas, we will use a basic time-series, where y_t, $t = 1, 2, \ldots, N$, are our data points and $\hat{y}_t$ will be our results, the estimated points on the spectral estimate. Then

$$\hat{y}_t(\omega) = \frac{1}{\pi}\left(c_0 + 2\sum_{k=1}^{N-1} c_k \cos \omega k\right)$$

where

$$c_k = \sum_{t=1}^{N-k} \frac{(y_t - \bar{y})(y_{t+k} - \bar{y})}{N}$$

Methods of performing spectral analysis vary due to the choice of weighting functions that compensate for the fact that the accuracy of c_k decreases as k increases. The two most popular techniques for adjusting for this problem introduce an estimator λ_k called a *lag window* and a truncation point $M < N$ so that the values of c_k for $M < k < N$ are no longer used and the values of c_k for $k \leq M$ are weighted by λ_k.

The spectral analysis approximation is then written

$$\hat{y}_t(\omega) = \frac{1}{\pi}\left(\lambda_0 c_0 + 2\sum_{k=1}^{M} \lambda_k c_k \cos \omega k\right)$$

where λ_k can be either of the following:

(a) *Tukey window*

$$\lambda_k = \frac{1}{2}\left(1 + \cos\frac{\pi k}{M}\right) \quad k = 0, 1, \ldots, M$$

(b) *Parzen window*

$$\lambda_k = \begin{cases} 1 - 6\left(\frac{k}{M}\right)^2 + 6\left(\frac{k}{M}\right)^3 & 0 \leq k \leq \frac{M}{2} \\ 2\left(1 - \frac{k}{M}\right)^3 & \frac{M}{2} \leq k \leq M \end{cases}$$

OTHER METHODS FOR FINDING SEASONAL EFFECTS

Most commodities are subject to noticeable seasonal effects, also termed *secular trends*, resulting from supply or demand. The seasonal patterns of crops are more noticeable than those of metals to most speculators because of the association with the growing year. We can understand the anticipation before planting, the weather problems during growing, and the usual abundance of crops at harvest. It is also clear that storage of an old crop into the harvest of the next season would cause the old crop to take on the value of the new crop, losing the advantage of availability just prior to harvest as well as its premium price, which included carrying charges (storage, interest, etc.).

United States production is our standard for "seasonal," although a wheat crop is harvested all year in different parts of the world. We expect prices to be lower during the United States harvest and highest during the middle of the growing season. The influence of world stocks and anticipated harvest from other major growing countries will serve an overall dampening or inflating effect on prices, rather than change the seasonal pattern. Costs of transporting grain to the United States would restrict its direct price competition, but the world market will be affected in its selection of a supplier at the best price. This has a first-order impact on the United States market that alters its local price based on export demand.

Other commodities have seasonal price variation based on demand. Silver, used as an electrical conductor, as jewelry, or as a general hedge against inflation, varies primarily according to its photographic application and is more heavily consumed during the summer months. Almost half of all copper is used in electrical and heat conductivity, much of it in the form of an alloy with nickel and silver. Its seasonality is heavily related to the housing industry, which requires it for both electrical and water systems. The production rates of copper and silver, as well as other metals, are relatively constant. New sources of ore are introduced infrequently and the anticipation of discovery or expansion rarely enters price movement as short-term anticipation. The primary supply problems are related to labor as well as social and political changes in the producing countries.

We will concentrate primarily on United States crops since the seasons are well-defined and examples will be clear. The price of corn rises and falls with the general economic trends of inflation and recession as well as the seasonality and world stockpile. Although there are other factors involved in corn prices, these three account for the primary components of its movement. These components may all depress or inflate corn prices at the same time or they might offset one another, but to understand and predict price movement we should be able to isolate each of the three and watch its movement independent of the others.

Finding The Seasonal Pattern

Seasonal patterns are easier to find than the longer-term cycles or economic trends, since we know they repeat each year. Although any 12-month period could be used to find the seasonal pattern, it will be more convenient and useful to use the crop year, beginning at harvest when prices tend to be lowest. With this approach we will also be able to eliminate the carrying charges, which increase steadily throughout the crop year. A study that uses the last old crop futures price will serve to eliminate this carrying-charge bias, since all prices will contain the proper discounted costs. For uniformity, our analysis will not consider carrying charges and will always use a calendar year, under the assumption that we have no knowledge of where the beginning of a "season" starts—which is true for commodities other than crops.

Yearly Averages

The most common way of measuring or describing the seasonal trend is by the monthly variation from the yearly or crop average, usually calculated as a ratio. Using the price of corn in 1975 we can see the results of this technique in Table 8-3.

Table 8-3 Ratio of Monthly Corn Prices to Average

	Avg	Jan	Feb	Mar	Apr	May	Jun	Jul	Aug	Sep	Oct	Nov	Dec
Price[a]	2.70	3.07	2.86	2.67	2.68	2.66	2.68	2.72	2.95	2.76	2.62	2.33	2.37
Ratio	1.00	113.7	105.9	98.9	99.2	98.5	99.2	100.7	109.2	102.2	97.0	86.3	87.8

[a] Mid-month U.S. farm price, 1975.

Table 8-4a Corn Cash Prices

Year	Avg	Jan	Feb	Mar	Apr	May	Jun	Jul	Aug	Sep	Oct	Nov	Dec
1956[a]	1.30	1.14	1.16	1.19	1.32	1.41	1.44	1.45	1.46	1.45	1.12	1.22	1.23
1957	1.25	1.22	1.16	1.18	1.18	1.20	1.20	1.21	1.22	1.13	1.04	.98	1.01
1958	1.10	.97	.98	1.04	1.18	1.20	1.23	1.23	1.24	1.15	1.02	.94	1.04
1959	1.09	1.05	1.06	1.08	1.17	1.18	1.19	1.17	1.17	1.09	.96	1.00	.99
1960	1.03	1.03	1.04	1.04	1.09	1.11	1.11	1.11	1.09	1.07	.97	.82	.92
1961	1.01	.99	1.03	1.04	.98	1.04	1.04	1.06	1.04	1.02	1.00	.91	.94
1962	.98	.94	.95	.96	.98	1.03	1.03	1.02	1.01	1.00	.94	.91	1.00
1963	1.11	1.03	1.05	1.06	1.09	1.12	1.19	1.21	1.21	1.23	1.04	1.02	1.20
1964	1.13	1.12	1.09	1.13	1.15	1.18	1.17	1.14	1.14	1.17	1.05	1.04	1.14
1965	1.18	1.16	1.17	1.19	1.22	1.25	1.26	1.24	1.20	1.18	1.10	1.04	1.13
1966[b]	1.25	1.19	1.20	1.17	1.19	1.21	1.20	1.27	1.34	1.35	1.29	1.26	1.29
1967	1.17	1.28	1.26	1.28	1.26	1.25	1.26	1.21	1.11	1.12	1.04	.97	1.03
1968	1.04	1.04	1.06	1.06	1.06	1.09	1.07	1.04	.99	1.01	.96	1.04	1.05
1969	1.12	1.08	1.09	1.09	1.12	1.19	1.18	1.08	1.18	1.15	1.12	1.07	1.09
1970	1.24	1.12	1.14	1.13	1.15	1.18	1.21	1.24	1.27	1.38	1.34	1.29	1.39
1971	1.27	1.42	1.43	1.43	1.41	1.38	1.43	1.36	1.19	1.11	1.00	.97	1.08
1972	1.17	1.09	1.09	1.10	1.13	1.15	1.13	1.14	1.15	1.22	1.19	1.20	1.42
1973	1.86	1.39	1.35	1.37	1.42	1.16	1.99	2.03	2.68	2.15	2.17	2.18	2.39
1974	2.92	2.59	2.76	2.68	2.41	2.45	2.57	2.91	3.37	3.30	3.45	3.32	3.27
1975	2.70	3.07	2.86	2.67	2.68	2.66	2.68	2.72	2.95	2.76	2.62	2.33	2.37
Average		1.30	1.30	1.29	1.31	1.32	1.38	1.39	1.45	1.40	1.32	1.28	1.34
1976		2.44	2.48	2.50									

[a] 1956–1965 Mid-month Illinois Farm Prices (U of I).
[b] 1966–1975 Mid-month U.S. Farm Prices (CRB Yearbook).

Table 8-4b Corn Price as Percentage Average (Annual)

Year	Avg	Jan	Feb	Mar	Apr	May	Jun	Jul	Aug	Sep	Oct	Nov	Dec
1956	1.30	87.6	89.2	91.5	101.5	108.5	110.8	111.5	112.3	111.5	86.1	93.8	94.6
1957	1.25	97.6	92.8	94.4	94.4	96.0	96.0	96.8	97.6	86.9	86.9	75.4	80.8
1958	1.10	88.2	89.1	94.5	107.3	109.1	111.8	111.8	112.7	88.5	92.7	85.4	94.5
1959	1.09	96.3	97.2	99.1	107.3	108.2	109.2	107.3	107.3	100.0	88.1	91.7	90.1
1960	1.03	100.0	101.0	101.0	105.8	107.8	107.8	107.8	105.8	103.9	94.2	79.6	89.3
1961	1.01	98.0	102.0	103.0	97.0	103.0	103.0	104.9	103.0	101.0	99.0	90.1	93.1
1962	.98	95.9	96.9	97.9	100.0	105.1	105.1	104.1	103.1	102.0	95.9	92.8	102.0
1963	1.11	92.8	94.6	95.5	98.2	101.0	107.2	109.0	109.0	110.8	93.7	91.9	99.1
1964	1.13	99.1	96.5	100.0	101.8	104.4	103.5	100.9	100.9	103.5	92.9	92.0	100.9
1965	1.18	98.3	99.1	100.8	103.4	105.9	106.8	105.1	101.7	100.0	93.2	88.1	95.8
1966	1.25	95.2	96.0	93.6	95.2	96.8	96.0	101.6	107.2	108.0	103.2	100.8	103.2
1967	1.17	109.4	107.7	109.4	107.7	106.8	107.7	103.4	94.9	95.7	88.9	82.9	88.0
1968	1.04	100.0	101.9	101.9	101.9	104.8	102.9	100.0	95.2	97.1	92.3	100.0	101.0
1969	1.12	96.4	97.3	97.3	100.0	106.2	105.3	96.4	105.3	102.7	100.0	95.5	97.3
1970	1.24	90.3	91.9	91.1	92.7	95.2	97.6	100.0	102.4	111.3	108.1	104.0	112.1
1956–1970 Avg		96.3	96.9	98.1	100.9	103.9	104.7	104.0	103.9	101.5	94.3	90.9	96.1
1971	1.27	111.8	112.6	112.6	111.0	108.7	112.6	107.1	93.7	87.4	78.7	76.4	85.0
1972	1.17	93.2	93.2	94.0	96.6	98.3	96.6	97.4	98.3	104.3	101.7	102.6	121.4
1973	1.86	74.7	72.6	73.6	76.3	62.4	107.0	109.1	144.1	115.6	116.7	117.2	128.5
1974	2.92	88.7	94.5	91.8	82.5	83.9	88.0	99.6	115.4	113.0	118.1	113.7	112.0
1975	2.70	113.7	105.9	98.9	99.2	98.5	99.2	100.7	109.2	102.2	97.0	86.3	87.8
1971–1975 Avg		96.4	95.8	94.2	93.1	90.1	100.7	102.8	112.1	104.5	102.4	99.2	106.9

Table 8-5a Soybean Cash Prices

Year	Avg	Jan	Feb	Mar	Apr	May	Jun	Jul	Aug	Sep	Oct	Nov	Dec
1956[a]	2.46	2.27	2.33	2.46	2.73	3.06	2.96	2.49	2.38	2.09	2.10	2.33	2.33
1957	2.23	2.37	2.29	2.30	2.28	2.25	2.20	2.28	2.35	2.15	2.09	2.10	2.14
1958	2.11	2.12	2.12	2.16	2.21	2.18	2.19	2.18	2.20	2.00	1.98	1.96	2.04
1959	2.07	2.07	2.09	2.11	2.15	2.19	2.15	2.10	2.01	1.93	1.99	2.06	2.03
1960	2.03	2.05	2.02	2.03	2.06	2.05	2.02	2.02	2.04	2.01	1.99	1.99	2.07
1961	2.55	2.31	2.54	2.76	3.14	3.05	2.62	2.46	2.50	2.25	2.27	2.33	2.35
1962	2.37	2.36	2.36	2.38	2.44	2.42	2.39	2.40	2.38	2.26	2.28	2.35	2.39
1963	2.53	2.46	2.54	2.54	2.49	2.52	2.53	2.48	2.48	2.47	2.59	2.69	2.60
1964	2.54	2.70	2.60	2.59	2.48	2.40	2.38	2.37	2.40	2.56	2.61	2.66	2.69
1965[b]	2.82	2.96	3.03	3.01	3.04	2.86	2.97	2.89	2.75	2.68	2.49	2.54	2.66
1966	3.13	2.84	2.91	2.86	2.98	3.08	3.38	3.59	3.73	3.19	2.96	2.99	3.00
1967	2.80	2.96	2.91	2.91	2.88	2.87	2.90	2.83	2.81	2.69	2.60	2.61	2.64
1968	2.66	2.69	2.73	2.71	2.71	2.74	2.71	2.71	2.72	2.61	2.46	2.53	2.59
1969	2.59	2.63	2.64	2.64	2.69	2.72	2.69	2.70	2.61	2.49	2.38	2.42	2.47
1970	2.76	2.55	2.59	2.58	2.64	2.70	2.71	2.89	2.79	2.81	2.95	3.00	2.93
1971	3.11	3.03	3.06	3.04	2.91	3.03	3.21	3.38	3.29	3.12	3.12	3.00	3.08
1972	3.48	3.09	3.18	3.37	3.49	3.49	3.47	3.51	3.55	3.48	3.33	3.64	4.13
1973	6.95	4.46	5.80	6.24	6.52	8.94	10.87	8.47	9.00	6.00	5.62	5.57	5.92
1974	6.75	6.17	6.35	6.29	5.59	5.47	5.51	7.11	7.76	7.64	8.30	7.54	7.23
1975	5.42	6.38	5.69	5.60	5.55	5.23	5.16	5.60	6.02	5.57	4.90	4.74	4.60

[a] 1956–1964: Illinois Agricultural Statistics.
[b] 1965–1975: CRB Yearbook.

Table 8-5b Soybean Price as Percentage Average (Annual)

Year	Jan	Feb	Mar	Apr	May	Jun	Jul	Aug	Sep	Oct	Nov	Dec
1956	92.2	94.7	100.0	110.9	124.3	120.3	101.2	96.7	84.9	85.3	94.7	94.7
1957	106.2	102.6	103.1	102.2	100.8	98.6	102.2	105.3	94.6	93.7	94.1	95.9
1958	100.4	100.4	102.3	104.7	103.3	103.7	103.3	104.2	94.7	93.8	92.8	96.6
1959	100.0	100.9	101.9	103.8	105.7	103.8	101.4	97.1	93.2	96.1	99.5	98.0
1960	100.9	95.5	100.0	101.4	100.9	99.5	99.5	100.4	99.0	98.0	98.0	101.9
1961	90.5	99.6	108.2	123.1	119.6	102.7	96.4	98.0	88.2	89.0	91.3	92.1
1962	99.5	99.5	100.4	102.9	102.1	100.8	101.2	100.4	95.3	96.2	99.1	100.8
1963	97.2	100.3	100.3	98.4	99.6	100.0	98.0	98.0	97.6	102.3	106.3	102.7
1964	106.2	102.3	101.9	97.6	94.4	93.7	93.3	94.4	100.7	102.7	104.7	105.9
1965	104.9	107.4	106.7	107.8	101.4	105.3	102.4	97.5	95.0	88.2	90.0	94.3
1966	90.7	92.9	91.3	95.2	98.4	107.9	114.7	119.1	101.9	94.5	95.5	95.8
1967	105.7	103.9	103.9	102.8	102.5	103.5	101.0	100.3	96.0	92.8	93.2	94.2
1968	101.1	102.6	101.8	101.8	103.0	101.8	101.8	102.2	98.1	92.4	95.1	97.3
1969	101.5	101.9	101.9	103.8	105.0	103.8	104.2	100.7	96.1	91.8	93.4	95.3
1970	92.3	93.8	93.4	95.6	97.8	98.1	104.7	101.0	101.8	106.8	108.6	106.1
1956–1970 Avg	99.3	100.15	101.1	102.5	103.9	102.9	101.7	101.0	95.8	94.9	97.1	98.1
1971	97.4	98.3	97.7	93.5	97.4	103.2	108.6	105.7	100.3	100.3	96.4	99.0
1972	88.7	91.3	96.8	100.2	100.2	99.7	100.8	102.0	100.0	95.6	104.5	118.6
1973	64.1	83.4	89.7	93.8	141.5	156.6	121.8	129.4	86.3	80.8	80.1	85.1
1974	91.4	94.0	93.1	82.8	81.0	81.6	105.3	114.9	113.1	122.9	111.7	107.1
1975	117.7	104.9	103.3	102.3	96.4	95.2	103.3	111.0	102.7	90.4	87.4	84.8
1971–1975 Avg	91.9	94.4	96.1	94.5	103.3	107.3	108.0	112.6	100.5	98.0	96.0	98.9

123

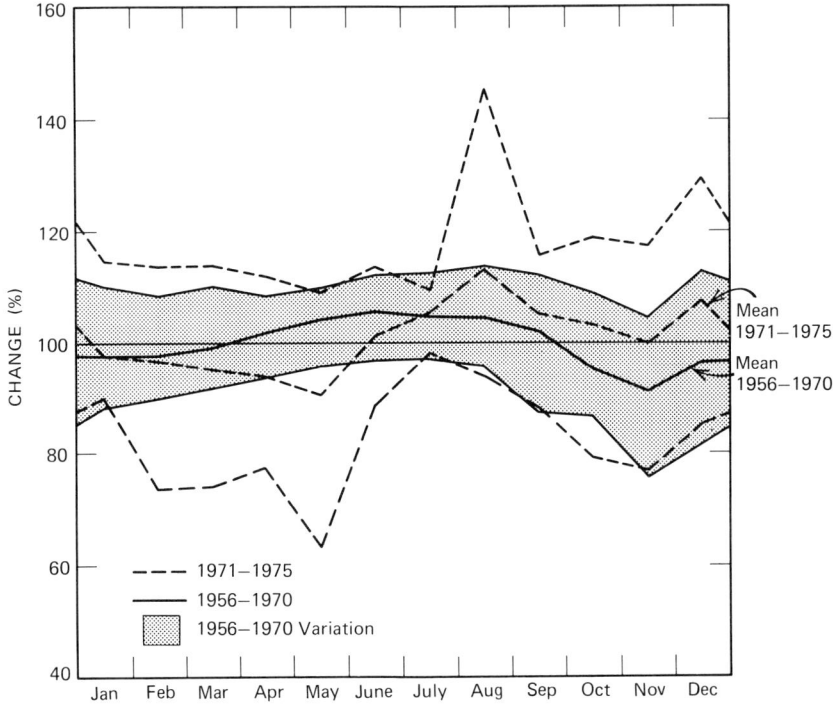

Diagram 8-6 Corn: changes in volatility and seasonal patterns.

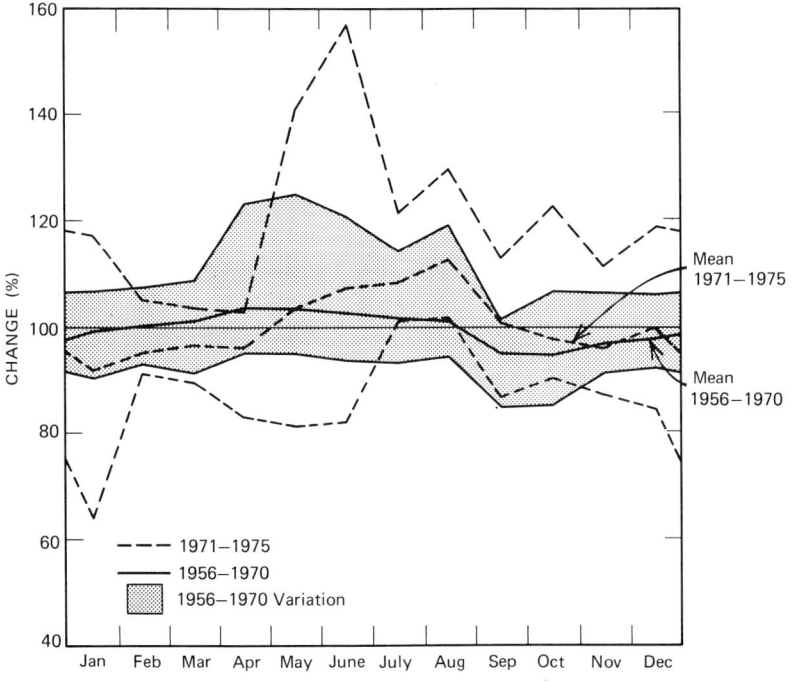

Diagram 8-7 Soybean: changes in volatility and seasonal patterns.

CYCLES AND SECULAR TRENDS

It is apparent that the highest prices occur in January and August and the lowest at harvest, conforming to our intrinsic knowledge of the corn season. We can also see the extent of the variation throughout the year. By applying this method for a number of years we get results shown in Tables 8-4a, 8-4b, 8-5a, and 8-5b for corn and soybeans.

Graphically we can show the long-term seasonality by averaging the monthly ratios; the highest and lowest are also plotted to show the possible variation from the seasonal pattern. For both corn and soybeans we have separated the data into the periods 1956–1970 and 1971–1975 to point out the volatility and slight change in pattern. In both crops, the highest and lowest points remained about the same, but the sharper fluctuations were reduced to intervals of shorter duration.

A fault in the use of annual average prices is its inability to reflect the long-term trend of the economy within the monthly variations. If the rate of inflation in the United States is 6%, then each month contributes about $\frac{1}{2}$%, reducing the first and increasing the last. The only prices not affected would be in the center of the yearly period. Trying to relate the end of our season to the beginning of another would be especially bad.

The Method of Link Relatives

Another interesting and important way of identifying the seasonal price variations and separating them from other price components involves the use of *link relatives*. Each month is expressed as a percentage by taking the ratio of that average monthly price to the average price of the preceding month. Using 1960 and 1961 corn prices from Table 8-4a we get the results shown in the first two lines of Table 8-6.

After the initial calculation of 1960 and 1961 link relatives it is necessary to find the average or median (preferred if an adequate sample is used) of the monthly ratios expressed in rows (1) and (2). The average in row (3) represents monthly variation in terms of a shifting base, since each calculation is a function of the preceding month. In order to establish a fixed base, *chain relatives* are constructed using January as 100; each monthly chain relative is calculated by multiplying its average link relative by the average link relative of the preceding month—the March chain relative is $1.005 \times 1.025 = 1.030$, and February remains the same since it used January as a base.

By multiplying the December chain relative (4) by the January average link relative we can determine any constant trend throughout our test period. If prices were uniform, showing no tendency for either upward or downward movement, the results of our multiplication would be 1.00; but we know that inflation should cause an upward bias and therefore expect the results to be higher. From line (4) the December entry times the January entry on line (3) gives $.946 \times 1.047 = .990$, leaving a negative factor of .1% unaccounted. This means that the 1960–1961 years showed a .1% deflation or that the standard inflationary rate was offset by some other economic cycle, such as the accumulation of grain stocks by the United States government.

The chain relatives must be corrected by adding the negative bias back into the values, using the same technique as in computing compound interest. For example, from 1967 to 1977 the Consumer Price Index increased from 100 to 175, a total of 75% in 10 years. To calculate the annual compounded rate of growth for that period, we apply the formula

$$\text{Compound rate of growth} = \sqrt[n]{\frac{\text{ending value}}{\text{starting value}}} - 1$$

Table 8-6 Corn Prices Expressed as Link Relatives

Jan	Feb	Mar	Apr	May	Jun	Jul	Aug	Sep	Oct	Nov	Dec	
1.040	1.010	1.000	1.048	1.018	1.000	1.000	.982	.982	.907	.845	1.122	(1)
1.053	1.040	1.010	.942	1.061	1.000	1.019	.981	.981	.980	.910	1.031	(2)
1.047	1.025	1.005	.995	1.040	1.000	1.010	.982	.982	.944	.878	1.077	(3)
1.000	1.025	1.030	1.000	1.035	1.040	1.010	.992	.964	.927	.829	.946	(4)
1.000	1.024	1.028	.997	1.032	1.036	1.005	.986	.958	.920	.822	.937	(5)
1.022	1.046	1.050	1.019	1.054	1.058	1.027	1.007	.979	.940	.840	.957	(6)

(1) 1960
(2) 1961
(3) Average
(4) Chain relatives
(5) Corrected chain relatives
(6) Indices of seasonal variations

CYCLES AND SECULAR TRENDS   127

where n is the number of years or the number of periods over which we are compounding the growth.

$$R = \sqrt[10]{\frac{175}{100}} - 1$$
$$= 1.05755 - 1$$
$$= .05755$$

This indicates a compounded rate of inflation equal to 5.75% per year. If our rate had been greater than 1.00 instead of .990 we would subtract the growth rate from each month to offset the upward bias. For this case we will add our results back into the chain relative to compensate for the negative influence. A .1% decline, compounded over 12 entries in our table gives

$$R = \sqrt[12]{\frac{.99}{1.00}} - 1$$
$$= .99916 - 1$$
$$= -.00084$$

This is a compounded deflation of about $\frac{8}{100}$ of 1%. We calculate the corrected chain relative by multiplying the February entry by .99916 or $(1 + R)$, March by .99832 or $(1 + R)^2$, and the December by .99076, which is $(1 + R)^{11}$.

The chain relatives have been calculated on a base of January, which was important in order to correct the compounded bias throughout the test period. Our final step is to switch the corrected chain relatives to a base of the average value. We find the arithmetic mean (.97875) of line (5) and create line (6), taking the ratio of the corrected chain relative entries to their average. The final result is the Index of Seasonal Variation. The accuracy of this result can be proved by averaging the entries of line (6), which will be 1.00.

The Moving-Average Method

We referred earlier to the use of the moving average as a popular means for determining seasonal patterns. Going back to our table of corn prices, take the average quarterly prices for the years 1960 through 1965, rounded to the nearest cent, for a simple example.

We have the advantage of knowing that every four entries completes a season and we can calculate a 4-point moving average and record the results so that they lag $2\frac{1}{2}$ points, corresponding to the center of the 4 points used in the calculation. Column (2) of Table 8-7 shows the 4-point moving average positioned properly; Diagram 8-8 is a plot of both the quarterly corn prices and the lagged moving average. Because of the use of the exact number of entries in the seasonal pattern, the line representing the moving average shows no effects of the seasonal trend; it is now only the results of the other time-series components.

Because the moving average used was of an even number of points, each calculation falls between two original data points. Column (3) of Table 8-7 is constructed by averaging every two adjacent entries in column (2) and placing them in a position corresponding to the original data points. The difference of column (1) minus column

Table 8-7 Seasonal Adjustment by the Moving-Average Method

		Average quantity price	4-point moving average	Corresponding 4-point values	Seasonal adjustment factor	Seasonal index
1960	Jan–Mar	104				
	Apr–Jun	110				
	Jul–Sep	109	$103\frac{1}{4}$	103	$+6$	1.06
	Oct–Dec	90	$102\frac{3}{4}$	$101\frac{3}{4}$	$-11\frac{3}{4}$	.88
1961	Jan–Mar	102	$100\frac{3}{4}$	$100\frac{1}{8}$	$+1\frac{7}{8}$	1.02
	Apr–Jun	102	$99\frac{1}{2}$	$100\frac{1}{8}$	$+1\frac{7}{8}$	1.02
	Jul–Sep	104	$100\frac{3}{4}$	$99\frac{7}{8}$	$+4\frac{1}{8}$	1.04
	Oct–Dec	95	99	$98\frac{7}{8}$	$-3\frac{7}{8}$	.96
1962	Jan–Mar	95	$98\frac{3}{4}$	$98\frac{3}{8}$	$-3\frac{3}{8}$	.96
	Apr–Jun	101	98	98	$+3$	1.03
	Jul–Sep	101	98	$99\frac{1}{4}$	$+1\frac{3}{4}$	1.02
	Oct–Dec	95	$100\frac{1}{2}$	102	-7	.93
1963	Jan–Mar	105	$103\frac{1}{2}$	$106\frac{1}{8}$	$-1\frac{1}{8}$	.99
	Apr–Jun	113	$108\frac{3}{4}$	$110\frac{3}{4}$	$+2\frac{1}{4}$	1.12
	Jul–Sep	122	$112\frac{1}{4}$	$113\frac{1}{4}$	$+8\frac{3}{4}$	1.08
	Oct–Dec	109	$113\frac{3}{4}$	$114\frac{1}{4}$	$-5\frac{1}{4}$	.95
1964	Jan–Mar	111	$114\frac{3}{4}$	$113\frac{7}{8}$	$-2\frac{7}{8}$	.97
	Apr–Jun	117	113	$113\frac{7}{8}$	$+4\frac{1}{8}$	1.04
	Jul–Sep	115	$112\frac{3}{4}$	$112\frac{7}{8}$	$+1\frac{1}{2}$	1.01
	Oct–Dec	108	$114\frac{1}{4}$	$113\frac{1}{2}$	$-7\frac{1}{8}$	.94
1965	Jan–Mar	117	116	$116\frac{3}{4}$	$-\frac{1}{4}$	1.00
	Apr–Jun	124	$117\frac{1}{2}$	$117\frac{5}{8}$	$+6\frac{3}{8}$	1.05
	Jul–Sep	121	$117\frac{3}{4}$			
	Oct–Dec	109				

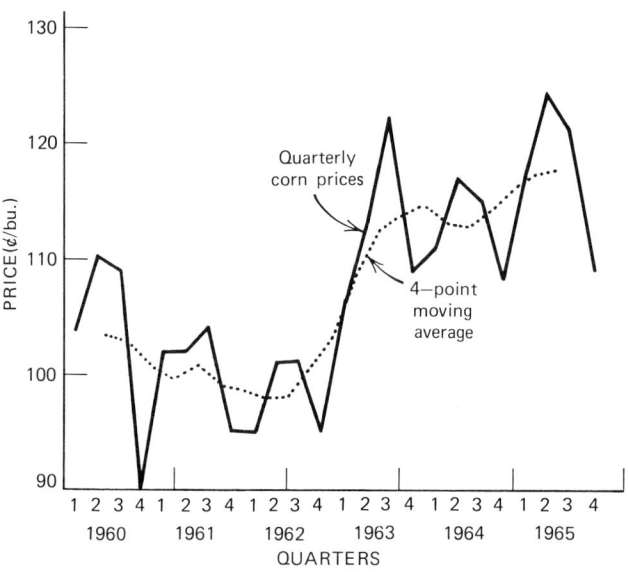

Diagram 8-8 Detrending corn with a moving average.

Table 8-8 Average Seasonal Variation Using the Moving-Average Method

Average of all years	Seasonal adjustment factor	Seasonal index
Jan–Mar	−1.15	.988
Apr–Jun	+3.53	1.052
Jul–Sep	+4.43	1.042
Oct–Dec	−7.00	.932

(3) is the seasonal adjustment factor (4) in cents per bushel; the seasonal index (5) is taken as the ratio of column (1) divided by column (3). The periodic fluctuation of prices becomes obvious once these values have been recorded. A generalized seasonal-adjustment factor and seasonal index is calculated by taking the average of the quarterly entries for the 5 complete years (Table 8-8).

Advanced Methods

A more complex solution to forecasting prices with a seasonal component is a self-generating, heuristic approach called *Winter's method*.[3] It assumes that the only relevant characteristics of price movement are the trend and seasonal components, which are represented by the formula

$$X_t = (a + bt)S_t + \varepsilon_t$$

where X_t is the estimated value at time t, $(a + bt)$ is a line that represents the trend, S_t is the seasonal weighting factors, and ε_t is the related error at each point. If each season is represented by L data points, S_t repeats every L entries and

$$\sum_{t=1}^{L} S_t = L$$

The unique feature of Winter's model is that each new observation is used to correct the previous components a, b, and S_t. Without that feature it would have no applicability to commodity-price forecasting. Starting with 2 or 3 years of price data, the yearly (seasonal) price average can be used to calculate both a and b of the linear trend. Each subsequent year can be used to correct the equation $a + bt$ using any regressive analysis. Winter's method actually uses a technique similar to exponential smoothing to estimate the next components a and b individually. The seasonal weighting factors (seasonal adjustments) are assigned by calculating the average variance from the linear component, expressed as a ratio, at each point desired. As more

---
[3] Winter's method, as well as other advanced models, can be found in Montgomery and Johnson (1976).

observations are made each component can be refined. Consequently, it will take on the form of the general long-term seasonal trend.

The latest developments in time-series analysis, including seasonal studies, are called *Box–Jenkins models*, due to the work of Box and Jenkins. Serious students of seasonal components or the decomposition of prices into elementary forms must study their methods. It considers the fact that successive observations in many time-series are highly *dependent*, and it offers ways to use this relationship. Regression and autoregressive methods such as multivariate analysis and exponential smoothing do not take advantage of this dependency. The Box–Jenkins models treat the "random" component of a time series as sequentially dependent.

SEASONALS FOR TRADING

Whatever method is used to find the seasonal trend, it is equally important to use it properly for speculation. There are many sources of seasonal studies that have already been completed using some of the simpler methods stated earlier in this section, while some others are unique. It is worth repeating that studies based on current cash market prices of crops have no bias due to carrying charges; the cash price each day excludes an added amount in consideration of storage costs and interest. Using one futures contract for all comparisons will include an increase due to the inclusion of all daily carrying charges. This applies to all futures contracts, whether agricultural, metals, or others. Even though the cash price may show the "true" seasonal pattern, trades entered will use futures and should therefore analyze the futures.

Select a commodity that has a dominant seasonal pattern. The crops always qualify, although the potato pattern is known not to react to the usual harvest depression. Livestock tend to be more complex than other commodities, because of the joint dependency of the prices on both feed-grain trends as well as livestock production and consumption. Both crops and livestock have primarily supply-oriented seasonal trends, depressed at harvest and highest during the summer months before harvest—or depressed in the fall when demand for meat falls off and the supply becomes greatest due to liquidation before winter. Metals patterns are caused by demand, since the product has no dependence on weather or development. The summer months still see highest prices due to increased consumption—copper in housing, silver in photography.

Exceptions occur in seasonal patterns as they do in any generalized or probabilistic model. In this case the years that do not conform tend to be easier to identify than with other, more mathematical, methods. When a harvest depression only brings prices down slightly from the highs of the preharvest season, a major shortage is apparent and prices should increase through the next crop season, or until an adequate new crop is assured that will meet demand. In 3 consecutive years, 1972 through 1974, corn prices increased steadily with only small adjustments in September and October. Once this variation occurs it is necessary to wait until another season has established the normal pattern. Using seasonal patterns during the exceptional years would require additional analysis of the dominant cyclic component of price movement.

The systems and methods that follow are based entirely on seasonal patterns, and may be used alone or as a filter with trending methods.

CYCLES AND SECULAR TRENDS

Key Dates

Some commodities have traditional and reliable rallies following an extremely depressed period in their seasonal trend. While the grains are lowest at harvest, they do not necessarily begin their best rise until the summer growing months, when threats of drought become a factor. Livestock patterns are all similar and can all be traded within a short time period over the early summer. Long positions taken in hogs, bellies, broilers, or eggs in about May will show all their profit by August if the seasonal pattern is consistent. Cattle varies somewhat from the other proteins, although the same pattern is true to a lesser degree. The primary rise in cattle prices is during the winter, from mid-December to about March, when the supply of beef is lowest. The increased demand following the winter generally offsets the increased availability, causing a slow rise or sideways price movement throughout the spring and summer.

The seasonal rise in grain prices is not as noticeable as the harvest declines. There is rarely a season where a short sale during July of corn, soybeans, cotton, or sugar will not net a good profit in 2 months when harvests begin. Potatoes have a distinct price trend not related to harvest since the demand for fall potatoes does not materialize until the winter months. Maine and Idaho potatoes are committed to storage in order to meet demand through late winter and spring, when no new fresh potatoes are available. Trading centers around the May U.S.D.A. stocks report which tells whether the remaining stored potatoes are enough to meet the next few months demands before the new southern crop is harvested. The potato seasonal pattern shows a sharp rise from December through May in anticipation of the report. A closer look at those patterns will show extreme variability that merits caution.

Seasonal Probability

A simple tool for using the seasonal trend as a trading filter is the historic probability of a higher or lower price on a month-to-month basis. If the price of corn were higher in December than in November for every year observed, it would be a strong argument against taking a short position or holding one during December. During the 20 years from 1956 through 1975 the percentage of incidence of corn prices being higher in one month than during the preceding month is shown as follows:

Table 8-9 Likelihood of Corn Prices Higher Than Prior Month

Jan	Feb	Mar	Apr	May	Jun	Jul	Aug	Sep	Oct	Nov	Dec
79	75	85	80	80	75	60	55	35	10	25	90

Historically, it is evident that a rise in price is most likely in December, with continued increase through June. The probability of a decline becomes greater in September and continues until November. The months of July and August are considered neutral. The profit to be gained during the highly seasonal months cannot be determined by this type of an analysis and, in fact, the greatest price moves are during the

THE CYCLE

We have dealt with the cycle mathematically, using trigonometric curves, and then shown some simpler methods of finding the seasonal adjustment factor. All the methods used for seasonal variation can be applied to cycles if the periods are known and well-defined. The copper chart (Diagram 8-3) at the beginning of the chapter shows peaks at 4-year intervals: 1966, 1970, and 1974. For quarterly data, the *moving-average method* used for identification of seasonals can be applied using a 16-point (4-year) moving average. The *cyclic adjustment factor* will be the result of such calculation. As we have discussed, the frequencies of cycles are not as regular as we would want, and fixing the period at 4 years might be an unreasonable restriction.

The important characteristic of a cycle is the simplest—its up-and-down movement caused by shortage and adequate supply. An analysis of the cycle might be most useful if it only determines the tops and bottoms that can be expected from such movement. For example, the diagram of scrap copper shows prices ranging from 22¢ per pound in late 1963 to 70¢ in the beginning of 1974. What could normally be expected? The data must first be detrended as we did with copper prices, and then the average distance between tops and the average distance between bottoms must be measured. This will give us an approximate period for the cycle. By using a moving average of this period we can determine whether the cycle is in an upward or downward trend and verify that information by its relationship to the detrended bottom price level. If a change occurs from a down trend to an up trend near the bottom level it is reasonably certain that the cycle is turning up.

The peaks are not as simple to place, since they do not have the bounds of the lower levels. It would still be a cautious move to consider the first downward sign in the cycle's moving average as an indication of a change of direction when it is near or above the average cycle peak. Although prices may go higher it is always safe to stand aside in unknown areas. If prices move above the average peak level, wait until they come back down before considering a continuation of the cycle. Applying this technique to cycles reduces it to a situation similar to an oscillator that is overbought or oversold.

Holt–Winters Method Of Components

The exponential smoothing that has been discussed has treated prices as a trending element. In actuality the speed of the smoothing and its relation to the long-term trend, cyclic component, seasonal component, or the smaller movements will determine the characteristics identified and followed by the smoothing method. The Holt–Winters method does not leave this to chance. It separates the time-series components, then smooths and updates each individually using an exponential technique.

Consider the situation where m_t represents the mean to date (the average of all data this year versus last year), which might be the long-term trend; c_t will be the intermediate trend representing the cyclic element, and s_t will be the seasonal component.

CYCLES AND SECULAR TRENDS

Each data element x_t will be monthly in order to identify the longer-term components. Then if the seasonal variation is multiplicative the updating equations will be

$$m_t = \frac{ax_t}{s_{t-12}} + (1-a)(m_{t-1} + c_{t-1})$$

$$s_t = \frac{bx_t}{m_t} + (1-b)s_{t-12}$$

$$c_t = d(m_t - m_{t-1}) + (1-d)c_{t-1}$$

where a, b, and d are exponential smoothing constants.

If the seasonal variation is additive we have

$$m_t = a(x_t - s_{t-12}) + (1-a)(m_{t-1} + c_{t-1})$$

$$s_t = b(x_t - m_t) + (1-b)s_{t-12}$$

$$c_t = d(m_t - m_{t-1}) + (1-d)c_{t-1}$$

The three smoothing constants must be chosen to correspond to the components they serve to isolate. For example, the constant b, which smooths the seasonal element, must be such that

$$\sum_{i=t}^{t+11} s_t = 12$$

This is a property that we have seen before. An alternative is to calculate its value from past data in a least-squares manner, recording the sum of the squares of the differences of the actual and estimated data for different choices of smoothing constants. The other constants, a and d, must also be selected with care.

CHAPTER 9
Advanced Charting

Charting is a most popular and practical form for evaluating commodity-price movement. There are so many approaches to graphing and interpreting prices that a major work would be necessary to do them justice. In this part we will summarize some of the more popular approaches to charting and then consider the topic in terms of advanced concepts of both the standard charting methods and systems directly related to its behavioral implications. A price chart is often considered a representation of human behavior. The goal of any chart analyst is to find consistant patterns that are reliable enough to be predictive. In the basic approaches to charting we find consolidation forms, trend channels, top-and-bottom formations, and a multitude of other patterns that can only be created by the same repeated action of large groups of people in similar circumstances.

At this time there has not been an explicit study of the psychology of behavior behind these chart formations that may make some more reliable than others. The philosophy of trading that is treated in most of the well-read literature in both stocks and commodities may be the cause of repeated patterns. Beginning speculators approach the problem with great enthusiasm and often some rigidity in an effort to stick to the rules. They will sell double and triple tops, buy breakouts, and generally do everything to propagate the standard formations. In that sense it is wise to know what are the most popular and well-read techniques and act accordingly. In *The Money Game* "Adam Smith" asks the question: "What is everyone else doing?" It certainly would make your planning easier if you knew. "Contrary opinion" is a longstanding approach to the behavior problem and a quasi-numerical answer to Adam Smith's question. It will be discussed later in this part of the book.

There are many habits of speculators taken as a whole that can be used to interpret charts and help trading. The typical trader not on the exchange floor will place an order at an even number, 5–10¢ increments in the grains, 10–50 points in other products. Who would think of buying corn at $278\frac{3}{4}$? The public is also known to enter in the bull markets always at the wrong time. Once the major media such as television news and syndicated newspapers and radio carry stories of outrageous prices in cattle, sugar, or coffee the public enters in what W. D. Gann calls the "grand rush," causing the final runaway move before the collapse; this behavior is easily identifiable on a chart. Gann also talks of "lost motion," the effect of momentum that carries you slightly past your goal. A common notion of the professional trader who is close to the market is that a move may carry 10% over its objective. A downward swing of soybeans from 8.00 to a support level of 7.50 could violate the bottom by 5¢ without being considered a break.

The behavioral aspects of prices are also rational. In the great bull markets, the repeated price patterns and variations from chance movement are indications of the effects of mass psychology. The greatest single source of information on this topic is Mackay's *Extraordinary Popular Delusions and the Madness of Crowds* originally published in 1841. In the preface to the edition of 1852 the author says:

> We find that whole communities suddenly fix their minds on one object, and go mad in its pursuit; that millions of people become simultaneously impressed with one delusion....

Not very long ago sugar was being rationed in supermarkets at the highest price ever known. The public was so concerned that there would not be enough at any price that they would buy (and horde) as much as possible. This extreme case of public demand coincided with the peak prices, and shortly afterwards the public found itself with an abundant supply of high-priced sugar in a rapidly declining market.

Charting is a broad topic; the chart paper itself and its scaling are sources of controversy. A standard bar chart (or line chart) representing highs and lows can be plotted for daily, weekly, or monthly intervals in order to smooth out the price movement over time. In the other direction, large increments representing price levels will reduce the volatile appearance of price fluctuations. Bar charts have been drawn on logarithmic and exponential scales,[1] where the significance of greater volatility at higher price levels is put into proportion with the quieter movement in the low ranges. Each variation gives the chartist a unique representation of price action. The shape of the box and its value of height/width will alter subsequent interpretations based on angles. Standard techniques applied to bar graphs, point-and-figure charts, and other representations use support and resistance trend lines, frequently measured at 45° angles (and in more complex theories at various other angles). Selection of the charting paper may have a major effect on the results. In our examples we will consider daily price charts unless otherwise noted and always plot using square boxes.

Following a review of bar charting, including the more advanced trading techniques and concepts, there is an extensive chapter on the point-and-figure method. This section emphasizes variations from the standard rules and concludes with a complete study on the creation of a variable-scale point-and-figure chart. It is hoped that the analytic procedure as well as the results will help a serious point-and-figure chartist complete the work for other commodities and serve as an exercise in analysis. For those of you that do not need the exercise, the results are summarized.

It may be a concern to today's chartist that the principles and rules that govern chart interpretations were based on the early stock market, and averages instead of individual contracts. This will be discussed in the beginning of the next chapter. For now we refer to Edwards and Magee, who said that the similarity of an organized exchange trading "anything whose market value is determined solely by the free interplay of supply and demand" will form the same graphic representation. They continue to

---
[1] Schabacker (1930) pp. 595–600.

say that the aims and psychology of speculators in either a stock or commodity environment would be essentially the same; the effect of postwar government regulations have caused a "more orderly" market in which these same charting techniques can be used.[2]

After these two basic charting systems we move to commodity systems based on charts but not requiring the plotting of lines or X's. The Taylor trading method, Eugene Nofri's congestion phase system, and Keltner's minor trend rule are all examples of chart interpretation by well-defined rules.

We then look into an area of pure behavior where some of the applications are not clearly defined. The theory of games is explained because of its behavioral implications. While no application to commodities markets has been published, its use in solving practical behavioral problems is only a matter of a short time. In keeping with this direction we review the techniques and principles of contrary opinion and then move into the controversial area of astrological forecasting. Since phases of the moon play such an important part in our lives the reader is left to judge for himself.

The next section includes some important theories, but requires background in areas approaching the mystical. R. N. Elliot's wave principle discusses Fibonacci numbers, a phenomenon of mathematics and nature, founded on a study of the great pyramid of Gizeh. Elliot's application is a combination of mathematics and behavior, as is W. D. Gann's treatment of geometric support and resistance lines. The works of both men are unique and yet related by their studies in defining human behavior by mathematics; their theories are sophisticated and extensive.

The last chapter of this advanced charting topic involves pattern recognition using a computer. If behavior of masses repeats itself, then the probabilities can be measured against some known event or time. Three sections measure the probability of a price moving up or down during a single week, over a weekend, or following a "key reversal" day. Although statistically tested, the interpretation is purely behavioral.

---

[2] Edwards and Magee (1948) Chapter XVI.

CHAPTER 10
Interpreting The Bar Chart

The *bar chart*, also called the *line chart*, became known through the theories of Charles H. Dow, who expressed them in the editorials of the *Wall Street Journal*. Dow first formulated his ideas in 1897 when he created the stock averages for the purpose of evaluating the movements of stocks as they were related in groups. After Dow's death in 1902 William P. Hamilton succeeded him and continued the development of his work into the theory that we know today. Those of you who have used charts extensively and understand their weak and strong points might be interested in just how far our acceptance has come. In the 1920s a New York newspaper was reported to have written:

One leading banker deplores the growing use of charts by professional stock traders and customers' men, who, he says, are causing unwarranted market declines by purely mechanical interpretation of a meaningless set of lines. It is impossible, he contends, to figure values by plotting prices actually based on supply and demand; but, he adds, if too many persons play with the same set of charts, they tend to create the very unbalanced supply and demand which upsets market trends. In his opinion, all charts should be confiscated, piled at the intersection of Broad and Wall and burned with much shouting and rejoicing.[1]

Since then charting has become part of the financial industry, whether the analyst is interested in the fundamentals of supply and demand or pure price movement. The earliest authoritative works on chart analysis are long out-of-print, and most of the essential material has been recounted in newer publications. If, however, a copy should cross your path, read the original *Dow Theory* by Robert Rhea;[2] most of all, you should read Richard W. Schabacker's outstanding work *Stock Market Theory and Practice*, which is probably the basis for most subsequent texts on the use of the stock market as an investment or speculative medium. The most available book that

---
[1] Wyckoff (1933) p. 105.
[2] Published by Vail–Ballou, Binghamton, N.Y. in 1932.

is both comprehensive and well written is *Technical Analysis of Stock Trends* by Robert D. Edwards and John Magee, which is confined entirely to chart analysis with related management implications and a small section on commodities. For the reader who prefers concise information with few examples, the monograph by W. L. Jiler, *Forecasting Commodity Prices with Vertical Line Charts*, and a complementary piece, *Volume and Open Interest, A Key to Commodity Price Forecasting*, are available.[3]

In its basic form the Dow theory is still the foundation of chart interpretation and applies equally to commodities as to stocks. Its major premise is that averages discount all extraneous motion; Dow's averages were groups of stocks while commodity averages could be individual products. The difficulty with interpreting stock movement is in the thinness of a specific issue; its fixed number of shares and light volume made the movement on one stock an unreliable indicator of an economic turn. Taken in total it would be improbable to move the average by the manipulation of a single issue; hence the averages became the subject of analysis. Commodities, expecially the grains, differ from stocks in their enormous volume; trading can be distributed in one or more contracts with little distortion because of "local spreading." The possibility of cornering a grain market is remote to the point of no concern; a single grain can substitute for a stock-related group average.

The Dow theory defines price motion, as represented by the average, in three distinct primary, secondary, and minor trends. These elements have often been compared to the tide, the wave, and the ripple. The primary trend denotes the main move and will exceed a magnitude of 20% of the original price; the secondary trend is an adjustment or correction and the minor movements are day-to-day fluctuations. The theory emphasized the main move. As Angas said: "Be simple. Take the grand view." It is easier to identify the dominant trend than to worry about every change in direction.

Accumulation and distribution are the beginning phases of a bull or bear market. Accumulation is the period where the insiders begin to acquire a long position in anticipation of a bull move. In charting, this is traditionally a wide formation at a low price with increasing open interest and erratic peaks in volume representing large purchases. The distribution phase serves the same function for anticipated bear moves.

A unique part of the Dow theory that distinguishes it from application in commodities is the principle of confirmation, requiring that a signal be produced by more than one average. There has been some criticism with regard to the relationship of an industrial group being confirmed by a rail, but the principle may not be unreasonable. If the purpose of the Dow theory is to identify major trends in the economy, then it is unlikely that the average of one stock group would be going up and the other group down in a well-defined inflationary or deflationary period. In the same way you would not expect the price of corn to increase and the price of wheat to decrease in absolute terms. A period of inflation should uniformly affect stocks and commodities; any items varying from the total pattern should be justified on an individual basis.

The relationship of sales to motion is characterized by saying that "volume expands with the trend." Whether a bull or bear market, activity increases as the trend becomes clear. In commodities the open interest has been treated in the same manner,

---

[3] Two newer works worth studying are Appel (1974) and Appel and Zweig (1976).

INTERPRETING THE BAR CHART

with increased positions, especially during the accumulation and distribution phases, a sign of a new move forming.

The Dow theory has other points that have been incorporated into most other chart interpretations. The exclusive use of closing prices is important for two reasons: they are most closely followed by the typical speculator, and they discount the effects of any positions taken by floor traders for 1-day profits. Support and resistance lines were introduced as a substitute for the secondary move, which may have been difficult to define. Lastly, the theory expressed some trading philosophy by stating that a trend should be assumed to be intact until a reversal occurred.

Chart analysis uses both trend lines and geometric formations extensively. Rather than discuss the placement and identification of these elements we will summarize them and then describe their use in trading situations.

Trend Lines

A support line is drawn to connect the bottom points of a price move.

A resistance line is drawn across the peaks of a trend.

A channel is the area between the support and resistance lines that contains a sustained price move.

Geometric Formations for Accumulation (Distribution)

- Head and shoulders bottom (top)
- Common rounded upwards (downwards) turn
- Triangular bottom (top) of an ascending, descending or symmetric shape
- Ascending bottom (top)
- Double bottom (top)
- Complex bottom (top) including a triple bottom (top) or a combination of other formations
- Broadening bottom (top)

The basic charting course also includes a variety of gap formations and a definition of a top based on irregularities of increasing magnitude. We will consider these rules, lines and formations and discuss applications to trading, including use of price objectives, and then offer some observation about charts.

TRADING RULES

The simplest formations to recognize are the most commonly used: horizontal support and resistance lines, bullish and bearish support and resistance lines, and channels. Once your support and resistance lines have been drawn, you can use the trend line (plus or minus some error factor) as your buy or sell point. When a breakout occurs you will be stopped into a position at your predetermined point. Because of the basic charting rule—"Once broken, a resistance level becomes a support level and a support level becomes a resistance level"—you can use the original trend line as your stop-loss. If you are stopped out of your trade, you have suffered a false breakout;

prices are now back within your previous formation and your original trend lines are still valid.

Experienced traders often wait for the first pullback after the breakout before entering their position. This technique results in a higher percentage of profitable trades, because the position is placed at a test of the old support or resistance levels (and your theoretic stop-loss). If the test fails, which occurs frequently, you do not get filled and you have saved yourself a loss. Unfortunately, most of the biggest profits occur on breakouts that never pull back. If you catch only one of these breakouts you compensate for all the small losses due to false signals. Many professional traders may be steady winners, but they do not often find the big move.

The same basic rules can be applied to trading during a single day, but with more critical timing and an unforgiving nature. It is common practice to buy or sell a breakout from the opening range as though it were bounded on the top and bottom by resistance and support lines. After the initial entry prices form what is considered the main trend, the position is closed out or reversed when the bullish support line or bearish resistance line is broken.

TOPS AND BOTTOMS

Most of the formations important to bar charting can be traded using a penetration of the support or resistance lines as a signal. But of all these the most interesting and potentially profitable trades occur on breakouts from major top or bottom formations, if you can recognize them in time. We will discuss them in detail. The simplest of all bottom formations as well as one that offers great opportunities is the extended rectangle at contract lows. Fortunes have been made by applying patience, some available capital, and the following plan:

1. Find the commodity with a long consolidating base and reduced volume (with increasing open interest).
2. Buy whenever there is a test of its major support level, placing a stop-loss to liquidate all positions on a new low price.
3. Buy again when prices pull back to the original resistance line (now a support level) after the initial breakout. Close out all positions if prices penetrate back into the consolidation area and start again at (2).
4. Buy whenever there is a major price adjustment in the bull move.
5. Liquidate all positions at a prior major resistance point, a top formation, or the breaking of a major bullish support line.

Building positions in this way can be done with a relatively small amount of capital and risk. The closer you let the price come to major support the shorter the distance from your stop-loss, but the fewer positions you can place. Stanley Kroll, in his book *The Professional Commodity Trader*, discussed "The Copper Caper—How We're Going to Make a Million," using a similar technique for building positions. It can be done, but it requires patience, planning, and capital. The opportunity is always there.

We have notably avoided discussions and examples of compounded positions in a bear market. There is money to be made on the short side of the market, but it is usually a faster move and doesn't permit the building of large positions. There is also

INTERPRETING THE BAR CHART 141

more risk, the possibility of false breakouts at higher levels caused by greater volatility, and the problem of "how high can it go?" In consolidation areas at low levels you have a basic underlying demand for a product, the cost of production, price support (for agricultural products), and low volatility. You also have a well-defined trend line that may have been tested many times. You won't find the careful trader entering a large position at an anticipated top, but you will find growing volume and open interest at a well-defined major support area.

HEAD AND SHOULDERS

This classic top-and-bottom formation is the "head and shoulders," accepted as a major reversal indicator. This pattern, well known to chartists, appears as a left shoulder, head, and right shoulder (Diagram 10-1).

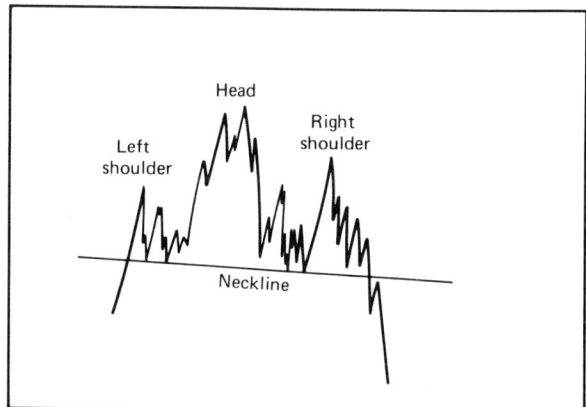

Diagram 10-1   Head-and-shoulders formation.

The head-and-shoulders top is developed in the following way:

1. A strong upward breakout, reaching new highs on increased volume. The move appears to be the continuation of a long-term bull move.
2. A consolidation area formed with diminishing volume. This can look much like a descending flag, predicting an upward breakout, or a descending triangle, anticipating a downward breakout.
3. An upward breakout on continued reduced volume forms the head. This is the key point of the formation. The new high is not confirmed by increased volume and prices fall off quickly.
4. Another descending flag or descending triangle on further reduced volume followed by a minor breakout without increased volume. This last move forms the right shoulder and is the third attempt at new highs for the move.
5. The lowest points of the two flags, pennants, or triangles become the "neckline" of the formation. A sale is indicated when this neckline is broken. Some chartists wait for the first rally back to the neckline to sell, but this approach is subject to the prior discussion of risk, and confirmation, and may mean lost opportunity.

Trading Rules For Head and Shoulders

There are three approaches for trading a head-and-shoulders top formation, involving increasing degrees of anticipation:

1. Sell when the final dip of the right shoulder penetrates the neckline. This represents the completion of the head-and-shoulders formation. Place a stop-loss just above your entry if you only want to stay with the trade on a sharp break, or place the stop-loss above the right shoulder or above the head in order to liquidate on new strength.
2. Sell when the right shoulder is being formed. A key place would be when prices have retraced their way halfway to the prior height of the head. A stop-loss can be placed above the top of the head.
   Another approach is to wait until the top of the right shoulder is formed and sell with a stop either above the high of the right shoulder or above the high of the head.
   Both of these techniques allow positions to be taken well in advance of the neckline penetration, with significant logical stop-loss points. If the high of the head can is used for a protective stop you gain added confidence from the old rule: "Always sell a triple top."
3. Sell when the head is forming, with a stop-loss at about the high of the move. This has less chance of success, although small risk. It is for traders who like to find tops and are willing to suffer frequent small losses to do it. Even if the current prices become the head of the formation, there may be numerous small corrections that will look like "absolute tops" to an anxious seeker.

OTHER TOP-AND-BOTTOM FORMATIONS

The experienced trader is most successful when prices are testing a major support or resistance level, usually a contract or seasonal high or low. The more often they are tested the less likely they are to break through to a new level without changing supply and demand factors.

Repeated tests of tops are visually clearer but not as exact as bottoms because of the added volatility of the higher prices. The *double top* is a more speculative trade than successive multiple tops; it is more frequent than the other formations, and is the first opportunity you have of picking the top of a bull move, and it is easy to position a stop-loss above the previous highs. As with other chart patterns, you might feel more confident if the volume declined after the formation of the first top and before each additional test of the top.

Triple tops are reliable opportunities for selling. Because they are popular formations, there is frequently anticipation, which causes the third top to look more like a right shoulder, lower than previous highs. Traders waiting for a near-test of the highs to afford less risk could find themselves with no position at all. Among professionals the fourth top is considered the final test; whichever direction prices turn at that time will determine a new major trend.

Sharp double and triple bottoms also occur, but generally of lesser magnitude than tops; if close together, double bottoms will have lower volatility. It is easier to find

INTERPRETING THE BAR CHART

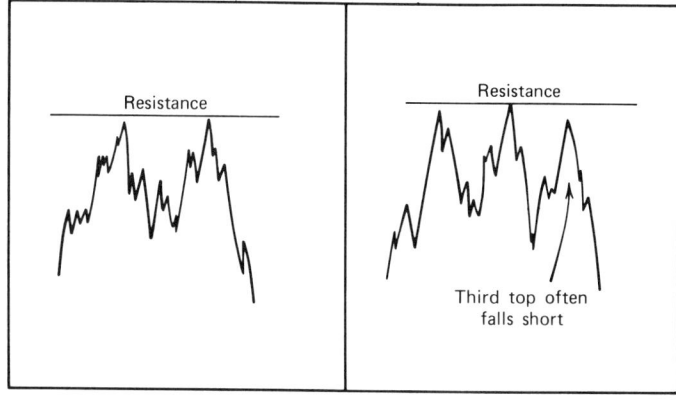

Diagram 10-2   Double and triple tops.

frequent testing of a long-term consolidated base (in a rectangle pattern), with better buying opportunities for the patient speculator.

NOW YOU SEE IT, NOW YOU DON'T!

The "V-top" (actually an inverted V) is probably the most difficult top formation to anticipate and consequently to trade. Its frequency in the 1974 markets tended to deceive new speculators. V-tops are caused by critical shortage and demand with public awareness. In 1974 they were caused by a combination of domestic crop shortage, severe pressure on the United States dollar abroad, and foreign purchases of United States grain. The news was so well publicized that novice commodity traders withdrew their funds from their declining stock portfolios and bought any commodity available as a hedge against inflation.

It could not go on forever. When the top came in soybeans, sugar, and others, there was no trading for days in locked-limit markets; paper profits dwindled faster than they were made and the late entrants found their investments unrecoverable. The public always seems to enter at the wrong time. Consider a simplified example:

> Live cattle is a familiar commodity, with prices based on a combination of consumer demand, other foods, and the price of various feed grains. During 1973, as the price of feed increased, led by soybeans, cattle prices moved steadily from under 40¢ per pound to almost 54¢ in August. Prior to that, live beef prices had never been over 37¢ (in 1952). The price of soybean meal, used as a high-protein feed, continued to move prices higher. How high could it go? Between August and October, live-cattle prices formed a V-top, and declined back under 40¢, giving up the 8-month gain in 2 months. How could the supply-and-demand factors change so quickly?

Consumers expect continued inflation and are not inclined to object to minor fluctuations in price. In the case of beef, they do not tend to consider pork, fowl, or fish as an actual substitute and so they will bear noticeably increased costs when necessary. As prices got near the top, the following changes occurred:

- The cost became a major impact on the standard household budget
- Rising prices received more publicity
- Movements for public boycotts of beef began
- Grain prices declined due to the new harvest

We call this the *elastic theory*. It can be applied to the 1973 soybean market and gold markets as well. The elastic theory is based on the principle:

When prices get high enough a number of phenomena occur:

1. Previously higher-priced substitutes become practical (e.g., synthetics for cotton).
2. Competition becomes more feasible (sugar substitutes, corn sweeteners).
3. Inactive operations start up (southwest gold mines).
4. Consumers would rather do without the product (beef).

Consequently, the demand disappears suddenly.

Announcements of new production, more acreage, new products, boycotts—all coming at once—cause highly inflated prices to sharply reverse, forming a V-top that is virtually impossible to anticipate. Further impact is given to the reversal because of the scramble to liquidate after the first reversal day, followed by those latecomers or pyramiders who put their most recent position on near the top and cannot sustain a continued adverse move. The rush to close out long positions, put on new shorts, and liquidate deficit accounts only prolongs the sharpness of the V-top.

GAPS

A gap is a formation caused by the price movement of a single day and is noted for its relationship to both trends and support and resistance lines. It is an open area on a chart created by prices trading entirely above or below the prior trading range. Gaps will usually occur outside the formations we have studied and may be caused by either extreme demand (upside gap) or supply (downside gap) or by a lack of speculators willing to take an opposing position, causing a thinly traded market. In most situations, the *common gap* is the result of many stop orders placed at new highs or lows or at major trend lines as protection against unfavourable breakouts of current positions or as an entry to a new position. The common gap, which can occur anywhere, might correctly indicate a new or continued trend, but usually is caused by speculative interest rather than the fundamentals of supply and demand.

There are a variety of terms given to gaps appearing at different places on a chart. These can be studied in any of the recommended readings.

There are no well-defined trading rules for gaps. The *island reversal* is a form of V-top that has been continually elusive to speculators. The *breakaway gap* that penetrated a support or resistance line offers the only opportune time to enter a position. If the breakout is then on light volume, you can wait for a pullback to the

INTERPRETING THE BAR CHART

prior trend line; you can then buy or sell using the trend line as a stop-loss point. If the breakaway gap is on high volume, you should enter at the first opportunity. The risk will be high, but the move should be fast and long.

PRICE OBJECTIVES FOR BAR-CHARTING

There is some satisfaction in having a price objective for a trade you have just entered. If this objective can be determined to a reliable degree in advance, you might select the trade having the best profit potential as compared to the risk. It is also comforting to know that at a specific point you will liquidate your position and take your profits. Unfortunately, prices sometimes don't recognize the price objective you have set and react in a way contrary to your plans.

The simplest and most logical price objective is a major support or resistance level, established by previous trading. When entering a long position, look at the most well-defined resistence levels above your entry point. The testing of those levels by the current price move will probably cause one of the top formations we have reviewed; when those prior levels are tested there is generally a technical adjustment or a reversal. In the case of a strong upward market, the volatility often causes a short penetration before the setback occurs. Placing your price objective a reasonable distance below the prior major resistance level will always be safe; the intermediate resistance levels can be used for adding positions on technical reversals. The downside objective can be handled in a similar manner: find the major support level and place a stop just above it.

When using both the support and resistance price objectives you must carefully watch for a violation of the current trend; don't be rigid about your position. You may

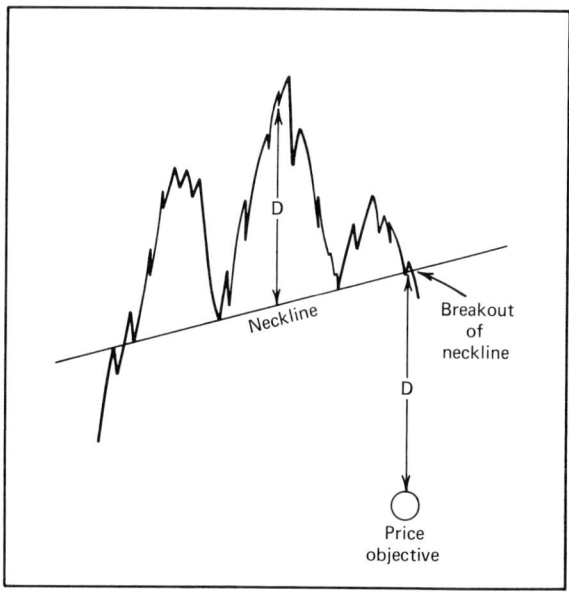

Diagram 10-3 Head-and-shoulders top price objective.

take advantage of each reaction to add to your position, but if the major trend line is broken before your objective is reached, get out. On the other hand, if you reach your goal and prices react as predicted, then reverse and break through the previous highs or lows; you can reenter the market with a new trade on the breakout and calculate a new price objective if possible.

There are other, more analytic, ways to determine the objective of a trade. Bear in mind that these methods are considered guidelines and are not expected to be precise; if the price objective falls very near a support or resistance level, that level should be substituted in the manner described in the first approach.

The *head-and-shoulders top* has a downside objective associated with the formation; it is a measure of volatility. This objective is measured from the point of penetration of the right shoulder through the neckline and is equal to the distance from the top of the head to the neckline. For a major top, this goal seems quite modest, but it will be a good measure of an initial reaction from the head-and-shoulders formations, and will generally be safe even if the top is broken later (see Diagram 10-3).

A *consolidation area*, both top and bottom, has a counting method based on the width of the rectangle or consolidation. For a basing formation, measure the width using a ruler and then place your objective the same distance above the congestion area, when measured from the point of the support line. For downside objectives, measure downward from the resistance line forming the upper bound of the congestion area. This technique seems to say: "The longer within a consolidation area, the bigger the move"; you will find this same method used later in point-and-figure charting (see Diagram 10-4).

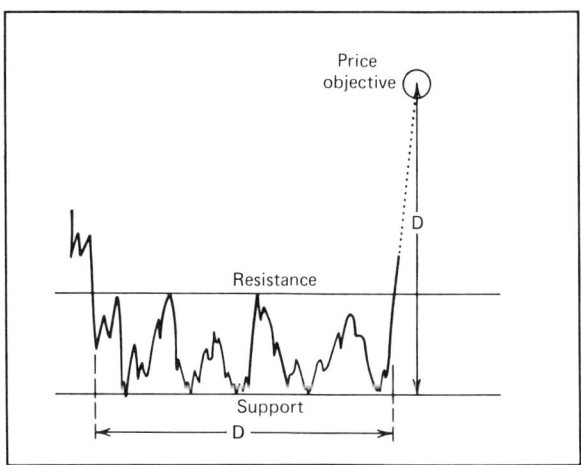

Diagram 10-4   Consolidation price objective.

Trend lines can also be used to measure the expected price move. The following are some accepted ways:

1. The channel width surrounding a trending move will determine the price objective when measured from the point of breakout of the channel (Diagram 10-5).

INTERPRETING THE BAR CHART 147

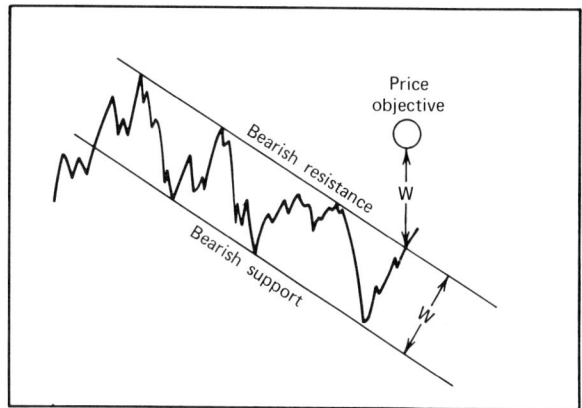

Diagram 10-5 The channel width as a price objective.

2. Once a breakout of a channel has occurred, try to construct a new descending channel. This can be done by connecting the major high prices since the recent decline began (for bottoms, connect the major lows); you then have a preliminary but fairly shallow trend line for the new move. Draw a line parallel to the new trend line from the last reaction prior to the top or bottom. This will be a bearish resistance line for a descending move or a bullish resistance line for an ascending move, and it will signal your first reaction and price objective.

In Diagram 10-6, the original channel around the bull move was broken at the point marked by the black dot, followed by prices moving down to point *a* and reacting back up to point *b*. When a new high is not made at point *b*, a resistance line (1R) can be drawn from the prior high, *h*, to the top of the latest move, *b*. A line parallel to 1R can be constructed at point *a*, forming the initial downward channel. Price objective #1 is on the support line of the new channel (1S) and is used once the top at *b* is determined. Price objective #1 cannot be expected to be too precise due to the early development of the move. If prices continue to point *c* and then rally to *d* we can now define a more reasonable channel using

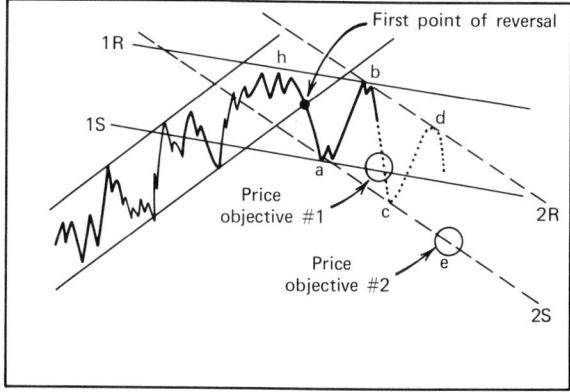

Diagram 10-6 Forming new channels to determine objectives.

trendlines 2R and 2S. The support line will again become the point where we can place our new price objective, #2. You can continue refining your upper and lower trend line as the new high and low reactions occur. Each time, the major trend line is drawn first and then your new price objective becomes a point on the minor parallel trend line.

Price objectives sometimes take on an air of the mystical when they precisely determine the extent of a trade, although this never happens with regularity. The best methods for setting objectives are the ones that get popular support and can be confirmed by other calculations, they are more likely to be accurate when they fall within the prior range of trading and can be associated with a previous support or resistance level. Most of the methods for determining objectives are in some sense measures of volatility; the width of a channel and the height of a head-and-shoulders formation are simple evaluations of market activity, and as such seem more reasonable.

USING THE BAR CHART

This section is meant to leave you with a realistic, but not negative, opinion of bar charting as a trading tool. Since it is not publicized as precise, the construction of trend lines and other geometric formations can be performed with some latitude. As a guideline, bar charting analysis serves the useful function of identifying support and resistance levels and allowing you to formulate a trading plan.

But this is more an art than a science. Some people don't have an eye for patterns; others will see formations where no one else would. Additional variables in both the construction and reading of the charts are the time element and scale. How much of the chart do you use? By choosing a shorter time interval we may be able to draw a trend line where none was possible over a longer time period; an entire sequence of lines may form a pennant while the most recent part forms a triangle; we may have broken a short-term trend line, but not a long-term one. Are the formations different if the scale is expanded or reduced?

The timeliness of identification is another major problem. Can you interpret the formation in time to act on a breakout, or do you always see the pattern afterwards? At different stages of development the lines may appear to be quite different patterns. Before you use this method, practice on a large bar chart, simulating the day-to-day development of prices as follows:

1. Hold a piece of paper over the right side of the chart, covering the most recent months.
2. Look at the chart and analyze the formations.
3. Determine what your actions will be based on your interpretation (be specific).
4. Move the paper one day to the right.
5. Record any orders that would have been filled. Don't cheat.
6. Determine whether the new day's price would have altered your formations and plans.
7. Continue at step (3).

By doing this simple exercise you might save a lot of money—but don't get discouraged. As you practice you will get much better at finding and using formations and you will select the ones that work best for you. Very few traders base their trading decisions entirely on bar charts. Quite a few consult the charts for confirmation of another technical or fundamental analysis of the market. The general acceptance of analysis by bar charting as a guideline makes it a lasting tool.

CHAPTER 11
The Point-And-Figure Method

Point-and-figure charting is credited to Charles Dow, who is said to have used it just prior to the turn of the century; at that time it had a different appearance than the familiar boxes of X's and 0's. The earliest published book containing the subject is reported to be *The Game in Wall Street and How to Play it Successfully*, published by Hoyle (not Edmond Hoyle, the English writer) in 1898. The first definitive work on the subject was by Victor de Villiers, who in 1933 published *The Point and Figure Method of Anticipating Stock Price Movement*. De Villiers worked with Owen Taylor to publish and promote a weekly point-and-figure service, maintaining their own charts; he was impressed by the simple scientific methodology. As with many of the original technical systems, the application was intended for the stock market, and the rules required the use of every change in price appearing on the ticker. The rationalization for a purely technical system has been told many times by now, but an original source is often refreshing. De Villiers said:

"The Method takes for granted:

1. That the price of a stock at any given time is its correct valuation up to the instant of purchase and sales (a) by the concensus of opinion of *all* buyers and sellers in the world and (b) by the verdict of *all* the forces governing the laws of supply and demand.
2. That the last price of a stock reflects or crystalizes *everything* known about or bearing on it from its first sale on the Exchange (or prior), up to that time.
3. That those who know more about it than the observer *cannot* conceal their future intentions regarding it. Their plans will be revealed in time by the stock's subsequent action."[1]

---
[1] de Villiers (1933) p. 8.

THE POINT-AND-FIGURE METHOD

The unique aspect of the point-and-figure method is that it ignores the passage of time. Unlike bar charts, you do not make a single vertical mark and then move to the right a uniform distance. Each column of a point-and-figure chart can represent any length of time. The measurement of a significant change in price direction alone determines the pattern of the chart.

The original "figure charts" were plotted with only dots or with the exact price in each box or with a combination of X's and occasional digits (usually 0's and 5's every five boxes) to help keep the chart aligned. A geometric representation was also created by connecting the points in each column with a vertical line and closing the gap between columns with a crossbar on top for a reversal down and a bar at the bottom if the next column goes up. Charts using one, three, and five points were popular, where each point represented a minimum price move. In the five-point method no entry was recorded unless the price change spanned five points.

The current three-box method of plotting point-and-figure charts can be used to follow intraday price moves or long-term trends. Diagram 11-1 shows the steps

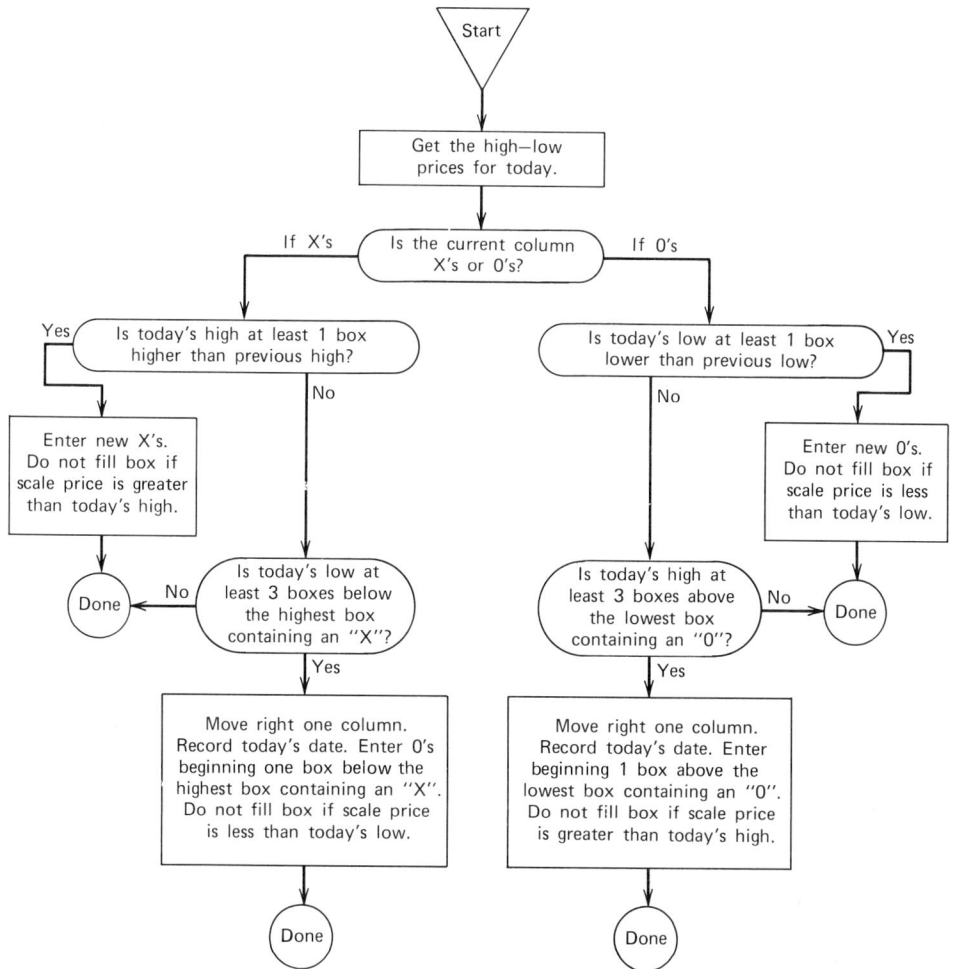

Diagram 11-1 Point-and-figure daily rules.

necessary to plot a daily chart, requiring only the high and low prices of the day. It would be impossible for the average speculator to follow the original method of recording every change in price. Those charts when applied to stocks became so lengthy that interpretations similar to the line chart were necessary in an attempt to select the best trades. In 1965 Robert E. Davis published *Profit and Profitability*, a point-and-figure study that detailed eight unique *buy* indicators and their corresponding *sell* signals. The study covered two stocks for the years 1914 through 1964 and 1100 for 1954 through 1964. The intention was to find specific bull and bear patterns that resulted in greater chances of a successful trade. The best buy signal was an ascending triple top and the best sell signal was the breakout of a triple bottom.

```
        Ascending Triple Top        Breakout of a Triple Bottom
               X ←BUY                    X   X
             X X                       0 X 0 X 0
        X    X 0 X                     0 X 0 X 0
        X 0 X 0 X                      0   0   0
        X 0 X 0                                0 ←SELL
        0
```

Diagram 11-2 Best Formations from Davis' study.

Plotted daily, commodity prices do not offer the variety of formations available in the stock market. Limited sets of commodities and the high correlation of movement between many of the delivery months makes signal selection impractical. It is necessary to limit the trading rules to the simple buy signal, an X in the current column going one box above the highest X in the last column of X's, and the simple sell signal, which requires 0 to be plotted below the lowest 0 of the last descending column. The variability in the system lies in the size of the box; the smaller the size the more sensitive the chart will be to price moves. In 1933 Richard Wyckoff noted that it was advisable to use a chart with a different box size when the price of stock varied substantially.[2]

In 1970 Charles C. Thiel, Jr., with Robert E. Davis completed the first purely commodity point-and-figure study[3] that calculated profitability of good samples of commodites by varying both the value of a box and the reversal criteria (the number of boxes necessary to start a new column). With the standard three-box reversal and only simple buy and sell formations the tests showed 799 signals of which 53% were profitable; the average net profit on all trades was $311 realized in approximately 50 days. The period studied was 1960 through 1969. More recently Zieg and Kaufman[4] performed a computerized study using the same rules but limiting the test period to 6 months ending May 1974, an extremely active market period. For the 22 commodities tested 375 signals showed 40% of the trades were profitable; the net profit over all the trades was $306 and the average duration was 12.4 days. It is interesting to note that the most significant difference in the results of the two studies is in the

---

[2] Wyckoff (1933) p. 89.
[3] Thiel and Davis (1970).
[4] Zieg and Kaufman (1975) contains completed tabularized results of both point-and-figure tests.

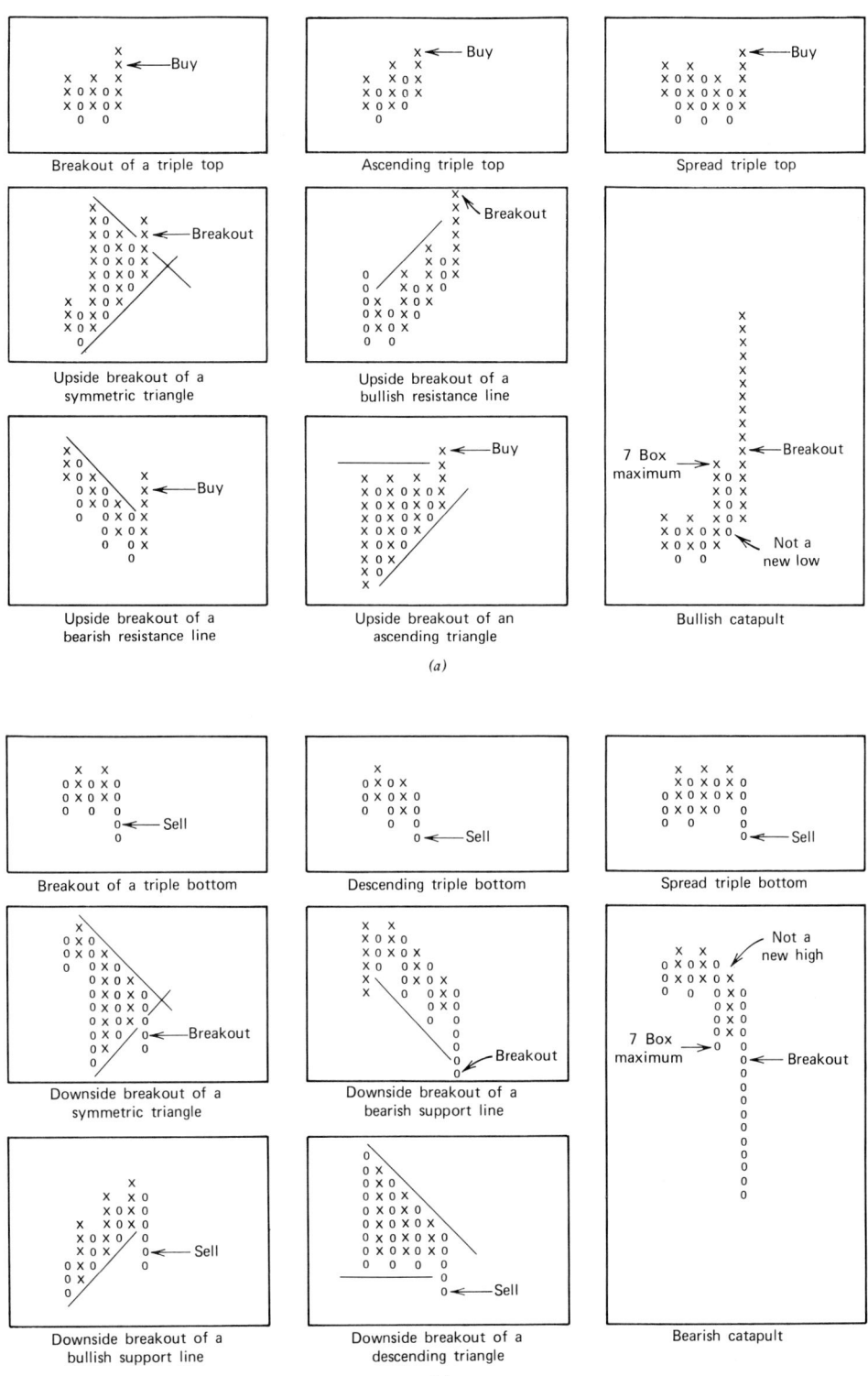

Diagram 11-3 (a) Compound point-and-figure buy signals; (b) compound point-and-figure sell signals.

average length of a trade, from 50 to 12.4 days, indicating a change potentially induced by more volatile markets. Although the two tests varied in many of the details, the results are a strong argument for the consistency of the point-and-figure method as a trading tool.

In its current role, point-and-figure differs from other forms of charting because it provides a rigid set of rules for entering long and short positions. Many of the formations are still subjected to interpretation and are frequently used in the original sense by floor traders; but as a tool for the speculator without access to intraday prices and the experience to understand the subtleties of chart analysis, point-and-figure fills an important gap. It will tell the trader exactly what penetration of a resistance or support level is necessary to generate a buy or sell signal, and exactly where he should place his stop-loss order to limit his risk. It is this well-defined nature of point-and-figure charting that allows computer testing and evaluation.

The basic study of the point-and-figure method involves rules of charting, buy and sell signals, trend lines, geometric formations, and price objectives. Since these points have been covered effectively in at least two books currently available[5] we will not repeat them here. We will discuss some of the more advanced topics using point-and-figure, including its relationship to bar charting, alternate plotting rules, risk-limited trading, and the problem of varying the box size.

THE POINT-AND-FIGURE BOX SIZE

The box size used in a point-and-figure chart determines the sensitivity of the method and will allow the identification of trends and trading ranges of various durations. At the present time there are services offering periodic charts of standard or changing box sizes according to current price levels or computerized testing. It is important to find the right chart to match your trading goals; if you keep these charts yourself be sure to reevaluate the box size as prices go up and down. It is as important to increase the size of the box at low levels as it is to reduce it at higher prices. In a later section we will discuss the variations in more detail. Table 11-1 shows older and current box sizes for well-known services in the United States and the United Kingdom using a standard three-box reversal method. Note the increase in box size in 1975 and the subsequent decrease in early 1977 for the United Kingdom service while the United States charts maintained the prior box size while most prices declined from the 1975 levels.

THE PROBLEM OF RISK

Jesse Livermore once said to Richard Wyckoff:

I go long or short as close as I can to the danger point, and if the danger becomes real I close out and take a small loss.[6]

The point-and-figure method has been shown to be successful by enough independent sources for us to accept the results. Then why is it necessary to modify the basic

---

[5] Cohen (1972), and Zieg and Kaufman (1975).
[6] Wyckoff (1933), p. 2.

Table 11-1a Point-and-Figure Box Sizes for Commodities on U.S. Exchanges[a]

Commodity	Prior to 1975[b] Year	Prior to 1975[b] Box size	1975[c] Box size	1977[c] Box size	1977[d] Box size
Broilers	1971	20 pts	100 pts	20 pts	
Cattle	1967	20 pts	20 pts	20 pts	
Cocoa	1964	20 pts	100 pts	100 pts	50 (50) pts
Coffee	----	(20 pts)	100 pts	100 pts	50 (50) pts
Copper	1964	20 pts	100 pts	100 pts	20 (50) pts
Corn	1971	$\frac{1}{2}$¢	2¢	2¢	1 (2) ¢
Cotton	----	(20 pts)	100 pts	100 pts	
Eggs	1964	20 pts	100 pts	20 pts	
Gold	----	----	50 pts	100 pts	
Hogs	1968	20 pts	20 pts	20 pts	
Lumber	----	(100 pts)	100 pts	100 pts	
Oats	1965	$\frac{1}{2}$¢	1¢	1¢	
Orange juice	1968	20 pts	20 pts	100 pts	
Platinum	1968	200 pts	100 pts	200 pts	100 (200) pts
Plywood	1971	100 pts	100 pts	100 pts	
Pork bellies	1965	20 pts	20 pts	20 pts	
Potatoes	1968	5 pts	10 pts	10 pts	
Silver	1971	100 pts	200 pts	200 pts	200 (400) pts
Silver coins	----	(10 pts)	20 pts	20 pts	
Soybeans	1971	1¢	10¢	10¢	2 (5) ¢
Soybean meal	1964	50 pts	500 pts	500 pts	
Soybean oil	1965	10 pts	20 pts	20 pts	
Sugar	1965	5 pts	20 pts	20 pts	10 (20) pts
Wheat	1964	1¢	2¢	2¢	2 (2) ¢

[a] All box sizes use a three-box reversal and apply to individual contracts except as noted in footnote d.
[b] Cohen (1972); (---- pts) indicates approximate values.
[c] Courtesy of Chartcraft Commodity Service, Chartcraft, Inc., Larchmont, N.Y.
[d] Chart Analysis Limited, Bishopsgate, London. (----) indicates long-term continuation chart box sizes; other values are single contracts.

signal, and use trending and geometric formations to interpret new signals? The answer involves the risk of an individual trade. If you look at a line chart and a corresponding point-and-figure chart for the same time period you can see the difference in treatment of the same formation. The line chart uses support and resistance trend lines to define a rectangle; when the resistance line is penetrated a long position is taken and a stop-loss placed below the resistance line in order to close out the position in the event of a false breakout. An alternate place for the stop-loss could have been below the support line, allowing the new bull move some latitude to develop. The interpreted line chart makes the selection of the entry point and the placement of stops seem obvious. In trading you discover that the placement of the support and

Table 11-1b Point-and-Figure Box Size, Currencies

Currencies[a]	1975 Box size[b]	1977 Box size[c]
Australian dollar	.010	----
Austrian Schilling	.050	----
Belgian franc	.100	----
British pound	----	.001
Canadian dollar	.001	.002
Dutch guilder	.010	----
French franc	.010	----
German deutschmark	.010	.002
Hong Kong dollar	.010	----
Italian lira	1.000	----
Japanese yen	.100	.002
Mexican peso	----	.020
Norwegian kronor	.010	----
South African rand	.001	----
Swiss franc	.010	.002

[a] Plotted in value to U.S. dollar—.01 = 1¢.
[b] Source: Chart Analysis, London. Box size did not change from 1975 to 1977 with the exception of the Australian dollar, plotted as .002 in 1977.
[c] Source: Chartcraft Commodity Service, Larchmont, N.Y.

Table 11-1c Point-and-Figure Box Size, Commodity Indices

Index	1975–1977 Box size
London Financial Times	1 pt
Reuters	5 pts
Dow–Jones spot	2 pts
Dow–Jones futures	2 pts
Moody's	5 pts

resistance lines is not clear, that you are not certain how long to wait after a breakout before you enter the trade, and that your choice of the position for the stop depends on the volatility of prices and the risk you are willing to assume in order to let the price move materialize.

In contrast to the ambiguity of the line chart the point-and-figure method defines exactly where the support and resistance levels are, establishes a point to buy in advance, and designates the position for the stop-loss at the bottom of the rectangular congestion area. The rigidity of the method allows only one place for your stop and fixes your risk as the difference between the support and resistance lines.

Table 11-1*d* Point-and-Figure Box Size, Foreign Products Traded Outside the United States[a]

Commodity	Box size 1975[b]		Box size 1977[b]	
	Individual	Continuation	Individual	Continuation
Barley	20 p	40 p	10 p	40 p
Cocoa	£2	£4	£10	£20
Coffee	£2	£5	£10	£20
Palm oil	£2	----	----	----
Potatoes	Fls 0.2	----	----	----
Rubber	20 p	40 p	20 p	40 p
Soybean meal	50 p	£1	----	----
Sugar	£2	£4	50 p	£1
Wheat	20 p	40 p	10 p	40 p
Wool	2 p	5 p	1 p	2 p

[a] Source: Chart Analysis, London.
[b] Abbreviations: p (pence), £ (pounds sterling), Fls (guilders).

Table 11-1*e* Point-and-Figure Box Sizes, Metals Traded Outside the United States[a]

Metals	1975[b]	1977[b]
Aluminum	£2	£2
Antimony	£20	£20
Bismuth	10¢	10¢
Cadmium	2¢	2¢
Copper wirebars	£1 or £2	£1 or £2
Gold	50¢ or $1	50¢ or $1
Lead	£1 or £2	£1 or £2
Nickel	1¢	1¢
Palladium	50 p	50 p
Platinum	50 p	50 p
Selenium	25¢	25¢
Silver	1 p or 2 p	1 p or 2 p
Tin	5¢ or £10	5¢ or £10
Wolfram	25 p	50 p
Zinc	£2 or £5	£2 or £5
Coins		
New sovereigns	25¢	50¢
Old sovereigns	25¢	50¢
Double eagles	$2	$2
Krugerrand	50 p or $1	50 p or $1

[a] Source: Chart Analysis, London.
[b] Abbreviations: p (pence), £ (pounds sterling).

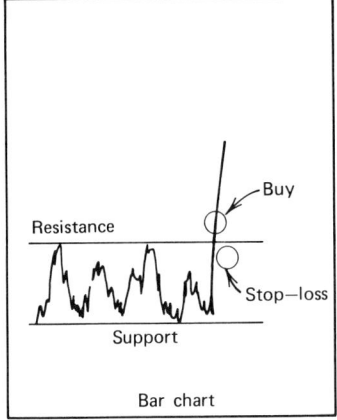 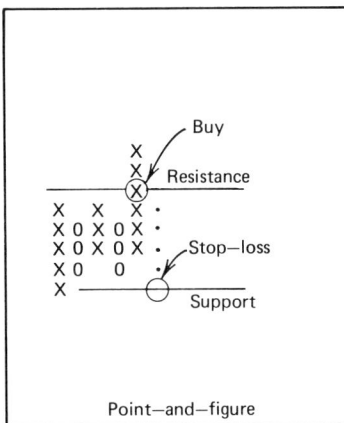

Diagram 11-4 Placement of a stop-loss.

In Diagram 11-4 the risk of the point-and-figure method is seen to be the width of the congestion formation plus two boxes, for a total of five boxes. In the line chart the risk might have been held to the equivalent of two boxes. One way to limit the risk of an individual trade is to diversify into a well-balanced portfolio; the risk of a specific trade will be hidden among the varying daily profits and losses.

TRADING TECHNIQUES

For limited investments or for those speculators interested in higher returns than diversification can offer, there are alternate methods for selecting entry and exit points. Buying or selling on a pullback, after an initial point-and-figure signal, is one of the more common modifications to the system, since it can limit risk to an individualized level and still maintain a logical stop-loss point. Of course, the smaller the risk you look for, the fewer trades you will find. There are two approaches that are recommended for entering on limited risk:

1. Wait for a reversal back to within your acceptable risk, then buy or sell immediately with the normal point-and-figure stop.

    Diagram 11-5 shows various levels of risk using the Board of Trade corn contract (5000 bushels or $50 for each 1¢ move). The initial buy signal is at 258 with the simple sell signal for liquidation at 249, giving a risk of 9¢ or $450 per contract. You can wait for a reversal following the breakout and buy when the low for the day penetrates the box corresponding to the predetermined risk. When you buy into a declining market you are anticipating the support level to hold, preventing the stop-loss point from being reached. Because of this you would want the base of the formation to be as broad as possible. The testing of a triple bottom or a spread triple bottom after a simple buy signal is a more reasonable place to go long than a simple buy after a small reversal in the middle of a contract price range.

    It is not advisable to reduce your risk by entering on the simple buy signal and and placing your stop-loss at the point of the first reversal (three boxes below the

THE POINT-AND-FIGURE METHOD 159

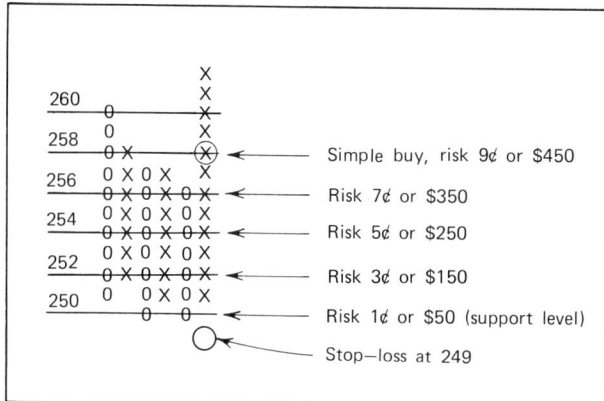

Diagram 11-5 Entering on a pullback.

highs). The advantage of waiting for the pullback is that it uses the logical support level as a stop—or the resistance level for short positions. A stop-loss placed in a tight position at the beginning of a breakout has no logical basis and will usually result in a short, losing trade.

2. Enter the market on the second reversal back in the direction of the original signal. As in Diagram 11-6, the first reversal following a signal may not pull back to within your allowable risk, but by placing an entry order at the point-and-figure reversal point you will enter on a confirmation of the original direction and have your stop-loss **at the minimum four-box distance.**

This technique is frequently used by traders who firmly believe that a reversal follows immediately after a breakout situation, and this approach prevents both high risk and false signals. If the pullback after the breakout continues in an adverse direction and penetrates the other support or resistance level, triggering the original system stop-loss, you will be able to pass the signal entirely, saving a substantial whipsaw loss.

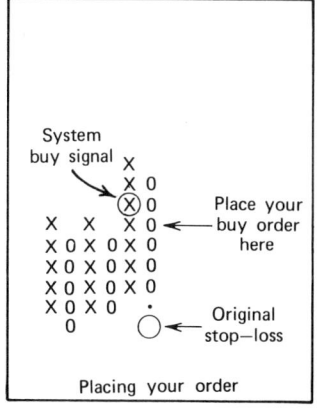 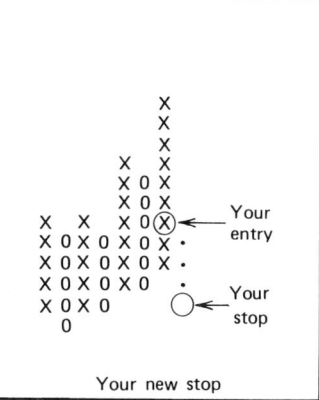

Diagram 11-6 Entering on a confirmation of the new trend.

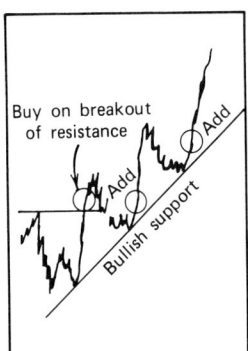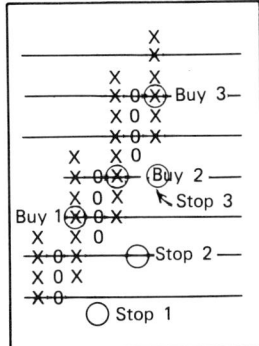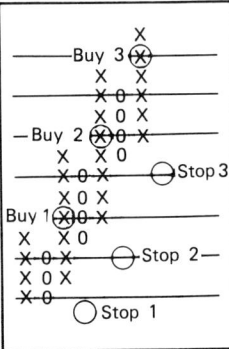

Diagram 11-7   Three ways to compound positions.

The reversal principle used in (2) can also be effective for building positions. In bar charting, a pullback to a bullish support line or a bearish resistance line was a point for adding to your position with a risk limited to a penetration of the major trend line. The equivalent procedure in point-and-figure trading is to add on each reversal back in the direction of the move, using the newly formed stop-loss point to exit the entire position, as shown in Diagram 11-7.

TAKE IT AND RUN...!

There comes a point in most sustained moves where you are more than satisfied with the current profit and apprehensive about how much of the paper profit you will return before the system close-out signal is reached. There is some varied thinking about what to do.

If the profit you are currently holding in open positions is enough to sustain a life of leisure, a home in the mountains or South Seas with ample money for the country club and a small investment in a hotel or restaurant to occupy your time, then take it and run ... but do not come back.

If you cannot sleep nights because you must have the money to meet personal commitments and you have just the right amount in open profits, and one or two adverse days would ruin the opportunity, then take the profit and start all over. If you want a logical place to cash in on current open profits, but you have some time and latitude, as long as you do not lose more than 10–25% of the existing profits, then use the point-and-figure reversal criterion. The reversal criterion of three boxes is meant to indicate a significant contrary move and can be used as an objective indication of a change of direction. One approach to taking your profits is shown in Diagram 11-8.

In Diagram 11-8a we use a trailing three-box reversal criterion for our stop-loss once we have a sustained move of at least ten boxes. To reenter the move in the same direction, we can use the same technique, shown in Diagram 11-8b, and add another four boxes of profits to our trade while also keeping our risk and give-up small. In Diagram 11-8c this method lost four boxes of the potential profits when the reversal was short-lived.

And finally, if you intend to stay with commodities as a long-term plan for compounding your money, then taking profits is a disaster. Naturally, if you can show that your modification to the system is profitable over enough tests on representative

THE POINT-AND-FIGURE METHOD 161

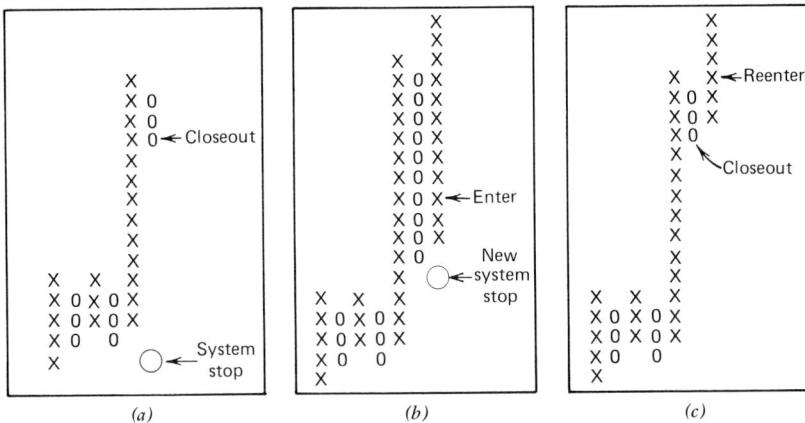

Diagram 11-8 Cashing in on profits.

data, then change your plans so that it is always included. But to selectively alter a system in this way would be to limit your potential profits, but do nothing to limit your losses.

ALTERNATE TREATMENT OF REVERSALS

There are certain reversal days that present a problem for the user of the point-and-figure method. If the current price trend is up and the next day has a new high, causing one or more additional X's to be placed, and also a low which would also have caused a three-box reversal, you are in doubt about the proper move (see Diagram 11-9). Should the reversal or trend continuation take precedence? Some of these days can be identified as key reversals after the fact and some are false reversals. Tests on the March 77 Soybean contract provided interesting results. In order to take a preliminary look (preliminary because we are looking at only one chart) at what might have happened if we had entered a reversal instead of the usual continuation on those days, we establish the following alternate rules:

If today's high-low results in a continuation of the current trend ...

and

If a reversal from the current trend is possible (ignoring the continuation of today) ...

and

If today's closing price was in the reverse direction of the current trend, relative to yesterday's close ...

then

(Option 1) Enter the continuation of the current trend, then enter the reversal as a new trend ...

or

(Option 2) Enter the reversal and ignore the continuation boxes for the current trend (making the reversal stop closer).

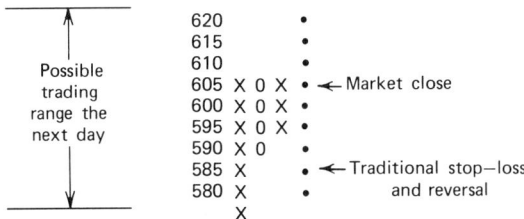

Diagram 11-9 A point-and-figure situation in which both an advance or reversal could occur.

There are more alternatives than the rules presented here, but these are well-defined and satisfy the current problem. Since the first option records both the continuation of the current trend and the new reversal, the extent of the current trend column will appear the same as a standard chart; consequently, a new buy or sell signal caused by the reversal will have the same stop-loss point as the traditional charting method. This modified technique does offer the possibility of a signal caused by a reversal occurring sooner. According to the standard point-and-figure rules you cannot reverse your position if prices continued in the direction of the current trend by at least the value of one box. On days when both a continuation and reversal are possible, the trader cannot enter a stop-loss for fear of being stopped out of his current trade while the commodity experienced an intraday adjustment only.

Option 1 allows the trader to enter the sell order in advance, since the reversal will be taken even if a new high is reached. The results of this modification on the single contract of March 77 Soybeans was not enlightening. There were no changes in any of the buy or sell signals and consequently the profitability was unchanged. This may be an optimistic result since, if it proved consistent, it would allow point-and-figure users to enter their reversal orders regardless of the possibility of the next day's high-low range causing both a new high and a reversal. It may also mean that the occurrence of a reversal, even when accompanied by a new high, results in a change in the direction of the trend. For those using chart formations, these rules did change the top formation from a symmetric triangle on the standard chart to a descending triangle. This would have resulted in an improvement in the predictive quality of the chart formations.

The second modification (Option 2), in which the reversal took precedence, had a notable effect on both the performance and interpretation of the original March 77 Soybean chart. By applying the basic buy and sell signals we find that four reversals caused the stop-loss point to be advanced 10¢, 10¢, 5¢, and 15¢, respectively. This change caused an improvement in a buy signal on October 22, 1976.

Example 11-1

Original method			Option 2		
	Profit/Loss			Profit/Loss	
Sell	655		Sell	655	
Buy	675	−20	Buy	660	−5
Sell	655	−10	Sell	665	+5

Example 11-1 shows the improvement of 30¢ on a combination of two consecutive trades. In addition, four secondary buy and sell signals were advanced and two secondary signals were created, all of which showed improvements in the position based on those signals. The effect of this modification is to make the chart more sensitive to reversals. In the case of our single test on March 77 Soybeans there was consistent improvements with no offsetting negative results; Option 2 also includes the benefits of Option 1 since it permits the trader to enter all reversal orders in advance. This approach should be worth examining using a representative sample of commodities.

PRICE OBJECTIVES

Point-and-figure charting has two unique definitive methods for calculating price objectives, called the *horizontal* and *vertical counts*. Before discussing them you should recall the bar-charting objectives using major support and resistance, since it applies equally here. A previous contract high or low should always be used as an objective if the other technical methods indicate enough potential strength (or weakness) in a move to cause a test of the highs or lows. There are very few cases of a commodity price penetrating major support or resistance levels in one nonstop move from a distant point. In all methods of setting price objectives the trader should keep in mind other popular techniques since confirmation or conflict with these other methods must be considered in the reliability of your own calculations.

The Horizontal Count

The time that a commodity spends in a consolidation area is considered an important element in determining its potential move. In bar charting one technique for calculating price objectives was to measure the width of the consolidation and project the same measurement up or down as the potential limits of the move. The point-and-figure horizontal-count method is a more exact approach to the same idea.

The upside price objective is calculated as

$$H_U = P_L + (W \times RV)$$

where H_U is the upside horizontal-count price objective
P_L is the price of the lowest box of the base
RV is the reversal value of the commodity (number of boxes times the value of one box)

In order to complete this formula we need to identify the base, count the number of columns (W) not including the breakout column, and multiply that width by the value of a minimum reversal (RV); then add that result to the bottom point of the base and you get the upper price objective. The base can always be identified after the break has occurred. For example, Diagram 11-10 shows the March 74 contract of London Cocoa (£4 box) forming a very long but clear base. The reversal value is £12 and the width of the base is 19 columns (not counting the last column, which resulted in a breakout). Added to the lowest point of the base (£570), that gives an objective of

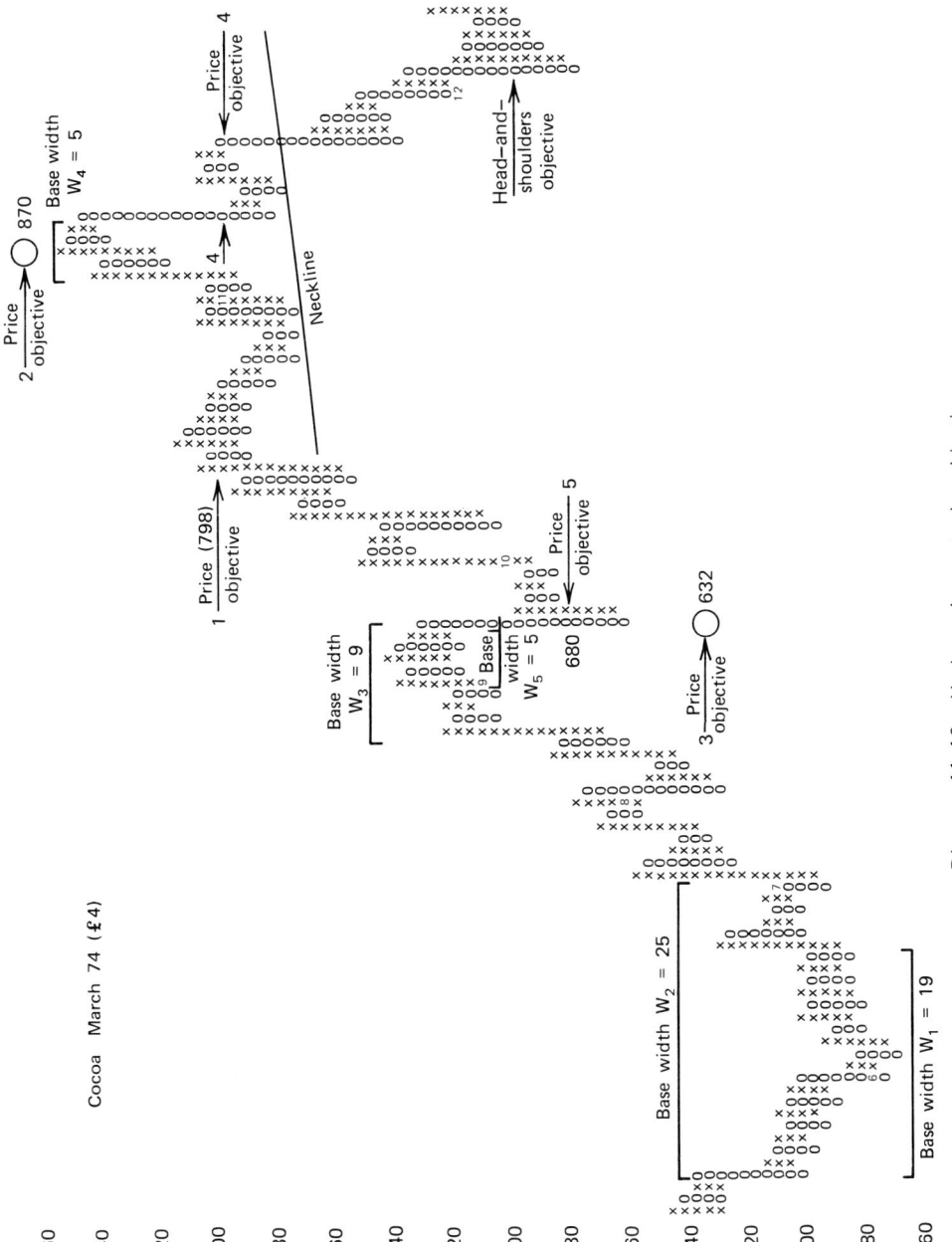

Diagram 11-10 Horizontal-count price objectives.

THE POINT-AND-FIGURE METHOD

£798, reached on the left shoulder of the topping formation. Another alternative is the wider base, marked as $W_2 = 25$. Using this selection we get a price objective of £870, by adding $25 \times £12 = 300$ to £570, the lowest point of the base.

The downside objective is calculated in the same manner as the upside objective:

$$H_D = P_H - (W \times RV)$$

where H_D is the downside horizontal-count price objective
P_H is the price of the highest box of the top formation
W is the width of the top
RV is the reversal value

Some examples are given for downside objectives in the same Cocoa diagram, Diagram 11-10. A small correction top could be isolated at the £720 level and two possible top widths, W_3 and W_5, could be chosen. W_3, the broader top, has a width of nine and a downside objective of £632 and W_5 has a smaller width of five and a downside objective of £680. Although the lesser objective, calculated from W_5, is easy to reach, the farther one is reasonable because it coincides with a strong intermediate support level at about £640.

The very top formation was small and only produced a nearby price objective, similar to that first downside example; there would be no indication that prices were ready for a major reversal. The top also forms a clear head and shoulders, which could be used in the same manner as in bar charting to find an objective. The height of the top of the head to the point on the neckline directly below is 20 boxes; then the downside price objective is 20 boxes below the point where the neckline was penetrated by the breakout of the right shoulder, at £776, giving £696 as an objective.

The Vertical Count

The vertical count is a simpler and more definitive calculation than the horizontal count; there are less subjective elements. As with the horizontal count, there is adequate time to identify the formations and establish a price objective before it is reached. The vertical count is a measure of volatility, the amount of rebound from a top or bottom, and can be used to determine the size of a retracement after a major price move. To calculate the upside vertical-count price objective you locate the first reversal column after a bottom. To do this you would have to establish a bottom with one or more tests, or have had a breakout of a major resistance line. You then get the vertical-count price objective by multiplying the value of the first reversal column following the bottom by the minimum reversal value of the chart (three boxes times the value of the box), and add the result to the lowest point of the bottom formation.

In simpler terms, the upside vertical-count price objective is three times the length of the first reversal after the bottom added to the bottom. This calculation is easier to do using boxes rather than values:

$$V_U = \text{lowest box} + (\text{number of boxes in first reversal}) \\ \times (\text{minimum number of boxes in a chart reversal})$$

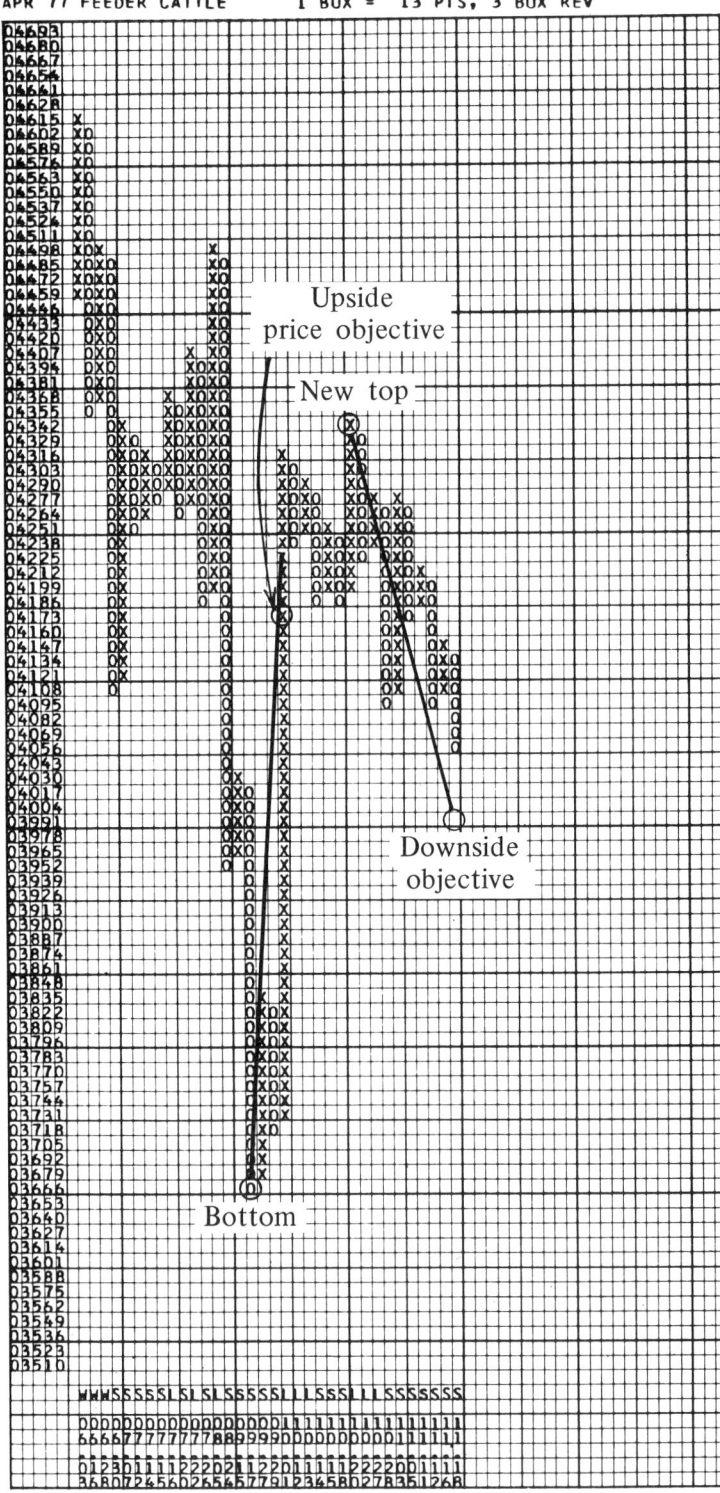

Diagram 11-11(a)　April 77 Feeder Cattle point-and-figure chart.

THE POINT-AND-FIGURE METHOD

The downside vertical-count price objective is just the opposite:

$$V_D = \text{highest box} - (\text{number of boxes in first reversal}) \\ \times (\text{minimum number of boxes in a chart reversal})$$

Examples illustrating the vertical count are easy to find. Consider the following cases:

1. The April 77 Feeder Cattle chart (Diagram 11-11a) has an obvious bottom at 36.66 and a 13-box reversal immediately following it. Using the vertical count we should get a retracement of three times the primary reversal (13 boxes) added to the low of the bottom. Our price objective is then 41.73, 39 boxes above the low.
2. Following that upward move in April 77 Feeder Cattle we can identify a top of 43.42, followed by a downward column of 9 boxes. Our price objective becomes 27 boxes below the high or 39.91, a likely goal on the chart since it represents the center of the only technical adjustment during the downtrend.
3. The February 77 Hog chart (Diagram 11-11b) shows a top at 44.08 with a subsequent six-box reversal. Our downside objective is calculated as 18 boxes below the high, or 37.24, the center of the first support level.

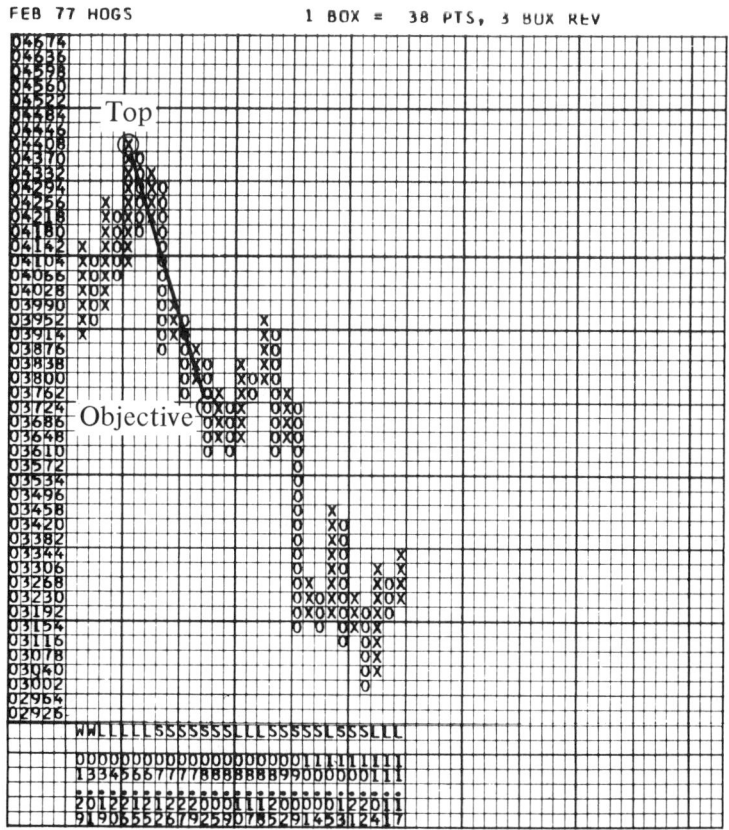

Diagram 11-11(b) February 77 Hogs point-and-figure chart.

4. May 77 Corn (Diagram 11-11c) topped at $312\frac{1}{2}$ and had an 11-box reversal in the next column; the price objective is 33 boxes lower, at $271\frac{1}{4}$. While that goal fell short of the lows by quite a distance, it netted about a 27¢ profit from the system-sell signal. Earlier in the contract there was an intermediate bottom at $278\frac{3}{4}$ with a six-box reversal. The price objective of $301\frac{1}{4}$ was in the center of the prior major resistance level and resulted in another good trade.

As much as it might be desirable for this technique to point out the ultimate bottom or top of a move, it is far from perfect. As a simple measurement tool from contract highs or lows it seems to have some reliability once the bottom or top becomes clear. When using this method, do not expect more from its results than is realistic.

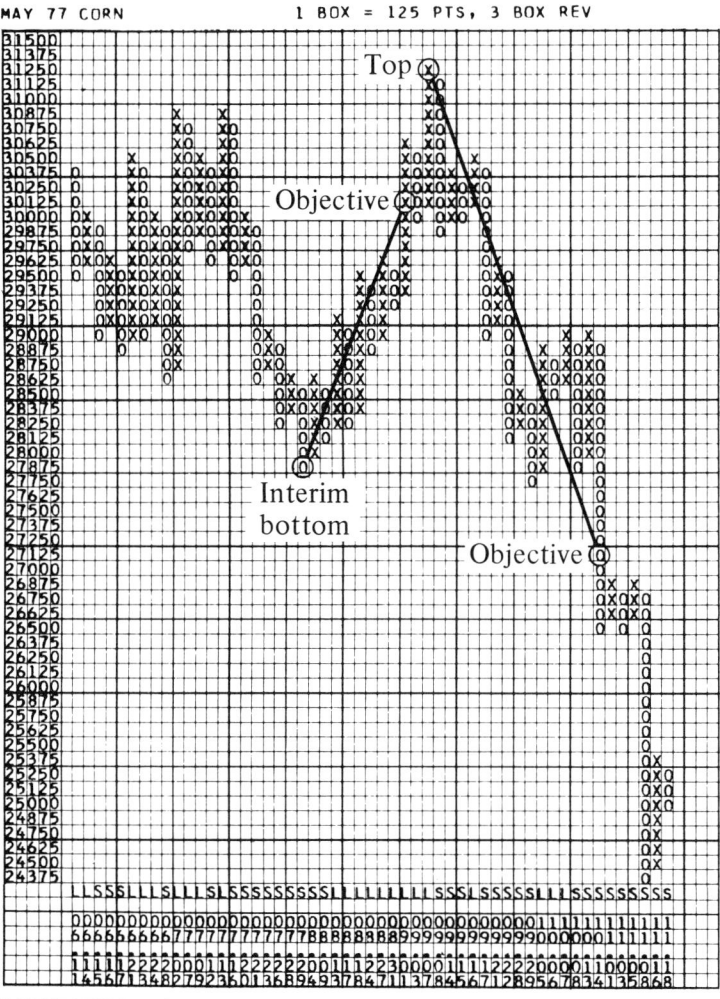

Diagram 11-11(c) May 77 Corn point-and-figure chart.

A STUDY IN POINT-AND-FIGURE OPTIMIZATION

Throughout the point-and-figure discussion there has been constant reference to "reversal criteria" or "three-box reversal" although there was no explicit suggestion of any alternative. In looking back at Table 11-1, it can be seen that the box sizes used prior to 1971 were generally smaller than the 1975 box sizes. You will also see that Table 11-1 uses two box sizes, larger for long-term (continuation charts) and smaller for individual contracts of maximum term 1 to $1\frac{1}{2}$ years. These differences are due to changing price levels and volatility, as Wyckoff had suggested.

Prior to 1971, prices had been steadily increasing, but at a much slower rate than 1974 through 1976. In a single year the price fluctuation of any one commodity was not extreme and the range was easy to anticipate. Appendix 7 shows the price range and average price for selected commodities since 1969 in absolute values and in percent of fluctuation. Not only have the prices increased but the annual volatility (the percentage of fluctuation) has increased accordingly.

In 1969, sugar prices were plotted on a five-point scale while prices ranged from 2.86¢ to 3.95¢ per pound; the possible span of point-and-figure boxes that could be filled was 22. In 1973, sugar prices went to almost 60¢ per pound, approximately twenty times their 1969 price. The daily limits were expanded from $\frac{1}{2}$¢ to 1–2¢—more than the price used to move in one year. A 5¢ point-and-figure box ceased to be practical; it would result in a new reversal column any day the market failed to continue its prior direction, and it no longer served the function of smoothing the price movement. It also took 1200 boxes (10 feet of graph paper with 10 boxes per inch) to record the moves all the way up to 60¢.

One reason why the scale changed for sugar from 5¢ boxes to 20¢ boxes, or for soybeans from 1¢ to 10¢, was the practical need to fit the point-and-figure chart on a single page. Oddly enough, rescaling to fit a piece of paper of constant size has considerable merit. Let us look at soybeans in 1970. The range of the January 71 futures contract was $251\frac{5}{8}$ to 315 and required a page of graph paper with only 64 boxes and an assigned value of 1¢ per box. Table 11-2 shows what happens if you keep the same number of boxes each year and change the scale to correspond. The reversal value is forced to increase so that the size of the point-and-figure chart and formations will look the same regardless of the price level. This is called *keeping the sensitivity constant*.

Table 11-2 Soybeans (January Futures Contract) Keeping the Size of the Chart the Same

Jan	High	Low	Average	Box size	Reversal	Total no. of Boxes	Reversal value	Reversal as percentage of average
1971	315	$251\frac{5}{8}$	$283\frac{1}{4}$	1¢	3	64	3¢	1.06%
1972	346	$282\frac{1}{8}$	314	1¢	3	64	3¢	.95%
1973	444	300	372	$2\frac{1}{4}$¢	3	64	$6\frac{3}{4}$¢	1.81%
1974	915	349	632	9¢	3	63	27¢	5.27%
1975	961	509	735	7¢	3	65	21¢	2.86%
1976	705	$439\frac{1}{2}$	$572\frac{1}{4}$	4¢	3	66	12¢	2.10%
1977	782	490	636	$4\frac{1}{2}$¢	3	65	$13\frac{1}{2}$¢	2.12%

The point-and-figure method with its increased reversal value due to larger box size will generate about the same number of reversals and buy and sell signals at any price level. Had prices increased without the box size increasing the system would have had more frequent reversals, as in the sugar example, and it would be considered *more sensitive* to price changes.

The relationship of reversal value to the average price for the contracts 1971 through 1977 gives you a price-volatility relationship, shown in the last column of Table 11-2. It is important to know to what degree prices will fluctuate as prices advance and decline. This can become a valuable risk management tool.

Before going on, certain questions must be asked of this method:

- Why were soybeans started with a 1¢ box ... why not ½¢ or 5¢?
- Does this price-volatility relationship represent the best approach to rescaling?
- How can you use it?

The first question is difficult to answer. It can only be assumed that the original selection of a box was a combination of both a smoothing attempt (chosen as a multiple of the minimum move) and convenience. The convenience part is easy to see, since all the box sizes in Table 11-1 were ½¢, 1¢, 10¢, 5 pts, 10 pts, 20 pts, 50 pts, 100 pts, and 200 pts in the earlier years. Accuracy was considered "within reason." The first point-and-figure charts were drawn using the smallest allowable move and later refined to larger increments to identify long-term trends and major support and resistance levels. It is necessary to find a more logical selection of starting parameters.

To answer the second question, you must understand the impact of rescaling on trading. As prices rise, boxes become larger and the minimum risk becomes proportionately greater. The risk of trading one contract increases at the same rate at the volatility expressed as a percent of the average price. If the box sizes are not increased when prices rise, risk can be kept small but frequent losses will occur waiting for a sustained move, and trading would be based on extremely short-term trends.

There are few alternatives to rescaling, the two most reasonable being:

1. Rechart at new price levels using larger box values in order to keep the size of the chart constant and the sensitivity fixed, as in Table 11-2.
2. Increase the box value at a rate based on a fixed percentage of the current price so that a chart with a box value of three points at a price of 300 (1% value) would have a six-point box at a price of 600.

Both approaches are similar because they effectively increase the box value and risk while reducing the sensitivity of the chart to reversals as prices increase.

Solving the Scaling Problem

Before the price-volatility method can be used it is necessary to perform a linear regression on the average price and box size to get the approximate relationship.

THE POINT-AND-FIGURE METHOD

Since the values in Table 11-2 were calculated after the price range was known, it would be unrealistic to select a box size in advance that would represent the average price of soybeans for the coming year. The relationships that we get are based on a three-box reversal:[7]

$$100 \times volatility = -28.8 + .485 \times average\ price$$

$$box\ size = -3.347 + .0147 \times price$$

We get the following exact figures for the box size corresponding to specific price levels:

Table 11-3 Point-and-Figure Price-Volatility Relationship (Method 1)

Average price	250	300	350	400	450	500	550	600
Percentage volatility	92	117	140	165	189	214	240	262
Box size	.328	1.06	1.80	2.54	3.20	4.01	4.75	5.49
Average price	650	700	750	800	850	900	950	1000
Percentage volatility	286	311	335	359	383	408	432	456
Box size	6.22	6.96	7.70	8.43	9.17	9.91	10.65	11.38

Understanding that the figures we are working with are probabilistic and that box sizes must be in practical increments, we can construct a variable-box point-and-figure chart that changes box size as the price increases according to our table. Assigning realistic values at computed price levels we get the following values for boxes on a soybean chart:

Table 11-4 Point-and-Figure Variable-Box Size for Specific Price Levels (Method 1)

Box	Price	Box	Price	Box	Price	Box	Price	Box	Price
$\frac{1}{4}$	245	$2\frac{1}{4}$	380	$4\frac{1}{4}$	516	$6\frac{1}{4}$	652	$8\frac{1}{4}$	787
$\frac{1}{2}$	262	$2\frac{1}{2}$	397	$4\frac{1}{2}$	533	$6\frac{1}{2}$	669	$8\frac{1}{2}$	804
$\frac{3}{4}$	279	$2\frac{3}{4}$	414	$4\frac{3}{4}$	550	$6\frac{3}{4}$	686	$8\frac{3}{4}$	821
1	295	3	431	5	567	7	703	9	838
$1\frac{1}{4}$	312	$3\frac{1}{4}$	448	$5\frac{1}{4}$	584	$7\frac{1}{4}$	720	$9\frac{1}{4}$	855
$1\frac{1}{2}$	329	$3\frac{1}{2}$	465	$5\frac{1}{2}$	601	$7\frac{1}{2}$	736	$9\frac{1}{2}$	872
$1\frac{3}{4}$	346	$3\frac{3}{4}$	482	$5\frac{3}{4}$	618	$7\frac{3}{4}$	753	$9\frac{3}{4}$	889
2	363	4	499	6	634	8	770	10	906

[7] It would be worth looking at the nonlinear techniques for this relationship, but for the purposes of our study a least-squares approximation will be sufficient.

The second choice of scaling involves solving the first question posed: "Why were soybeans started with a 1¢ box?" In order to increase the box size at a constant rate we must first establish a beginning size at a specific price. The long-term charts show that prior to 1970 prices were relatively stable, fluctuating between normally accepted ranges. By finding the proper box size to be used for this time interval we have a basis for continuing into more volatile years. In 1970, Charles C. Thiel, Jr., and Robert E. Davis published a study intitled *Point and Figure Commodity Trading: A Computer Evaluation*. In this analysis they approach the problem of variable box size and reversal criteria (number of boxes for a reversal) from a strict scientific background, defining the rules and objectives. They proceeded to test a good sampling of commodities, varying both the box size and reversal criteria, and recorded the resulting profits or losses and the reliability of the combination (percentage of profitable trades). For example, the January 66 Soybean contract test results were presented:

Table 11-5 Thiel and Davis' Results, January 66 Soybeans

Box size	Reversal boxes	Results		
		Profitability	Profit	Per trade
0.500	4	2 of 12	−14.874	−1.239
0.500	5	2 of 12	−14.874	−1.239
0.500	6	2 of 10	−15.124	−1.512
⋮	⋮	⋮	⋮	⋮
1.000	4	1 of 2	3.00	1.500
⋮	⋮	⋮	⋮	⋮
4.000	1	1 of 1	7.25	7.25
⋮	⋮	⋮	⋮	⋮

The study included the years 1960–1969 with data supplied by Dunn and Hargitt.[8] This coincides exactly with the time interval needed to determine our basic box size and reversal. In their study Thiel and Davis draw conclusions and present alternatives for their selections of box sizes and reversals, but the interests of this analysis are slightly different, and Table 11-6 shows the final choice. The most important part of Table 11-6 is the reversal value, expressed as a percentage of the 10-year fluctuation. This figure represents the best choice of a value for rescaling as a fixed percentage of the average price of a commodity. The proper reversal criteria for each price level can now be selected using the rate of increase shown in the first and second formulas and the base price from Table 11-6.

It is assumed that distribution of reversal value into box size and reversal criteria is not important, and therefore all box sizes will be chosen to correspond to the standard three-box reversal. In general, a reversal value of 6¢ in soybeans would be profitable if plotted on a scale of 2 × 3, 3 × 2, 6 × 1, or 1 × 6, where the first number is the box size and the second is the number of boxes for a reversal. By having the

---
[8] Dunn and Hargitt Financial Services, Inc., W. Lafayette, IN.

Table 11-6 Optimum Box and Reversal Criteria for 10 Years—1960–1969
(Davis and Thiel)

	Approximate price range 1960–1969	Average	Box size	Reversal	Reversal value	10-year fluctuation (%)
Wheat	113–225	169.0	$1\frac{1}{2}$¢	3 boxes	$4\frac{1}{2}$¢ = $225	2.66
Corn	88–154	121.0	$1\frac{1}{2}$¢	4 boxes	6¢ = $300	4.95
Soybeans	196–309	252.0	2¢	3 boxes	6¢ = $300	2.38
Soybean meal	48–102	75.0	75 pts	2 boxes	150 = $150	2.00
Soybean oil	7.3–12.3	9.8	25 pts	1 box	25 = $150	2.55
Cattle	19–34	26.5	20 pts	2 boxes	40 = $160	1.50
Pork bellies	18–55	36.5	25 pts	6 boxes	150 = $540	4.10
Potatoes	1.9–8.4	5.15	5 pts	3 boxes	15 = $75	2.91
Copper	29–52	40.5	50 pts	4 boxes	200 = $500	4.93
Sugar	2–12	7.0	10 pts	5 boxes	54 = $560	7.14
Cocoa	12–51	31.5	25 pts	7 boxes	175 = $525	5.55
Silver	85–245	165.0	100 pts	2 boxes	200 = $200	1.21

percentage reversal value, the box and reversal criteria can be varied in a logical manner as the prices rise or decline. Using the January Soybean contract we can assign box sizes in such a way that the reversal value, using a three-box reversal, is close to 2.38% of the annual range (taken from Table 11-6). We get the following parameters:

Table 11-7 Holding the Chart to a 2.38% Reversal Value[a]

Soybean contract	Highest price	Lowest price	Annual range	Reversal value	Box size
Jan 71	315	$251\frac{5}{8}$	$63\frac{3}{8}$	$1\frac{1}{2}$	$\frac{1}{2}$
Jan 72	346	$284\frac{7}{8}$	$61\frac{1}{8}$	$1\frac{1}{2}$	$\frac{1}{2}$
Jan 73	444	300	144	$3\frac{1}{2}$	$1\frac{1}{8}$
Jan 74	915	$354\frac{1}{4}$	$560\frac{3}{4}$	$13\frac{3}{8}$	$4\frac{1}{2}$
Jan 75	961	509	452	$10\frac{3}{4}$	$3\frac{1}{2}$
Jan 76	705	$439\frac{1}{2}$	$265\frac{1}{2}$	$6\frac{3}{8}$	$2\frac{1}{8}$
Jan 77	$782\frac{1}{2}$	490	$292\frac{1}{2}$	7	$2\frac{3}{8}$

[a] All values in cents.

Variable-Scale Comparative Results

A simple way of determining the best selection of scaling is to plot the results. The choice of equal-percentage increases presented no problem. A standard point-and-figure chart was drawn with incremental price ranges assigned the necessary box size as follows:

Price range (¢/bu)	Box size (¢/bu)
240–286	2¢
286–351	2½¢
351–417	3¢
417–480	3½¢
480–544	4¢
544–598	4½¢
598–648	5¢
648–725	5½¢
725–917	6¢

Once the master chart is constructed it will never have to be changed. If prices rise above the top of the scale additional boxes can be numbered with larger increments. Using the standard three-box method of charting, each January Soybean futures contract was plotted and the results shows in Table 11-8. The profits were consistently good except for 1976. It should be noted that the number of trades increased as the average price increased throughout the test period. This can be expected since the box size does not increase as quickly at higher prices as does the price-volatility relationship. Because of this steady lag the sensitivity of the system will increase noticeably at peak levels.

The chart based on the price-volatility approximation taken from Tables 11-3 and 11-4 is much smaller than the one used for equal percentage increases. Because the box sizes increase so rapidly the formations appear more uniform at all price levels

Table 11-8 Results Using Equal Percentage Increases (Method 2)

	Trades		Net P/L[a] (¢/bu)
	Total	Profitable	
January 1966	2	1	+22
January 1971	4	3	+21
January 1972	3	2	+8½
January 1973	2	1	+93⅝
January 1974	20	9	+23⅝
January 1975	12	7	+554⅝
January 1976	16	7	−175¼
		Total	+548⅛

[a] 1¢ commissions deducted.

THE POINT-AND-FIGURE METHOD

and the number of trades occurring during each contract was reasonably constant. The results of this method show that its application to a long-term chart would be more practical. Any one contract contained only a small number of reversals and was able to generate from one to three trades. Often part of a trend was missed because of the time needed to generate the first entry signals. While neither method showed profits over the entire test span, the continuation approach was evidently the best for this technique.

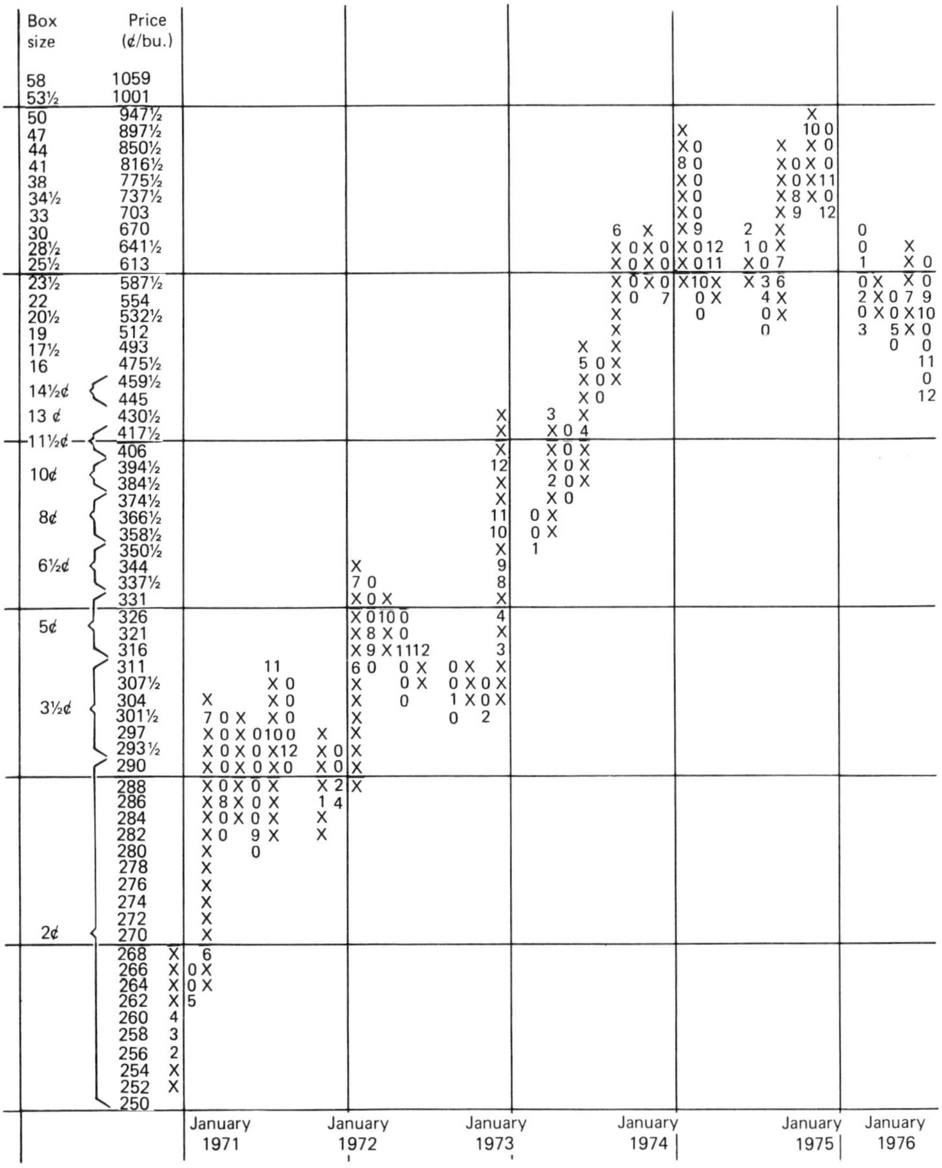

Diagram 11-12 Point-and-figure chart for January soybeans using price-volatility scaling.

Table 11-9 Results Using Price-Volatility Scaling

Individual contracts	Trades		Net P/L[a] (¢/bu)
	Total	Profitable	
January 1971	3	1	−28
January 1972	2	1	$+\frac{1}{4}$
January 1973	1	1	+109
January 1974	2	1	+32
January 1975	1	0	−24
January 1976	3	1	−234
		Total	$-144\frac{3}{4}$
Continuous trading 1971–1976	10	5	−70

[a] 1¢ commission deducted.

The plotted results appear to be much better than the tabulated results. This can be attributed to the increased risk at higher price levels. While the number of boxes in a losing reversal remained small, the value of the loss increased by a factor of 25 from the bottom to the top of the chart. The few profits and losses that occur at higher price levels will be so significant in the final results that the earlier trading performance is unimportant.

Both variable-box approaches offer unique possibilities for identifying trends but increase the problems of risk management. Some of these effects can be offset by reducing the invested margin as prices rise. Other techniques are discussed in Chapter 17.

CHAPTER 12
Systems Founded On Charting Patterns

The principles of trading from chart patterns do not always require the presence of a chart. It is not necessary to see an ascending bottom since a simple calculation or observation of the prices are self-evident. The following systems and ideas were developed from observations of price charts but refined into rules that use price only. They concentrate primarily on the highest or lowest prices occurring within a recent time period. The ability to penetrate these high and lows gives us the rules.

WILLIAM DUNNIGAN AND "THE THRUST METHOD"

Dunnigan's work in the early 1950s is based on chart formations and is purely technical. Although an admirer of others' ability to perform fundamental analysis, his practical approach is represented by these statements:

"If the economists are interested in the price of beans, they should, first of all, learn all they can about the *price of beans*." Then, by supporting their observations with the fundamental elements of supply and demand they will be "certain that the bean *prices will reflect these things*." [1]

Dunnigan did extensive research before his major publications in 1954. A follower of the Dow theory, he originally created a "breakaway system" of trading stocks and commodities but was forced to drop this approach because of long strings of losses, while the net results of his system were profitable. He was also disappointed when his "$2\frac{3}{8}$ swing method" failed after its publication in *A Study in Wheat Trading*. But good

[1] Dunnigan (1954) p. 7.

often comes from failure and Dunnigan had realized by now that different measurements applied to each commodity at different price levels. His next system, the *Percentage Wheat Method*, used a combination of a $2\frac{1}{2}\%$ penetration and a 3-day swing, introducing the time element into his work and perhaps the first notion of *thrust*, a substantial move within a predefined time interval. With the $2\frac{1}{2}\%$ 3-day swing a buy signal was generated if the price of wheat came within 2% of the lows, then reversed and moved up at least an additional $2\frac{1}{2}\%$ over a period of at least 3 days.

For Dunnigan the swing method of charting[2] represented a breakthrough; it allowed each commodity to develop its natural pattern of moves, more or less volatile than any other commodity. He had a difficult time trying to find a criterion for his charts that satisfied all commodities, or even all grains, but established a $2 swing for stocks where Rhea's *Dow Theory* used only $1 moves. His studies of percentage swings were of no help.

The Thrust Method

Dunnigan's final development of the *thrust method* combined both the use of percentage measurements with the interpretation of chart patterns, later modified with some mathematical price objectives. He defines a *downswing* as a decline in which the current day's high and low are both lower than the corresponding high and low of the highest day of the prior *upswing*. If we are currently in an upswing, a higher high or higher low will continue the same move. The reverse effect of having both a higher high and low would take us from a downswing to an upswing. The "top" and "bottom" of a swing are the highest high of an upswing and the lowest low of a downswing, respectively. It should be noted that a broadening or consolidation day, in which the highs and lows are both greater or both contained within any previous day of the same swing, has no effect on the direction.

In addition to the swings, Dunnigan defines the five key buy patterns:

1. *Test of the bottom*, where prices come within a predetermined percentage of a prior low.
2. *Closing-price reversal*, a new low for the swing followed by a higher close than the prior day.
3. *Narrow range*, where the current day's range is less than half of the largest range for the swing.
4. *Inside range*, where both the high and low fall within the prior range.
5. *Penetration of the top* by any amount, conforming to the standard Dow theory buy signal.

All of these conditions can be reversed for the sell patterns. An entry buy signal was generated by combining the patterns, indicating a preliminary buy, with a thrust the next day confirming the move. The *thrust* was defined as a variable price gain based on the level of the commodity (in 1954 wheat, this was $\frac{1}{2}-1\frac{1}{2}¢$). Dunnigan's system attempted to enter the market long near a bottom and short near a top, an improvement on the Dow theory. Because of the risks, the market was asked to give evidence

---

[2] W. D. Gann (1976) devotes a large section to swing charts and includes many examples of markets prior to Dunnigan's work.

SYSTEMS FOUNDED ON CHARTING PATTERNS   179

of a change of direction by satisfying two of the first four patterns followed by a thrust on the next day. Any variance would not satisfy the conditions and an entry near the top or bottom would be passed.

The same buy and sell signals applied for changes in direction that did not occur at prior tops and bottoms but somewhere within the previous trading range. In the event all the conditions were not satisfied and prices penetrated either the top or bottom, moving into a new price area, the fifth pattern satisfied the preliminary signal and a thrust could occur on any day, not being restricted to the day following the penetration. So that if nothing else happened, Dunnigan followed the rules of the Dow theory to insure not missing a major move.

It has been said by followers of Dunnigan's method that his *repeat* signals are the strongest part of his system; even Dunnigan states that they are more reliable, although they restrict the size of the profit by not taking full advantage of the trend from its start. Repeat signals use relaxed rules, not requiring a new thrust, because the trend has already qualified. Two key situations for repeat buy signals are:

1. A test of the bottom followed by an inside range (market indecision).
2. A closing price reversal followed by an inside range.

"One-Way Formula"

Dunnigan worked on what he hoped would be a generalized version of his successful *thrust method* and called it the *one-way formula*. Based on his conclusions that the thrust method was too sensitive, causing more false signals than he was prepared to accept, he modified the confirmation aspect of the signal, and made the thrust into the preliminary signal. He also emphasized longer price trends.

With the upswing and downswing remaining the same, Dunnigan modified the thrust to have its entire range outside the range of the prior day. For a preliminary buy the low of the day must be above the high of the prior day. This is a stronger move than his original thrust but only constitutes a preliminary buy. The confirmation occurs only if an additional upthrust occurs after the formation of, or test of, a previous bottom. We must have a double bottom or ascending bottom followed by a thrust to get a buy signal near the lows. If the confirmation does not occur after the first bottom of an adjustment, it may still be valid on subsequent tests of the bottom.

For the *one-way formula*, repeat signals are identical to original confirming signals. Each one occurs on a pullback and test of a previous bottom, or ascending bottom, followed by an upthrust. Both the initial and repeat signals allow the trader to enter after a reaction to the main trend. The Dow approach to penetration is still allowable in the event all else fails. The refinement of the original thrust method satisfied Dunnigan's problem of getting in too soon.

The Square-Root Theory

Both methods we have discussed show a conspicuous preponderance of entry techniques and an absence of ways to exit. Although it is valid to reverse positions when an opposite entry condition appears, Dunnigan spends a great effort in portfolio management[3] and risk-reward conditions that were linked to exits. By his own definition his technique would be considered "trap forecasting," taking a quick or calculated profit rather than letting the trend run its course (the latter was called "continuous forecasting").

A fascinating calculation of risk evaluation and profit objectives is the *square-root theory*. He strongly supported this method, thinking of it as the "golden"[4] key, and claiming recognition by numerous esoteric sources such as *The Journal of the American Statistical Association*, *The Analysts Journal*, and *Econometrica*. The theory claims that prices move in units of the square root. For example, a commodity trading at 81 (or 9^2) would move to 64 (or 8^2) or 100 (or 10^2); either would be one point up or down based on the square root. The rule also states that a price may move to a level that is a multiple of its square root.

NOFRI'S CONGESTION-PHASE SYSTEM

It is undisputed that, when viewed closely, commodity markets spend the greater part of their time in nontrending motions, moving up and down within a range determined by an unstable equilibrium of supply and demand. Most followers of trending systems often complain about the unpleasant state of affairs when markets fail to move continuously in one direction; but their systems are designed to conserve capital during these periods in order to be around for the "big move." Eugene Nofri's system, presented by Jeanette Nofri Steinberg, is used during the long period of congestion, returning steady but small profits. Nofri's system does not concern itself with the long move, and with time on his side the user of the congestion-phase system can wait to be certain of a well-defined congestion area before beginning his trading sequence.

The system can be used on its own for 1-day profits or it can complement a longer-term method by improving on entry and exit fills, where applicable. The basis of the system is a third-day reversal; if prices are within a congestion range and have closed in the same direction for 2 consecutive days you do the opposite on the close of the second day, anticipating a reversal. If you are right, you take your profit on the close of trading the next (third) day. Nofri claims a 75% probability of success using this technique and the theory of runs would support that figure. If there is a 50% chance of a move either up or down on one day, there is a 25% chance of the same move 2 days in sequence and a $12\frac{1}{2}$% chance the third day ($\frac{1}{2}^3$). Considering both commissions and the distortion of this distribution due to behavioral effects, an assumption of 75% is reasonable.

The congestion-phase system is only applied to markets within a trading range specifically defined by Nofri. Users are cautioned not to be too anxious to trade in a newly formed range until adequate time has elapsed or a test of the bounds has failed. The top of a congestion area is defined as a high price immediately followed by 2 consecutive days of lower closing prices; the bottom of a congestion area is a low price followed by 2 higher days. A new high or low price cancels the congestion area. Any 2 consecutive days with prices closing almost unchanged ($\frac{1}{2}$¢ for the grains) are considered 1 day for the purposes of the system. These ranges occur frequently and can

---

[3] Each of his writings on systems contained examples of multiple-fund management of varied risk.
[4] Refers to the Greek description of Fibonacci ratios.

SYSTEMS FOUNDED ON CHARTING PATTERNS   181

be found by starting your plotting with only the last ten closing prices. In cases where the top or bottom has been formed following a major breakout or price run, it is suggested that you wait 10 additional days to insure the continuance of the congestion area and limit the risk during more volatile periods. Remember, systems that trade only within ranges have enough opportunity to allow you to exercise patience without loss.

A congestion area is not formed until both a top and bottom can be identified. Penetration of a previous top and formation of a new top redefines the range without altering the bottom point; the opposite case can occur for new bottoms. If a false breakout occurs lasting 2 or 3 days, a waiting period of 7 days is suggested with the idea of safety first. Logical stops are also possible, the most obvious places being the top and bottom of the current congestion area, but closer stops could be formulated by measuring price volatility.

The congestion-phase system can stand alone as a short-term trading method or can be used to complement any longer technique. When trying to improve entry or exit fills the system qualifies as a timing device, but only within the congestion areas defined by the rules. It should not be used in all situations, regardless of current price patterns. The converse of the system should tell you that an entry signal given outside of a congestion area should be taken immediately, since longer periods of prolonged movement in one direction are more likely. But in a trading range the congestion-phase system may turn a moving-average technique from a loser to a winner.

The congestion-phase system presented here is not to be considered the entire program. It is no doubt the most basic element and the easiest to explain; it is a market pattern based on statistical frequency and trading experience. There are other patterns more complex that may be taken separately or in a compound nature with this one; a detailed study of charts may uncover them. The essence of the system is twofold— use mathematics to define the method and patience to make it work.

KELTNER'S MINOR-TREND RULE

One of the classic trading systems is the minor trend rule published by Keltner in his book *How to Make Money in Commodities*. It is followed closely to this date by a great part of the agricultural community and should be understood at least for its potential impact on markets.

Keltner defines an upward trend by the failure to make new lows (comparing today's low with the prior day) and a downtrend by the absence of new highs. This notion is consistent with chart interpretation of trend lines by measuring upward moves along the bottom and downward moves along the tops. The minor-trend rule is a plan for using the daily trend as a trading guide. The rule states that the *minor trend* turns up when the *daily trend* sells above its more recent high; the *minor trend* stays up until the *daily trend* sells below its most recent low, when it is considered to have turned down. In order to trade using the minor-trend rule, you buy when the minor trend turns up and sell when the minor trend turns down; you always reverse your position.

The minor-trend rule is a simple short-term trading tool, buying on new highs and selling on new lows. It is a breakout method much like a band around a moving average except that it is not smoothed and uses the exact market prices to determine entry and exit points. It requires frequent trading in most markets, with risk varying according to the volatility of the commodity. You will find Keltner's minor-trend rule the basis for a number of current technical systems that vary the time period over which prior highs and lows are established and consequently increase the interval between trades and the risk of each trade. An advantage of the Keltner approach is that it imposes no arbitrary restrictions on the analysis of prices (e.g., breakouts of 100 points).

DONCHIAN'S FOUR-WEEK RULE

Playboy's *Investment Guide* reviewed Donchian's 4-week rule as "childishly simple... was recently discovered to rank premiere among a dozen widely followed mechanical techniques." And the rules are simple:

1. Go long (and cover shorts) when the current price exceeds the highs of the previous 4 full calendar weeks.
2. Go short (and liquidate longs) when the current price falls below the lows of the previous 4 full calendar weeks.
3. Roll forward if necessary into the next contract on the last day of the month preceding expiration.

In 1970 *The Traders Note Book*, available from Dunn and Hargitt Financial Services, rated the 4-week rule as the best of the popular systems of the day. Based on 16 years of history, the best performers were December Wheat, June Cattle, May Copper, August Bellies, January Soybean Oil, and May Potatoes.

The system satisfies the basic concepts of trading with the trend, limiting your losses and following well-defined rules. It bears a great resemblance to the principle of Keltner's minor-trend rule, modified to avoid trading too often. The system is so simple that the only comments about it must also be simple: can a 4-week rule work for all commodities? If the volatility of a commodity increases dramatically, then the high and low for a 4-week period could become astronomical while at the same time lower prices could cause narrow ranges in another commodity. The solution may be a price-level-modified rule that reduces the number of weeks (or days) in the high-low measured period as prices and volatility increase. A change of this sort would keep risk on a more even level but still relate to the basic volatility principle of the original system. The concept is easy enough to test by any trader without need of a computer.

Modified for the Final 3 Months

An actual system based on the 4-week rule uses only the last 3 months of each contract. Beginning 3 months before the delivery month, plot the highs and lows according to the 4-week rule. For example, if you are trading December Silver, start on September 1 and plot for 4 weeks. The first time the market price crosses the high or low of that 4-week period take the appropriate long or short position and place a stop-loss of $2\frac{1}{2}\%$ of the entry price. If you are not stopped out, liquidate your position on the last day of the month prior to delivery. If you are stopped out you can reenter a new position, using the high and low established during the original 4 weeks.

SYSTEMS FOUNDED ON CHARTING PATTERNS   183

The theory behind the modification is that breakouts are "truer" and larger in the period just prior to delivery. An advantage of the system is that it trades very little and has a low commission burden. The disadvantage is that when tested over a diversified market it showed 6 profits out of 23 trades and netted a loss of $6900.

ACTION AND REACTION

The human element in the market is not responsible for the ultimate rise and fall of prices, but for the way in which prices find their proper level. Each move is a series of overreactions and adjustments. Many stock and commodity analysts have studied this phenomenon and based entire systems and trading rules on their observations. Elliot's *wave principle* is the clearest of the theories founded entirely on this notion; Tubbs' *Stock Market Correspondence Course* is the first to define the magnitude of these reactions in the *law of proportion*; and more recently the trident system has been based on both the patterns and the size of the action and reaction.

Retracement of a major bull campaign is the most familiar of the market reactions, and the one to which almost every theory applies. It is virtually unanimous that a 100% retracement, back to the beginning of the move, encounters the most important support level. The 100% figure itself has been discussed in terms of unity, referring to its behavioral significance. The next most accepted retracement level is 50%, strongly supported by Gann and commonly discussed by experienced speculators. The other significant levels vary according to different theories:

Schabacker accepts an adjustment of $\frac{1}{3}$ or $\frac{1}{2}$, considering anything larger a trend reversal.

Angas anticipates 25% reaction for intermediate trends.

Dunnigan and Tubbs look at the larger $\frac{1}{2}$, $\frac{2}{3}$, or $\frac{3}{4}$ adjustment.

Gann takes inverse powers of 2 as behaviorally significant: $\frac{1}{2}$, $\frac{1}{4}$, $\frac{1}{8}$, ...

Elliot based his projections on the Fibonacci ratio and its complement (.618 and .382).

Predicting advances into new ground is also based on prior moves. Gann believed in multiples of the lowest historic price as well as even numbers; prices would find natural resistance at $2, $3, ..., at intermediate levels of $2.50, $3.50, ..., or at twice or three times the base price level. Elliot looked at moves of 1.618% based on a Fibonacci ratio.

Tubbs' "Law of Proportion"

The technical point of Tubbs' course in stock market trading is heavy chart interpretation. The "law of proportion" presented in Lesson 9 is a well-defined action-and-reaction law. In cases where the nearby highs or lows of a swing were not broken,

Tubbs claims four out of five successful predictions with this principle. The law states:

Aggregates and individual stocks tend to run on half, two-thirds, three-fourths of previous moves. First in relation to the next preceding move which was made. Then in relation to the move preceding that.

Graphically, we see an initial move from $4 to $6 in silver, reacting $\frac{1}{2}$ to $5, $\frac{2}{3}$ to $4.67 or $\frac{3}{4}$ to $4.50. Tubbs does allow for support as a major obstacle to the measured price move, and so we may consider unity in addition to the three proportions. Diagram 12-1 shows subsequent reactions to the silver move just described; the second reversal could be any of three magnitudes (or back to major support at $4.00), ending at $4.50, a $\frac{3}{4}$ reversal. Reversals 3, 4, and 5 are shown with their possible objectives. The last reversal, 5, becomes so small that the major support levels are considered as having primary significance (horizontal and broken lines), along with proportions of moves 1 and 2. We see that major support at $4.00 coincides with $\frac{1}{2}$ of move 1 and $\frac{2}{3}$ of move 2. This would normally be sufficient to nominate that point as the most likely to succeed. Tubbs indicates that these points rarely occur with exactness, but proportions serve as a valuable guideline. The principle is one of reaction in relationship to an obvious preceding action.

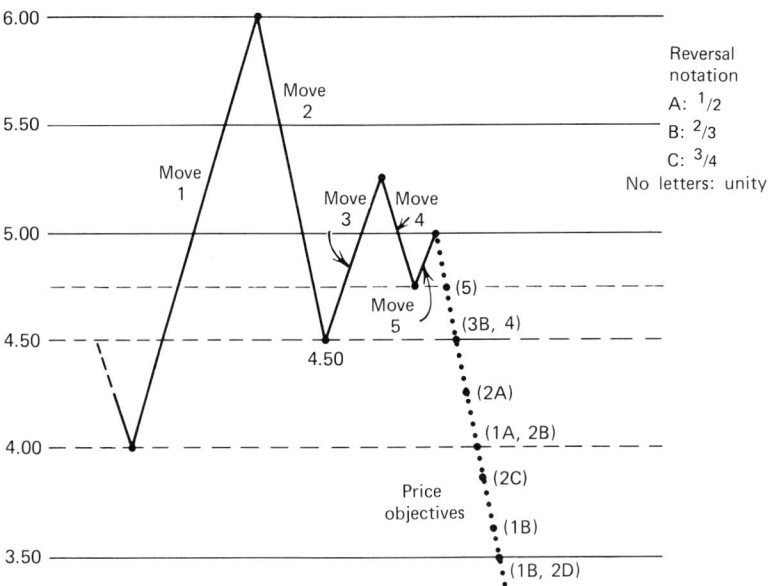

Diagram 12-1   Tubbs' law of proportion.

Trident

The Trident commodity-trading system has received its fair share of publicity since its introduction at the beginning of 1975. An article in the 1977 *Dow Jones Commodities Handbook* has an excellent review of the background of the system and some of the conflicts surrounding its presentation and subsequent successes and failures. The system itself is not unique in concept, but in its implementation. It is based upon the principle of price action and reaction with formations similar to the "waves" of R. N. Elliot. For each price move there is a point of undervalue and overvalue with subsequent reaction, or adjustments, in price as it moves irregularly in the direction determined by the ultimate balance of supply and demand.

The object of the system is to trade in the direction of the main trend but take advantage of the reaction (or waves) to get favorable entry and exit points. The concept of trading with the trend and entering on reactions is discussed in commodity technical analysis as early as 1942 by W. D. Gann and in the preceding section on action and reaction. The key to that goal is to predict where the reactions will occur and what profit objective to set for each trade.[5] Trident's approach is easy to understand: each wave in the direction of the main trend will be equal in length to the previous wave in the same direction. The target is calculated by adding this distance to the highest or lowest point of the completed reaction. As with Elliot's principle, the determination of the tops and bottoms of the waves is dependent on the time element used; the complex form of primary and intermediate waves would hold true with Trident.

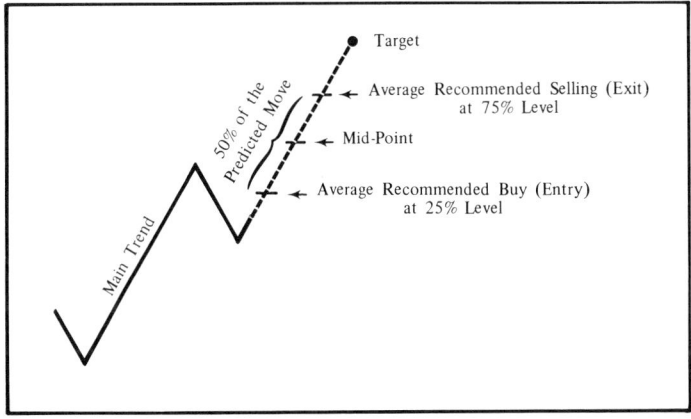

Diagram 12-2   Trident entry-exit.

Since there are inaccuracies in the measurement of behavioral phenomena, Trident emphasizes the practical side of its theory by offering latitude in its choice of entry and exit points. By entering at an average point of 25% of the anticipated move and exiting 25% before the target, there is ample time to determine that the downward reaction has ended before your position is taken, and enough caution to exit well before the next reaction. A critical point in each main trend is midway between the start of the move and the target. If the midpoint is not reached we have a change in direction of the main trend causing a reevaluation and reassignment of the main trend and the reactions. A change of direction is considered conclusive if a reversal equal in size to 25% of the last reaction occurs during what was expected to be an extension of the

---

[5] Gann's work also discusses this topic specifically.

main trend. That 25% value becomes the trailing stop-loss on any trade in the event your objective is not reached.

This discussion is not intended to be a complete representation of the Trident system, but a brief description of its essential ideas. The actual system has substantial refinements and subleties in target selection for major and minor trends and corrective moves; it includes points to reverse your position based on the trailing stop.

In a later bulletin to Trident users, it was suggested that a modification to the system be implemented with respect to money management. Using a technique similar to the Martingale system, discussed in this book under the *theory of runs*, each loss is followed by an increase in the number of positions traded. The trader only has to continue to extend his positions and stay with the system until he wins. A comprehensive version of this classic gambling approach can be found in the *theory of runs*. The Trident concepts are all reasonable and generally accepted by experienced traders: advance and retracement; trade the trend; don't pick tops and bottoms but take the center out of each move; and use a trailing stop. It is more carefully defined than most charting systems and it should be interesting to follow its publicized performance (operated by Commodity Timing, Monterey, CA).

CHAPTER 13
Behavioral Techniques

There are some approaches to commodity trading that are more directly dependent on human behavior than the purely mathematical techniques. Most systems when used in the short-term will be more representative of behavior than economic factors, but the concepts presented in this chapter deal specifically with human reactions. *Measuring the news* covers an area that has been greatly overlooked by technicians and offers the greatest single opportunity for research. *Contrary opinion* takes the form of a poll or consensus of opinions of traders and commodity publications. It may help answer the question "what is everyone else doing?", or at least "what are they thinking of doing?"

The principal works of Elliot and Gann are covered in the envelope of *mathematics and the mystic*. It is not intended that these two approaches be taken lightly, but some of the assumptions upon which these systems are based are abstract and not capable of being substantiated other than by the success of the systems themselves. Both are fascinating and open areas of creativity essential to commodity traders. They are grouped together with discussions of natural phenomena and astrological forecasting, all of which should leave you thinking.

MEASURING THE NEWS

If you can keep your head when all about you are losing theirs, maybe you haven't heard the news.

Rudyard Kipling[1]

The news is one of the greatest single elements affecting all free markets. As a medium it carries both fundamental and technical information about all commodities, directly or indirectly, and is indispensable. If not objective, the news services could materially alter any opinion by the inclusion or omission of relevant information.

---
[1] Adam Smith (1967), p. 48.

The impact of news is so great that a speculator holding a market position according to a purely technical system would do best not reading, listening to, watching, or in any sense being exposed to news that might cause him to deviate from the system. In a study commissioned by the *Wall Street Journal* it was shown that 99% of the financial analysts polled read the paper regularly and 92% considered it the "most valuable" publication they read.[2]

As an element of a program or as an indicator of its own, the news is invaluable. If we could measure the impact of unexpected news, the importance of the *Wall Street Journal* or the wire service articles, the USDA crop reports and the CFTC positions reports, and the anticipation of news, we might know the direction of the markets. But first we must be aware of the complications of analyzing the news. There is the problem of objectively selecting which items are relevant to our purpose and which sources are most important. The most difficult problem is quantifying the news—how do you rank each item for measurement, and on what scale do you determine cumulative importance? Some news items are known to have more of an affect on the market—weather disasters, major trade agreements, key crop reports—but these must be ranked against themselves and other issues to produce a numerical system of analysis. On a single day you might have an address by the President about foreign relations ranked as a "+6", a continued lack of rain in the west as a "+2", large grain stocks as "−4", and a key article in the *Wall Street Journal* on the improved Russian harvest as "−5", giving a net score of "−1" to the news—interpreted as neutral. Such a ranking scheme would be considered analytic in nature since it tries to weigh relevance on a predetermined scale without knowledge of individual effects.

Klein and Prestbo attempted such a study by assigning values of 3, 2, and 1 to articles in the *Wall Street Journal* of decreasing importance. Their interest was the stock market, but their work was straightforward and some of the conclusions general in nature. They showed a direct correlation between the relevant positive and negative news articles and the direction of the stock market. As it was scored over 6-week intervals before and after major turning points in the Dow Jones Industrial Averages, the news would stay about 70% favoring the current market direction. Having eliminated the possibility of the market influencing the news, they could conclude that, in retrospect, the market reflected the nature of the news.

The sources that influence commodity prices are different from those that move the stock market because of the fewer, more specific, items, and the purpose of those trading commodities. Specific news releases and economic reports are an implicit part of commodity prices; newspaper releases become important in the last phase of a long move. The most important news items in commodities are:

- Government reports on production and stocks
- Unexpected news of any type from any medium
- Wire-service news
- Weather
- In-depth studies by the *Wall Street Journal*
- Front-page news articles (or television, etc.) on high prices, strikes, etc.
- Market letters and research reports from accepted authorities and known organizations

[2] Klein and Prestbo (1974) p. 53.

The problem of ranking and assigning values to news items requires a knowledge of how others see the news. Klein and Prestbo also studied this problem for the stock market and concluded that about 90% of the *Wall Street Journal* readers perceived news in the same way (bullish, bearish, or neutral). We could assume the same relationship for commodities. A reason for the uniform interpretation of the news articles in any field is the publicized analysis. Shortly after the release of a USDA stocks report the wire serives begin to quote independent and poll opinions of the meaning of the report, then transmit those interpretations over their news media to be relayed to most traders. The "professional analysis" is taken as correct and later discussions based on that interpretation serve to solidify the opinion.

News can also be measured empirically, by studying the immediate impact of an expected or surprise news item. It is necessary to make the assumption for this type of measurement that the effects of a news release are most important in the short term, and that their influence on the market is diluted daily. A place to start in assigning a quantitative value to this reduced influence would be with a modification of the standard physics formula

$$I = \frac{1}{D^2}$$

where I is the net influence and D is the elapsed days since the release of the news. In science this phenomenon of a sharp decline in effect as distance increases is applicable to many areas.

Measured empirically, the USDA and CFTC reports are worth studying. The CFTC releases its *Commitments of Traders* report each month on the 10th, accurate as of the last day of the previous month. It tells the distribution of holdings among large and small speculators and hedgers as a percent of total open interest. This report is watched because it is assumed that the small speculators are always wrong and the large hedgers right. You can study the shift in positions that occurs after each report is released and see that the initial reaction to these reports is consistently contrary to the direction prices take a week or two later.[3]

It is important to understand the difference between the analytic and emprical approach to news. In the analytic method, you determine in advance the value of specific events, and then when they occur you verify their preassigned value against the effects. Using the empirical method you measure the effects of each event for a fair sample and then apply your results to subsequent news items.

The analytic approach has the advantage of working in an environment where multiple events are occurring simultaneously; the sum of all news items can be calculated for a new measurement. When testing the empirical approach we may be measuring the event of interest as well as other news of importance occurring at the same time. Getting a pure measurement may be impossible. The primary disadvantage of the analytic approach is that it does not account for the discounting or anticipation of the news. An event of modest importance may become neutral or very significant relative to other concurrent or anticipated events; the empirical method would not be subject to that problem since it measures reaction and not expectation.

---

[3] This study was performed at Economic Research, Inc., Decatur, Il., on a modest sample and represents what is believed to be an accurate conclusion. Complications in such a study are other government reports being released on the same day.

Trading on the News

Even without a sophisticated method of measurement there are many professional speculators who trade on the news. When a bullish news item or report is introduced and the market fails to respond upward, the experienced trader looks for a place to sell. It shows that there is too much apprehension about higher prices and possibly a large numbers of sellers over the market. Similarly, opening calls, available for most commodities, are transmitted via wire services within half an hour of the opening bell. Regardless of the means for determining the opening direction, an experienced trader may take advantage of a higher opening call to place a sell order. There are frequent cases of so many traders wanting to sell a higher opening that the influx of orders after a call, before the opening, has changed the direction from higher to sharply lower on the open.

Weather markets are purely news reactions. Traders with long positions wait for the 5-day forecast hoping for no rain; they anticipate a loss of a specific number of bushels per acre for every dry day once the rainfall is below a given level. Weather markets are nervous and are characterized by evening-up on weekends; they rely heavily on anticipation and emotion. It is said that a farmer loses his crop three times each year, once for drought, once for disease, and once for frost. In 1976 the news carried numerous articles on the desperate wheat crop in the western states, showing films of virtually barren fields, and yet the United States harvested one of their largest wheat crops on record, showing the danger in using weather for long-term predictions.

The discounting of news is well-known by "insiders," but the public remains unaware. An old saying in the market, "Buy the rumor, sell the fact," implies that anticipation drives the price past the point where it would realistically adjust to news. When the actual figures are released, there is invariably an adjustment back to their proper level.

The news could be the next area of concentrated study for the analyst; it is an intrinsic part of all market activity and its presentation has an obvious effect on price movement. Think of what would happen if you knew that there was a true shortage of some commodity and no one else knew—you might be a buyer, the only one.

CONTRARY OPINION[4]

The contrarian lies somewhere in between the fundamentalist and the technician, basing has actions on the behavior of crowds, in this case the commodity speculator. Klein and Prestbo claim that the two traditional schools "talk themselves into severe cases of tunnel vision," but the principles of contrary thinking have more substance. In his observation the contrarian sees the end of a bull market occurring where everyone is bullish; hence his opportunities always lie in the reverse direction from crowd thinking.

Contrary opinion alone is not meant to signal a new entry into a position; it identifies situations that qualify. It is more of a filter than a trading system, a means of finding an opportunity. In every prolonged bull or bear move there is a point where

---

[4] For the most definitive work see Humphrey Neill (1960). Neill is credited with having first formulated the concept.

the direction is generally accepted as the major trend. After that traders wait for a reversal to reenter in the direction of the trend at a more favorable price. These adjustments become smaller or disappear when everyone wants to "buy a lower open" or "sell a higher open" until you have the ultimate "blow-off" and reversal of a major bull or bear market. The dynamic end is generally credited to the entrance of the public; when the masses are unanimously convinced that prices are going higher, who is left to buy?

The other important ingredient to a contrarian is that all the facts cannot be known. The widely accepted belief that "prices will go higher" must be based on presumptions; if the final figures were out the market would adjust to the proper level. This idea is older than *The Art of Contrary Thinking*. Schabacker in 1930 talked about cashing out a long position if the market rallied on future news that was not specific but general.

The practical application of the theory of contrary opinion is the *Bullish Consensus* and the *Market Sentiment Index*,[5] created from a poll of market letters prepared by the commodity departments of brokerage firms and professional advisors. In the Bullish Consensus these opinions are weighted according to the estimated exposure of these letters until a final index value is determined. This value will range from 0 to 100%, indicating an increasingly bullish attitude. Because of the psychology of the novice commodity trader, the neutral consensus point is 55%. The normal range is considered from 30 to 80%, although each commodity must be individually evaluated.

The principle of contrary opinion does not require the user always to look for a trade in the opposite direction of the current price movement. Within the normal range the contrarian will take a position in the direction of the trend. Frequently the Bullish Consensus will begin increasing prior to the price's turning higher, indicating that the attitude of the trader is becoming bullish. It is considered significant when the index changes 10% in a 2-week period. Once the Bullish Consensus reaches 90% during an upward move or 20% during a bear move, the commodity is considered overbought or oversold and the contrarian looks for a convenient point to exit from his current trade. He would not reverse his position until prices shows that they would not continue in the original direction. This could be identified using a moving average. Remembering Schabacker's advice, the occasion of a general news release that moves the market further in the direction of the general opinion would be an opportune moment to enter a contrary trade; specific news that fails to move prices would be a good indication of an exhausted trend when the consensus is overbought or oversold.

Contrary thinking is important for all traders. Even if they never enter a trade according to the Market Sentiment Index, they should be wary when the overwhelming majority agrees with their position and look for a place to exit a current trade. A contrary position entered on a dip after a long bear move has the added advantage of low risk with a fill near the bottom of the move.

R. Earl Hadady said about the system that he sponsors: "The principle of contrary opinion, by definition, works 100% of the time. The problem is getting an accurate concensus."[6] Timeliness is another problem with an index; if 60 to 70 market letters are reviewed, read, and weighted to form an index to be published, the results may be dated before they can be used. The theory of contrary opinion also emphasized its

---

[5] The *Bullish Consensus* is a product of Sibett–Hadady, Pasadena; a Market Sentiment Index is published in *Consensus*, Kansas City.
[6] George Angell (1976).

use as a timing device, to enter trades at an opportune moment and to filter out the ambigous trades; the theory is not readily applicable to exiting a position, since you cannot always wait for a confirmation to exit a trade.

The principles of contrary opinion are sound, but it may never be refined enough to be considered technical, and perhaps it never should. It serves as an essential reminder not to fall in love with your position.

MATHEMATICS AND THE MYSTIC

Even though we may not understand the cause underlying a particular phenomenon, we can, by observation, predict the phenomenon's recurrence.

R. N. Elliot[7]

History is a great record of achievement in the face of disbelief: the explorations of Columbus, Magellan, Marco Polo; the science of da Vinci, Galileo, Copernicus; and the philosophy of Socrates and other men now known to be great. We are more observant today and less apt to condemn those who delve into areas still unknown. Of these, astrology is the most obvious; but its acceptance may be partly because of its harmless nature—in its common form it attempts to classify personality and behavioral traits. If the predictive aspect of astrology were emphasized, there would be fewer that would accept its premises. And still, the positions of our moon and planets, the energy given off, the gravitational phenomenon, are directly responsible for physical occurrences of tides and weather—should they not have a measureable affect on behavior? We will consider this in the following section.

Let us look first at the fascinating subject of symmetry in nature. Science is familiar with the symmetric shapes of crystalline substances, snowflakes, the spherical planets, and the human body. The periodicity of the universe—sun spots, eclipses, and other cyclic phenomena—is also understood, but its bearing on human behavior is not yet accepted. Recent work in biorhythms is only at the point of being a curiosity; the relationship of behavior to nonbiological functions, such as planetary positions, is too abstract.

In 1904, Arthur H. Church wrote about phyllotaxis, the leaf arrangement of plants,[8] showing its relationship to a mathematical series based on the works of Leonardo Pisano (Fibonacci).[9] Our interest is in whether this mathematical series of numbers can represent human behavior. To do this we will present examples that may be considered "interesting coincidences" with enough intrinsic justification to merit further study.

Fibonacci and Human Behavior

It is not certain how Fibonacci conceived his summation series. His greatest work, *Liber Abaci*, written in the early part of the 13th century, was not published until

---

[7] Elliot (1964), p. 4.
[8] A. H. Church (1904).
[9] In the appendices to Jay Hambridge (1931) pp. 146–161, there is a full discussion of the evolution of this number series within science and mathematics, together with further references.

1857.[10] It contained a description of a situation involving the reproduction of rabbits, in which the following two conditions hold: every month each pair produces a new pair, which, from the second month on, becomes productive; deaths do not occur. We then have the famous *Fibonacci summation series*

$$1, 2, 3, 5, 8, 13, 21, 34, 55, 89, 144, \ldots$$

(more currently written 1, 1, 2, 3, ...). It can be easily seen that each element of the series is the sum of the two previous entries.

Those who have studied the life of Fibonacci often attribute the series to his observations of the Great Pyramid of Gizeh. This pyramid, dating from a preliterary, prehieroglyphic era, contains many features said to have been observed by Fibonacci. In the geometry of a pyramid there are 5 surfaces and 8 edges, for a total of 13 surfaces and edges; there are 3 edges visible from any one side. More specifically, the Great Pyramid of Gizeh is 5813 inches high (5-8-13, and the inch is the standard Egyptian unit of measure); and the ratio of the elevation to the base is .618.[11] The coincidence of this ratio is that it is the same as the ratio that is approached by any two consecutive Fibonacci numbers; for example,

$$\tfrac{2}{3} = .667, \quad \tfrac{3}{5} = .60, \quad \tfrac{5}{8} = .625, \quad \ldots, \quad \tfrac{89}{144} = .618$$

It is also true that the ratio of a side to a diagonal of a regular pentagon is .618.

Another phenomenon of the pyramid is that the total of the 4 edges of the base, measured in inches, is 36524.22, which is exactly 100 times the length of the solar year. This permits interpretations of the Fibonacci summation series to be applied to time.

The Greeks showed a great fascination for the ratios of the Fibonacci series, noting that while $F_n/F_{n+1} = .618$, the reverse $F_{n+1}/F_n = 1.618$ was even more amazing. They expressed these relationships as "golden sections" and used them either consciously or not, in the proportions of such works as the Parthenon, the sculpture of Phidias, and classic vases. Leonardo da Vinci consciously employed the ratio in his art. It has always been a curiosity that the great mathematician, Pythagoras, left behind a symbol of a triangle with the words "The Secret of the Universe" inscribed below.

Church, in his work in phyllotaxis, studied the sunflower, noting that one of normal size (5 to 6 inches) has a total of 89 curves, 55 in one direction and 34 in another. In observing sunflowers of other sizes he found that the total curves are Fibonacci numbers (up to 144) with the two previous numbers in the series describing the distribution of curves. The chambered nautilus is also considered a natural representation of a "golden spiral," based on the proportions of the Fibonacci ratio.

Up to now we have discussed aspects of the Fibonacci series that are intriguing, but here we take a step beyond. The numbers in the series represent frequent or coincidental occurrences:

- The human body has 5 major projections; both arms and legs have 3 sections; there are 5 fingers and toes, each with 3 sections (except the thumb and great toe). There are also 5 senses.
- In music an octave means eight, with 8 white keys and 5 black, totaling 13.

[10] *Il Liber Abaci di Leonardo Pisano*, publicato da Baldassare Boncompagni, Roma, 1857.
[11] Jay Hambridge (1931) pp. 27–38.

- There are 3 primary colors.
- The United States had 13 original states and 13 is an unlucky number.
- The legal age was 21 and the highest salute in the army is a 21-gun salute.
- The human emotional cycle has been determined at 33 to 36 days by Dr. R. B. Hersey.[12]
- The wholesale price index of all commodities is shown to have peaks of 50–55 years according to the Kondratieff wave: 1815 after the war of 1812, 1965 after the Civil War, 1920 after the World War I, and about 1975 after ...[13]

These examples are not meant to prove anything in the strict sense, but to open an area that may not have previously existed for you. Human behavior is not yet a pure science and probes of this sort may lead the way to further understanding. The following sections deal with ideas such as these—sometimes reasonable and other times seeming to stretch your imagination.

ELLIOT'S "WAVE PRINCIPLE"

R. N. Elliot was responsible for one of the more highly regarded and complex forms of market analysis currently available to technicians. The Elliot wave theory is a sophisticated method of price motion analysis, and has received careful study by A. H. Bolton (1960) and later with Charles Collins. A condensed interpretive rendition of the theory was printed by David Harahus in 1977 in support of an advisory service based on the work; brief summaries of the analysis appear in some of the comprehensive books on commodities.[14] This presentation of Elliot's technique will include both the original principles and extensions with examples.

The wave theory is an analysis of behavioral patterns based on mathematics and implemented using price charts; its original application was stocks and it is credited with some predictive ability with respect to the Dow Jones Industrial Averages that is second only to the occurrence of Haley's comet. It is understood that Elliot never intended to apply his principle to individual stocks, perhaps because the thinness of trading might reduce the expected patterns caused by mass behavior. If so, there are few commodities markets that would have satisfied his requirement. The successes of the Elliot wave theory are fascinating and reinforce the use of the technique; most summaries of Elliot's work recount them and the reader is encouraged to read them. We will assume the seriousness of the work. The "waves" referred to in the theory are price peaks and valleys, not the formal oscillations of sound waves or harmonics described in the science of physics. The waves of price motion are overreactions to both supply and demand factors within major bull moves developed in five waves and corrected in three. His broad concept was related to "tidal wave bull markets" that has such large upward thrusts that each wave could be divided into five subwaves satisfying the same principle. After each primary wave of the major bull trend there was a major corrective move of three waves, which could also be divided into subwaves of three.

[12] Elliot (1946) p. 55. Elliot quotes other human emotional relationships.
[13] *Cycles*, January 1976, p. 21; see also *The Kondratieff Wave: The Future of America Until 1981 and Beyond*, Dell, New York, 1974, which is based on the theory developed by the Russian economist early in this century.
[14] Merrill (1966) Appendices E and F contains one of the more thorough summaries and analysis of the basic wave theory, including performance.

BEHAVIORAL TECHNIQUES

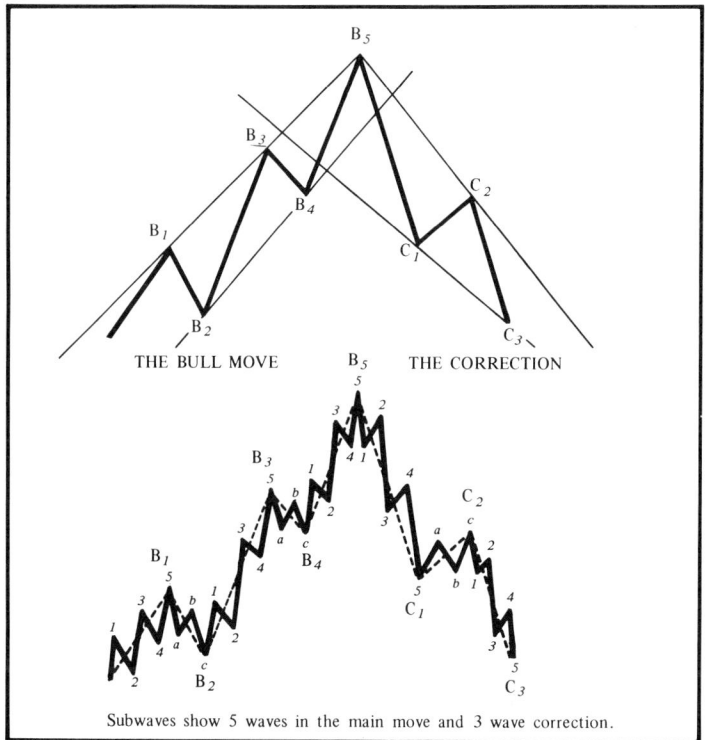

Diagram 13-1 Basic Elliot wave.

The types of waves could be classified into the broad categories of trianges and ABC's representing a main trend and a correction, respectively. The term triangle was taken from the consolidating or broadening shape that the waves form within trend lines, although in later work Elliot eliminated the expanding form of triangle.

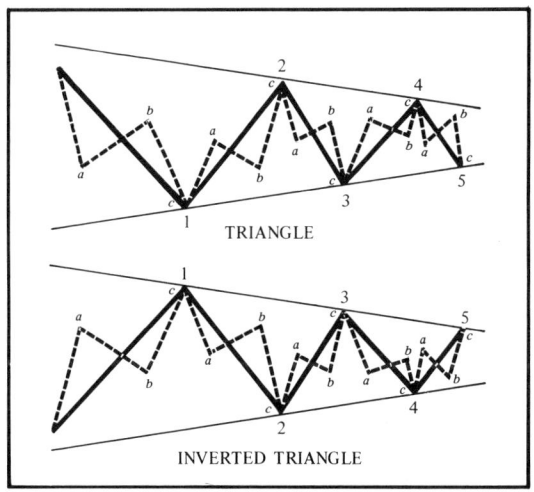

Diagram 13-2 Triangles and ABCs.

An interesting aspect of the theory is its compound-complex nature, by which each sequence of triangles can occur as well in subwaves within waves. More recent work suggests that in commodities a three-wave development is more common than one involving five and should therefore be watched carefully.

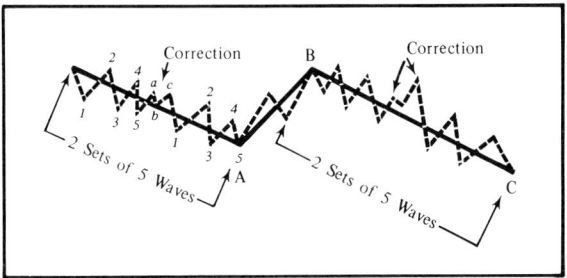

Diagram 13-3 Compound correction wave.

One point to remember when applying an intricate set of rules is that an exact fit will not occur often. The best trading opportunities that will arise will be for those price patterns that fit best as the move is progressing; each successful step will serve as positive reinforcement for continuing. The critical period in the identification process is the fifth wave. The failure of the fifth wave to form indicates that that last correction of three waves will be retraced. In a bull market, an extension of the fifth wave is often followed by a corrective three-wave formation that may restore prices back to the level of the nonextended five-wave formation. In addition, the recognition of a five-wave sequence should be followed by further analysis to determine whether that cycle was part of a complex series. One of the difficulties in the method is the orientation of your current position to the wave formation; the multitude of primary and secondary waves makes some of the situations subjective until further developments clarify the position. Anyone interested in the further complexities of wave formation should refer directly to Bolton's work.

The application of the Elliot wave theory is unique in its use of the Fibonacci series. Besides the natural phenomena mentioned earlier, the summation series has the mathematical properties that

- The ratio of any number to its successor (F_i/F_{i+1}) approaches .618.
- The ratio of any number to its previous element (F_{i+1}/F_i) approaches 1.618
- The ratio of F_{i+2}/F_i is 2.618
- The two ratios (F_i/F_{i+1}) × (F_{i+1}/F_i) = .618 × 1.618 = 1

Elliot was also able to link certain measurements of the Great Pyramid to the Fibonacci series and connect the number of days in the year as well as the geometric figure of a circle to his theory. Both time and the circle will play a role in Elliot wave analysis.

While Elliot used the lower end of the Fibonacci series to describe the patterns in the stock market, it should be noted that there are increasingly larger gaps between successive entries as the series increases. To be consistent with the original principle each gap could be subdivided into another Fibonacci series in the same manner that the waves take on a complex formation. Harahus offers an alternate approach to filling these spaces by use of Lucas numbers, formed in the same way as the Fibonacci summation beginning with (1, 3) and resulting in (1, 3, 4, 7, 11, 18, 29, 47, 76, 123, 199, ...). The two sets are combined, eliminating common numbers, to form (*1*, 2, *3*, 4, *5*, 7, 8, *13*, 18, *21*, 29, *34*, 47, *55*, 76, *89*, 123, *144*, 199, *233*, ...). The Fibonacci numbers have been italicized since they will receive the most emphasis, while the Lucas numbers will serve as intermediate levels of less significance. The numbers themselves are applied to predict the length in days of a price move. A bull move that lasts for more than 34 days should meet major resistance or reverse on the 55th day or on the 89th day (considering Fibonacci numbers only). It is suggested that a penetration of the 89th day should permit the series to start again with the beginning of the series added to 89 (e.g., ..., 94, 96, *97*, *102*, 107, *110*, 118, *123*, 136, ...), including the more important Lucas and Fibonacci numbers from the original series. This effect is similar to the complex wave-within-a-wave motion.

The same numbers are used to express key levels in a trend reversal. For example a bull move that carries prices up for about 47 days before a reversal, should meet resistance at the price level on the 34th day. If that price does not stop the reversal, either the behavioral implications of the number series do not hold for this situation or you are in a different part of the cycle.

With the introduction of Lucas numbers (L) there are some additional key ratios. In the combined Fibonacci-Lucas series (FL) we denote an element with j if it is the first element of the other series following the entry i; L_j is the first Lucas number entry following F_i that is a Fibonacci number. We then have the ratios $F_i/L_j = .72$, $L_i/F_j = .854$, and $F_i/F_{i+2} = L_i/L_{i+2} = .382$.

The important ratio of a Fibonacci number to its following entry can be represented by the ratio of successive numbers ($\frac{1}{2}, \frac{2}{3}, \frac{3}{5}, \frac{5}{8}, \frac{8}{13}, \frac{13}{21}, \frac{21}{144}, \ldots$). When expressed in decimal, these ratios approach the number .618 in a convergent oscillating series (1.000, .500, .667, .625, .615, .619, ...). These ratios, the key Fibonacci-Lucas ratios, and the alternate-entry ratios represent the potential resistance levels (in terms of percentage) for price adjustments within a well-defined move. For example, a price advance of $1.00 in silver to $5.00 might correct 100%, 50%, or 62%, to $4.00, $4.50, or $4.38, respectively, according to the most important ratios.

Fibonacci numbers are a unique and interesting phenomenon of mathematics having important implications in physical science. Examples of its use can be found in any of the works relating directly to Elliot's theory or in general source material. Harahus shows some interesting constructions using Fibonacci ratios; they are referred to as the "golden rectangle," "golden triangle," and "golden spiral." There is no doubt of its importance, but its application to markets is not trivial. As a behavioral model any technique is subject to gross inaccuracy at times. In using a method as sophisticated as the Elliot wave theory, it is necessary to select situations that are representative examples of the phenomenon described by the FL sequence. Confirmation of such action can only be found by careful monitoring and the development of an awareness of the nature of the price motion important to the system.

Elliot also knew that there was great variability in this adherence to waves and ratios. The appearance of the waves is not regular in either length or duration and should not be expected to continually increase as they develop, although the fifth wave is generally the longest. The waves must be identified by peaks only. Elliot introduced a channel into his theory in order to determine the direction of the wave being analyzed as well as to establish intermediate price objectives. Looking back at the diagram of the basic wave, we can see the channel drawn touching the peaks and bottoms of the bull move. For every two peaks we can draw a channel that will serve as a trend line for price objectives. This same technique is covered in detail in a later section of Chapter 10. The lower trend line in the bull move will serve to tell when a correction has begun.

The Elliot wave theory is very intricate and should not be attempted without careful study of the original material, but some rules are presented here in order to help you understand the nature of the method:

1. Identify a main trend.
2. Determine the current status of the main trend by locating the major peaks and bottoms that will form the five key waves.
3. Look for three wave corrections and five wave subtrends or extensions.
4. Draw trend lines to determine the direction.
5. Measure the length of the waves in days to determine its adherence to the Fibonacci–Lucas sequence; measure the size of reactions as compared to FL ratios.
6. Watch for reactions at points predicted by the FL sequence and corresponding to the patterns described by the five-wave main trend and three-wave correction.
7. Use the ratios, day counts, and trend lines as predictive devices to select price objectives.
8. Use the trend lines to determine changes of direction.

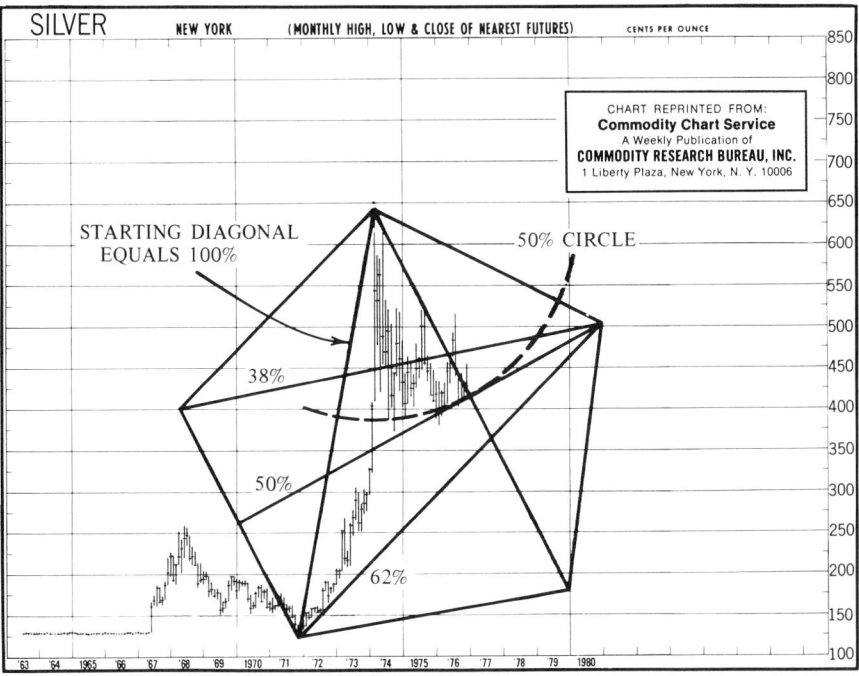

Diagram 13-4(a)   Pentagon constructed from one diagonal.

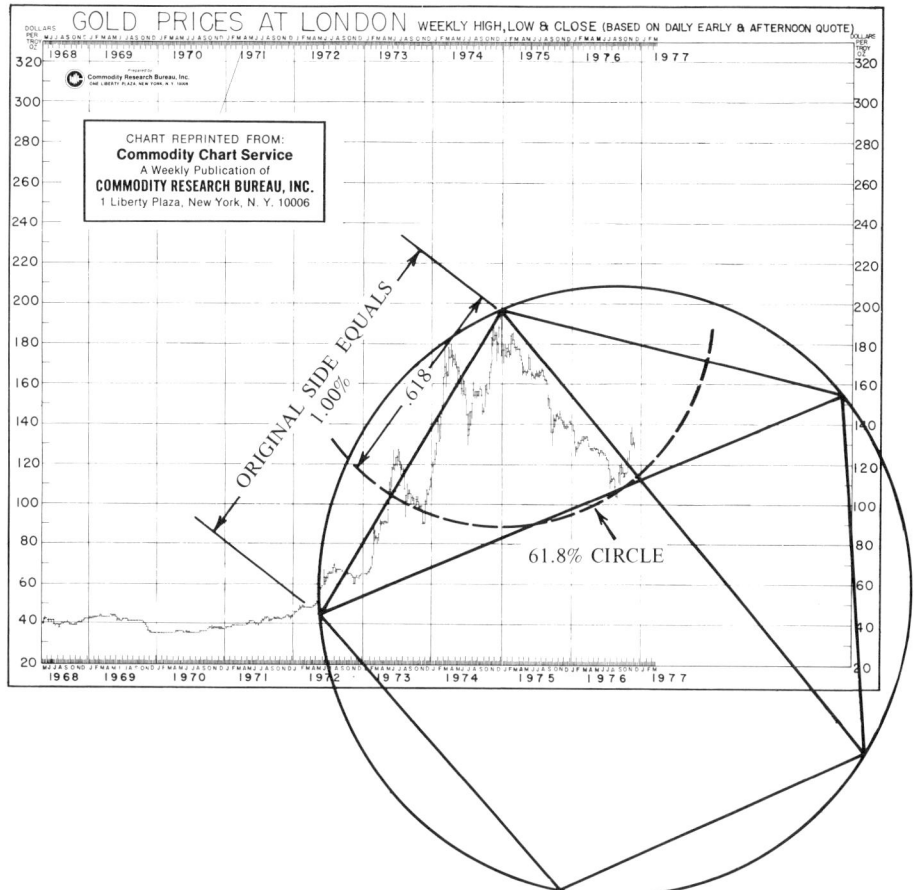

Diagram 13-4(b)   Pentagon constructed from one side.

Harahus further introduces the regular pentagon as a tool for measuring correction. This geometric figure has the property that any diagonal is 1.618 times the length of a side, exactly a Fibonacci ratio.

By constructing a regular pentagon so that the major trend falls along one diagonal (or one side), the other line connecting the corners of the pentagon will serve as support or resistance to price moves. In addition, the circumscribed and inscribed circle will serve as a measurement of support and/or resistance.

Harahus further extends the charting techniques of the Elliot wave theory using circles and arcs. A circle drawn from the top or bottom of a wave, representing the 38%, 50%, or 62% levels serves as a convenient measurement of either elapsed time or a price adjustment, either of which could occur within the bounds of the rules.

Prices are expected to meet resistance at any attempt to penetrate the key circles formed about either *A* or *B* in Diagram 13-5.

The Elliot wave theory is highly regarded although it is an odd combination of mathematics and chart interpretation, bordering slightly on the mystic. Since it is primarily based on chart patterns it has been criticized as being too interpretive, not

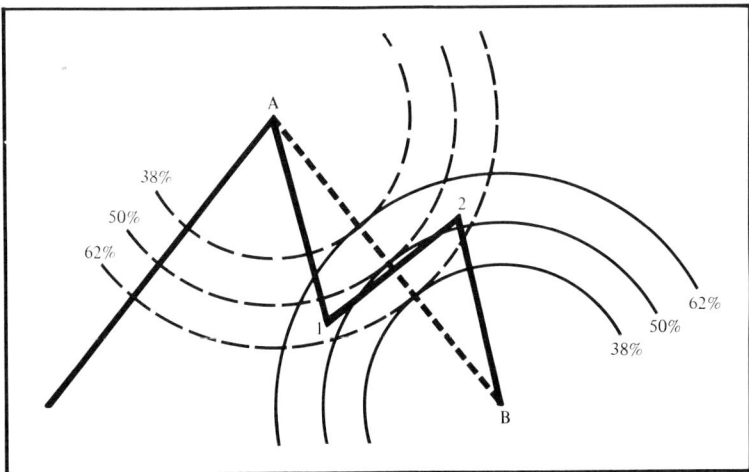

Diagram 13-5   Using circles to find support and resistance.

specific enough. The development of the fifth wave received the most comment—sometimes it never develops while at other times it must be extended into another subset of waves. In an analysis by Merrill, it is shown that the median stock market bull move has seven legs and the bear move has five legs; but this is also interpretive, although it may account for the need for the compound form of the Elliot wave. Those analysts who find this study of interest, should also read the available works of W. D. Gann and Edson Gould, both of whom concentrated on mathematical approaches to charting.

W. D. GANN, "TIME AND SPACE"

The works of W. D. Gann cannot be explained with any thoroughness in a few words, but some of his main ideas have been selected and presented in this section. Gann was a pure technician using charts for all his analyses. His methods varied substantially from our conventional charting techniques, but his philosophy was one of a professional trader: conserve your capital and wait for the right time. Gann traded the markets, primarily grains, for many years and in his writings he attempted to summarize these dominant observations; some of them are reminiscent of other well-known market lore.

Price moves are never exact. Gann was a believer in support and resistance lines, but expected some violation of the objectives because of "lost motion," his way of accounting for the momentum that carries prices higher or lower than their likely goals. Nearly a cross between Elliot's "waves" and Angas' "cycles," Gann classifies bull and bear moves into four "stages," each one compared to a trending move and a subsequent reversal, culminating in a major top or bottom. He observed that bull markets last longer than bear markets. He concluded that reversal patterns must reduce in magnitude as the move develops and persists. A similar argument is expressed in the "theory of contrary thinking." Much of Gann's work is related in 1940

BEHAVIORAL TECHNIQUES

cents—if you intend to study it on your own, find an economic inflator to keep close at hand.

Gann's techniques combine mathematics and geometry with time and space; he finds duration as important as the distance covered. One of his principles reflects the idea of a longer consolidation period resulting in a longer resulting price move after a breakout. One of the approaches to price objectives in bar charting is exactly this idea.

Time and Prices

Gann's idea was that there are certain natural divisions, expressed as percents. Zero and 100% are the most important of these. Based on behavioral awareness, he considered a potential resistance level at 100% of the original point of the move or 100% of the highest or lowest (the best guide) price of that commodity. In a reversal, 100% was a full retracement of the original move. The rationale for this theory is behavioral, as is his conclusion that most traders like even numbers; for this reason orders in grains are most often placed at 5–10¢ levels.

After the 100% level, decreased importance goes to increments of 50%, 25%, $12\frac{1}{2}$%, and so on. For a grain this would mean that major resistance could be expected at the even dollar levels, with the next resistance at 50¢ intervals, then every 25¢, and so on; after a bull move of $1, the major support would be $1 lower, then 50¢, 25¢ and 75¢, and so on. The use of succesive halving of intervals was also extended to time. A year is a full cycle of 360° that makes a half of a year (26 weeks), a quarter of a year (13 weeks), an eighth of a year (45 days), and a sixteenth of a year ($22\frac{1}{2}$ days) of similar significance. In cases of conflict, time always took precedence over price. The combination of a key price level (percentage move) occurring at a periodic time interval is the basis for much of Gann's work.

Geometric Angles

One approach that Gann used for relating price and time was geometric angles. By using square graph paper it was not necessary to know the exact angle, because the construction was based on boxes up versus boxes to the right. A 1 × 1 angle (45°) was drawn diagonally from the bottom of the lowest point of a price move through the intersection 1 box up and 1 box to the right. This is the primary bullish support line. A bearish resistance line is drawn down from left to right from the highest price using the 1 × 1 angle. The next most important angles in order of significance are 2 × 1, 4 × 1, and 8 × 1; for lower support areas there is also 1 × 2, 1 × 4, and 1 × 8. Places where the support and resistance lines cross are of special significance, indicating a major congestion area.

Diagram 13-6 is taken from Gann's private papers and shows the use of geometric angles in an actual trading situation. Lines were first drawn where Gann expected a bottom, then redrawn again. The initial upward move followed the primary 45° line; the second important support line, 1 × 2, met the primary downward line at the point of wide congestion at the center of the chart. The highest point on this congestion phase became the pivot point for the next 45° downward angle, defining the next breakout.

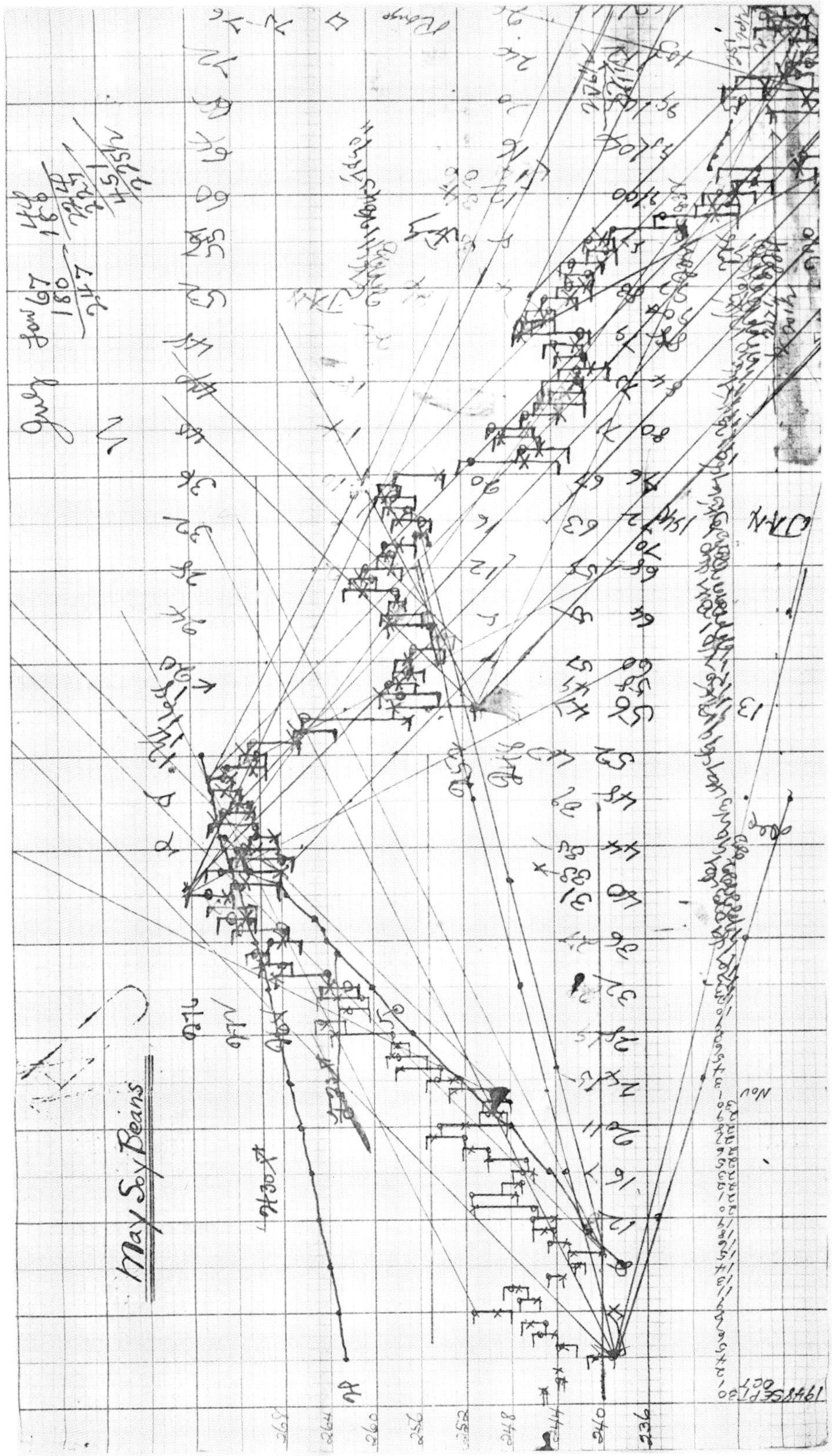

Diagram 13-6　Gann's soybean worksheet.

BEHAVIORAL TECHNIQUES   203

Gann combined this method with a more remarkable technique, the *squaring of price and time*. We were fortunate to find a chart that complemented Diagram 13-6, based on the lowest recorded cash price of soybeans, 44¢ per bushel. Diagram 13-7 shows how Gann constructed this square, beginning with the lowest price at the center and moving one square to the right, circling counterclockwise and continuing the process. The basic geometric lines (the horizontal, vertical and diagonal) indicate the major support and resistance price levels, the most important one being 44, the junction of all lines.

Relating the square to the price chart showing geometric lines, we see the first support level exactly at 240 (upper left diagonal), the major resistance at 276 (right horizontal), the next minor support at 268 (lower right diagonal), congestion area support at 254 and 262 (1 box off), and back down to support at 240. Notice that the distance between the lines on the square become wider as prices increase, conforming

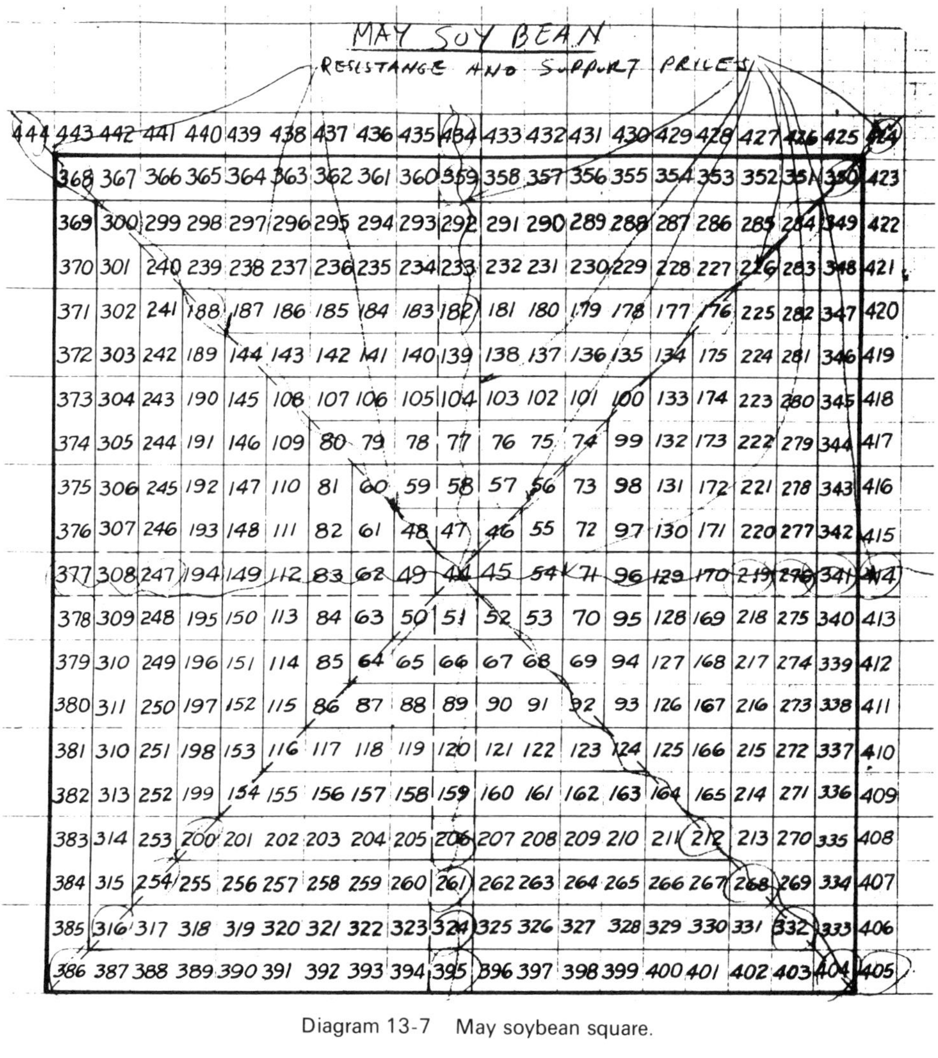

Diagram 13-7   May soybean square.

to our current notion of volatility. We would also expect Soybeans at $10 to have some "lost motion" near these key support and resistance levels.

The Hexagon Chart

Gann generalized his "squaring method" to include both geometric angles and the main cyclic divisions of 360°. By combining these different behavioral concepts we can isolate the strongest levels of support and resistance where all three coincide. The generalized construction for this purpose is "the master calculator," based on aligning the chart at a point representing a multiple of the lowest historic price for that commodity; crisscrossing angles will then designate support and resistance for the specific commodity. Other time charts of importance are the *square of twelve*, one corner of the master calculator, the *hexagon chart*, and *the master chart of* 360°. As an example of a combined effect we will look at the hexagon chart.

As you can see in Diagram 13-8 the inner ring begins with six divisions, giving Gann the basis for the chart name. Each circle gains six additional numbers

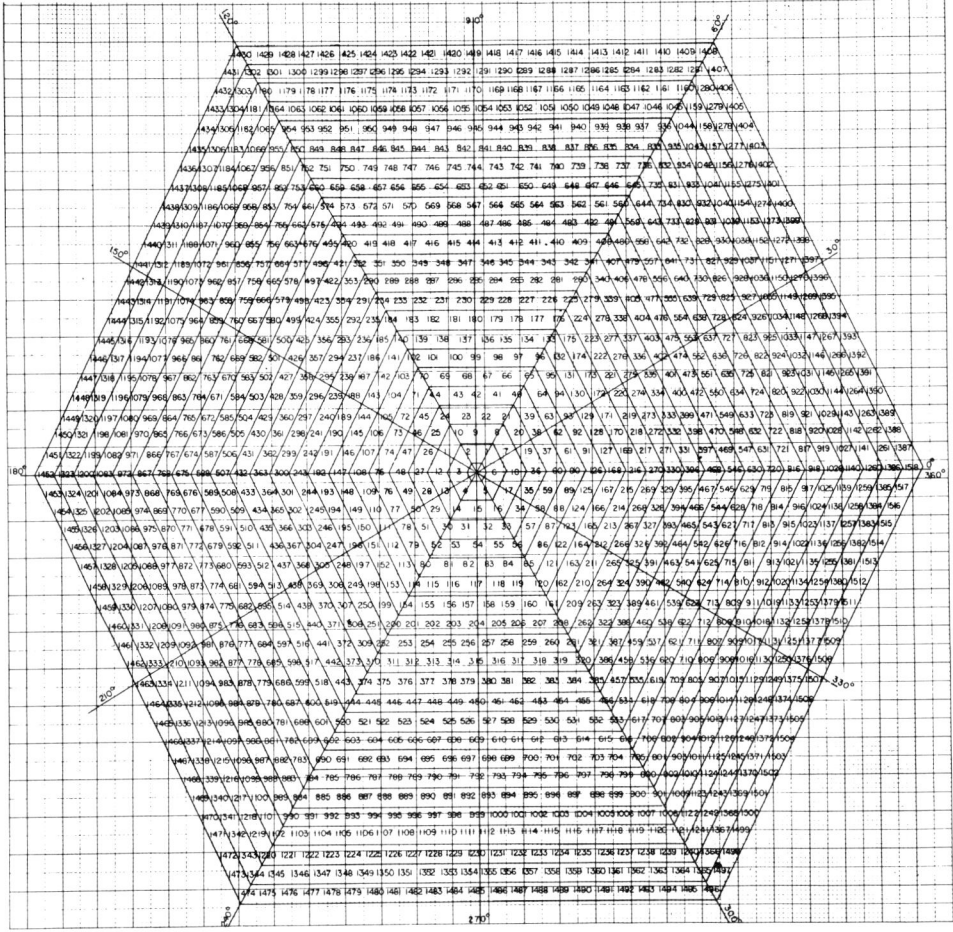

Diagram 13-8 The hexagon chart.

as we proceed outward, which relates to the overall continuity of the construction. In using the hexagon, the degrees represent time and the numbers in the circle are price; a major support or resistance point exists when both time and price occur simultaneously.

For example, consider the 360° of the hexagon relating to the calendar year, or perhaps the crop year for grains. In his own work on grain, Gann equated 0° to March 20, near to the first day of spring, when the sun crosses the equator going north. Then the 45° line is on May 6, 90° on June 21 (the first day of summer), 180° on September 23 (fall), and 270° on December 21 (winter). These primary divisions also represent the most significant places for price support or resistance. The other lines represent secondary levels.

When looking at the prices and times together on the hexagon chart we see that the distance between the major degree lines become greater as prices increase, showing the importance of volatility. Using the price of November 77 Soybeans, we can interpret the chart to say that between 90° and 180°, or June 21 to September 23, 1977, the price of soybeans should show support at 567 and then move its major support level to 507 and its major resistance to 588 with next higher and lower support and resistance at 432 and 675, respectively. As it turned out this was a very accurate prediction, but one observation does not make the method infallible.

Gann's work is more difficult to grasp than most methods; his tools are unique to the field. If we were able to ask Gann for a word of advice, there is no doubt that he would caution to patience, stating: *When price meets time, a change is imminent.*

The Moon: "Buy Full, Sell New"

As long as you have read this far, you may as well continue. We know that the moon's effect on our planet is great—it is vitally connected with the movement of all fluids. The moon is also believed to affect human behavior in strange ways, especially during a new or full moon.

In an experiment conducted on an arbitrary set of commodities for the year 1972[15] it was shown that short-term movements of prices react with some uniformity with respect to the phases of the moon. In fact, the commodities chosen for observation—silver, wheat, cattle, cocoa, and sugar—showed an uncanny ability to form a rising market following a full moon and a falling market after a new moon.

"Corn is Rising"

Astrology seeks a common bond in human behavior, similar to the work in biological rhythms and cycles. At this point in its development its values and applications must be individually evaluated. The impact of astrology on civilization has been great; observations of the periodicity of the moon is traced back 32,000 years, star charts were known to have been in Egypt about 4200 B.C., and the earliest written ephemerides were in the 7th century B.C.[16] The pyramids at Ghiza are said to have sloping

---

[15] Todd Lofton (July 1974) writes about his observations.
[16] Parker and Paricor (1971), p. 12.

corridors leading from the faces to the interior that were used as sighting tubes for Egyptian astrologers for making accurate forecasts. The acceptance of astrology throughout history is widespread, including virtually all civilizations. Can these beliefs relating to behavior be used to predict the movements of prices?

Jack Perrine in an article entitled "Taurus the Bullish" presented an adaptation that may be a start of a new predictive approach to trading. The method considers each planet as representative of one or more commodities as well as traits; for example, Mars is cattle, heavy industry and railrods; Uranus is corn, revolution, change, and larger corporations; and the moon is gold and silver. The positions of the planets are also significant. The "aspect," a measurement of the angular separation between two planets as seen from the Earth, are termed "hard" and "soft" for scarce and plentiful. Aspects reach peak effectiveness at specific positions: very hard at 90° and very soft at 120°; they seem to oscillate in their interpretation as they continue in one direction.

The "signs" are associated with angular sectors in the geocentric system of astrology. Beginning with Aries in the spring we have the twelve familiar signs related to varying degrees of bullish and bearish influence. The months alternating with Aries (April) are bearish, with the exception of December, which is bullish instead of bearish. The relationship of the "signs" to the market is not apparent to the casual observer.

Perrine uses his rules to predict the turns in the markets for a near and a long-term forecast. Some of the aspects are interpreted as:

- Jupiter in conjunct to Pluto—very bearish for the financial world
- Jupiter square to Neptune—sky-high interest rates[17]

In subsequent analyses by Perrine, he says: "... Mars will be square to the Sun, a friendly sign for precious metals." However, a strong bearish influence approaching may cause many commodities that are otherwise strong to "get swept down in their powerful bearish currents."

Are you going to be the one to say that this won't work? Behaviorally, this is the same as telling a child that there is no Santa when he *knows* that he gets presents every year.

---

[17] Perrine (1974) p. 36.

CHAPTER 14
Pattern Recognition

So much in commodity trading can be classified by the term *pattern* that it is necessary to restrict its use to a specific category of price movement. This chapter will be concerned with a mathematical pattern recognition; the justification of this comes from very nonmathematical observations. In order to be successful, speculators look for patterns in market price movement; because they were not equipped with high-powered tabulating equipment their conclusions are considered market lore rather than fact. They are handed down from generation to generation as proverbs of the following sort: "Up on Monday, down on Tuesday," "Locals even-up on Fridays," and "Watch for key reversals." Since these three sayings have survived for so long they are candidates for analysis in the section at the end of this chapter.[1]

The earliest technical systems using patterns were of the general form "if after a sharp rise the market fails to advance for three days, sell." Although not specific or mathematical, it is definitely a pattern and clearly understood. In recent years the extreme mathematical approach has also been taken. By observing the closing prices starting at an arbitrary day, it is possible to record *all* patterns of higher and lower closes and their tendency to repeat periodically. You would not want to do this manually, but a computer is well equipped to perform this task. First you eliminate the two-day pattern, and possibly the three-day pattern, from your study, since the recurrence of up-down or down-up would be too frequent to be meaningful; then you start scanning closing prices for occurrences of your pattern. For example, if you are looking for up-up-down-up-down-up you must look at every six consecutive prices and record the intervals between these occurrences. From these results you can decide whether these patterns can be predicted in advance or whether they precede price moves that can be predicted.

Pattern recognition seems more like a game than a business, but it is a source of many valuable ideas. A graph of the New York Stock Exchange from 1854 to 1959 shows the simplification of patterns to the point where it is difficult not to count the recurrences of the more obvious patterns and look for the formations that precede them in order to see whether they could be predictive. For example, in 1922, 1924, and

---

[1] The only other work discovered that deals with patterns similar to these, although for the stock market, is by Merrill (1966).

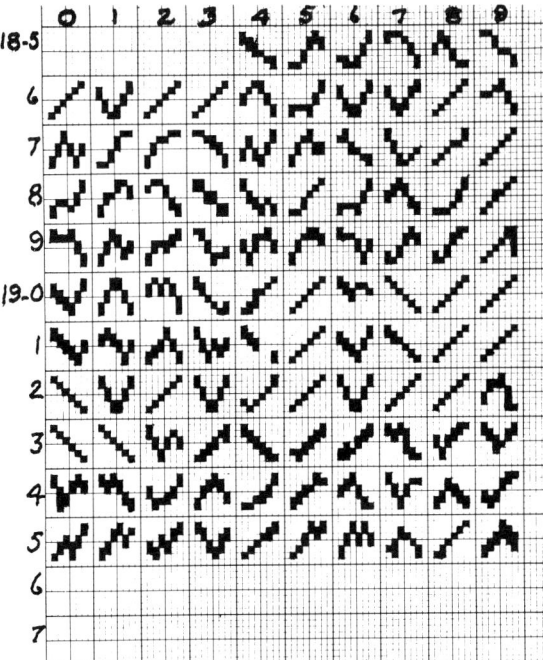

Diagram 14-1   Graph of the New York Stock Market.

1927 we had sharp advances in the market; the years preceding those all showed an identical U pattern. It would be interesting to see whether another occurrence of a symmetric U was followed by a similar rise. Another pattern that stands out is that of two consecutive years of sharp rise, 1862–1863, 1908–1909, 1918–1919, and 1927–1928; in no case was there a third consecutive year, but neither the preceding nor following years seem consistent.

Patterns frequently provide the foundation for a trading method or the justification for beginning work in developing a method. They have been applied in many ways in commodity analysis, from the time of day to place an order to the compound relationship of price, volume, and open interest. The first section that follows deals with patterns occurring during a single day, identifying them by time. The second section is concerned with more restrictive patterns based on the strength or weakness of the daily opening price. These are also considered in conjunction with the time of day. From there we look at weekly and weekend traits and finally at the types of reversals and the nature of their influence. These techniques can be considered as complementary when used sequentially, or they can verify the validity of another test when they overlap. Both situations are included as the studies are developed.

TIME OF DAY

Floor traders, and those who watch the momentary fluctuations of prices, develop habits en masse that can be distinguished in the periodic movement of prices throughout the day. Angas called these the "tides of the daily prices." Over the years the great increase in participants may have uniformly added liquidity to each pit, but certain patterns still persist.

There are a number of reasons for the regular movement of prices. Since we are dealing with day trading most of the positions taken on any day are also liquidated that same day; a trade entered in the morning will be closed out by the afternoon so that no margin must be put up by an exchange member. Scalpers, who do not hold positions for more than a few minutes, add liquidity to the trading and during mid-morning frequently have coffee together; you would sometimes do best having your coffee break with them rather than trying to get a good fill. All traders develop habits of trading at particular times. Many orders placed through wire houses go in Market-on-Open. Other speculators may wait for the reaction which follows the opening trading. More recently, larger funds and managed accounts have been using close-only orders.

As a day trader there are key times to watch. The opening ring is an opportunity to evaluate the situation, but not to place an order. On a strong open a day trader will sell and on a weak open he will buy; this means that he will have to "even up" later and reinforce the opening direction with his own liquidating position. On a strong open without a downward reaction all local selling is absorbed by the market and later attempts of the locals to liquidate will hold the prices up. In any event, you can always expect the floor to take the opposite position to the opening direction, usually causing a reversal early in the session.

Tubbs' Stock Market Correspondence Lessons (#13) explains the dominant patterns in the stock market (given a 10:00-to-3:00 session).

1. If a rally after the open has returned to the opening price by 1:00 o'clock, the day is expected to close weaker.
2. If the market is strong from 11:00 to 12:00 it will continue from 12:00 to 1:00.
3. If a reversal from 1:00 to 1:30 finds support at 1:30, it will close strong.
4. If the market has been bullish until 2:00 o'clock it will probably continue until the close and into the next day.
5. A rally that continues for 2 or 3 days as in (4) will most likely end on an 11:00 o'clock reversal.
6. In general, a late afternoon reaction down after a strong day shows a pending reversal.

Putting these together we get the following possibilities (among others):

A strong open with a reversal at 11:00 not reaching the opening price, then strength from 11:00 to 1:00, a short reversal until 1:30 and a strong close; according to (5) another strong open the following day

A strong open that reverses by 11:00, continuing lower until 1:00, reverses again until 1:30 and then closes weak

Merrill's work shows the hourly pattern of the stock market as in Table 14-1. The chart clearly indicates a bullish bias, with 1963 the most obvious. The pattern is uniform and similar in nature to what we would expect: early trending, an adjustment, and some fluctuation up and down. Contrary to commodities, these 4 years show extremely consistent strength on the opening with a sell-off on the close.

Table 14-1 Merrill's Hourly Stock Market Patterns

	Time during trading session					
	10:00	11:00	12:00	1:00	2:00	3:00
1962	−	+	−	−	+	−
1963	+	+	+	+	+	−
1964	+	+	−	−	+	−
1965	+	+	−	−	−	−

Commodity prices may have regular patterns, but these patterns may occur with downward moves as well as upward ones. You are just as likely to see an opening sell-off with a rally on the close. The studies here will combine these patterns into one.

In commodities the patterns are similar, with their own personality due to shorter, earlier hours (9:30 to 1:15 for the Chicago Board of Trade). Knowing the daily time patterns would not only help a day trader, but also aid any speculator to time his entry to better advantage. Diagram 14-2 shows the time pattern for the Chicago Mercantile Exchange Live Cattle contract (open from 9:05 to 12:45). 76 consecutive trading days were tabulated for the June 75 contract from February 1 through May 31, 1975, an active period for cattle. The left scale of the chart shows the number of

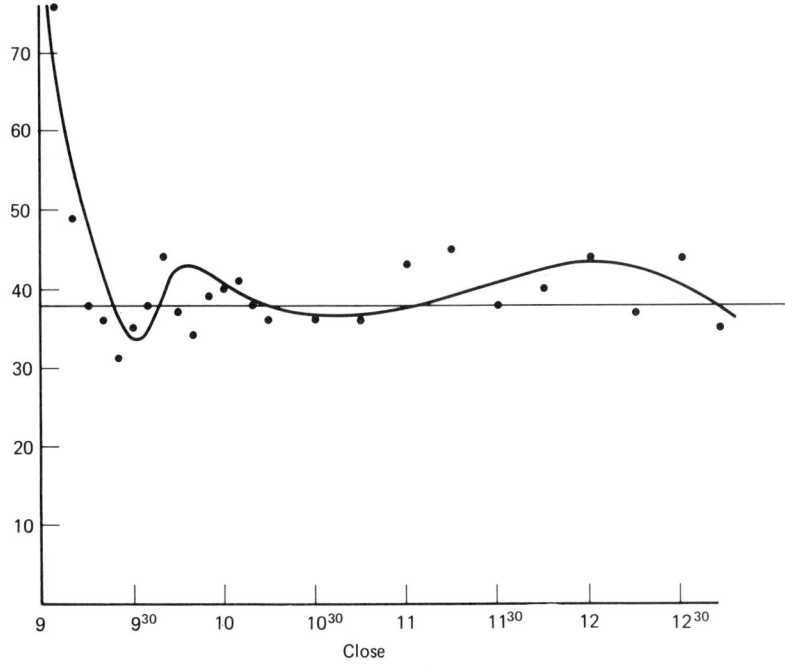

Diagram 14-2 Intraday time patterns, June 75 Cattle.

PATTERN RECOGNITION   211

occurrences out of the total 76 days and the bottom shows the time of day. The line appearing in the top half of the chart indicates price movement in the direction of the opening price (from the prior close); the lower half shows a reversal trend. Measurements were initially taken every five minutes and later every fifteen minutes, since an entry into a new position would be likely to occur early in the day.

The diagram shows that trading in the direction of the opening price slows down immediately until by 9:30, 25 minutes after the open, the price direction has usually reversed. There is a subsequent steady change in direction back and forth throughout the day.

By showing 2 consecutive days of cattle price movement, Table 14-2 demonstrates how the data were accumulated.

Table 14-2   Accumulating Time-of-Day Data

Time		Price	Direction from last	Direction from open
		Monday		
9:05	(1)	45.15	+	O
9:30	(2)	45.25	+	O
10:00	(3)	45.10	−	X
10:30	(4)	45.05	−	X
11:00	(5)	45.20	+	O
11:30	(6)	45.30	+	O
12:00	(7)	45.40	+	O
12:30	(8)	45.30	−	X
		Tuesday		
9:05	(9)	45.25	−	O
9:30	(10)	45.35	+	X
10:00	(11)	45.45	+	X
10:30	(12)	45.40	−	O
11:00	(13)	45.50	+	X
11:30	(14)	45.40	−	O
12:00	(15)	45.20	−	O
12:30	(16)	45.05	−	O

Although the table actually used 5-minute intervals from 9:00 to 10:15 A.M. and then 15-minute intervals from 10:15 until the close at 12:45, Table 14-1 is expressed in half-hour increments. If Friday's closing price was 45.00, Monday's open of 45.15 was indicated by a "+" for absolute direction and an "O" for opening direction. Any half-hour interval showing a price rise was marked with a relational symbol "O" and a reversal with an "X"; Tuesday opened lower but the opening direction is still given as "O." Every interval with lower prices is in the opening direction and is marked "O." By adding the 76 test days together we get the following score:

Table 14-3 Time Reversal Patterns[a]

9:05	76	9:35	38	10:05	35	11:15	31
9:10	27	9:40	32	10:10	38	11:30	38
9:15	38	9:45	39	10:15	40	11:45	36
9:20	40	9:50	42	10:30	40	12:00	32
9:25	45	9:55	37	10:45	40	12:15	39
9:30	41	10:00	36	10:00	33	12:30	32
						Close	41

[a] A more recent look at June 1976 Cattle showed very similar results.

Knowing the direction of the price movement does not mean that trading these intervals will be profitable. In order to evaluate the potential we also need to know the anticipated size of the move; we can then select the interval with the greatest potential for movement in the direction of the time-of-day pattern. By observing Diagram 14-2 we can pick the intervals to study from the tops and bottoms of the cycles:

Example 14-1 Selected Time Intervals

a. Opening to 9:20
b. 9:20 to 10:00
c. 10:00 to 11:00
d. 9:20 to 11:00
e. 9:20 to 12:00
f. 12:00 to closing

For each interval, we measured the average range from high to low (volatility) and the net result of this span (additive bias) as it related to absolute higher or lower prices without considering the "relative direction" that we used to create the curve of time patterns (Diagram 14-1). The results, shown in Table 14-4, indicated that the narrowest ranges, (b) and (c), were early, moving only over a total range of 14 points.

Table 14-4 Summarized Time Data

Time	Average volatility	Additive bias	Points moved in direction of open
a. Open–9:20	17.3	+4.9	+4.4
b. 9:20–10:00	14.3	+1.5	+.6
c. 10:00–11:00	14.2	+3.7	+3.9
d. 9:20–11:00	21.7	+5.3	+4.6
e. 9:20–12:00	25.8	+7.2	+3.3
f. 12:00–Close	19.6	+3.2	−1.2

PATTERN RECOGNITION

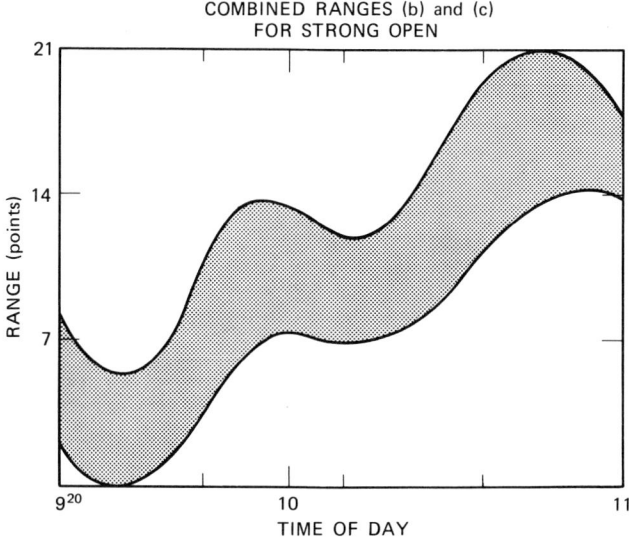

Diagram 14-3   Cattle price ranges 9:20 A.M.–11:00 A.M.

We draw this conclusion from (d), which points out that the two intervals from 9:20 to 10:00 and from 10:00 to 11:00 were of generally the same direction, since (d), which represented the total period, was 21.7 points, 50% greater. Diagram 14-2 describes the likely combination of the intervals.

This results in a midmorning drift that nets a total of 4.6 points in the direction of the opening price and a probable maximum potential of 21 points by entering a position between 9:20 and 10:00 and then liquidating between 10:00 and 11:00. For cattle during the test period the magnitude of the move did not appear worth the risk, but the same pattern might be profitably traded in a more volatile market.

When trying to find other market patterns it is suggested that you restrict your acceptable data to stronger or weaker openings. For example, a gap open higher or lower by 5 to 20 points in cattle would indicate a potentially more volatile day and allow greater price reactions. We can expect more uniform results because of our other work in constructing the table of price variation, which appears later in this chapter. Restricting your trading to days of higher price volatility will reduce your trading possibilities but should improve your results.

Wait 20 To 30 Minutes

If you want to trade against the trend the best opportunity would be 5 minutes after the open. You have the advantage of the opening momentum carrying prices further in the opening directions and you have reduced the time you must wait for a reversal to occur. By waiting 20 to 30 minutes you will find an opening reversal, which will allow you to enter in the same direction of the opening but at a more favorable price.

RELATING THE OPENING TRADE TO THE PRIOR DAY

Another analysis performed on the time-pattern chart was a correlation to determine whether the period from market open to 9:20 (15 minutes), related to the prior day's direction, could help predict the direction of the "tides" during the current day. The 15-minute interval was chosen as enough time to react to results and place an order. The two situations distinguished were the relationship of the first trade to the prior day's direction and the direction of the early trading, using the first 15 minutes. Since the same 76 days of cattle trading were used, it must be noted that the conclusions are based on a small sample and, while we expect them to be valid, there should be some variation between these results and those based on a large sample.

Table 14-5 Likelihood of Movement in the Same Direction as the Open

	Cases			
	(1)	(2)	(3)	(4)
Open– 9:20	39%	—	—	—
9:20–10:00	52%	57%	58%	50%
10:00–11:00	43%	40%	35%	48%
9:00–11:00	45%	47%	43%	48%
9:20–12:00	43%	49%	43%	44%
12:00–Close	46%	53%	48%	42%

Four cases were observed, using the time intervals shown in Table 14-5. The percentages are calculated as the likelihood of movement in a specific direction relative to the conditions of the opening trade and opening interval:

1. The opening trade continued in the direction of the prior close.
2. The opening 15-minute interval was consistent with the direction of the opening trade.
3. The opening trade and opening interval both continued the direction of the prior close.
4. The opening trade and opening interval both continued opposite to the direction of the prior close.

You can notice that most of the intervals observed moved in the direction opposite to the opening trade. This will support the more extensive trading study presented in the table of price variation. The two most extreme entries are the 39% in column 1 and the 35% in column 3. The first shows that by 9:20 there have been reversals of 61%, further supporting our previous conclusions. The second case, in column 3, shows that an opening and opening interval that continues in the direction of the prior close has reversed 65% of the time in the 10:00-to-11:00 A.M. interval.

Highs and Lows of the Day

In selecting a place to enter the market during a single day trade, it would be a great advantage to know the time of day at which the highest or lowest price is likely to occur. To understand this, Diagram 14-4 presents a combined tabulation of both the daily highs and lows positioned at the time they occurred. The pattern is very clear, indicating that the opening and closing ranges are most likely to be highest or lowest,

PATTERN RECOGNITION

with 11:00 o'clock as the only midday possibility. No attempt was made to determine whether a high at the open had a low at 11:00 o'clock or at the close; nor was any relative positioning of the high-low observed. Separate charts of only highs and only lows proved that there was no distinction in the patterns—highs were just as likely to occur at the three peaks as were lows.

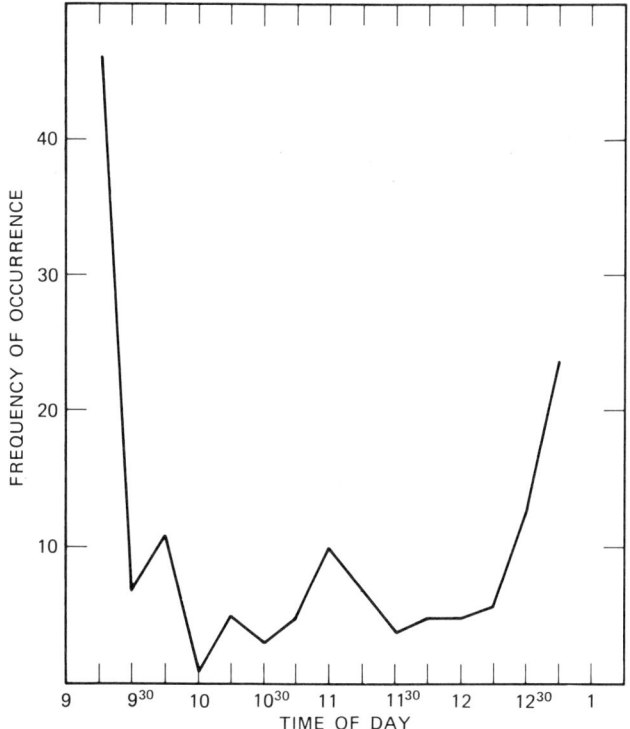

Diagram 14-4 Combined occurrence of highs and lows.

There are simple ways in which this small piece of information could be of advantage. After the opening range has been formed, watch for the breakout of the range and assume the other direction is a high or low. For our example, the breakout will occur to the upside and the bottom of the range will be considered the daily low. You can *buy* the opening breakout with a stop below the opening range. Look for the high of the day at 11:00 o'clock. If there is a test of the highs at 11:00, liquidate your position, assuming that the resistance will hold. If there is another upside breakout, buy again and anticipate the highs of the day at the close. If no test of the highs occur at 11:00 hold your position until the close; if support is broken, close out or reverse and expect the lows of the day at the close.

DAILY PRICE VARIATION

The ability of a commodity price to fluctuate widely may be related to the strength or weakness of the daily opening. A gap opening of considerable strength allows a correspondingly greater reaction after the opening range and may show more consistency

Table 14-6 Table of Price Variation—Soybeans

Open from prior close	Continued same direction	Close			Trading range			Next day open	Number of cases
		Adjusted from open	Reversed from open	Crossed prior close	Adjusted after open	Continued from open		Direction same as prior	
25.00	20.00	60.00	20.00	26.67	46.67	26.67		60.00	15
24.00	.00	.00	.00	.00	.00	.00		.00	0
23.00	100.00	.00	.00	.00	100.00	.00		100.00	1
22.00	.00	.00	.00	.00	.00	.00		.00	0
21.00	.00	.00	.00	.00	.00	.00		.00	0
20.00	.00	88.89	11.11	16.67	11.11	72.22		77.78	18
19.00	.00	.00	.00	.00	.00	.00		.00	0
18.00	100.00	.00	.00	.00	100.00	.00		100.00	1
17.00	100.00	.00	.00	.00	100.00	.00		100.00	1
16.00	.00	.00	100.00	100.00	.00	.00		100.00	1
15.00	12.50	75.00	12.50	37.50	25.00	37.50		62.50	8
14.00	60.00	20.00	20.00	40.00	20.00	40.00		40.00	5
13.00	50.00	25.00	25.00	25.00	75.00	.00		50.00	4
12.00	40.00	40.00	20.00	20.00	80.00	.00		40.00	5
11.00	75.00	.00	25.00	25.00	75.00	.00		25.00	4
10.00	16.67	66.67	16.67	25.00	33.33	41.67		58.33	12
9.00	44.44	55.56	.00	22.22	44.44	33.33		77.78	9
8.00	33.33	26.67	40.00	53.33	46.67	.00		46.67	15
7.00	.00	.00	100.00	100.00	.00	.00		25.00	4
6.00	76.47	11.76	11.76	23.53	70.59	5.88		64.71	17
5.00	84.21	10.53	5.26	36.84	52.63	10.53		31.58	19
4.00	44.00	24.00	32.00	68.00	28.00	4.00		36.00	25
3.00	59.26	11.11	29.63	37.04	33.33	29.63		59.26	27
2.00	61.11	11.11	27.78	66.67	22.22	11.11		44.44	36
1.00	61.90	11.90	26.19	52.38	35.71	11.90		47.62	42

0.00	.00	.00	.00	.00	.00	.00	65
−1.00	40.51	11.39	48.10	84.81	7.59	7.59	54.43	79
−2.00	69.70	.00	30.30	57.58	33.33	9.09	45.45	33
−3.00	47.06	5.88	47.06	76.47	20.59	2.94	44.12	34
−4.00	56.25	9.38	34.38	56.25	34.38	9.38	62.50	32
−5.00	45.83	20.83	33.33	62.50	29.17	8.33	54.17	24
−6.00	58.33	20.83	20.83	50.00	41.67	8.33	54.17	24
−7.00	41.67	25.00	33.33	58.33	25.00	16.67	66.67	12
−8.00	71.43	.00	28.57	28.57	71.43	.00	57.14	7
−9.00	58.33	33.33	8.33	41.67	58.33	.00	50.00	12
−10.00	75.00	12.50	12.50	12.50	62.50	25.00	75.00	8
−11.00	80.00	20.00	.00	.00	100.00	.00	60.00	5
−12.00	25.00	25.00	50.00	50.00	50.00	.00	100.00	4
−13.00	33.33	.00	66.67	66.67	33.33	.00	33.33	3
−14.00	.00	.00	.00	.00	.00	.00	.00	0
−15.00	57.14	42.86	.00	.00	85.71	14.29	71.43	7
−16.00	100.00	.00	.00	.00	50.00	50.00	50.00	2
−17.00	100.00	.00	.00	.00	100.00	.00	.00	1
−18.00	.00	.00	.00	.00	.00	.00	.00	0
−19.00	50.00	33.33	16.67	16.67	50.00	33.33	50.00	6
−20.00	13.33	80.00	6.67	6.67	33.33	60.00	46.67	15
−21.00	.00	100.00	.00	.00	100.00	.00	100.00	1
−22.00	.00	.00	.00	.00	.00	.00	.00	0
−23.00	.00	.00	.00	.00	.00	.00	.00	0
−24.00	.00	.00	.00	.00	.00	.00	.00	0

in later direction than does a quiet open. To do this we created a table of daily price variation.[2] The table was constructed in such a way that we could determine the magnitude of the continuation and reaction to large opening gaps, and the relationship to the closing price. A strong open followed by a stronger close would allow a speculator to buy on a reaction while a consistent weak close after a strong open would allow him to sell. The time of day for these trades can be selected by considering the previous section.

We read the daily price variation table (shown as Table 14-6) from left to right as follows:

Opening price is the number of points or cents in the gap opening; the zero value separates higher openings (above) from the lower openings (below). All data on that line refers only to the specific gap and are not the accumulation of all larger or smaller gaps.

Closing price—continued is a tabulation of days in which the close was above the higher open or below the lower open (in percent).

Closing price—adjusted indicates that a percentage of those gap openings closed in the range between the opening gap and the prior closing price. For strong openings it implies that the opening was extreme but the direction was consistent.

Closing price—reversal shows the percentage of cases in which the opening gap was followed by a closing change of direction.

The *closing price—adjusted and reversal* columns added together give the total percentage of all cases in which the opening gap was followed by a closing reversal.

As an example of how to read the table, consider a soybean open of 5.80 following a prior close of 5.70; the entire entry will be placed on the +10 row. Had the opening been 5.65 the entry would have been on the row starting −5. The next three columns marked "closing price" show the relative distribution of the closing price. For 10¢ gaps in soybeans we have only 16.67% of the cases closing higher, 66.67% adjusting. A total of 83.34% closed lower than the open, indicating that a short position at the opening price or better is a likely winner. Notice that in 100% of the cases of a gap opening of 20¢ (the limit at the time) the subsequent closing price was lower. The situations with a high percentage of continuation (17¢ and 18¢) were only based on one case and is difficult to determine their relevance.

The total number of cases in Table 14-6 of 10¢ gaps or better were 59, with 75% of them closing lower. By combining the observations stated in the previous section we can wait 10 to 15 minutes after the opening session and expect prices to continue higher before entering a sell order. Any price higher than the open increases your chances of success about 75% and reduces your risk. All positions should be liquidated by the close. Since the overall results do not favor the closing price below the prior close it might be practical to place an order to buy back the position below the prior close.

The limit open of 20¢ in our example is of particular interest. Of the 18 cases qualifying, all 18 closed off the limit, two of them closing lower than the prior close. While this becomes an attractive trade it also merits extreme caution, which can be imple-

---

[2] The complete results are presented in Appendix 10.

mented by placing a sell-stop slightly below the limit with a liquidation order if prices go back to the 20¢ limit.

The next three columns, the fifth through seventh, allow you to identify the type of movement expected each day. The fifth column, "crossed prior close," shows the percent of times that soybeans crossed below the prior close after opening higher (looking at the 10¢ row). The 25% entry means that three out of twelve times the opening of 10¢ higher was followed by trading below the prior close. Tying this to the suggestion of shorting when the prices opened strong we can expect profits in excess of the prior close in 25% of the cases. The sixth and seventh columns give "adjusted after open" and "continued from open" data. The first shows the frequency of pullbacks after strong openings to between the prior close and today's opening. The "continued from open" column includes only those trades for which the opening was also the low—all trading was higher for the day.

The eighth column, "next opening direction same as prior," offers some interesting possibilities. As you may expect, it shows the probability of the next day's opening being in the same direction as today's opening. The results are also expected—the more extreme (stronger or weaker) the opening, the more likely the next opening will be in the same direction. If you trade against the trend by selling short after a strong opening, this tells you to be sure to liquidate your position by the close of trading because tomorrow's opening will be against you. If you're trading with the trend, use the next day to your advantage. An alternative to the first trading method is waiting until the closing session to take a long position, then expect a gap opening in your favor the next day. If the open tomorrow is also strong, short after the opening and buy on the close in order to recycle into the price-variation chart.

Each commodity may have a pattern of its own. The grains seem to be different from some other commodities. Cocoa represents another pattern where the smaller gap openings reverse and the larger ones continue in the opening direction for both the current closing price and the direction of the next opening. It would be advantageous to study each chart for this turning point.

THREE STUDIES IN MARKET MOVEMENT— WEEKLY, WEEKEND, AND REVERSAL PATTERNS

The next three sections are concerned with longer periods of time than the previous ones. The first, on *weekly patterns*, looks only at the closing prices during a 5-day week from Monday through Friday in order to find recurring close-only patterns. In the same manner as we considered a single day, a week has its own integrity and can be considered independent of the long-term trend or seasonal influences. The study attempts to isolate predictive patterns; for example, if Monday through Thursday were all up, what is the possibility of Friday being up also? If the weekly trend can be clearly identified, should we expect a correction on Friday due to "evening up?" Since patterns only represent human behavior, we would expect to find interesting results.

The weekend patterns are considered independently in the second study. The opening direction on Monday could restore the trend of the prior week if those traders who liquidate on Friday intend to resume their positions. The weekend is also an extended period for unexpected news or a build-up of public interest. The study will attempt to relate the direction of the Monday opening price to some pattern of the preceding week.

Reversal patterns are not as clear nor as conclusive as the other two analyses, but can be used to explain and confirm other patterns. It also provides a filter and timing device for other methods.

A Study in Weekly Patterns

During their constant exposure to the market, professional traders often observe patterns in price movement. Although instinctual and not scientifically based, the acceptance of these patterns are as old as the market itself. In *Reminiscences of a Stock Operator* the fictional character Larry Livingston (assumed to be Jesse Livermore) begins his career recording prices on a chalk board above the floor of the New York Stock Exchange, finally becoming aware of patterns within these prices. The most accepted occurrence of a pattern is the Tuesday reversal, which is taken as commonplace by close observers of the market. When questioned why a strong soybean market on the first of the week is followed by a weak day, a member of the Board of Trade would shrug his shoulders and quote: "Up on Monday, down on Tuesday." If this is true, there is a trading opportunity.

If a commonly accepted idea is not enough to be convincing, consider the additional rationalization about human behavior: the weekend allows a build-up of sentiment, which should result in higher activity on Monday; coupled with adding back positions that were liquidated prior to the weekend, this may cause a disproportionate move on Monday, especially early in the session. With this overbought or oversold condition, it is likely that Tuesday would show an adjustment. So much for hypothesizing.

The first aspect of the test was to define the weekly pattern. We did this in terms of the Friday-to-Monday move (close to close). Monday always received the value X, regardless of whether its direction from Friday was up ($+$) or down ($-$). For each day that closed in the same direction as the Friday-to-Monday move, we used another X; when the close reversed direction, we used an O. Therefore XOXXO means that Tuesday and Friday, represented by O, closed in opposite directions from the prior Friday-to-Monday move, while Wednesday and Thursday were in the same direction. This could have meant either of the situations:

Example 14-2

		(1)	(2)
Monday	X	Up	Down
Tuesday	O	Down	Up
Wednesday	X	Up	Down
Thursday	X	Up	Down
Friday	O	Down	Up

PATTERN RECOGNITION

It could be that there is a distinction between the cases that start up on Monday compared to down, but in trying to analyze what we considered market psychology, we combined the situations. Since there are 16 possible combinations of patterns using our notation we tested all of them for the following commodities and contracts:

Table 14-7 Weekly Pattern Tests

Contract	Period	Commodity
Jun	1970–1975	Cattle
Dec	1970–1975	Cocoa
Dec	1970–1975	Copper
Dec	1970–1975	Cotton
May	1970–1975	Potatoes
Dec	1973–1975	Soybean meal
Jly	1974	Soybeans
Aug	1975	Soybeans
Sep	1970–1975	Sugar
Dec	1972–1975	Swiss franc
Sep	1974–1976	Wheat

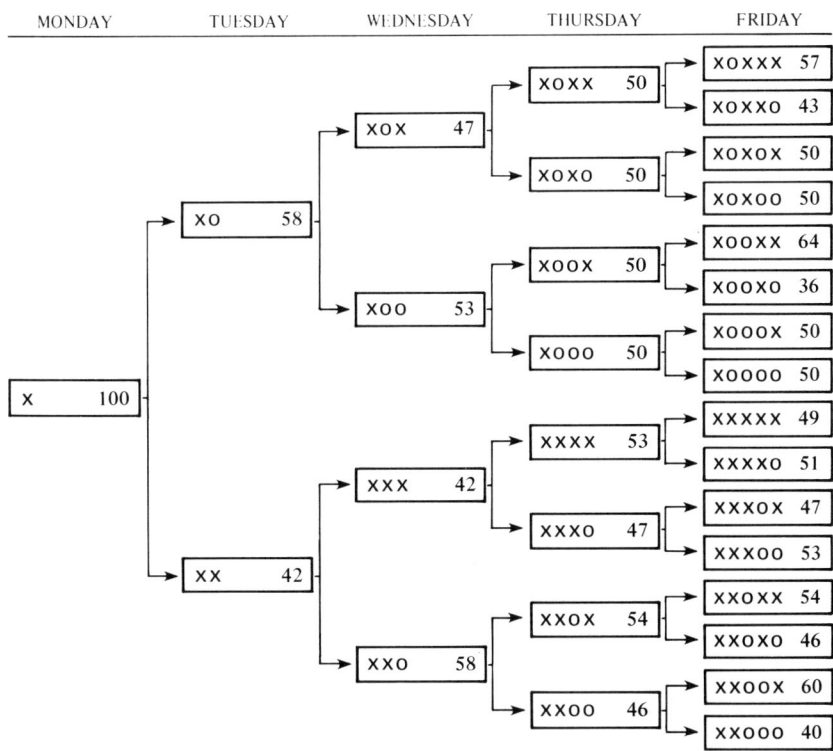

Chart 14-1 23 commodities 1976 (873 weeks tested).

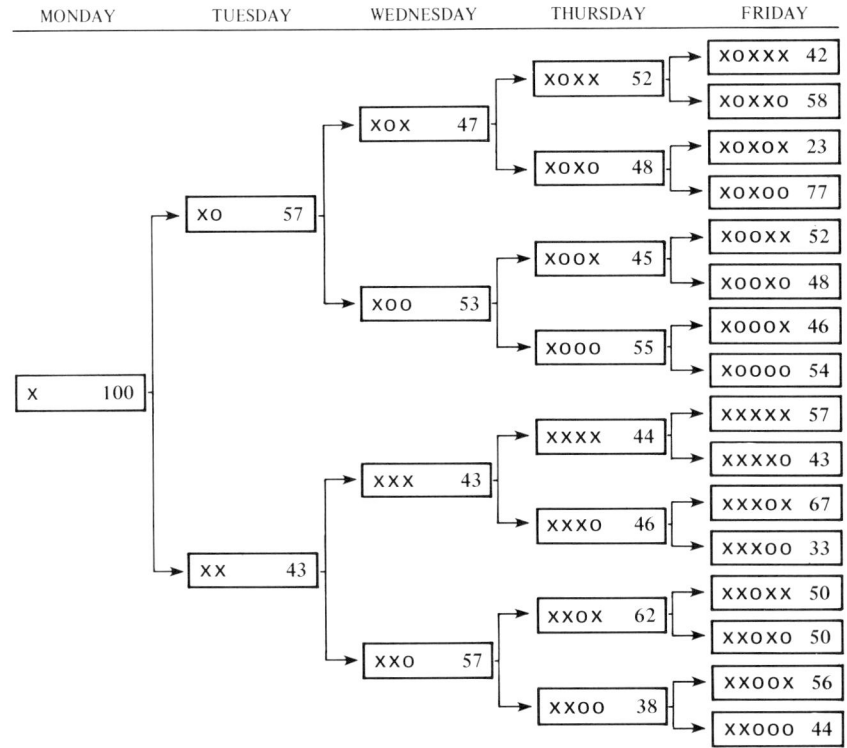

HIGH PROBABILITY TRADES:
IF **XX** THEN EXPECT **O**; IF **XXO** THEN REVERSE AND EXPECT **XXOX**
IF **XXX** THEN C/O
IF **XXXO** THEN EXPECT **X**
IF **XOXO** THEN EXPECT **O**

Chart 14-2   1976 metals (171 weeks tested).

The results of these tests are shown in Appendix 8. Although we never found a use for our groupings, we did coin the words "single," "blocked," and "staggered" reversals to represent similar types of patterns. Once tested, we formed probability charts representing the likelihood of a continued or reversed close the next day. This was done by counting the number of cases that reversed on Tuesdays (XO) and those that did not reverse (XX). We continued in the same way, asking: "If a particular pattern has occurred through today, what is the probability of a reversal or continuation tomorrow?" Charts 14-1 through 14-8 show the results of these calculations for specially selected commodities and groupings:

- 23 combined commodities (1976)
- 4 combined metals (1976)
- Grains and soybean complex (1976)
- Cattle, potatoes, copper, cotton, cocoa (individually)

PATTERN RECOGNITION

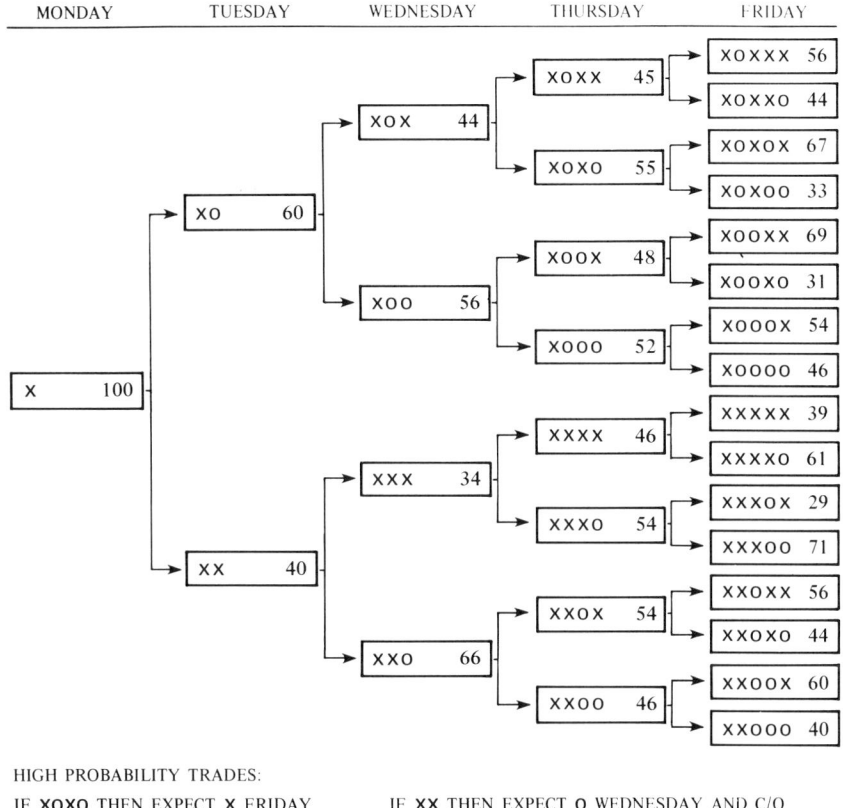

HIGH PROBABILITY TRADES:
IF XOXO THEN EXPECT X FRIDAY
IF XOOX THEN EXPECT X FRIDAY
IF XXXX THEN EXPECT O FRIDAY
IF XXXO THEN EXPECT O FRIDAY
IF XXOO THEN EXPECT X FRIDAY

IF XX THEN EXPECT O WEDNESDAY AND C/O

ALSO REVERSE MONDAY ON OPEN, C/O TUESDAY
IF ANOTHER REVERSAL, OR ELSE C/O WEDNESDAY
ON THE CLOSE.

Chart 14-3 1976 grains and soybeans complex.

Before going on to an analysis of trading possibilities, recall the original Tuesday reversal. From the charts just mentioned we can calculate the past occurrences of this reversal.

Table 14-8 Pattern Continuation

Commodity	History of continuation (percent)			
	Tues	Wed	Thurs	Fri
23 combined	43	44	51	54
4 Metals	43	46	44	48
Grains & Soybean complex	40	40	48	57

224   COMMODITY TRADING SYSTEMS AND METHODS

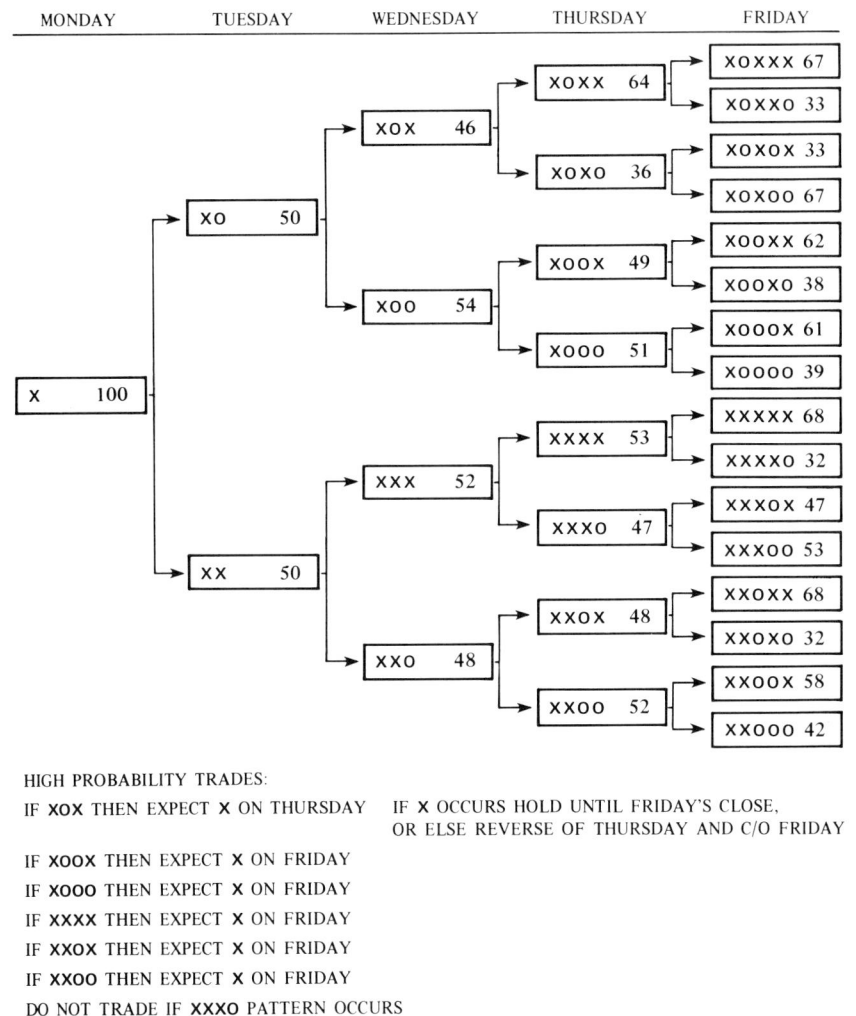

HIGH PROBABILITY TRADES:
IF **XOX** THEN EXPECT **X** ON THURSDAY   IF **X** OCCURS HOLD UNTIL FRIDAY'S CLOSE,
                                                                                OR ELSE REVERSE OF THURSDAY AND C/O FRIDAY
IF **XOOX** THEN EXPECT **X** ON FRIDAY
IF **XOOO** THEN EXPECT **X** ON FRIDAY
IF **XXXX** THEN EXPECT **X** ON FRIDAY
IF **XXOX** THEN EXPECT **X** ON FRIDAY
IF **XXOO** THEN EXPECT **X** ON FRIDAY
DO NOT TRADE IF **XXXO** PATTERN OCCURS

Chart 14-4   Cattle 1970–1975.

It is evident that Tuesday is the most likely candidate for a reversal, with Wednesday close behind. Each successive day becomes more likely to return to the original Monday direction. Individual commodities should be studied with caution and not expected to perform in line with a group pattern. For less liquid items you might find the behavioral characteristics readily changing based on the dominant influences in the market. Maine potatoes, related to other commodities as a "food," shows no tendency to reverse with the weekly pattern of .51, .51, .55, .52 for Tuesday through Friday.

The reversal patterns offer opportunities for trading profits. Consider the cattle chart, Chart 14-4. By scanning all the entires we see seven combinations with over 60% probability of occurrence (provided we get in the day before). In order to take advantage of these situations, we would have to place close-only orders on the prior day. Since six of the situations occur on Friday, Thursday becomes the day for placing

PATTERN RECOGNITION

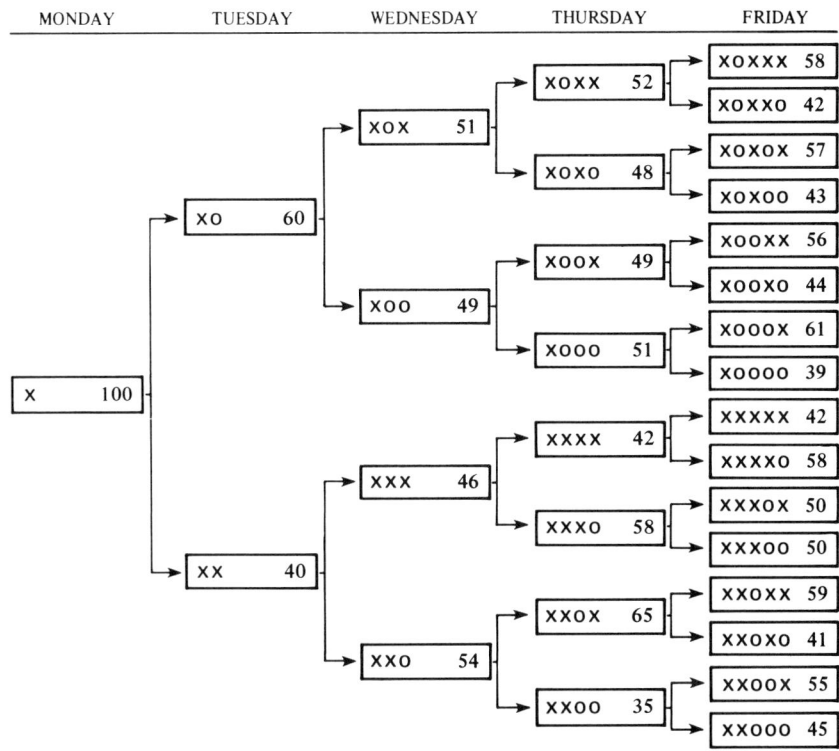

HIGH PROBABILITY TRADES:

IF X OCCURS THEN EXPECT O AND C/O
IF XXO OCCURS THEN EXPECT X; IF YES, THEN HOLD AND C/O FRIDAY
IF XOOO OCCURS THEN EXPECT X

Chart 14-5   Cocoa 1970–1975.

specific orders. It is coincidental that five situations—XOXX, XOOX, XOOO, XXXX, and XXOX—all show a strong tendency to be followed by an X on Friday. By following through a sample week, you can see the technique needed to implement this approach.

1. *Monday* closed up from Friday's close (X). Since the probability of a reversal on Tuesday is 50%, we do nothing.
2. *Tuesday* closed down from Monday's close (XO) forming a reversal pattern. We now follow the upper branch.
3. *Wednesday* continues the downward trend (XOO). We must now plan our order for Thursday if we are to take advantage of Friday.

Assuming that X means up for this example, we can conclude that regardless of whether Thursday closes up (XOOX) or down (XOOO) there is better than a 60% probability that there will be an up (X) move on Friday. This can be seen by looking at the fifth and seventh entries in the Friday column. Note that both combinations end in X, indicating a Friday move in the same direction as Monday. To trade this properly, place an order to buy, Market-on-Close (MOC), Thursday, and liquidate the trade Friday, MOC.

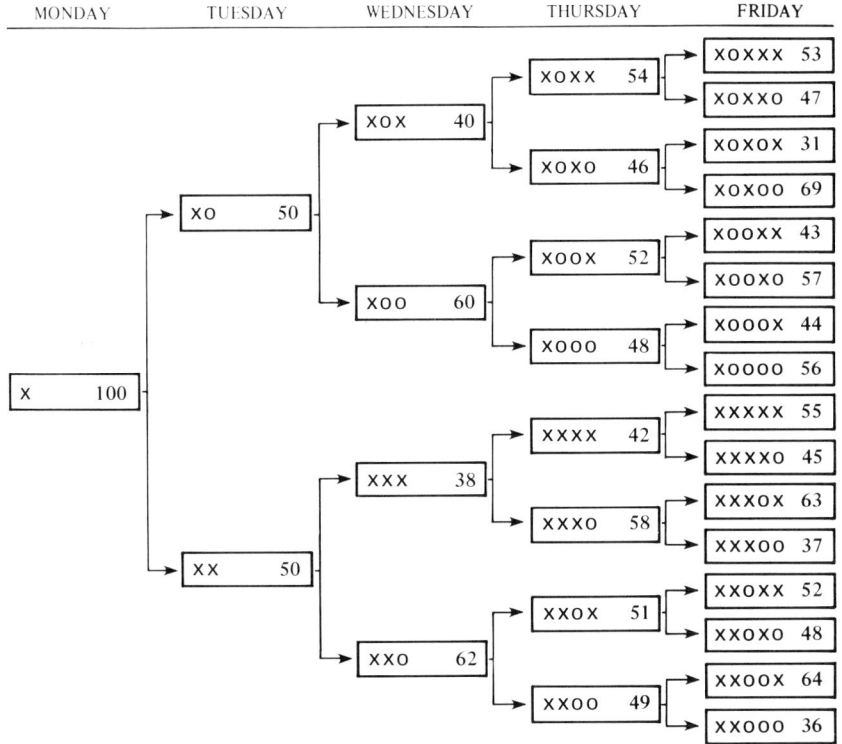

HIGH PROBABILITY TRADES:
IF XX OR XO THEN O ON WEDNESDAY, THEN C/O
IF XOXO THEN EXPECT O ON FRIDAY
IF XXXO THEN EXPECT X ON FRIDAY
IF XXOO THEN EXPECT O ON FRIDAY

Chart 14-6   Copper 1970–1975.

Consider a more complicated example using the same cattle chart, Chart 14-4:

1. *Monday* opens up (X).
2. *Tuesday* reverses (XO).
3. *Wednesday* reverses again (XOX), closing up from Tuesday.

Again we must plan for the two Friday possibilities, entries 1 and 4. In this case, the added problem is that the first entry is profitable if the Friday move is up (the same as Monday), while the fourth entry is profitable if prices go down (reverse of Monday). An order placed on Thursday would be to buy MOC, if Thursday closes above Wednesday; or sell MOC, if Thursday closes below Wednesday. When in doubt, wait until Friday. Remember to close out either trade on Friday, MOC.

An alternate possibility is to wait until Friday. If Thursday prices closed above Wednesday, at 45.00 for example, place an order Friday to buy at 45.00 or better (OB). If you can beat the price, you have increased your profits—if you miss, you have destroyed the purpose of a high-probability study.

One last example. The Thursday cattle combination of XOXX yielded 64%, a high probability that should also be used for trading. In order to combine the Thursday

PATTERN RECOGNITION

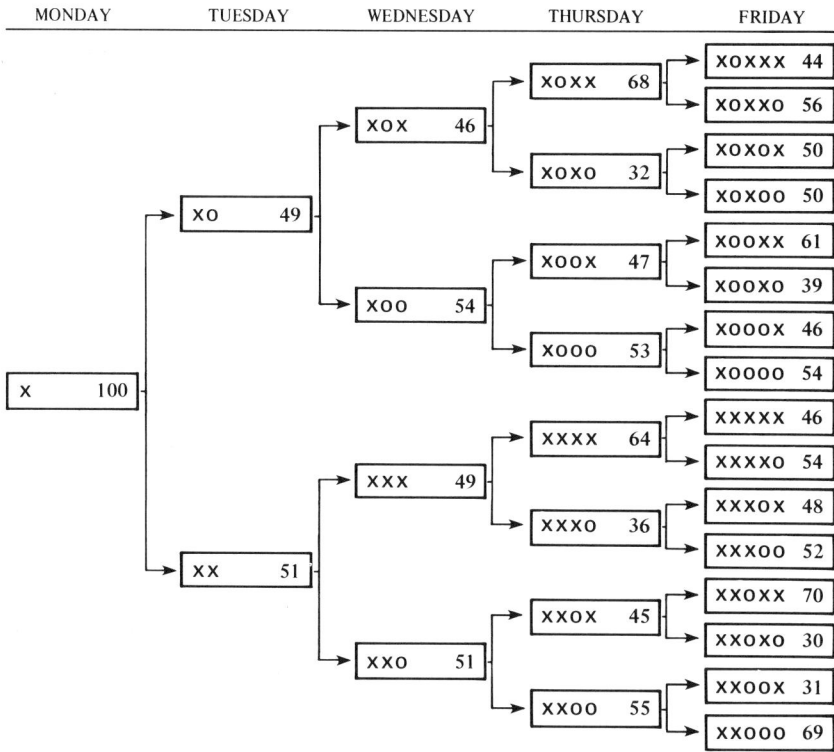

HIGH PROBABILITY TRADES:
IF **XOX** OCCURS, EXPECT **X** THURSDAY AND C/O
IF **XXX** OCCURS, EXPECT **X** THURSDAY AND C/O
IF **XOOX** OCCURS, EXPECT **X** FRIDAY
IF **XXOX** OCCURS, EXPECT **X** FRIDAY
IF **XXOO** OCCURS, EXPECT **O** FRIDAY
MAXIMUM OF 1 TRADE PER WEEK

Chart 14-7 Cotton 1970–1975.

and Friday patterns, we proceed as follows:

1. *Monday* closes up from Friday (X).
2. *Tuesday* reverses (XO).
3. *Wednesday* becomes the key day for this pattern, since we must act on the prior close. In this case, if Wednesday closes up from Tuesday, forming an XOX pattern, we wait to buy on the close on Wednesday, in expectation of prices continuing up on Thursday.
4. *Thursday* has two courses of action. If we were successful in predicting a price increase we have an XOXX pattern and there is a 67% chance of another increase on Friday. We can take advantage of our current long position and hold that position through Friday, liquidating MOC. If we were wrong about Thursday, and now have an XOXO pattern, we reverse our position and take the 76% chance of a continuing price decline, closing out the trade Friday, MOC.

On the bottom of each chart are rules developed from observing the high-probability situations. Since probability does not mean profitability, these rules had to be tested

228   COMMODITY TRADING SYSTEMS AND METHODS

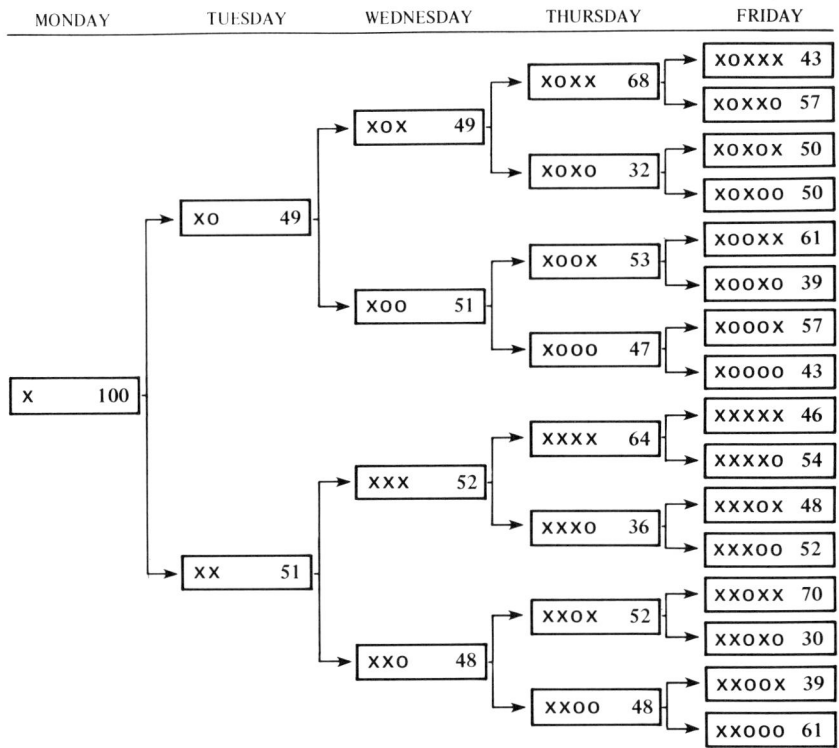

HIGH PROBABILITY TRADES:
IF XOX, THEN EXPECT X, IF YES THEN REVERSE AND EXPECT O ON FRIDAY
IF XXX, THEN EXPECT X AND C/O
IF XOOX, THEN EXPECT X AND C/O
IF XXOX, THEN EXPECT X AND C/O
IF XXOO, THEN EXPECT O AND C/O

Chart 14-8   Maine Potatoes 1970–1975.

on a trade-by-trade basis. For cattle, we tested the February 76 contract from February 24, 1975, through December 31, 1975, recording the day the trade was initiated, the date, position (long or short), entry and exit price, and the profit or loss in points. The commission was omitted because of the great variance in fees due to the nature of the person trading; commissions based on minimum exchange rates were subtracted after profits were calculated. The results on contracts tested were:

Table 14-9a   Results of Using Weekly Patterns

	Number of trades	Reliability (%)	Gross Profit	Commission	Net Profit
February 76 cattle	33	70	$2756	$1320	$1436
January 76 copper	53	64	$4325	$2226	$2099
March 76 soybeans	66	68	$4850	$3300	$1550
March 76 wheat	52	67	$3537	$2600	$ 937

Table 14-9b February 76 Cattle Trades, 2-24-75 through 12-31-75

Day	Date	Position	Entry	Exit	Points P/L
Wednesday	3-05-75	Short	35.15	35.30	− .15
Thursday	3-06-75	Long	35.50	35.45	+ .15
Thursday	3-13-75	Long	36.70	36.75	+ .05
Wednesday	3-19-75	Long	37.15	38.10	+ .95
Thursday	4-03-75	Long	38.40	38.50	+ .10
Thursday	4-10-75	Long	38.22	38.25	+ .03
Thursday	4-17-75	Long	38.60	38.75	+ .15
Thursday	4-24-75	Long	39.00	39.40	+ .40
Thursday	5-01-75	Long	39.30	39.80	+ .50
Thursday	5-08-75	Short	37.95	37.10	+ .85
Thursday	5-15-75	Long	39.10	38.60	− .50
Wednesday	6-11-75	Long	40.10	40.57	+ .52
Wednesday	6-18-75	Long	42.05	41.60	− .25
Thursday	6-19-75	Short	41.70	41.02	+ .68
Thursday	6-26-75	Long	41.12	39.90	−1.22
Thursday	7-10-75	Short	40.00	40.32	− .32
Thursday	7-17-75	Long	39.62	39.90	+ .32
Thursday	7-24-75	Long	41.40	42.22	+ .82
Thursday	7-31-75	Long	40.52	40.40	− .12
Thursday	8-07-75	Short	42.30	41.85	+ .45
Thursday	8-14-75	Long	41.92	42.90	+ .98
Thursday	8-21-75	Short	44.22	44.67	− .45
Thursday	8-28-75	Short	44.15	43.82	+ .33
Thursday	9-18-75	Long	45.12	45.12	.00
Thursday	9-25-75	Long	44.32	45.35	+1.03
Thursday	10-02-75	Short	44.77	44.55	+ .22
Thursday	10-16-75	Short	41.35	40.62	+ .73
Thursday	10-23-75	Long	40.85	41.70	+ .85
Thursday	10-30-75	Long	39.50	40.17	+ .67
Thursday	11-20-75	Long	45.35	44.95	− .40
Thursday	12-04-75	Long	46.00	46.07	+ .07
Thursday	12-11-75	Short	43.40	42.87	+ .40
Thursday	12-18-75	Short	42.35	43.30	− .95

Results

	Points	Dollars
Total profits from trades =	+ 6.87	$2756
Less commissions .10 × 33 =	− 3.30	$1320
Profits minus commissions =	+ 3.57	$1436

70% Reliability, 33 trades

Table 14-9c January 76 Copper Trades, 1-06-75 through 12-31-75

Day	Date	Position	Entry	Exit	Points P/L
Tuesday	1-07-75	Long	59.00	59.20	+ .20
Tuesday	1-14-75	Long	60.40	59.30	− 1.10
Tuesday	1-21-75	Short	58.20	57.80	+ .40
Tuesday	1-28-75	Short	59.20	58.50	+ .70
Tuesday	2-04-75	Short	58.70	58.10	+ .60
Tuesday	2-25-75	Long	62.50	62.90	+ .40
Thursday	2-27-75	Short	63.60	64.00	− .40
Tuesday	3-05-75	Long	62.00	63.40	+ 1.40
Tuesday	3-11-75	Long	62.60	62.30	− .30
Thursday	3-13-75	Long	62.60	62.60	.00
Tuesday	3-18-75	Long	62.70	64.80	+ 2.10
Tuesday	4-02-75	Short	67.10	66.80	+ .30
Tuesday	4-08-75	Short	64.10	63.80	+ .30
Thursday	4-10-75	Long	60.80	61.80	+ 1.00
Tuesday	4-15-75	Long	62.50	62.60	+ .10
Tuesday	4-22-75	Long	62.00	61.50	− .50
Tuesday	4-29-75	Short	61.00	60.10	+ .90
Thursday	5-01-75	Long	59.40	58.60	− .80
Tuesday	5-06-75	Long	59.20	59.20	.00
Tuesday	5-20-75	Short	59.60	60.10	− .30
Thursday	5-22-75	Long	60.00	60.00	.00
Tuesday	6-03-75	Long	58.10	57.50	− .60
Tuesday	6-10-75	Short	55.50	55.00	+ .50
Tuesday	6-17-75	Short	56.20	55.30	+ .90
Thursday	6-19-75	Long	55.00	56.00	+ 1.00
Tuesday	6-24-75	Long	55.50	57.00	+ 1.50
Tuesday	7-08-75	Long	57.90	58.70	+ .80
Tuesday	7-15-75	Short	59.50	59.60	− .10
Thursday	7-17-75	Short	59.00	59.00	.00
Tuesday	7-22-75	Short	61.00	59.70	+ 1.30
Tuesday	7-29-75	Short	61.70	60.80	+ .90
Tuesday	8-05-75	Short	59.60	59.20	+ .40
Tuesday	8-12-75	Short	61.10	61.10	.00
Thursday	8-14-75	Long	60.90	61.20	+ .30
Tuesday	8-19-75	Short	62.90	63.60	− .70
Thursday	8-21-75	Long	62.70	63.80	+ 1.10
Tuesday	8-26-75	Short	63.00	62.90	+ .10
Tuesday	9-09-75	Long	58.20	58.20	+ .60
Tuesday	9-16-75	Long	57.10	57.10	.00
Tuesday	9-23-75	Short	58.20	58.60	− .40
Thursday	9-25-75	Long	57.60	58.00	+ .40
Tuesday	9-30-75	Long	57.10	57.20	+ .10
Tuesday	10-07-75	Long	57.00	56.90	− .10
Tuesday	10-21-75	Short	55.30	54.30	+ 1.00
Thursday	10-23-75	Long	53.70	54.10	+ .40
Tuesday	10-28-75	Short	54.50	55.70	− 1.20
Tuesday	11-18-75	Long	54.20	54.90	+ .70
Thursday	11-20-75	Short	53.90	53.30	+ .60

Table 14-9c (continued)

Day	Date	Position	Entry	Exit	Points P/L
Tuesday	12-02-75	Long	53.00	52.80	− .20
Thursday	12-04-75	Long	53.10	53.90	+ .80
Tuesday	12-09-75	Long	52.60	52.90	+ .30
Thursday	12-11-75	Short	53.60	52.80	+ .80
Tuesday	12-16-75	Long	52.80	53.90	+1.10

Results

	Points	Dollars
Total profits from trades =	+17.30	$4325
Less commissions .17 × 53 =	− 9.01	$2226
Profits minus commissions =	8.29	$2099
64% Reliability, 53 trades		

Table 14-9d March 76 Soybean Trades, 3-03-75 through 2-12-76

Day	Date	Position	Entry	Exit	Points P/L
Monday	3-03-75	Short	535	547	−12
Thursday	3-06-75	Short	567½	560	+ 7½
Monday	3-10-75	Long	555	575	+20
Thursday	3-13-75	Short	572½	562	+10½
Monday	3-17-75	Short	571	553	+18
Monday	3-24-75	Short	585	607	−22
Thursday	3-27-75	Short	597	609	−12
Monday	4-07-75	Long	577	581½	+ 4½
Thursday	4-10-75	Short	572½	575	− 2½
Monday	4-14-75	Long	574	575	+ 1
Thursday	4-17-75	Short	574½	569	+ 5½
Monday	4-21-75	Long	563	544½	−18½
Monday	4-28-75	Long	530	531	+ 1
Monday	5-05-75	Long	505	504	− 1
Monday	5-12-75	Short	506	517½	−11½
Thursday	5-15-75	Short	511	509½	+ 1½
Monday	5-19-75	Short	513½	528	−14½
Thursday	5-22-75	Short	529	525	+ 4
Monday	6-02-75	Long	494½	499	+ 4½
Thursday	6-05-75	Short	497¾	493¼	− 4½
Monday	6-09-75	Short	502¾	501	+ 1¾
Thursday	6-12-75	Long	497¼	500½	+ 3¼
Monday	6-16-75	Short	507½	515	− 8½
Monday	6-23-75	Long	523½	521¼	− 2¼
Thursday	6-26-75	Long	522¼	515	− 7¼
Monday	7-07-75	Long	523¼	543¼	+20
Monday	7-14-75	Long	570	571	+ 1

Table 14-9d (*continued*)

Day	Date	Position	Entry	Exit	Points P/L
Thursday	7-17-75	Short	569	555	+14
Monday	7-21-75	Short	575	572	+ 3
Monday	7-28-75	Short	632	614	+18
Thursday	7-31-75	Long	$602\frac{1}{2}$	$607\frac{1}{2}$	+ 5
Monday	8-04-75	Short	$627\frac{1}{2}$	621	+ $6\frac{1}{2}$
Monday	8-11-75	Long	618	$632\frac{1}{4}$	+$14\frac{1}{2}$
Thursday	8-14-75	Short	635	655	−20
Monday	8-18-75	Long	635	653	+18
Thursday	8-21-75	Short	638	$641\frac{1}{4}$	− $3\frac{1}{4}$
Monday	8-25-75	Long	$640\frac{1}{2}$	615	−25
Thursday	8-28-75	Long	595	587	− 8
Monday	9-08-75	Long	$574\frac{1}{4}$	$584\frac{3}{4}$	+$10\frac{1}{2}$
Monday	9-15-75	Long	590	$601\frac{3}{4}$	+$11\frac{3}{4}$
Thursday	9-18-75	Short	$613\frac{1}{4}$	$610\frac{1}{2}$	+ $2\frac{3}{4}$
Monday	9-22-75	Long	593	593	0
Thursday	9-25-75	Short	602	$597\frac{3}{4}$	+ $4\frac{1}{4}$
Monday	9-29-75	Long	$583\frac{1}{2}$	$589\frac{1}{2}$	+ 6
Thursday	10-02-75	Short	572	$567\frac{1}{2}$	+ $4\frac{1}{2}$
Monday	10-06-75	Long	$562\frac{1}{4}$	$565\frac{1}{4}$	+ 3
Monday	10-12-75	Long	$552\frac{1}{2}$	$553\frac{3}{4}$	+ $1\frac{1}{4}$
Thursday	10-16-75	Short	$559\frac{3}{4}$	$549\frac{1}{2}$	+$10\frac{1}{4}$
Monday	10-20-75	Long	$547\frac{3}{4}$	529	−$18\frac{3}{4}$
Monday	10-27-75	Long	$501\frac{1}{2}$	$508\frac{1}{4}$	+ $6\frac{3}{4}$
Monday	11-03-75	Long	$500\frac{1}{2}$	505	+ $4\frac{1}{2}$
Monday	11-10-75	Long	$505\frac{1}{2}$	495	−$10\frac{1}{2}$
Monday	11-17-75	Long	$489\frac{1}{4}$	475	−$14\frac{1}{4}$
Thursday	11-20-75	Short	$475\frac{1}{2}$	$483\frac{1}{4}$	− $7\frac{3}{4}$
Monday	12-01-75	Long	$494\frac{3}{4}$	$504\frac{1}{4}$	+ $9\frac{1}{4}$
Thursday	12-04-75	Short	$500\frac{3}{4}$	493	+ $7\frac{3}{4}$
Monday	12-08-75	Long	474	$477\frac{1}{2}$	+ $3\frac{1}{2}$
Thursday	12-11-75	Short	$476\frac{1}{2}$	$459\frac{1}{2}$	+17
Monday	12-15-75	Long	455	$464\frac{1}{2}$	+ $9\frac{1}{2}$
Monday	1-05-76	Short	$469\frac{1}{4}$	465	+ $4\frac{1}{4}$
Monday	1-12-76	Short	$487\frac{3}{4}$	$483\frac{1}{4}$	+ $4\frac{1}{2}$
Monday	1-19-76	Short	$493\frac{1}{2}$	$490\frac{1}{2}$	+ 3
Thursday	1-22-76	Long	$475\frac{1}{2}$	$476\frac{3}{4}$	+ $1\frac{1}{4}$
Monday	1-26-75	Long	$456\frac{3}{4}$	$458\frac{1}{2}$	+ $1\frac{3}{4}$
Monday	2-02-76	Short	$476\frac{3}{4}$	$474\frac{1}{2}$	+ $2\frac{1}{4}$

Results

	Points	Dollars
Total profits from trades =	+97.00	$4850
Less **commissions** 1.0 × 66 =	−66.00	$3300
Profits minus **commissions** =	+31.00	$1500

68% Reliability, 66 trades

Table 14-9e March 76 Wheat Trades, 3-19-75 through 12-31-75

Day	Date	Position	Entry	Exit	Points P/L
Monday	3-31-75	Short	$398\frac{1}{2}$	390	$+\ 2\frac{1}{2}$
Thursday	4-03-75	Long	$386\frac{1}{2}$	$387\frac{1}{2}$	$+\ 1$
Monday	4-07-75	Long	$381\frac{1}{2}$	383	$+\ 1\frac{1}{2}$
Monday	4-14-75	Long	366	359	$-\ 6$
Thursday	4-17-75	Short	$362\frac{3}{4}$	361	$+\ 1\frac{3}{4}$
Monday	4-21-75	Long	356	353	$-\ 3$
Thursday	4-24-75	Short	356	358	$-\ 2$
Monday	4-28-75	Short	359	$354\frac{1}{4}$	$+\ 4\frac{3}{4}$
Monday	5-05-75	Long	$332\frac{1}{2}$	$333\frac{1}{2}$	$+\ 1$
Thursday	5-08-75	Short	335	336	$-\ 1$
Monday	5-12-75	Long	335	334	$-\ 1$
Thursday	5-15-75	Long	330	$327\frac{3}{4}$	$-\ 2\frac{1}{4}$
Monday	5-19-75	Short	324	342	$+\ 2$
Monday	6-02-75	Long	$317\frac{1}{2}$	$323\frac{1}{2}$	$+\ 6$
Thursday	6-05-75	Long	321	320	$-\ 1$
Monday	6-09-75	Short	$327\frac{1}{2}$	325	$+\ 2\frac{1}{2}$
Monday	6-16-75	Short	$330\frac{1}{2}$	$341\frac{3}{4}$	$-11\frac{3}{4}$
Thursday	6-19-75	Long	$338\frac{1}{2}$	352	$+13\frac{1}{2}$
Monday	6-23-75	Long	$344\frac{1}{4}$	$349\frac{1}{2}$	$+\ 5\frac{1}{4}$
Monday	7-07-75	Short	$329\frac{1}{2}$	356	$-26\frac{1}{2}$
Thursday	7-11-75	Short	372	$389\frac{1}{2}$	$-17\frac{1}{2}$
Monday	7-14-75	Long	$370\frac{1}{2}$	386	$+15\frac{1}{2}$
Thursday	7-17-75	Short	$386\frac{1}{2}$	376	$+10\frac{1}{2}$
Monday	7-21-75	Short	383	$379\frac{1}{2}$	$+\ 3\frac{1}{2}$
Monday	7-28-75	Short	$414\frac{3}{4}$	407	$+\ 7\frac{3}{4}$
Thursday	8-01-75	Long	$391\frac{1}{2}$	$396\frac{1}{2}$	$+\ 5\frac{1}{2}$
Monday	8-04-75	Short	398	395	$+\ 3$
Monday	8-11-75	Long	$410\frac{1}{4}$	$423\frac{1}{4}$	$+13$
Monday	8-18-75	Long	$442\frac{3}{4}$	$453\frac{1}{4}$	$+10\frac{1}{2}$
Monday	8-25-75	Long	$472\frac{1}{2}$	$454\frac{1}{2}$	-18
Monday	9-08-75	Long	$443\frac{3}{4}$	$435\frac{1}{4}$	$+\ 2\frac{1}{2}$
Monday	9-15-75	Long	$439\frac{3}{4}$	$441\frac{3}{4}$	$+\ 2$
Thursday	9-18-75	Short	$449\frac{3}{4}$	$450\frac{1}{2}$	$-\ \frac{3}{4}$
Monday	9-22-75	Long	$446\frac{1}{2}$	440	$-\ 6\frac{1}{2}$
Thursday	9-25-75	Short	$451\frac{1}{2}$	$449\frac{3}{4}$	$+\ 1\frac{3}{4}$
Monday	9-29-75	Long	443	444	$+\ 1$
Monday	10-06-75	Short	$432\frac{1}{4}$	$428\frac{1}{4}$	$+\ 4$
Monday	10-13-75	Long	420	$427\frac{1}{4}$	$+\ 7\frac{1}{4}$
Thursday	10-16-75	Short	$423\frac{3}{4}$	$419\frac{1}{4}$	$+\ 4\frac{1}{2}$
Monday	10-20-75	Short	$425\frac{1}{2}$	$410\frac{1}{2}$	$+15$
Thursday	10-23-75	Long	$407\frac{1}{2}$	$405\frac{1}{2}$	$-\ 2$
Monday	10-27-75	Long	$394\frac{1}{4}$	399	$+\ 4\frac{3}{4}$
Monday	11-03-75	Long	$389\frac{1}{4}$	$393\frac{3}{4}$	$+\ 4\frac{1}{2}$
Thursday	11-06-75	Short	$387\frac{1}{4}$	$384\frac{3}{4}$	$+\ 2\frac{1}{2}$
Monday	11-10-75	Long	378	$363\frac{1}{2}$	$-14\frac{1}{2}$
Thursday	11-13-75	Long	$360\frac{1}{4}$	$363\frac{1}{2}$	$+\ 3\frac{1}{4}$

Table 14-9e (*continued*)

Day	Date	Position	Entry	Exit	Points P/L
Monday	11-17-75	Short	365	$355\frac{3}{4}$	$+ 9\frac{1}{4}$
Monday	12-08-75	Long	$344\frac{1}{2}$	$347\frac{1}{4}$	$+ 2\frac{3}{4}$
Thursday	12-11-75	Short	$347\frac{3}{4}$	$334\frac{3}{4}$	$+13$
Monday	12-15-75	Long	$322\frac{1}{2}$	$332\frac{1}{2}$	$+ 4\frac{1}{4}$
Thursday	12-18-75	Short	$336\frac{1}{4}$	343	$- 6\frac{3}{4}$

Results

	Points	Dollars
Total profits from trades =	$+70.75$	$3537
Less commisions $1.0 \times 52 =$	-52.00	$2600
Profits minus commissions =	$+18.75$	$ 937
67% Reliability, 52 trades		

At full commission, this may be a broker's dream, since fees account for better than 50% of the gross profit. But still, the high reliability has its appeal.

Weekend Patterns

Of all the pattern studies, this test was the most interesting. Intuitively, we suspected that the supposed "Friday liquidation," combined with the 2-day delay, would provide better trading opportunities than the weekly probabilities. We were not disappointed. Tests were performed on the combination of contracts:

Table 14-10

24 U.S. commodities (combined)	1 1976 contract each
8 London commodities (combined)	1 contract each
Cattle	June 1970–June 1975
Cocoa	December 1970–December 1975
Copper	December 1970–December 1975
Cotton	December 1970–December 1975
Potatoes	May 1970–May 1975
Silver—NY	December 1970–December 1975
Soybean meal	December 1973–December 1975
Soybean oil	December 1973–December 1975
Sugar	September 1970–September 1975
Swiss franc	December 1970–December 1975

PATTERN RECOGNITION   235

Not knowing what to expect, but anticipating combining the results with the study in weekly patterns, we tested as many unique situations as possible. It was necessary to determine the "trend" of the prior week in order to relate the weekend move. Possibilities were limited to close-only prices of the following combinations:

Prior Friday to Monday direction. The probability of this Friday-to-Monday (closing prices only) direction compared to the prior Friday-to-Monday direction. For example, May 76 Wheat moved in the same direction 62% of the time.

Friday-to-Friday direction (measured in points). Is this Friday-to-Monday move related to the increase or decrease in the price from the prior Friday to the current Friday? The calculated number represents the probability of the current Friday to Monday moving in the same direction as the price during the prior week.

Most frequent direction last week. Regardless of the net change in price of the prior week, we asked whether the number of days in one direction (either up or down) predicted the move over the current weekend.

Direction of Friday from Thursday. Will the weekend move be a continuation of the Friday move (direction determined as the net change in price from the close on Thursday to the close on Friday)?

Weekend move following a weekly pattern. Compare the weekend move on the Wednesday-Thursday-Friday pattern of the prior week. The seven combinations possible in the 3 days are presented with the probability of a weekend move in the same direction as Friday. For example, using May 76 Wheat again, the OOX case shows a 71% likelihood of continuing in the same direction as Friday (another X).

The most interesting results from these tests are summarized in Table 14-11.[3]

Since all the continuation patterns presume an X in the Monday position, we have X-XXX, X-XXO, X-XOX, X-OXX, X-XOO, X-OOX, X-OOO.[4] The first four continuations each have four X's, automatically categorizing them as most frequently in the X direction. The last case is in the O direction and the remaining two cases are determined by the Tuesday direction.

In order to increase our success, we want to combine the high probability of the direction of the most frequent move and also use the best Wednesday-Thursday-Friday continuation possibilities for trading over the weekend. Selecting cocoa because of its highest score relative to the most frequent direction, we summarize the combinations in Table 14-12.

We conclude from Table 14-12 the best possibilities for predicting the Monday direction, and combine them with the Friday probabilities using the weekly pattern study for cocoa.

In order to use this technique, we select out the most favorable situation, marked with an "*a*", and place an order on Thursday's close to hold through Monday's

---

[3] A complete set of results appears in Appendix 9.
[4] For an explanation of this notation or the pattern, see the prior study on weekly patterns.

Table 14-11 Summary Results of Weekend Moves

	Most frequent direction	Continuation patterns[a]							
		WTF XXX	WTF XXO	WTF XOX	WTF OXX	WTF XOO	WTF OOX	WTF OOO
24 U.S. commodities	63	59	49	56	61	57	48	52
8 London commodities	61	70	45	40	50	59	60	57
Cattle	60	59	52	61	60	44	60	73
Cocoa	65	46	55	69	58	64	50	72
Copper	58	48	42	62	61	28	52	46
Cotton	61	64	53	60	58	50	51	58
Potatoes	65	66	55	70	53	57	55	51
Silver (NY)	63	77	53	54	56	56	51	47
Soybean meal	68	70	66	88	66	27	55	22
Soybean oil	66	70	54	77	66	37	58	46
Sugar	55	53	50	51	51	46	67	39
Swiss franc	69	65	16	80	42	61	38	64
	(The following calculations exclude the 24 U.S. commodities)							
Mean	62.8	62.5	49.2	64.7	56.5	48.1	54.3	52.3
Standard deviation	4.3	9.9	12.6	13.9	7.2	12.9	7.4	14.9

[a] Figures represent percentage of situations of next Monday close in "X" direction.

PATTERN RECOGNITION 237

Table 14-12 Summary of Most Frequent Weekly Direction with Best WTF Continuation: Cocoa

MTWTF	Most frequent direction	Continuation probabilities
X–XXX	X	46%
X–XXO	X	45%
X–XOX	X	69%[a]
X–OXX	X	58%[a]
XXXOO	X	36%
XOXOO	O	64%[a]
XXOOX	X	50%
XOOOX	O	50%
X–OOO	O	72%[a]

[a] Indicates best trading possibilities.

close. The three situations we look for are (Monday through Thursday):

MTWT
XOXO
XOOX
XXOX

In all three cases we expect the Friday and Monday price movements to be in the direction of both the Thursday-to-Friday and the prior Monday move (X). If the prior Monday was up, we then buy on Thursday's close and watch the closing

Table 14-13 Combining Best Cocoa Weekly and Weekend Results with Friday Probability

Weekly pattern[b] MTWTF		Probability of continuing in same direction
XOXXX	58%	46% favors X Monday
XOXOX	57%	68% favors X Monday[a]
XOOXX	56%	58% favors X Monday[a]
XOOOX	61%	50% favors X Monday
XXXXO	58%	45% favors O Monday
XXOXX	59%	58% favors X Monday[a]
XXOOX	55%	50% favors X Monday

[a] Indicates best trading possibilities.
[b] For explanation see Chart 14-5 (Cocoa).

session Friday. If we have a profit, we continue to hold until Monday on the close, if Friday moved against us, we close out our position Friday. There is also a 60% probability of the cocoa prices reversing on Tuesday. If we hold the trade that was initiated on Thursday into Monday and the Monday move is unfavorable, there is a 60% chance of recovering at least part of that loss by holding onto the position for another day. When we combine all these situations we have the following trades:

Table 14-14 Rules for Combined Weekly-Weekend Cocoa Trading

Pattern MTWT	Actual directions	Buy or sell	Entry day on close	C/O Friday if	Hold Friday if	C/O Monday if	Hold Monday if
1 (up) XOXO	+ − + −	Buy	Thurs	−	+	+	−
(down)	− + − +	Sell	Thurs	+	−	−	+
2 (up) XOOX	+ − − +	Buy	Thurs	−	+	+	−
(down)	− + + −	Sell	Thurs	+	−	−	+
3 (up) XXOX	+ + − +	Buy	Thurs	−	+	+	−
(down)	− − + −	Sell	Thurs	+	−	−	+

Close out all positions Tuesday

Using the May 76 Cocoa contract the calculated results were recorded in Table 14-15. When evaluating this, note that weekends following a short week are not traded but that the prior week is traded. The first and second trading days of the week are considered Monday and Tuesday for liquidation purposes.

A Comment on Holidays

Because these tests were performed using a computer, the occurrence of a holiday was not treated as a special situation. For the weekly pattern study, a series of 5 consecutive days qualified as a week and the prior trading day as the previous "Friday." It may have happened that the prior "Friday" was really a Thursday and a 3-day weekend separated it from the next week. For the weekend pattern, only 2-day weekends were used, and therefore no account of holidays has been attempted.

It is commonly accepted that the reaction prior to holidays is the same as those before weekends, since the rationale seems to be similar. The only available work in this area is by Merrill, whose results, based on the stock market, show a strong bullish tendency before a holiday with a weak day immediately after. Remembering the bullish bias of the stock market (about 54% of all days were higher from January 1897 through January 1964), we have Merrill's results as shown in Table 14-16.

Table 14-15 Results of Weekly-Weekend Cocoa Trades

Date Monday	Pattern	Direction	Thursday entry	Friday action	Monday action	Tuesday action	P/L
3-17-75	XOOX	+ − − +	Buy 55.90	C/O 55.45			− .45
3-31-75	XOOX	− + + −	Sell 55.25	C/O 55.65			− .40
4-21-75	XOOX	− + + −	Sell 50.85	Hold	C/O 48.80		+2.05
4-28-75	XOXO	− + − +	Sell 48.50	Hold	C/O 46.80		+1.70
6-19-75	XOXO	− + − +	Sell 42.15	Hold	C/O 41.65		+ .50
6-26-75	XOXO	− + − +	Sell 41.75	C/O 42.13			− .38
7-07-75	XXOX	+ + − +	Buy 47.50	Hold	C/O 51.40		+3.90
7-14-75	XOXO	+ + − −	Buy 50.50	Hold	C/O 53.60		+3.00
7-21-75	XXOX	+ + − +	Buy 55.20	C/O 54.70			− .50
7-28-75	XXOX	− − − +	Sell 49.85	Hold	Hold	C/O 49.32	+ .53
8-07-75	XOXO	+ + − −	Buy 49.80	Hold	Hold	C/O 49.70	+ .10
9-18-75	XOOX	+ − − +	Buy 48.40	C/O 48.30			− .10
9-22-75	XXOX	+ + − +	Buy 51.25	C/O 50.55			− .70
9-29-75	XOXO	+ − + −	Buy 50.20	C/O 49.70			− .50
10-31-75	XXOX	− − + −	Sell 54.85	C/O 56.20			−1.45
1-08-76	XOOX	− + + −	Sell 62.55	Hold	C/O 61.95		+ .60
1-19-76	XOOX	− + + −	Sell 59.30	C/O 60.28			− .98
2-06-76	XOXO	+ − + −	Buy 64.75	Hold	C/O 65.55		+ .80
3-08-76	XOOX	+ − − +	Buy 64.84	C/O 64.70			− .14

19 trades, 8 profitable   13.08 point profit — 5.80 point loss
2.25 P/L ratio   7.28 net profit
            1.63 average profit
            .52 average loss

Table 14-16 Merrill's Holiday Results

Period tested	Holiday or holiday period	% upward moves
1897–1964	Day prior to all holidays	67.9%
1897–1964	Day after all holidays	50.8%
1897–1964	Thanksgiving to New Year	74%
1897–1964	July 4th to Labor Day	69%
1931–1965	Before Christmas	74%
1931–1965	Before New Year	75%

In relationship to commodity trading this would indicate the possibility of a sharp trending move prior to, or throughout, a holiday season.

Combining Weekly and Weekend Patterns for Cattle and Soybeans

In the same manner in which cocoa evolved, the weekly and weekend patterns can be combined for cattle as well as all other commodities. From the weekly and weekend charts we can list the patterns that resulted in Friday and Monday moves of at least 60% probability.

Table 14-17 Selection of Weekly and Weekend Patterns for Cattle

	Weekly			Weekend	
(1)	XOXXX	(67%)			
(2)	XOXOO	(67%)	(A)	X-XOX	(61%)
(3)	XOOXX	(62%)	(B)	X-OXX	(61%)
(4)	XOOOX	(61%)	(C)	X-OOX	(60%)
(5)	XXXXX	(68%)	(D)	X-OOO	(73%)
(6)	XXOXX	(68%)			

To use these results together for a highly predictive method we must find corresponding patterns. It should be possible to take a position on Thursday in anticipation of a Friday move and hold that trade through the weekend. The weekly and weekend patterns can be matched up as 3-B, 4-C, and 6-B; all other patterns are distinct from one another. If the proper direction for Friday does not materialize, the trade is liquidated before the weekend. One exception could be made when using combination 4-C: a reverse position taken Thursday on the close that is not profitable by the Friday close becomes weekend pattern (D) of highest reliability and can still be held instead of liquidated.

To test the possibilities of this combined approach, we use the weekly grain charts combined with the general condition of the next Monday move consistent with the

PATTERN RECOGNITION

direction of the prior Monday move. The best weekly grain patterns are XOXOX, XOOXX, XXOOX, XXXXO, and XXXOO, which also correspond to the "most frequent direction" results. We choose the first three situations in order to be able to enter a new trade before Friday and hold through the weekend, giving a potentially longer price move. If the Friday direction fails, we liquidate before the weekend. The results of this technique using March 76 Soybeans from March through December are shown in Table 14-18.

Table 14-18 March 76 Soybeans—Results of Combining Weekly and Weekend Trades

Day	Date	Short or long	Weekly trade Entry	Weekly trade Exit	P/L	Weekend trade Exit	Weekend trade P/L	Total P/L
TH	3-13	S	$572\frac{1}{2}$	562	$+10\frac{1}{2}$	571	-9	$+1\frac{1}{2}$
TH	4-10	S	$572\frac{1}{2}$	575	$-2\frac{1}{2}$			$-2\frac{1}{2}$
TH	4-17	S	$574\frac{1}{2}$	569	$+5\frac{1}{2}$	563	$+6$	$+11\frac{1}{2}$
TH	6-05	S	$497\frac{3}{4}$	$493\frac{1}{4}$	$+4\frac{1}{2}$	$502\frac{3}{4}$	$-9\frac{1}{2}$	-5
TH	6-12	L	$497\frac{1}{4}$	$500\frac{1}{2}$	$+3\frac{1}{4}$	$507\frac{1}{2}$	$+7$	$+10\frac{1}{4}$
TH	7-17	S	569	555	$+14$	575	-20	-6
TH	7-31	L	$602\frac{1}{2}$	$607\frac{1}{2}$	$+5$	$627\frac{1}{2}$	$+20$	$+25$
TH	8-14	S	635	655	-20			-20
TH	8-21	S	638	$641\frac{1}{4}$	$-3\frac{1}{4}$			$-3\frac{1}{4}$
TH	9-18	S	$613\frac{1}{4}$	$610\frac{1}{2}$	$+2\frac{3}{4}$	593	$+17\frac{1}{2}$	$+20\frac{1}{4}$
TH	9-26	S	602	$597\frac{3}{4}$	$+4\frac{1}{4}$	$583\frac{1}{2}$	$+14\frac{3}{4}$	$+18\frac{1}{4}$
TH	10-16	S	$559\frac{3}{4}$	$549\frac{1}{2}$	$+10\frac{1}{4}$	$547\frac{3}{4}$	$+1\frac{3}{4}$	$+12$
TH	11-20	S	$475\frac{1}{2}$	$483\frac{1}{4}$	$-7\frac{3}{4}$			$-7\frac{3}{4}$
TH	12-04	S	$500\frac{3}{4}$	493	$+7\frac{3}{4}$	474	$+19$	$+26\frac{3}{4}$
TH	12-11	S	$476\frac{1}{2}$	$459\frac{1}{2}$	$+17$	455	$+4\frac{1}{2}$	$+21\frac{1}{2}$

A selection of the patterns to be used for all grains can be accomplished by starting with the weekly pattern table and eliminating all patterns that do not have at least three X's; then eliminate all patterns that end with XXO or XOO, which are poor predictions of an X-direction on Monday. The remaining nine combinations can be used. Table 14-19 shows the progression of improvement using these filters on January 76 Soybeans for the entire year of 1975. Using all patterns we start with a 41% reliability. By selecting the most frequent direction we increase results to $\frac{24}{41}$, then to $\frac{22}{32}$ by choosing only the X-direction, and finally $\frac{20}{26}$ by eliminating the Wednesday-through-Friday patterns XXO and XOO. The result is 77% reliability and a profit of $1.57 per bushel on 26 trades.

Reversal Patterns

The last of the three studies is on the nature of reversals. The intention is to find a pattern in the open, high, low, and closing price of the day that will help predict the

Table 14-19 January 76 Soybeans

Date Friday	Position	Most frequent direction P/L	Filter with last Monday direction P/L	Not W, T, F XXO, XOO
1-10	Long	−14	−14	−14
1-17	Short	+15	+15	+15
1-24	Long	−20		
1-31	Short	+ 9	+ 9	+ 9
2-07	Long	− 9		
2-14	Short	+20	+20	+20
2-28	Short	−11	−11	−11
3-07	Long	− $5\frac{1}{2}$	− $5\frac{1}{2}$	
3-14	Short	− 9	− 9	− 9
3-21	Long	+ $5\frac{1}{2}$	+ $5\frac{1}{2}$	+ $5\frac{1}{2}$
4-04	Short	+ $10\frac{1}{2}$		
4-25	Short	+ $14\frac{1}{4}$	+ $14\frac{1}{4}$	+ $14\frac{1}{4}$
5-02	Short	+ $16\frac{1}{2}$	+ $16\frac{1}{2}$	+ $16\frac{1}{2}$
5-09	Long	+ $1\frac{1}{2}$		
5-16	Long	+ 3	+ 3	
5-23	Long	−20	−20	
6-06	Short	− $10\frac{1}{2}$	− $10\frac{1}{2}$	− $10\frac{1}{2}$
6-13	Long	+ 7	+ 7	+ 7
6-20	Long	− $4\frac{3}{4}$	− $4\frac{3}{4}$	− $4\frac{3}{4}$
6-27	Short	+ $1\frac{1}{2}$	+ $1\frac{1}{2}$	+ $1\frac{1}{2}$
7-11	Long	−11		
7-18	Short	−20	−20	−20
7-25	Long	+20	+20	+20
8-01	Long	+20	+20	+20
8-08	Long	−16	−16	
8-15	Long	−18		
8-22	Long	− $\frac{1}{2}$		
8-29	Short	+ 6	+ 6	+ 6
9-12	Short	+ 5	+ 5	+ 5
9-19	Short	+ $16\frac{1}{4}$	+ $16\frac{1}{4}$	+ $16\frac{1}{4}$
9-26	Short	+ $16\frac{1}{4}$	+ $16\frac{1}{4}$	+ $16\frac{1}{4}$
10-03	Short	+ 6	+ 6	+ 6
10-10	Short	+20	+20	+20
10-17	Short	+ $\frac{1}{4}$	+ $\frac{1}{4}$	+ $\frac{1}{4}$
10-24	Short	+ $17\frac{3}{4}$	+ $17\frac{3}{4}$	+ $17\frac{3}{4}$
10-31	Long	−13		
11-07	Long	− $8\frac{3}{4}$		
11-14	Short	+ $5\frac{3}{4}$	+ $5\frac{3}{4}$	+ $5\frac{3}{4}$
11-21	Short	−20	−20	
12-12	Short	+ $4\frac{1}{4}$	+ $4\frac{1}{4}$	+ $4\frac{1}{4}$
12-19	Short	+ $1\frac{3}{4}$	+ $1\frac{3}{4}$	
	Reliability	24/41 = 59%	22/32 = 69%	20/26 = 77%
Without commission	P/L	+32	+$100\frac{1}{4}$	+157

Table 14-20 Reversal Patterns (in Percent)

	Commodity	Trend continued			Key reversal			Minor reversal		
		Times	Open	Close	Times	Open	Close	Times	Open	Close
Jan 76	Broilers	74	52.70	43.24	50	36.00	42.00	33	36.36	54.55
Feb 76	Cattle	107	57.94	45.79	66	59.09	46.97	25	40.00	44.00
Jun 76	Hogs	67	58.21	53.73	53	39.62	49.06	23	47.83	39.13
Feb 76	Pork bellies	124	66.94	59.68	62	54.84	43.55	23	52.17	56.52
Mar 76	Corn	125	55.20	38.40	75	53.33	49.33	28	32.14	46.43
Mar 76	Oats	69	60.87	39.13	55	49.09	41.82	23	30.43	52.17
Jan 76	Soybeans	122	58.20	45.90	81	49.38	48.15	29	58.52	58.62
Jan 76	Soybean meal	107	53.27	42.99	65	49.23	41.54	36	41.67	50.00
Jan 76	Soybean oil	110	54.55	45.45	74	52.70	51.35	34	47.06	55.88
Mar 76	Wheat	101	51.49	48.51	67	65.67	53.73	27	59.26	59.26
May 76	Sugar (world)	106	60.38	53.77	70	61.43	52.86	57	49.12	56.14
May 76	Potatoes (Maine)	85	58.82	54.12	63	60.32	61.90	19	42.11	47.37
Mar 76	Orange juice	112	55.36	47.32	75	48.00	50.67	31	58.06	45.16
May 76	Cocoa (NY)	122	51.64	46.72	73	54.79	47.95	50	56.00	56.00
Mar 76	Coffee 'C'	86	48.84	53.49	65	56.92	49.23	40	40.00	55.00
May 76	Cotton	126	46.83	37.30	65	52.31	47.69	39	41.03	43.59
Jan 76	Lumber	88	55.68	50.00	57	50.88	36.84	20	35.00	70.00
Jan 76	Plywood	101	45.54	39.60	59	50.85	49.15	27	48.15	62.96
Apr 76	Silver CBT	116	51.72	39.66	79	41.77	41.77	34	50.00	41.18
Mar 76	Silver NY	120	47.50	40.83	87	49.43	40.23	44	59.09	59.09
Jly 76	Silver coins	98	43.88	31.63	63	42.86	49.21	46	39.13	43.48
Apr 76	Platinum	94	56.38	48.94	72	44.44	44.44	45	57.78	53.33
Jan 76	Copper	116	48.28	44.83	55	47.27	38.18	40	50.00	42.50

next day's pattern or direction. One reversal of special interest is termed a *key reversal* and is generally defined to be a day on which prices opened higher, making new highs of a bull move, but closed below the prior close. Since these specific situations are not common and difficult to identify automatically via a computer, the reversals and patterns analyzed in this study were defined as follows:

Trend continued—the current opening price was above (below) the prior closing price and the current close was above (below) the current open. The market has continued to rise (or fall) steadily.

Key reversal—the current open was above (below) the prior close, and the current close was below (above) the prior close. This is not as strong as the standard definition of key reversal, since it does not account for a preceding bull or bear move with relative new highs or lows.

Minor reversal—the current open was above (below) the prior close, but the close was between the current open and prior close.

The three reversal forms tested related a current to a prior trading day and was used to predict movement in the next day's opening or closing price. Specifically, we tested for a continuation of the next day's movement: up if the trend was up, down if a key or minor reversal changed from a higher open to lower close. Table 14-20 contains a summary of the 23 contracts tested and the results. During the 1-year period observed the average of all contracts relative to the subsequent opening and closing prices was:

Table 14-21 Next Day's Movement Based on Prior Day's Patterns (in Percent)

	Open	Close
Trend continued	53.9	45.7
Key reversal	50.9	46.9
Minor reversal	46.6	51.8

The results show that the trading day following any of the tested formations did not have a remarkable tendency to continue or reverse its direction taken as a group. There was a noticeable tendency to change direction during the next day following a trend day—an opening score of 53.9% and a closing score of 45.7%. For a large sampling of data these results may be of interest in showing the nature of the market; however, for a speculator these results do not differ enough from the norm to use for trading. On an individual basis, some of the commodities showed predictive possibilities (positive correlation).

The commodities were listed in order of correlation strength. Since our tests only analyze the one day following the defined situation, we will consider the use of these

PATTERN RECOGNITION

Table 14-22 Best Continuation Possibilities

		Open	Close
Trend continued	Pork bellies	66.94	59.68
	Oats	60.87	39.13
	Sugar	60.38	53.77
Key reversal	Wheat	65.67	53.73
	Sugar	61.43	52.86
	Potatoes	60.32	61.90
Minor reversal	Lumber	35.00	70.00
	Plywood	48.15	62.96

Best contrary continuation (a nontrending feature)

		Open	Close
Trend continued	Corn	55.20	38.40
	Oats	60.87	39.13
	Cotton	46.83	37.30
	Plywood	45.54	39.60
	Silver (CBOT)	51.72	39.66
	Silver coins	43.88	31.63
Key reversal	Lumber	50.88	36.84
	Copper	47.27	38.18
	Broilers	36.00	42.00
	Hogs	39.62	49.00
Minor reversal	Broilers	36.36	54.55
	Hogs	47.83	39.13
	Corn	32.14	46.43
	Oats	30.43	52.17
	Lumber	35.00	70.00
	Silver coins	39.13	43.48

results for a single day trade. The best opportunities are in using oats and lumber, which showed the greatest tendency to change direction during the day. Oats opened in the direction consistent with a prior trending day 60.87% but only closed in that direction 39.13%; lumber was more extreme, contradicting the continuation of a minor reversal on the open, but strongly confirming it by the close—a change from 35% to 70%. For example, the pattern of lumber prices starting with a Monday close might be:

Table 14-23 Lumber Pattern

Monday	Close	135.00
Tuesday	Open	141.00—Up 6.00
Tuesday	Close	138.00—Minor reversal
Wednesday	Open	Up —65% possibility
Wednesday	Close	Down—70% possibility

By selling on a higher open Wednesday, we have confirmed half of the predicted pattern; there is now only the 70% possibility of a lower close and a profitable liquidation of the trade.

Since oats had higher predictability in trend following, trading is different than with lumber. A trending oats sequence might be:

Table 14-24 Oats Pattern

Monday	Close	165
Tuesday	Open	167 — Up 2¢
Tuesday	Close	$168\frac{1}{2}$ — Continued up $1\frac{1}{2}$¢
Wednesday	Open	Up — 61% possibility
Wednesday	Close	Down — 61% possibility

Following an upward trend day we wait for a higher opening and then sell, expecting a lower close for liquidating the same day. The results of day trading oats using this technique is presented in Table 14-25.

Reversal patterns may be used for entry or exit timing in addition to the day-trading applications. The same rules can be followed if prices satisfy one of the more predictive patterns and you are waiting for an adjustment after a trending day.

Combining Reversal and Weekly Patterns

The reversal patterns that have been derived from a prior day's open and closing price direction can be related to the general direction previously developed in the study of weekly patterns. With the exception of Monday, the direction of the close of

Table 14-25 Results of Combining Reversal and Weekly Patterns May 76 Oats

Day of the week	Date	Position	P/L	Anticipated weekly pattern
Wednesday	6-18-75	Short	$-1\frac{1}{2}$	
Thursday	6-24-75	Long	0	60%
Wednesday	7-09-75	Short	$+\frac{1}{2}$	44%
Friday	7-11-75	Short	$-1\frac{1}{2}$	54%
Monday	7-14-75	Short	$+3\frac{1}{2}$	
Friday	7-18-75	Long	$-3\frac{1}{4}$	31%
Monday	7-21-75	Long	$+\frac{1}{2}$	
Tuesday	7-22-75	Short	$+2$	60%
Thursday	7-24-75	Long	$+1\frac{1}{2}$	48%
Friday	7-25-75	Short	$-1\frac{1}{2}$	31%
Monday	7-28-75	Short	$-2\frac{1}{2}$	
Tuesday	7-29-75	Short	$+4$	40%
Thursday	7-31-75	Long	$-1\frac{1}{2}$	54%

Table 14-25 (*continued*)

Day of the week	Date	Position	P/L	Anticipated weekly pattern
Friday	8-01-75	Short	0	40%
Tuesday	8-05-75	Short	$-\frac{1}{2}$	60%
Friday	8-08-75	Short	$-1\frac{3}{4}$	44%
Monday	8-18-75	Short	$+5$	
Thursday	8-21-75	Short	$-\frac{1}{4}$	48%
Wednesday	8-27-75	Long	$+2$	44%
Thursday	9-03-75	Long	$+2$	60%
Friday	9-05-75	Long	$+1\frac{1}{2}$	55%
Thursday	9-11-75	Short	$+\frac{1}{4}$	54%
Friday	9-12-75	Long	$+2\frac{1}{2}$	44%
Wednesday	9-17-75	Short	-4	44%
Friday	9-19-75	Long	$-\frac{3}{4}$	31%
Friday	9-26-75	Short	-1	54%
Friday	10-03-75	Long	$-\frac{1}{2}$	56%
Thursday	10-14-75	Long	$+2\frac{1}{2}$	60%
Friday	10-17-75	Short	$+1\frac{3}{4}$	67%
Monday	10-27-75	Short	$+3\frac{1}{2}$	
Tuesday	11-04-75	Long	$+1\frac{1}{4}$	60%
Wednesday	11-05-75	Short	$-2\frac{1}{4}$	44%
Thursday	11-06-75	Short	$+1\frac{1}{2}$	48%
Monday	11-10-75	Long	-1	
Tuesday	11-11-75	Long	$-4\frac{1}{2}$	40%
Thursday	11-20-75	Long	$+\frac{1}{4}$	48%
Monday	11-24-75	Short	$-3\frac{1}{2}$	
Tuesday	11-25-75	Short	$+3\frac{3}{4}$	60%
Thursday	11-28-75	Short	$+2\frac{3}{4}$	
Tuesday	12-02-75	Short	$-\frac{1}{2}$	60%
Wednesday	12-03-75	Short	$+3$	66%
Monday	12-08-75	Long	-4	
Tuesday	12-09-75	Long	$+1$	60%
Wednesday	12-10-75	Short	$+\frac{3}{4}$	44%
Thursday	12-11-75	Long	$-\frac{1}{2}$	55%
Monday	12-15-75	Long	$-2\frac{3}{4}$	
Tuesday	12-16-75	Long	$-\frac{1}{2}$	60%
Wednesday	12-24-75	Long	$+3\frac{3}{4}$	44%
Friday	1-02-76	Short	$-\frac{1}{4}$	
Tuesday	1-06-76	Short	$+\frac{1}{4}$	60%
Thursday	1-08-76	Short	$+2$	55%
Wednesday	1-28-76	Short	$-\frac{1}{2}$	44%
Tuesday	2-03-76	Short	$-1\frac{3}{4}$	60%
Friday	2-13-76	Short	$-\frac{1}{2}$	54%
Tuesday	2-24-76	Short	$+2\frac{1}{2}$	60%
Friday	2-27-76	Long	$+2\frac{1}{2}$	67%
Tuesday	3-09-76	Long	$-\frac{1}{2}$	60%

28/57 Profitable trades = 49%

each day has been related to the directions of the other days in the week. A comparison of the anticipated reliability of the reversal pattern using the weekly probabilities might serve as a filter for unreliable results on a specific day of the week or due to a previous weekly formation not considered in the reversal tests.

Table 14-25 contains all the trades based on reversal patterns for the May 76 Oats contract. Since these are day trades the entry and exit prices have been omitted (they were the open and close respectively) and only the profit or loss in cents listed. The far right column is the probability of success based on the weekly pattern of the chart "1976 Grain and Soybean Complex" (Chart 14-3). The omissions occur on Mondays, for which there is no corresponding probability.

By grouping the weekly pattern probabilities into lowest to highest percentile groups and adding the trading results, we get an idea of the potential of this filter:

Table 14-26 Filtering Reversal and Weekly Patterns for May 76 Oats

Weekly pattern probability	Reliability Prof/Total trades	Profit or loss	Profit/Loss ratio
30–30%	$\frac{0}{3} = .00$	$- 5\frac{1}{2}$	0.0
40–49%	$\frac{9}{15} = .60$	$+ 4\frac{1}{4}$	.84
50–59%	$\frac{3}{9} = .33$	$- 1\frac{3}{4}$	1.36
60–69%	$\frac{11}{17} = .65$	$+19\frac{1}{4}$	3.79

Although these groups are large and the number of trades small, the correlation between anticipated success and profits can be seen. Even within the 60–69% group, the only losses occurred at the lower, 60%, level.

CHAPTER 15

Day Trading

The techniques discussed in such rigid form in Chapter 14 are put to use by the day trader. Day trading requires extreme discipline and depth of knowledge. The need for fast response to changing situations tends to exaggerate any bad trading habits that you have acquired. As in other fields, the faster you work, the more chance for error.

In order to keep mistakes to a minimum, daily strategy must be planned in advance. It should account for all the likely situations that might occur based on the nature of the current price movement. It should also have alternatives for the extreme unexpected moves in either direction. If prices closed sharply higher yesterday, you must know what to do in advance if there is a continued higher open, or a lower open, or some reversal following the open. You must decide on a plan and stick to it. Making spot decisions during market hours will cause more frequent errors.

ONE-DAY-ONLY TECHNIQUES

If a trading plan requires holding positions for only one day it is best to be a member of the exchange that is being used. The nonmember commissions will restrict the trading of many commodities. As a member, the fee is so small that it can be ignored as a deterrent. Table 15-1 presents brief evaluation of the significance of the commission for various commodities. The *daily range* in points and dollars shows the maximum potential move in one day. It will also be useful to calculate the average trading range (daily high minus low price) for the current month to get a realistic picture of the normal daily move. A reasonable substitute might be 35% of the maximum range. From Table 15-1 it can be seen that the higher-priced commodities—soybeans, coffee, and cocoa—all have the smallest relative commission. Since commissions do not change often, it will generally be true that those commodities in extreme demand will offer the best fluctuations for day trading. Potatoes and sugar are examples of depressed prices in which the commission becomes disproportionately large. It would be very difficult to offset the impact of commissions for those commodities.

The value of a contract can also be a help in determining the potential fluctuations. The commission taken as a percentage of the value should be in the same order as the

Table 15-1 Relative Impact of Commissions

Commodity	Commission[a]	Maximum daily range		Commission as percentage of range	Spot[b] price	Contract value	Commission as percentage of value	Range as percentage of value
		In points	In dollars					
Cattle	$45	4.00	$1600	2.8	40.25	$16100	.28	9.9
Cocoa	66	12.00	3600	1.8	198.30	59490	.11	6.1
Coffee	80	12.00	4500	1.7	205.00	76875	.10	5.9
Copper	46	4.00	1000	4.6	53.10	13275	.35	7.5
Corn	45	20¢	1000	4.5	1.95	9750	.46	10.3
Cotton	57	4.00	2000	2.8	54.90	27450	.21	7.3
Gold (IMM)	45	20.00	2000	2.3	146.70	14670	.31	13.6
Hogs	40	3.00	900	4.4	43.20	12960	.31	6.9
Pork bellies	50	4.00	1440	3.5	52.60	18936	.26	7.6
Potatoes	42	1.00	500	8.4	6.45	3225	1.30	15.5
Silver (CBT)	45	40.00	2000	2.3	455.00	22750	.20	8.8
Soybeans	45	60¢	3000	1.5	6.05	30250	.15	9.9
Soybean meal	45	20.00	2000	2.3	145.30	14530	.31	13.8
Soybean oil	45	2.00	1200	3.8	21.40	12840	.35	9.3
Sugar	68	1.00	1120	6.1	7.80	8736	.77	12.8
Wheat	45	40¢	2000	2.3	2.23	11150	.40	17.9

[a] Approximate minimum exchange commissions mid-1977.
[b] Closing price of nearest futures contract (except May potatoes).

DAY TRADING

commission with respect to the maximum range. Occasionally the daily range is not expanded or reduced when prices change and the calculation using the actual value of the contract will be a more accurate guide. It can be seen that the three most opportune are still the same, but now in the following order: coffee, cocoa, and soybeans.

Occasionally a sharp price rise is not followed by a timely increase in the daily trading limits and frequent locked-limit days occur. A day trader does not want to be locked into an undesirable position overnight. The daily range taken as a percentage of the contract value will indicate the potential problems with regard to limit moves. The commodities with the highest relative range—wheat, potatoes, gold, soybean meal, and so on—are least likely to have this problem while coffee, cocoa, and hogs are most likely.

To get an idea of the importance of the relative levels, when the pork bellies daily range became about 3.5% of its value in 1975 there were nearly 20 consecutive limit days. At the same time the cattle range was 6.6% of its value and it had 13% limit days with 4% of those days closing at the limit. Considering those situations it seems that the best selections would be commodities in which the range exceeded 7% of the value. A day trader must find a compromise between the two problems of high relative commissions and potential limit moves. This evaluation method will help select the best and eliminate the worst. Since prices can change rapidly it will require periodic reevaluation.

LIQUIDITY

The importance of liquidity is magnified in day trading. A $100 execution skid in soybeans may seem small when you are taking a $2000 profit from a position held for a month, but frequent deductions of $100 from an average profit objective of $300 in a day trade may be critical. It will be easier to get in and out of a cattle contract when 4000 lots are traded than a broiler contract with only 25 lots of total sales.

There are some advantages to trading a few lots of a thinly traded commodity. The lack of liquidity causes extreme moves, especially in the deferred contracts. Using the more liquid near-term options for analysis and trading in a manner contrary to the current price direction, it is possible to sell at a much higher price or buy at a lower one in a different contract. Getting out of that position may, of course, force a return of these additional profits.

POINT-AND-FIGURE AS A DAY-TRADING METHOD

The first method to be considered for day trading is point-and-figure charting. Because of the limitations of the daily trading range it is necessary to choose a small box size for our charts. A standard three-box reversal will be used. Using the Chicago Mercantile Exchange's hog contract, with a 3¢ (300 point) maximum range, we chose a five-point box size to be used for the charts. For soybeans $\frac{1}{2}$¢ might be selected, or for corn $\frac{1}{4}$¢. Diagram 15-1 illustrates three general situations that might occur in order to get buy or sell signals. It is assumed that a new chart is started each day.

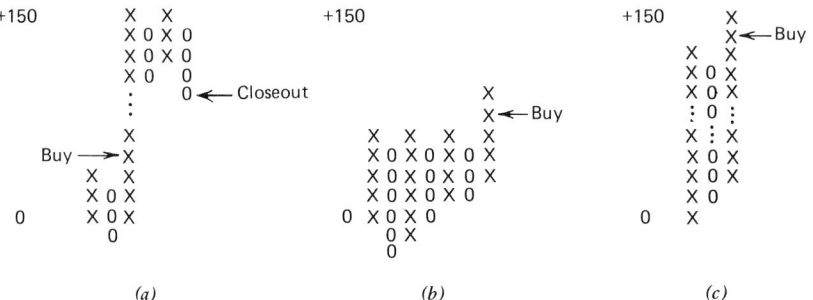

Diagram 15-1 Point-and-figure intraday formations.

Example (a) is ideal, generating a buy signal after an unchanged open with a minimum number of reversals and boxes. Similarly, the closeout of that position occurred as close to the limit as possible. In this case the buy signal occurred three boxes above the open (+15 points) and the sell five boxes below the limit (−25 points). This leaves a maximum profit of 110 points less 12 points of commission, or 98 points, about $300. But a normal trading day only ranges about 100 points out a possible 300, which gives a maximum potential profit of 48 points once the 40 points are subtracted for point-and-figure entry and exit as well as 12 points for commission. Realistically, this leaves a minimum opportunity with this method.

The other two examples, (b) and (c), are more common developments of the first point-and-figure signals. Each shows that an appreciable amount of points can be missed before that signal occurs. In many cases there would not be enough potential in the trade to merit taking the signal.

MOVING AVERAGES

The intrinsic time dependency of a moving average makes it less adaptable to day trading. In earlier discussions it was pointed out that the prices in a time-series must be recorded at equal intervals. During the trading day it must be decided what intervals are practical to allow reliable recording of prices and enough time to calculate the averages required.

To consider the problems involved in such a moving-average method, assume that prices are recorded every 5 minutes and that a 10-point moving average is used. Then the first calculation will be made 50 minutes after the open, and a signal will occur only when the prices change direction. That is a natural conclusion from the standard rule that causes a buy or sell signal when prices cross the moving average line. Using that rule, the first signal must occur in the opposite direction from the initial opening move. The first position will usually be contrary to the major trend and therefore should be used with caution.

INTERDAY VARIATIONS

The limited potential for a systematic approach to trading during a single day causes many traders to hold overnight positions. With this concession most of the standard

DAY TRADING 253

technical systems can be adapted to short-term trading by considering the days as continuous. If the point-and-figure method is used the trader is no longer restricted to plotting increments of the minimum move in order to get the first signal, when a larger box size might isolate an intermediate trend. With this in mind, the meat futures —cattle, hogs and pork bellies—show good formations with 10-point boxes and a four- or five-box reversal. Each day would generate between one and five reversals, not enough to use for a single day's trading, but much more sensitive than the standard point-and-figure method described in Chapter 11.

Support and Resistance

The concept of support and resistance levels is important to the short-term trader. If prices start to move higher, slow down, and finally reverse, it is natural to consider the top price as a resistance point. Prices are thought to have been stretched to their extreme at that level. Any subsequent attempt to approach the previous high price will be met with professional selling in anticipation of prices stopping again at the same point. In addition, it is common for the same traders and others to place orders above the previous high prices in order to take new long positions or close out shorts taken below the resistance level.

This method of trading, very popular among floor brokers and active speculators, tends to create and emphasize the support and resistance price levels until they define a clear *trading range*. Within a 1- to 3-day period these ranges can be narrow and yet effectively contain price movement. During the life of the trading range it will continue to narrow as the levels become clear to more traders and the anticipation of a reversal at those levels becomes imminent.

To take advantage of the smaller ranges caused in this manner it is necessary to enter positions during the middle of a trading session, frequently holding that trade until the middle of the next session. An example using the Chicago Board of Trade December 75 Silver contract, during August of 1975, will help to illustrate the problem. Prices on 4 consecutive days were:

Table 15-2 December 75 CBT Silver

	Open	High	Low	Close
August 21	500.50	505.00	493.00	498.20
22	501.00	504.00	494.50	500.00
25	501.00	594.50	496.00	503.80
26	502.50	504.00	483.80	483.80

The opening and closing prices for the first 3 days do not indicate any opportunity for trading. Prices were generally in the middle of the daily range. By using the high and low of the previous day this situation can be traded either of two ways.

Thursday, August 21, forms a range of 505 to 493, closing near the center of the range. After the next open, you can buy just above 493 and sell just below 505 in order to be certain of entering and exiting your position. For protection a stop can be entered at about 506 and 492 to reverse your position on a breakout.

Had this procedure been followed, entering 2¢ (200 points) before the bounds of the range, the following trades would have been executed:

Table 15-3 Trading December 75 Silver Using Support and Resistance

		Profit/Loss
August 22	Sold at 503.00	
	Closed out short and bought at 495.00	+ 8.00
August 25	Closed out long and sold at 502.00	+ 7.00
	Closed out short and bought at 496.50	+ 5.50
August 26	Closed out long and sold at 502.0	+ 5.50
	Closed out short and bought at 498.00	+ 4.00
	Closed out long and sold at 495.00	− 3.00
	Open position	+11.20

In each case the entry was 200 points before the point where prices had reversed on the prior day. The stop-loss was placed to limit losses to a 100-point penetration. While this is an ideal situation, it does happen this way and professional traders frequently use this method. It can be seen that the support levels did actually rise from 493.00 to 494.50 and then to 496.00. When support was penetrated, prices rapidly broke to new lows of 483.80, down to the permissible limit. Similarly, the resistance level remained intact going from 505.00 to 504.00, 504.50, and, finally, 504.00. It is generally accepted that the resistance level represents a more volatile area, which must be watched closely for false breakouts.

Support and resistance levels gain importance the more time they remain intact. The high and low of the prior day are not as significant as the weekly or the monthly range. Each can be traded using the same technique. The major support and resisttance levels are contract highs and lows, which rarely allow breakouts with less than one attempt. Longer-term price objectives can be identified using a continuation chart. This chart plots only the nearest (spot) futures contract of a specific commodity to allow the location of support and resistance levels when the current contracts are in a new high or low area.

Very few systems have been written on day trading because of the difficulties in finding a large enough audience and an experienced trader willing to set down his knowledge. The following method is a valuable part of the available literature.

THE TAYLOR TRADING TECHNIQUE

In 1950 George Douglass Taylor published his *book method* of day trading, which he had been using for many years in both the stock and grain markets. The method is one that requires the experience of discipline and timing, but is carefully set down and offered to the public in its full measure of sophistication and in a simplified state. The system is intrinsically cyclic, anticipating 3-day movements in the grains. These 3 days can vary in character when they are within an uptrend or a downtrend, but remain essentially consistent. Taylor's explanation of his method is thorough and includes many valuable thoughts for traders interested in working with the market full-time. The summary and analysis presented here cannot replace a reading of the original material.

Taylor developed his approach to trading through experience and a belief in a basic rhythm in the market. The dominant pattern is seen to be a 3-day repetition with occasional, although regular, intervals of 4- to 5-day patterns. Taylor's cycles are evaluated as continuous trading days, without regard to weekends or holidays. The 3-day cycle varies slightly if prices are in an uptrend or downtrend. The uptrend is defined as having higher tops and bottoms over some predefined time period, involving weekly, monthly, or even seasonal observations. A downtrend is the reverse. During an uptrend we can expect the following sequence:

A buying day objective where prices stop declining and we can purchase before a rally begins

A selling day objective at which we close out our long position

A short sale day objective where prices meet resistance and we can sell prior to a reversal

Following the third day where we enter our short position we begin again with the buying day. For the 3-day cycle within an uptrend Taylor has given extra latitude to the long position, with part of a day reserved to allow it to exhaust its upward move prior to a short sale. For downtrends we can do the opposite, expecting some added time necessary for the downward move to finish before mustering a rally.

The objectives themselves are extremely short-term support and resistance levels, usually only the prior day's high and low prices or occasionally the high and low of the 3-day cycle, which may be the same prices. On a buying day the objective is a test or a penetration of the prior day's low price, buy only if it occurs first, before a test of the prior highs. Taylor's method is then a short-term contra-trend technique, which looks for prices to continuously reverse direction. His belief was that speculation caused these erratic, sometimes large, cyclic variations about the long-term trend.

Taylor places great emphasis on the order of occurrence of the high and low on each day. If we are looking to buy, the low must occur first. If this is a buying day and we are in an uptrend, we will buy after any lower opening, whether the prior low is not reached or is penetrated. An uptrend will generally be stronger towards the close and the first opportunity must be taken on a buying day. However, if a high is reached first and prices then decline, so that they are near their lows towards the end of trading, no long position is entered. This pattern is indicative of a lower opening the next day, which will then provide a better opportunity for a buy. During a downtrend period these violations of the lows, or penetrations towards the close, are more common and by waiting until the next day to make our purchase we switch the 3-day cycle to favor the short sale.

Consider the same problems with regard to closing out a long and selling during an uptrend. After the buying day we have a long position that we are looking to liquidate. If it happens that on the same day that we purchased prices rallied sharply, touching or penetrating the prior highs, we would expect a higher opening the next day, at which time we would close out our position. Because of the uptrend we might then

Table 15-4 November 1975 Soybeans

1975		Open	High	Low	Close	D	R	BH	BU	Net
March										
M	10	540	x542	535	540½					
T	11	435	560¼	x535	560¼	7		18¾	0	
W	12	560	x572	552	571½		37			
H	13	568	x577	559	560½					
F	14	553	559	√549	549½	28		0	10	+2¾
M	17	548	√560	548	558		11			
T	18	555	x558	538	538½					
W	19	530	546	x529	545¼	29		0	9	
H	20	543	√555	540	547½		26			
F	21	547½	√567½	547½	567½					−1½
M	24	573	581	√561	573	6½		13½	0	
T	25	573	x575	564	574		14			
W	26	577	√594	574	594					
H	27	587	590	√579	585	15		0	0	+31½
M	31	592	√603½	589	595½		24½			
April										
T	1	599	x599	584	591½					
W	2	589	591½	√575	575¾	24		0	9	
H	3	570	√573	565	566¾		0			
F	4	570	√578	567	576¾					−12

DAY TRADING   257

Table 15-4 (*continued*)

1975		Open	High	Low	Close	D	R	BH	BU	Net
M	7	577	577	ⓥ562	565¾	16		0	5	
T	8	566	ⓥ579½	563	568¼		17½			
W	9	565	ⓥ574	561½	573½					
H	10	571	575	ⓥ556	561¾	18		1	5½	
F	11	560	ⓧ564½	558	563½		8½			−9
M	14	561	ⓧ568	555½	561½					
T	15	565	569½	ⓥ560½	563½	7½		1½	0	
W	16	562	ⓧ566	553	559¼		5½			
H	17	560	ⓥ565	558	563½					
F	18	563	563	ⓥ557	559	8		0	1	−1

expect a small set back and another test of the highs. We would wait another day to be sure that the strength was exhausted. If we tested the highs of the selling day on the next short sale day open, we would immediately sell, entering a new position. If the short sale day opened lower and finished higher we would wait.

Faster reactions to price moves are expected when we take a long position on a buy day, or on the next open, when we are in a downtrend. If the opportunity arises and prices rally sharply on the same day that our position was entered, we liquidate at once and take the profit. This is an important point to remember, since we are trading against a known trend and do not have the opportunity to profit by waiting. Time would be playing against our position.

Taylor called this his "book method" because he recorded all the information necessary for trading in a small 3 × 5 spiral notebook that he carried. The organization of the book is simple and shown in Table 15-4, an example that uses the November 75 Soybean contract. Of course, in Taylor's book there would be only one month per page, due to its size. The first five columns contain the date and day, and the open, high, low, and closing prices. The first 10 days are used to determine where the cycle begins. Scanning the daily lows, circle the lowest of the first 10 days, in this case March 19. Then work backward and forward, circling every third low price. This is your buying day. The sequences of 2 days in between are circled in the high column and indicate the selling day and the short sale day, respectively.

In order to judge the opportunities for buying and selling, the next columns, marked D and R, indicate the number of points in the *decline* from the short sale day to the buying day and the number of points in the *rally* from the buying day to the selling day. In both columns the differences are taken using the highs and lows only. These values represent the maximum number of points that could have been made during those trades, provided that the highs and lows occurred in the proper order. An "x" or a "√" in the circle next to the high or low means that the opportunity to buy or sell occurred first (if an x) or last (if a √). In the case of the first, the trade would have been entered that day and in the other case we would have waited.

The next two columns, BH and BU, show the adversity and opportunity of that day's prices to our buying objective. BH means a *buying-day high* and is entered with the number of points that the day traded above the prior day's high (the short sale day), and BU shows the opportunity to *buy under*, by recording the number of points by which the day sold under the low of the prior day—an area in which you would buy if the low occurred first. If neither situation occurred, zeros were entered.

A wide column on the right is used to indicate the net weekly change in direction by taking the difference between the prior Friday's closing price and the current Friday's price. This should be used to compare with your own performance.

By observing columns D and R in Table 15-4 it can be seen that there was ample opportunity for substantial profits on both the long positions and short sales, with only one case of a zero entry on April 3. The trades that would have been entered or liquidated can be approximated using the BH and BU columns and the x and √ notations. For consistency you might assume that the √ indicates a position was taken on the next open. In either case, the results would have been good.

Taylor's daily method requires a care in monitoring the market of which only a professional trader is fully equipped. You must observe when the highs and lows occur and whether the new low is going to penetrate or fail to penetrate the prior lows. You must time your trades carefully for maximum profit. In addition, it would be helpful to combine this method with long- and short-term trends and cycles as well as seasonal patterns to increase your sensitivity to price movement.

For those who cannot watch the market constantly, Taylor offers a rigid *3-day trading method*, which is a modification of his overall daily method. The cycles remain the same, but the buying and selling objectives are entered into the market in advance. This method is expected to work on balance, as are other well-defined systems. What is primarily lost by this approach is the order of occurrence of the highs and lows; otherwise the concept of the system remains intact.

It is interesting that this technique expects and profits from penetration of support and resistance levels. Most other methods consider a breakout of prior highs and lows as a major trending indication, but Taylor views it as a better opportunity to do the opposite. It is one of the few examples of such an approach and could only succeed in the short term, where the behavioral aspects of trading are dominant.

CHAPTER 16

Practical Considerations

There are areas of technical and mathematical analysis that cannot be regarded as systems, but are essential to the successful trader. This chapter covers some of the important items, emphasizing the correct use of computers, the combining of systems, gambling techniques, and some other interesting material. While not everyone will use a computer, most traders will be strongly influenced by computer analysis in the form of other systems or predictive information. It is best to know what you are dealing with and what mistakes and omissions could have occurred on the way to getting an answer. Because a computer was used doesn't mean that its results are correct, even though we recognize that the computer was necessary to process enough information to consider the answer to a test as reliable.

The second section, on the theory of runs, is actually an application of gambling techniques, primarily Martingale, to commodities trading. What would seem more reasonable than assuming that the odds are against you in the commodities market and treating it as a gambling situation? The third section is on filtering, which is an unavoidable tendency of all traders to eliminate their losses. Instead, many eliminate their capital. Filtering has been overlooked as a well-defined strategy, but we hope to shed some light on it here. The next section is a short analysis of trading limits to show some of the problems and flaws in its operating environment. The last section is an attempt to teach a lesson by pointing out a bad example; anyone that sees the problem has come a long way.

USE AND ABUSE OF THE COMPUTER

Make sure your present report system is reasonably clean and effective before you automate. Otherwise your new computer will just speed up the mess.

Robert Townsend[1]

Computers are not a substitute for thinking, only for calculating or filing, and even then you can only get out information as accurate as that which was entered. But you are convinced that even with these handicaps you must use a computer if you want some evaluation of your original technical ideas. This chapter will consider both good and bad ways to approach a computer problem, none of which can be credited to or blamed on the machine, but on the expertise of those responsible for organization, implementation, and testing of the problem. As a calculator a computer can't be beat; many of the systems, advancements, and refinements presented in this book could not have been considered without it.

Computers come in many shapes and sizes, owned and borrowed. Their packaging is becoming second only to the car. The average time period between computer "generations" is about 10 years and no one keeps the old machine when a new model is announced. Most computers are justified by their efficient generation of invoices and statements, which in turn produces income for their users. When time is still available in the computer day, other accounting functions are applied, then marketing and sales reports, then other operations, and, finally, research and development (between 2:00 and 4:00 in the morning). If you have a computer on hand, but fall into the "no priority" group, or if you have no computer, you will find it cheaper and more convenient to find a small company with extra time available to rent on their computer. Most small businesses will appreciate any income from an outside source in order to defer their basic costs.

The specification of the computer you need will vary according to both the data base and the system you intend to develop. In some cases, the data base that you use or purchase will be adaptable only to specific machines—select which data base you want in advance, but do not purchase it until your system has passed preliminary testing. Your system design might also require a computer of certain memory size with either disk or tape drives. Rent a machine that will allow for expansion, but don't pay for features you can't use. Most service bureaus bill according to the specific equipment accessed by your program. Computers differ in the relationship of size to speed of operation. You can usually operate your program on a large computer in a short time or on a small computer at a slow speed, but both will work.

Once you have access to a computer and have made arrangements to pay, you are ready to start. You know that you want to test different simply moving averages of 5 days, 6 days, and so on, up to 50 days. What next? You need two essential elements: a programmer and test data.

Programming and Personnel

He who has not worked in a computer environment may be in for a rude awakening—computer programmers and other personnel are a different breed. Perhaps it's working

---
[1] Townsend (1970), p. 36.

PRACTICAL CONSIDERATIONS

with the machines so long, or not working with people, but programmers are extreme individualists with distinctive nonconformist traits. Getting a programmer to tell you "how much" or "how long" it will take to solve a problem is impossible. If one did venture to give you an estimate, you would be safe to double it. Even competant managers of a programming staff have difficulty figuring a schedule based on the performance of varied personalities. It's not that a programmer means to mislead you, but his unfailing optimism in his ability to solve a "simple" problem results in a drastically wrong estimate of completion. At any stage of the work his response to "How much longer?" will be "It will be ready after this one last error is found." If you're going to contract your work or hire a programmer, do it on a "fixed-price" contract and avoid the problems that will occur later.

Keep your programmer on a schedule. Establish a working plan with your programmer in advance, starting with the end product, the input, then the intermediate steps, in the following way:

1. Define what you want out of this program—for example, a report showing results of various moving averages, including:
   - Profitability
   - Number of total trades
   - Number of profitable trades
   - Worst losing streak
2. Simulate the form of the output report, *exactly* as it should appear.
3. Ask the question, "What do I need to put into this program to get the results I want?"
4. Write a technical description of how the results are calculated, using only the input data.
5. Draw a flow chart of the logic involved in handling data, calculations, and so on (standard program flow chart).
6. Write the program.
7. Test the program with simply cases that you can verify by hand.
8. Run the tests that will generate your desired answers.
9. Thank the computer people for their help.

Remember that most programmers won't understand your interest in using the results in the real world. To most programmers, solving the problem is its own reward.

The Data Base

Now we have a program that works. It calculates the profits, losses, and some other statistics about simple moving averages. What do we use as data for testing and how much data do we need? If your requirements are small—for example, only one commodity related to your business—you may find the data in the Chicago Board of Trade Statistical Annual or the Chicago Mercantile Exchange Yearbook. Both books go back for a number of years and include all data necessary for testing. Using sample data from one of these sources (or the *Wall Street Journal* or *Journal of Commerce*) can be an inexpensive way to do preliminary testing; if your ideas are a flop, you haven't made a major investment in a data base. The form and procedures for entering this interim data should be the same as the permanent data base you anticipate purchasing; otherwise you will have additional work later on in the form of conversion.

There are only a few services that provide historic data on commodities, the most popular being Dunn and Hargitt Financial Serives in W. Lafayette, Indiana, Remote Computing Corp. in Roslyn, New York, and, more recently, Comtrend in Stamford, Connecticut. The Dunn and Hargitt service sells data in any format on most media; Remote Computing provides a real-time charting service with programming capability and system generation; and Comtrend has the new Videcom graphics display with the most detailed, sophisticated, and expensive access. These companies provide data as part of a monthly service. In any case, the data are available if you can determine how much you want and how you want them organized. Be sure that you get daily open, high, low, and closing prices (some services omit the open) as well as volume and open interest; sometimes you can get the day of the week but it is not essential since it can be calculated.

Looking Into the Past

Your selection of how many years to use in your test is a function of the number of trades and its predictive qualities. As you use more data you will find that the faster moving averages have a lower reliability (percentage of profitable to total trades) than the slower moving averages. The profitability may vary differently than the reliability since it may only take one good trade out of ten to be a winner.

The predictive qualities of test durations are more complicated to uncover and can only be calculated by a forward extrapolation. In other words, you can perform the following tests:

1. One-year test—
   - Test moving averages for 1970, then use the best results on simulated trading for 1971
   - Repeat using 1971 results for simulating 1972 trading, and so on
2. Two-year test—
   - Find the best moving average for 1971–1972, then simulate 1973 trading
   - Repeat for larger combinations

These simulated trading results will give you the number of years of testing necessary to find the best predictive quality. The technique may be a simplistic approach, but computers won't tire of repeating the same calculations over and over again.

Poor Use of Data

In a 1975 publication of trading systems there was a well-organized approach to the testing of a single commodity. The life of each contract was 18 months and 15 individual contracts ranging from July 1968 delivery to January 1972 were selected. Reasonable? Apparantly so, but in actuality not very scientific.

PRACTICAL CONSIDERATIONS 263

While in this instance the distribution of data proved unfavorable to the author, it is necessary to follow the principles for proper selection in order for the reader to have a reasonable attempt at objective evaluation.

The contracts selected for the test were:

July 1968	Dec 1967	Sept 1968	May 1970
July 1969	Dec 1968	Sept 1969	Jan 1971
July 1970	Dec 1969	Sept 1970	
July 1971	Dec 1970	Sept 1971	
	Dec 1971		

In a seasonal or cyclic commodity there is a good reason for selecting more than one delivery month during each year; new and old crop or production cycles can cause substantially unique price patterns during the same time period for different deferred deliveries. Even the proper overlapping of a traditionally nonseasonal product may pick up deviations due to antipation or extreme short-term demand or surplus. But this commodity was not seasonal or cyclic, and the 18-month contract duration caused the overlapping time intervals show in Diagram 16-1.

Once you see the number of tests being performed at any one time it is easy to construct a distribution (Diagram 16-2) by counting the horizontal bars at specific points. This distribution will show the testing bias due to duplication. In the diagram

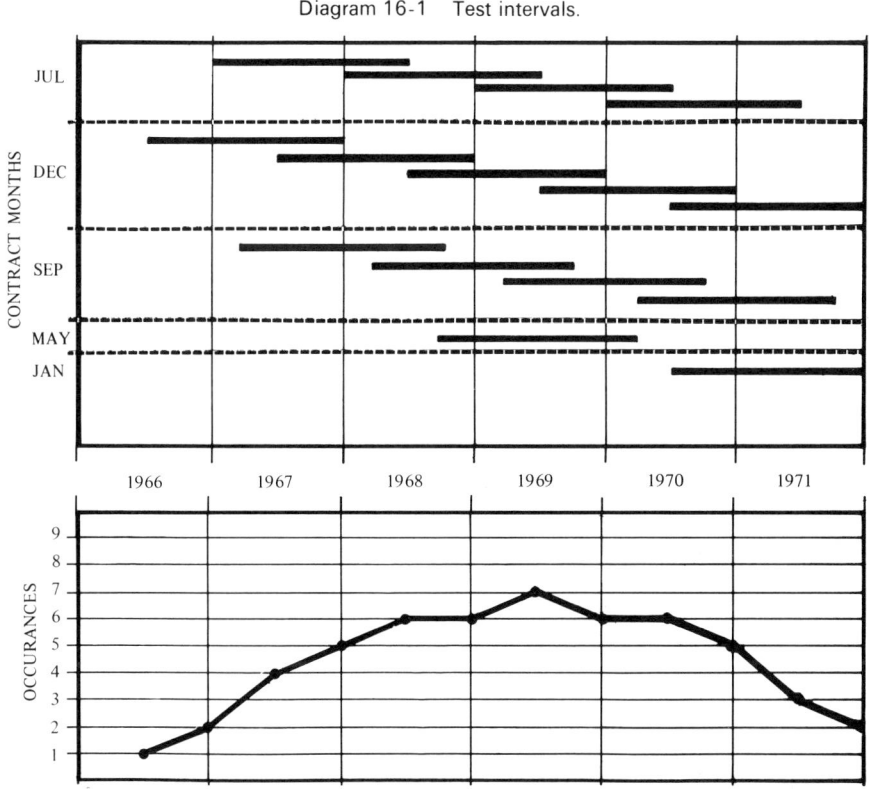

Diagram 16-1 Test intervals.

Diagram 16-2 Distribution of testing.

shown, we can see that there was only one delivery month tested in the last half of 1966, while there were six contracts being tested through the middle period, tapering off to two contracts at the end of 1971.

Whether this selection of data is favorable to the author or not, or whether it is the proper time period to test this commodity, the reader should be aware of the duplicate use of data that has a high degree of similarity. When testing your own system it would benefit you to avoid this problem.

What Is the Price of Knowledge?

By the time you invest in a data base (worth at least $5000) and a programmer to implement your ideas (at about $20/hour minimum) and the computer time to "debug" and test your programs (another 10 hours at $25/hour on a small computer) you have an investment of no less than $7000. What do you have for your money? Your hard work has resulted in proving one of four things:

1. The system is profitable.
2. The system is not profitable.
3. The system can't be implemented effectively.
4. Computer testing is too expensive.

If you've run out of money, or feel that what you have could be better spent, then your trading philosophy is due to be reexamined. If the third situation occurred you must either continue until you have succeeded in implementing the rules or admit that much of your technique is subjective. That can be an important and valuable discovery. Many spectators believe that they are very clinical about their rules—they know exactly what they will do in every circumstance and therefore think that their approach can be well-defined in writing. When you implement these rules on a computer there are no "maybes" and no "wait and see" and no exceptions whatsoever. With the exception of a single losing trade there are many speculators who would have been rich.

The second possible result is that you would have proved that the system will not work using either the rules or the variables imposed by the program. If you have tested various moving averages in the range of 20 through 50 days, you now should try moving averages of less than 20 days. If your stop-loss points were too big or too small (judging by the size of your losses) try different sizes. Systems don't always work as you would like (or expect), and their performance is related to price movement. Perhaps a slight modification to your theory is necessary? Negative results are important feedback. They show you where you might have gone wrong and help you correct before it is too late. After all, if you knew it was going to work in advance, all this would be unnecessary.

A Winner in Disguise

One important twist on performance should not be overlooked: a consistently bad performer can become a consistent winner by doing just the opposite. If you have

PRACTICAL CONSIDERATIONS 265

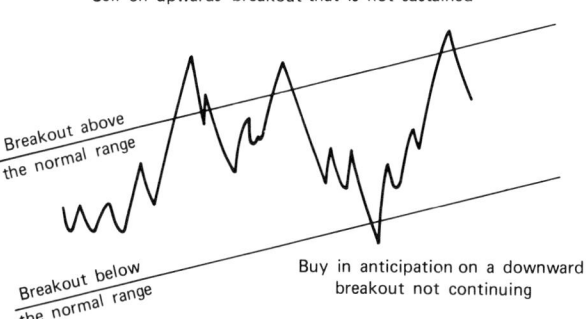

Diagram 16-3   Reversing the trading rules.

ever studied the trending characteristics of the frozen orange juice market you may have concluded that it is a hopeless case and should be ignored; on the other hand, steady losses means that the price movement consistently stays within a trading range, and every buy signal and sell signal actually represents an overbought and oversold condition, predictive of a change in direction. (See Diagram 16-3.)

The first and best result is that your method does actually work. Now you must probe a little farther and ask:

- Can the rules be followed exactly as the computer program was implemented?
- Did I account for normal market execution problems: gaps, skids, and locked-limit days?
- What investment would be necessary to survive the worst losing streak with excess-margin money?
- Do I have the discipline to follow the system rigorously?
- Do I have the confidence in both the results and the skill of the programmer to know that the results I have are what I asked for?
- Is there a better system than the one I have created?

And most of all, before you begin a monumental task of designing and testing your own system, you should know yourself. If you solve the problem scientifically, will you still have doubts about following the system with actual money?

Can You Find Happiness With a 5-, 10-, or 20-Day Moving Average?

There are very few alternatives open to a speculative trader. One possibility is to select a well-known service or published system that you can calculate yourself. Let's use as an example a 5- and 10-day moving average. The rules are:

- Buy when the 5-day moving average crosses above the 10-day moving average
- Sell when the 5-day moving average crosses below the 10-day moving average
- Liquidate when the prices move into the neutral area between the 5- and 10-day moving averages

There is more than one well-known system of this design, with either different moving averages or slightly modified rules. The basic questions to be asked about this or any other system are:

- Does it work?
- Will it continue to work?
- Why were 5- and 10-day averages chosen?
- Why were these rules used?

There are usually no answers to these questions. At best you might discover that "this is a basic trading approach that everyone believes," or, "the 5- and 20-day moving averages were chosen because they work." Profitable results will justify the means in most cases, but there may be no way of telling what investment would have been necessary to actually realize the published results. If you must follow such a system, use as little margin as possible and keep the largest reserve possible until you have some experience with it.

Whenever you see a system using 5-, 10-, or 20-day averages or other simple numbers (100-point boxes or 1% stops) be wary of the fact that these may be "convenient" numbers that were selected and then tested and subsequently resulted in a profit. The 5-, 10-, and 20-day selections seem reasonable because they represent 1, 2, and 4 weeks, a likely place to start if you're not using a computer to test all combinations.

The other alternatives open to you as a speculator are to find someone who has properly tested a method or to do the testing yourself. Since it is your money, take your choice.

It seems only reasonable that the same test that determines trending ability also indicates nontrendinding features. Learning how to use your test results is an important step toward a successful system.

Just Because It Doesn't Work in Practice Doesn't Mean It Won't Work in Theory

You thought you followed all the rules, that is:

1. Precisely defined the system.
2. Tested using enough data.
3. Evaluated performance by forward extrapolation.
4. Invested enough to survive the worst losing streak.
5. Traded a diversified portfolio.
6. Followed every signal.

And still you lost all your money ... What happened? It's not unusual to have a novice technician complain about how he did everything right, but still lost. There are two possibilities that could have caused his problem. The first is that he was not disciplined enough to follow the rules, although he thought he was. Many new traders only test their ideas "in general" by spot checking a few selected commodities during years that seem to have "interesting" or "typical" movement. They assume that their shortcuts do not affect the results of the system; some even believe that they are being harder on the system than if they had performed complete testing. The advantage of computerized testing is that *all* years can be tested easily—the only valid procedure.

In evaluating their own results, there is a temptation to "make" a system work if it failed because of one or two large losses. An analyst can impose a filter on the selected trades to eliminate those that would have caused the major losses. Some technicians may just assume that circumstances would have caused them to "pass" the trade, rather than buy or sell in an "obviously" adverse market. If you have lost your investment by following a system, you owe it to yourself to have some well-disciplined friend review your rules and your trades to see that you actually did follow the system.

Suppose you did follow all the rules. The most common problem is to misjudge the volatility of the market. If you average the size of the losses in your testing and compare them with the size of your real trading losses, you may find that the actual losses are substantially larger than the theoretical ones. That's not surprising. On the average, prices are higher now than they have been in the past. The higher the price and the more volatile, the larger the losses. Consequently, a long losing streak will eat up more money. Execution prices also become worse in faster moving markets and commissions may be higher than in your original testing. The combination of volatility and skids may cause a bigger impact on even the most carefully followed methods.

People Win, Systems Go On . . .

Start slowly. You can't get hurt if you trade a ridiculously small portfolio—one that you can afford to lose ten times over. Get the feel for the system; see if it is performing the way it was tested. Check the size and frequency of your losses; see how much of your profits are given up before your positions are liquidated; watch your equity cycle. When you know what to expect you can increase your investment slowly. Patience will make you succeed where even the most clever fail.

An even safer way to win is to combine your plan with true discipline by turning the day-to-day following of your system over to someone else. It is the only way you can be certain that the rules will be followed precisely. In addition, take a trip and don't leave an address. Tell your broker to liquidate your account if your equity decreases by 50%, or whatever level your system calls for. If you can't do that and you want to be successful you should know why.

GAMBLING TECHNIQUE—THE THEORY OF RUNS

The application of gambling theory to commodity trading satisfies two important conditions. First, it presumes no statistical advantage in the results but concerns itself with the probable patterns that occur. A gambler never believes that a roulette wheel is skew or that the dice are off balance enough to favor some numbers more then others. You could treat each day of commodity trading as an occurrence of red or black—up or down price moves. Or you can treat the profits and losses of your trading as red or black occurrences. We will apply our work to the latter.

Secondly, gambling theory is the art of money management under adverse conditions. A successful professional gambler and a commodities trader must both be highly disciplined. This section will look at a gambler's approach to money management and risk, using the *theory of runs*.

If you make the assumption that each day of commodity trading is unrelated to the previous day or that each day prices have an equal chance of going up or down, you have a situation closely related to roulette. In Monte Carlo the roulette wheel has 37 compartments: 18 black, 18 red, and 1 white, assuring a loss of 2.7% in the same way that you consider brokerage cost of trading as a handicap. If you were to continuously bet on only red or black you would find yourself even, less the 2.7%, over long betting periods. The only alternative to changing the chances is in the management of money—varying the size of the bet. The most well-known method for winning in a gambling situation is based on the probability of successive wins, the theory of runs.

On each spin of the wheel, the likelihood of the same color (red or black) occurring again is 50% or ½ (ignoring the zero slot). We define a run of three reds occuring at the center of five events,

Black-Red-Red-Red-Black

If each color had a 50% chance of occurring, the probability of a run of three is

$$\tfrac{1}{2} \cdot \tfrac{1}{2} \cdot \tfrac{1}{2} \cdot \tfrac{1}{2} \cdot \tfrac{1}{2} = (\tfrac{1}{2})^5$$

We then know that we can expect one run of three for 32 spins of the wheel (coups). Extending that to runs of n consecutive reds, we have $(\tfrac{1}{2})^{n+2}$. For 256 *coups*, which is both a power of 2 and the approximate number of trading days in a year, we have the following possibilities for runs of red:

Run of length	Probability of occurrence	Expected number of occurrences	Total appearances of red
1	$\tfrac{1}{8}$	32	32
2	$\tfrac{1}{16}$	16	32
3	$\tfrac{1}{32}$	8	24
4	$\tfrac{1}{64}$	4	16
5	$\tfrac{1}{128}$	2	10
6	$\tfrac{1}{256}$	1	6
		Total appearances	120

Any specific run of greater than six cannot be expected to occur and yet the total appearances of red is only 120, short eight, without accounting for the white slot. These eight appearances could increase any of the runs from one through six or appear as a longer run. The likelihood of a run greater than six is calculated using geometric progression to get the sum of all probabilities greater than six, or $(\tfrac{1}{2})^{n+2}$ where $256 \geq n \geq 7$:

$$P = (\tfrac{1}{2})^9 + (\tfrac{1}{2})^{10} + \cdots + (\tfrac{1}{2})^{256}$$

$$= \frac{(\tfrac{1}{2})^9}{1 - \tfrac{1}{2}} = \frac{1}{256}$$

There is a single chance that we have a run greater than six in our 256 tries, which is what we would have expected, since we had already accounted for all the other combinations. The average length of a run greater than six turns out to be eight, based on the decreasing probability of occurrence of longer runs. The average length of all runs greater than n will be $n + 2$. That makes our table of runs complete, with the number of occurrences of red equal to 128.

Martingale and Anti-Martingale

The classic application of the theory of runs is by Martingale. His approach was to double the bet each time he lost and begin again after each win. To demonstrate how this works, we can use a table of uniform random numbers (Appendix 5) and let all those numbers starting with digits 0 through 4 be assigned to red and 5 through 9 to black. Diagram 16-4, read left to right, where open squares are red and the solid

COUPS GENERATED FROM RANDOM NUMBERS

	1	2	3	4	5	6	7	8	9	10	11	12	13	14	15
1	□	□	□	□	■	■	■	□	■	□	□	□	□	□	■
2	□	■	□	■	■	□	■	□	□	□	■	■	■	□	□
3	□	□	□	□	■	□	■	□	□	□	■	■	■	□	□
4	□	■	□	□	■	■	■	□	■	□	■	□	□	□	□
5	■	□	■	■	□	□	■	■	■	■	■	□	■	□	□
6	□	■	■	■	□	□	□	□	■	■	■	■	□	■	□
7	■	□	□	□	■	■	□	□	■	■	□	■	■	■	■
8	□	■	□	□	□	□	■	■	□	■	■	■	□	■	□
9	□	■	□	□	□	□	■	□	■	■	□	□	□	■	■
10	■	■	□	□	□	□	□	■	□	■	■	■	□	■	■
11	■	□	□	■	□	■	■	□	■	□	□	■	■	■	□
12	■	□	■	■	■	□	□	■	■	□	■	■	□	□	■
13	■	■	□	■	□	□	■	■	□	■	□	■	□	□	□
14	□	■	■	■	■	■	□	■	□	□	■	■	□	■	■
15	□	■	□	□	□	□	■	□	■	□	■	□	■	■	□
16	□	□	■	□	■	□	□	■	■	□	■	□	□	■	□
17	■	□	□	□	□	□	□	□	□	■	□	□	□	□	□
18	□	■													

Diagram 16-4 Coups generated from random numbers.

squares are black, shows the first 257 assignments. Assuming that we are betting on black we will be concerned with the largest possible run that red might have. We want to make our bet as large as possible and still withstand the longest run of red that is likely to occur. By using the results from the analysis of the length of runs, we know that in 256 coups the likelihood is that only one run greater than six might occur, and that run would most probably be of eight in length. The probability of a run of nine occurring is $(\frac{1}{2})^{11}$ or 1 in 1024. In only 256 coups the odds are about 3 to 1 against a run of nine reds occurring.

Having decided that your capital must withstand a run of eight reds, you can figure that a bet of \$1 doubled eight times is \$128. Divide the amount of money that you are willing to risk by 128 and you get the size of your initial bet. A \$1000 limit divided by 128 gives 7.8125 rounded down to \$7; on the eighth consecutive occurrence of red you will be betting $897. If you count the occurrences of runs in our simulated roulette table, you find:

Table 16-1 Random Occurrences of Red and Black

Red	Black
35 Runs of 1	35 Runs of 1
12 Runs of 2	14 Runs of 2
7 Runs of 3	11 Runs of 3
7 Runs of 4	3 Runs of 4
2 Runs of 5	2 Runs of 5
2 Runs of 6	
1 Run of 8	
138 Total occurrences	118 Total occurrences

The results are within a reasonable approximation to what was expected, and no runs greater than eight occurred in either red or black. The betting would then proceed as follows, using an initial amount of $1. The numbers in the squares represent winning bets.

	1	2	3	4	5		6	7	8	9	10		11	12	13	14	15
1	1	2	4	8	[16]		[1]	[1]	1	[2]	1		2	4	8	16	[32]
2	1	[2]	1	[2]	[1]		1	[2]	1	2	4		[8]	[1]	[1]	1	2
3	4	8	16	32	[64]		1	[2]	1	2	4		[8]	[1]	[1]	1	2
4	4	[8]	1	2	[4]		[1]	[1]	1	[2]	1		[2]	1	2	4	8
5	[16]	1	[2]	[1]	1		2	[4]	[1]	[1]	[1]		[1]	1	[2]	1	2

Diagram 16-5 Martingale betting pattern.

Each time black occurs we win, and although we actually win up to $64 on a single black coup, each sequence of runs of red nets only the initial bet. In the 256 coups represented in Table 16-1 there were a total of 65 distinct runs resulting in a profit of $65 (based on $1 bets), about half of your capital. Had you bet equally on the black to win you would have lost $20 with this same sequence. The Martingale system gives you a good chance of winning a reasonable amount.[2]

The anti-Martingale approach gives you a small chance of winning a large amount; it is exactly the opposite of the Martingale system. Instead of doubling each losing bet, we will double the winners until we get a run long enough to reach our goal. What length run should we expect? We know that there is an excellent chance of one run of six in 256 coups and a similar chance of a longer run, probably of length eight. A run

---

[2]The Martingale system is likely to work if the player could withstand adverse runs of 11, but casinos tend to limit bets equal to amounts less than 2^{10} times the minimum bet.

of six would return $32 on a bet of $1 and a run of eight would net $128. If we bet on black for either six or eight we would have lost in our test sequence. Since there were 138 red coups we would have lost $138. If we had bet on red for a run of six we would have won three times for $94 and lost $118 on the total appearances of black. Had we waited for a run of eight we would have won $128 and lost $117 on black by stopping right after our win. The success of the anti-Martingale method depends on how soon your long run appears. In 4096 coups a run of 11 will occur once, returning $1024 on a bet of $1. In the same 4096 spins, you will have lost 2048 times, showing that if your long run happens in the middle of your playing, you will break even, and if sooner you will come out ahead.

The Theory of Runs Applied to Commodities

Before applying either Martingale or anti-Martingale systems to commodity markets we must determine whether the movement of prices up or down is as uniform as it is in the case of roulette. A simple test was performed on a combined set of 21 diverse commodity contracts as well as individual commodity sequences. The combined results of all up and down runs are shown in Table 16-2. The expected occurrences of both up and down were twice the probability of either a red or black coup occurring.

Certain differences between the expected and actual results should be noted in Table 16-2. Commodities consistently have fewer runs of one, and more frequent runs of two, with a tendency also to fluctuate in a narrowing pattern about the expected length of a run (see Diagram 16-6). This oscillation would be more dramatic if the actual was plotted as a percentage of the expected amount, but for the small sample the results might not be valid.

The applications of the theory of runs in commodities requires a great deal of new research to be decisive. You could use the probabilities to decide the chances of the next trading day continuing the prior day's trend, noting that a 4-day run is as long as you might expect before a reversal day. The most interesting applications are in the betting strategies of the Martingale and anti-Martingale systems, applied to futures markets. The following two sections show the possibilities.

Day Trading

Trade the daily open to close, considering a buy as a bet on black and a sell as a bet on red. Follow the Martingale system by doubling the number of contracts traded after each loss; start again with the initial amount after each win. For the anti-Martingale approach, reinvest all your winnings after each profitable trade, and continue until you have won consecutively for a predetermined run length. The obvious problems with these applications are the commissions, which are disproportionately large if you are not an exchange member, as well as the variability in the size of profits and losses. In order to work around these factors, consider the average move from open-to-close as the potential profit or loss on any trade and assume that any abnormally large or small profit or loss will adjust after enough trading. You might simply double your next positions for each loss or profit with the Martingale or anti-Martingale methods, respectively. The problem of commissions is not as easily

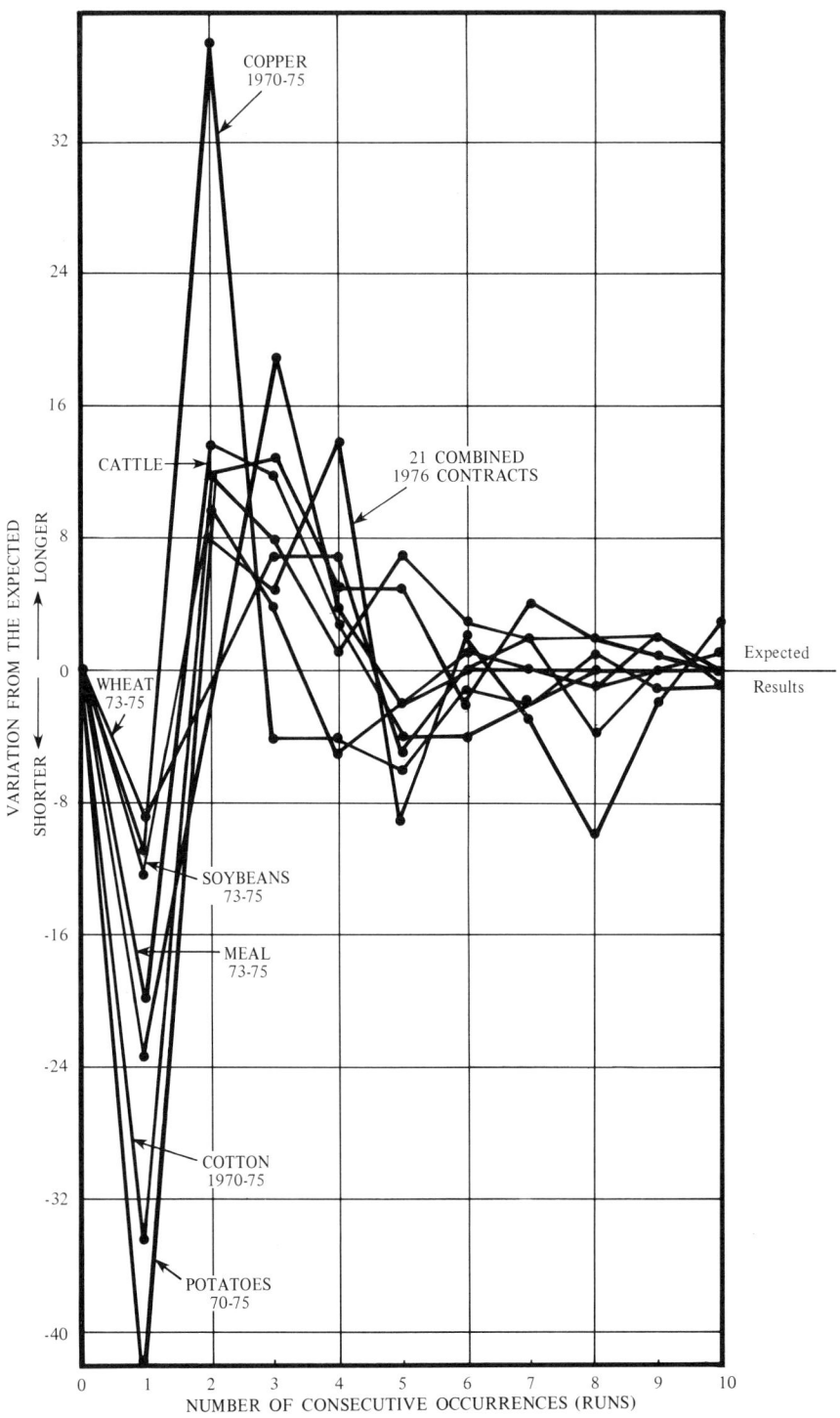

Diagram 16-6 Actual commodity movement related to the theory of runs.

Table 16-2 Length of Commodity Runs

Length of run	Probability of occurrence	21 combined 1976 occurrences		Cotton (6 years)		Copper (6 years)		Potatoes (6 years)	
		Expected	Actual	Expected	Actual	Expected	Actual	Expected	Actual
1	$\frac{1}{2}$	1225	1214	369	346	382	380	329	295
2	$\frac{1}{4}$	612	620	185	183	196	229	165	177
3	$\frac{1}{8}$	306	311	92	111	98	92	82	90
4	$\frac{1}{16}$	153	167	46	50	49	44	41	42
5	$\frac{1}{32}$	77	67	23	21	24	18	21	28
6	$\frac{1}{64}$	38	41	12	12	12	11	10	7
7	$\frac{1}{128}$	19	16	6	8	6	4	5	9
8	$\frac{1}{256}$	10	5	3	5	3	4	3	7
9	$\frac{1}{512}$	5	3	1	1	2	1	1	2
≧10	$\frac{1}{1024}$	4	5	1	1	1	0	1	1
Total tested			2449		738		783		658

handled, since a $35 Chicago Board of Trade commission is greater than the effect of the white slot ($\frac{1}{37}$) on the roulette wheel. The only offsetting help to the burden of commissions would be to increase the probability of your trade winning, or to have a proportionately larger ratio of dollar profit to losses, thereby lessening the impact of the commissions. Trading in the direction of the long-term trend or using a well-defined plan may be the selective process necessary.

System Trading

A standard trend-following system has between 30% and 40% successful trades (reliability) of varying profitability, which can be defined in terms of a profit/loss ratio. In considering the Martingale or anti-Martingale systems it should be noted that the lower probability of occurrence of profitable trades would make the wait for a long run of profits less attractive. If we expect 35% successful trades with a profit/loss ratio of 3/1 we find that with equal amounts of contracts traded we have the following breakdown, assuming $750 each profit and $250 each loss:

$$
\begin{array}{lll}
\text{total trades} & 100 \times \$35 \text{ (comm.)} & = \$-3500 \\
\text{profitable trades} & 35 \times \$750 & = +26250 \\
\text{losing trades} & 65 \times \$250 & = -16250 \\
& \text{(note \$65 per trade only)} & + \$6500
\end{array}
$$

Taking these same figures and applying Martingale's system against a uniform sequence of two losses and one profit, we get $285 as the first loss ($250 plus as $35 commission), $570 for the second loss, then $2145 for the profit, netting $1290 for three trades, which would have returned $145 with equal contracts traded.

The disadvantage to the Martingale approach in commodities is that a long run of losing trades requires a large amount of capital. The decision is one of money management. If it is necessary to keep a large reserve in the event of a series of losing trades, then why not just trade a larger number of contracts equally, without the Martingale system? Commodity trading differs from a pure gambling situation because you will win with specific systems in the long term while you will lose at roulette. The results show that trading a larger number of contracts equally will return a higher profit than an application of the Martingale system requiring the same available capital.

FILTERING

Filtering seems to be an unavoidable part of human behavior when dealing with the success and failure of commodity trading. No trader ever wants to lose, but some handle failure worse than others; in commodities failure can be fast and thorough. The beginning speculator has his own special prejudicial filter, which works with a variety of flexibility. It prevents him from using certain techniques that go against his intuitive senses. It allows him to use judgment, to resist taking a small profit from the center of a move when he can get it all, and to interpret all news in his favor and

PRACTICAL CONSIDERATIONS

to stick with a trade until it shows a profit. If he succeeds in getting past the first year of trading he has learned not to take a loss personally, to establish a modus operandi, and to stick to it and filter *out* the influences and opinions of others.

The experienced trader keeps on filtering. His goal is to eliminate all the losing trades by prior examination and enter only those that will be profitable. The more complex technical systems are attempts to qualify each trade in such a way to increase the odds of success. The object of this exercise is good, but the results may be disappointing. Consider a combination of moving averages traded in the same manner as the double moving-average system discussed earlier. A fast-moving average enters a trade shortly after prices reverse, then exits on a similarly small adjustment to the move; it has frequent positions. As a smoothing method becomes slower it requires a longer price move to show profits, since the entry and exit both occur after an increasingly larger reversal. If you consider the fastest average as the timing filter and the slowest as the major trend and the others as intermediate trends, and if they are all in a long position at the same time, you may experience the greatest bull move in history. It is more likely that you will filter yourself out of the market completely.

When used properly, filtering can be a valuable tool in constructing a trading system or plan. This is demonstrated by most technical systems, which rarely consist of just one element. When selecting what to use as a filter, do not use other systems—stay with pure elements. Not knowing everything about a system that you use may cause duplication of a specific feature; you may give unnecessary weight to a faster moving average, a 3-day run or some other criterion. You can only know and balance all the ingredients of your program if they are clearly identifiable; the Deluxe Forecasting Service may already include the day of the week or a high volatility filter in its predictions.

Look for unique elements to combine, and use them only once. The selection of the speed of a moving average will be more important than how many moving averages to use. There may be an advantage to the double moving average approach, but a third, fourth, and so on, lose their significance. A momentum indicator bears a close resemblance to a moving average when its rules are to buy or sell on a move through the zero line. Both are heavily based on standard characteristics of a time-series and will not offer enough variance if both are applied to the same data. The methods should be fundamentally different. A technique that does not consider time would be a better complement to a moving average. A point-and-figure system or a support-and-resistance analysis of a charting nature would satisfy the requirements. The more complicated cycle and wave theories, contrary opinion, and other methods all view price movement in a completely different way than a moving average, even when applied to the same data. Two moving averages can be used without duplication when evaluating distinctly different data. A moving average of the closing price and one of the volume or open interest have no relationship other than the implications of the speed selection.

Filtering is a tool not restricted to price analysis, but applicable to money management, reliability, risk, portfolio selection, and other aspects of a trading program. The selection of which commodities to trade and how many contracts to enter is as important as the buy and sell signals. If the system itself corrects for high volatility markets by decreasing the distance of the stop-loss point (keeping the risk constant), it would be redundant to trade fewer positions of that commodity, thereby reducing the effects of any profits or losses relative to other commodities in a portfolio.

The Commodex Method of Filtering

The *Commodex system* was first presented in 1959 and claims a successful 18-year real-time trading record; it is still an active system, published daily by *Commodity Futures Forecast* in New York. Commodex filters together the components most acceptable to the experienced trader in a unique weighting method of its own. It combines moving averages, price momentum, volume, and open interest to calculate a trend index.

The most interesting aspect of the Commodex system is its ranking process, intended to produce a relative strength value for each trend. Using a 10- and 20-day double moving average, the system scores the current market performance to establish the value of the trending component. Bullish and bearish values are calculated by looking at three situations independently: the simple moving-average signals derived from both the long- and short-term trends, and the double moving average signal generated by combining the two trends. The two techniques of single and double moving averages are exactly as treated in this book in Chapter 5. The most important of the three factors is the long-term trend; second is the short-term trend, and last the relative position of the fast to the slow moving average. The strongest upward moving trend is generated when current prices are above both the faster and slower moving averages and the faster average is below the slower. The opposite positions would result in the strongest downward trending component. Trends are considered neutral if the most important element, the long-term moving average, conflicts with the other two factors.

The rate of change in open interest is considered a secondary reinforcement of the trend. Using a concept different from the usual charting techniques, Commodex considers it a bullish implication if there is an increasing growth momentum in open interest combined with rising prices. The growth momentum is the difference between the rate of increase of the open interest and the 20-day moving average of the open interest. The concept of continuing a bull move with rising prices and rising open interest is a classic concept of charting. The bear move is confirmed with increasing open interest and falling prices. Commodex also considers a drop in open interest along with falling prices to be a bullish factor. The movement of volume is treated in the same manner as open interest and can confirm a bull or bear trend. An increasing volume momentum with rising prices is support of an upward move, while other combinations indicate bear trends.

Added together the signals range from a strong "buy" to a strong "sell" with lesser degrees in between. The system must be given credit for the quantification and balancing of these elements, which are generally treated as highly interpretive charting techniques. The rules for applying the daily signals to trading combine both the individual strength of the signal with the movement of the Commodex trend index. The trend index itself acts as an overbought-oversold indicator, encouraging profits at specified levels and considering a position reversal in more extreme situations; stops are placed using the 20-day moving average with predetermined band penetrations. Additional objectives are based on the profits accrued for a trade, with a 50% return justifying a protective stop on part of the positions, and a 100% profit requiring the liquidation of half your position. These money-management concepts are an important aspect of any system and tend to round out Commodex.

The Commodex system has been used as an example of combining techniques that have been studied individually in previous sections. It is a good example because each element is simple to understand and avoids duplication; it has single and double moving averages (with and without bands), momentum indicators derived from volume and open interest, an overbought-oversold indicator formed from a combination of all elements, trading stops and liquidation based on money management and inverse pyramiding.

COMBINING TRENDS AND TRADING RANGES

Trends and trading ranges represent two distinct philosophies of technical analysis. A trend is concerned with a periodic tendency of prices to persist in their movement in one direction with unrestricted goals, while a trading range is a definition of price containment. The time element of the two approaches is quite different since the trend must advance with regularity (time-series) while prices within a trading range can move in any direction with varying speed as long as the upper or lower bounds are not violated.

The reasons for the existence of each principle are simple to explain but require a personal acceptance, since mathematical proof is ambiguous. We have discussed the nature and identification of trends in the more technical sense earlier in the book; the trend is most obvious in the long term by looking at the inflationary tendencies as defined by both the buying power of the United States dollar and the Consumer Price Index. In these cases we see a slow but steady decline in the value of the dollar and a rise in costs. These long-term trends are easily related to fundamental economic factors and can be predicted with more or less accuracy for some years in advance. In the shorter time period of 2 to 10 years we see the prices of commodities vary according to overall industrial production and contemporary national policy. If copper prices are high we can expect a shift within the industry to satisfy the demand by increasing production. The start up of new mines and increased refining may take 2 years; therefore we can predict that 2 years after higher copper prices we can expect demand to be satisfied (to a greater or lesser degree) and lower prices at that time. The converse would also be true in the event of copper prices that were too low. A reduction in production would eventually move prices higher by cutting the supply. This production cycle, applicable to most industries, causes what we observe as a trend of medium duration. The fastest price movement is considered trending because of psychological reactions to short impact news. If there is a large slaughter of cattle for a few days in a row the declining prices will persist for an extra day or two, giving the appearance of a natural smoothing effect on prices. In all, trends can be caused by a variety of factors that result in a continued price move in one direction.

A trading range is a description imposed by the speculator on a natural phenomenon. It is a frequent occurrence for prices to move back and forth between two price levels. The lower level, called support, becomes the price at which the seller is no longer interested in merchandising. In the first part of 1977 the price of corn fell to $2.35 per bushel in central Illinois. There were isolated days when the price was lower, even down to $2.00, but those were few. Whenever prices tried to move below $2.35 they recovered because farmers were not interested in selling for less. They had worked that year for $2.20 per bushel, and were going to resist taking such a small profit for their labors. It is impossible to know at what level *country movement* will stop and a price support level form. Each year is different; costs vary, political events and government policies influence the thinking of the producer. If support levels became high and the crop and stocks were large, any price would be good and there would be little chance of a bull market, but a great possibility of sustained lower prices.

The top of a trading range is not as well-defined as the bottom because of the inherently greater volatility with high prices. The top, or resistance level, will be a broader range of prices and therefore of less use as a decision-making tool. But even with the broad formation there is a clear point at which prices have gone higher and are no longer within the trading range. Demand has finally outweighed supply.

It often happens that the two techniques of price trend and trading ranges are in conflict: the trend is up and a resistance level is encountered, or the downtrend is stopped by a support level. If you accept the philosophies of both approaches to price analysis there is still latitude to use both methods without contradiction. The simplest is to use the trading range while prices are within that area and follow the trend when prices break out either above or below (see Diagram 16-7).

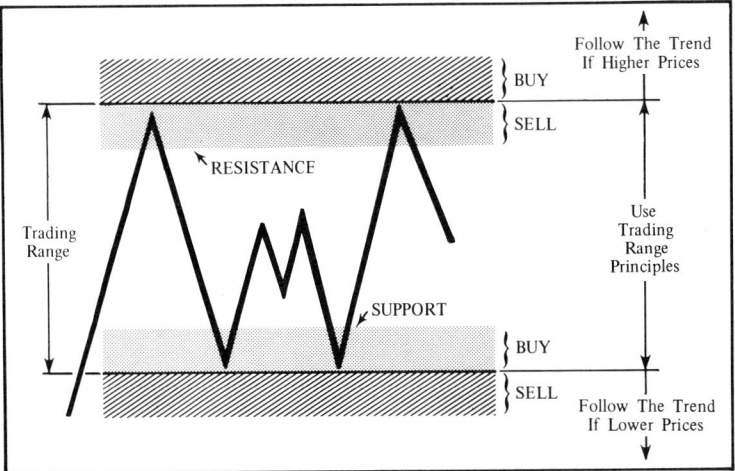

Diagram 16-7 Combining the trend and trading range.

The exact rules followed depend on the size of the trading range. If the range is narrow, a moving average buy or sell signal invariably occurs at the resistance or support level and is met with an initial reversal. For a larger range a medium speed moving-average signal may occur closer to the center of the range and allow some opportunity for profit with the trending system. For very wide ranges there may be ample latitude for a moving average to signal entry and closeout without the interference of support or resistance levels. One method of filtering the two techniques together is to use whichever signal is generated, regardless of the system. The following combinations are possible for medium width ranges:

Enter a new short position when the moving average turns down

or

Enter a new short position when prices penetrate the sell zone around the resistance level or

Enter a new short position when prices fall below the support area, then close out a short position when the moving average turns up

or

Close out a short position when prices enter the buy zone around the support level

or

Close out a short position when prices break through a resistance level moving up.

The same rules in reverse would apply to long positions. The advantage of this filtering method is that new short trades are not entered at support levels, which causes immediate losses or prolonged trades of little profit or loss. It is necessary to give up some of the potential profit in a trade in order to improve your overall reliability of performance.

TRADING LIMITS—A DAMPENING EFFECT

The existence of trading limits in United States markets has always been the concern of novice speculators who seem convinced that their first entry into the market will result in an adverse locked-limit move, stripping them of their future and happiness overnight. There is no doubt that many people have suffered from being "caught" on the wrong side of a move, but trading limits would tend to protect rather than harm them. The limits established by the exchanges were intended to allow free trading within the normal ranges of price fluctuation. If properly established these limits should rarely be reached. As prices rise the volatility of the market increases and so the limits must be expanded to correspond to the level. At this point the risks become proportionately greater and margins are raised.

The purpose of limits is to prevent an immediate reaction to unexpected news from moving prices to unjustifiable levels. The first reaction to bad news is usually more extreme than is realistic and when proper assessment of the problem is completed, the results are rarely as bad as initially thought. For example, among commercial grain traders it is generally understood that farmers lose their crops three times before harvest—once because of drought, another time for disease and then for frost—and still the United States finds itself with about the same size crop as the year before. Rather than prices jumping 50¢ or $1.00 per bushel in one bound, limits on corn allow only a 10¢ move; in 5–10 trading days a more accurate evaluation of damage or other surprising news can be made. If the results are actually bad, the higher price is reached before trading comes "off the limit"; if the damage is modified downward, the trader can exit at a better adjusted level than would have originally been possible without limits.

Limits

Looking at sugar prices, which had a spectacular rise in 1974, we can examine the most extreme case of changing volatility. The first trading day that could be found to have closed at the daily limit for the New York Sugar contract was on December 22, 1971. Our search started at the beginning of July 1969, a total of 486 trading days earlier. At that time the September 1972 contract ran up to over 9¢ and 19 out of the next 137 trading days closed at the 50¢ limit; prices had moved from the 3¢ range to the 7–8¢ level. After that, limit closes became more common. Without duplicating calendar days, Table 16-3 lists the activity of the September sugar contracts (not including the delivery month).

Table 16-3 Frequency of Limit Moves

	Total days examined	Days closing limit	Percentage of limit closes	Range of closing prices	Limits
Sep 70	248	0	.0	2.91–4.01	.50
Sep 71	249	0	.0	2.74–5.08	.50
Sep 72	240	18	7.5	4.26–9.17	.50
Sep 73	239	9	3.8	5.44–10.50	.50
Sep 74	239	40	16.7	7.56–28.15	.50–2.00
Sep 75	239	54	22.6	11.51–50.82	1.00–2.00
Sep 76	238	3	1.3	12.07–18.65	1.00

The obvious conclusion to be drawn from the pattern of the sugar market is that limits do not expand quickly enough at higher price levels. In 1975, 22.6% of all trading days closed at the limit, while at low price levels the limits were of no consequence. The 1974 price of sugar increased by 15 times its 1969 price while the limits only expanded from 50 to 200 points, a factor of four. The use of a trading system tested in a market with few limit closes should not be expected to operate effectively in a limit-intense situation; speculators should be wary of these markets.

The only realistic way of comparing the effects of limit moves against a limitless market is to compare the United States and London exchanges. Using the May 77 Coffee contract for the month of February 1977 we can show three separate examples of limit moves in the United States contracts and the corresponding London action. Diagram 16-8 illustrates the closing prices of markets on the same day. Two problems must be considered: the conversion of sterling to United States dollars, which was fixed at $1.70 for the entire comparison, and the overlapping hours of the New York Coffee and Sugar Exchange and the London Sugar Exchange. The exchange hours may have some difference in the daily price, but should not appreciably effect the comparison.

The first United States locked-limit day was on February 7, when the New York Coffee prices for the May 77 contract moved to 230.82 (up 300 points). On the same day London prices for the May 77 contract moved from 218.80 to 230.56 (actually 2883 to 3038 sterling). A trader who closed out his position on the open in the London market would have taken a fill of 2850 and a loss of 12.67 points relative to the United States market. The traders locked into their New York position could have gotten out on the open on February 8 at 233.50, a loss of 568 points. Had both the United

PRACTICAL CONSIDERATIONS 281

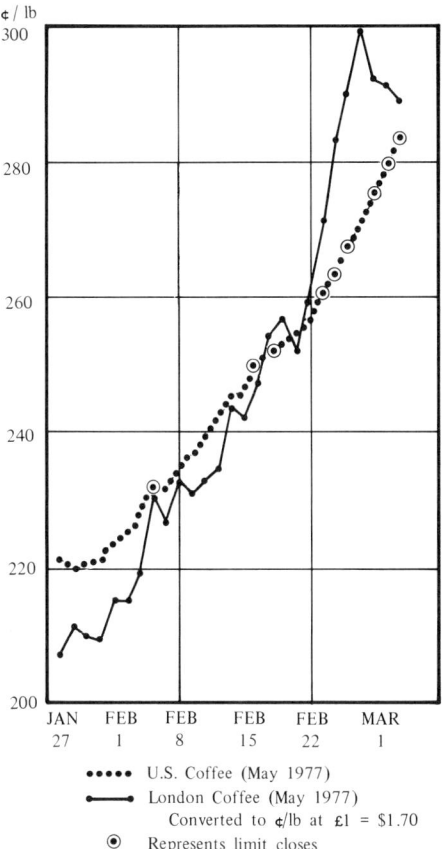

Diagram 16-8 Limit moves, May 77 Coffee.

States and London traders waited for the closing prices as shown in the diagram, the corresponding losses would have been reduced to 1176 points in London and 318 points in New York.

The second case was on February 17 and 18 when the United States market stayed locked at the limit for two days. A trader entering the market in London on the prior day at 241.91 (3187.50 sterling) could have gotten out on the next day at 247.07 (3255.07) for a loss of 516 points. The corresponding New York trader would have entered at 246.00 and exited at 254.50 for a loss of 810 points.

Remarkably, the London coffee prices had moved to 252.04 by the time the New York market was trading again. London prices had gained 1013 points during the time that a locked limit United States market gained only 850 points. In both cases the volatility of the London market with no limits was much greater than the United States equivalent and the results do not show any disadvantage to trading limits.

The third case of locked-limit moves occurred on February 24 and continued. On the day prior to the first locked-limit day the United States market traded actively even after the London Exchange moved up an equivalent of 698 points. There should have been ample time that day or even the prior day, when the United States market traded at the limit but closed lower for any trader to exit an undesirable position. The diagram shows the larger moves of the London market peaking and starting down to meet the plodding United States prices. The market with no limits has overreacted to the bullish news by at least 1000 points. Of course, if you didn't get out of New York coffee soon enough the overreaction of the London market would not be very gratifying.

A satisfactory test of a trading method must include a combination of different price patterns with respect to trading limits. It should be a comforting feeling to a speculator to know that his analysis will be equally reliable if the next day traded quietly, closed at the limit, or had all limits taken off.

GOING TO EXTREMES

Every profession has its conservative and extreme elements, and perhaps commodity trading balances out towards the extreme. In 1974 public awareness of inflation caused an overwhelming interest in all forms of hedging, with large numbers of naive investors purchasing silver and gold coins and bullion for its value as currency protection. More sophisticated investors turned to media that offered leverage on their purchases, such as the futures markets; some learned how to use the market themselves, while others relied on advice.

Since 1974 a great number of methods have been sold that promised profitable returns on investment; some of them worked and others didn't. With intense pressure to protect their savings and with no real expertise of their own, most investors were forced to rely on the research and creditability of professionals. A summary of one such investment system using the futures market is presented here. At the time it was published it had always worked and it might still work—time will tell. The sponsor of the system stood behind it with his name and reputation.

The principles of the system are:

1. Trade silver futures because of their intrinsic value, historic performance, potential, and fundamental demand with short supply.
2. Use the futures contract between 3 and 7 months from delivery to combine the advantages of liquidity and duration.
3. Always buy, never sell, because it always succeeds.
4. Begin whenever you like. Although you can use any sophisticated methods you want to decide on exactly when to buy, it won't matter in the long run—any guess will do just as well. Follow the same method for adding to your position or re-entering after closing out a trade.
5. Close out your position when you have a profit—not before.
6. Meet all margin calls—don't let the market beat you.
7. Invest $5000 per contract (5000 troy ounces)—that will allow a $1.00 per ounce adverse move (silver was $4.50 per ounce then).
8. Whenever you need reinforcement, reread the reasoning behind this system.
9. Do not let anyone or anything interfere with following this system.

How would you have done using this system? As with most systems, it depends greatly on when you start; there are opportunities for profits using any technique if your timing is good. As far as being foolproof, it has its problems. Looking at the years

Table 16-4 Reinvesting Profits

		1975											Adj	1976											Net P/L (¢)
Jan	Feb	Mar	Apr	May	Jun	Jul	Aug	Sep	Oct	Nov	Dec	+8	Jan	Feb	Mar	Apr	May	Jun	Jul	Aug	Sep	Oct	Nov		
466	−18	0	−18	−15	−12	+6	+57	−18	−6	−45	−60	−52	−3	−23	−19	−25	−1	+27	+55	−19	−27	−21	−25	−25
	448	+18	0	+3	+6	+24	+75	0	+12	−27	−42	−34	+15	−5	−1	−7	+17	+45	+73	−1	−9	−3	−7	−7
		466	−18	−15	−12	+6	+57	−18	−6	−45	−60	−52	−3	−23	−19	−25	−1	+27	+55	−19	−27	−21	−25	−25
			448	+3	+6	+24	+75	0	+12	−27	−42	−34	+15	−5	−1	−7	+17	+45	+73	−1	−9	−3	−7	−7
				451	+3	+21	+72	−3	+9	−30	−45	−37	+12	−8	−4	−11	+14	+42	+70	−4	−13	−6	−10	−10
					454	+18	+69	−6	+6	−27	−14	−40	+9	+11	−7	−14	+11	+39	+67	−7	−16	−9	−13	−13
						472	+51	−24	−12	−51	−66	−58	−9	−29	−25	−32	−7	+21	+49	−25	−34	−27	−31	−31
							523	−75	−63	−102														−100
								448	+12	−27	−42	−34	+15	−5	−1	−7	+17	+45	+73	−1	−9	−3	−7	−7
									460	−39	−54	−46	+3	−17	−13	−19	+5	+33	+61	−13	−21	−15	−19	−19
										421	−15	−7	+42	+10	+26	+20	+44	+72	+100	+26	+18	+24	+20	+20
											406	+8	+57	+25	+41	+35	+59	+77	+105	+31	+23	+29	+25	+25
													455	−32	−16	−32	−8	+10	+38	−26	−34	−28	−32	−32
														423	+16	+10	+34	+52	+80	+16	+8	+14	+10	+10
															439	−6	+18	+36	+64	0	−8	−2	−6	−6
																433	+24	+42	+70	+6	−2	+4	0	0
																	457	+18	+42	−18	−26	−20	−24	−24
																		485	+28	−46	−54	−48	−52	−52
																			513	−74	−82	−76	−80	−80
																				439	−8	−2	−6	−6
																					431	+6	+2	+2
																						437	−4	−4
																							433	0

Entry price

Table 16-5 Taking Profits Out

	Jan	Feb	Mar	Apr	May	Jun	Jul	Aug	Sep	Oct	Nov	Dec	Adj +8	Jan	Feb	Mar	Apr	May	Jun	Jul	Aug	Sep	Oct	Nov	Net P/L (¢)	# Prof. trades
						1975													1976							
	466	−18	0	−18	−15	−12	(+6)	(+51)	−75	−63	−102	—	—	—	—	—	—	—	—	—	—	—	—	—	−43	2
		448	(+18)	−18	−15	−12	(+6)	(+51)	−75	−63	−102	—	—	—	—	—	—	—	—	—	—	—	—	—	−23	3
			466	−18	−15	−12	(+6)	(+51)	−75	−63	−102	—	—	—	—	—	—	—	—	—	—	—	—	—	−43	2
				448	(+3)	(+3)	(+18)	(+51)	−75	−63	−102	—	—	—	—	—	—	—	—	—	—	—	—	—	−37	4
					451	(+3)	(+18)	(+51)	−75	−63	−102	—	—	—	—	—	—	—	—	—	—	—	—	—	−40	3
						454	(+18)	(+51)	−75	−63	−102	—	—	—	—	—	—	—	—	—	—	—	—	—	−43	2
							472	(+51)	−75	−63	−102	—	—	—	—	—	—	—	—	—	—	—	—	—	−49	1
								523	−75	−63	−102	—	—	—	—	—	—	—	—	—	—	—	—	—	−100	0
									448	(+12)	−39	−54	−46	(+3)	−32	−16	−32	−8	(+10)	(+28)	−74	−82	−76	−80	−27	4
										460	−39	−54	−46	(+3)	−32	−16	−32	−8	(+10)	(+28)	−74	−82	−76	−80	−37	3
											421	−15	−7	(+42)	−32	−16	−32	−8	(+10)	(+28)	−74	−82	−80	−80	0	3
												406	(+8)	(+57)	−32	−16	−32	−8	(+10)	(+28)	−74	−82	−76	−80	+15	3
													455	−32	−16	−32	−8	(+10)	(+28)	−74	−82	−76	−80	−41	2
														423	(+16)	−6	(+18)	(+18)	(+28)	−74	−82	−76	−80	0	4
															439	−6	(+18)	(+18)	(+28)	−74	−82	−76	−80	−16	3
																433	(+24)	(+18)	(+28)	−74	−82	−76	−80	−10	3
																	457	(+18)	(+28)	−74	−82	−76	−80	−34	2
																		485	(+28)	−74	−82	−76	−80	−52	1
																			513	−74	−82	−76	−80	−80	0
																				439	−8	−2	−6	−6	0
																					431	+6	−4	+2	1
																						437	−4	−4	0
																							433	0	0

Entry price

284

PRACTICAL CONSIDERATIONS

1975 through 1976 we can evaluate the performance by assuming that one new investor entered the silver futures market (December New York contracts) on the first of each month beginning January 2, 1975, and ending December 1, 1976. The results of their investments have been presented two ways:

1. Table 16-4 shows the accumulated profit or loss if the investor left his money in the market from the time of his investment until December 1, 1976. Considering that the rules of the system allow the investor to close out and reenter any time, the effect of continuous trading (with good and bad selection of entry-exit points) would be the same as a continuous investment. In addition, the user was not instructed *when* to take profits; so his choice of letting his investment grow is acceptable.

    The results of this approach are an average loss of 18¢ per contract. Of the 22 investors with a 1-month to 22-month duration, four showed profits ranging from 2¢ to 25¢ ($100 to $1250, without commissions) and 18 showed losses of 0¢ to $1.00 ($0 to $5000), the average being a 25¢ loss.

2. Considering a most profitable use of the system rules, we can liquidate any position which has a profit at the beginning of the month (circled in Table 16-5). This satisfies most investors by reducing their maximum loss by the accumulated profits that they have by liquidation. From the table we can see that there were frequent profits taken, although only two investors out of 22 had net gains of 2¢ and 15¢. The other 20 had average losses of 34¢ ranging from 0¢ to $1.00. Of the 22 total investors, eight lost in excess of $1.00 per contract or $5000 on a single trade, which required complete withdrawal.

In trying to understand how a system such as this can have a chance of reaching the public, we must remember the time it was introduced. With the price of everything increasing drastically, food shortages and publicity over the devaluing United States dollar abroad, the rationale of the system seemed justifiable. Unfortunately, public awareness usually marks the most volatile period just prior to the climax of any price move, and this was no exception. Since early 1974 silver prices, along with overall inflation, have been declining. There have been opportunities for profit on the long side of the market, but realizing those profits require more sophistication than this system offers.

CHAPTER 17

System Management

A trading system alone will not assure success without an overall management program. Systems have losing streaks that will ruin an investor with inadequate resources; a speculator must decide how much money to invest at the beginning, when to add, and when not to add. This chapter deals with capital and shows why many traders will be winners for months, building outstanding profits, and then lose everything in only a few days. It will explain the choices in pyramiding and offer alternatives of less risk. The last section analyzes when a system is performing properly and when it is not living up to its reputation.

CAPITAL

Success does not depend on having enough capital, but in using it properly.

Dixon G. Watts

Your beginning capital, the need for that capital, and the desire to make money will determine your trading strategy. Regardless of your ambition, a speculator using new methods or systems should start with a relatively minimal investment. Every system has its own profit-and-loss cycle, depending on what aspect of price motion or behavior it is measuring. A simple moving average will return profits in a trending market and losses in a nontrending one; a system that operates within a trading range defined by support and resistance levels will return the opposite results in trending and nontrending situations.

It is commonly accepted that prices spend 70–80% of their total time in nontrending motion. If you are using a system based on a trending concept, it is most likely and desirable that you will begin your system in a nontrending period. Because you may not have a realistic appraisal of the downside risk of your system in a sustained trendless market, you should begin with a minimum investment and yet not modify any of the characteristics of the system; you should have enough capital to follow your entire plan using only 20% of the money available. In the worst case, a loss of 100% of margin would leave you with a 20% total loss and a better idea of the risks of the method; in the best case your profits will be less than if you had been fully invested. When dealing with an unknown, a new system or risks, remember that you cannot keep trading if you lose all your money.

Set a guideline for your maximum margin, based on your experiences of the losses during the nontrending markets. If you are still uncertain, keep your total margin account well under 50% of available capital. In the following sections, we review ways of compounding profits in an orderly manner.

Diversification reduces both risk and potential. Using a well-distributed portfolio for a system whose risks are known, a larger portion of the total capital can be allocated to margin. Advantages of statistics become apparent in the netting out of profits and losses daily or weekly; the majority of trades will move in a direction favorable to you a majority of the time. The volatility of your portfolio will be dampened by this netting effect; a trade with a slow upward trend and a distant stop-loss will be offset by a slow downward trending position in another contract.

A speculator with small starting capital cannot use an extensively diversified system and will therefore be increasing his risk. The most obvious case is the trader with only enough money to trade one contract of one commodity. A single losing trade ends his account since he will no longer be able to meet initial margin on a new trade. Being in a position where one or two successive losses will be fatal to your chances requires a different, low-risk approach to each trade. A long-term trend, no matter how correct, will at some point probably require additional margin that will not be available. A system of low-risk, close stop-loss points must be used; such a method will also restrict you from capturing profits from the sustained moves since any adjustment will touch your protective stop. Small capital requires small risk; many writers on trading have suggested maximum risk of ten percent of your investment. If your system falls in line with normal performance standards you should have one out of three profits with a higher than 3:1 profit-to-loss ratio. You should have adequate opportunity to start winning if you can follow the 10% rule, although your own system will have its special requirements.

There are two important rules in managing your own account. The first, *don't meet margin calls*, implies that a margin call represents an objective identification of a wrong trade, or a system that is not performing to specifications. There should be few exceptions, if any, to the rule. A margin call represents a time to reflect on your trading. *Liquidate your worst position* if you must lighten up. The profitable trades have proved that they are trending or performing as they should for your system; the losing trades have proved they are not. Stay with the good positions and liquidate the worst.

The successful performance of a system does not always result in profits; the management of capital is equally important to the outcome. We have discussed the selection of systems that have different characteristics relating to the risk and portfolio of a speculator, but at some point every trader wants to compound his profits. A system that has returned 200% each year will yield 1000% of the original investment in 5 years, but attempts at 3200% compounded profits are usually unsuccessful, and sometimes disastrous. The next two sections present a traditional and a conservative approach to the problems of compounding and increased leverage.

PYRAMIDING

At some point in a speculator's career he will find himself pyramiding, by choice or by accident. Pyramiding is the action of adding to one's position as profits increase. There are a number of techniques used by experienced traders, but the time to pyramid must be carefully selected. The situation chosen must have potential for a long move with limited risk; the sustained consolidation period of a commodity that is priced near its historic lows would be a candidate. No matter how well chosen, each method will result in having your largest holdings at the highest (or lowest) price; when the market reverses you will be losing on a larger base than you began and profits will disappear instantly. Pyramiding is very fragile hard work and must be watched cautiously for a changing market; there are enough stories of speculators who pyramided small capital into a large fortune in less than a year's time and then lost it all in a week. That is the risk of pyramiding that balances the opportunities.

The Scaled-Down Pyramid

The standard pyramid has a larger base than top to take advantage of the beginning of a trend. The largest portion of profits are developed over a longer time and an adverse price move is not as likely to be disastrous. The profit-compounding effect of this technique is comparably reduced. A favorite scaling method of this type has the characteristic of adding half of the prior position at each subsequent opportunity. For this reason you must plan ahead to decide the maximum number of contracts you would want to hold. Your total position, if followed to completion, will be about twice the number of contracts that you initially entered; starting with 20 lots you would add 10, 5, 2, and 1, respectively. An advantage of this or any other pyramiding method is that an initial loss will be based on a smaller number of contracts than your maximum commitment. If you had intended to trade 40 contracts from the start, you may be reducing your losses on most trades.

Adding Equal Positions

As you add larger commitments, your risk of an immediate loss in a short reversal becomes greater. Adding of an equal number of contracts reduces your original commitment in the event the trend does not materialize, but it increases your exposure later in the trade. The shift of risk can only be determined by the trader. With this approach as well as the next inverted pyramid methods, the speculator should follow the rule that *no unsuccessful secondary purchase should offset the entire profits of a prior purchase.*

Adding Equal Amounts

To offset the effects of disproportionate risk, subsequent positions can be added based on the new value of the commodity being traded. Comparing this to the previous method of equal contracts, this would reduce the number of purchases in a rising

SYSTEM MANAGEMENT

market and increase them in a declining market. The effect of increased volatility at higher levels would substantiate this approach to adding as a means of maintaining the same relative effect of each new position to the prior ones.

Maximum-Leverage Pyramiding

The greatest risk and the most potential is in adding to your position using all the profits accumulated to date. To do this you must work closely with the margin department of the brokerage firm that you are using. They might even want to install a direct line. When you accumulate enough for a new position you add, considering it a confirmation of the trend. Being completely leveraged is a tenuous position, requiring constant monitoring of the market; you must have a well-defined realistic price objective and you must liquidate when you reach it since an early reversal would be dangerous.

EQUITY CYCLES

Every system has profit-loss cycles that can be seen clearly by plotting the daily or weekly equity of the account in which you are only following that system. Using a trending technique we find that in a short interval once or twice each year there will be a major increase in profits corresponding to a trending market; and at other times there will be a steady depletion and then a stabilizing pattern to the total equity. For a system to operate as it is expected, you must keep your investment in the market constant. If you increase your positions as your equity increases in a trending cycle, you will always be fully invested at the top of the cycle, when you begin to lose. You will then lose on a larger base than you won; consequently your equity will drop much faster than it had increased.

The same effect can occur at the bottom of an equity cycle, after a nontrending market period. A sustained losing streak may cause a speculator to reduce his investment in proportion to his dwindling capital. If this happens the result will be entering into a profitable period with a smaller investment than the prior losing period. The system must have disproportionately larger profits to both recover the losses and achieve a net gain. An example of a typical system is shown using a 100% gain for each profitable cycle followed by a 50% loss cycle. We will assume this cycle is repeated twice each year. In one year we would expect the following equity pattern:

Example 17-1 Expected Equity Pattern

	Change in equity	Total equity	
Original margin		$10,000	
Gain of 100%	+10,000	20,000	First 6 months
Loss of 50%	−5000	15,000	
Gain of 100%	+10,000	25,000	Second 6 months
Loss of 50%	−5000	20,000	

This leaves a net gain of 100% for the year. Each 100% profit was $10,000 and losses were $5000, the rate of return always being based on the original margin. Had we started with the losing phase of the cycle we would only show a profit of 50% for the first year but 100% for each subsequent year.

In reality, most traders would not net 100% each year from a system that performs as the one in the example. As their profits increased during the period of gain, their committed margin would increase in proportion, so that at the time the original $10,000 margin is worth $20,000, their current margin requirements would also be $20,000. The 50% loss is then applied to the total equity:

Example 17-2   Pattern of Equity if Fully Invested

	Change in equity	Total equity	
Original margin		$10,000	
Gain of 100%	+10,000	20,000	First 6 months
Loss of 50%	−10,000	10,000	
Gain of 100%	+10,000	20,000	Second 6 months
Loss of 50%	−10,000	10,000	

Trading commodities is a great deal of effort for no return.

Holding your investment constant as in Example 17-1 can be viewed differently by studying the growth and decline of the account excess, which we call the *reserve*. The size of the reserve relative to total equity tells us the key to successful management.

Example 17-3   Equity Pattern Using a Reserve Account

	Change in equity	Margin	Reserve	Total equity	Reserve/ equity
Original investment		10,000	10,000	20,000	50%
Gain of 100%	+10,000	10,000	20,000	30,000	67%
Loss of 50%	− 5000	10,000	15,000	25,000	60%
Gain of 100%	+10,000	10,000	25,000	35,000	71%
Loss of 50%	− 5000	10,000	20,000	30,000	67%

We started with a reserve of 50%, equal amounts in required margin and surplus, increasing the reserve during profitable periods and decreasing it during losing periods; we trade more of total equity as we lose and less as we win. The reserve is the proper measure of profits. In this example our base margin remains the same, but we see the concept of *winning on a larger commitment than the previous losing commitment*.

A direct means to implementing this plan is to plot the equity, determining the position of the profit-loss cycles. Each time we experience the profit phase we maintain

SYSTEM MANAGEMENT

our fixed margin and allow reserves to build; we continue this procedure through the loss phase. When the expected loss of paper profits is complete and we have entered a stable equity period, we can redistribute the current total equity into margin and reserve according to our original 50% formula. In Example 17-4 we have two profit-loss cycles. At the end of the first we show a total equity of $25,000, allocated 40% to margin and 60% to reserve. Instead of continuing with the same margin of $10,000 based on an original investment of $20,000, we now redistribute the equity so that $12,500 is in each of the margin and reserve accounts. This maintains the 50% reserve and increases the margin account following an expected losing phase. We are now in a position to enter a profit phase with a larger base than our previous losing one.

Example 17-4   Equity Change Using Redistribution

	Change in equity	Margin	Reserve	Total equity	Reserve/ equity
Original investment		10,000	10,000	20,000	50%
Gain of 100%	+10,000	10,000	20,000	30,000	67%
Loss of 50%	−5000	10,000	15,000	25,000	60%
Redistribute		12,500	12,500	25,000	50%
Gain of 100%	+10,000	12,500	25,000	37,500	67%
Loss of 50%	−5000	12,500	18.750	31.250	60%
Redistribute		15,625	15,625	31,250	50%

This last example, compared to Example 17-3, shows the gradual increase in profits that might result from properly timed increases in margin. Each system has a natural cycle that may be substituted for the 100% and 50% cycle that was used in the examples; cycles might also be longer or shorter, and the ratio of margin to reserve will vary with your intended risk, but the principle of adding after a losing phase does not change.

Trading on Equity Cycles

A unique use of equity in system management involves its analysis in the same fashion as the system whose performance it represents. If you are trading a moving average technique, we have mentioned that the equity will fluctuate with the trending nature of the market. By applying a moving-average analysis to the equity itself you can identify the trending and nontrending periods by the "buy" and "sell" signals that the equity analysis would produce.

Any equity "buy" means that the commodities market has begun trending and that we may expect some continued periods of such trending; the length of this anticipated period depends on the speed of your moving average. A "sell" signal means that we are passing out of a trending market. These signals can be taken as "buy the system" or "short the system," that is, enter all positions that the system currently holds or liquidate your entire portfolio and hold cash. An equity "buy" could also be taken as the point to redistribute you equity into the original ratio of margin to reserve.

Whichever way it might be used, a record of equity is a key for understanding the performance and personality of your system.

Just because 10% is the initial requirement does not imply that 10% is all the capital that the prudent speculator should have behind the trade.

John Moody

SYSTEM EVALUATION

One aspect in the development of an economic model or trading system is the selection of elements for analysis and subsequent evaluation of their performance. Deciding which available data is useable as a predictive tool may not be possible until the model is complete and tested. Often the results of these tests are given in terms of profit/loss ratios, annual percentage profits, expected reliability (percentage of profitable trades to total trades), and maximum potential risk. Although these statistics are common, neither the developer nor the user of the model knows the accuracy of the figures. On occasion these results are generated by a sample that is too small, and usually they are not the results of a predictive but an historic test. This does not mean that the model will not be successful, but that the pattern of success might vary far from the profit/loss ratio, reliability, and risk. In actual trading every speculator has experienced a series of losses far exceeding anything that he expected; at that point he would like to know whether this situation could occur within the realm of the system's predicted results. For example, a moving-average system is expected to have $\frac{1}{3}$ profitable trades (reliability of 33%) with a profit/loss ratio of 4:1. But the first ten trades of the system are losers. Should you stop using the system because it does not work as you were told?

It has been shown in the section on the theory of runs that commodity-market price motion bears a strong resemblance to random motion with some short-term distortion. To have accurate comparative figures you should test a system with both commodity data and random data. Even if the system fails on the random data you have your own proof that the model is isolating certain nonrandom features of commodity prices. You also get statistics based on random movement that will help later evaluation of its performance.

Binomial Probability

Consider the application of a random-number sequence to the trading model. We would like to know what is the probability of l losses in n tries when the probability of a loss is p. Most of the work in this area of probability is credited to Bernoulli, whose study of a random walk is called a Bernoulli process. A clear representation of a random walk is shown by the Pascal triangle, where each box represents the probability of being in a particular position at a specific time in a forward random walk. The result of this process is called a binomial distribution. (See Diagram 17-1.)

The forward random walk has an analogy to price movement, with the far edges of Pascal's triangle showing the probability of a continuous sequence of wins or losses using random numbers. The sequence $\frac{1}{2}, \frac{1}{4}, \frac{1}{8}, \ldots, (\frac{1}{2})^n$ is exactly the same as in the

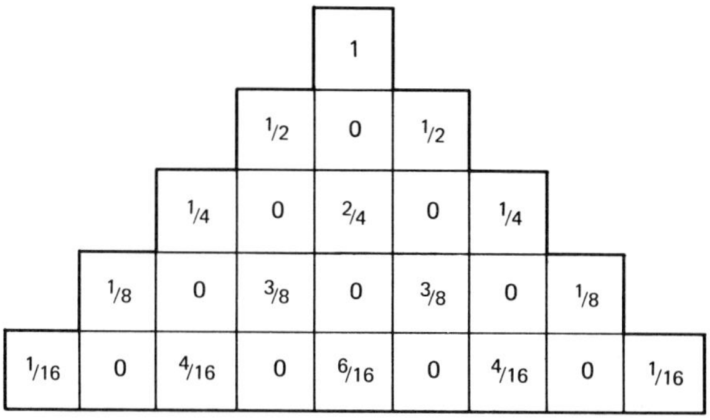

SYSTEM MANAGEMENT

				1				
			½	0	½			
		¼	0	2/4	0	¼		
	⅛	0	3/8	0	3/8	0	⅛	
1/16	0	4/16	0	6/16	0	4/16	0	1/16

Diagram 17-1 Pascal's triangle.

discussion of the theory of runs. The probability for successive losses can be calculated as the likelihood of a run of the same length, $(\frac{1}{2})^{n+2}$.

A binomial distribution is useful in considering the total number of losses that can occur in any order within a sequence of trades; in other words, it is the probability of getting to a specific point at the base of Pascal's triangle when there is a higher probability of moving to the left (losses) rather than the right (profits). The formula for the binomial probability is

$$B(l:p, n) = \frac{n!}{l!(n-l)!} p^l (1-p)^{n-l}$$

where

  l is the number of losses
  n is the total number of tries
  p is the probability of a loss

and the symbol "!" represents factorial (e.g., $5! = 5 \times 4 \times 3 \times 2 \times 1$).

Consider the first five trades of a system with a probability of success of $\frac{1}{3}$. How many losses should we expect? To answer the question we must solve the binomial probability B for all possibilities and form a distribution function. Let $l = 4$. Then

$$B(4:.667, 5) = \frac{5!}{4!1!} (.667)^4 (.333)^1$$

$$= \frac{120}{24} \times (.19792)(.333)$$

$$= 5 \times .0659 = .32954$$

The binomial probability of having four losses out of the first five trades is about 33%. The following table shows the probability of losses for the first five, ten, and fifteen trades of a system with a $\frac{1}{3}$ predicted reliability. Results show the highest probability of occurrence of loss is at the $\frac{2}{3}$ point (mean) for each sequence, but the standard deviation gives the range of variance about the mean, so that we reasonably can expect from 2.28 to 4.38 losses in five trades, 5.17 to 8.17 out of ten trades, and 8.175 to 11.825 losses in fifteen trades.

Note that in the 5-trade example the chances of no losses is only 1% and there is a 13% chance of all losses. For the purposes of evaluation it is easier to look at the

Table 17-1 The Probability of a Specific Number of Losses[a]

5 Trades		10 Trades				15 Trades			
Losses	Probability (%)	Losses	Probability (%)	Losses	Probability (%)	Losses	Probability (%)	Losses	Probability (%)
0	1	0	0	6	23	0	0	6	2
1	4	1	0	7	26	1	0	7	6
2	16	2	0	8	19	2	0	8	11
3	33	3	2	9	9	3	0	9	18
4	33	4	5	10	2	4	0	10	21
5	13	5	14			5	1		
								11	20
								12	13
								13	6
								14	2
								15	0
$m^b = 3\frac{1}{3}$		$m = 6\frac{2}{3}$				$m = 10$			
$sd^c = 1.05$		$sd = 1.5$				$sd = 1.825$			

[a] These figures were calculated using a binomial distribution program on a Texas Instruments SR-56 pocket calculator.
[b] Mean.
[c] Standard deviation.

SYSTEM MANAGEMENT

maximum rather than the minimum number of losses. For fifteen trades there is an 8% probability of thirteen or more losses; if your system has produced more than twelve losses in that period, there is something wrong with the reliability that you were given.

Note: More advanced probability functions that may have application to system evaluation are the Pascal distribution, the Poisson distribution, and various skewed distribution functions, all of which are explained in readily available texts on probability and statistics.

χ^2—CHI-SQUARE TEST

If you have already followed a system and have accumulated some data that gives a performance profile, a simple correlation between your actual results and your expected results can be found using the chi-square test. Your first concern is whether you have enough data for a relevant answer. From our section on sampling, we have the formula for error as $1/\sqrt{N}$ where N is the number of items sampled. If you have 25 trades, the expected error in our calculation is $1/\sqrt{25} = 20\%$; 100 trades would give results accurate to 10%.

Let us assume that our own information is accurate, and that we have results showing that our trading reliability was 20% (1 out of 5) while our expected reliability was 35%. What are the chances of getting these results and are they significant? The chi-square test is

$$\chi^2 = \frac{(O - E)^2}{E}$$

where O is the observed, or actual result and E is the expected or theoretical result.

For our particular case we have

$$\chi^2 = \frac{(20 - 35)^2}{35} + \frac{(80 - 65)^2}{65}$$

$$= \frac{(-15)^2}{35} + \frac{(-15)^2}{65}$$

$$= \frac{225}{35} + \frac{225}{65} = 6.428 + 3.46$$

$$= 9.89$$

We compared the percentage of winning trades with the anticipated winning trades and the losing trades with the expected losing trades. The answer must be looked up in Table 17-2, which gives the distribution of χ^2. The numbers that are of interest to us are in the first row.

The reason for the probability being distributed unequally in the table is that the results are only significant if the probability is small, showing less likelihood of the results occurring by chance. For this simple two-element test your results are classified as (where P is the result of the χ^2 test):

- *highly significant*   if $P \geq 10.83$ (.1% or $\frac{1}{1000}$)
- *significant*   if $P \geq 6.64$ (1% or $\frac{1}{100}$)
- *probably significant* if $P \geq 3.84$ (5% or $\frac{1}{20}$)

Table 17-2 Distribution of χ^2

Cases Less 1	Probability of occurring by chance								
	.70	.50	.30	.20	.10	.05	.02	.01	.001
1	.15	.46	1.07	1.64	2.71	3.84	5.41	6.64	10.83
2	.71	1.39	2.41	3.22	4.61	5.99	7.82	9.21	13.82
3	1.42	2.37	3.67	4.64	6.25	7.82	9.84	11.34	16.27
4	2.20	3.36	4.88	5.99	7.78	9.49	11.67	13.28	18.47
5	3.00	4.35	6.06	7.29	9.24	11.07	13.39	15.09	20.52
6	3.82	5.35	7.23	8.56	10.65	12.59	15.03	16.81	22.46
7	4.67	6.35	8.38	9.80	12.02	14.07	16.62	18.48	24.32
8	5.53	7.34	9.52	11.03	13.36	15.51	18.17	20.09	26.13
9	6.39	8.34	10.66	12.24	14.68	16.92	19.68	21.67	27.88
10	7.27	9.34	11.78	13.44	15.99	18.31	21.16	23.21	29.59

The answer $\chi^2 = 9.89$ is closer to .1% than to 1%, showing us that the results are significant. For a large sample you should not have had a 20% reliability when you expected 35%.

The chi-square test can also be used to compare a set of actual data points with the results of a regression analysis to determine the actual relationship to the approximation, or the distribution of trading within a price range can be tested against standard distribution curves. Actual price movement can be compared with random movement to see whether there is appreciable variation. In the section that discussed the theory of runs, the following comparison was shown:

Table 17-3 Results from Analysis of Runs

Length of run	Expected results (E)	Actual results (O)
1	1225	1214
2	612	620
3	306	311
4	153	167
5	77	67
6	38	41
7	19	16
8	10	5
9	5	3
≥ 10	4	5
≥ 8[a]	19	13

[a] The last groups were combined in order not to distort the results based on a small sample.

For the eight classifications for length of run we get the calculation

$$\chi^2 = \sum_{n=1}^{8} \frac{(O_n - E_n)^2}{E_n}$$

$$= \frac{(1214 - 1225)^2}{1225} + \frac{(620 - 612)^2}{612} + \frac{(311 - 306)^2}{306}$$

$$+ \frac{(167 - 153)^2}{153} + \frac{(67 - 77)^2}{77} + \frac{(41 - 38)^2}{38}$$

$$+ \frac{(16 - 19)^2}{19} + \frac{(13 - 19)^2}{19}$$

$$= \overset{(1)}{.09877} + \overset{(2)}{.10457} + \overset{(3)}{.08169} + \overset{(4)}{1.2810} + \overset{(5)}{1.2987}$$

$$\overset{(6)}{.23684} + \overset{(7)}{.47368} + \overset{(8)}{1.8947}$$

$$= 5.470$$

Looking up the χ^2 value in Table 17-2 we find the probability about 55% for eight cases. The results are both nonsignificant and near random. The theory of runs shows that all cases taken together give the same results as chance movement. Looking at individual terms in the calculation we can find χ^2 for sets of two and three adjacent cases to decide whether there is a significant distortion of the expected distribution. In both cases the results are more probable but not yet mathematically significant. The two runs that differed the most were 4 to 5 days, which showed a probability of 11%, while the best three consecutive runs of 4, 5, and 6 days showed only a 25% probability of having occurred by chance.

The chi-square test is simple and practical for comparing known with theoretical results. More complex examples and uses can be found in any statistics book, along with a complete table of distribution.

CHAPTER 18

Personal Management

I have seen the future and it works.

Lincoln Steffens

Speculating is both a science and an art. Trading in commodities must be a total commitment; it is not possible to enter a position and then place it in a safety-deposit box with your other valuables and investment certificates. The market must be watched. The dedication to this objective is more important than the technique. As you develop a rapport with commodities markets you will find your best way of trading; it could be following a computerized system for a diversified portfolio or trading a single commodity. Each of the famous speculators had his own particularly important trading rules that continually appear throughout their writings. Jesse Livermore had a general technique of "testing the market," a tool used by the large trader to find the current state of the market, its resistance or acceptance to increased buying or selling. W. D. Gann preferred support and resistance levels that were halfway points and helped support the classic 50% retracement theory. Of course, Gann and others had many rules that they considered important, but prior highs and lows and the 50% level were probably the foremost.

Richard Wyckoff, who edited *The Magazine of Wall Street* and acted as an advisor during the 1920s and 1930s, talked repeatedly of limiting your risk. Wyckoff was both prolific and humorous and had no trouble expressing his opinion; and he emphasized risk in these terms:

Trading without scientifically limiting your risk is like wearing your pants without a belt or suspenders.[1]

---

[1] Wyckoff (1933) p. 80.

The older legends of Wall Street, such as Harriman, Keene, and Livermore, also believed in limiting losses and letting profits run. L. L. B. Angas, a specialist in foreign exchange and monetary markets during the 1930s, was an early advocate of long-term positions based on business and economic cycles.

The advice that follows is not original, but extracted from the writing of many traders. Few professionals ever discuss their techniques with anyone outside of their intimate group; some of these traders may not be able to define what they do, that is, when to trade and when to stand aside. Let us just say that they are fine-tuned to price movement. Since the available writings contain many rules and extensive philosophy, you must understand that the selections are those that the author personally considered important. They are not geared to the beginning trader, but to those who need to be reminded on occasion that there are good and bad ways to operate; and that the bad ways seem to reoccur even when we are watchful.

A point of special importance must be emphasized before the rest. It is one of tolerance and is best related by a quote from Adam Smith's *Money Game*:

"Everyone makes mistakes, my boy," he said, "it's nothing to worry about. It's all part of learning part of the great panorama of life." Then he tried to push me out of the window.

Concentrate on what to do if things go wrong. Profits have a way of taking care of themselves. Most of the serious problems occur from not knowing when to close out a losing trade—or not closing it out at all. Before entering a new position you should know what your risk is and identify the point at which you must exist. A margin call might help you realize that your trade is not going the right way—do not meet the call, liquidate your worst position (or positions) and stay with the ones that are profitable.

Don't ignore your emotions. Emotions can play no part in a wholly mechanical or computerized system, but everywhere else are important. There is always an element of anxiety in every risk situation, but each trader can define the level he considers normal and the point of being uncomfortable. This feeling is a warning that something is wrong. It may be that there are a lot of small elements in your trade that don't seem to be working—nothing specific, but nevertheless there. Listen to yourself and close out the trade; later you can look back and decide what happened.

Don't overextend yourself. If the risk is too high you may not act rationally at the key times. You might take profits too soon just to be out of the trade or hold a losing position to make back the loss. You cannot function at your best if you're overcommitted.

Take a rest. If you make a mistake trading, don't go back into the market to prove that you can beat it. Take a break until you feel rested and can handle yourself. You can never win if you get vindictive about a loss.

Don't blame losses on others. A losing trade can happen even when "all systems are go." They just do. We trade commodities because of the difficulty and the opportunity. No one can successfully move a market and hold it there if the price can't be justified by supply-and-demand factors. If the price of cattle declines below where you expected it to go and you went long while prices continued lower, then you made a mistake. No one manipulator or group of manipulators could hold down any market. If meat packers and processors aren't buying, it is because there is no demand at the current price. If cattle feeders are still selling, then they can make a profit (or hold their losses) at this level. Prices reflect fundamentals with few exceptions. The next time you hear a rally attributed to "short coverings" or "locals evening up" look to see if it continues.

Don't listen to rumors and tips. Information posed as reliable can only harm your trading. A bull tip cannot be evaluated or weighted properly and can therefore not be incorporated into your method unless you can verify the information personally. Why would an insider from a major grain merchandiser release a rumor that they will be buying one hundred million bushels of soybeans for export? It seems obvious that it could only harm their purchasing efforts. Anyone receiving that information prior to the purchasing and knowing its truth would also act on it before telling anyone else. When the rumor finally reaches the public the insiders have already bought what they wanted and are anxiously waiting for the public to start buying in order to add value to their prior purchases. Rumors are more likely devices to benefit persons who originated the tip. If you held a great quantity of potato shorts in the market and decided that the market had gone as low as possible for the present conditions, you certainly would not want to start a rumor about the poor quality of potatoes available for delivery or about a potato embargo. You would be interested in having everyone believe that there is a surplus or that exports have been slow or that there is a bumper crop coming up in Europe. Once the public becomes sellers but the fundamental news actually remains unchanged, you can unload all your positions at a profit.

The big money is in the big moves. Every trader finds a trading speed that he is most comfortable with. Day trading is for smaller risk and immediate action. But in order to have big profits you need a large position and a long move. The potential for the big move may be easier to identify but requires planning and a long-term investment.

Don't trade against the long-term trend. If you are trading the big positions, then the long term trend will be your position; but even with shorter plans, the overall market direction is difficult to withstand. You must be counting on profiting from price reactions that can be fast and sharp, almost the same as a V-top or bottom. The main advantage of the long-term move is that there is a bias in that direction. Not that you won't suffer some severe setbacks; but you have the fundamentals on your side and the market will usually come back in your direction.

Don't fall in love with your position. Markets change. The situations that may have put you into an outstanding trade change daily. Most times these changes are not significant enough to alter your position; other times they are obviously altered and you should exit immediately. Most often the changes fall into a gray area where you become unsure of the position. Then you must decide how comfortable you are with the position. If you fall in love with a trade you won't see these changes; you go around telling all your friends what a great position you have taken in the market until you have convinced yourself that it will last foreever. By the time you come to your senses your profits are gone.

Being right at the wrong time isn't rewarding. No amount of market analysis will help if you don't act at the right time. Waiting too long to enter a position after you have determined the potential of the move negates all your work. When you're right you must act.

Enter positions when prices are moving in your direction. A move in the direction that you want is a confirmation that you are right. It may be impractical to enter major positions in thin markets once prices turn in your direction, but only a minor position should be entered as long as prices move against you. Once these positions show a profit you can add the remaining positions in order to keep prices moving with you. The advantages of trading the big move is that there is room in the move to add and still get large profits. For small-lot long-term trades your positions should all wait until prices are moving in your direction.

Be able to understand the difference between your trading objective and your personal-profit goals. The market doesn't understand your financial position; the right time to exit from the market may not correspond to the amount of money you expected to make from the trade. Don't be influenced by your desire for profits; if the time to get out is here, do it now!

Test the market. It is very rare to get advice from a successful trader that relates to what really happens in the market. The only source at the present time is the long-out-of-print *Reminiscences of a Stock Operator*. The advice tends to be philosophic and is related by examples of actual market events, but an experienced trader finds it easy to apply to his own methods. For large-position traders looking for long-term trends, the constant references to "testing the market" makes it an essential element of trading technique. In order to determine the attitude of a commodity market toward being either bullish or bearish a test order is entered of sufficient volume to most nearly absorb orders or cause a noticeable "skid" during execution. It should be placed as a market order and the impact on prices should be watched. If the order is for a sell and it is absorbed with no effect on the current price level, then the trend of the market is up since there are adequate buyers below the current level looking for better prices. If the market had fallen erratically on the test selling it would show a lack of support and a confirmation of a further price decline. Similar market reactions can be useful to the observant trader throughout a move. A slow steady price rise with intermittent collapses should show a lack of adequate support, and consequently is indicative of a price top and an impending decline. Prices take the path of least resistance.

Look at the overall picture. This is another way of looking at the long-term trend. The overall picture lets you get the full potential out of a trade. Know what's going on. Do your own research.

"It's not the losing money that hurts in trading—it's being wrong." Another philosophic observation by Larry Livingston worth remembering is to be certain that losing doesn't affect your trading. Taking a loss doesn't hurt you when it's part of the plan, but not taking a loss when you should have acted causes personal damage.

A few ideas from W. D. Gann can be quoted without additional explanation:

If you don't know stand aside.
Trade on knowledge.
The time to act is when others show signs of tire.
Do not expect abnormal profits in normal markets.
When the time is right, sell at the market.
When the bad news is out it is time to buy, and when the good news is out it is time to sell.

In a narrow trading market, there is no benefit in trying to anticipate the next move. Wait until it happens before you enter a position. Until then you might use your money more effectively and avoid getting whipsawed in a narrow range.

Take advantage of a pleasant surprise. If you have analyzed everything correctly and taken your position you should have beaten the public to the punch. When the newspaper finally prints an article confirming your position, the public will jump in and move the market sharply in your direction. Take advantage of it and get out as fast as you can.

Don't be disturbed by conditions beyond your control. Even the best plans can go wrong by the advent of conditions that could never be reasonably anticipated. New regulations, politics, and disasters are beyond the scope of planning. Once they occur you can be wary in the future and take the loss as an exception.

Get out of a trade that doesn't develop. You have better uses for your time and capital than waiting for a bull or bear move to develop on cue. Try something else and come back to this trade when you have a significant change in the pattern.

It is harder to get out of a position than into one. Trading a large position is similar to sticking your foot in your mouth; once committed it often takes more skill to extricate yourself. Entering a trade allows you to select just the right time, placing orders in your own style. If things don't go quite right or if they feel uncomfortable you can stand aside. Once committed, much of the choice is gone. If everything goes perfectly you'll know exactly what to do; otherwise your hand is forced and you must have a full complement of contingent plans, including immediate liquidation.

Keep in top physical condition. You can't think properly if you don't feel well. Trading is as demanding as any activity you will ever encounter. Good food, fresh air, and exercise will be a refreshing break to the constant thinking during market hours and will keep you thinking clearly.

You can't trade without money. Conserve your capital. When you begin trading start small and experiment on money you can afford to lose without impact on your overall investment. When you start out at the beginning or after a long break your chances of losing are greater and should be considered as such. It is better to take a smaller profit at first than to lose your entire capital before your timing has developed.

APPENDIX 1

Least-Squares Method Using Normal Equations

The properties of least squares are

$$\sum (y - \hat{y}) = 0 \qquad (1)$$

$$\sum (y - \hat{y})^2 = \text{minimum} \qquad (2)$$

where y is the original data point, $\hat{y}$ is the corresponding data point on the approximation line, and $\sum$ represents $\sum_{i=1}^{n}$ where n is the total number of data points.

Since the equation for a straight line is

$$y = a + bx$$

we need to find values for a and b satisfying equations (1) and (2). If we have n data points formed by related x and y values, we can sum the equations

$$y_1 = a + bx_1 \qquad (3\text{-}1)$$

$$y_2 = a + bx_2 \qquad (3\text{-}2)$$

$$\vdots$$

$$y_n = a + bx_n \qquad (3\text{-}n)$$

and get

$$\sum y = na + b \sum x \qquad (3)$$

Multiplying each of equations (3-1), (3-2), ..., (3-n) by x, we then get

$$\sum xy = a \sum x + b \sum x^2 \qquad (4)$$

CORN–SOYBEAN SOLUTION 1956–1972

Using Table 3-1, we can substitute values for 1956–1972 into equations (3) and (4) to get

$$19.15 = 17a + 43.63b \qquad (3')$$

$$49.34 = 43.63a + 113.94b \qquad (4')$$

Solving for b we get

$$b = \frac{19.15 - 17a}{43.63} = .4389 - .3896a$$

and substituting back into (4') gives

$$49.34 = 43.63a + 113.94(.4389 - .3896a)$$

or

$$a = .879$$

Resubstituting into (3'):

$$19.15 = 17(.879) + 43.63b$$

$$b = .0964$$

The final equation for the line approximation is

$$y = .879 + .0964x$$

which can be plotted by solving for even values of x:

Table A1-1 Corn-Soybean Results 1956–1972

x (soybeans)	1.00	2.00	3.00	4.00
y (corn)	.97	1.07	1.17	1.26

CORN–SOYBEAN SOLUTION 1965–1975

Starting again with equations (3) and (4) we substitute values for the entire 1956–1975 period.

$$26.29 = 20a + 62.30b \qquad (3')$$

$$93.83 = 62.30a + 230.15b \qquad (4')$$

Solving for a in (3') we get

$$a = \frac{26.29 - 62.30b}{20} = 1.3145 - 3.115b$$

and substituting a into (4') gives

$$93.83 = 62.30(1.3145 - 3.115b) + 230.15b$$

$$b = .311$$

Replacing b in (3') we get

$$26.29 = 20a + 62.30(.331)$$
$$a = .2835$$

Our final equation is then

$$y = .2835 + .331x$$

and for the selected values of x:

Table A1-2 Corn-Soybean Results 1956–1975

x (soybeans)	1.00	3.00	5.00	6.00
y (corn)	.61	1.28	1.94	2.27

APPENDIX 2
Statistical Programs

a. FORTRAN PROGRAM FOR LEAST SQUARES (TWO VARIABLES)

The following FORTRAN program will read n sets of data (x, y) and compute the coefficients of the linear equation
$$y = a + bx$$
by solving the least-square equations
$$b = \frac{n \sum xy - \sum x \sum y}{n \sum x^2 - (\sum x)^2}$$
$$a = \frac{\sum y - b \sum x}{n} = \bar{y} - b\bar{x}$$

Other statistical data will be calculated as well.

b. PROGRAMS FOR THE TEXAS INSTRUMENTS SR-52 HAND-HELD PROGRAMMABLE CALCULATOR

Program number	Description
1	Simultaneous linear equations, matrix solution (3 × 4)
2	Least-squares approximation for a time-series
3	Detrending data from a linear approximation
4	Single-frequency trigonometric curve-fitting—least-squares solution for α
5	Single-frequency trigonometric curve-fitting—sums of normal equations
6	Single-frequency trigonometric curve-fitting—predicted results
7	Two-frequency trigonometric curve-fitting—solution of α and ω
8	Two-frequency trigonometric curve-fitting—sums of normal equations
9	Simultaneous linear equations, matrix solution (4 × 5)
10	Two-frequency trigonometric curve-fitting—predicted results

```fortran
LC2VAR
// SEQ40 UNITNO-10,BLOCKSIZE-128
*PROCESS SOURCE,NOOBJECT,LINK(R,LIB(F2))
      PROGRAM LC2VAR
      IMPLICIT INTEGER*2(I-N)
C---- LINEAR CORRELATION FOR 2 VARIABLES USING LEAST SQUARES
      INTEGER*4 DESCY(4),DESCX(4),DESCT(4),IX(100),IY(100),FYPRED(51),
     1          IYAXIS(51),TIME(100,4),HEADER(10),DATE(4),IXAXIS(51)
      DIMENSION X(100),Y(100),LINE(51),YAXIS(51),XAXIS(51)
      REAL*4 SX,SY,SXM,SYM,SXY,SYE
      COMMON DATE,NPAGE,HEADER,N,X,Y,
     1       DESCY,DESCX,XMIN,XMAX,YMIN,YMAX
      DATA MAX/98/, IBLANK/' '/,LINES/55/,IDOT/'.'/,LX/'X'/,
     1 SYE,SX,SY,SXY,SXM,SYM/6*0./,LOOP/0/
      NPAGE=0
      N=0
      READ(10,1000,END=900)HEADER,DATE
 1000 FORMAT(14A4)
C---- READ DESCRIPTIONS OF TIME INTERVAL, DEPENDENT VARIABLE (Y), AND
C---- INDEPENDENT VARIABLE (X)
      READ(10,1001,END=900)DESCT,DESCY,DESCX
 1001 FORMAT(4A4,4X,4A4,4X,4A4)
C---- HEADER
      NPAGE = 1
      WRITE(3,3000)DATE,NPAGE,HEADER,DESCT,DESCY,DESCX
 3000 FORMAT('1ECONOMIC RESEARCH, INC',25X,4A4,5X,'PAGE',I2//20X,10A4//
     1       15X,4A4,4X,4A4,4X,4A4/)
C---- READ DETAIL CARDS AND SUM
      I = 1
   30 READ(10,1002,END=50)(TIME(I,J),J=1,4),TY,TX
 1002 FORMAT(4A4,2F10.2)
      Y(I) = TY
      X(I) = TX
      IF(I.GT.1)GO TO 31
      YMAX = TY
      YMIN = TY
      XMAX = TX
      XMIN = TX
   31 IF(N.GT.MAX)GO TO 40
      N = N+1
C---- SUMS FOR CALCULATION
      SX = SX+TX
      SY = SY+TY
      IF(TY.GT.YMAX)YMAX=TY
      IF(TX.GT.XMAX)XMAX=TX
      IF(TY.LT.YMIN)YMIN=TY
      IF(TX.LT.XMIN)XMIN=TX
      WRITE(3,3001)N,(TIME(I,J),J=1,4),TY,TX
 3001 FORMAT(12X,I2,1X,4A4,2X,F10.3,10X,F10.3)
      I = I+1
      GO TO 30
C---- EXCEEDED MAXIMUM DATA
   40 PAUSE 20
C---- ALL DATA READ, CALCULATE COEFFICIENTS
C---- PRINT SIMPLE SUMS OF EACH COLUMN
   50 WRITE(3,3002)SY,SX
 3002 FORMAT(/10X,'SUMS',19X,F10.2,10X,F10.2)
      NPAGE = NPAGE+1
      WRITE(3,3030)DATE,NPAGE,HEADER
 3030 FORMAT('1ECONOMIC RESEARCH, INC',25X,4A4,5X,'PAGE',I2//20X,10A4//
```

```
      1         ' LEAST SQUARES LINEAR APPROXIMATION')
 3003 FORMAT(//' INTERMEDIATE VALUES'// 5X,'S Y = ',E12.5,4X,'S XY = ',
     1          E12.5,4X,'S YM = ',E12.5/ 5X,'S X = ',E12.5, 4X,'S XM = ',
     2          E12.5,4X,'S YE = ',E12.5)
C---- CALCULATE VALUES OF A AND B
      XBAR=SX/N
      YBAR=SY/N
      DO 55 I=1,N
      XDIF=X(I)-XBAR
      YDIF=Y(I)-YBAR
      SXM=SXM+XDIF*XDIF
      SYM=SYM+YDIF*YDIF
   55 SXY=SXY+XDIF*YDIF
      B = SXY/SXM
      A = (SY-B*SX)/N
C---- PRINT LINEAR EQUATION
 3004 FORMAT(//' RESULTING EQUATION IS   Y = A + BX    WHERE    A =',
     1          F10.3/40X,'AND    B =',F10.3)
C---- CORRELATION COEFFICIENT
      DO 58 I=1,N
      XDIF=A+B*X(I)
      YDIF=Y(I)-XDIF
   58 SYE=SYE+YDIF*YDIF
      C = SQRT(1.0-SYE/SYM)
      WRITE(3,3003)SY,SXY,SYM,SX,SXM,SYE
      WRITE(3,3004)A,B
      WRITE(3,3005)C
 3005 FORMAT( '0LINEAR CORRELATION COEFFICIENT IS   C =',F10.3)
C---- STANDARD DEVIATION FROM FITTED LINE
      YSUM = 0.
      DO 60 I = 1,N
      FY = A+B*X(I)
      Y2 = (FY-Y(I))**2
      FYSUM = FYSUM+FY
   60 YSUM = YSUM+Y2
      SD =        (YSUM/N)**.5
      WRITE(3,3006)SD
 3006 FORMAT('0STANDARD DEVIATION FROM LINE IS    SD =',F10.3)
C---- PLOT TWO VARIABLE RESULT
   65 LOOP=LOOP+1
      NPAGE = NPAGE+1
      WRITE(3,3010)DATE,NPAGE,HEADER,DESCY
 3010 FORMAT('1ECONOMIC RESEARCH, INC',25X,4A4,5X,'PAGE',I2//20X,10A4/
     1          6X,4A4)
C---- SCALE X-AXIS, ALLOW 50 COLUMNS, CALCULATE INCREMENTS
      XSPAN = XMAX-XMIN
      XINT = XSPAN/50.
C---- CALCULATE Y-AXIS SCALING
      YSPAN = YMAX-YMIN
      YINT = YSPAN/50.
C---- INTERVALS CALCULATED ON 51X50 MAP
      WRITE(3,3011)
 3011 FORMAT(14X,53('.'))
C---- CALCULATE LOWER SCALE
C---- CHECK IF EXPANDED SCALE
      IF(XINT.GE.1.)GO TO 470
      DO 70 I = 1,51
      XAXIS(I) = XMIN+XINT*(I-1)
      TX=XAXIS(I)
      FY=A+B*TX
```

```
      IF(LOOP .NE. 2) GO TO 68
      FY=LOG(A)+B*LOG(TX)
      FY=EXP(FY)
   68 IF(LOOP .NE. 3) GO TO 69
      FY=LOG(A)+        B*TX
      FY=EXP(FY)
   69 FYPRED(I) = (FY            -YMIN)/YINT+1.5
   70 IXAXIS(I) = XAXIS(I)*100.+.5
      XMA1 = XMAX*100.
      GO TO 320
  470 DO 475 I = 1,51
      IXAXIS(I) = XMIN+XINT*(I-1)+.5
C---- FIND FY-PREDICTED FOR EACH X VALUE
      TX=IXAXIS(I)
      FY=A+B*TX
      IF(LOOP .NE. 2) GO TO 474
      FY=LOG(A)+B*LOG(TX)
      FY=EXP(FY)
  474 IF(LOOP .NE. 3) GO TO 475
      FY=LOG(A)+        B*TX
      FY=EXP(FY)
  475 FYPRED(I) = (FY            -YMIN)/YINT+1.5
      XMA1=XMAX
C---- SCAN VALUE OF X AND Y AND ROUND OFF BOX VALUE
C---- CONVERT X-VALUES TO BOX LOCATION
  320 DO 330 I = 1,N
  330 IX(I) = (X(I)-XMIN)/XINT+1.5
C---- CALCULATE SCALE FOR Y-AXIS
      FACTOR = 1.
C---- FRACTIONAL SCALE
      IF(YINT.LE.1)FACTOR=100.
C---- INTEGER SCALE
      DO 346 I = 1,51
  346 IYAXIS(I) =(YMIN+YINT*(I-1))*FACTOR+.5
C---- CONVERT Y-VALUES TO BOX LOCATION
      DO 360 I = 1,N
  360 IY(I) = (Y(I)-YMIN)/YINT+1.5
C---- PLOT EACH ROW
      J = 51
  390 DO 400 I = 1,51
  400 LINE(I) = IBLANK
      DO 410 I = 1,N
      IF(IY(I).NE.J)GO TO 410
      K = IX(I)
      LINE(K) = LX
  410 CONTINUE
C---- ENTER DOTS TO REPRESENT FITTED LINE
      DO 415 I = 1,51
      IF(FYPRED(I).NE.J)GO TO 415
C---- DO NOT PLACE DOT OVER PRIOR SYMBOL
      IF(LINE(I).EQ.IBLANK)LINE(I)=IDOT
  415 CONTINUE
C---- PRINT ROW
      WRITE(3,3013)IYAXIS(J),LINE
 3013 FORMAT( 8X,I5,1X,'.',51A1,'.')
C---- TEST END OF PLOT
      IF(J.EQ.1)GO TO 460
      J = J-1
      GO TO 390
C---- END OF PLOT
```

```
      460 DIGITS = 10000
          WRITE(3,3011)
C---- SCALE DOWN IF MORE THAN 2 DIGITS
      465 IF(XMA1/DIGITS.LT.10)GO TO 480
          DO 466 I = 1,51
      466 IXAXIS(I) = IXAXIS(I)/10
          XMA1 = XMA1/10
          GO TO 465
      480 IF(XMA1/DIGITS.GT.1.)GO TO 500
      490 IF(DIGITS.LE.1)GO TO 600
          DIGITS = DIGITS/10
          GO TO 480
C---- SCALE AND PRINT INTERVALS
      500 DO 510 I = 1,51
          LINE(I) = IXAXIS(I)/DIGITS
      510 IXAXIS(I) = IXAXIS(I)-LINE(I)*DIGITS
          WRITE(3,3015)LINE
     3015 FORMAT(15X,51I1)
          GO TO 490
C---- SCALING COMPLETED
      600 WRITE(3,3020)DESCX
          IF(LOOP .GE. 2) GO TO 850
     3020 FORMAT(/30X,4A4)
C---- LOGARITHMIC APPROXIMATION
          CALL LCLN(A,B)
          GO TO 65
C---- EXPONENTIAL APPROXIMATION
      850 IF(LOOP .GT. 2) GO TO 900
          CALL LCEXP(A,B)
          GO TO 65
      900 STOP
          END
```

ECONOMIC RESEARCH, INC   JULY 1977   PAGE 1

YEAR TO RATE OF INFLATION RELATIONSHIP

	YEARLY	INFLATION RATE	YEAR
1	1928	0.438	1.928
2	1933	0.340	1.933
3	1938	0.380	1.938
4	1947	0.669	1.947
5	1948	0.720	1.948
6	1949	0.714	1.949
7	1950	0.720	1.950
8	1951	0.778	1.951
9	1952	0.796	1.952
10	1953	0.802	1.953
11	1954	0.805	1.954
12	1955	0.803	1.955
13	1956	0.814	1.956
14	1957	0.842	1.957
15	1958	0.865	1.958
16	1959	0.873	1.959
17	1960	0.886	1.960
18	1961	0.896	1.961
19	1962	0.907	1.962
20	1963	0.917	1.963
21	1964	0.929	1.964
22	1965	0.945	1.965
23	1966	0.973	1.966
24	1967	1.000	1.967
25	1968	1.043	1.968
26	1969	1.098	1.969
27	1970	1.163	1.970
28	1971	1.213	1.971
29	1972	1.253	1.972
30	1973	1.331	1.973
31	1974	1.477	1.974
32	1975	1.612	1.975
33	1976	1.701	1.976
34	1977	1.811	1.977
SUMS		32.51	66.62

ECONOMIC RESEARCH, INC   JULY 1977   PAGE 2

YEAR TO RATE OF INFLATION RELATIONSHIP

LEAST SQUARES LINEAR APPROXIMATION

INTERMEDIATE VALUES

    S Y = 0.32514E+02   S XY = 0.12316E+00   S YM = 0.37767E+01
    S X = 0.66621E+02   S XM = 0.48304E-02   S YE = 0.63663E+00

RESULTING EQUATION IS   Y = A + BX   WHERE   A = -49.002
                                       AND   B = 25.496

LINEAR CORRELATION COEFFICIENT IS   C =   0.912

STANDARD DEVIATION FROM LINE IS   SD =   0.137

ECONOMIC RESEARCH, INC   JULY 1977   PAGE 3

```
              YEAR TO RATE OF INFLATION RELATIONSHIP
  INFLATION RATE
        ..............................................
    181 .                                            X.
    178 .                                             .
    175 .                                             .
    172 .                                             .
    169 .                                         X   .
    166 .                                             .
    163 .                                             .
    161 .                                       X     .
    158 .                                             .
    155 .                                             .
    152 .                                             .
    149 .                                     X       .
    146 .                                             .
    143 .                                             .
    140 .                                           ..
    137 .                                           .
    134 .                                    X..    .
    131 .                                     .     .
    128 .                                           .
    125 .                                  .X       .
    122 .                                  .X       .
    119 .                                 ..        .
    116 .                               .  X        .
    113 .                                           .
    110 .                              .  X         .
    108 .                              .            .
    105 .                            . X            .
    102 .                           ..              .
     99 .                          . XX             .
     96 .                         .  X              .
     93 .                         . XX              .
     90 .                        .XXX               .
     87 .                       .XX                 .
     84 .                     .. X                  .
     81 .              X XXXX                       .
     78 .              X .                          .
     75 .               .                           .
     72 .           XXX.                            .
     69 .            ..                             .
     66 .         X.                                .
     63 .          .                                .
     60 .         .                                 .
     58 .        .                                  .
     55 .       .                                   .
     52 .     ..                                    .
     49 .                                           .
     46 .                                           .
     43 .X        .                                 .
     40 .                                           .
     37 .     ..X                                   .
     34 .    X .                                    .
        ...........................................
        11111111111111111111111111111111111111111111
        99999999999999999999999999999999999999999999
        33333333444444444455555555556666666666777777777888
                              YEAR
```

ECONOMIC RESEARCH, INC   JULY 1977   PAGE 4

YEAR TO RATE OF INFLATION RELATIONSHIP

LOGARITHMIC APPROXIMATION

INTERMEDIATE VALUES

     S Y = 0.32514E+02   LNXLNY = 0.72567E-01   S X = 0.66621E+02
     LNYM= 0.45239E+01   LNXM= 0.12635E-02
                                                                       (LNY)E = 0.34729E+00

RESULTING EQUATION IS   Y = A(X**B)   WHERE   A = 0.15004E-16
                                                               AND   B = 0.57432E+02

COEFFICIENT OF CORRELATION IS   C =   0.953

STANDARD DEVIATION FROM CURVE IS   SD =   0.101

ECONOMIC RESEARCH, INC   JULY 1977   PAGE 5

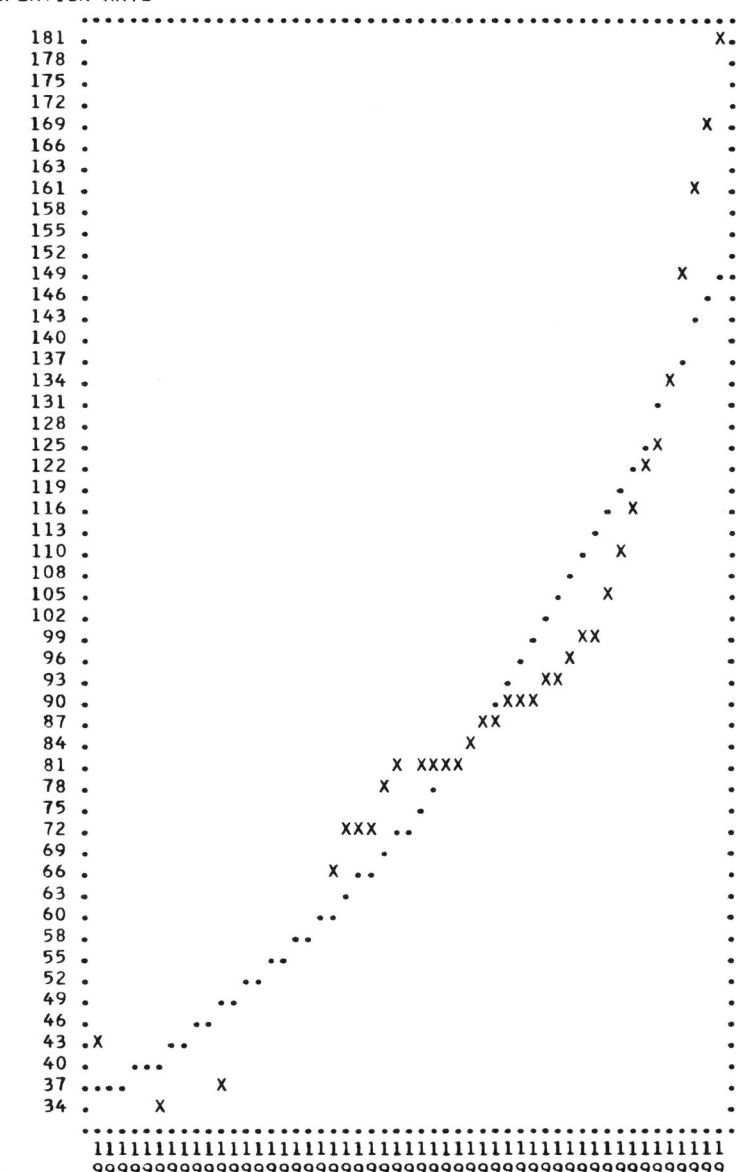

YEAR TO RATE OF INFLATION RELATIONSHIP

ECONOMIC RESEARCH, INC　　　　　　　　　　JULY 1977　　　　　　PAGE 6

YEAR TO RATE OF INFLATION RELATIONSHIP

EXPONENTIAL APPROXIMATION

INTERMEDIATE VALUES

$SX = 0.66621E+02$　　　$SX2 = 0.48304E-02$　　　$LNY = -0.36526E+01$

$(LNY)E = 0.34246E+00$

RESULTING EQUATION IS　　$Y = A(E^{**}BX)$　　WHERE　$A = 0.89617E-25$
　　　　　　　　　　　　　　　　　　　　　　　　 AND　$B = 0.29379E+02$

COEFFICIENT OF CORRELATION　　　　$C = 0.954$

STANDARD DEVIATION FROM CURVE IS　　$SD = 0.100$

ECONOMIC RESEARCH, INC   JULY 1977   PAGE 7

YEAR TO RATE OF INFLATION RELATIONSHIP

```
INFLATION RATE
       ..........................................................
  181 .                                              X.
  178 .                                               .
  175 .                                               .
  172 .                                               .
  169 .                                          X    .
  166 .                                               .
  163 .                                               .
  161 .                                        X      .
  158 .                                               .
  155 .                                               .
  152 .                                             ..
  149 .                                       X     .
  146 .                                           . .
  143 .                                             .
  140 .                                             .
  137 .                                         .   .
  134 .                                       X     .
  131 .                                       .     .
  128 .                                             .
  125 .                                      .X     .
  122 .                                     .X      .
  119 .                                             .
  116 .                                    . X      .
  113 .                                             .
  110 .                                   .  X      .
  108 .                                   .         .
  105 .                                  .  X       .
  102 .                                             .
   99 .                                 .  XX       .
   96 .                                .   X        .
   93 .                                .  XX        .
   90 .                               .XXX          .
   87 .                                XX           .
   84 .                                X            .
   81 .                          X XXXX             .
   78 .                          X  .               .
   75 .                             .               .
   72 .                      XXX ..                 .
   69 .                         .                   .
   66 .                     X ..                    .
   63 .                       .                     .
   60 .                     ..                      .
   58 .                                             .
   55 .                    ..                       .
   52 .                   ..                        .
   49 .                  ..                         .
   46 .                ..                           .
   43 .X             ..                             .
   40 .            ...                              .
   37 .....           X                             .
   34 .       X                                     .
       ..........................................................
        1111111111111111111111111111111111111111111111111
        9999999999999999999999999999999999999999999999999
        333333334444444444555555555566666666667777777777888
                            YEAR
```

Program 1: Simultaneous Linear Equations—Matrix Solution (3 × 4)

Find the unknowns x, y, and z of the three simultaneous linear equations of the form

$$a_{11}x + a_{12}y + a_{13}z = a_{14}$$
$$a_{21}x + a_{22}y + a_{23}z = a_{24}$$
$$a_{31}x + a_{32}y + a_{33}z = a_{34}$$

Registers

0	1 a_{11}	2 a_{12}	3 a_{13}	4 a_{14}
5 a_{21}	6 a_{22}	7 a_{23}	8 a_{24}	9 a_{31}
10 a_{32}	11 a_{33}	12 a_{34}	13	14
15	16	17	18	19

To Run Program #1

Step	Procedure	Enter	Display	Press keys
1	Enter program			
2	Initialize			*CMs, *rset
3	Enter data points a_{11} thru a_{34} into correct registers	a_{ij}		
4	Start program			RUN
5	Program will halt and answers will be displayed		x	RUN
			y	RUN
			z	
6	Restart next problem at step 2			

* indicates second function.

Program Instructions

Step	Enter	Step	Enter	Step	Enter	Step	Enter
001	RCL 01	026	×	051	=	076	*rset
002	INV*PROD 04	027	RCL 09	052	INV SUM 12	077	
003	INV*PROD 03	028	=	053	RCL 07	078	
004	INV*PROD 02	029	INV SUM 11	054	×	079	
005	RCL 04	030	RCL 02	055	RCL 10	080	
006	×	031	×	056	=	081	
007	RCL 05	032	RCL 09	057	INV SUM 11	082	
008	=	033	=	058	RCL 11	083	
009	INV SUM 08	034	INV SUM 10	059	INV*PROD 12	084	
010	RCL 03	035	RCL 06	060	RCL 12	085	
011	×	036	INV*PROD 08	061	×	086	
012	RCL 05	037	INV*PROD 07	062	RCL 03	087	
013	=	038	RCL 08	063	=	088	
014	INV SUM 07	039	×	064	INV SUM 04	089	
015	RCL 02	040	RCL 02	065	RCL 12	090	
016	×	041	=	066	×	091	
017	RCL 05	042	INV SUM 04	067	RCL 07	092	
018	=	043	RCL 07	068	=	093	
019	INV SUM 06	044	×	069	INV SUM 08	094	
020	RCL 04	045	RCL 02	070	RCL 04	095	
021	×	046	=	071	HLT	096	
022	RCL 09	047	INV SUM 03	072	RCL 08	097	
023	=	048	RCL 08	073	HLT	098	
024	INV SUM 12	049	×	074	RCL 12	099	
025	RCL 03	050	RCL 10	075	HLT	100	

* indicates second function; follows INV when both occur.

Program 2: Least-Squares Approximation For A Time-Series

This program will calculate the values for a and b in the equation $y = a + bx$. The method of least squares requires the solution to the equation

$$a = \frac{1}{N}\left(\sum y - b \sum x\right)$$

$$b = \frac{N \sum xy - \sum x \sum y}{N \sum x^2 - (\sum x)^2}$$

where N is the number of data points to be entered. The independent variable x must be time based, requiring equal intervals, and will be calculated automatically by the program.

Registers

0	1	2	3	4
$N \to 0$	N	x_0	y_n	x increment
5	6	7	8	9
$\sum x$	$\sum y$	$\sum xy$	$\sum x^2$	$(\sum x)^2$
10	11	12	13	14
b	a	x_n		
15	16	17	18	19

To Run Program #2

Step	Procedure	Enter	Display	Press keys
1	Enter program			
2	Initialize			*CMs, *rset
3	Start program			RUN
4	Enter first x value,	x_0		RUN
	number of data points,	N		RUN
	x increment	I		RUN
5	Enter other data.	y_n		RUN
	Repeat step 5 until all N values for y have been entered			
6	Program will halt		b	RUN
			a	RUN
7	Enter any value of x to get y	X_n		RUN
8	Program will halt. Repeat step 7 as required to get results of least-square approximation.		Y_n	RUN

* indicates second function.

Program Instructions

Step	Enter	Step	Enter	Step	Enter	Step	Enter
001	HLT	026	STO 09	051	RCL 05	076	
002	STO 02	027	(	052	)	077	
003	STO 12	028	RCL 01	053	÷	078	
004	HLT	029	×	054	RCL 01	079	
005	STO 00	030	RCL 07	055	=	080	
006	STO 01	031	−	056	STO 11	081	
007	HLT	032	RCL 05	057	RCL 10	082	
008	STO 04	033	×	058	HLT	083	
009	*LBL A	034	RCL 06	059	RCL 11	084	
010	HLT	035	)	060	*LBL B	085	
011	STO 03	036	÷	061	HLT	086	
012	SUM 06	037	(	062	×	087	
013	×	038	RCL 01	063	RCL 10	088	
014	RCL 12	039	×	064	+	089	
015	=	040	RCL 08	065	RCL 11	090	
016	SUM 07	041	−	066	=	091	
017	RCL 12	042	RCL 09	067	GTO B	092	
018	SUM 05	043	)	068		093	
019	*x^2	044	=	069		094	
020	SUM 08	045	STO 10	070		095	
021	RCL 04	046	(	071		096	
022	SUM 12	047	RCL 06	072		097	
023	*dsz A	048	−	073		098	
024	RCL 05	049	RCL 10	074		099	
025	*x^2	050	×	075		100	

* indicates second function; follows INV when both occur.

Program 3: Detrending

Calculate the difference between the original data points (y_n) of a time-series (x_n) and the straight-line equation $y = a + bx$. The values for a and b are found using the least-squares approximation (Program #2). The results will be detrended data.

Registers

0	1	2 a	3 b	4 x_0
5 x increment	6 $y_n - \hat{y}_n$	7	8	9
10	11	12	13	14
15	16	17	18	19

To Run Program #3

Step	Procedure	Enter	Display	Press keys
1	Enter program			
2	Initialize			*rset
3	Start program			RUN
4	Enter initial data	a		RUN
		b		RUN
	First x value	x_0		RUN
	x increment	I		RUN
5	Enter y values	y_n		RUN
6	Program will halt and display answer. Continue with Step 5.		$y_n - \hat{y}_n$	RUN

* indicates second function.

Program Instructions

Step	Enter	Step	Enter	Step	Enter	Step	Enter
001	HLT	026		051		076	
002	STO 02	027		052		077	
003	HLT	028		053		078	
004	STO 03	029		054		079	
005	HLT	030		055		080	
006	STO 04	031		056		081	
007	HLT	032		057		082	
008	STO 05	033		058		083	
009	*LBL A	034		059		084	
010	HLT	035		060		085	
011	−	036		061		086	
012	(	037		062		087	
013	RCL 02	038		063		088	
014	+	039		064		089	
015	RCL 03	040		065		090	
016	×	041		066		091	
017	RCL 04	042		067		092	
018	)	043		068		093	
019	=	044		069		094	
020	STO 06	045		070		095	
021	RCL 05	046		071		096	
022	SUM 04	047		072		097	
023	RCL 06	048		073		098	
024	GTO A	049		074		099	
025		050		075		100	

* indicates second function; follows INV when both occur.

Program 4: Single-Frequency Trigonometric Curve Fitting— Least-Squares Solution For α

The value of α is defined by the equation

$$\alpha y_n = y_{n-1} + y_{n+1}$$

The solution requires the sums in the equation

$$\alpha \sum c^2 = \sum cd$$

Registers

0 $N-2$	1 y_{n-1}	2 y_n	3 y_{n+1}	4 $\sum c^2$
5 $\sum cd$	6	7	8	9
10	11	12	13	14
15	16	17	18	19

To Run Program #4

Step	Procedure	Enter	Display	Press keys
1	Enter program			
2	Initialize			*CMs, *rset
3	Enter initial data			
	1st data point	y_1		RUN
	2nd data point	y_2		RUN
	No. data points -2	$N-2$		RUN
4	Enter next data.	y_n		RUN
	Repeat step 4 until complete			
5	Program will halt and display answer		α	
6	Next solution will continue at step 2			RUN

* indicates second function.

Program Instructions

Step	Enter	Step	Enter	Step	Enter	Step	Enter
001	HLT	026	RCL 05	051		076	
002	STO 01	027	÷	052		077	
003	HLT	028	RCL 04	053		078	
004	STO 02	029	=	054		079	
005	HLT	030	*rset	055		080	
006	STO 00	031		056		081	
007	*LBL A	032		057		082	
008	HLT	033		058		083	
009	STO 03	034		059		084	
010	RCL 02	035		060		085	
011	$*x^2$	036		061		086	
012	SUM 04	037		062		087	
013	RCL 01	038		063		088	
014	+	039		064		089	
015	RCL 03	040		065		090	
016	=	041		066		091	
017	×	042		067		092	
018	RCL 02	043		068		093	
019	=	044		069		094	
020	SUM 05	045		070		095	
021	RCL 02	046		071		096	
022	STO 01	047		072		097	
023	RCL 03	048		073		098	
024	STO 02	049		074		099	
025	*dsz A	050		075		100	

* indicates second function; follows **INV** when both occur.

Program 5: Single-Frequency Trigonometric Curve Fitting

Find the sums necessary to solve the equations

$$a \sum \cos^2 \omega t + b \sum \cos \omega t \sin \omega t = \sum y_t \cos \omega t$$
$$a \sum \sin \omega t \cos \omega t + b \sum \sin^2 \omega t = \sum y_t \sin \omega t$$

where ω is known, y_t is the input data (detrended), and $t = 1, 2, \ldots, n$.

Registers

0	1	2	3	4
	ω	$\sum \cos \omega t \sin \omega t$	$\sum \cos^2 \omega t$	$\sum \sin \omega^2 t$
5	6	7	8	9
$\sum y_t \cos \omega t$	$\sum y_t \sin \omega t$	y_t	t (date)	ωt
10	11	12	13	14
$\sin \omega t$	$\cos \omega t$	date increment		
15	16	17	18	19

To Run Program # 5

Step	Procedure	Enter	Display	Press keys
1	Enter program			
2	Initialize			*CMs, *rset
3	Start program			RUN
4	Enter initial data	ω		RUN
	date	t		RUN
	date increment	I		RUN
5	Enter detrended data. Repeat step 5 until complete.	y_t		RUN
6	Answers will be in registers			

* indicates second function.

Program Instructions

Step	Enter	Step	Enter	Step	Enter	Step	Enter
001	HLT	026	STO 11	051		076	
002	STO 01	027	$*x^2$	052		077	
003	HLT	028	SUM 03	053		078	
004	STO 08	029	RCL 11	054		079	
005	HLT	030	×	055		080	
006	STO 12	031	RCL 07	056		081	
007	*LBL A	032	=	057		082	
008	HLT	033	SUM 05	058		083	
009	STO 07	034	RCL 10	059		084	
010	RCL 08	035	×	060		085	
011	×	036	RCL 11	061		086	
012	RCL 01	037	=	062		087	
013	=	038	SUM 02	063		088	
014	STO 09	039	RCL 12	064		089	
015	sin	040	SUM 08	065		090	
016	STO 10	041	GTO A	066		091	
017	$*x^2$	042		067		092	
018	SUM 04	043		068		093	
019	RCL 10	044		069		094	
020	×	045		070		095	
021	RCL 07	046		071		096	
022	=	047		072		097	
023	SUM 06	048		073		098	
024	RCL 09	049		074		099	
025	cos	050		075		100	

* indicates second function; follows INV when both occur.

Program 6: Single-Frequency Trigonometric Curve Fitting

Find the results of the equation

$$y_t = a \cos \omega t + b \cos \omega t$$

where variables a, b, ω, and t are known and t changes.

Registers

0	1 a	2 b	3 ω	4 ωt
5	6	7	8	9
10	11	12	13	14
15	16	17	18	19

To Run Program # 6

Step	Procedure	Enter	Display	Press keys
1	Enter program			
2	Initialize			*rset
3	Start program			RUN
4	Enter initial data			
	amplitude 1	a		RUN
	amplitude 2	b		RUN
	frequency	ω		RUN
5	Enter date or other independent variable	t		RUN
6	Program will halt to display answer. Repeat step 5 until complete		y_t	RUN

* indicates second function.

Program Instructions

Step	Enter	Step	Enter	Step	Enter	Step	Enter
001	HLT	026		051		076	
002	STO 01	027		052		077	
003	HLT	028		053		078	
004	STO 02	029		054		079	
005	HLT	030		055		080	
006	STO 03	031		056		081	
007	*LBL A	032		057		082	
008	HLT	033		058		083	
009	×	034		059		084	
010	RCL 03	035		060		085	
011	=	036		061		086	
012	STO 04	037		062		087	
013	cos	038		063		088	
014	×	039		064		089	
015	RCL 01	040		065		090	
016	+	041		066		091	
017	RCL 04	042		067		092	
018	sin	043		068		093	
019	×	044		069		094	
020	RCL 02	045		070		095	
021	=	046		071		096	
022	GTO A	047		072		097	
023		048		073		098	
024		049		074		099	
025		050		075		100	

* indicates second function; follows INV when both occur.

Program 7: Two-Frequency Trigonometric Curve Fitting

Solve the two-frequency trigonometric curve-fitting problem for α_1 and α_2, where

$$\alpha_1(y_n + y_{n+2}) + \alpha_2 y_{n+1} = y_{n-1} + y_{n+3}$$

For convenience, the following notation is used:

$$c = (y_n + y_{n+2})$$
$$d = (y_n + y_{n+2})(y_{n+1})$$
$$p = (y_{n-1} + y_{n+3})$$

Then the least-squares solution is written

$$\alpha_1 \sum c^2 + \alpha_2 \sum cd = \sum cp$$
$$\alpha_1 \sum cd + \alpha_2 \sum d^2 = \sum dp$$

Both α_1 and α_2 can be found by direct substitution:

$$\alpha_1 = \frac{\sum cp - \alpha_2 \sum cd}{\sum c^2}$$

$$\alpha_2 = \left(\sum d^2 - \frac{\sum cd \sum cp}{\sum c^2}\right) \bigg/ \left(\sum d^2 + \frac{(\sum cp)^2}{\sum c^2}\right)$$

Registers

0 $N-4$	1 y_{n-1}	2 y_n	3 $y_{n+1} = d$	4 y_{n+2}
5 y_{n+3}	6 c	7 p	8 $\sum c^2$	9 $\sum cd$
10 $\sum cd$	11 $\sum cp$	12 $\sum d^2$	13 $\sum dp$	14 α_1
15 α_2	16	17	18	19

To Run Program #7

Step	Procedure	Enter	Display	Press keys
1	Enter program			
2	Initialize			*CMs, *rset
3	Start program			RUN
4	Enter initial data	y_1		RUN
	first 4 detrended	y_2		RUN
	data points	y_3		RUN
		y_4		RUN
	Enter number of data			RUN
	points minus 4	$N-4$		
5	Enter remaining data.	y_i		RUN
	Repeat step 5 until nth			
	data item is entered			
6	Program will halt		α_1	RUN
	to display answers		α_2	RUN
7	Return to step 2 for a			
	new problem.			

* indicates second function.

Program Instructions

Step	Enter	Step	Enter	Step	Enter	Step	Enter
001	HLT	026	×	051	*dsz A	076	RCL 11
002	STO 02	027	RCL 03	052	(	077	=
003	HLT	028	=	053	RCL 13	078	÷
004	STO 03	029	SUM 13	054	−	079	RCL 09
005	HLT	030	RCL 03	055	RCL 10	080	=
006	STO 04	031	×	056	×	081	STO 14
007	HLT	032	RCL 07	057	RCL 11	082	HLT
008	STO 05	033	=	058	÷	083	RCL 15
009	HLT	034	SUM 10	059	RCL 09	084	HLT
010	STO 00	035	RCL 06	060	)	085	*rset
011	*LBL A	036	×	061	÷	086	
012	HLT	037	RCL 07	062	(	087	
013	STO 05	038	=	063	RCL 12	088	
014	RCL 02	039	SUM 11	064	+	089	
015	+	040	RCL 03	065	RCL 10	090	
016	RCL 04	041	$*x^2$	066	$*x^2$	091	
017	=	042	SUM 12	067	÷	092	
018	STO 06	043	RCL 02	068	RCL 09	093	
019	$*x^2$	044	STO 01	069	)	094	
020	SUM 09	045	RCL 03	070	=	095	
021	RCL 01	046	STO 02	071	STO 15	096	
022	+	047	RCL 04	072	×	097	
023	RCL 05	048	STO 03	073	RCL 10	098	
024	=	049	RCL 05	074	+/−	099	
025	STO 07	050	STO 04	075	+	100	

* indicates second function; follows INV when both occur.

Program 8: Two-Frequency Trigonometric Curve Fitting

Find the sums of the factors of a_1, b_1, a_2, and b_2 in the normal equations

$$a_1 \sum \cos^2 \omega_1 t + b_1 \sum \cos \omega_1 t \sin \omega_1 t + a_2 \sum \cos \omega_1 t \cos \omega_2 t$$
$$+ b_2 \sum \cos \omega_1 t \sin \omega_2 t = \sum y_t \cos \omega_1 t$$

$$a_1 \sum \sin \omega_1 t \cos \omega_1 t + b_1 \sum \sin^2 \omega_1 t + a_2 \sum \sin \omega_1 t \cos \omega_2 t$$
$$+ b_2 \sum \sin \omega_1 t \sin \omega_2 t = \sum y_t \sin \omega_1 t$$

$$a_1 \sum \cos \omega_2 t \cos \omega_1 t + b_1 \sum \cos \omega_2 t \sin \omega_1 t + a_2 \sum \cos^2 \omega_2 t$$
$$+ b_2 \sum \cos \omega_2 t \sin \omega_2 t = \sum y_t \cos \omega_2 t$$

$$a_1 \sum \sin \omega_2 t \cos \omega_1 t + b_1 \sum \sin \omega_2 t \sin \omega_1 t + a_2 \sum \sin \omega_2 t \cos \omega_2 t$$
$$+ b_2 \sum \sin^2 \omega_2 t = \sum y_t \sin \omega_2 t$$

Registers

0	1	2	3	4
y_t	$\sum \cos^2 \omega_1 t$	$\sum \cos \omega_1 t \sin \omega_1 t$	$\sum \cos \omega_1 t \cos \omega_2 t$	$\sum \cos \omega_1 t \sin \omega_2 t$
5	6	7	8	9
$\sum \sin^2 \omega_1 t$	$\sum \sin \omega_1 t \cos \omega_2 t$	$\sum \sin \omega_1 t \sin \omega_2 t$	$\sum \cos^2 \omega_2 t$	$\sum \cos \omega_2 t \sin \omega_2 t$
10	11	12	13	14
$\sum \sin^2 \omega_2 t$	$\sum y_t \cos \omega_1 t$	$\sum y_t \sin \omega_1 t$	$\sum y_t \cos \omega_2 t$	$\sum y_t \sin \omega_2 t$
15	16	17	18	19
ω_1	ω_2	$\omega_1 t$	$\omega_2 t$	t

To Run Program #8

Step	Procedure	Enter	Display	Press keys
1	Enter program			
2	Initialize			*CMs, *rset
3	Start program			RUN
4	Enter initial data	ω_1		RUN
		ω_2		RUN
5	Enter time element	t		RUN
	Enter data	y_t		RUN
	Repeat step 5 for as many sets of (t, y_t) as necessary			
6	Registers will contain answers when complete.			

* indicates second function.

Program Instructions

Step	Enter	Step	Enter	Step	Enter	Step	Enter
001	HLT	026	sin	051	cos	076	RCL 00
002	STO 15	027	=	052	=	077	×
003	HLT	029	SUM 02	053	SUM 06	078	RCL 17
004	STO 16	029	RCL 17	054	RCL 17	079	cos
005	*LBL A	030	cos	055	sin	080	=
006	HLT	031	×	056	×	081	SUM 11
007	STO 19	032	RCL 18	057	RCL 18	082	RCL 00
008	×	033	cos	058	sin	083	×
009	RCL 15	034	=	059	=	084	RCL 17
010	=	035	SUM 03	060	SUM 07	085	sin
011	STO 17	036	RCL 17	061	RCL 08	086	=
012	cos	037	cos	062	cos	087	SUM 12
013	$*x^2$	038	×	063	$*x^2$	088	RCL 00
014	SUM 01	039	RCL 18	064	SUM 08	089	×
015	HLT	040	sin	065	RCL 18	090	RCL 18
016	STO 00	041	=	066	cos	091	cos
017	RCL 19	042	SUM 04	067	×	092	=
018	×	043	RCL 17	068	RCL 18	093	SUM 13
019	RCL 16	044	sin	069	sin	094	RCL 00
020	=	045	$*x^2$	070	=	095	×
021	STO 18	046	SUM 05	071	SUM 09	096	RCL 18
022	RCL 17	047	RCL 17	072	RCL 18	097	sin
023	cos	048	sin	073	sin	098	=
024	×	049	×	074	$*x^2$	099	SUM 14
025	RCL 17	050	RCL 18	075	SUM 10	100	GTO A

* indicates second function; follows INV when both occur.

Program 9: Simultaneous Linear Equations—Matrix Solution (4 × 5)

Find the unknowns w, x, y, z of the four simultaneous linear equations of the form

$$a_{11}w + a_{12}x + a_{13}y + a_{14}z = a_{15}$$
$$a_{21}w + a_{22}x + a_{23}y + a_{24}z = a_{25}$$
$$a_{31}w + a_{32}x + a_{33}y + a_{34}z = a_{35}$$
$$a_{41}w + a_{42}x + a_{43}y + a_{44}z = a_{45}$$

If Program #8 was used to calculate the value of the a's, the registers from that problem would appear in the following order:

$$
\begin{array}{ccccc}
R_{01} & R_{02} & R_{03} & R_{04} & R_{11} \\
R_{02} & R_{05} & R_{06} & R_{07} & R_{12} \\
R_{03} & R_{06} & R_{08} & R_{09} & R_{13} \\
R_{04} & R_{07} & R_{09} & R_{10} & R_{14}
\end{array}
$$

The program is written in two parts due to its extreme length.

Registers

0	1	2	3	4
a_{11}	a_{12}	a_{13}	a_{14}	a_{15}
5	6	7	8	9
a_{21}	a_{22}	a_{23}	a_{24}	a_{25}
10	11	12	13	14
a_{31}	a_{32}	a_{33}	a_{34}	a_{35}
15	16	17	18	19
a_{41}	a_{42}	a_{43}	a_{44}	a_{45}

To Run Program #9

Step	Procedure	Enter	Display	Press keys
1	Enter program, part 1			
2	Initialize			*CMs, *rset
3	Enter data into proper registers	a_{ij}		
4	Start program			RUN
5	When halts, enter program, part 2			
6	Start program			*rset, RUN
7	Answers will be displayed		w	RUN
			x	RUN
			y	RUN
			z	
	Program must be restarted at step 1			

* indicate second function.

Program Instructions, Part 1

Step	Enter	Step	Enter	Step	Enter	Step	Enter
001	RCL 00	026	RCL 10	051	RCL 15	076	×
002	INV*PROD 04	027	×	052	×	077	RCL 08
003	INV*PROD 03	028	RCL 04	053	RCL 03	078	=
004	INV*PROD 02	029	=	054	=	079	INV SUM 03
005	INV*PROD 01	030	INV SUM 14	055	INV SUM 18	080	RCL 01
006	RCL 05	031	RCL 10	056	RCL 15	081	×
007	×	032	×	057	×	082	RCL 07
008	RCL 04	033	RCL 03	058	RCL 02	083	=
009	=	034	=	059	=	084	INV SUM 02
010	INV SUM 09	035	INV SUM 13	060	INV SUM 17	085	HLT
011	RCL 05	036	RCL 10	061	RCL 15	086	
012	×	037	×	062	×	087	
013	RCL 03	038	RCL 02	063	RCL 01	088	
014	=	039	=	064	=	089	
015	INV SUM 08	040	INV SUM 12	065	INV SUM 16	090	
016	RCL 05	041	RCL 10	066	RCL 06	091	
017	×	042	×	067	INV*PROD 09	092	
018	RCL 02	043	RCL 01	068	INV*PROD 08	093	
019	=	044	=	069	INV*PROD 07	094	
020	INV SUM 07	045	INV SUM 11	070	RCL 01	095	
021	RCL 05	046	RCL 15	071	×	096	
022	×	047	×	072	RCL 09	097	
023	RCL 01	048	RCL 04	073	=	098	
024	=	049	=	074	INV SUM 04	099	
025	INV SUM 06	050	INV SUM 19	075	RCL 01	100	

* indicates second function; follows INV when both occur.

Program Instructions, Part 2

Step	Enter	Step	Enter	Step	Enter	Step	Enter
001	RCL 11	026	RCL 16	051	RCL 13	076	RCL 13
002	×	027	×	052	=	077	×
003	RCL 09	228	RCL 07	053	INV SUM 08	078	RCL 19
004	=	029	=	054	RCL 17	079	=
005	INV SUM 14	030	INV SUM 17	055	×	080	INV SUM 14
006	RCL 11	031	RCL 12	056	RCL 14	081	RCL 04
007	×	032	INV*PROD 14	057	=	082	HLT
008	RCL 08	033	INV*PROD 13	058	INV SUM 19	083	RCL 09
009	=	034	RCL 02	059	RCL 17	084	HLT
010	INV SUM 13	035	×	060	×	085	RCL 14
011	RCL 11	036	RCL 14	061	RCL 13	086	HLT
012	×	037	=	062	=	087	RCL 19
013	RCL 07	038	INV SUM 04	063	INV SUM 18	088	HLT
014	=	039	RCL 02	064	RCL 18	089	
015	INV SUM 12	040	×	065	INV*PROD 19	090	
016	RCL 16	041	RCL 13	077	RCL 03	091	
017	×	042	=	067	×	092	
018	RCL 09	043	INV SUM 03	068	RCL 19	093	
019	=	044	RCL 07	069	=	094	
020	INV SUM 19	045	×	070	INV SUM 04	095	
021	RCL 16	046	RCL 14	071	RCL 08	096	
022	×	047	=	072	×	097	
023	RCL 08	048	INV SUM 09	073	RCL 19	098	
024	=	049	RCL 07	074	=	099	
025	INV SUM 18	050	×	075	INV SUM 09	100	

* indicates second function; follows INV when both occur.

Program 10: Two-Frequency Trigonometric Curve Fitting

Calculate values of the complex trigonometric curve and its two frequency components

$$y_t = a_1 \cos \omega_1 t + b_1 \sin \omega_1 t + a_2 \cos \omega_2 t + b_2 \sin \omega_2 t$$

where the components are

$$y'_t = a_1 \cos \omega_1 t + b_1 \sin \omega_1 t$$
$$y''_t = a_2 \cos \omega_2 t + b_2 \sin \omega_2 t$$

Registers

0	1 ω_1	2 ω_2	3 a_1	4 a_2
5 b_1	6 b_2	7 t	8 $\omega_1 t$	9 $\omega_2 t$
10 y'_t	11	12	13	14
15	16	17	18	19

To Run Program #10

Step	Procedure	Enter	Display	Press keys
1	Enter program			
2	Initialize			*rset
3	Start program			RUN
4	Enter initial data	ω_1		RUN
	frequencies	ω_2		RUN
	amplitudes	a_1		RUN
		a_2		RUN
		b_1		RUN
		b_2		RUN
5	Enter next value of t	t_i		RUN
6	Program will halt		y'_t	RUN
	with answers		y''_t	RUN
			y_t	RUN
	Continue with step 5			

* indicates second function.

Program Instructions

Step	Enter	Step	Enter	Step	Enter	Step	Enter
001	HLT	026	cos	051	HLT	076	
002	STO 01	027	×	052	GTO A	077	
003	HLT	028	RCL 03	053		078	
004	STO 02	029	+	054		079	
005	HTL	030	RCL 08	055		080	
006	STO 03	031	sin	056		081	
007	HLT	032	×	057		082	
008	STO 04	033	RCL 05	058		083	
009	HLT	034	=	059		084	
010	STO 05	035	STO 10	060		085	
011	HLT	036	HLT	061		086	
012	STO 06	037	RCL 09	062		087	
013	*LBL A	038	cos	063		088	
014	HLT	039	×	064		089	
015	STO 07	040	RCL 04	065		090	
016	×	041	+	066		091	
017	RCL 01	042	RCL 09	067		092	
018	=	043	sin	068		093	
019	STO 08	044	×	069		094	
020	RCL 07	045	RCL 06	070		095	
021	×	046	=	071		096	
022	RCL 02	047	HLT	072		097	
023	=	048	+	073		098	
024	STO 09	049	RCL 10	074		099	
025	RCL 08	050	=	075		100	

* indicates second function; follows INV when both occur.

c. PROGRAMS AVAILABLE ON COMPUTERS

Statistical subroutines are available on most major computer systems. One such system, the Control Data 6000 series, has the following programs available to users:

1. *Basic descriptive statistics*, which includes: mean; second, third, and fourth moments about the mean; variance; standard deviation; skewness; and kurtosis.
2. *Deletion and standardization of variables*, which are steps in the solution of a coefficient matrix used with multiple linear equations.
3. *Correlation matrix*—data elements of a matrix can be normalized and the mean and standardization taken.
4. *Rank order standardized observation*, which will order any specified column of a matrix of data values.
5. *Multiple regression analysis*, which calculates a least-square approximation between the dependent variable (y) and the multiple independent variables $(x_1, \ldots, x_n)$.
6. *Stepwise regression analysis*, which allows the user to proceed step-by-step through the multiple regression analysis, including intermediate values.
7. *Autoregression and spectral analysis*, which takes a stationary time-series for equally spaced points and calculates the autocorrelation coefficients, power spectrum (spectral densities), and various intermediate quantities.
8. *Analysis of variance*, which analyzes the relationship between data from an equal number of equal-weight designs.
9. *Uniform random numbers*, generating a sequence of random numbers that can be used for statistical testing.

The use of these programs is explained, as well as the mathematical techniques implemented. They tend to be efficient and should be used if at all possible.

APPENDIX 3

Matrix Solution To Linear Equations

a. GENERAL FORM

A matrix is a rectangular arrangement of elements into rows and columns. A matrix A is said to be $m \times n$ (m by n) if there are m rows and n columns in A.

$$a_{m \times n} = \begin{pmatrix} a_{11} & a_{12} & \cdots & a_{1n} \\ a_{21} & a_{22} & \cdots & a_{2n} \\ \vdots & \vdots & & \vdots \\ a_{m1} & a_{m2} & \cdots & a_{mn} \end{pmatrix}$$

Certain properties of a matrix make it a valuable tool for solving simultaneous linear equations. These elementary matrix operations, called transformations, allow you to alter the rows (which will represent equations) without changing the solution. There are three basic row operations:

1. Multiplication or division of all elements of the row by any number.
2. Interchanging of any two rows (and consequently of all rows).
3. The addition or subtraction of the elements of one row with the corresponding elements of another.

In order to relate the matrix to simultaneous linear equations, consider a three-equation example:

$$a_{11}x_1 + a_{12}x_2 + a_{13}x_3 = a_{14} \tag{1}$$

$$a_{21}x_1 + a_{22}x_2 + a_{23}x_3 = a_{24} \tag{2}$$

$$a_{31}x_1 + a_{32}x_2 + a_{33}x_3 = a_{34} \tag{3}$$

This is the same as the multivariate approximation in three variables once the sums are substituted and only the coefficients remain as unknowns.

The three elementary row operations can now be interpreted in terms of simple operations on an equation:

1. When both sides of an equation are multiplied or divided by the same value, the results are equal.
2. Any two equations in a system of equations can be interchanged with no effect.
3. When two equals are added or subtracted, the results are equal.

Putting these rules into use, we write the coefficients of the three simultaneous linear equations as a 3×4 coefficient matrix,

$$\begin{pmatrix} a_{11} & a_{12} & a_{13} & a_{14} \\ a_{21} & a_{22} & a_{23} & a_{24} \\ a_{31} & a_{32} & a_{33} & a_{34} \end{pmatrix}$$

with the objective of reducing the matrix to the form

$$\begin{pmatrix} 1 & 0 & 0 & A_1 \\ 0 & 1 & 0 & A_2 \\ 0 & 0 & 1 & A_3 \end{pmatrix}$$

which would mean that $x_1 = A_1$, $x_2 = A_2$ and $x_3 = A_3$ since

$$1 \cdot x_1 + 0 \cdot x_2 + 0 \cdot x_3 = A_1$$
$$0 \cdot x_1 + 1 \cdot x_2 + 0 \cdot x_3 = A_2$$
$$0 \cdot x_1 + 0 \cdot x_2 + 1 \cdot x_3 = A_3$$

To achieve our results, we perform the following steps. Divide the first equation by a_{11}, the first element, leaving

$$\left(1 \quad \frac{a_{12}}{a_{11}} \quad \frac{a_{13}}{a_{11}} \quad \frac{a_{14}}{a_{11}} \right) \tag{1-1}$$

and then multiply by a_{21} to get the first elements in rows one and two the same:

$$\left(a_{21} \quad \frac{a_{12}(a_{21})}{a_{11}} \quad \frac{a_{13}(a_{21})}{a_{11}} \quad \frac{a_{14}(a_{21})}{a_{11}} \right) \tag{1-2}$$

Now we can subtract (1-2) from (2) and get

$$\left(0 \quad a_{22} - \frac{a_{12}(a_{21})}{a_{11}} \quad a_{23} - \frac{a_{13}(a_{21})}{a_{11}} \quad a_{24} - \frac{a_{14}(a_{21})}{a_{11}} \right) \tag{2-1}$$

That successfully eliminates the first element a_{21} of the second equation. By going back and multiplying (1-1) by a_{31} and subtracting the resulting equation from (3) we can eliminate a_{31} from equation (3). Now column 1 looks like

$$\begin{pmatrix} 1 \\ 0 \\ 0 \end{pmatrix}$$

MATRIX SOLUTION TO LINEAR EQUATIONS 343

We can operate upon column two or any column in the same manner as the first column:

- Divide row n by the element in position n (a_{nn}), thereby setting $a_{nn} = 1$
- Multiply row n by the corresponding element in row $i \neq n$, so that $a_{nn} \times a_{in} = a_{in}$
- Subtract row n from row i, resulting in $a_{in} = 0$, and all other elements reduced by the corresponding element in row n

Continue this procedure for each row i until all elements

$$a_{1n}, a_{2n}, \ldots, a_{i-1n}, a_{i+1n}, \ldots, a_{mn} = 0 \quad \text{and} \quad a_{in} = 1.$$

For example, consider

$$\begin{pmatrix} 2 & 4 & 8 & 34 \\ 6 & 5 & 2 & 22 \\ 3 & 6 & 5 & 30 \end{pmatrix}$$

Divide row 1 by 2 (position a_{11}):

$$\begin{pmatrix} 1 & 2 & 4 & 17 \\ 6 & 5 & 2 & 22 \\ 3 & 6 & 5 & 30 \end{pmatrix}$$

Multiply row 1 by 6 to get (6 12 24 102) and subtract the new calculated row from row 2:

$$\begin{pmatrix} 1 & 2 & 4 & 17 \\ 0 & -7 & -22 & -80 \\ 3 & 6 & 5 & 30 \end{pmatrix}$$

Multiply row 1 by the number 3 to get (3 6 12 51), then subtract the calculated row from row 3:

$$\begin{pmatrix} 1 & 2 & 4 & 17 \\ 0 & -7 & -22 & -80 \\ 0 & 0 & -7 & -21 \end{pmatrix}$$

We have now completed column 1. Divide Row 2 by -7 and get:

$$\begin{pmatrix} 1 & 2 & 4 & 17 \\ 0 & 1 & \dfrac{+22}{7} & \dfrac{+80}{7} \\ 0 & 0 & -7 & -21 \end{pmatrix}$$

Multiply row 2 by 2 and subtract the result (0 2 44/7 160/7) from row 1 in order to eliminate position 2 in the first row:

$$\begin{pmatrix} 1 & 0 & \dfrac{-16}{7} & \dfrac{-41}{7} \\ 0 & 1 & \dfrac{+22}{7} & \dfrac{+80}{7} \\ 0 & 0 & -7 & -21 \end{pmatrix}$$

Since the element in row 3 and column 2 is already 0, we can now work on row 3. Divide row 3 by -7 and get

$$\begin{pmatrix} 1 & 0 & \dfrac{-16}{7} & \dfrac{-41}{7} \\ 0 & 1 & \dfrac{+22}{7} & \dfrac{+80}{7} \\ 0 & 0 & 1 & 3 \end{pmatrix}$$

Multiply row 3 by $-16/7$ and subtract the result $(0 \quad 0 \quad -16/7 \quad -48/7)$ from row 1:

$$\begin{pmatrix} 1 & 0 & 0 & 1 \\ 0 & 1 & \dfrac{+22}{7} & \dfrac{+80}{7} \\ 0 & 0 & 1 & 3 \end{pmatrix}$$

Multiply row 3 by $+22/7$ and subtract $(0 \quad 0 \quad +22/7 \quad +66/7)$ from row 2:

$$\begin{pmatrix} 1 & 0 & 0 & 1 \\ 0 & 1 & 0 & 2 \\ 0 & 0 & 1 & 3 \end{pmatrix}$$

The results show that $x_1 = 1$, $x_2 = 2$, $x_3 = 3$.

There are other ways to reduce the matrix to the final representation, but this technique is well-defined and lends itself to being programmed on a computer.

b. SOLUTION TO WEATHER PROBABILITIES EXPRESSED AS A MARKOV CHAIN

Let $A = P(\text{CLEAR})_{i+1} = P(\text{CLEAR})_i$
$B = P(\text{CLOUDY})_{i+1} = P(\text{CLOUDY})_i$
$C = P(\text{RAINY})_{i+1} = P(\text{RAINY})_i$

since when they converge all ith elements will equal $(i + 1)$th elements. The equations are

$$A = .7A + .2B + .2C \tag{1}$$

$$B = .25A + .6B + .4C \tag{2}$$

$$C = .05A + .2B + .4C \tag{3}$$

We also have

$$A + B + C = 1 \tag{4}$$

MATRIX SOLUTION TO LINEAR EQUATIONS

To solve this system of equations using matrices, we convert and add equation (3) to (4),

$$-.3A + .2B + .2C = 0 \qquad (1')$$
$$.25A - .4B + .4C = 0 \qquad (2')$$
$$1.05A + 1.2B + .4C = 1 \qquad (3')$$

which becomes the matrix

$$\begin{pmatrix} -.3 & .2 & .2 & 0 \\ .25 & -.4 & .4 & 0 \\ 1.05 & 1.2 & .4 & 1 \end{pmatrix} \begin{matrix} (1') \\ (2') \\ (3') \end{matrix}$$

The following are key steps in the solution:

1. Reduce the first row,

$$\begin{pmatrix} 1 & -.6667 & -.6667 & 0 \\ .25 & -.4 & .4 & 0 \\ 1.05 & 1.2 & .4 & 1 \end{pmatrix}$$

and make the leading entries of rows 2 and 3 zero:

$$\begin{pmatrix} 1 & -.6667 & -.6667 & 0 \\ 0 & -.2333 & .5667 & 0 \\ 0 & 1.9000 & 1.1000 & 1 \end{pmatrix}$$

2. Reduce the second row,

$$\begin{pmatrix} 1 & -.6667 & -.6667 & 0 \\ 0 & 1 & -2.4291 & 0 \\ 0 & 1.9000 & 1.1000 & 1 \end{pmatrix}$$

and make the second entries of rows 1 and 3 zero

$$\begin{pmatrix} 1 & 0 & 2.2857 & 0 \\ 0 & 1 & -2.4291 & 0 \\ 0 & 0 & 5.7143 & 1 \end{pmatrix}$$

3. Reduce the third row,

$$\begin{pmatrix} 1 & 0 & 2.2862 & 0 \\ 0 & 1 & -2.4291 & 0 \\ 0 & 0 & 1 & .1750 \end{pmatrix}$$

and make the third entry of rows 1 and 2 zero:

$$\begin{pmatrix} 1 & 0 & 0 & .4000 \\ 0 & 1 & 0 & .4250 \\ 0 & 0 & 1 & .1750 \end{pmatrix}$$

Then $A = .4000$, $B = .4250$, and $C = .1750$.

APPENDIX 4

Construction Of A Pentagon

a. CONSTRUCTION OF A PENTAGON FROM ONE FIXED DIAGONAL

Establish the diagonal *D* by connecting the top and bottom of a major price move by a straight line. This diagonal will be toward the left and top of the pentagon to be constructed. (See Diagram A4-1.)

1. Measure the length of the diagonal *D*. This diagonal connects two points of the pentagon.
2. With a compass point at one end of the diagonal and the tip on the other, draw a long arc to the right; placing the point on the other end of the diagonal, draw another arc to the right. These arcs should not cross to avoid confusion.
3. The length of a side of a regular pentagon is calculated from the diagonal by the formula

$$S = .618 \times D$$

   Using a ruler, set the compass to the length of a side and place the point at one end of the diagonal. Draw an arc on both sides, crossing the arc on the right; do the same for the other end of the diagonal. The two new arcs will cross on the left. The three new crossings are the missing points of the pentagon.
4. The center of the pentagon can be found by bisecting any two sides. The point at which the two bisecting lines cross is the center. Use this point to circumscribe a circle around the pentagon.

CONSTRUCTION OF A PENTAGON

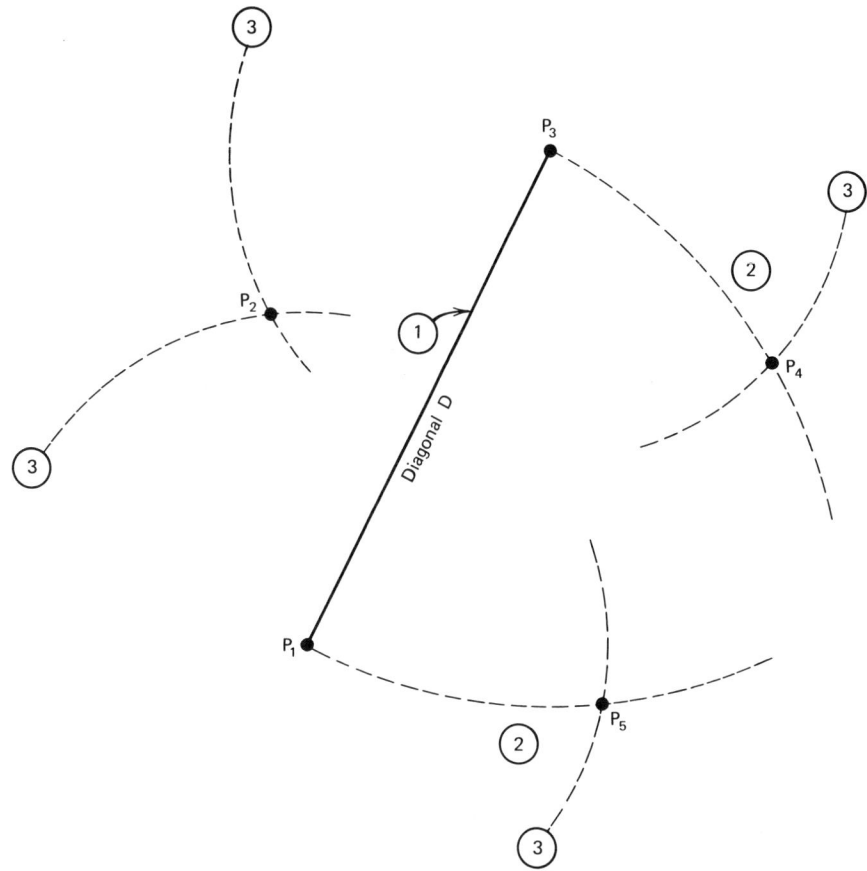

Diagram A4-1   Construction of a pentagon from one diagonal.

b. CONSTRUCTION OF A PENTAGON FROM ONE SIDE

Establish the side S by connecting the top and bottom of a major price move with a straight line. As in the previous example this side will be toward the top and left of the pentagon, which will extend down and to the right. (See Diagram A4-2.)

1. Calculate the length of the diagonal D by applying the formula $D = S/.618$. This will require a ruler to determine the length of S.
2. Using a ruler again, set your compass to the length of the diagonal calculated in the first step. Draw wide arcs of radius D from the endpoints of S crossing to the lower right of S. The place of crossing will be the third point of the pentagon P_4, opposite side S.
3. Set the compass back to length S and place the point P_4. Cross the inner arcs drawn in step 2 with a small arc drawn on either side of P_4. These crossing will be the two remaining points of the pentagon.
4. The perpendicular bisectors of any two sides will cross at the center of the pentagon and allow you to circumscribe a circle around the pentagon.

348　COMMODITY TRADING SYSTEMS AND METHODS

The perpendicular bisector of any side is constructed by setting the compass to any length greater than half of the line being bisected, then placing the point at one end of the line. Draw an arc on both sides of the line in the area above the center of the line. Do the same by placing the point of the compass at the other end and crossing the arcs already drawn. A line through the two crosses will be the perpendicular bisector of the original line.

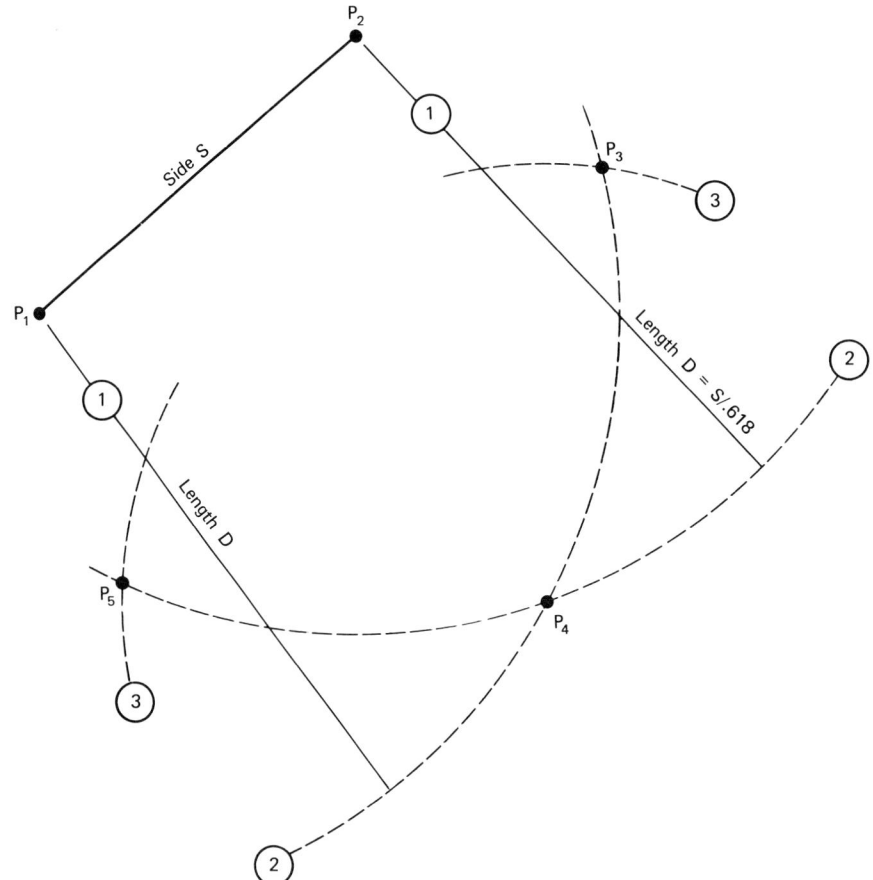

Diagram A4-2　Construction of a pentagon from one side.

APPENDIX 5
Uniform Random-Number Table

From Francis F. Martin, *Computer Modeling and Simulation*, p. 288. Copyright © 1968 by John Wiley & Sons, Inc. Reprinted by permission.

	1	2	3	4	5	6	7	8	9	10	11
1	10480	15011	01536	02011	81647	91646	69179	14194	62590	36207	20969
2	22368	46573	25595	85393	30995	89198	27982	53402	93965	34095	52666
3	24130	48360	22527	97265	76393	64809	15179	24830	49340	32081	30680
4	42167	93093	06243	61680	07856	16376	39440	53537	71341	57004	00849
5	37570	39975	81837	16656	06121	91782	60468	81305	49684	60672	14110
6	77921	06907	11008	42751	27756	53498	18602	70659	90655	15033	21916
7	99562	72905	56420	69994	98872	31016	71194	18738	44013	44840	63213
8	96301	91977	05463	07972	18876	20922	94595	56869	69014	60045	18425
9	89579	14342	63661	10281	17453	18103	57740	84378	25331	12566	58678
10	85475	36857	53342	53988	53060	59533	38867	62300	08158	17893	16439
11	28918	69578	88231	33276	70997	79936	56865	05859	90106	31595	91547
12	63553	40961	48235	03427	49626	69445	18663	72695	52180	20847	12234
13	09429	93969	52636	92737	88974	33488	36320	17617	30015	07272	84115
14	10365	61129	87529	85689	48237	52267	67689	93394	01511	26358	85104
15	07119	97336	71048	08178	77233	13916	47564	81056	97735	85977	29372
16	51085	12765	51821	51259	77452	16308	60756	92144	49442	53900	70960
17	02368	21382	52404	60268	89368	19885	55322	44819	01188	65255	64835
18	01011	54092	33362	94904	31273	04146	18594	29852	71585	85030	51132
19	52162	53916	46369	58586	23216	14513	83149	98736	23495	64350	94738
20	07056	97628	33787	09998	42698	06691	76988	13602	51851	46104	88916
21	48663	91245	85828	14346	09172	30168	90229	04734	59193	22178	30421
22	54164	58492	22421	74103	47070	25306	76468	26384	58151	06646	21524
23	32639	32363	05597	24200	13363	38005	94342	28728	35806	06912	17012
24	29334	27001	87637	87308	58731	00256	45834	15398	46557	41135	10367
25	02488	33062	28834	07351	19731	92420	60952	61280	50001	67658	32586
26	81525	72295	04839	96423	25878	82651	66566	14778	76797	14780	13300
27	29676	20591	68086	26432	46901	20849	80768	81536	86645	12659	92259
28	00742	57392	39064	66432	84673	40027	32832	61362	98947	96067	64760
29	05366	04213	25669	26422	44407	44048	37937	63904	45766	66134	75470
30	91921	26418	64117	94305	26766	25940	39972	22209	71500	64568	91402
31	00582	04711	87917	77341	42206	35126	74087	99547	81817	42607	43808
32	00725	69884	62797	56170	86324	88072	76222	36086	84637	93161	76038
33	69011	65795	95876	55293	18988	27354	26575	08625	40801	59920	29841
34	25976	57948	29888	88604	67917	48708	18912	82271	65424	69774	33611
35	09763	83473	73577	12908	30883	10317	28290	35797	05998	41688	34952
36	91567	42595	27958	30134	04024	86385	29880	99730	55536	84855	29080
37	17955	56349	90999	49127	20044	59931	06115	20542	18059	02008	73708
38	46503	18584	18845	49618	02304	51038	20655	58727	28168	15475	56942
39	92157	89634	94824	78171	84610	82834	09922	25417	44137	48413	25555
40	14577	62765	35605	81263	39667	47358	56873	56307	61607	49518	89565

APPENDIX 6
String Lengths (Sequences Of Runs)

		String lengths (days)									03 Feb 76
		One	Two	Three	Four	Five	Six	Seven	Eight	Nine	Ten or more
Dec 70	Cotton	51	26	17	14	2	4	2	0	0	0
Dec 71	Cotton	46	37	26	3	4	1	1	0	0	1
Dec 72	Cotton	58	31	15	11	3	0	1	2	1	0
Dec 73	Cotton	48	26	9	9	5	4	3	3	0	0
Dec 74	Cotton	73	27	24	7	2	2	1	0	0	0
Dec 75	Cotton	70	36	20	6	5	1	0	0	0	0
Totals		346	183	111	50	21	12	8	5	1	1

		String lengths (days)									03 Feb 76
		One	Two	Three	Four	Five	Six	Seven	Eight	Nine	Ten or more
May 70	Potatoes (Maine)	41	38	18	9	3	1	1	0	0	0
May 71	Potatoes (Maine)	46	31	17	7	7	1	1	1	0	0
May 72	Potatoes (Maine)	62	24	10	10	5	0	3	4	0	0
May 73	Potatoes (Maine)	56	32	22	5	5	0	0	2	0	1
May 74	Potatoes (Maine)	38	20	7	5	2	1	3	0	1	0
May 75	Potatoes (Maine)	52	32	16	6	6	4	1	0	1	0
Totals		295	177	90	42	28	7	9	7	2	1

		String lengths (days)									03 Feb 76
		One	Two	Three	Four	Five	Six	Seven	Eight	Nine	Ten or more
Mar 76	Corn	68	29	16	13	6	0	0	0	0	0
Mar 76	Cotton	71	25	26	5	5	2	1	0	0	0
Mar 76	Wheat	53	32	14	6	3	3	1	0	0	0
Mar 76	Oats	57	26	10	8	1	2	0	0	0	1
Mar 76	Soybeans	73	39	15	8	0	5	0	0	0	0
Mar 76	Soybean oil	57	35	12	10	5	2	0	0	0	0
Mar 76	Soybean meal	65	34	19	5	1	3	1	0	0	0
Mar 76	Plywood	64	29	13	6	3	2	1	0	0	0
Feb 76	Eggs	12	6	6	2	2	1	0	0	0	0
Feb 76	Cattle	60	29	14	10	3	1	2	1	1	0
Feb 76	Pork bellies	55	27	13	8	6	4	2	1	0	0
Feb 76	Hogs	58	32	20	9	1	3	2	0	0	0
Mar 76	Lumber	36	22	13	3	2	3	0	1	0	0
Mar 76	Copper	56	36	13	10	7	2	0	0	0	0
Mar 76	Sugar (world)	60	34	15	13	4	1	1	0	0	0
Mar 76	Coffee 'C'	52	29	11	10	3	1	1	1	1	0
Apr 76	Platinum	65	28	16	9	2	2	3	0	0	1
May 76	Potatoes (Maine)	36	18	15	10	6	1	2	0	0	3
Feb 76	Silver CBOT	78	37	20	7	1	1	1	0	0	0
Mar 76	Gold—IMM	64	37	16	7	3	2	0	0	0	0
Mar 76	Cocoa (NY)	74	36	14	8	4	0	0	1	1	0
Totals		1214	620	311	167	67	41	16	5	3	5

		String lengths (days)									03 Feb 76
		One	Two	Three	Four	Five	Six	Seven	Eight	Nine	Ten or more
Dec 70	Copper	67	33	21	6	2	2	1	0	1	0
Dec 71	Copper	68	45	15	5	1	1	2	1	0	0
Dec 72	Copper	69	44	16	7	1	2	1	0	0	0
Dec 73	Copper	57	34	13	10	4	1	0	0	0	0
Dec 74	Copper	69	36	13	6	2	3	0	3	0	0
Dec 75	Copper	50	37	14	10	8	2	0	0	0	0
Totals		380	229	92	44	18	11	4	4	1	0

		String lengths (days)										03 Feb 76
		One	Two	Three	Four	Five	Six	Seven	Eight	Nine	Ten or more
Jun 70	Cattle	44	33	26	5	6	2	0	1	0	0
Jun 71	Cattle	56	34	20	5	6	0	2	0	1	0
Jun 72	Cattle	37	20	9	1	4	1	2	1	1	0
Jun 73	Cattle	44	22	16	7	4	1	1	1	1	0
Jun 74	Cattle	56	30	12	10	5	3	2	0	0	0
Jun 75	Cattle	50	38	12	8	1	1	2	2	0	1
Totals		287	177	95	46	26	8	9	5	4	1

APPENDIX 7
Annual Price Fluctuations

	1969				1970				1971			
Commodity	High	Low	Average	%	High	Low	Average	%	High	Low	Average	%
Broilers (¢/lb)	32.4	26.1	28.7	22	28.2	24.6	26.2	14	30.0	24.1	26.8	22
Cattle ($/cwt)	29.40	23.80	26.2	21	29.00	24.40	27.1	17	33.92	28.83	32.03	16
Cocoa (¢/lb)	50	43.3	45.8	15	39.5	28.6	34.1	32	30.9	23.4	26.8	28
Coffee (¢/lb)	55.9	39.9	45	36	59.4	52.5	56.4	12	52.4	47.8	49.3	9
Copper (¢/lb)	52.1	43.0	47.4	19	60.1	53.1	58.1	12	52.9	50.4	52.1	5
Corn (¢/bu)	130	115	121	12	152	122	135	22	159	107	139	37
Cotton (¢/lb)	22.5	21.4	21.9	5	23	22	22.6	4	29.6	22.8	25.4	27
Eggs (¢/doz)	62.7	33.4	46	64	61.1	33	42.5	66	37.2	29.1	33.2	24
Hogs (¢/lb)	27.4	20.1	24.0	30	28.2	15.0	21.9	61	20.0	15.8	18.4	23
Lumber (¢/10 board ft)	147.1	94.3	113.5	47	95.0	90.3	92.2	5	130.2	91.5	117.7	33
Oats (¢/bu)	70½	59⅝	65	17	74	63½	68.5	15	77½	62	68.5	23
Orange juice (¢/lb)	49.3	44	45	12	44	36.4	39	19	46.9	36.7	43.3	24
Platinum (¢/troy oz)	132.5	122.5	124.2	8	132.5	132.5	132.5	0	129	122.5	123.0	5
Plywood (¢/10 board ft)	139	78	108.5	56	89	75	82	17	101	81	92	22
Potatoes—Maine (¢/lb)	4.9	2.9	3.8	54	6.0	3.2	4.4	63	5.6	3.6	4.3	49
Silver—NY (¢/troy oz)	197.9	161.8	179.1	20	189.6	163.5	177.1	15	172.6	132	154.6	26
Soybeans—May (¢/bu)	271¼	257⅝	264	5	270	244⅜	257	10	322	286½	304	12
Soybean meal (¢/20 lb bag)	82	74.2	79.1	10	92.5	76.2	84.4	19	90.3	79.3	83.7	13
Soybean oil (¢/lb)	10.9	7.8	9.1	34	14.0	9.6	12	37	14.5	11.2	12.6	26
Sugar (¢/lb)	3.95	2.86	3.37	32	4.18	3.12	3.75	28	5.95	3.99	4.52	43
Wheat (¢/bu)	148	127	134	16	177	141	157	23	175	145	162	19

	1972				1973				1974				1975			
Commodity	High	Low	Average	%	High	Low	Average	%	High	Low	Average	%	High	Low	Average	%
Broilers (¢/lb)	29.8	25.6	27.9	15	60.0	32.5	41.6	66	41.8	33.8	38.1	21	50.9	39.8	44.8	25
Cattle ($/cwt)	37.6	33.3	35.4	12	53.1	38.6	43.5	33	47.1	37.2	41.8	23	51.8	34.7	44.6	38
Cocoa (¢/lb)	38.5	25.6	32.2	40	87	36.9	63.6	79	119.3	64.8	98.2	55	89.5	59.5	75.9	40
Coffee (¢/lb)	63.8	50.1	56.7	24	76.1	69.1	72.7	10	82.2	72.4	77.9	13	100.9	65.8	81.7	43
Copper (¢/lb)	52.7	50.4	51.4	4	66.6	52.4	59.5	24	86.3	68.7	77.06	23	68.9	63.0	64.5	9
Corn (¢/bu)	153	121	130	25	298	155	219	65	375	269	323	33	316	263	292	18
Cotton (¢/lb)	34.8	23.3	30.1	38	65.7	28.1	45.9	82	67.1	33.9	47.1	71	51.6	31.1	40.6	50
Eggs (¢/doz)	49.8	28	33.8	65	76.9	43.1	61.0	55	75	44.5	59.8	51	73.8	51.3	59.4	38
Hogs (¢/lb)	29.3	22.6	26.6	25	55.3	31.3	40.1	60	39.3	25.4	34.8	40	61.2	38.2	47.7	48
Lumber (¢/10 board ft)	151.3	135	144.3	11	209.9	152.5	181.9	32	186.2	133.2	158.8	33	169.8	138.4	158.9	20
Oats (¢/bu)	91	66	72.5	35	132	84	105	46	187	126	160	38	178	149	165	18
Orange juice (¢/lb)	84	46.9	47.6	2	48	46.9	47.6	2	48.9	47.3	48	3	52.9	49.8	51.3	6
Platinum ($/troy oz)	132.5	122.5	127.1	8	160.5	132.5	152.2	18	195	162.7	185	18	195	160	169.9	21
Plywood (¢/10 board ft)	156	107	135.8	36	184	107	140.4	55	151	107	125.7	35	156	116	135	30
Potatoes—Maine (¢/lb)	5.3	3.5	4.5	39	11.4	6.2	8.3	63	16.1	4.7	9.5	120	13.4	4.3	7.4	124
Silver—NY (¢/troy oz)	197.6	147.3	168.5	30	133.7	201.7	256	44	543.2	363.7	470.8	38	470.5	408.5	442	14
Soybeans—May (¢/bu)	$361\frac{1}{4}$	$309\frac{1}{2}$	335	15	1020	$328\frac{1}{8}$	674	102	906	521	713	53	971	$487\frac{1}{4}$	729	66
Soybean meal (¢/20 lb bag)	180.6	88.6	111.09	83	418.9	166.2	245	103	178.8	107.1	148.3	48	143.4	125	132.5	14
Soybean oil (¢/lb)	11.9	9.6	10.6	22	33.5	10.1	19.6	119	43.3	28.2	35.8	42	33.6	16.8	25.4	66
Sugar (¢/lb)	9.08	6.28	7.43	37	11.83	8.89	9.61	30	15.17	15.32	29.99	139	38.32	13.29	20.49	122
Wheat (¢/bu)	260	146	183	62	584	237	371	94	650	348	482	63	502	303	361	27

SOURCE OF PRICES USED

All prices are taken from Commodity Research Bureau Year Book average monthly price tables unless otherwise noted.

- BROILERS: wholesale price (grade A) delivered at Chicago
- CATTLE: prior to 1971, average price received by farmers; 1971–1975 beef prices, Omaha
- COCOA: spot cocoa bean prices in New York
- COFFEE: average price Columbian "Manizales" coffee in New York
- COPPER: producers prices of electrolytic (wirebar) copper, New York refinery equivalent
- CORN: average price of #3 yellow at Chicago
- COTTON: average spot price of strict low Middling 1" cotton at designated United States markets
- EGGS: average wholesale prices of shell eggs delivered in Chicago
- HOGS: 1969 monthly average barrows & gilts (*Statistical Annual*); 1970–1975 average wholesale price of hogs (all grades) at Sioux City
- LUMBER: average price of Douglas fir softwood lumber dimension, constructed, dried, 2 × 4, random lengths
- OATS: average cash price of #2 extra heavy white oats at Minneapolis
- ORANGE JUICE: wholesale price of frozen orange concentrate
- PLATINUM: average price of platinum in New York
- PLYWOOD: Douglas fir, 1/2" std exterior, west coast (*Statistical Annual*)
- POTATOES: Wholesale price of potatoes at New York (Maine) white, eastern origin
- SILVER: average price of .999 fine silver in New York
- SOYBEANS: May soybean futures prices on the Chicago Board of Trade
- SOYBEAN MEAL: (44%) average Chicago price bagged
- SOYBEAN OIL: average price in tank cars, FOB Decatur (crude)
- SUGAR: average wholesale refined cane sugar prices in New York
- WHEAT: average price of #2 soft red winter wheat at Chicago

APPENDIX 8
Weekly Pattern Tables

Weekly patterns 03 Feb 76

		Single reversals					Blocked reversals						Staggered reversals					Total
		XXXXX	XXXOX	XXOXX	XOXXX	OXXXX	XXOOX	XOOXX	OOXXX	XOOOX	OOOXX	OOOOX	XOXOX	OOXOX	OXOOX	OXOXX	OXXOX	
Mar 76	Corn	0	5	1	0	0	5	5	5	3	2	7	4	1	2	2	2	44
Mar 76	Cotton	2	5	5	1	1	4	2	2	6	1	1	3	6	1	0	2	42
Mary 76	Wheat	2	2	3	0	1	4	4	0	5	2	3	3	3	2	2	3	39
Mar 76	Oats	1	2	1	1	1	4	3	2	1	4	3	4	2	2	2	1	34
Mar 76	Soybeans	2	1	5	2	2	6	2	1	4	2	2	6	1	2	3	3	44
Mar 76	Soybean oil	0	2	5	1	5	6	3	1	4	1	4	3	0	2	3	2	42
Mar 76	Soybean meal	0	2	3	1	1	4	2	4	4	2	3	5	1	2	6	2	42
Mar 76	Plywood	3	5	1	1	2	3	4	0	2	0	0	2	1	4	4	6	38
Feb 76	Eggs	2	2	2	1	0	0	0	1	1	0	1	1	0	0	0	1	12
Feb 76	Cattle	3	2	2	3	2	7	2	2	5	2	4	2	4	4	2	0	42
Feb 76	Pork bellies	3	4	0	2	2	6	1	1	2	4	4	3	5	2	1	1	44
Feb 76	Hogs	0	2	3	3	3	4	5	2	4	3	1	3	5	1	1	1	42
Mar 76	Lumber	0	3	3	1	5	3	5	1	1	1	3	0	1	1	0	1	29
Mar 76	Copper	3	2	3	5	1	2	4	2	4	1	6	0	4	0	3	1	41
Mar 76	Sugar (world)	2	3	3	2	4	4	3	1	2	2	2	3	4	2	1	3	41
Mar 76	Coffee 'C'	2	4	2	2	2	4	2	2	1	3	2	2	2	4	1	1	36
Apr 76	Platinum	2	2	3	1	3	4	1	2	4	2	6	1	5	3	3	2	44
May 76	Potatoes (Maine)	9	4	6	0	3	2	3	2	2	2	4	1	2	0	1	2	43
Feb 76	Silver CBOT	1	3	2	4	1	3	1	0	3	2	2	0	5	3	6	8	44
Mar 76	Soybean meal	0	2	3	1	1	4	2	4	4	2	3	5	1	2	6	2	42
Mar 76	Gold—NY	0	0	0	0	0	1	0	1	1	0	0	0	1	0	0	1	5
Mar 76	Gold—IMM	2	3	3	2	1	3	3	2	2	2	3	4	3	5	1	3	42
Mar 76	Cocoa (NY)	1	6	4	0	1	3	3	1	2	0	3	4	2	5	4	2	41
	Totals	40	66	63	34	42	86	60	39	67	40	67	59	59	48	53	50	873
	Grains	7	19	73	6	11	33	21	15	27	14	23	28	14	13	18	15	287
	Metals	8	10	13	12	6	12	9	6	13	7	17	5	17	11	13	14	171

Overall "X" M — T 43 W 44 T 51 F 54

Weekly patterns   03 Feb 76

		Single reversals					Blocked reversals						Staggered reversals					Total
		XXXXX	XXXOX	XXOXX	XOXXX	OXXXX	XXOOX	XOOXX	OOXXX	XOOOX	OOOXX	OOOOX	XOXOX	OOXOX	OXOOX	OXOXX	OXXOX	
Jul 74	Soybeans	2	2	2	1	0	2	2	3	3	2	0	3	1	4	2	2	31
Aug 75	Soybeans	5	1	5	2	3	4	3	3	3	1	3	3	4	1	1	1	43
	Totals	7	3	7	3	3	6	5	6	6	3	3	6	5	5	3	3	74

Weekly patterns   03 Feb 76

		Single reversals					Blocked reversals						Staggered reversals					Total
		XXXXX	XXXOX	XXOXX	XOXXX	OXXXX	XXOOX	XOOXX	OOXXX	XOOOX	OOOXX	OOOOX	XOXOX	OOXOX	OXOOX	OXOXX	OXXOX	
Sep 74	Wheat	0	5	2	4	2	5	4	1	2	0	3	1	4	4	1	1	39
Sep 75	Wheat	2	4	4	1	1	5	3	1	4	2	3	1	3	2	2	3	41
Sep 76	Wheat	0	1	0	0	1	0	1	0	3	0	3	0	1	1	1	0	12
	Totals	2	10	6	5	4	10	8	2	9	2	9	2	8	7	4	4	92

03 Feb 76

Weekly patterns

	Single reversals					Blocked reversals						Staggered reversals					Total
	XXXXX	XXXOX	XXOXX	XOXXX	OXXXX	XXOOX	XOOXX	OOXXX	XOOOX	OOOXX	OOOOX	XOXOX	OOXOX	OXOOX	OXOXX	OXXOX	
Dec 73 Soybean meal	2	2	2	0	3	1	2	1	2	0	0	0	1	0	0	1	17
Dec 74 Soybean meal	2	2	3	1	0	7	5	2	3	3	1	2	3	4	0	2	40
Dec 75 Soybean meal	0	2	5	3	2	6	1	1	5	5	3	3	3	3	3	1	43
Totals	6	6	10	4	5	14	8	4	10	8	4	5	7	7	3	4	100

19 Mar 76

Weekly patterns

	Single reversals					Blocked reversals						Staggered reversals					Total
	XXXXX	XXXOX	XXOXX	XOXXX	OXXXX	XXOOX	XOOXX	OOXXX	XOOOX	OOOXX	OOOOX	XOXOX	OOXOX	OXOOX	OXOXX	OXXOX	
Dec 70 Cocoa (NY)	2	1	3	0	3	2	3	5	4	1	3	2	3	3	2	4	41
Dec 71 Cocoa (NY)	1	3	3	4	1	3	2	3	6	2	1	2	3	5	1	1	41
Dec 72 Cocoa (NY)	2	3	5	4	4	3	1	3	3	0	1	2	1	2	2	4	40
Dec 73 Cocoa (NY)	2	2	1	3	2	3	3	2	2	0	2	6	1	0	5	2	36
Dec 74 Cocoa (NY)	0	7	5	2	1	3	0	0	4	5	2	2	2	3	2	3	41
Dec 75 Cocoa (NY)	1	6	3	0	0	5	1	0	3	0	5	6	5	2	2	2	41
Totals	8	22	20	13	11	19	10	13	22	8	14	20	15	15	14	16	240

Weekly patterns   19 Mar 76

		Single reversals					Blocked reversals						Staggered reversals					Total
		XXXXX	XXXOX	XXOXX	XOXXX	OXXXX	XXOOX	XOOXX	OOXXX	XOOOX	OOOXX	OOOOX	XOXOX	OOXOX	OXOOX	OXOXX	OXXOX	
Dec 70	Copper	1	3	2	2	2	3	3	2	0	4	2	3	5	3	2	4	41
Dec 71	Copper	2	1	3	6	2	3	5	1	1	2	1	1	1	2	7	2	40
Dec 72	Copper	2	2	2	2	1	3	4	2	4	2	2	2	2	6	2	2	40
Dec 73	Copper	0	2	6	1	4	1	5	1	3	1	4	0	3	2	3	0	36
Dec 74	Copper	3	4	2	3	0	4	2	3	3	2	3	1	2	5	2	3	42
Dec 75	Copper	3	2	5	3	0	2	4	1	4	2	7	0	2	3	2	1	41
Totals		11	14	20	17	9	16	23	10	15	13	19	7	15	21	18	12	240

Weekly patterns   19 Mar 76

		Single reversals					Blocked reversals						Staggered reversals					Total
		XXXXX	XXXOX	XXOXX	XOXXX	OXXXX	XXOOX	XOOXX	OOXXX	XOOOX	OOOXX	OOOOX	XOXOX	OOXOX	OXOOX	OXOXX	OXXOX	
Sep 70	Sugar (world)	3	3	1	5	3	4	3	4	3	1	1	2	1	2	4	2	41
Sep 71	Sugar (world)	2	1	4	2	1	6	4	2	5	3	4	1	2	1	3	3	42
Sep 72	Sugar (world)	3	2	3	4	1	4	5	2	2	2	4	0	3	1	0	5	41
Sep 73	Sugar (world)	2	3	7	1	1	3	1	2	2	2	2	6	3	1	2	2	40
Sep 74	Sugar (world)	3	3	2	1	3	1	2	6	1	2	5	4	2	3	1	1	40
Sep 75	Sugar (world)	3	3	4	3	4	0	2	3	1	3	4	2	3	2	2	1	40
Totals		16	15	21	16	13	18	17	19	14	13	20	14	14	10	10	14	244

Weekly patterns

19 Mar 76

		Single reversals						Blocked reversals						Staggered reversals					Total
		XXXXX	XXXOX	XXOXX	XOXXX	OXXXX	XXOOX	XOOXX	OOXXX	XOOOX	OOOXX	OOOOX	XOXOX	OOXOX	OXOOX	OXOXX	OXXOX	
Dec 72	Swiss Franc	1	3	2	0	0	0	0	4	3	3	2	1	2	2	1	0	24
Dec 73	Swiss Franc	10	0	0	2	2	1	1	2	1	1	3	0	2	1	1	0	27
Dec 74	Swiss Franc	3	3	2	1	3	6	3	2	4	2	0	2	4	3	4	2	44
Dec 75	Swiss Franc	4	2	2	2	2	6	1	1	5	3	0	2	2	3	1	3	39
	Totals	18	8	6	5	7	13	5	9	13	9	5	5	10	9	7	5	134

03 Feb 76

		Single reversals						Blocked reversals						Staggered reversals					Total
		XXXXX	XXXOX	XXOXX	XOXXX	OXXXX	XXOOX	XOOXX	OOXXX	XOOOX	OOOXX	OOOOX	XOXOX	OOXOX	OXOOX	OXOXX	OXXOX	
May 70	Potatoes (Maine)	2	0	5	2	2	1	6	1	1	4	1	0	3	4	2	5	39
May 71	Potatoes (Maine)	4	1	4	1	3	4	1	4	4	2	4	1	1	1	1	5	41
May 72	Potatoes (Maine)	6	2	2	1	4	2	1	4	2	2	4	4	2	3	3	2	44
May 73	Potatoes (Maine)	2	6	2	3	3	7	1	3	3	2	2	2	1	0	2	5	44
May 74	Potatoes (Maine)	3	3	3	2	2	3	1	0	1	5	1	1	0	1	0	1	27
May 75	Potatoes (Maine)	2	5	5	2	8	2	1	0	5	2	0	1	2	3	1	4	43
	Totals	19	17	21	11	22	19	11	12	16	17	12	9	9	12	9	22	238

03 Feb 76

Weekly patterns

		Single reversals					Blocked reversals						Staggered reversals					Total
		XXXXX	XXXOX	XXOXX	XOXXX	OXXXX	XXOOX	XOOXX	OOXXX	XOOOX	OOOXX	OOOOX	XOXOX	OOXOX	OXOOX	OXOXX	OXXOX	
Dec 70	Cotton	3	3	6	2	5	2	1	3	2	4	2	2	3	4	1	1	44
Dec 71	Cotton	1	2	3	1	1	5	3	1	8	2	5	0	4	2	2	1	41
Dec 72	Cotton	2	0	2	5	2	2	4	3	1	5	4	2	1	3	3	2	41
Dec 73	Cotton	5	5	2	4	3	2	4	4	2	2	1	1	2	1	1	2	41
Dec 74	Cotton	2	3	2	4	3	2	2	5	2	2	1	3	1	3	4	4	43
Dec 75	Cotton	0	6	4	1	0	4	4	2	4	3	0	3	3	3	2	4	43
	Totals	13	19	19	17	14	17	18	18	19	18	13	11	14	16	13	14	253

03 Feb 76

Weekly patterns

		Single reversals					Blocked reversals						Staggered reversals					Total
		XXXXX	XXXOX	XXOXX	XOXXX	OXXXX	XXOOX	XOOXX	OOXXX	XOOOX	OOOXX	OOOOX	XOXOX	OOXOX	OXOOX	OXOXX	OXXOX	
Jun 70	Cattle	5	4	1	6	1	3	4	4	3	4	2	2	0	2	1	2	44
Jun 71	Cattle	4	1	7	0	3	3	1	3	4	3	2	1	2	4	4	2	44
Jun 72	Cattle	3	3	2	4	4	4	2	3	2	1	5	0	0	1	1	1	36
Jun 73	Cattle	4	6	2	1	1	1	3	3	3	1	0	1	3	3	1	3	36
Jun 74	Cattle	4	5	4	1	1	1	5	2	4	2	1	3	5	1	2	3	44
Jun 75	Cattle	3	5	3	2	1	8	3	1	4	2	3	0	4	1	0	1	41
	Totals	23	24	19	14	11	20	18	16	20	13	13	7	14	12	9	12	245

APPENDIX 9
Weekend Pattern Tables

Weekend patterns[a]   05 Feb 76

	Last Friday to Monday direction	Friday–Friday point trend	Most frequent direction last week	Direction of Friday	WHF XXX	WHF XXO	WHF XOX	WHF OXX	WHF XOO	WHF OOX	WHF OOO	Cases
May 76 Wheat	60	48	57	51	50	50	33	66	0	62	40	33
May 76 Corn	53	53	71	56	60	66	50	87	100	33	28	39
May 76 Soybeans	70	56	54	62	100	40	75	63	0	100	50	37
May 76 Oats	48	58	67	64	100	100	75	60	50	42	66	31
May 76 Soybean oil	65	56	68	59	100	40	100	71	100	40	28	32
May 76 Soybean meal	78	71	71	75	100	100	60	100	50	100	25	28
Apr 75 Cattle	57	50	67	53	50	0	66	100	75	25	40	28
Apr 76 Hogs	56	62	70	48	66	50	62	57	50	40	0	37
May 76 Pork bellies	38	66	56	51	0	100	40	60	40	50	100	39
Mar 76 Broilers	46	61	46	53	100	0	33	50	0	100	100	13
Mar 76 Eggs	53	38	61	61	50	0	100	50	50	66	66	13
Apr 76 Platinum	58	69	66	52	75	0	0	71	62	50	42	36
May 76 Copper	56	51	64	45	20	33	100	60	50	50	33	37
May 76 Silver NY	37	46	59	50	33	77	0	42	60	33	25	32
Mar 76 Gold—IMM	38	48	43	38	50	50	0	28	50	40	50	39
May 76 Lumber	40	59	53	53	50	50	50	25	66	50	100	32
May 76 Plywood	46	53	53	50	42	57	50	75	0	33	100	30
Mar 76 Orange juice	48	54	60	57	33	33	100	50	50	71	75	33
May 76 Cocoa (NY)	54	64	64	54	60	25	80	50	66	33	60	31
May 76 Coffee 'C'	36	70	70	60	100	100	66	25	100	12	75	30
May 76 Sugar (world)	42	44	68	50	28	75	25	80	100	44	42	38
May 76 Potatoes (Maine)	59	63	70	75	100	60	100	57	75	57	75	44
May 76 Cotton	58	74	66	63	80	33	66	77	37	14	100	39
Mar 76 Swiss franc	50	66	70	43	50	0	25	25	75	62	66	30
Totals	52	58	63	54	59	49	56	61	57	48	52	781

[a] Entries in the tables of this Appendix represent the percentage of situations where the following Monday closing price was a continuation of the same direction; for WHF indicates the "X" direction.

367

		Weekend patterns				Monday move after pattern								05 Feb 76
		Last Friday to Monday direction	Friday–Friday point trend	Most frequent direction last week	Direction of Friday	WHF XXX	WHF XXO	WHF XOX	WHF OXX	WHF XOO	WHF OOX	WHF OOO	Cases
Mar 76	Coffee (London)	48	60	54	45	75	0	28	40	66	50	60	35
Mar 76	Cocoa (London)	48	65	60	54	66	60	50	50	37	33	100	35
Mar 76	Sugar (London)	51	42	62	51	100	100	33	50	66	60	33	35
3 mo.	Silver (London)	55	62	70	51	50	50	100	50	66	50	25	27
3 mo.	Copper (London)	48	64	61	58	80	50	40	50	60	50	100	31
3 mo.	Tin (London)	51	45	51	63	50	57	50	66	60	83	62	33
3 mo.	Lead (London)	62	55	72	51	60	0	100	50	50	66	50	29
3 mo.	Zinc (London)	43	62	62	65	100	60	0	50	83	75	60	32
	Totals	50	57	61	55	70	45	40	50	59	60	57	257

		Weekend patterns				Monday move after pattern								19 Mar 76
		Last Friday to Monday direction	Friday–Friday point trend	Most frequent direction last week	Direction of Friday	WHF XXX	WHF XXO	WHF XOX	WHF OXX	WHF XOO	WHF OOX	WHF OOO	Cases
Jun 70	Cattle	56	63	48	53	22	33	75	75	25	71	66	41
Jun 71	Cattle	54	62	54	57	40	60	100	66	20	60	80	35
Jun 72	Cattle	44	41	55	44	66	60	25	33	66	25	33	34
Jun 73	Cattle	65	53	75	68	60	50	100	100	50	83	100	32
Jun 74	Cattle	60	75	70	70	88	50	50	100	57	55	100	41
Jun 75	Cattle	46	66	61	58	75	50	50	36	50	57	100	39
	Totals	54	61	60	59	50	52	61	60	44	60	73	222

Weekend patterns   19 Mar 76

		Last Friday to Monday direction	Friday–Friday point trend	Most frequent direction last week	Direction of Friday	Monday move after pattern								
						WHF XXX	WHF XXO	WHF XOX	WHF OXX	WHF XOO	WHF OXO	WHF OOX	WHF OOO	Cases
Dec 70	Cocoa (NY)	52	50	77	66	66	71	50	80	62	71	50	36
Dec 71	Cocoa (NY)	51	54	68	65	25	100	66	83	50	62	100	35
Dec 72	Cocoa (NY)	44	50	61	52	40	50	50	50	75	50	100	36
Dec 73	Cocoa (NY)	54	58	74	58	50	25	77	75	100	20	50	31
Dec 74	Cocoa (NY)	41	55	47	50	42	50	75	37	50	25	71	36
Dec 75	Cocoa (NY)	51	56	64	62	57	50	83	50	60	50	80	37
Totals		49	54	65	59	46	55	69	58	64	50	72	211

Weekend patterns   19 Mar 76

		Last Friday to Monday direction	Friday–Friday point trend	Most frequent direction last week	Direction of Friday	Monday move after pattern								
						WHF XXX	WHF XXO	WHF XOX	WHF OXX	WHF XOO	WHF OXO	WHF OOX	WHF OOO	Cases
Dec 70	Copper	66	58	55	52	50	0	60	100	42	66	66	36
Dec 71	Copper	51	58	54	54	66	75	57	33	0	66	66	31
Dec 72	Copper	65	62	68	50	50	0	75	80	50	50	25	32
Dec 73	Copper	35	58	51	45	0	75	0	57	25	25	80	31
Dec 74	Copper	68	54	60	48	71	66	75	50	0	60	20	35
Dec 75	Copper	55	38	61	47	20	100	66	57	33	62	33	36
Totals		57	54	58	49	48	42	62	61	28	52	46	201

Weekend patterns   19 Mar 76

		Last Friday to Monday direction	Friday–Friday point trend	Most frequent direction last week	Direction of Friday	WHF XXX	WHF XXO	WHF XOX	WHF OXX	WHF XOO	WHF OOX	WHF OOO	Cases
Dec 70	Cotton	43	48	58	64	50	83	75	50	83	66	50	39
Dec 71	Cotton	59	67	59	54	66	50	100	50	20	63	57	37
Dec 72	Cotton	54	54	54	51	100	25	57	25	50	60	55	35
Dec 73	Cotton	61	64	66	61	80	60	60	75	33	50	66	39
Dec 74	Cotton	51	54	60	45	50	28	57	50	66	25	33	35
Dec 75	Cotton	50	68	68	60	50	75	50	87	40	37	100	38
Totals		53	59	61	56	64	53	60	58	50	51	58	223

Weekend patterns   19 Mar 76

		Last Friday to Monday direction	Friday–Friday point trend	Most frequent direction last week	Direction of Friday	WHF XXX	WHF XXO	WHF XOX	WHF OXX	WHF XOO	WHF OOX	WHF OOO	Cases
May 70	Potatoes (Maine)	48	48	75	66	50	85	50	66	100	71	20	33
May 71	Potatoes (Maine)	50	60	47	42	20	37	50	42	20	60	66	38
May 72	Potatoes (Maine)	45	59	70	59	75	40	60	50	66	0	83	37
May 73	Potatoes (Maine)	61	61	66	52	50	50	60	77	25	50	25	42
May 74	Potatoes (Maine)	69	73	73	65	100	33	100	50	0	50	50	26
May 75	Potatoes (Maine)	51	48	64	66	85	66	100	28	100	66	50	39
Totals		53	58	65	58	66	55	70	53	57	55	51	215

Weekend patterns   19 Mar 76

		Last Friday to Monday direction	Friday–Friday point trend	Most frequent direction last week	Direction of Friday	Monday move after pattern							
						WHF XXX	WHF XXO	WHF XOX	WHF OXX	WHF XOO	WHF OOX	WHF OOO	Cases
Dec 70	Silver NY	51	54	62	51	100	20	100	50	50	41	100	35
Dec 71	Silver NY	57	60	68	57	100	66	33	83	50	55	33	35
Dec 72	Silver NY	57	45	54	48	100	100	50	33	20	80	0	35
Dec 73	Silver NY	54	60	71	60	75	25	71	66	100	25	40	35
Dec 74	Silver NY	62	71	65	65	88	33	50	66	50	100	66	35
Dec 75	Silver NY	39	36	60	54	25	70	50	50	75	50	0	33
Totals		53	54	63	56	77	53	54	56	56	51	47	208

Weekend patterns   19 Mar 76

		Last Friday to Monday direction	Friday–Friday point trend	Most frequent direction last week	Direction of Friday	Monday move after pattern							
						WHF XXX	WHF XXO	WHF XOX	WHF OXX	WHF XOO	WHF OOX	WHF OOO	Cases
Dec 73	Soybean meal	58	64	70	58	100	75	0	66	0	25	0	17
Dec 74	Soybean meal	61	61	66	61	50	100	75	70	40	62	33	36
Dec 75	Soybean meal	72	56	70	54	50	33	100	63	25	66	16	37
Totals		65	60	68	57	70	66	88	66	27	55	22	90

	Last Friday to Monday direction	Friday–Friday point trend	Most frequent direction last week	Weekend patterns								Monday move after pattern					
				Direction of Friday	WHF XXX	WHF XXO	WHF XOX	WHF OXX	WHF XOO	WHF OXO	WHF OOX	WHF OOO	Cases
Dec 73 Soybean oil	75	81	87	75	100	0	100	100	0	50	100	16
Dec 74 Soybean oil	56	73	73	65	72	75	100	57	60	50	60	41
Dec 75 Soybean oil	64	46	51	48	60	60	50	55	0	71	16	39
Totals	62	63	66	60	70	54	77	66	37	58	46	96

19 Mar 76

	Last Friday to Monday direction	Friday–Friday point trend	Most frequent direction last week	Weekend patterns								Monday move after pattern					
				Direction of Friday	WHF XXX	WHF XXO	WHF XOX	WHF OXX	WHF XOO	WHF OXO	WHF OOX	WHF OOO	Cases
Sep 70 Sugar (world)	54	54	51	45	66	20	20	20	66	83	0	35
Sep 71 Sugar (world)	47	60	63	65	33	75	66	70	50	55	85	38
Sep 72 Sugar (world)	47	47	50	45	20	50	50	42	40	57	50	40
Sep 73 Sugar (world)	67	54	51	51	80	66	71	50	0	66	25	37
Sep 74 Sugar (world)	57	51	51	57	66	100	40	66	50	100	28	35
Sep 75 Sugar (world)	60	54	65	42	40	20	60	50	66	66	14	35
Totals	55	53	55	51	53	50	51	51	46	67	39	220

19 Mar 76

					Weekend patterns								
	Last Friday to Monday direction	Friday–Friday point trend	Most frequent direction last week	Direction of Friday				Monday move after pattern					
					WHF XXX	WHF XXO	WHF XOX	WHF OXX	WHF XOO	WHF OOX	WHF OOO	Cases
Dec 72 Swiss franc	42	52	80	57	75	0	100	50	83	0	40	21
Dec 73 Swiss franc	54	83	75	66	70	0	100	0	66	50	100	24
Dec 74 Swiss franc	62	59	64	48	66	20	100	37	33	57	50	37
Dec 75 Swiss franc	48	57	62	45	50	20	50	50	66	33	66	35
Totals	52	62	69	52	65	16	80	42	61	38	64	117

APPENDIX 10
Tables Of Price Variation

COMMODITY INVESTORS RESEARCH GROUP TABLE OF PRICE VARIATION - BROILERS PAGE 8

OPEN FROM PRIOR CLOSE	CONTINUED SAME DIRECTION	CLOSE ADJUSTED FROM OPEN	REVERSED FROM OPEN	CROSSED PRIOR CLOSE	TRADING RANGE ADJUSTED AFTER OPEN	CONTINUED FROM OPEN	DIRECTION SAME AS PRIOR	NO. OF CASES
2.00	0.00	0.00	0.00	0.00	0.00	0.00	0.00	0
1.90	0.00	0.00	0.00	0.00	0.00	0.00	0.00	0
1.80	0.00	0.00	0.00	0.00	0.00	0.00	0.00	0
1.70	0.00	0.00	0.00	0.00	0.00	0.00	0.00	0
1.60	0.00	0.00	0.00	0.00	0.00	0.00	0.00	0
1.50	0.00	0.00	0.00	0.00	0.00	0.00	0.00	0
1.40	0.00	0.00	0.00	0.00	0.00	0.00	0.00	0
1.30	0.00	0.00	0.00	0.00	0.00	0.00	0.00	0
1.20	0.00	0.00	0.00	0.00	0.00	0.00	0.00	0
1.10	0.00	0.00	0.00	0.00	0.00	0.00	0.00	0
1.00	0.00	0.00	0.00	0.00	100.00	0.00	0.00	1
0.90	0.00	0.00	0.00	0.00	0.00	0.00	0.00	0
0.80	0.00	0.00	0.00	0.00	0.00	0.00	0.00	0
0.70	0.00	0.00	0.00	0.00	0.00	0.00	0.00	0
0.60	0.00	0.00	0.00	0.00	0.00	0.00	50.00	2
0.50	50.00	50.00	0.00	50.00	50.00	0.00	50.00	2
0.40	100.00	100.00	0.00	100.00	100.00	0.00	80.00	5
0.30	50.00	50.00	0.00	40.00	40.00	20.00	33.33	6
0.20	7.41	40.00	40.67	33.33	33.33	33.33	33.33	27
0.10	50.00	33.33	44.44	51.85	9.09	30.00	30.00	6
-0.00	22.73	22.73	54.55	68.18	41.18	22.73	54.55	22
-0.10	41.18	41.18	17.65	23.53	35.29	58.82	17
-0.20	18.75	18.75	18.75	37.50	50.00	12.50	56.25	16
-0.30	0.00	52.50	0.00	0.00	0.00	0.00	0.00	2
-0.40	0.00	100.00	0.00	0.00	100.00	0.00	100.00	0
-0.50	0.00	0.00	0.00	0.00	0.00	0.00	0.00	0
-0.60	0.00	0.00	0.00	0.00	0.00	0.00	0.00	0
-0.70	0.00	0.00	0.00	0.00	0.00	0.00	0.00	0
-0.80	0.00	0.00	0.00	0.00	0.00	0.00	0.00	0
-0.90	0.00	0.00	0.00	0.00	0.00	0.00	0.00	0
-1.00	0.00	0.00	0.00	0.00	0.00	0.00	0.00	0
-1.10	0.00	0.00	0.00	0.00	0.00	0.00	0.00	0
-1.20	0.00	0.00	0.00	0.00	0.00	0.00	0.00	0
-1.30	0.00	0.00	0.00	0.00	0.00	0.00	0.00	0
-1.40	0.00	0.00	0.00	0.00	0.00	0.00	0.00	0
-1.50	0.00	0.00	0.00	0.00	0.00	0.00	0.00	0
-1.60	0.00	0.00	0.00	0.00	0.00	0.00	0.00	0
-1.70	0.00	0.00	0.00	0.00	0.00	0.00	0.00	0
-1.80	0.00	0.00	0.00	0.00	0.00	0.00	0.00	0
-1.90	0.00	0.00	0.00	0.00	0.00	0.00	0.00	0
-2.00	0.00	0.00	0.00	0.00	0.00	0.00	0.00	0

COMMODITY INVESTORS RESEARCH GROUP TABLE OF PRICE VARIATION - CATTLE Dec 73, 74, 75 PAGE 1

OPEN FROM PRIOR CLOSE	CONTINUED SAME DIRECTION	CLOSE ADJUSTED FROM OPEN	REVERSED FROM OPEN	CROSSED PRIOR CLOSE	TRADING RANGE ADJUSTED AFTER OPEN	CONTINUED FROM OPEN	DIRECTION SAME AS PRIOR	NO. OF CASES
1.60	0.00	0.00	0.00	0.00	0.00	0.00	0.00	0
1.50	0.00	0.00	0.00	0.00	0.00	0.00	0.00	0
1.40	0.00	0.00	0.00	0.00	0.00	0.00	0.00	0
1.30	0.00	0.00	0.00	0.00	0.00	0.00	0.00	0
1.20	100.00	0.00	0.00	0.00	100.00	0.00	0.00	1
1.10	0.00	0.00	0.00	0.00	0.00	0.00	0.00	0
1.00	0.00	96.43	3.57	14.29	42.86	42.86	53.57	28
0.90	50.00	50.00	0.00	50.00	50.00	0.00	100.00	2
0.80	50.00	25.00	25.00	37.50	50.00	12.50	50.00	8
0.70	33.33	50.00	16.67	50.00	33.33	16.67	16.67	6
0.60	28.57	28.57	42.86	42.86	42.86	14.29	57.14	7
0.50	63.16	31.58	5.26	31.58	47.37	21.05	47.37	19
0.40	36.84	36.84	26.32	47.37	47.37	5.26	52.63	19
0.30	51.22	29.27	19.51	46.34	43.90	9.76	56.10	41
0.20	51.52	24.24	24.24	54.55	24.24	21.21	54.55	33
0.10	52.78	12.50	34.72	51.39	27.78	20.83	54.17	72
0.00	22.12	0.00	37.50	59.62	0.00	0.00	18.27	104
-0.10	46.55	8.62	44.83	77.59	15.52	0.90	41.38	58
-0.20	49.02	19.61	31.37	66.67	19.61	13.73	56.86	51
-0.30	50.00	19.23	30.77	65.38	15.38	19.23	65.38	26
-0.40	48.72	23.08	28.21	43.59	41.03	15.38	51.28	39
-0.50	54.55	27.27	18.18	45.45	45.45	9.09	59.09	22
-0.60	46.15	23.08	30.77	46.15	38.46	15.38	30.77	13
-0.70	70.00	20.00	10.00	10.00	80.00	10.00	60.00	10
-0.80	62.50	25.00	12.50	12.50	87.50	0.00	25.00	8
-0.90	66.67	0.00	33.33	33.33	33.33	33.33	66.67	3
-1.00	2.86	91.43	5.71	17.14	45.71	37.14	60.00	35
-1.10	0.00	100.00	0.00	0.00	55.56	44.44	100.00	9
-1.20	0.00	50.00	50.00	50.00	50.00	0.00	0.00	2
-1.30	0.00	0.00	0.00	0.00	0.00	0.00	0.00	0
-1.40	0.00	0.00	0.00	0.00	0.00	0.00	0.00	0
-1.50	0.00	0.00	0.00	0.00	0.00	0.00	0.00	0
-1.60	0.00	0.00	0.00	0.00	0.00	0.00	0.00	0

COMMODITY INVESTORS RESEARCH GROUP TABLE OF PRICE VARIATION - COCOA (NY) PAGE 5

OPEN FROM PRIOR CLOSE	CLOSE CONTINUED SAME DIRECTION	CLOSE ADJUSTED FROM OPEN	REVERSED FROM OPEN	CROSSED PRIOR CLOSE	TRADING RANGE ADJUSTED AFTER OPEN	CONTINUED FROM OPEN	DIRECTION SAME AS PRIOR	DIRECTION	NO. OF CASES
2.00	50.00	50.00	0.00	0.00	0.00	100.00	100.00	100.00	2
1.90	0.00	0.00	0.00	0.00	0.00	0.00	0.00	0.00	0
1.80	100.00	0.00	0.00	0.00	0.00	100.00	0.00	100.00	1
1.70	100.00	0.00	0.00	0.00	100.00	0.00	0.00	100.00	1
1.60	0.00	0.00	0.00	0.00	0.00	0.00	0.00	0.00	0
1.50	0.00	50.00	50.00	50.00	50.00	0.00	0.00	100.00	2
1.40	100.00	0.00	0.00	0.00	100.00	0.00	0.00	100.00	1
1.30	50.00	0.00	50.00	50.00	50.00	0.00	0.00	0.00	2
1.20	33.33	66.67	0.00	0.00	66.67	33.33	33.33	0.00	3
1.10	66.67	33.33	0.00	0.00	0.00	33.33	33.33	66.67	3
1.00	0.00	66.67	100.00	100.00	0.00	0.00	0.00	100.00	3
0.90	66.67	0.00	33.33	33.33	66.67	0.00	0.00	100.00	3
0.80	66.67	0.00	0.00	0.00	33.33	66.67	66.67	33.33	3
0.70	100.00	0.00	0.00	0.00	0.00	66.67	66.67	33.33	3
0.60	66.67	33.33	0.00	0.00	33.33	0.00	0.00	33.33	3
0.50	14.29	57.14	28.57	28.57	71.43	0.00	0.00	28.57	7
0.40	60.00	20.00	20.00	20.00	20.00	60.00	60.00	0.00	5
0.30	54.55	18.18	27.27	45.45	0.00	54.55	54.55	27.27	11
0.20	60.00	20.00	20.00	40.00	10.00	20.00	50.00	60.00	10
0.10	58.33	0.00	41.67	66.67	0.00	33.33	33.33	41.67	12
0.00	27.27	0.00	18.18	45.45	0.00	0.00	0.00	36.36	11
-0.10	45.45	27.27	27.27	63.64	9.09	27.27	27.27	27.27	11
-0.20	41.18	11.76	47.06	70.59	5.88	23.53	23.53	50.82	17
-0.30	54.55	36.36	9.09	45.45	27.27	27.27	27.27	45.45	11
-0.40	55.56	22.22	22.22	22.22	33.33	44.44	44.44	44.44	9
-0.50	46.15	30.77	23.08	30.77	46.15	23.08	23.08	61.54	13
-0.60	54.55	36.36	9.09	18.18	27.27	54.55	54.55	45.45	11
-0.70	50.00	25.00	25.00	25.00	25.00	50.00	50.00	100.00	4
-0.80	40.00	0.00	40.00	40.00	20.00	40.00	40.00	40.00	5
-0.90	100.00	0.00	0.00	0.00	100.00	100.00	100.00	25.00	4
-1.00	100.00	25.00	0.00	0.00	100.00	0.00	0.00	100.00	1
-1.10	0.00	0.00	0.00	0.00	100.00	0.00	0.00	0.00	2
-1.20	100.00	100.00	0.00	0.00	0.00	0.00	0.00	0.00	1
-1.30	0.00	0.00	0.00	0.00	0.00	0.00	0.00	0.00	1
-1.40	0.00	0.00	0.00	0.00	0.00	0.00	0.00	0.00	0
-1.50	0.00	0.00	0.00	0.00	0.00	0.00	0.00	0.00	0
-1.60	0.00	0.00	0.00	0.00	0.00	0.00	0.00	0.00	0
-1.70	0.00	0.00	0.00	0.00	0.00	0.00	0.00	0.00	0
-1.80	0.00	0.00	0.00	0.00	0.00	0.00	0.00	0.00	0
-1.90	0.00	0.00	0.00	0.00	0.00	0.00	0.00	0.00	0
-2.00	0.00	0.00	0.00	0.00	0.00	0.00	0.00	0.00	0

COMMODITY INVESTORS RESEARCH GROUP   TABLE OF PRICE VARIATION - COFFEE 'C'   PAGE 4

OPEN FROM PRIOR CLOSE	CONTINUED SAME DIRECTION	CLOSE ADJUSTED FROM OPEN	REVERSED FROM OPEN	CROSSED PRIOR CLOSE	TRADING RANGE ADJUSTED AFTER OPEN	CONTINUED FROM OPEN	CONTINUED SAME AS PRIOR	DIRECTION	NO. OF CASES
2.00	0.00	100.00	0.00	0.00	25.00	75.00		87.50	8
1.90	0.00	100.00	0.00	0.00	0.00	100.00		100.00	1
1.80	0.00	0.00	0.00	0.00	0.00	0.00		0.00	0
1.70	0.00	0.00	0.00	0.00	0.00	0.00		0.00	0
1.60	0.00	0.00	0.00	0.00	0.00	0.00		0.00	0
1.50	0.00	0.00	100.00	100.00	0.00	0.00		0.00	1
1.40	0.00	0.00	0.00	0.00	0.00	0.00		0.00	0
1.30	33.33	33.33	33.33	33.33	33.33	33.33		33.33	3
1.20	0.00	0.00	0.00	0.00	0.00	0.00		0.00	0
1.10	0.00	50.00	0.00	0.00	0.00	0.00		0.00	2
1.00	50.00	0.00	0.00	0.00	100.00	0.00		50.00	2
0.90	0.00	0.00	0.00	0.00	0.00	0.00		0.00	0
0.80	0.00	0.00	0.00	0.00	0.00	0.00		0.00	0
0.70	50.00	50.00	0.00	0.00	50.00	50.00		50.00	2
0.60	40.00	0.00	0.00	20.00	60.00	20.00		60.00	5
0.50	0.00	50.00	50.00	100.00	0.00	0.00		100.00	2
0.40	100.00	0.00	0.00	0.00	0.00	100.00		100.00	2
0.30	55.56	33.33	11.11	22.22	11.11	66.67		77.78	9
0.20	33.33	16.67	50.00	50.00	0.00	16.67		33.33	6
0.10	33.33	22.22	44.44	55.56	0.00	44.44		66.67	9
-0.00	33.33	0.00	33.33	66.67	0.00	0.00		33.33	3
-0.10	33.33	0.00	66.67	100.00	0.00	0.00		33.33	6
-0.20	50.00	0.00	50.00	50.00	0.00	50.00		50.00	2
-0.30	50.00	20.00	20.00	20.00	25.00	20.00		20.00	5
-0.40	25.00	25.00	50.00	75.00	0.00	0.00		0.00	4
-0.50	33.33	0.00	66.67	66.67	0.00	33.33		0.00	3
-0.60	0.00	100.00	0.00	0.00	100.00	0.00		100.00	1
-0.70	0.00	100.00	0.00	0.00	100.00	0.00		100.00	1
-0.80	100.00	0.00	0.00	0.00	100.00	100.00		0.00	1
-0.90	0.00	0.00	0.00	0.00	100.00	0.00		0.00	3
-1.00	0.00	100.00	0.00	0.00	0.00	0.00		33.33	3
-1.10	0.00	0.00	0.00	0.00	0.00	0.00		0.00	0
-1.20	100.00	0.00	0.00	0.00	0.00	100.00		0.00	1
-1.30	0.00	0.00	0.00	0.00	0.00	0.00		0.00	0
-1.40	100.00	0.00	0.00	0.00	0.00	0.00		0.00	0
-1.50	0.00	0.00	0.00	0.00	0.00	0.00		0.00	0
-1.60	0.00	0.00	0.00	0.00	0.00	0.00		0.00	0
-1.70	0.00	0.00	0.00	0.00	0.00	0.00		0.00	0
-1.80	0.00	0.00	0.00	0.00	0.00	0.00		0.00	0
-1.90	0.00	0.00	0.00	0.00	0.00	0.00		0.00	0
-2.00	0.00	0.00	0.00	0.00	0.00	0.00		0.00	0

YESTERDAYS CLOSE - TODAYS OPEN OUT OF RANGE   53.30   50.30

COMMODITY INVESTORS RESEARCH GROUP TABLE OF PRICE VARIATION - COPPER PAGE 9

OPEN FROM PRIOR CLOSE	CONTINUED SAME DIRECTION	CLOSE ADJUSTED FROM OPEN	REVERSED FROM OPEN	CROSSED PRIOR CLOSE	TRADING RANGE ADJUSTED AFTER OPEN	CONTINUED FROM OPEN	DIRECTION SAME AS PRIOR	NO. OF CASES
3.00	0.00	0.00	0.00	0.00	0.00	0.00	0.00	0
2.80	0.00	0.00	0.00	0.00	0.00	0.00	0.00	0
2.60	0.00	0.00	0.00	0.00	0.00	0.00	0.00	0
2.40	0.00	0.00	0.00	0.00	0.00	0.00	0.00	0
2.20	0.00	0.00	0.00	0.00	0.00	0.00	0.00	0
2.00	0.00	0.00	0.00	0.00	0.00	0.00	0.00	0
1.80	0.00	0.00	0.00	0.00	0.00	0.00	0.00	0
1.60	0.00	0.00	0.00	0.00	0.00	0.00	0.00	0
1.40	0.00	0.00	0.00	0.00	0.00	0.00	0.00	0
1.20	0.00	0.00	0.00	0.00	0.00	0.00	0.00	0
1.00	0.00	100.00	0.00	0.00	0.00	0.00	0.00	1
0.80	75.00	25.00	0.00	0.00	100.00	0.00	0.00	4
0.60	50.00	40.00	10.00	10.00	70.00	20.00	40.00	10
0.40	58.33	25.00	16.67	41.67	25.00	33.33	33.33	12
0.20	58.33	16.67	25.00	33.33	33.33	33.33	20.00	12
0.00	6.67	0.00	33.33	40.00	0.00	0.00	13.33	15
-0.20	33.33	19.05	47.62	66.67	14.29	19.05	52.38	21
-0.40	81.82	18.18	0.00	0.00	45.45	54.55	54.55	11
-0.60	68.75	25.00	6.25	18.75	62.50	18.75	50.00	16
-0.80	33.33	66.67	0.00	0.00	100.00	0.00	100.00	3
-1.00	100.00	0.00	0.00	0.00	100.00	0.00	0.00	1
-1.20	0.00	0.00	0.00	0.00	0.00	0.00	0.00	0
-1.40	0.00	0.00	0.00	0.00	0.00	0.00	0.00	0
-1.60	0.00	0.00	0.00	0.00	0.00	0.00	0.00	0
-1.80	0.00	0.00	0.00	0.00	0.00	0.00	0.00	0
-2.00	0.00	0.00	0.00	0.00	0.00	0.00	0.00	0
-2.20	0.00	0.00	0.00	0.00	0.00	0.00	0.00	0
-2.40	0.00	0.00	0.00	0.00	0.00	0.00	0.00	0
-2.60	0.00	0.00	0.00	0.00	0.00	0.00	0.00	0
-2.80	0.00	0.00	0.00	0.00	0.00	0.00	0.00	0
-3.00	0.00	0.00	0.00	0.00	0.00	0.00	0.00	0

COMMODITY INVESTORS RESEARCH GROUP   TABLE OF PRICE VARIATION - CORN   PAGE 10

OPEN FROM PRIOR CLOSE	CLOSE CONTINUED SAME DIRECTION	CLOSE ADJUSTED FROM OPEN	REVERSED FROM OPEN	CROSSED PRIOR CLOSE	TRADING RANGE ADJUSTED AFTER OPEN	TRADING RANGE CONTINUED FROM OPEN	DIRECTION SAME AS PRIOR	NO. OF CASES
10.00	0.00	0.00	0.00	0.00	0.00	0.00	0.00	0
9.00	100.00	0.00	0.00	0.00	100.00	0.00	0.00	1
8.00	100.00	0.00	0.00	0.00	0.00	0.00	0.00	1
7.00	0.00	0.00	0.00	0.00	100.00	0.00	0.00	0
5.00	100.00	0.00	0.00	0.00	0.00	0.00	0.00	2
4.00	100.00	0.00	0.00	0.00	50.00	100.00	50.00	2
3.00	50.00	11.11	22.22	33.33	44.44	22.22	50.00	9
2.00	25.00	0.00	75.00	75.00	25.00	0.00	37.50	8
1.00	42.31	11.54	46.15	73.08	7.69	19.23	57.69	26
-1.00	6.67	26.67	13.33	60.00	33.33	50.00	33.33	15
-2.00	50.00	16.67	16.67	16.67	33.33	0.00	33.33	6
-3.00	33.33	66.67	33.33	0.00	100.00	100.00	33.33	3
-5.00	50.00	0.00	33.33	33.33	33.33	33.33	50.00	2
-6.00	0.00	100.00	100.00	100.00	0.00	0.00	100.00	1
-7.00	0.00	0.00	0.00	0.00	0.00	0.00	0.00	1
-9.00	100.00	0.00	0.00	0.00	0.00	0.00	100.00	1
-10.00	0.00	0.00	0.00	0.00	0.00	0.00	0.00	0

COMMODITY INVESTORS RESEARCH GROUP TABLE OF PRICE VARIATION - EGGS PAGE 11

OPEN FROM PRIOR CLOSE	CONTINUED SAME DIRECTION	CLOSE ADJUSTED FROM OPEN	REVERSED FROM OPEN	CROSSED PRIOR CLOSE	TRADING RANGE ADJUSTED AFTER OPEN	CONTINUED FROM OPEN	DIRECTION SAME AS PRIOR	NO. OF CASES
2.00	0.00	0.00	0.00	0.00	0.00	0.00	0.00	0
1.90	0.00	0.00	0.00	0.00	0.00	0.00	0.00	0
1.80	0.00	0.00	0.00	0.00	0.00	0.00	0.00	0
1.70	0.00	0.00	0.00	0.00	0.00	0.00	0.00	0
1.60	0.00	0.00	0.00	0.00	0.00	0.00	0.00	0
1.50	0.00	0.00	0.00	0.00	0.00	0.00	0.00	0
1.40	0.00	0.00	0.00	0.00	0.00	0.00	0.00	0
1.30	0.00	0.00	0.00	0.00	0.00	0.00	0.00	0
1.20	0.00	0.00	0.00	0.00	0.00	0.00	0.00	0
1.10	0.00	0.00	0.00	0.00	0.00	0.00	0.00	0
1.00	0.00	0.00	0.00	0.00	100.00	0.00	100.00	1
0.90	0.00	100.00	0.00	0.00	0.00	0.00	0.00	2
0.80	0.00	50.00	50.00	50.00	50.00	0.00	25.00	2
0.70	0.00	50.00	50.00	50.00	50.00	0.00	25.00	4
0.60	50.00	50.00	0.00	50.00	100.00	50.00	100.00	2
0.50	50.00	50.00	50.00	50.00	100.00	50.00	100.00	3
0.40	33.33	66.67	66.67	66.67	0.00	33.33	66.67	3
0.30	57.14	28.57	14.29	28.57	64.29	7.14	50.00	14
0.20	58.33	8.33	33.33	66.67	16.67	16.67	50.00	12
0.10	4.55	0.00	22.73	27.27	0.00	0.00	9.09	22
-0.10	33.33	25.00	75.00	75.00	16.67	25.00	33.33	6
-0.20	50.00	16.67	50.00	50.00	16.67	33.33	16.67	6
-0.30	100.00	0.00	33.33	33.33	0.00	100.00	0.00	2
-0.40	0.00	0.00	100.00	100.00	0.00	0.00	0.00	1
-0.50	0.00	50.00	0.00	0.00	0.00	0.00	50.00	2
-0.60	50.00	0.00	0.00	0.00	100.00	0.00	0.00	2
-0.70	0.00	0.00	0.00	0.00	0.00	0.00	0.00	0
-0.80	0.00	0.00	0.00	0.00	0.00	0.00	0.00	0
-0.90	0.00	0.00	0.00	0.00	0.00	0.00	0.00	0
-1.00	0.00	100.00	0.00	0.00	100.00	0.00	0.00	1
-1.10	0.00	0.00	0.00	0.00	0.00	0.00	0.00	0
-1.20	0.00	0.00	0.00	0.00	0.00	0.00	0.00	0
-1.30	0.00	0.00	0.00	0.00	0.00	0.00	0.00	0
-1.40	0.00	0.00	0.00	0.00	0.00	0.00	0.00	0
-1.50	0.00	0.00	0.00	0.00	0.00	0.00	0.00	0
-1.60	0.00	0.00	0.00	0.00	0.00	0.00	0.00	0
-1.70	0.00	0.00	0.00	0.00	0.00	0.00	0.00	0
-1.80	0.00	0.00	0.00	0.00	0.00	0.00	0.00	0
-1.90	0.00	0.00	0.00	0.00	0.00	0.00	0.00	0
-2.00	0.00	0.00	0.00	0.00	0.00	0.00	0.00	0

COMMODITY INVESTORS RESEARCH GROUP TABLE OF PRICE VARIATION - GOLD-IMM PAGE 1

OPEN FROM PRIOR CLOSE	CONTINUED SAME DIRECTION	CLOSE ADJUSTED FROM OPEN	REVERSED FROM OPEN	CROSSED PRIOR CLOSE	TRADING RANGE ADJUSTED AFTER OPEN	CONTINUED FROM OPEN	DIRECTION SAME AS PRIOR	NO. OF CASES
10.00	0.00	100.00	0.00	0.00	100.00	0.00	100.00	1
9.00	0.00	0.00	0.00	0.00	0.00	0.00	0.00	0
8.00	0.00	0.00	0.00	0.00	0.00	0.00	0.00	0
7.00	0.00	0.00	0.00	0.00	0.00	0.00	0.00	0
6.00	0.00	0.00	0.00	0.00	0.00	0.00	0.00	0
5.00	0.00	0.00	0.00	0.00	0.00	0.00	0.00	0
4.00	0.00	0.00	0.00	0.00	100.00	0.00	0.00	1
3.00	0.00	100.00	0.00	0.00	100.00	0.00	100.00	4
2.00	25.00	75.00	0.00	33.33	44.44	22.22	33.33	18
1.00	33.33	50.00	16.67	0.00	0.00	0.00	42.86	42
0.00	52.50	22.50	15.00	25.00	27.50	47.50	36.36	40
-1.00	27.27	63.64	9.09	18.18	63.64	18.18	42.86	11
-2.00	57.14	42.86	0.00	0.00	28.57	71.43	0.00	7
-3.00	0.00	0.00	0.00	0.00	0.00	0.00	0.00	0
-4.00	0.00	100.00	0.00	0.00	100.00	0.00	0.00	1
-5.00	0.00	0.00	0.00	0.00	0.00	0.00	0.00	0
-6.00	0.00	0.00	0.00	0.00	0.00	0.00	0.00	0
-7.00	0.00	0.00	0.00	0.00	0.00	0.00	0.00	0
-8.00	0.00	0.00	0.00	0.00	0.00	0.00	0.00	0
-9.00	0.00	0.00	0.00	0.00	0.00	0.00	0.00	0
-10.00	0.00	0.00	0.00	0.00	0.00	0.00	0.00	0

COMMODITY INVESTORS RESEARCH GROUP TABLE OF PRICE VARIATION - LUMBER PAGE 2

OPEN FROM PRIOR CLOSE	CLOSE		RANGE		TRADING RANGE		NO. OF CASES
	CONTINUED SAME DIRECTION	ADJUSTED FROM OPEN	REVERSED FROM OPEN	CROSSED PRIOR CLOSE	ADJUSTED AFTER OPEN	CONTINUED FROM OPEN	DIRECTION SAME AS PRIOR
5.00	0.00	0.00	0.00	0.00	0.00	0.00	0.00	0
4.50	0.00	0.00	0.00	0.00	0.00	0.00	0.00	0
4.00	0.00	0.00	0.00	0.00	0.00	0.00	0.00	0
3.50	0.00	0.00	0.00	0.00	0.00	0.00	0.00	0
3.00	0.00	0.00	0.00	0.00	0.00	0.00	0.00	0
2.50	0.00	0.00	0.00	0.00	0.00	0.00	0.00	0
2.00	0.00	50.00	50.00	50.00	0.00	50.00	100.00	2
1.50	50.00	50.00	0.00	25.00	0.00	25.00	75.00	4
1.00	20.00	16.67	33.33	33.33	50.00	66.67	50.00	6
0.50	12.50	25.00	62.50	62.50	12.50	25.00	0.00	8
0.00	0.00	0.00	37.50	0.00	0.00	37.50	25.00	17
-0.50	37.50	25.00	33.33	62.50	0.00	0.00	0.00	6
-1.00	0.00	66.67	33.33	33.33	66.67	0.00	33.33	3
-1.50	0.00	100.00	0.00	0.00	66.67	0.00	33.33	3
-2.00	100.00	0.00	0.00	0.00	100.00	0.00	0.00	1
-2.50	0.00	0.00	0.00	0.00	0.00	0.00	0.00	0
-3.00	0.00	0.00	0.00	0.00	0.00	0.00	0.00	0
-3.50	0.00	0.00	0.00	0.00	0.00	0.00	0.00	0
-4.00	0.00	0.00	0.00	0.00	0.00	0.00	0.00	0
-4.50	100.00	0.00	0.00	0.00	100.00	0.00	100.00	1
-5.00	0.00	0.00	0.00	0.00	0.00	0.00	0.00	0

COMMODITY INVESTORS RESEARCH GROUP TABLE OF PRICE VARIATION - OATS PAGE 3

OPEN FROM PRIOR CLOSE	CONTINUED SAME DIRECTION	CLOSE ADJUSTED FROM OPEN	REVERSED FROM OPEN	CROSSED PRIOR CLOSE	TRADING RANGE ADJUSTED AFTER OPEN	CONTINUED FROM OPEN	DIRECTION SAME AS PRIOR	NO. OF CASES
6.00	0.00	0.00	0.00	0.00	0.00	0.00	0.00	0
5.50	0.00	100.00	0.00	0.00	100.00	0.00	0.00	1
5.00	100.00	0.00	0.00	0.00	0.00	100.00	100.00	2
4.50	100.00	0.00	0.00	0.00	100.00	0.00	50.00	2
4.00	0.00	0.00	0.00	0.00	0.00	0.00	100.00	1
3.50	50.00	50.00	0.00	0.00	0.00	100.00	50.00	2
3.00	0.00	100.00	0.00	0.00	0.00	100.00	0.00	2
2.50	40.00	60.00	0.00	0.00	40.00	80.00	80.00	5
2.00	33.33	33.33	33.33	66.67	33.33	0.00	33.33	3
1.50	57.14	14.29	28.57	42.86	0.00	57.14	42.86	7
1.00	0.00	0.00	100.00	100.00	0.00	0.00	0.00	1
0.50	0.00	0.00	0.00	0.00	0.00	0.00	0.00	2
-0.50	66.67	33.33	0.00	66.67	0.00	33.33	40.00	3
-1.00	50.00	0.00	40.00	40.00	20.00	40.00	40.00	6
-1.50	0.00	80.00	50.00	50.00	33.33	16.67	33.33	5
-2.00	0.00	0.00	20.00	40.00	100.00	40.00	0.00	1
-2.50	0.00	100.00	0.00	0.00	0.00	0.00	100.00	1
-3.00	100.00	0.00	0.00	0.00	0.00	100.00	100.00	1
-3.50	0.00	0.00	0.00	0.00	0.00	0.00	0.00	0
-4.00	100.00	100.00	0.00	0.00	100.00	100.00	100.00	1
-4.50	0.00	0.00	100.00	0.00	0.00	0.00	0.00	1
-5.00	0.00	0.00	0.00	0.00	0.00	0.00	0.00	0
-5.50	0.00	0.00	0.00	0.00	0.00	0.00	0.00	0

YESTERDAYS CLOSE - TODAYS OPEN OUT OF RANGE   56.50   56.50

COMMODITY INVESTORS RESEARCH GROUP TABLE OF PRICE VARIATION - ORANGE JUICE PAGE 12

OPEN FROM PRIOR CLOSE	CLOSE CONTINUED SAME DIRECTION	CLOSE ADJUSTED FROM OPEN	REVERSED FROM OPEN	CROSSED PRIOR CLOSE	TRADING RANGE ADJUSTED AFTER OPEN	CONTINUED FROM OPEN	DIRECTION SAME AS PRIOR	NO. OF CASES
3.00	0.00	0.00	0.00	0.00	0.00	0.00	0.00	0
2.80	0.00	0.00	0.00	0.00	0.00	0.00	0.00	0
2.60	0.00	0.00	0.00	0.00	0.00	0.00	0.00	0
2.40	0.00	0.00	0.00	0.00	0.00	0.00	0.00	0
2.20	0.00	0.00	0.00	0.00	0.00	0.00	0.00	0
2.00	0.00	0.00	0.00	0.00	0.00	0.00	0.00	0
1.80	0.00	0.00	0.00	0.00	0.00	0.00	0.00	0
1.60	0.00	0.00	0.00	0.00	0.00	0.00	0.00	0
1.40	0.00	0.00	0.00	0.00	0.00	0.00	0.00	0
1.20	100.00	0.00	0.00	0.00	0.00	0.00	0.00	1
1.00	0.00	100.00	0.00	0.00	0.00	100.00	100.00	1
0.80	0.00	100.00	0.00	100.00	100.00	0.00	0.00	1
0.60	50.00	50.00	0.00	25.00	25.00	50.00	75.00	4
0.40	37.04	44.44	18.52	33.33	33.33	33.33	48.15	27
0.20	34.92	15.79	49.21	84.13	33.33	0.00	39.68	63
-0.00	45.61	15.79	38.60	47.37	10.53	42.11	47.37	57
-0.20	43.75	18.75	37.50	37.50	18.75	43.75	50.00	16
-0.40	33.33	33.33	33.33	33.33	22.22	44.44	66.67	9
-0.60	33.33	66.67	0.00	0.00	50.00	50.00	66.67	6
-0.80	50.00	50.00	0.00	0.00	50.00	50.00	0.00	2
-1.00	100.00	0.00	0.00	0.00	0.00	0.00	100.00	1
-1.20	0.00	0.00	100.00	100.00	0.00	0.00	0.00	1
-1.40	0.00	0.00	0.00	0.00	0.00	0.00	100.00	1
-1.60	0.00	0.00	0.00	0.00	0.00	0.00	0.00	0
-1.80	0.00	0.00	0.00	0.00	0.00	0.00	0.00	0
-2.00	0.00	100.00	0.00	0.00	100.00	0.00	0.00	1
-2.20	0.00	0.00	0.00	0.00	0.00	0.00	0.00	0
-2.40	0.00	0.00	0.00	0.00	0.00	0.00	0.00	0
-2.60	0.00	0.00	0.00	0.00	0.00	0.00	0.00	0
-2.80	0.00	0.00	0.00	0.00	0.00	0.00	0.00	0
-3.00	0.00	0.00	0.00	0.00	0.00	0.00	0.00	0

COMMODITY INVESTORS RESEARCH GROUP TABLE OF PRICE VARIATION - PLYWOOD PAGE 13

OPEN FROM PRIOR CLOSE	CLOSE CONTINUED SAME DIRECTION	CLOSE ADJUSTED FROM OPEN	REVERSED FROM OPEN	CROSSED PRIOR CLOSE	TRADING RANGE ADJUSTED AFTER OPEN	CONTINUED FROM OPEN	SAME AS PRIOR DIRECTION	NO. OF CASES
7.00	0.00	0.00	0.00	0.00	0.00	0.00	0.00	0
6.50	0.00	0.00	0.00	0.00	0.00	0.00	0.00	0
6.00	0.00	0.00	0.00	0.00	0.00	0.00	0.00	0
5.50	0.00	0.00	0.00	0.00	0.00	0.00	0.00	0
5.00	0.00	0.00	0.00	0.00	0.00	0.00	0.00	0
4.50	0.00	0.00	0.00	0.00	0.00	0.00	0.00	0
4.00	0.00	0.00	0.00	0.00	0.00	0.00	0.00	0
3.50	0.00	0.00	0.00	0.00	0.00	0.00	0.00	0
3.00	0.00	100.00	0.00	0.00	0.00	0.00	0.00	2
2.50	42.86	57.14	0.00	0.00	0.00	50.00	75.00	4
2.00	21.43	57.14	35.71	0.00	0.00	42.86	71.43	7
1.50	27.27	36.36	30.36	45.45	18.18	14.29	71.43	14
1.00	23.08	38.46	38.46	69.23	15.38	15.38	30.77	13
0.50	0.00	0.00	0.00	0.03	7.69	0.00	38.46	13
-0.00	53.85	0.00	46.15	76.92	7.69	15.38	8.33	13
-0.50	50.00	41.67	8.33	8.33	50.00	41.67	8.33	12
-1.00	80.00	20.00	0.00	0.00	40.00	50.00	20.00	5
-1.50	50.00	50.00	0.00	0.00	0.00	0.00	50.00	2
-2.00	0.00	0.00	0.00	0.00	0.00	100.00	0.00	1
-2.50	50.00	50.00	0.00	0.00	0.00	100.00	0.00	2
-3.00	100.00	100.00	0.00	0.00	0.00	0.00	0.00	1
-3.50	0.00	0.00	0.00	0.00	0.00	0.00	0.00	0
-4.00	0.00	0.00	0.00	0.00	0.00	0.00	0.00	0
-4.50	0.00	0.00	0.00	0.00	0.00	0.00	0.00	0
-5.00	100.00	0.00	0.00	0.00	100.00	0.00	0.00	1
-5.50	0.00	0.00	0.00	0.00	0.00	0.00	0.00	0
-6.00	0.00	0.00	100.00	100.00	0.00	0.00	100.00	1
-6.50	0.00	0.00	0.00	0.00	0.00	0.00	0.00	0
-7.00	0.00	0.00	0.00	0.00	0.00	0.00	0.00	0

YESTERDAYS CLOSE - TODAYS OPEN OUT OF RANGE   23.85   24.75

COMMODITY INVESTORS RESEARCH GROUP TABLE OF PRICE VARIATION - PORK BELLIES PAGE 1

OPEN FROM PRIOR CLOSE	CONTINUED SAME DIRECTION	CLOSE ADJUSTED FROM OPEN	REVERSED FROM OPEN	CROSSED PRIOR CLOSE	TRADING RANGE ADJUSTED AFTER OPEN	CONTINUED FROM OPEN	DIRECTION SAME AS PRIOR	NO. OF CASES
2.00	0.00	100.00	0.00	100.00	0.00	0.00	100.00	1
1.90	0.00	0.00	0.00	0.00	0.00	0.00	0.00	0
1.80	100.00	0.00	0.00	0.00	0.00	100.00	100.00	1
1.70	0.00	0.00	0.00	0.00	0.00	0.00	0.00	0
1.60	0.00	0.00	0.00	0.00	0.00	0.00	0.00	0
1.50	0.00	96.23	3.77	15.09	30.19	54.72	73.58	53
1.40	50.00	25.00	25.00	25.00	75.00	0.00	75.00	4
1.30	57.14	28.57	14.29	14.29	57.14	28.57	42.86	7
1.20	33.33	50.00	16.67	50.00	16.67	33.33	33.33	6
1.10	62.50	12.50	25.00	37.50	62.50	0.00	50.00	8
1.00	50.00	30.00	20.00	40.00	50.00	10.00	70.00	10
0.90	50.00	33.33	16.67	33.33	66.67	0.00	33.33	6
0.80	78.57	0.00	21.43	28.57	71.43	0.00	78.57	14
0.70	60.00	10.00	30.00	40.00	60.00	0.00	60.00	10
0.60	60.00	5.00	35.00	50.00	40.00	10.00	45.00	20
0.50	58.33	13.89	27.78	63.89	30.56	5.56	61.11	36
0.40	61.54	15.38	23.08	42.31	50.00	7.69	53.85	26
0.30	58.54	9.76	31.71	48.78	24.39	26.83	56.10	41
0.20	46.00	22.00	32.00	66.00	26.00	8.00	36.00	50
0.10	52.83	13.21	33.96	73.58	11.32	15.09	43.40	53
-0.00	28.77	0.00	23.29	52.05	0.00	0.00	21.92	73
-0.10	45.71	5.71	48.57	85.71	2.86	11.43	62.86	35
-0.20	52.00	16.00	32.00	69.33	14.67	16.00	40.00	75
-0.30	50.00	20.00	30.00	56.00	20.00	24.00	52.00	50
-0.40	50.00	16.67	33.33	54.17	37.50	8.33	62.50	24
-0.50	91.76	8.82	29.41	55.88	35.29	8.82	58.82	34
-0.60	59.09	13.64	27.27	45.45	40.91	13.64	36.36	22
-0.70	50.00	12.50	37.50	50.00	41.67	8.33	41.67	24
-0.80	66.67	11.11	22.22	50.00	27.78	22.22	44.44	18
-0.90	44.44	22.22	22.22	55.56	33.33	11.11	55.56	9
-1.00	50.00	40.00	10.00	40.00	40.00	20.00	60.00	10
-1.10	25.00	0.00	75.00	75.00	0.00	25.00	50.00	4
-1.20	60.00	20.00	20.00	20.00	60.00	0.00	80.00	5
-1.30	57.14	42.86	0.00	0.00	71.43	28.57	42.86	7
-1.40	3.57	50.00	16.67	50.00	50.00	0.00	50.00	6
-1.50	3.57	96.43	0.00	7.14	57.14	35.71	53.57	28
-1.60	0.00	100.00	0.00	0.00	0.00	100.00	100.00	3
-1.70	0.00	0.00	0.00	0.00	0.00	0.00	0.00	1
-1.80	0.00	0.00	0.00	0.00	0.00	0.00	0.00	0
-1.90	0.00	0.00	0.00	0.00	0.00	0.00	0.00	0
-2.00	0.00	0.00	0.00	0.00	0.00	0.00	0.00	0
ALL								

COMMODITY INVESTORS RESEARCH GROUP TABLE OF PRICE VARIATION - SOYBEAN MEAL PAGE 7

OPEN FROM PRIOR CLOSE	CLOSE CONTINUED SAME DIRECTION	CLOSE ADJUSTED FROM OPEN	REVERSED FROM OPEN	CROSSED PRIOR CLOSE	TRADING RANGE ADJUSTED AFTER OPEN	TRADING RANGE CONTINUED FROM OPEN	DIRECTION SAME AS PRIOR	NO. OF CASES
10.00	0.00	0.00	0.00	0.00	0.00	0.00	0.00	0
9.00	0.00	0.00	0.00	0.00	0.00	0.00	0.00	0
8.00	0.00	0.00	0.00	0.00	0.00	0.00	0.00	0
7.00	100.00	0.00	0.00	0.00	100.00	0.00	0.00	1
6.00	0.00	100.00	0.00	0.00	100.00	0.00	100.00	1
5.00	0.00	66.67	33.33	33.33	66.67	0.00	33.33	3
4.00	33.33	66.67	0.00	33.33	33.33	33.33	0.00	3
3.00	16.67	66.67	16.67	16.67	66.67	16.67	66.67	6
2.00	33.33	50.00	16.67	16.67	50.00	33.33	50.00	6
1.00	45.83	37.50	16.67	41.67	37.50	20.83	54.17	24
0.00	0.00	0.00	0.00	0.00	0.00	0.00	0.00	44
-1.00	47.50	20.00	32.50	47.50	20.00	32.50	47.50	40
-2.00	36.36	45.45	18.18	31.82	63.64	4.55	59.09	22
-3.00	42.86	42.86	14.29	21.43	57.14	21.43	71.43	14
-4.00	100.00	0.00	0.00	0.00	50.00	50.00	0.00	2
-5.00	100.00	0.00	0.00	0.00	100.00	0.00	100.00	1
-6.00	100.00	0.00	0.00	0.00	100.00	0.00	100.00	1
-7.00	0.00	0.00	0.00	0.00	0.00	0.00	0.00	0
-8.00	0.00	100.00	0.00	100.00	0.00	0.00	0.00	1
-9.00	0.00	0.00	0.00	0.00	0.00	0.00	0.00	0
-10.00	0.00	0.00	0.00	0.00	0.00	0.00	0.00	0

COMMODITY INVESTORS RESEARCH GROUP   TABLE OF PRICE VARIATION - SOYBEAN OIL   PAGE 14

OPEN FROM PRIOR CLOSE	CONTINUED SAME DIRECTION	CLOSE ADJUSTED FROM OPEN	REVERSED FROM OPEN	CROSSED PRIOR CLOSE	TRADING RANGE ADJUSTED AFTER OPEN	CONTINUED FROM OPEN	DIRECTION SAME AS PRIOR	NO. OF CASES
1.00	0.00	100.00	0.00	0.00	100.00	0.00	33.33	3
0.90	0.00	100.00	0.00	0.00	100.00	0.00	0.00	1
0.80	50.00	50.00	0.00	0.00	100.00	0.00	0.00	2
0.70	0.00	0.00	0.00	0.00	0.00	0.00	0.00	0
0.60	60.00	20.00	20.00	20.00	40.00	40.00	60.00	5
0.50	0.00	66.67	33.33	33.33	50.00	16.67	50.00	6
0.40	50.00	50.00	0.00	16.67	33.33	50.00	50.00	6
0.30	40.00	30.00	30.00	50.00	40.00	10.00	80.00	10
0.20	33.33	20.00	46.67	73.33	13.33	13.33	46.67	15
0.10	55.56	11.11	33.33	55.56	22.22	22.22	55.56	18
-0.00	21.21	0.00	21.21	42.42	0.00	0.00	9.09	33
-0.10	62.50	0.00	37.50	75.00	12.50	12.50	50.00	8
-0.20	56.00	12.00	32.00	60.00	20.00	20.00	36.00	25
-0.30	50.00	42.86	7.14	42.86	42.86	14.29	57.14	14
-0.40	37.50	37.50	25.00	37.50	37.50	25.00	37.50	8
-0.50	40.00	60.00	0.00	0.00	80.00	40.00	40.00	5
-0.60	50.00	25.00	25.00	25.00	75.00	0.00	25.00	4
-0.70	100.00	0.00	0.00	50.00	50.00	0.00	50.00	2
-0.80	0.00	100.00	0.00	0.00	0.00	100.00	0.00	1
-0.90	0.00	100.00	0.00	100.00	0.00	0.00	0.00	1
-1.00	0.00	0.00	100.00	100.00	0.00	0.00	0.00	1

COMMODITY INVESTORS RESEARCH GROUP TABLE OF PRICE VARIATION - SOYBEANS PAGE 1

OPEN FROM PRIOR CLOSE	CONTINUED SAME DIRECTION	CLOSE ADJUSTED FROM OPEN	REVERSED FROM OPEN	CROSSED PRIOR CLOSE	TRADING RANGE ADJUSTED AFTER OPEN	CONTINUED FROM OPEN	DIRECTION SAME AS PRIOR	NO. OF CASES
25.00	20.00	60.00	20.00	26.67	46.67	26.67	60.00	15
24.00	0.00	0.00	0.00	0.00	0.00	0.00	0.00	0
23.00	100.00	0.00	0.00	0.00	100.00	0.00	100.00	1
22.00	0.00	0.00	0.00	0.00	0.00	0.00	0.00	0
21.00	0.00	0.00	0.00	0.00	0.00	0.00	0.00	0
20.00	0.00	88.89	11.11	16.67	11.11	72.22	77.78	18
19.00	0.00	0.00	0.00	0.00	0.00	0.00	0.00	0
18.00	100.00	0.00	0.00	0.00	100.00	0.00	100.00	1
17.00	100.00	0.00	0.00	0.00	100.00	0.00	100.00	1
16.00	0.00	0.00	100.00	100.00	0.00	0.00	0.00	1
15.00	12.50	75.00	12.50	37.50	25.00	37.50	62.50	8
14.00	60.00	20.00	20.00	40.00	20.00	40.00	50.00	5
13.00	50.00	25.00	25.00	25.00	75.00	0.00	50.00	4
12.00	40.00	40.00	20.00	40.00	80.00	0.00	40.00	5
11.00	75.00	0.00	25.00	25.00	75.00	0.00	25.00	4
10.00	16.67	66.67	16.67	25.00	33.33	41.67	58.33	12
9.00	44.44	55.56	0.00	22.22	44.44	33.33	77.78	9
8.00	33.33	26.67	40.00	53.33	46.67	0.00	46.67	15
7.00	76.47	11.76	11.76	100.00	70.59	5.88	64.71	17
6.00	84.21	10.53	5.26	36.84	52.63	10.53	31.58	19
5.00	44.00	24.00	32.00	68.00	28.00	44.00	36.00	25
4.00	59.26	11.11	29.63	37.04	33.33	29.63	59.26	27
3.00	61.11	11.11	27.78	66.67	22.22	11.11	44.44	36
2.00	61.90	11.90	26.19	52.38	35.71	11.90	47.62	42
1.00	0.00	0.00	0.00	0.00	0.00	0.00	0.00	65
-1.00	40.31	11.39	48.10	84.81	7.59	7.59	54.43	79
-2.00	69.70	0.00	30.30	57.58	33.33	9.09	45.45	33
-3.00	47.06	5.88	47.06	76.47	20.59	2.94	44.12	34
-4.00	56.25	9.38	34.38	56.25	34.38	9.38	62.50	32
-5.00	45.83	20.83	33.33	62.50	29.17	8.33	54.17	24
-6.00	58.33	20.83	20.83	50.00	41.67	8.33	66.67	12
-7.00	41.67	25.00	33.33	58.33	25.00	16.67	57.14	7
-8.00	71.43	0.00	28.57	28.57	71.43	0.00	50.00	7
-9.00	58.33	33.33	8.33	41.67	58.33	0.00	75.00	12
-10.00	75.00	12.50	12.50	62.50	12.50	25.00	60.00	8
-11.00	80.00	20.00	0.00	50.00	100.00	0.00	100.00	5
-12.00	25.00	25.00	50.00	50.00	50.00	0.00	33.33	4
-13.00	33.33	0.00	66.67	66.67	33.33	0.00	71.43	3
-14.00	0.00	0.00	0.00	0.00	0.00	0.00	0.00	7
-15.00	57.14	42.86	0.00	0.00	85.71	14.29	50.00	2
-16.00	0.00	0.00	0.00	0.00	100.00	50.00	0.00	1
-17.00	100.00	0.00	0.00	0.00	100.00	0.00	50.00	0
-18.00	100.00	0.00	0.00	0.00	50.00	0.00	0.00	6
-19.00	50.00	33.33	16.67	16.67	50.00	33.33	46.67	15
-20.00	13.33	80.00	6.67	6.67	33.33	60.00	100.00	1
-21.00	0.00	0.00	0.00	0.00	100.00	0.00	0.00	0
-22.00	0.00	0.00	0.00	0.00	0.00	0.00	0.00	0
-23.00	0.00	0.00	0.00	0.00	0.00	0.00	0.00	0
-24.00	0.00	0.00	0.00	0.00	0.00	0.00	0.00	0

COMMODITY INVESTORS RESEARCH GROUP TABLE OF PRICE VARIATION - SUGAR (WORLD) PAGE 1

OPEN FROM PRIOR CLOSE	CLOSE CONTINUED SAME DIRECTION	CLOSE ADJUSTED FROM OPEN	CLOSE REVERSED FROM OPEN	CROSSED PRIOR CLOSE	TRADING RANGE ADJUSTED AFTER OPEN	CONTINUED FROM OPEN	DIRECTION SAME AS PRIOR	NO. OF CASES
2.50	0.00	100.00	0.00	0.00	100.00	0.00	50.00	2
2.40	0.00	0.00	0.00	0.00	0.00	0.00	0.00	0
2.30	0.00	0.00	0.00	0.00	0.00	0.00	0.00	0
2.20	0.00	100.00	0.00	0.00	100.00	0.00	100.00	1
2.10	0.00	0.00	0.00	0.00	0.00	0.00	0.00	3
2.00	0.00	87.50	12.50	25.00	25.00	50.00	75.00	8
1.90	0.00	0.00	0.00	0.00	0.00	0.00	0.00	0
1.80	100.00	0.00	0.00	50.00	50.00	0.00	0.00	2
1.70	0.00	0.00	0.00	0.00	0.00	0.00	0.00	0
1.60	0.00	0.00	100.00	100.00	0.00	0.00	0.00	1
1.50	0.00	0.00	0.00	0.00	0.00	0.00	0.00	0
1.40	0.00	0.00	0.00	0.00	0.00	0.00	0.00	0
1.30	100.00	0.00	0.00	100.00	100.00	0.00	0.00	1
1.20	100.00	0.00	0.00	0.00	50.00	50.00	100.00	1
1.10	50.00	50.00	0.00	5.00	40.00	55.00	55.00	20
1.00	50.00	20.00	5.00	0.00	66.67	33.33	100.00	6
0.90	33.33	50.00	16.67	50.00	50.00	0.00	83.33	6
0.80	57.14	42.86	0.00	0.00	85.71	14.29	71.43	7
0.70	66.67	16.67	16.67	16.67	50.00	33.33	83.33	6
0.60	47.06	41.18	11.76	29.41	64.71	5.88	58.82	17
0.50	66.67	16.67	16.67	16.67	61.11	22.22	72.22	18
0.40	51.61	25.81	22.58	32.26	48.39	19.35	61.29	31
0.30	60.78	23.53	15.69	29.41	60.78	9.80	74.51	51
0.20	50.00	23.47	26.53	44.90	42.86	12.24	58.16	98
0.10	40.34	0.00	50.57	90.91	0.00	0.00	36.93	176
0.00	47.65	19.46	32.89	68.46	24.16	7.38	46.98	149
-0.10	56.14	24.56	19.30	33.33	56.14	10.53	30.60	57
-0.20	47.83	30.43	21.74	47.83	47.83	4.35	56.52	23
-0.30	45.45	36.36	18.18	18.18	72.73	9.09	45.45	11
-0.40	43.75	25.00	31.25	37.50	56.25	6.25	25.00	16
-0.50	40.00	40.00	20.00	20.00	80.00	0.00	40.00	5
-0.60	44.44	22.22	33.33	44.44	55.56	0.00	44.44	9
-0.70	14.29	71.43	14.29	14.29	71.43	14.29	42.86	7
-0.80	33.33	66.67	0.00	0.00	66.67	33.33	66.67	3
-0.90	25.00	62.50	12.50	12.50	50.00	37.50	75.00	8
-1.00	0.00	100.00	0.00	0.00	66.67	33.33	33.33	3
-1.10	0.00	50.00	50.00	50.00	50.00	0.00	100.00	2
-1.20	0.00	0.00	0.00	0.00	0.00	0.00	0.00	0
-1.30	0.00	0.00	0.00	0.00	0.00	0.00	0.00	0
-1.40	100.00	0.00	0.00	50.00	100.00	0.00	100.00	2
-1.50	0.00	50.00	50.00	50.00	50.00	0.00	50.00	2
-1.60	100.00	0.00	0.00	100.00	0.00	100.00	100.00	1
-1.70	0.00	0.00	0.00	0.00	0.00	0.00	0.00	0
-1.80	0.00	0.00	0.00	0.00	0.00	0.00	0.00	0
-1.90	0.00	0.00	0.00	0.00	0.00	0.00	90.00	1
-2.00	0.00	95.00	5.00	20.00	20.00	50.00	0.00	2
-2.10	0.00	0.00	0.00	0.00	0.00	0.00	0.00	0
-2.20	0.00	100.00	0.00	0.00	100.00	0.00	100.00	1
-2.30	0.00	0.00	0.00	0.00	0.00	0.00	0.00	0
-2.40	0.00	0.00	0.00	0.00	0.00	0.00	0.00	0

COMMODITY INVESTORS RESEARCH GROUP   TABLE OF PRICE VARIATION - WHEAT   PAGE 6

OPEN FROM PRIOR CLOSE	CLOSE CONTINUED SAME DIRECTION	CLOSE ADJUSTED FROM OPEN	CLOSE REVERSED FROM OPEN	TRADING RANGE CROSSED PRIOR CLOSE	TRADING RANGE ADJUSTED AFTER OPEN	TRADING RANGE CONTINUED FROM OPEN	DIRECTION SAME AS PRIOR	NO. OF CASES
20.00	0.00	0.00	0.00	0.00	0.00	0.00	0.00	0
19.00	0.00	0.00	0.00	0.00	0.00	0.00	0.00	0
18.00	0.00	0.00	0.00	0.00	0.00	0.00	0.00	0
17.00	0.00	0.00	0.00	0.00	0.00	0.00	0.00	0
16.00	0.00	0.00	0.00	0.00	0.00	0.00	0.00	0
15.00	0.00	0.00	0.00	0.00	0.00	0.00	0.00	0
14.00	0.00	0.00	0.00	0.00	0.00	0.00	0.00	0
13.00	0.00	0.00	0.00	0.00	0.00	0.00	0.00	0
12.00	100.00	0.00	0.00	0.00	0.00	0.00	0.00	1
11.00	50.00	50.00	0.00	0.00	100.00	0.00	50.00	2
10.00	0.00	0.00	100.00	0.00	100.00	0.00	0.00	1
9.00	0.00	0.00	0.00	0.00	0.00	0.00	0.00	0
8.00	0.00	0.00	0.00	0.00	0.00	0.00	0.00	0
7.00	100.00	0.00	0.00	0.00	100.00	0.00	66.67	3
6.00	100.00	0.00	0.00	0.00	60.00	20.00	100.00	5
5.00	60.00	0.00	20.00	20.00	57.14	14.29	85.71	7
4.00	57.14	28.57	14.29	28.57	33.33	0.00	33.33	3
3.00	33.33	16.67	16.67	33.33	50.00	16.67	50.00	6
2.00	66.67	0.00	0.00	0.00	0.00	0.00	0.00	5
1.00	0.00	0.00	0.00	0.00	14.29	28.57	42.86	7
-1.00	28.57	14.29	57.14	57.14	37.50	12.50	50.00	8
-2.00	50.00	50.00	50.00	50.00	50.00	0.00	25.00	4
-3.00	75.00	25.00	0.00	50.00	0.00	0.00	0.00	0
-4.00	0.00	0.00	0.00	0.00	0.00	0.00	0.00	2
-5.00	50.00	0.00	50.00	50.00	0.00	50.00	50.00	2
-6.00	50.00	0.00	50.00	50.00	0.00	0.00	0.00	0
-7.00	0.00	0.00	0.00	0.00	0.00	0.00	0.00	0
-8.00	0.00	0.00	0.00	0.00	0.00	0.00	0.00	0
-9.00	0.00	100.00	100.00	100.00	100.00	0.00	100.00	1
-10.00	0.00	0.00	0.00	0.00	0.00	0.00	0.00	0
-11.00	0.00	0.00	0.00	0.00	0.00	0.00	0.00	0
-12.00	0.00	0.00	0.00	0.00	0.00	0.00	0.00	0
-13.00	0.00	0.00	0.00	0.00	0.00	0.00	0.00	0
-14.00	0.00	0.00	0.00	0.00	0.00	0.00	0.00	0
-15.00	0.00	0.00	0.00	0.00	0.00	0.00	0.00	0
-16.00	0.00	0.00	0.00	0.00	0.00	0.00	0.00	0
-17.00	0.00	0.00	0.00	0.00	0.00	0.00	0.00	0
-18.00	0.00	0.00	0.00	0.00	0.00	0.00	0.00	0
-19.00	0.00	0.00	0.00	0.00	0.00	0.00	0.00	0
-20.00	0.00	0.00	0.00	0.00	0.00	0.00	0.00	0

Bibliography

Andrews, W. S. *Magic Squares and Cubes*, Dover, New York, 1960.

Angas, L. L. B. *Investment For Appreciation*, Somerset, New York, 1936.

Angell, George. "Thinking Contrarily," *Commodities Magazine*, November 1976. (An interview with R. Earl Hadady.)

Appel, Gerald, and Martin E. Zweig. *New Directions in Technical Analysis*, Signalert, Great Neck, NY, 1976.

Appel, Gerald, *Winning Market Systems: 83 Ways to Beat the Market*, Signalert, Great Neck, NY, 1974.

Arms, Richard W., Jr. "Equivolume—A New Method of Charting," *Commodities Magazine*, April 1973.

Barnett, Eugene H. *Programming Time—Shared Computers in BASIC*, Wiley–Interscience, New York, 1972.

Beyer, William H., Ed. *Standard Mathematical Tables*, 24th ed. CRC Press, Cleveland, OH, 1976.

Bolton, A. Hamilton. *The Elliot Wave Principle, A Critical Appraisal*, Bolton, Tremblay & Co., Montreal, 1960.

Box, G. E. P., and G. N. Jenkins, *Time Series Analysis, Forecasting and Control*, Holden–Day, San Francisco, 1970.

Chatfield, C. *The Analysis of a Time Series: Theory and Practice*, Chapman and Hall, London, 1975.

Church, A. H. *On the Relation of Phyllotaxis to Mechanical Laws*, Williams and Newgate, London, 1904.

Cleeton, Claude. *The Art of Independent Investing*, Prentice–Hall, Englewood Cliffs, NJ, 1976.

Cohen, A. W. *How to Use The Three-Point Reversal Method of Point and Figure Stock Market Trading*, Chartcraft, Larchmont, NY, 1972.

Commodity Traders Club. *Comparative Performances*, Messena, NY, 1969. (A reprint).

Commodity Yearbook 1975. Commodity Research Bureau, New York, 1975.

Control Data Corporation. *Control Data 6000 Series Computer Systems Statistical Subroutines Reference Manual*, St. Paul, 1966.

Cootner, Paul, ed. *The Random Character of Stock Market Prices*, MIT Press, Cambridge, MA., 1964.

"Speculation and Hedging," *Food Research Institute Studies, Vol. VII: 1967 Supplement*, Stanford University Press, Stanford, 1967.

Cycles, Foundation for the Study of Cycles, Pittsburgh, January 1976.

Davis, Robert Earl. *Profit and Profitability*, R. E. Davis, West LaFayette, IN, 1969.

Davis, R. E., and C. C. Thiel, Jr. *A Computer Analysis of the Moving Average Applied To Commodity Futures Trading*, Ouiatenon Management Co., West Lafayette, IN, 1970. (A research report)

DeVilliers, Victor. *The Point and Figure Method of Anticipating Stock Price Movements*, Trader Press, NY, 1966. (Reprint of 1933 edition)

Dewey, Edward R. and Og Mandino. *Cycles*, Hawthorn Books, New York, 1971.

Donchian, Richard D. "Donchian 5- and 20-Day Moving Averages," *Commodities Magazine*, December 1974.

Downie, N. M., and R. W. Heath. *Basic Statistical Method*, 3rd ed., Harper & Row, New York, 1970.

Dunn, Dennis. *Consistent Profits in June Live Beef Cattle*, Dunn & Hargitt, West Lafayette, IN, 1972.

Dunnigan, William. *One Way Formula*, Dunnigan, Palo Alto, CA, 1955.

——— *Select Studies in Speculation*, Dunnigan, San Francisco 1954. (Includes "Gain in Grains," and "The Thrust Method in Stocks")

——— *117 Barometers for Forecasting Stock Price*, Dunnigan, San Francisco, 1954.

Earp, Richard B. "Correlating Taylor and Polous," *Commodities Magazine*, September 1973.

Edwards, Robert D., and John Magee. *Technical Analysis of Stock Trends*, John Magee, Springfield, MA, 1948.

Elliot, R. N. *Nature's Law, The Secret of the Universe*, Elliot, New York, 1946.

——— *The Wave Principle*, Elliot, New York, 1938.

Floss, Carl William. *Market Rhythm*, Investors Publishing Co., New York, 1955.

Fuller, Wayne A. *Introduction to Statistical Time Series*, Wiley, New York, 1976.

Fults, John Lee. *Magic Squares*, Open Court, La Salle, IL, 1974.

Gann, William D. *The Basis of My Forecasting Method For Grain*, Lambert–Gann, Pomeroy, WA, 1976. (Originally 1935.)

——— *Forecasting Grains By Time Cycles*, Lambert-Gann, Pomeroy, WA, 1976. (Originally 1946)

——— *Forecasting Rules for Cotton*, Lambert–Gann, Pomeroy, WA, 1976.

——— *Forecasting Rules for Grain-Geometric Angles*, Lambert–Gann, Pomeroy, WA, 1976.

——— *How to Make Profits In Commodities*, Lambert–Gann, Pomeroy, WA, 1976. (Originally 1942)

——— *Master Calculator for Weekly Time Periods to Determine the Trend of Stocks and Commodities*, Lambert–Gann, Pomeroy, WA, 1976.

——— *Master Charts*, Lambert–Gann, Pomeroy, WA, 1976.

——— *Mechanical Method and Trend Indicator for Trading in Wheat, Corn, Rye or Oats*, Lambert–Gann, Pomeroy, WA, 1976. (Originally 1934)

——— *Rules for Trading in Soybeans, Corn, Wheat, Oats and Rye*, Lambert–Gann, Pomeroy, WA, 1976.

——— *Speculation A Profitable Profession (A Course of Instruction In Grains)*, Lambert–Gann, Pomeroy, WA, 1976. (Originally 1955)

——— *45 Years in Wall Street*, Lambert–Gann, Pomeroy, WA, 1949.

Gies, Joseph, and Frances Gies. *Leonard of Pisa and The New Mathematics of the Middle Ages*, Thomas M. Crowell, New York, 1969.

Gilchrist, Warren. *Statistical Forecasting*, Wiley, London, 1976.

Gotthelf, Edward B. *The Commodex System*, Commodity Futures Forecast, New York, 1970.

Gotthelf, Philip, and Carl Gropper. "Systems Do Work . . . But You Need a Plan" *Commodities Magazine*, April 1977.

Gould, Bruce G. *Dow Jones–Irwin Guide to Commodities Trading*, Dow Jones–Irwin, Homewood, IL, 1973.

Hallberg, M. C., and V. I. West. *Patterns of Seasonal Price Variations for Illinois Farm Products*, Circular 861, U. of Illinois College of Agriculture, Urbana, 1967.

Hambridge, Jay. *Dynamic Symmetry, The Greek Vase*, Yale University Press, New Haven, 1931.

——— *Practical Applications of Dynamic Symmetry*, Yale University Press, New Haven, 1938.

Harahus, David. ". . . *on Market Speculation* . . . ," Harahus Analysis, Ferndale, MI, 1977.

Haze, Van Court, Jr. *Systems Analysis: A Diagnostic Approach*, Harcourt, Brace & World, New York, 1967.

Hieronymus, Thomas A. *Economics of Futures Trading*, Commodity Research Bureau, New York, 1971.

——— *When to Sell Corn-SoyBeans-Oats-Wheat*, University of Illinois College of Agriculture, Urbana, 1967.

Hildebrand, F. B. *Introduction to Numerical Analysis*, McGraw–Hill, New York, 1956.

Hurst, J. M. *The Profit Magic of Stock Transaction Timing*, Prentice–Hall, Englewood Cliffs, NJ, 1970.

Jiler, William L. *Forecasting Commodity Prices With Vertical Line Charts*, Commodity Research Bureau, New York, 1966.

———— *Volume and Open Interest A key to Commodity Price Forecasting*, Commodity Research Bureau, New York, 1967.

Kaufman, Perry J. "Market Momentum Re-examined," Unpublished Article, November 1975.

Kaufman, Perry J., and Kermit C. Zieg, Jr. "Measuring Market Movement," *Commodities Magazine*, May 1974.

Keltner, Chester W. *How to Make Money in Commodities*, The Keltner Statistical Service, Kansas City, 1960.

Kemeny, John G., and J. Laurie Snell. *Finite Markov Chains*, Springer–Verlag, New York, 1976.

Kemeny, John G., and Thomas E. Kurtz. *Basic Programming*, 2nd ed., John Wiley & Sons, New York, 1971.

Klein, Frederick C., and John A. Prestbo. *News and the Market*, Henry Regnery Co., Chicago, 1974.

Knuth, Donald E. *The Art of Computer Programming, Vol. 2: Seminumeric Algorithms*, Addison–Wesley, Reading, MA, 1971.

Kroll, Stanley. *The Professional Commodity Trader*, Harper & Row, New York, 1974.

Kroll, Stanley, and Irwin Shishko, *The Commodity Futures Market Guide*, Harper & Row, New York, 1973.

Kunz, Kaiser S. *Numerical Analysis*, McGraw–Hill, New York, 1957.

Labys, Walter C. *Dynamic Commodity Models: Specification, Estimation, and Simulation*, Lexington Books, Lexington, MA, 1973.

Lefevre, Edwin. *Reminiscences of a Stock Operator*. Doran, New York, 1923.

Lofton, Todd. "Chartists Corner," *Commodities Magazine*, December 1974. (Two series of articles.)

———— "Moonlight Sonata," *Commodities Magazine*, July 1974.

Luce, R. Duncan, and Howard Raiffa. *Games and Decisions*, John Wiley & Sons, New York, 1957.

MacKay, Charles. *Extraordinary Popular Delusions and The Madness of Crowds*, Noonday Press (Farrar, Straus and Giroux), New York, 1932.

Macon, Nathaniel. *Numerical Analysis*, John Wiley & Sons, New York, 1963.

Martin, Francis F. *Computer Modeling and Simulation*, John Wiley & Sons, New York, 1968.

Maxwell, Joseph R., Sr. *Commodity Futures Trading with Moving Averages*, Speer, Santa Clara, CA, 1974.

McKinsey, J. C. C. *Introduction to the Theory of Games*, McGraw–Hill, New York, 1952.

Mendenhall, William, and James E. Reinmuth. *Statistics for Management and Economics*, 2nd ed., Duxbury Press, North Scituate, MA, 1974.

Merrill, Arthur A. *Behavior of Prices on Wall Street*, The Analysis Press, Chappaqua, NY, 1966.

Mills, Frederick Cecil. *Statistical Methods*, Henry Holt & Co., New York, 1924.

Montgomery, Douglas C., and Lynwood A. Johnson. *Forecasting and Time Series*, McGraw–Hill, New York, 1976.

Morney, M. J., "On The Average and Scatter," in *The World of Mathematics*, Vol. 3 (James R. Newman, Ed.), Simon & Schuster, New York, 1956.

Neill, Humphrey. *The Art of Contrary Thinking*, The Caxton Printers, Caldwell, OH, 1960.

Oster, Merrill J. "How the Young Millionaires Trade Commodities," *Commodities Magazine*, March and April 1976.

Parker, Derek, and Julia Paricor. *The Compleat Astrologer*, McGraw–Hill, New York, 1971.

Perrine, Jack. "Taurus the Bullish," *Commodities Magazine*, September 1974.

Polous, E. Michael. "The Moving Average As A Trading Tool," *Commodities Magazine*, September 1973.

Powers, Mark J. *Getting Started in Commodity Futures Trading*, Investors Publications, Waterloo, Iowa, 1975.

Reiman, Ray. "Handicapping the Grains," *Commodities Magazine*, April 1975.

Rockwell, Charles S. "Normal Backwardation, Forecasting, and the Returns to Commodity Futures Traders," *Food Research Institute Studies, Vol. VII: 1967 Supplement*, Stanford University Press, Stanford, 1967.

Schabacker, R. W. *Stock Market Theory and Practice*, B. C. Forbes, New York, 1930.

Shaw, John E. B. *A Professional Guide to Commodity Speculation*, Parker Publ., West Nyack, NY, 1972.

Smith, Adam. *The Money Game*, Random House, New York, 1967.

Springer, Clifford H., Robert E. Herlihy, and Robert I. Beggs. *Advanced Methods and Models*, Richard D. Irwin, Homewood, IL, 1965.

———. *Probabilistic Models*, Richard D. Irwin, Homewood, IL, 1968.

Statistical Annual, Chicago Board of Trade, Chicago, 1969–1975 eds.

Steinberg, Jeanette Nofri. "Timing Market Entry and Exit," *Commodities Magazine*, September 1975.

Taylor, George Douglass. *The Taylor Trading Technique*, Lilly Pub. Co., Los Angeles, 1950.

Taylor, Robert Joel. "The Major Price Trend Directional Indicator," *Commodities Magazine*, April 1972.

Teweles, Richard J., Charles V. Harlow, and Herbert L. Stone. *The Commodity Futures Game, Who Wins? Who Uses? Why?*, McGraw-Hill, New York, 1974.

Thiel, Charles, and R. E. Davis. *Point and Figure Commodity Trading: A Computer Evaluation*, Dunn & Hargitt, West LaFayette, IN, 1970.

Thiriea, H., and S. Zionts, Eds. *Multiple Criteria Decision Making*, Springer-Verlag, Berlin, 1976.

Thorp, Edward O. *Beat the Dealer*. Vintage, New York, 1966.

Tippett, L. C. "Sampling and Standard Error," *The World of Mathematics*, Vol. 3 (James R. Newman, Ed.), Simon & Schuster, New York, 1956.

Townsend, Robert. *Up the Organization*, Knopf, New York, 1970.

Tubbs. "Tubbs' Stock Market Correspondence Lessons." (Chap. 13, Tape Reading.)

Turner, Dennis, and Stephen H. Blinn. *Trading Silver—Profitably*, Arlington House, New Rochelle, NY, 1975.

Von Neumann, John, and Oskar Morgenstern. *Theory of Games and Economic Behavior*, Princeton University Press, Princeton, 1953. (First published 1943)

Waters, James, J., and Larry Williams. "Measuring Market Momentum," *Commodities Magazine*, October 1972.

Watling, T. F., and J. Morley. *Successful Commodity Futures Trading*, Business Books Ltd., London, 1974.

Watson, Donald S., and Mary A. Holman. *Price Theory and Its Uses*, 4th ed., Houghton Mifflin, Boston, 1977.

Williams, Edward E., and M. Chapman Findlay III. *Investment Analysis*, Prentice-Hall, Englewood Cliffs, NJ, 1974.

Williams, J. D. *The Complete Strategyst*, McGraw-Hill, New York, 1966.

Williams, Larry R. *How I Made One Million Dollars . . . Last Year . . . Trading Commodities*, Conceptual Management, Carmel Valley, CA, 1973.

Williams, Larry, and Charles Lindsey. *The Trident System*, Lindsey, O'Brien & Co., Thousand Oaks, CA, 1975. (A report).

Williams, Larry, and Michelle Noseworthy. "How Seasonal Influences Can Help You Trade Commodities," *Commodities Magazine*, October 1976.

Winski, Joseph N. "A Sure Thing?" *The Dow Jones Commodities Handbook 1977*, Dow-Jones Books, Princeton, NJ, 1977.

Working, Holbrook. "Test of a Theory Concerning Floor Trading on Commodity Exchanges," *Food Research Institute Studies, Vol. VII: 1967 Supplement*, Stanford University Press, Stanford, 1967.

Wyckoff, Richard D. *The Richard D. Wyckoff Method of Trading and Investing in Stocks*, Wyckoff Associates, Inc., Park Ridge, IL, 1936. (Originally 1931)

Wyckoff, Richard D. *Stock Market Technique, Number One*, Wyckoff, New York, 1933.

———. *Wall Street Ventures and Adventures Through Forty Years*, Harper & Brothers, New York, 1930.

Zieg, Kermit C., Jr., and Perry J. Kaufman. *Point and Figure Commodity Trading Techniques*, Investors Intelligence, Larchmont, NY, 1975.

Index

Acceleration, 6, 95-99
   see also Momentum; Velocity
Accumulation/distribution, 138, 139
Amplitude, 107
Angas, L. L. B., 1, 183, 200, 208, 299
Angell, G., 191
Appel, G., 138
Astrology, 192, 205-206
Autoregression, 53
   see also Trend
Averages, 9-22
   arithmetic mean, 9, 15, 16, 54
   characteristics, 16
   geometric mean, 10, 11
   harmonic mean, 10, 11
   law of averages, 21-22
   weighted, 10, 11, 22
   see also Moving averages

Background, 1, 5
Band, price:
   for momentum, 88
   rules for use, 77-79
   as stop-loss, 80
   variations, 76
   see also Moving average systems; Price channels
Basic concepts, 6, 9-24
Behavioral methods, 7, 187-206
   astrology, 205-206
   contrary opinion, 190-192
   Elliot, "wave principle," 194-200
   as filter, 274
   Gann, "Time and Space," 200-205
   mystic, 192-194
   news, 187-190
Bernoulli process, 292
"Best fit," *see* Regression analysis

Binomial probability (distribution), 292-295
Blinn, S. H., 84-85
Bolton, A. H., 194, 196
Book method, 257
Box, G. E. P., 26
Box-Jenkins methods, 130
Breakout:
   false, 77
   trendline, 140
   see also Penetration
Broilers, table of daily price variation, 375
Bullish concensus, 191

Calculator, programmable:
   statistical programs, 306, 318-339
      detrending, 322-323
      least-squares method, 320-321
      matrix solutions, 318-319, 335-337
      simultaneous linear equations, 318-319
      single frequency trigonometric curve fit, 324-329
      two-frequency trigonometric curve fit, 330-339
   use of, 6
Capital, conservation of, *see* Management
Cattle, frequency distribution, 13, 15
   hourly price patterns, 210
   mean deviation, 18
   point-and-figure vertical count, 166
   price variation, table of daily, 376
   seasonal variation, 131
   sequence of runs, 354
   v-top, 143
   weekend patterns, 368
   weekly patterns, 224, 229, 365
   weekly-weekend patterns, 240
Chance (price movement), 22
   see also Random

Chart analysis, 6, 134-136
  gaps, 144-145
  geometric formations, 139
    angles, 201-204
    pentagon and circle, 198-200
  head and shoulders, 141-142
  line or bar, 7, 137-149
  point-and-figure method, 4, 150-176
  price objectives, 145-148
  readings, 137-138
  tops and bottoms, 140-144
  trading rules, 139-140
  trend lines, 139, 146
Charting, systems based on, 177-186
  Donchian, four-week rule, 182-183
  Dunnigan, 177-180
    one-way formula, 179
    square root theory, 179-180
    thrust method, 177-179
  Keltner, minor-trend rule, 181-182
  Trident, 184-186
  Tubbs', law of proportion, 183-184
Chart paper, 135
Chatfield, C., 116
Chi-square test, 295-297
Church, A. H., 192-193
Circle:
  relationship to seasonals, 205
  use in charting, 198-200
Cleeton, C., 109
Closing price:
  direction, 215-219
  penetration of prior, 219
  reversal, 215-219, 241-248
Cocoa, frequency distribution, 13, 14
  mean deviation, 17
  opening price patterns, 219
  point-and-figure price objectives, 163-165
  price variation, table of daily, 377
  weekend patterns, 237, 369
  weekly patterns, 225, 362
Coffee:
  limit moves analysis, 280-282
  price variation, table of daily, 378
Cohen, A., 154
Collins, C., 194
Commissions, brokerage, 7
  day trading, 249-251
  effects of, 234
Commodex system, 276-277
Commodities Magazine, 5
Commodity Timing, Inc., 186
Compounding, *see* Pyramiding
Computer, 7
  costs, 264
  data base, 260-264
  personnel, 260-261
  programming, 260-261
  programs:
    available, 340
    regression analysis, 306-317
  selection of, 260
  services, 260-261
  use of, 259, 260-267
Computerized studies (testing):
  development, 261
  evaluating results, 265-267
  historic testing, 262
  moving averages, 82-83
  point-and-figure:
    Theil and Davis, 172
    Zieg and Kaufman, 152
  use of data, 262-264
Comtrend, 262
Conservation of capital, 269
Consolidation area, 146
Contrary opinion, 134, 187, 190-192, 200
Contra-trend, *see* Overbought/oversold
Cootner, P., 4
Copper:
  cycle analysis, 110-116
  dealers buying price, no. 2 heavy, 110
  detrended prices, 110-111
  moving average plot, 61-63
  price variation, table of daily, 379
  regression predictive error analysis, 55-56
  sequence of runs, 354
  weekend patterns, 369
  weekly patterns, 226, 230, 363
  see also Metals
Corn:
  cash prices 1956-1975, 120
  cash prices as % of average, 121
  point-and-figure vertical count, 168
  price variation, table of daily, 380
  ratio of monthly price to average, 119
  regression analysis, 30-45, 304-305
  seasonal pattern, 124, 131
    method of link relatives, 126
    moving average method, 127-129
Correlation, *see* Regression analysis
Cotton, sequence of runs, 352
  weekend patterns, 370
  weekly patterns, 227, 365
Currencies, point-and-figure box size, 156
Cycles, 6, 26, 106-133, 299
  cyclic adjustment factor, 132
  least-squares sinusoidal, 48-49
  see also Regression
  in momentum, 89
  phase, 108
  using moving average phasing, 99-102
  use in Taylor trading technique, 155
  see also Waves

INDEX

Data, 21
  characteristics of time-series, 27-29
  exponential smoothing, 66
  law of averages, 21-22
  random, for testing, 292
  representative or sample, 21
  standard error, 23
  testing of significance, 21
  weighting, 22
Data base, 260-264
  availability, 262
Davis, R. E., 82-83
Davis–Thiel:
  moving average studies, 82-83
  point-and-figure studies, 152, 172-173
Day trading, 7, 209, 245, 249-258
  commission effects, 249-251
  gambling techniques, 271
  liquidity, 251
  Taylor trading technique, 254-258
  use of moving averages, 252
  use of point-and-figure, 251-252
  use of support-resistance, 253-254
Definitive, *see* Probability
Delay, 75
  see also Timing
Detrending, 109-111
Deviation, 16-19
DeVilliers, V., 150
Differentiation, 96-97
  of trigonometric functions, 108-109
Donchian, R., 82, 182
Dow, C., 2, 137, 150
Dow theory, 137, 138, 139, 178, 179
Dunn and Hargitt, 79, 172, 182, 262
Dunnigan, W., 7, 183

Econometrics, *see* Regression analysis
Economic Research, Inc., 189
Edwards, R. D., 5, 135, 138
Eggs, table of daily price variation, 381
Elliot, R. N., 187, 192
  retracements, 183, 185
  wave principle, 183, 194-200
Emotions, 299
Equity cycles, 289-292
Error analysis:
  expected performance, 295
  regression techniques, 43-45
  of trend prediction, 54-57
Error of bias, 22
Error of omission, 8
Error, standard, 21, 295
Exponential smoothing, *see* Moving averages
Extrema, 109

Fibonacci, 192-197
  applied to Elliot wave principle, 196
  number series, 193

ratios, 180, 183, 193, 196-197
Filtering, 7, 259, 274-279
  combining trends and trading ranges, 277-279
  commodex method, 276-277
  using contrary opinion, 191
  velocity filtering functions, 98-99
Five and twenty-day moving average, 82
Foreign products, point-and-figure box size, 157
Fourier analysis, 48, 116
Four-week rule, 182
Frequency (periodic motion), 107
Frequency distribution, 13-16
  see also Probability, distribution
Frequency density, 14-15
Fundamental analysis:
  compared with technical, 2
  news, 3, 187-190, 301
  supply and demand, 2
Fundamental factors, 3

Gambling techniques, 7, 259, 267, 274
  applied to trading systems, 274
  Martingale, 186
  theory of runs, 271
  use in day trading, 271
Gann, W. D., 134, 187, 298
  philosophy, 301
  retracements, 183, 185
  swing charts, 178
  "time and space," 200-205
Gaps, charting, 144-145
  close-to-open, 213
  opening, 213
  see also Price variation
Geometric formations, *see* Chart analysis
Gilchrist, W., 16
Gold, table of daily price variation, 382
  see also Metals
"Golden" sections, 193, 197
Gould, E., 200
Grains, weekly patterns, 223
Growth, compound rate of, 125

Hadady, R. E., 191
Hambridge, J., 192, 193
Hamilton, W. P., 137
Harahus, D., 194-200
Harlow, C. V., 5
Head and shoulders, 141-142
Hexagon chart, 204
Hogs, point-and-figure vertical count, 167
Holiday price patterns, 238-240
Horizontal count, 163-165
Hurst, J. M., 48, 99-102

Index, 19-21
  bullish concensus, 191

Index *(continued)*
  market sentiment, 191
  point-and-figure box size, 156
  simple aggregate, 20
  use in commodex, 276
  weighted aggregate, 20
Inflation, rate of, 127
  computer analysis, 311-317
Inside range, 178
"Insiders," 300
Intra-day trading, *see* Day trading
Investment, initial, 7, 286

Jenkins, G. N., 26
Jiler, W. L., 138
Johnson, L. A., 129

Kaufman, P. J., 5, 79, 152, 154
Keltner, C. W.:
  minor-trend rule, 181-182
  ten-day moving average, 80-81
Kemeny, J. G., 49
Key reversal, *see* Price patterns; Reversals
Klein, F. C., 188-189
Kondratieff wave, 194
Kroll, S., 5

Lag, 63, 75
  of moving average stop, 104
  in phasing, 101
Lead, 63, 75
Leap, 83
Least-squares method, *see* Regression analysis
Least-squares sinusoidal, 48
Lefevre, E., 5, 220
Leverage, 1, 289
Limits, effect on trading, 279-282
  frequency, 251, 279-282
  locked-limit, 94
Linear correlation, *see* Regression analysis
Liquidity, 251
Livermore, J., 4, 154, 229, 298, 299, 301
Locked-limit, *see* Limits
Lofton, T., 205
Long-term analysis, *see* Trend
Losses, 299, 301
  consecutive, 3
  evaluation of, 292-297
Lucas numbers, 197
Lumber:
  price reversal pattern, 245
  price variation, table of daily, 383

Mackay, C., 135
Magee, J., 5, 135, 138
Management:
  conservation of capital, 79, 286, 302
  money, 7, 302
    effects of volatility, 267
    poor example, 282-285
    see also Gambling techniques
  personal, 298-302
  portfolio, 180, 267, 275, 286-292
    diversification, 287
    use of moving averages, 103
    use of reserve, 290
  risk, 78, 286
    see also Gambling techniques
  system, 286-287
    capital, 286-287
    equity cycles, 289-292
    evaluation of performance, 292-297
    pyramiding, 288-289
Manipulation, 299
Margin calls, 287
Market sentiment index, 191
Markov chains, 49-52
Martingale, *see* Gambling techniques
Master calculator, 204
Matrix solutions:
  general, 341-345
  of Markov process, 344-345
  programmable calculator, 318-319, 335-337
Maxwell, J. R., 5, 82-84
Mean deviation, 17
Means (arithmetic, geometric, harmonic), *see* Averages
Median, 12, 15, 16
  see also Averages
Merrill, A. A.:
  Elliot wave performance, 194
  holiday price patterns, 238-240
  hourly price patterns, 209-210
  NYSE price patterns, 207
Metals:
  point-and-figure box sizes, 157
  weekend patterns, 368
  weekly patterns, 222
Minor-trend rule, 181-182
Mode, modal value, 14, 15, 16
  see also Averages
Model:
  deterministic, 32
  probabalistic, 32
Modeling, mathematical, *see* Regression analysis
Momentum, 6, 86-102
  in commodex, 276
  compared to moving averages, 87-88
  system rules, 88, 90-91
  see also Oscillators
Montgomery, D. C., 129
Moody, J., 292
Moon, *see* Astrology
Moving averages, 6, 57, 58-73, 103-105
  accumulative, 59, 61
  average-modified, 60, 61, 83

INDEX

compared with momentum, 87-88
comparing standard and exponential, 67-72
data to average, 59
exponential smoothing, 6, 64-73
 complex, 72-73
 double (2nd order), 66-67
 Holt-Winters method, 132-133
 significance of data, 66
 Winters method, 129
"front-loaded," 60
geometric, 6, 64
phasing, 63, 99-102
plotted, 62-63
 with lag, lead, 63
reset accumulative, 60
step-weighted, 61, 79
truncated, 60
used for equity, 291
used to find seasonal pattern, 106, 127-129
used in portfolios, 291
weighted, 60, 65, 83
see also Averages: Moving average systems
Moving average systems, 74-85
 commodex, 276
 comprehensive studies, 82-85
 computer evaluation, 265-266
 double moving averages, 81-82
 equity patterns, 286
 expectations, 103
 as filter, 275
 living with, 103-105
 multiple moving averages, 82
 rules, general, 74-77
 selection of single, 79, 104-105
 selection of speed, 103-105
 signals, 74
 single moving averages, 79-81
 use of band, 76-79
 use in day-trading, 252
 use with trading range, 104, 277-279
 5- and 20-day moving average, 82
 10-day moving average rule, 80-81
 see also Averages; Moving averages
MPTDI, 79

Neill, H., 190
News:
 measurement and ranking, 187-190
 services, 3
 used for trading, 190, 301
Nofri, E., 180-181
Nonlinear approximations, *see* Regression analysis
Nonrandom price movement, 5, 25
 Box-Jenkins models, 130
 see also Random price movement

Oats:
 price reversal pattern, 246
 price variation, table of daily, 384
 weekly-reversal patterns, 246-248
Orange juice, table of daily price variation, 385
"One-way formula," 179
Open interest, 276
Opening price, breakout, 215
 direction, 214
 movement, 213
 see also Price variation
Optimization study, *see* Point-and-figure method
Oscillators, 6, 86, 91-102
 A/D, 91-95
 applications, 91-95
 see also Momentum
Overbought/oversold, computer results, 265
 in commodex, 276
 in contrary opinion, 191
 in momentum, 89
 in Taylor trading technique, 255
Overcommitment, 299

Paricor, J., 205
Parker, D., 205
Pascal triangle, 293
Penetration, 78, 178
 of prior close, 219
 see also Band; Breakout; Support and resistance lines
Pentagon, construction, 346-348
 use in charting, 198-200
Performance, evaluation, 292-297
 significance, 295
Periodic movement, 48-49, 107
 see also Cycles; Regression analysis
Perrine, J., 206
Phasing, 6
 of cycles, 108
 to represent cycles, 99-102
 see also Moving averages
Philosophy, market, 7, 298-302
Physics, use of, *see* Velocity
Plywood, table of daily price variation, 386
Point-and-figure method, 4, 7, 150-176
 box size, 154-157
 day trading, 251-252
 as filter, 275
 formations, 152-153
 optimization, 169-176
 price objectives, 163-168
 reversals, alternate treatment, 161-163
 risk analysis, 154, 156, 158-160
 rules, 151
 trading techniques, 158-160
Pork bellies, table of daily price variation, 387
Potatoes, seasonal variation, 131
 sequence of runs, 352
 weekend patterns, 369

Potatoes *(continued)*
  weekly patterns, 228, 364
Prestbo, J. A., 188-189
Price channels, 84
  for determining price objectives, 146-148
  see also Chart analysis; Trend lines
Price fluctuations, table of annual, 355-358
  see also Volatility
Price high and low, daily order of occurrence, 255-258
  finding extrema, 109
  as support and resistance, 298
  time-of-day, 214-215
  see also Tops and bottoms
Price movement, components of, *see* Cycle; Price patterns; Random; Seasonal analysis; Time-series; *and* Trend
Price objectives, bar charting, 145-148
  in phasing, 101
  point-and-figure, 163-168
  using retracement, 184-186
  using support-resistance levels, 254
Price patterns (pattern recognition), 4, 207-248
  close-only, 219-248, 359-373
  holdiays, 238, 240
  hourly, 209-213
    used with opening direction, 218
    see also Price variation
  NYSE, 207-208
  reversal, 7, 219
    daily, 241-248
    hourly, 212
  weekend, 219-241, 366-373
  weekly, 219-234, 359-365
  weekly-reversal combined, 246-248
  weekly-weekend combined, 235-241
Price ratios, 6
Price reaction, 7, 78
  action and reaction, 183-186
  to specific levels, 201
  see also Elliot, wave principle; Price patterns; *and* Pullback
Price variation, table of daily, description, 213, 215-219
  tables, 374-392
Price-volatility relationship, 171
Price trend, *see* Trend
Probability (probabilistic), 23-24
  binomial, 292-295
  distribution, 24
    see also Frequency distribution
  in gambling, 269
  Markov chains, 49-52
  netword, 50
Pullback, 77
  from opening price, 219
  point-and-figure, 158-159
  test of lows, 179
  to trendline, 140

  see also Price reaction; Retracements; *and* Reversals
Pyramiding, 7, 288-289
  Dunnigan repeat signals, 179
  point-and-figure, 160

Random, binomial probability, 292-295
  component of time-series, 25-26
  data for testing, 292
  number table, uniform, 349-350
  price movement, 4, 25-26, 296
  walk, 292
  see also Chance
Rate of change, 86
  see also Acceleration; Momentum; *and* Velocity
Reading guide, 5-6
Regression analysis, 6, 29-49, 107-117
  comparison of methods, 42-45
  computer programs, 340
  Fourier, 48, 116
  least-squares method, 32-36, 110-111, 114
    computer program, 306-317
    normal equations, 303-305
    programmable calculator, 320-321
  least-squares sinusoidal, 48-49
  linear, 27, 29-37, 43-46
    correlation, 36-37, 56-57
    matrix solutions, 341-345
    multivariate (2 variables), 45-47
    generalized, 48, 107
  nonlinear, 37-45
    computer program, 306-317
    curvilinear, 38-40, 53
    exponential, 42-43, 53
    logarithmic (power), 40-42, 53
  polynomial, generalized, 107
  predictive error, 54-57
  spectral, 116-117
  trigonometric, 48-49, 107-117
    complex, 114-117
    programmable calculator, 324-339
  used in phasing, 101
  see also Trend
Remote computing, 262
Repeat signals, *see* Pyramiding
Reports, USDA, *Commitments of Traders,* 189
Research skills, 8
Research studies, 7
  pattern recognition, 207-248
  point-and-figure optimization, 169-176
  see also Moving average systems, comprehensive studies
Reserve, capital, 290-291
Resistance lines (levels), *see* Support and resistance lines
Retracements, *see* Price reaction
Reversal patterns, *see* Price patterns; Reversals

Reversals:
  closing price, 178
  entering on, 191
  point-and-figure, 158-163
Reversing your position, 78
Rhea, R., 135, 178
Risk, 78, 292
  analysis of point-and-figure, 154, 156, 158-160
  see also Gambling techniques; Management
Risk/reward ratio, 3, 180
Rumors, 300
Runs:
  sequence of, tables, 351-354
  theory of runs, 186, 259, 267-274, 293
  variation from random, 297

Sampling, see Data, representative or sample
Scaling into position, 288-289
Schabacker, R. W., 135, 137, 183, 191
Seasonal analysis, 6, 106, 117-133
  effects, 26
  finding seasonal patterns, 117-133
  Holt-Winters method, 132-133
  method of link relatives, 125-127
  method of yearly averages, 118-125
  moving average method, 127-129
  patterns of corn, soybeans, 124
  Winters method, 129
  use of circle, 205
Seasonal systems:
  key dates, use of, 131
  probability, 131-132
  trading rules, 130-132
Secular trends, see Cycles; Seasonals
Sequentially dependent, see Nonrandom price movement
Sequentially independent, see Random price movement
Shishko, I., 5
Short-term trading, see Day trading
Silver, trading system, 282-285
  use of trading range, 253-254
  weekend patterns, 371
  see also Metals
Sine (sinusoidal) wave, 107-113
Skids, 251, 301
Skip, 83
Slope, see Momentum
"Smith, Adam," 134, 187, 299
Smoothing, 59, 65
  see also Moving averages; Regression analysis
Smoothing constant, 64
Soybeans:
  cash prices 1956-1975, 122
    as percent of average, 123
  Gann's worksheet, 202
    square, 203

point-and-figure optimization, 169-176
price variation, table of daily, 216-217, 390
regression analysis, 30-48, 304, 305
seasonal patterns, 124
Taylor's *book method,* 256-257
weekly patterns, 231-232, 361
weekly-weekend patterns, 240-242
Soybean meal, table of daily price variation, 388
  weekend patterns, 371
  weekly patterns, 362
Soybean oil, table of daily price variation, 389
  weekend patterns, 372
Spectral analysis, 116-117
Speed, of moving average, 103
  price change, see Acceleration; Momentum; Velocity
Square-root theory, 179-180
Standard deviation, 18, 55
  in momentum, 89
  use of, 57
Stone, H. L., 5
Stop-loss, in momentum, 90
  in MPTDI, 80
  placement, see *individual systems*
Strings (string lengths), see Runs, sequence of
Sugar, frequency of limit moves, 280
  price variation, table of daily, 391
  weekend patterns, 372
  weekly patterns, 363
Supply and demand, 2
  elastic theory, 144
  see also Fundamental analysis
Support and resistance lines (levels), 139, 140, 143
  for day trading, 253-254
  effects of time, 254
  as filter, 275
  hexagon chart, 204
  soybean square, 203
  in Taylor trading technique, 255
  using circle, 198-200
  using pentagon, 198-200
  see also Chart analysis; Trend lines
Swiss franc:
  weekend patterns, 373
  weekly patterns, 364
System, performance evaluation, 292-297
  predictive qualities, 292
System development and testing, see Computer; Testing; *and individual systems*

Target price, see Price objectives
Taylor, G. D., 7, 254-258
Taylor, O., 150
Taylor, R. J., 79-80
Technical adjustment, 78, 145
  see also Price reaction; Pullback; Reversals

Technical analysis compared with fundamental analysis, 2
Ten-day moving average rule, 80-81
Testing, distribution, 263
  of moving average duration, 105
  of predictive qualities, 262
Test results, evaluation, 264-267, 292-297
  historic, 292
  see also Computer
Teweles, R. J., 5
Thiel, C. C., 82-83
Thorp, E. O., 6
Three-day trading method, 258
Thrust method, 177-179
Time charts, use of, 200-205
Time intervals, 5
  effect on support-resistance, 254
  variation, 27-29
Time patterns, *see* Price patterns
Time-of-day, *see* Price patterns, hourly
Time series, 25-26
  Box-Jenkins analysis, 130
  component analysis, 106-133
  data characteristics, 27-29
  variations in interval patterns, 27
  see also individual components
Timing:
  delay, 75, 83
  entry-exit, 75, 78, 298, 300-301, 302
Tops and bottoms, 140-144
  tests of, 178
  see also Chart analysis; Overbought/oversold
Townsend, R., 260
Trading ranges, 302
  applications, 180-181
  combined with trends, 7, 104, 277-279
  formation, 277
  see also Support and resistance lines
Trading systems, rules, *see individual systems*
Trap forecasting, 180
Trend, 25-52
  combined with contrary opinion, 191
  combined with trading ranges, 7, 277-279
  continuation test results, 245
  distortions, noise, 22
  forecasting, 53
  identification with moving averages, 103
  long-term, 6, 277, 300
  minor, 81
  model, 53-73
  reversal test results, 245
  short-term, 81
  time interval, 4
  trading against the trend, 95, 213
  see also Overbought/oversold
  see also Moving averages
Trend following, 5
  analysis of predictive error, 54-57
  predictive qualities, 53
  systems, *see* Moving average systems
  used with weekend patterns, 235
Trend lines, 139, 201
  for determining price objectives, 146-148
  as geometric angles, 201-204
Trident, 184-186
Trigonometric curve fitting, 107-117, 324-339
  least-squares sinusoidal, 48-49
Tubbs, 183-184, 209
Turner, D., 84-85

Variable box point-and-figure, 169-176
Variance, coefficient of, 19, 55
Velocity, 6, 95-99
  see also Acceleration; Momentum
Vertical count, 165-168
Volatility, 5-6
  applied in moving average system, 79-80
  of daily price range, 249, 252-253
  in Gann's time charts, 205
  of hourly patterns, 212-213
  of limits, 251
  in momentum, 90
  in penetration, 82, 145
  point-and-figure analysis, 169-176
  -price relationship, 171
  on size of losses, 267
Volume, 138, 251
  in commodex, 276

Waters, J., 91-95
Watts, D. G., 22, 286
Wave (wave motion), 6, 107
  Kondratieff, 194
  of price reaction, 185
  see also Cycles; Elliot, *wave principle*
Wavelength, 107
Wheat, table of daily price variation, 392
  weekly patterns, 233-234, 361
Wheat method, percentage, 178
Wheat trading, a study in, 177-178
Williams, L., 91-95
Wyckoff, R., 3, 5, 135, 152, 154, 169, 298

Yearly averages, method of, 118-125

Zieg, K. C., 5, 152, 154
Zweig, M. E., 138